7⁰⁰

THE ECONOMICS OF MONEY AND BANKING

The Economics
of
Money and Banking

THIRD EDITION

LESTER V. CHANDLER
Gordon S. Rentschler Professor of Economics
Princeton University

HARPER & BROTHERS, PUBLISHERS, NEW YORK

TO

MY FATHER

TO

MY FATHER

CONTENTS

FIGURES

FIGURES

TABLES

PREFACE

Though extensively revised and largely rewritten, this edition is quite similar in purpose, approach, and treatment to the two that preceded it. It is addressed primarily to college undergraduates who are just beginning their formal study of money and banking. In selecting and presenting materials, I have tried to keep their needs constantly in mind and have not written for my professional colleagues. This is not an exhaustive treatment of money and banking. Not even a book many times the size of this one could claim to deal exhaustively with the vast amount of theoretical, legal, institutional, and historical material that has accumulated in this field. Nor do I believe that the newcomer should be forced to wade through an encyclopedic treatment of this broad and complex subject. I have therefore selected what I believe to be the most important principles, processes, and problems and have attempted to deal with them fully enough to clarify their significance.

The ultimate central interest of this book is in policy. But policy cannot be understood without a theory of the interrelationships of money and banking and the functioning of the economy as a whole, a clear understanding of the institutions and processes involved, and an appreciation of the social and historical context within which policymakers operate and by which their policies are shaped. This book therefore employs theoretical, institutional, and historical approaches. It emphasizes an evolutionary view, attempting not only to explain how present-day structures, attitudes, and policies evolved but also to suggest some possible directions of future change.

While concentrating on the functioning of the monetary and banking system as a whole and its relationships with the rest of the economy, this book devotes relatively little attention to technical problems of operating and administering an individual bank. I am convinced that this is the most fruitful approach for the student whose interest in the field is purely cultural. I believe the same is no less true for those who aspire to be leaders in banking or finance. Through formal study or experience they must, of course, master the tools of their trade. But they will be better citizens if from the beginning they see their profession in its broad economic and social context and understand both the effects of their own actions on the functioning of the economy and the effects of government monetary and fiscal policies on the various parts of the economy, including the banks and other financial institutions.

In preparing this and the two preceding editions I have been helped by so many persons that I cannot mention all of them. Three persons have been especially helpful on this edition. Professor Lawrence Werboff of Pennsylvania State University read the entire manuscript and made many useful suggestions. Mr. Neal Albert, my undergraduate assistant at Princeton, displayed extraordinary ability and ingenuity in searching out materials. Miss Carol Search was of invaluable assistance in gathering materials, acting as critic, and otherwise putting the manuscript in shape for the publisher. They are not, however, responsible for any errors and shortcomings that remain; these are on me.

L. V. C.

January, 1959

THE ECONOMICS OF MONEY AND BANKING

CHAPTER 1

The Roles of Money

One need not be an economist to be acutely aware that money plays an important role in modern life; he need only think of his own experience and recall the headlines that have thrust themselves at him in recent years. From his personal experience he knows that the process of getting a living is a process of getting and spending money, and that how well he can live depends on how many dollars he can get and how many goods and services each dollar will buy. He also knows that dollars are harder to get at some times than at others, and that the buying power of each dollar has varied widely, sometimes to his benefit and sometimes to his injury.

When he recalls the events of recent decades, he is reminded that the behavior of money is also vitally important to the operation of the national and international economy. During the 1930's newspapers headlined stories relating to "deflation": the drastic decline of output, job opportunities, and prices accompanying the shrinkage of effective money demand; the widespread want and suffering while millions of unemployed workers and other productive facilities that were both willing and able to work were standing idle because of insufficient "demand"; and the wholesale failures of debtors to meet their obligations because of the decline of their money incomes and of the prices of their assets. Headlines in the 1940's told a different sort of story—not stories of deflation and shrunken employment, but stories of "inflation," of rising living costs, and of discontent and distress among those whose income and wealth were relatively fixed in terms of money. The 1950's were less unstable in the United States, but they included years of inflation, years of mild deflation, and years when unemployment was considerably above minimum levels.

In short, personal experience as well as some knowledge of history and economics makes it clear to almost everyone that money plays an important role in the economic system and that the behavior of money is somehow causally related to the behavior of employment, the rate of real output, price levels, the distribution of wealth and income, and so forth. What is not as clear, however, is the answer to such questions as these: Just what are the functions of money in the economy, and just how does money perform these functions? To what extent do economic disturbances "arise on the side of money and monetary policy"? To what extent do money and monetary policy amplify and spread through the economy disturbances originating in nonmonetary factors? What are the effects of the various types of money and monetary policies? Which ones promote economic objectives generally considered desirable, and which ones militate against the attainment of those objectives? With how much success can we use monetary policy to prevent unemployment, promote a steadily advancing level of output, and maintain a stable purchasing power of the dollar while preserving a basically free-enterprise economy?

Such questions are the central concern of this book. The primary interest throughout is in the functioning of the monetary, credit, and banking systems and in their relationships to the functioning of the economy as a whole. Though much space will be devoted to historical, structural, and legal aspects of the various institutions that create, transfer, and destroy money, these aspects will not be studied primarily for their own sakes, but rather for their contribution to our understanding of the functioning of the economic system.

THE BASIC FUNCTION OF MONEY

Money has but one fundamental purpose in an economic system: to facilitate the exchange of goods and services—to lessen the time and effort required to carry on trade. A man living and working in complete isolation from others has no use for money. He cannot eat it, or wear it, or use it to promote his productive processes; having no occasion to exchange either goods or services with others, he has no need for money. Even if a dozen persons lived together in isolation from all others, the use of money would be of only limited benefit to them; they could barter their goods and services among themselves with but little loss of time and effort. As groups become larger, however, and wish to increase their degree of specialization and the size of the trade area, they find the direct barter of goods and services increasingly inconvenient and increasingly wasteful of time and effort. They therefore search for something that will enable them to escape the wasteful processes of barter; they invent money.

We may say, then, that the sole purpose of money in the economic system is to enable trade to be carried on as cheaply as possible in order to make feasible the optimum degree of specialization, with its attendant increase of productivity. We are all familiar with the high degree of specialization that characterizes modern economies—specialization of persons, of business firms, of regions, and of types of capital. We know that without this high degree of specialization, which enables us to utilize the various regions to maximum advantage, to make the most advantageous use of native abilities, to develop skills, to amass huge amounts of specialized and useful knowledge, and to employ large aggregations of specialized capital, our productive power and living standards would be far below their present levels. But this specialization would be impossible without an equally highly developed system of exchange or trade. Money is productive, therefore, in the sense that it is an essential part of the modern exchange mechanism and thereby facilitates specialization and production.

BARTER EXCHANGE

We have carefully avoided saying that exchange is impossible without money. People can, of course, carry on trade by a direct bartering of goods and services. Primitive trade was often carried on in this way, and bartering is not unknown even now. Yet pure barter is so wasteful of time and effort that little trade would be feasible if this were the only available method of exchange. Since the shortcomings of pure or direct barter constitute the only reason for the invention and use of money, they will be described at some length.

The first serious shortcoming of pure barter, with neither money nor the concept of a monetary unit available, is the lack of any common unit in terms of which to measure and state the values of goods and services. (By the "value" of a good or service is meant its "worth," the quantity of other goods and services that it can command in the market.) In this situation the value of each article in the market could not be stated simply as one quantity, but would have to be stated in as many quantities as there were kinds and qualities of other goods and services in the market. For example, if there were 500,000 kinds and qualities of goods and services in the market, the value of each would have to be stated in terms of 499,999 others. Moreover, no meaningful accounting system would be possible. A balance sheet would consist of a long physical inventory of the kinds and qualities of the various goods owned and another inventory of those owed; consequently the net worth of the person or firm could be ascertained, if at all, only by a prolonged and tedious study of the numerous barter rates of exchange prevailing in the market. Profit and loss statements would be equally difficult to draw up and interpret. A firm could only list the various kinds and qualities of goods and services acquired during the period as income and those paid out as expenses, so that again the net results could be discovered, if at all, only by a laborious study of barter rates of exchange. It is almost inconceivable that even a small department store, not to mention General Motors Corporation, could keep meaningful accounts in the absence of a monetary unit.

The second serious disadvantage of barter is often called "the lack of a double coincidence of wants." Stated more simply, it would happen only rarely that the owner of a good or service that he wished to barter could easily find someone who both wanted his commodity more than anything else and also possessed the commodity that our trader wanted more than anything else. For example, suppose that he owns a three-year-old draft horse that he wishes to trade for a certain kind of two-wheeled cart. To find someone who already owns or can build with maximum economy exactly the kind of cart that he wants and who is willing to trade it, and who also wants more than anything else the kind of horse that is being offered, is likely to be a laborious and time-consuming process, if such a person exists at all. The horse owner will probably have to accept something that he wants less than the cart or else carry through a number of intermediate barter transactions; he may have to trade the horse for a cow, the cow for a boat, the boat for some sheep, and the sheep for the desired cart. Barter presents even more serious difficulties when the articles to be exchanged are not of the same value and cannot be divided without loss of value. Imagine, for example, the plight of the owner if he wanted to trade his horse for a pair of overalls, a hat for his wife, three dishes, an aluminum skillet, 50 cartridges, schoolbooks for his children, and numerous other inexpensive articles.

The third disadvantage of pure barter, the lack of any satisfactory unit in terms of which to write contracts requiring future payments, grows out of the two disadvantages already noted. Contracts involving future payments are an essential part of an exchange economy; individuals must enter into agreements as to wages, salaries, interest, rents, and other prices extending over a period of time. But in a pure barter economy these future payments would have to be stated in terms of specific goods or services. Though this would be possible, it would lead to three grave difficulties: (1) It would often invite controversy as to the quality of the goods or services to be repaid. (2) The two parties would often be unable to agree on the specific commodity to be used for repayment. (3) Both parties would run the risk that the commodity to be repaid would increase or decrease seriously in value over the duration of the contract. For example, wheat might rise markedly in value in terms of other commodities, to the debtor's regret, or decrease markedly in value, to the creditor's regret.

The fourth disadvantage of pure barter, which also results from its first two shortcomings, is the lack of any method of storing generalized purchasing power. People could store purchasing power for future use only by holding specific commodities or claims against specific commodities. This method of storing purchasing power has often been used and, as we shall see later, is used extensively even today. Yet it has serious disadvantages when it is the only method available. The stored commodity may deteriorate (or appreciate) in value, its storage may be costly, and it may be difficult to dispose of quickly without loss if its holder wishes to buy something else.

Because of the four disadvantages outlined above, pure barter is a highly inefficient means of trade. It was to overcome these difficulties that virtually every society invented some kind of money early in its development.

THE SPECIFIC FUNCTIONS OF MONEY

Money serves its basic purpose as "the great wheel of circulation, the great instrument of commerce" by performing four specific functions, each of which obviates one of the difficulties of pure barter described above. These functions are to serve as: (1) a unit of value, (2) a medium of exchange, (3) a standard of deferred payments, and (4) a store of value. The first two are usually called the *primary* functions of money. The last two are called *derivative* functions because they are derived from the primary functions.

Money as a Unit of Value

The first function of money has been given many names, of which the most common are "unit of value," "standard of value," "unit of account," "common measure of value," and "common denominator of value." Through all these names runs one common idea: The monetary unit serves as the unit in terms of which the "value" of all goods and services is measured and expressed. As soon as a group develops a monetary unit, such as a dollar, a peso, a franc, a pound sterling, or a pengö, the "value" of each good or service can be expressed as a "price," by which we mean the number of monetary units for which it will exchange. For example, we say that the "value" of a certain hat is $10, that beef of a certain grade has a "value" of $1 a pound, and so on. Ours is certainly a "pecuniary" society in the sense that values typically are measured and expressed in monetary units.

The practice of measuring the values of goods and services in monetary units unquestionably simplifies the problem of measuring the exchange values of things in the market. One has merely to compare their relative prices in terms of monetary units. For example, if carbon steel is $8 per hundredweight and corn is $2 per bushel, a hundredweight of steel is worth 4 bushels of corn. It also simplifies accounting. Assets of all kinds, liabilities of all kinds, income of all kinds, and expenses of all kinds can be stated in terms of common monetary units to be added or subtracted.

Money is not the only common unit of measurement employed in the economic system. Units such as feet, inches, and meters are used to measure linear distance; ounces, grams, pounds, and short tons to measure weight; gallons, liters, and barrels to measure liquid volume; and so on. These units of physical measurement are themselves constant quantities. Confusion would surely result if these units of physical measurement, such as pints, inches, and ounces, should shrink 25 percent one year and expand 10 percent the next. Yet the unit of value (money), perhaps the most important unit of measurement in the entire economic system, has too often undergone wide fluctuations. The dollar has had a high value at one time (that is, an ability to purchase large amounts of goods and services in the market) and much lower values at other times (that is, an ability to buy only smaller quantities of goods and services). To be a satisfactory measure of value, the monetary unit itself must maintain a relatively stable value, or purchasing power. Some of the consequences of a fluctuating monetary unit will be discussed later.[1]

Money as a Medium of Exchange

Various names have been given to the second function of money: "medium of exchange," "medium of payments," "circulating medium," and "means of payment." This function of money is served by anything that is generally (not necessarily universally, but very commonly) accepted by people in exchange for goods and services. The "thing" may be porpoise teeth, bits of gold, copper coins, pieces of paper, or credits on the books of a bank; the only essential requirement is that people in general be willing to accept it in exchange for their goods and services. When a group has developed such a mechanism, its members need no longer waste their time and energy in barter trade. Our horse owner can simply sell his horse to the person who will give him the most money for it and then buy the supplies that he most desires from those who will give him what he considers to be the best bargain. The Ford worker need not barter his bolt-tightening services directly for the various things that he needs; he can sell his services for money in the most favorable market and spend the money as he sees fit. In the last analysis all trade is, of course, barter; one good or service is traded indirectly for others, with money acting as the intermediary. But by serving this purpose money greatly increases the ease of trade.

Money is often referred to as "generalized purchasing power" or "a bearer of options." This emphasizes the freedom of choice that the use of money affords. The owner of a good or service need not secure his supplies from the people to whom he trades his good or service; he can use his money to buy the things he wants most, from the people who offer the best bargain, and at the time he considers the most advantageous.

Here, again, money can function properly only if it maintains a relatively stable purchasing power. If a dollar is a bearer of fluctuating amounts of generalized purchasing power it is likely to cause confusion and injustice in trade.

---

[1] The following sections implicitly assume that each of the "things" that actually circulate as money—that is used as a means of payment—is stated in terms of the unit of account and maintains a fixed market value in terms of the unit of account. For example, a certain piece of paper money is stated as $5 and actually passes in the market as five of these units of account. In such cases, a depreciation or appreciation of the purchasing power of the unit of account is accompanied by a proportional depreciation or appreciation of each of the things used as a means of payment. However, in some abnormal cases the things used as means of payment may fluctuate in value in relation to the unit of account. For example, a certain silver coin might be equal to one unit of account (say $1) at one time and to two units of account (say $2) at another time. In such cases the purchasing power of the unit of account and of each of the things used as a means of payment will not vary proportionally.

Money as a Standard of Deferred Payments

As soon as money comes into general use as a unit of value and a medium of payments, it almost inevitably becomes the unit in terms of which deferred or future payments are stated. Modern economic systems require the existence of a large volume of contracts of this type. Most of these are contracts for the payment of principal and interest on debts, in which future payments are stated in monetary units. Some of these contracts run for only a few days or a few months, many of them run for ten years or more, and some run for a hundred years or more. By the late 1950's, the volume of outstanding debt in the United States was well above $700 billion. There are also many contracts other than debts which require future payments that are fixed or semifixed in terms of monetary units: dividends on preferred stock, long-term leases on property, salary contracts, and so on.

The disadvantages of writing contracts for future payments in terms of specific commodities have already been noted. But money is a satisfactory standard of deferred payments only to the extent that it maintains a constant purchasing power through time. If money increases in value through time, it injures the groups who have promised to pay fixed amounts of money and gives windfall gains to those who receive these fixed amounts. If, on the other hand, money loses value through time, it injures those who have agreed to receive the fixed amounts and lightens the burden of payers. Suppose, for example, that in 1948 Reilly borrowed $1000 from MacGregor, promising to repay him in 1968. MacGregor transferred to Reilly a certain amount of purchasing power in 1948. If in 1968 a dollar will buy only half as much as it did twenty years earlier (if prices, in general, have doubled), Reilly will return to MacGregor only half as much purchasing power as was lent to him. The shoe will be on the other foot, however, if the value of the dollar doubles during the period (if prices, in general, fall by half); Reilly will have to return twice as much purchasing power as he borrowed. Because of the widespread prevalence of such contracts, and for many other reasons as well, variations in the value of money have serious social consequences.

Money as a Store of Value

We have already noted the disadvantages of holding specific commodities as a store of value. As soon as money comes to be used as a unit of value and as a generally acceptable means of payment, it is almost certain to be widely used as a store of value. The holder of money is, in effect, a holder of generalized purchasing power that he can spend through time as he sees fit for the things he wants most to buy. He knows that it will be accepted at any time for any good or service and that it will remain constant in terms of itself. Money is thus a good store of value with which to meet unpredictable emergencies and especially to pay debts that are fixed in terms of money. This does not mean that money has been a stable and wholly satisfactory store of value; it could meet this test only if its purchasing power remained constant. In actual practice it has performed this function most capriciously. Its value or purchasing power shrinks in periods of rising price levels and actually increases during periods of falling price levels.

Money is not, of course, the only store of value. This function can be served by any valuable asset. One can store value for the future by holding short-term promissory notes, bonds, mortgages, preferred stocks, household furniture, houses, land, or any other kind of valuable goods. The principal advantages of these other assets as a store of value are that they, unlike money, ordinarily yield an income in the form of interest, profits, rent, or usefulness (as in the case of an auto or a suit of clothes), and they sometimes rise in value in terms of money. On the other hand, they have certain disadvantages as a store of value, among which are the following: (1) They sometimes involve storage costs; (2) they may depreciate in terms of money; and (3) they are "illiquid" in varying degrees, for they are not generally acceptable as money and it may be possible to convert them into money quickly only by suffering a loss of value.

Every person and business firm is free to choose for himself the form in which he will store his value, to determine the proportions he will hold in the form of money and in various nonmonetary forms, and to alter these from time to time to achieve what seem to him the most advantageous proportions, taking into consideration income, safety, and liquidity. These decisions are much influenced by a person's expectations as to the future behavior of prices. If he comes to believe that the prices of other things are less likely to decline and more likely to rise, he will be inclined to hold less of his wealth in the form of money and more in the form of other things. But if he comes to believe that prices of other things are less likely to rise and more likely to fall, he will be inclined to hold an increased part of his wealth in the form of money and a smaller part in other forms.

We shall see later that this freedom of people and business firms to determine for themselves the distribution of their holdings as between money and other assets and to shift freely from one form of assets to another may initiate or aggravate fluctuations in the flow of money expenditures and in prices and business activity. Sometimes people as a group show a tendency that is variously described as a desire to hold more of their wealth in the form of money and less in other forms, to use more money as a store of value and less as a means of payment, to transfer money from active use to idle balances, to hoard money, to hold money longer before spending it, or to decrease the velocity or rapidity of circulation of money. But regardless of the name applied to it, such a development tends to decrease the flow of money expenditures for securities, goods, and services, thereby exerting a downward pressure on the national money income, employment, and price levels. On the other hand, a widespread tendency that has been variously described as a general movement to hold less wealth in the form of money and more in other forms, to use less money as a store of value and more as a means of payment, to transfer money from idle balances to active use, to dishoard money, to hold money only a short time before spending it, or to speed up the velocity or rapidity of circulation of money, serves to raise the rate of money expenditures and to raise money incomes, price levels, and, under some conditions, employment and real output. Such fluctuations in the velocity of money or the demand for money to hold will occupy a very important position in our later discussions of the relationships between money and the behavior of the economy.

THE UNPRECEDENTED IMPORTANCE OF MONEY

Money is by no means a recent invention. It is certainly as old as recorded history, and some form of it seems to evolve as soon as a group finds a significant amount of specialization and exchange advantageous, which is usually early in group life. Nor are monetary problems less ancient; historians have yet to find a society with a perfectly functioning money, and many of the ancient monetary disorders were serious. Yet money is of unprecedented importance in modern capitalistic economies. This is due to two interrelated factors: (1) the unprecedented extent of specialization and exchange, and (2) the nature of economic motivations under capitalism.

The rapid rise of specialization and trade in the United States has been outlined by Walton Hamilton:

In the United States in fewer decades than the fingers on the hands has occurred a social revolution. An economy of small farms and petty trade, with a bit of commerce on the fringe, has been converted into "the great industry." At the end of the Civil War there was a coastal plain with a few cities, a back country with a dotting of small towns, and a West which invited settlement. The small, all but isolated, farm was dominant. The family, committed to a subsistence agriculture, undertook to produce their own livings with their own hands and formed an all-but-priceless economy. The household group was well or poorly off as they were hard working, prudent, thrifty, and had the break of the seasons. The weather could bountifully give or stingily withhold; for, because of an undeveloped technique in agriculture, it was still nature and not the market which made years fat or lean. The face of the land was covered with these almost self-contained entities. Almost—for the town was near at hand, to which the farmer took his surplus of produce; discovered the strange phenomena of the market, money, and price; engaged in verbal combat in haggling over a bargain; established an indirect contact with places far removed; and brought away tobacco, tools, and the subscription to the county weekly.[2]

[2] Walton Hamilton, *Price and Price Policies*, McGraw-Hill, New York, 1938, p. 7.

Even in the period before the Civil War money was not unimportant in this country. The farmer's enjoyment of life, if not his possession of the necessities, depended to a considerable extent on the prices of farm products, the prices of the things he bought, and the real burden of his money debts. Moreover, there were already many people in the towns and cities whose dependence on money and markets was greater than that of the farmer. Yet, as Hamilton indicates, the farmers were to a considerable extent self-sufficient, and even the city dwellers were less dependent on money and markets than they are today. A social revolution has indeed occurred since that time. In 1840 about 70 percent of our people lived on farms; this figure has now dwindled to less than 15 percent and may fall still further. And farming itself has experienced a revolution. The self-sufficient farm family is now the rare exception; to a constantly increasing extent the farmer is a specialized businessman, producing for sale in the market and relying on the market for a large part of the equipment and supplies with which to carry on production, as well as for most of the things with which to satisfy his family's wants. He, too, gets a living by obtaining money for his production and spending the money for tractors, implements, building materials, gasoline, automobiles, clothing, food, and other supplies and services. Any lingering illusion that the American farmer was independent of the market vanished during the great depression following 1929. The great numbers of our people who are engaged in mining, manufacturing, transportation, communication, marketing, and service are almost completely dependent on markets and money. For them, getting a living is a process of securing money in return for their specialized goods or services and then spending it for the things they want. Anything that disrupts the flow of their money income is likely to cause serious suffering and frustration.

A second reason for the unprecedented importance of money in the United States and other countries with similar types of economic systems is to be found in the nature of economic motivations in a capitalistic system. Money and monetary policy cannot safely be neglected even in a collectivistic society such as Soviet Russia, which relies primarily on centralized physical planning and direction of employment, output, and distribution. Time after time central planners have been embarrassed by excessive or deficient money flows that create dissatisfaction and militate against the success of their master plan. But money and monetary policy are inescapably more powerful forces in a capitalistic free-market economy. The leaders in this system are the enterprisers— those who determine the policies of business firms, whether these are individual proprietorships, partnerships, corporations, or coöperatives. They are the ones who, at least in the first instance, determine whether or not to establish plants, the size and location of plants, the types of goods to be produced, the rate of output, the amount of employment to be offered, and the demand for capital equipment. Their motivation is to "make money," as much money as possible; and they make goods and services only to the extent that this process will contribute to their primary objective of making money profits. If the flow of money spendings for their output is so great relative to their costs as to enable enterprisers to maximize their money profits by using all the available productive factors, something like full employment will be attained. If, however, money spendings for their output are so small relative to their costs that they will maximize their profits or minimize their losses by stopping far short of full output, they are likely to leave large numbers in the ranks of the unemployed. If the flow of expenditures for their products rises when almost all available factors of production are already fully employed they are almost certain to raise their prices. Such fluctuations of money expenditures are likely to be accompanied by fluctuations not only in employment and real output but also in price levels. This brings us to the difficult subject of the causative role of money.

MONEY AS A CAUSATIVE FACTOR IN THE ECONOMY

We must neither underestimate nor overestimate the influence of money and monetary policy on the functioning of an economic system. Many of the writings of the so-called "classical economists" who dominated British and American economic thinking in the nineteenth and twentieth centuries tended to accord money only an unimportant causative role. Such a view of the significance, or rather the insignificance, of money was clearly stated by John Stuart Mill:

It must be evident, however, that the mere introduction of a particular mode of exchanging things for one another by first exchanging a thing for money, and then exchanging the money for something else, makes no difference in the essential character of transactions. . . .

There cannot, in short, be intrinsically a more insignificant thing, in the economy of society, than money; except in the character of a contrivance of sparing time and labor. It is a machine for doing quickly and commodiously, what would be done, though less quickly and commodiously, without it; and like many other types of machinery, it only exerts a distinct and independent influence of its own when it gets out of order.

The introduction of money does not interfere with the operation of any of the Laws of Value laid down in the preceding chapters. The reasons which make the temporary or market value of things depend on the demand and supply, and their average and permanent values upon their cost of production, are as applicable to a money system as to a system of barter. Things which by barter would exchange for one another, will, if sold for money, sell for an equal amount of it, and so will exchange for one another still, though the process of exchanging them will consist of two operations instead of only one. The relations of commodities to one another remain unaltered by money; the only new relation introduced is their relation to money itself; how much or how little money they will exchange for; in other words how the Exchange Value of money itself is determined.[3]

[3] John Stuart Mill, *Principles of Political Economy*, Book III, chap. 7, ¶3.

Before jumping to the conclusion that money deserves no more attention than each of the thousands of other labor-saving devices in the economy, we should note two aspects of Mill's statement. First, he concedes that money "exerts a distinct and independent influence of its own when it gets out of order." This suggests the importance of keeping the money "in order" to avoid disturbances. Second, he was speaking primarily of "equilibrium conditions"—those conditions which would rule after sufficient time had elapsed for all factors of production, output, and prices to be so adjusted that there would be no incentive for further changes.

Modern economists tend, for several reasons, to accord money and monetary policy a more prominent role in their analysis. In the first place, they believe that money is frequently, if not virtually always, "out of order," and that its "distinct and independent influences" may force conditions in the economy far away from those of long-run equilibrium. In the second place, economists now concentrate their attention to a greater extent on economic disequilibrium: on business cycles, periods of unemployment or inflation, and periods of transition from one equilibrium position to another. There can be no doubt that during such periods money can exert a great influence on the behavior of total real output, the volume of employment, prices, and the social distribution of real wealth and income. Public policy cannot afford to neglect such periods, for they are often long and a succession of such disturbances may even alter the long-run course of the economy. In extreme cases they may create so much dissatisfaction as to bring radical changes in the organization and control of the whole economic system.

To overemphasize the role of money and monetary policy can be as dangerous as to underemphasize it. Some reformers, noting that the ability of an individual to obtain goods and services depends on the amount of money he can command, have erroneously assumed that the same must always hold true for an entire nation. They would therefore abolish poverty and usher in the economic millennium by great expansions in the money supply. How wonderful it would be if we could all become rich in any real sense simply by creating great batches of money! Unfortunately, it is not all that easy. We have already noted that an expansion of money spendings may serve to expand real production if it occurs in a period of unemployment when the labor force and other productive factors are not working at full capacity. Economic policy must not ignore this fact. But neither can it safely ignore the fact that the most that monetary policy can do to promote production—and it may not accomplish this without the aid of other wise economic policies—is to achieve and maintain full employment. It cannot compensate for a paucity of natural resources, or a scarcity of capital goods, or a backward state of technology, or sluggish and unintelligent labor, or unimaginative and unenterprising economic management, or inefficiency in government economic activities. In other words, a wise monetary policy may help to raise and maintain the actually realized rate of production closer to potential productive capacity—though we should not assume that it can always achieve even this objective—but it is usually not one of the major determinants of this potential capacity. Nor is it by any means the only factor determining the distribution of income and wealth among the members of the community. We shall have wiser monetary policy, and certainly wiser economic policies as a whole, if we recognize its limitations as well as its power.

SELECTED READINGS

Sources of Recent and Current Information

Bank for International Settlements, Annual Reports.

Board of Governors of the Federal Reserve System:
> Annual Reports, 1914 to date.
> Federal Reserve Bulletin (monthly).
> > This is a highly valuable source of current information concerning monetary and banking developments both in the United States and abroad.
> Banking and Monetary Statistics (Through 1941. Current statistics in Federal Reserve Bulletins.)
> Miscellaneous publications.
> > See lists of these in Federal Reserve Bulletins.

Chase Manhattan Bank of New York, Monthly Bulletins.

Comptroller of the Currency, Annual Reports.

Council of Economic Advisors, Economic Indicators (monthly).

Federal Deposit Insurance Corporation, Annual Reports.
> These reports contain excellent statistics and analyses of the structure and condition of American banks.

Federal Reserve Banks, Annual Reports, Monthly Bulletins, and special publications.
> The Monthly Letter of the Federal Reserve Bank of New York is a rich source of information concerning conditions abroad and in the central financial markets.

International Bank for Reconstruction and Development, Annual Reports.
> See also its special studies.

International Monetary Fund, Annual Reports.
> Also valuable are its publications of staff papers and special studies.

Secretary of the Treasury:
> Annual Reports.
> Treasury Bulletins (monthly).

U.S. Congress:
> House Banking and Currency Committee, various hearings and reports.
> Senate Banking and Currency Committee, various hearings and reports.
> Joint Economic Committee, numerous hearings, special compilations of materials, and reports.

CHAPTER 2

Kinds of Money

MONEY STOCKS AND MONEY FLOWS

We should bear constantly in mind the distinction between the *supply* or *stock* of money and money *flows*. The supply of money is simply the stock of those things that are used as a medium of exchange or means of payments, the size of this stock being measured in terms of the country's unit of account or unit of value. Thus the money supply is stated as the stock in existence at a point of time. This stock may, of course, be increased or decreased from one point of time to another. On the other hand, money spendings or expenditures are *flows* per unit of time. These flows are usually expressed at annual rates. Thus we might say that spending for American output is at an annual rate of $500 billion. We may state these flows at annual rates even though we are speaking of a point of time. For example, the statement above that spending for output is at an annual rate of $500 billion might apply to "right now"; the rate may have changed by tonight.

To relate the stock of money to the rate of money flow, we must introduce some concept of the average "velocity" or "rapidity of turnover" of the money stock. An outstanding characteristic of money is that it has some durability and can be used over and over again. (You may not use again that dollar you spent last night but someone else can.) The flow of money expenditures varies with the size of the stock of money and its average velocity or rapidity of turnover. For example, if the money supply is $150 billion and if on the average each dollar of it is spent for output four times a year, the flow of expenditures for output will be at an annual rate of $600 billion. The same stock of money with each dollar of it spent for output on an average of only three times a year would produce a rate of expenditure for output of only $450 billion a year. Since the velocity of money is not constant, we cannot assume that the supply of money and the flow of money expenditures will always move proportionally.

It is the flow of money expenditures rather than the money supply that is most directly relevant to the behavior of output, employment, and prices. In determining their policies relative to output, hiring, and prices, producers and sellers are most interested in the current and prospective flow of money demand for their products. They have no such direct concern for the size of the money stock. Nevertheless, we shall for two reasons begin with a long section on the money supply. (1) The size of the stock of money is a major determinant of money flows. (2) Under the conventions of our society the stock of money is subject to more direct official control than is its velocity. The rapidity of turnover of money is determined by people's decisions as to holding versus spending their money receipts and as to how long they will hold money before spending it. Direct government control of these individual decisions is not considered acceptable. But it is generally conceded that governments should regulate, if not control with precision, the supply of money. From a public policy point of view it is sometimes useful to concentrate attention on those factors in a situation that are subject to control. Moreover, we shall see that it may be possible to regulate the money supply in such a way as to offset, at least in part, fluctuations emanating from changes in the velocity of money.

The definition of "money" and the things included in the money supply vary from place to place and from period to period. The crucial test is this: Is the thing generally used as a means of payment? Is it generally acceptable in exchange for goods and services? Anything that meets this test is money for that area and that period.

EXAMPLES OF MONEY

Anyone who begins his study of money with the belief that there is some one thing that "is by nature money" and that has been used as money at all times and in all places will find monetary history very disconcerting, for a most heterogeneous array of things has served as circulating media. An incomplete list of these is given in Table 1.

Some of these are animal, some vegetable, some mineral; some, such as

TABLE 1. An Incomplete List of Things That Have Served as Money

clay	goats	hoes	iron
cowry shells	slaves	pots	bronze
wampum	rice	boats	nickel
tortoise shells	tea	porcelain	paper
porpoise teeth	tobacco	stone	leather
whale teeth	pitch	iron	pasteboard
boar tusks	wool	copper	playing cards
woodpecker scalps	salt	brass	
cattle	corn	silver	debts of individuals
pigs	wine	gold	debts of banks
horses	beer	electrum	debts of governments
sheep	knives	lead	

debts, defy this classification. Some are as valuable for nonmonetary purposes as they are in their use as money; others are practically worthless for purposes other than money; still others are valuable for nonmonetary purposes, but not as valuable as in their monetary use. Some are quite durable, whereas others are much less so. About the only characteristic that all these articles have in common is the fact that each of them was able, at some time and place, to achieve general acceptability as a means of payment. And the reasons for their general acceptability certainly varied from place to place and from time to time.

The very heterogeneity in the forms of the various things that have served as money suggests, as was said earlier, that there is no one form of money that is best at all times, in all places, and under all physical and cultural conditions. Gold and silver may have served England well in the seventeenth century, but the Indians of the New World spurned them and used wampum. A native of Malaita would no more think of accepting a checking deposit as money than a New York broker would think of accepting porpoise teeth. What will serve best as money depends upon many things, such as the stage of economic development, the availability of the various things that may be used as money, the people's taste in ornaments, the nature of religious practices, the extent of literacy, the stage of development of financial institutions, the honesty and strength of the government, and past monetary experiences.

TYPES OF MONEY

Though the monetary systems of advanced countries show wide variations, their circulating media have been mainly of the following types: (1) checking deposits, (2) paper money issued by governments, central banks, and

TABLE 2.   Classifications of Money

I. Full-bodied money
II. Representative full-bodied money
III. Credit money
   A. Issued by government
      1. Token coins
      2. Representative token money
      3. Circulating promissory notes
   B. Issued by banks
      1. Circulating promissory notes issued by central banks
      2. Circulating promissory notes issued by other banks
      3. Demand deposits subject to check

---

privately owned banks, and (3) coins of various kinds. These are listed in the order of their present importance as means of payments. Most of our payments are made by transferring claims on banks from payers to payees, the bank debts being transferred by check. Next in importance as an exchange medium is paper money, which is usually a debt of a government, a central bank, or a privately owned bank. Coin is the least important of all; it is, in effect, the small change of the economic system. We must emphasize that our circulating medium is made up largely of debts (or credits) which are transferred from payers to payees. We shall see later that this is largely true even of coins.

A classification of modern money that is more useful for analytical purposes is given in Table 2. It is based on the relationship between the value of money as money and the value of money as a commodity for nonmonetary uses.

Full-Bodied Money

Full-bodied money is money whose value as a commodity for nonmonetary purposes is as great as its value as money. It is versatile money; it can desert its monetary job and take up other occupations without losing value, if too much of it does not leave monetary uses. There have been many examples of this type of money. Most of the early commodity moneys—such as cattle, rice, wool, and boats—were as valuable for nonmonetary purposes as they were in their monetary use. The principal full-bodied moneys in modern monetary systems have been coins of the standard metal that are issued when a country is on a metallic standard: a gold standard, a silver standard, or a bimetallic standard using gold and silver.

Full-bodied coins usually result when two conditions exist: (1) Money can be shifted from monetary to nonmonetary uses virtually without cost, and (2) the metal can be coined into money without limit and virtually without charge. The ability to shift coins from their monetary use without cost prevents their being worth more as a commodity than as money. Any tendency for the market price of the commodity in the coin to rise above its face value—its price as a coin—would lead to a melting down of coins and the sale of their contents as a commodity. This would continue to the extent necessary to hold the market price of the commodity down to the face value of the coin or until all such coins had been drained from the monetary system. Even the threat of death has usually proved incapable of preventing the melting down of coins when this was profitable.

On the other hand, when a metal may be coined into money without limit and virtually without charge it is impossible for the coins to have a higher value as money than as a material for other uses. Any tendency for the market price of the metal to fall below the face value of the coins into which it could be minted would be corrected by a diversion of the metal from the market to the mint. For example, for many years before 1933, the federal government stood ready to coin gold in unlimited amounts and with only a negligible charge; it gave a dollar for each 23.22 grains of fine (pure) gold offered to it. This amounted to setting a purchase price of $20.67 per ounce of fine gold, because an ounce of gold (480 grains) will yield 20.67 dollars of 23.22 grains each. The minimum price of gold in the market became $20.67 per ounce, because as long as the government stood ready to buy all the gold offered at this price no one would sell for less, no matter whether the gold was to be coined or used in dentistry.

In summary, the equality of the monetary and nonmonetary values of full-bodied money is usually maintained by these two flows. The option of converting the money freely into a commodity for nonmonetary use prevents the market price of the material in the coin from rising above its face value as long as coins are available for this purpose. No one would pay more than $20.67 an ounce for gold in the open market as long as he could melt down full-bodied gold coins. And the option of converting the material into money without limit and virtually without expense prevents the market price of the material from falling below the face value of the coins into which it could be converted.

Full-bodied money has in the past played an important role in the monetary system of the United States as well as in the systems of other countries. All coins issued by the federal government in the first few decades after the establishment of the mint were full bodied, and full-bodied gold coins were in circulation, though in decreasing quantities, until 1933. In that year, however, all gold was called in by the government and the coinage of gold was discontinued. No full-bodied money has circulated in the United States since 1933, and this type of money has for many years been a rarity in most other countries.

Despite the fact that full-bodied money has all but disappeared from modern monetary systems, many persons still feel that it is superior to the "flimsier" types of money. They believe that it is "safer" because of its ability to shift without loss of value to nonmonetary uses, such as jewelry, dentistry, gold plate, gold leaf, and so on. Most of these persons seem to think that the value of a full-bodied coin merely reflects the value of the material in it for industrial and artistic purposes, and that the value of the metal is determined solely by its supply and by its *demand for nonmonetary uses*. This is clearly an erroneous idea. The value of any metal, both for industrial purposes and as a full-bodied coin, depends on its supply and on the aggregate demand for it, and the aggregate demand is made up of two parts: (1) the demand for it for use as money, and (2) the demand for it in other uses, such as industry and art. As soon as a metal comes to be used as money, the monetary demand for it may easily become the larger part of the total demand, and the value of the metal may depend largely on the behavior of the monetary demand for it. This is especially true of gold. How much purchasing power would gold have if no important country would purchase any of the current output for monetary use, so that the only remaining demand was for nonmonetary purposes? What would be the value of gold if all countries demonetized it and threw on the industrial market the hundreds of millions of ounces that they now hold in their monetary gold stocks? The value of gold would surely decline as the monetary demand for it disappeared. This is particularly likely in view of the fact that the nonmonetary demand for gold is to such a large extent derived from its use for "conspicuous waste"—in jewelry, gold plate, and gold leaf. If gold lost its monetary use and depreciated seriously, people might well turn to other means of ostentation.

We are thus led to two important conclusions. The first is that though the value of a full-bodied coin as money is equal to its value as a commodity for nonmonetary uses, the value as money does not merely reflect a value determined by the supply and the nonmonetary demand. Instead, the value of the metal both as money and for other uses depends on the supply and on the aggregate demand for monetary and nonmonetary uses, and the monetary demand is often dominant. The second conclusion is that though small amounts of full-bodied money may be able to shift to nonmonetary uses without loss of value, this is not possible on any large scale. Mass attempts to convert full-bodied coins into bullion for other uses are likely to reduce the value of the metal.[1]

This fact is clearly brought out by the history of silver. Before the last quarter of the nineteenth century, many important countries stood ready to coin all the silver offered to them at a value equal to around $\frac{1}{15}$ or $\frac{1}{16}$ of the value of gold; hence the value of silver for both monetary and nonmonetary uses was fixed at that level. But after these countries had withdrawn from silver the privilege of unlimited coinage, thereby decreasing its demand for monetary purposes, its value fell precipitately. In the 1920's its value averaged only about $\frac{1}{30}$ of the value of gold. In the late 1950's its value was only about $\frac{1}{38}$ of the value of gold. There is no reason to believe that the value of gold would escape at least as great a decline if its monetary use were similarly curtailed.

Some persons favor the exclusive use of full-bodied money because of its automatic limitation upon the quantity of money that can be created. Fearing that irresponsible monetary authorities would resort to inflation if token coins, paper money, or other debts were used as money, they would define the monetary unit in terms of a metal and then limit the money supply to the amount of the metal or metals offered for coinage. Though this technique might prevent the most extreme inflations, it would not at all assure an appropriate behavior of the money supply or of the flow of money spendings. For example, new gold strikes or a decreased use of gold in industry and the arts could swell the money supply far beyond the amounts needed to carry on trade

[1] For a delightful passage in which a piqued bank note "tells off" haughty gold coins, see D. H. Robertson, *Money*, Harcourt, Brace, New York, 1929, pp. 49–50.

at stable prices, and the failure of gold production to rise sufficiently during periods of rapidly advancing production and trade could bring about a deficiency of money spendings, then falling prices and unemployment.

Another shortcoming of full-bodied money is its cost. To get the gold, silver, or other metal needed for full-bodied money, a nation must devote part of its productive power to mining and refining, or it must exchange part of its output of other goods and services for the metal of other nations. Credit money can be obtained more cheaply. Full-bodied money would probably be worth the extra cost, however, if in fact it performed monetary functions more satisfactorily than other types of money.

Representative Full-Bodied Money

Representative full-bodied money, which is usually made of paper, is in effect a circulating warehouse receipt for full-bodied coins or their equivalent in bullion. The representative full-bodied money itself has no significant value as a commodity, but it "represents" in circulation an amount of metal with a commodity value equal to the value of the money. Thus, the "gold certificates" that circulated in the United States before their recall from circulation in 1933 represented fully equivalent amounts of gold coin or gold bullion held by the Treasury as "backing" for them.

In some respects, representative full-bodied money is similar to full-bodied money. The amount of it that can be issued depends upon the quantity of full-bodied money or its bullion equivalent available as "backing," and the cost of the "backing" material is as great as that of full-bodied money. This type of money has certain advantages over full-bodied money. In the first place, its use obviates the expense of coining, though against this must be set the cost of providing and maintaining the pieces of representative paper. In the second place, it avoids ordinary abrasion as well as the deliberate sweating, clipping, and chipping to which circulating coins are sometimes subjected. In the third place, it is easier to transport than the full-bodied money that it represents. This was certainly true of the Swedish representative money that circulated in place of massive copper coins during the seventeenth and eighteenth centuries, of the warehouse receipts for tobacco that circulated in Virginia and some of the other colonies, and of the pre-1933 gold certificates. The principal disadvantages of this type of money as compared with full-bodied money are the ease of counterfeiting it if the representative paper money is not very distinctive, and its destructibility by fire.

Credit Money

All the money in circulation in the United States and almost all the circulating moneys in other countries are credit money. By credit money we mean any money, except representative full-bodied money, that circulates at a value greater than the commodity value of the material of which it is made. The principal modern types of credit money are token coins, paper money, and checking deposits. Each of these will be discussed in turn.

Token Coins. All of the circulating coins in the United States—silver dollars, half dollars, quarters, dimes, nickels, and pennies—are token money; their value as money is significantly greater than their value as materials in the commodity market. The market values of the materials in these coins are shown in Table 3. Silver would have an even lower value as bullion if it had been com-

TABLE 3.   Metallic Content and Commodity Values
of United States Coins

Coin	Total Weight in Grains	Composition	Market Value of Commodity Content of Coins at June, 1958, Prices (in Cents)
Dollar	412.5	90% silver, 10% copper	67.2
Half dollar	192.9	"	31.9
Quarter	96.45	"	16.0
Dime	38.58	"	6.4
Nickel	77.16	75% copper, 25% nickel	0.4
Penny	48.00	95% copper, 5% tin, and zinc	0.2

pletely deprived of its monetary use so that the only demand for it was for other purposes.

Why are people willing to accept these coins in payment at values far above the values of the materials out of which they are made? The fundamental reason is that the quantity of these coins is deliberately limited by the government. We saw that the value of full-bodied money cannot rise above the value of the materials of which it is made because of unlimited coinage at virtually no cost to the suppliers of metal. But the government does not permit free and unlimited coinage in the case of token coins. Instead, it purchases the required metals at its own option and itself determines the quantities of token coins that it will issue. By appropriate limitations on the supply of these coins it can maintain their monetary value well above their commodity value. It can also make a profit equal to the difference between the cost of the material in the market and the value of the coins made from it. For example, it can pay $90.50 for 100 ounces of silver in the market and coin it into $129, thereby making a $38.50 gross profit. These profits are usually called seigniorage.

To insure that token coins will remain at parity with other types of money, the monetary authorities often provide for the free exchange of token coins for other types of money on a dollar-for-dollar basis as well as for the free exchange of other types of money for token coins. They then limit their issues of token coins to the amounts that people want to use or hold on a parity basis. But though this free interchangeability of the various types of money is usually necessary to maintain these various types at strict parity with each other, it must be emphasized that the basic reason why token coins can circulate at a monetary value above the value of the materials of which they are made is the limitation on their issue.

The above arrangement under which the government issues token coins made of metal purchased at its own option and in quantities determined by itself is the one ordinarily used today. But there have also been token money systems in which governments coined all the metal offered to them, but only at a very high cost to the suppliers of it, the governments retaining the high margin as seigniorage. For example, suppose that the monetary unit of a country is the dinar and that a 1-dinar piece contains 100 grains of silver. The government might stand ready to coin all the silver offered to it, but to give only 1 dinar for each 200 grains of silver. The market price of silver could fall as low as 1 dinar for 200 grains of silver, the government purchase price. The 100 grains of silver in the dinar could be worth as little as half a dinar in the commodity market. This underlines the fact that unlimited coinage or purchase of a metal is not sufficient to make a coin full bodied; the coinage must also be virtually without cost to the supplier of the metal. The market value of the material in a coin can fall below the monetary value of the coin by the amount of any charge made for coinage.

Representative Token Money.   Representative token money, which is usually paper, is in effect a circulating warehouse receipt for token coins or for an equal weight of bullion that has been deposited with the government. It is like representative full-bodied money, except that the coin or bullion held as "backing" is worth less as a commodity than as money. Silver certificates are the only example of this type of money in the United States. These have been in circulation in varying amounts since 1878 and are "backed" by an equivalent number of silver dollars or by silver bullion of equivalent weight. Most of our $1 bills are silver certificates, as are some of our $2, $5, and $10 bills. Most economists see no advantage in having a paper money "backed" by silver with a commodity value far below its monetary value. They believe that the money function could be served fully as well by an equivalent amount of paper currency without specific backing. But silver producers, constantly on the alert for better markets for their product, take a different view.

Circulating Promissory Notes Issued by Governments.   Governments also issue credit money in a form that is usually, but sometimes inaccurately, called circulating promissory notes. These are usually made of paper and are sometimes called *fiat* money. Some of them carry the government's promise to redeem them in other types of money on demand; this is why this type of money is usually called circulating promissory notes. Others, however, lack this promise and in effect say, "This is a certain number of monetary units."

The only circulating promissory notes issued by the United States government and still in circulation are the United States notes, or "greenbacks," which were issued to assist in financing the Civil War. Over $400 million of them were originally issued, but they were reduced to $347 million by 1878 and have since remained at approximately that level.[2]

Many people oppose the use of government paper money, fearing that it will be issued in excessive amounts. Monetary history provides a real basis for this fear, because these issues provide an attractive source of revenue to governments. By spending a small amount for paper, engraving, and printing, a government can produce millions of dollars' worth of paper money, which can then be used to pay its debts or cover its expenses. The temptation to sacrifice proper monetary management to budgetary needs is often strong. It should be pointed out, however, that most of the excessive issues of paper money have occurred during war periods when nations felt that their very existence was at stake and when they were in dire need of more money to meet military requirements. There is no reason why a properly managed government paper money should not function well.

Circulating Promissory Notes Issued by Central Banks. A considerable part of the hand-to-hand currency that is used in most advanced countries is in the form of circulating promissory notes issued by central banks, such as our Federal Reserve banks, the Bank of England, and the Bank of France. The largest part of our paper money is made up of Federal Reserve notes, which are circulating evidences of debt issued by the twelve Federal Reserve banks. In some cases the paper money issued by central banks is redeemable in other types of money; in other cases it is irredeemable. Though the Federal Reserve banks will redeem their notes in token coins or other types of paper money, they are not obligated to redeem them in full-bodied money.

Circulating Promissory Notes Issued by Private Banks. Circulating promissory notes that are issued by privately owned banks have played an important role in monetary systems. Promissory notes issued by state-chartered banks and by the First and Second Banks of the United States provided a large part of the circulating medium in this country before the Civil War, and the national banks chartered by the federal government issued such notes from the Civil War until 1935, when their power of note issue was rescinded. Though most of the notes issued by privately owned banks have been retired in this country, they are still used extensively in some other areas. These notes, it must be em-

---

[2] The Treasury statements also list as outstanding $1 million of Treasury notes of 1890. Though these are government promissory notes, most of them are believed to have been destroyed, lost, or placed in collectors' boxes.

phasized, are only circulating evidences of bank debts—creditor claims against banks.

Checking Deposits at Banks. The major part of the money supply in this country, as well as that in most other advanced countries, is in the form of demand deposits at banks. These so-called "deposits" are merely bank debts payable on demand: claims of creditors against a bank that can be transferred from one person or firm to another by means of checks or other orders to pay. These claims against banks are generally acceptable in payment of debts and for goods and services. They are used almost exclusively in transactions involving large payments and very widely in small payments, such as those from customers to retailers and salaries and wages to employees.

The popularity of checking deposits can be traced to their advantages: (1) They are not so liable to loss or theft as other types of money. (2) They can be transported very cheaply, no matter how large the amount of the payment or how great the distance from payer to payee. (3) Checks can be written for the exact amount of the payment, thereby obviating the necessity of making change and counting bills and coins. (4) When endorsed by the payee, checks serve as a convenient receipt for payment. The principal disadvantage of checking deposits is that checks drawn on them may not be accepted from an unknown person, but this is largely remedied by such devices as certified checks, cashier's checks, and traveler's checks.

THE GENERAL ACCEPTABILITY OF MONEY

Though many countries, including the United States, have long used credit money and this credit money has often not been redeemable in gold, silver, or any other money with a substantial nonmonetary value, the feeling still persists in some quarters that pieces of money cannot be "good" or even generally acceptable unless they themselves have an equivalent value for nonmonetary purposes or are kept redeemable in other types of money that have an equivalent value for nonmonetary uses. At the risk of excessive repetition we must point out again that this view is erroneous. That token coins, paper money, and other circulating debts can be overissued, and on too many occasions have been, is undeniable. But if their issue is properly limited they can be given a scarcity value and can circulate at least as satisfactorily as any full-bodied money; in fact, with proper management their quantities can be adjusted to the needs of trade better than can the quantities of a gold or silver full-bodied money whose supply often reflects the capriciousness of gold or silver mining.

Money can have a value simply because it is limited in supply and is demanded for use as money. Barter, as we have seen, is inconvenient. To escape these inconveniences, people want some kind of "tokens" or "tickets" that can be used as means of payment. In determining whether or not to accept such tickets in payment of debt or for goods and services, each person is interested in only one question: "Can I pass them along to someone else in exchange and without loss of value for the things I want to buy?" He is interested in their acceptability as money, not in their usability for some other purpose.

Such things could come into general monetary use in a group that had no previous monetary experience. Let us imagine, for example, the Zanzabu tribe, whose chief is Fungo II. The members of the tribe have been trading among themselves, but only by means of crude barter. By democratic processes or by edict of the chief they establish a monetary system, using the pecunio as their monetary unit. The physical things used as money may be baked pieces of clay bearing the seal or other distinguishing mark of Fungo II and the notation "1 pecunio," "5 pecunios," or "10 pecunios." To assure limitation of "coinage" and to prevent the chief from converting the system to his own uses, a committee of elder statesmen may be appointed to supervise the "mint." Though they have no use for other purposes, these imprinted pieces of clay may be readily accepted in trade by the tribal members who are happy to escape the clumsiness of barter. The acceptability of pecunios may be expedited somewhat by an edict declaring them to be acceptable in payment of taxes, or declaring them to be legal tender in payment of debts, or giving them both powers. No trouble need arise if the tokens are issued in proper amounts.

After a while, however, Fungo II or the tradesmen may decide that the monetary system is inefficient; some of the able-bodied members of the tribe must spend their time imprinting and baking the pieces of clay, and the tokens are liable to theft and are heavy to transport in quantities. They may therefore decide that they will supplement the "coin" system with book credits. The tribal treasurer, or perhaps a reputable tradesman, will set up pecunio credits on his books, and these credits can be transferred by written order from one tribesman to another in payment. At first the tribesmen who receive claims against the treasurer or tradesman may demand that they be redeemed in "coin." Later, however, after they have become accustomed to the system, they may make virtually all their payments by transferring book credits from payers to payees. The volume of pecunio credits or debts available for transfer in making payments may become far greater than the volume of "coins" in existence. In fact, the "coins" may be discontinued entirely.

Though modern credit money systems could have arisen in the manner indicated above, they are actually the result of a long evolution that is still in process. "The longer history of money has shown an almost unbroken evolution from commonplace, concrete, and simple forms to the representative, incorporeal and abstract."[3] The general nature of this evolution was somewhat as follows. Let us start with the use of uncoined metals, such as copper, gold,

---

[3] F. D. Graham and C. R. Whittlesey, *Golden Avalanche*, Princeton University Press, Princeton, 1939, p. 215.

and silver, as circulating media. These metals probably came to be widely acceptable in payment because they were widely desired for ornamental and religious purposes, they did not deteriorate, they were relatively easy to transport, and so on. At this stage money was not differentiated at all from the material of which it was made; the metal flowed freely into and out of monetary uses. The use of bullion as money had serious disadvantages, however. Precision weighing apparatus was not widely available and assaying was both laborious and inaccurate. Coinage solved, at least in part, both of these problems. At first, coinage amounted merely to an official certification as to the purity and weight of the lump of metal. The imprint of the king's stamp meant in effect, "I hereby certify that this contains a certain weight of metal of a certain purity." The names of many monetary units—pounds, livres, lire, and shekels—which were originally units of weight attest to this fact.

Coinage was an important monetary innovation. It greatly expanded the use of metallic substances as money. More important, however, it was a long step toward the differentiation of money from its component material. Not metal but *coined metal* became money. People gradually ceased to think in terms of the *weights* of metal; they thought in terms of the *number* of *coins*—not the weight of silver in a payment, but the number of shekels or lire. Debts and other contracts came to be stated in monetary units. This habit often persisted after the pure metallic content of the coins was reduced through abrasion, clipping, chipping, sweating, or deliberate action of the sovereign. When coinage was limited, the value of the coins as money often rose above the commodity value of their reduced metallic content; token coins appeared. Token coins also came into circulation at times as tokens redeemable in full-bodied money. After the group had become accustomed to these tokens, they continued to be acceptable whether or not they were redeemable in other money.

The use of representative paper money probably arose out of governments' desires to save the costs of coinage and of keeping coins in good condition as well as from the greater ease of transporting pieces of paper. The pieces of paper may have been acceptable at first, largely because of confidence that they were fully "backed" and that they would be redeemed in full-bodied money on demand. But after attaining general acceptability they could retain their monetary use even though the right of redeemability was withdrawn. The same is true of circulating promissory notes, whether issued by a government or by a reputable bank or merchant. At first their acceptability probably rested largely on confidence that the issuer would pay them on demand in other types of money. Then they continued to circulate after the promise to pay other types of money was rescinded and the pieces of paper bore only the legend "This is X dollars." We shall see later that the use of checking deposits evolved in this same general way. At first people may have been willing to accept and hold claims against banks only because they believed that their claims were fully "backed" by full-bodied money. But after the practice of accepting and holding claims against banks became solidly established, people continued to be willing to accept and hold these claims even though they knew perfectly well that the banks held only very small amounts of coin and paper money and that the "deposits" were nothing but bank debts.

At the present stage of monetary evolution there can be no doubt that people in the principal nations of the world are fully accustomed to the use of credit money and that by far the larger part of their payments is made by the transfer of bank deposits and paper money. Coins are typically the "small change" of economic systems, and full-bodied money has all but disappeared from general circulation.

THE MONEY SUPPLY OF THE UNITED STATES

We shall define the money supply of the United States at any time as the total of coin, currency, and demand (checking) deposits owned by the American "public," that is, by all individuals, business firms, and state and local governments.[4] Table 4 shows the composition of the money supply of the United States as of April 30, 1958.[5] A study of this table brings out several important facts about our monetary system.

1. There is no full-bodied money in circulation, and the $33 million of representative full-bodied money (gold certificates) listed in the table have been lost, destroyed, or locked up in private hoards, for they may not legally circulate. The entire money supply is in the form of credit money. Or, since credit is merely debt looked at from the reverse side, all the money is debt money; it is in the form of a liability or debt of the issuer. This is clearly true of demand deposits; they are merely debts or liabilities of the commercial banks. Likewise, Federal Reserve notes are merely debts or liabilities of the twelve Federal Reserve banks, and the various types of Treasury paper money are but debts or liabilities of the Treasury. The token coins, which are stamped pieces of metal instead of stamped pieces of paper, are also debts or liabilities of the Treasury.

2. Ranked in order of size, the types of money are: checking deposits, paper money, and coins. Checking deposits make up more than three quarters of the money supply, and it is estimated that they are used to effect more than 90 percent of all money payments. Paper money represents about 22 percent of the total, and coins are indeed the "small change" of the system, consti-

---

[4] Coin, currency, and checking deposits owned by the federal government, the Federal Reserve and commercial banks, and foreigners are by this definition excluded from the money supply. This is partly to avoid difficulties of accounting and double-counting, and partly because these types of money seem to be less relevant to the rate of spending than is the money supply as defined in the text.

[5] For current data, see *Federal Reserve Bulletins*.

tuting only 1.5 percent of the total. It should be noted that this distribution represents the choice of the holders, for the banks and the Treasury stand ready to exchange the various types of money for each other on a dollar-for-dollar basis.

3. Ranked in order of size of their outstanding money issues, the issuers of money are: the commercial banks, the Federal Reserve banks, and the Treasury. The 13,500 commercial banks, which are privately owned and privately operated institutions, are the issuers and are liable for the type of debt that we call demand deposits, which makes up more than three quarters of the money supply. The Federal Reserve banks are the issuers and are liable for the debts called Federal Reserve notes, which make up about a fifth of the money supply.

TABLE 4. Kinds of Money in Circulation in the United States, April 30, 1958[6]
(In millions of dollars)

	Amount	Percent of Total
Full-bodied money	$ none	0.0
Representative full-bodied money (gold certificates)	33	—
Credit money issued by the Treasury		
Token coins	2,076	1.5
Representative token money (silver certificates)	2,119	1.5
Circulating promissory notes[a]	495	0.4
Credit money issued by Federal Reserve banks		
Circulating promissory notes (Federal Reserve notes)	25,845	18.8
Credit money issued by commercial banks		
Demand deposits subject to check	107,200	77.8
Total money supply	$137,768	100.0

[a] Includes U.S. notes (greenbacks) and national bank notes and Federal Reserve bank notes for which the Treasury has assumed liability.

The Treasury itself issues less than 4 percent of the money in actual circulation. Thus, the Federal Reserve and commercial banks together supply us with more than 96 percent of our actual circulating medium. This fact alone explains why it is impossible to discuss money and banking separately.

4. All types of circulating money in this country, except checking deposits, have full legal-tender powers. That is, they have the legal power to discharge debts; creditors may not insist on payment in any other type of money if the debt is stated in dollars. Though checking deposits are not themselves legal tender, the banks are obligated to redeem them on demand in legal-tender money. This lack of legal-tender power reduces the general acceptability of

[6] See *Federal Reserve Bulletin*, June, 1958, pp. 665–666. The figures for coins and paper money show amounts outside the Treasury and the Federal Reserve banks. They therefore overstate the amounts in actual circulation by the quantities in commercial banks and other countries.

demand deposits only in periods when people doubt the banks' ability to redeem their debts.

NEAR-MONEY

It is now necessary to raise some questions concerning our definition of money, which includes all coins, paper money, and checking deposits owned by American individuals, business firms, and state and local governments. There is little doubt that all these things should be included in the money category. They are all perfectly "liquid"—that is, they remain at par in terms of the monetary unit at all times—and they are in fact generally acceptable at face value in payment of debts and for the purchase of goods and services. However, some economists believe that this definition is perhaps too narrow and that it excludes some other assets that have a high degree of "moneyness" and that at least to some extent perform monetary functions. They also believe that the rate of spending by the public is affected by their holdings of these other highly liquid assets almost to the same extent as by their holdings of money as we have defined it.

Time and savings deposits at commercial, mutual savings, and postal savings banks are in fact highly liquid. These are debts of the issuing institutions, which usually are not legally payable on demand, as are checking deposits, but are legally payable only after the passage of a specified period of time. In practice, however, the banks in many cases waive this requirement and permit withdrawals on demand. In fact, therefore, these deposits are often almost perfectly liquid and have the attributes of money in serving as a store of value, with the added attraction that they usually bear interest. To a very limited extent they are even transferred by checks or other orders from payer to payee as a means of payment. This, however, is rather uncommon; in most cases one who wishes to surrender his time or savings deposit to make payments to others must first surrender it in exchange for some form of money as we have defined it, and then use this money to pay his bills.

There are other types of assets that remain so stable in terms of money that they may be considered to be "near-moneys." Short-term government securities (and sometimes even long-term securities) are cases in point. To the extent that their values are constant in terms of money, they have the qualities of money as a store of value and can be converted into money for spending purposes without loss. But they are not themselves commonly used as a means of payment.

It is worth remembering that many types of assets have the quality of moneyness in varying degrees. Nevertheless, we shall for several reasons stand by our earlier definition of money. (1) Only coins, paper money, and checking deposits are in fact generally used as means of payments. The other liquid assets, even those whose value in terms of money remains fixed, can ordinarily be employed as a means of payment only by being first converted into money as we have defined it. (2) From the point of view of monetary policy, it may at times be desirable to make more expensive the step of converting these other assets into money proper. For example, it may be desirable to force people to take losses if they try to convert government securities into money. (3) The rate of spending depends not only on the supply of money and other liquid assets, but also on many other things, such as the people's total wealth, both liquid and illiquid, and their expectations as to future incomes and price levels. To include these other liquid assets in the money supply simply because they exert an influence on the rate of spending would raise questions as to why other determinants of the spending rate were not also included. (4) Since all assets possess the quality of moneyness in varying degrees, any other definition would leave equally troublesome borderline cases.

For all these reasons we shall retain the earlier definition of money, though it will be well to remember that the dividing line between money and non-money is somewhat arbitrarily drawn.

SELECTED READINGS

Angell, N., *The Story of Money*, Stokes, New York, 1929.

Board of Governors of the Federal Reserve System, *Banking and Monetary Statistics*, Washington, 1943, pp. 34–35. (See *Federal Reserve Bulletins* for current statistics on the money supply.)

Del Mar, A., *The Science of Money*, Bell, London, 1885.

Graham, F. D., and Whittlesey, C. R., *Golden Avalanche*, Princeton University Press, Princeton, 1939.

Robertson, D. H., *Money*, Harcourt, Brace, New York, 1929.

CHAPTER 3

Debt and Credit

At first glance this chapter may appear to be a digression from the main purpose of this section of the book, which is to explain the behavior of the money supply and the functioning of our principal monetary institutions: the Treasury, the Federal Reserve System, and the commercial banking system. In fact, however, we can understand the functioning of our monetary institutions only if we understand the nature and functions of debt or credit and the instruments representing them. For example, we have already found that our money supply is composed of those particular types of debt that have somehow come to be generally acceptable as a means of payment. Moreover, we shall find later that our monetary institutions create or destroy money largely by purchasing or selling types of debt which are not themselves money. With little inaccuracy these institutions can be characterized as "dealers in debt" or as "monetizers and demonetizers of debt."

THE NATURE OF CREDIT OR DEBT

Debt and credit are merely the same thing looked at from two different points of view. They are an obligation to pay in the future and, since money is so widely used as a standard of deferred payments, they are usually obligations to pay a fixed sum of money. From the point of view of the person to whom the future payment is to be made the obligation is a credit; it is his claim against another for payment. But from the point of view of the one who is obliged to pay in the future the obligation is a debt. Since debt and credit are but the same thing looked at from different points of view, it is obvious that the amount of debt outstanding at any time is equal to the amount of outstanding credit, and that the amount of each is the sum of existing obligations to pay in the future.

Credit or debt usually originates in economic and financial transactions in which creditors surrender something of value at one point of time in exchange for debtors' promises to pay in the future. We ignore here debts that may arise out of gifts of promises to pay in the future. The "something of value" surrendered may be money, services, goods, or some sort of financial claim such as stocks or bonds. However, the resulting debt is usually payable in money. We are all familiar with the creation of debt by the sale of goods or services "on credit." For example, Mrs. Jones buys groceries, promising to pay at the end of the month. A corporation gets raw materials from its suppliers with the understanding that it will pay at the end of the quarter. Much of the outstanding debt at any time arose from such "extensions of credit" by sellers of goods and services. Most of the rest arose out of money-lending transactions in which creditors surrendered money at one point of time in exchange for promises of debtors to pay later, usually with interest. These money-lending transactions range all the way from the simple case in which Joe lends Bob $5 until payday to the much more complicated one in which a large public utility corporation borrows $500 million, giving in return its bonds, which carry its promise to pay the principal at the end of a stated number of years and to pay interest at 4 percent annually. Thus, it is often said that the creation of credit (or debt) involves the exchange of present goods or purchasing power against future goods or purchasing power, interest being paid by the borrower for the privilege of having the goods or purchasing power sooner.

The Bases of Credit

The ability of any person, business firm, or governmental unit to get credit depends on the potential creditors' faith that the borrower will be both able and willing to pay. The popular statement that "Smith's credit is worth half a million" means he is believed to be both able and willing to pay at least that amount. The statement that "his credit is bad" indicates lack of faith in either his ability or his willingness to pay. In determining an applicant's credit worthiness, credit analysts emphasize the three "C's"—character, capital, and capacity to acquire income. The relative importance of these elements varies from case to case.

Character is a major determinant of a debtor's ability to obtain credit. Creditors analyze carefully an applicant's past record in meeting his obligations, his general reputation for honesty, his police record, his likelihood of becoming involved in damage suits of any kind, his marital status, his drinking habits, and any other characteristics or associations that might bear upon his ability or willingness to pay. Anyone who acquires a reputation for paying his debts only when forced by the courts to do so is likely to lose his ability to command credit, no matter how rich he may be.

Credit analysts also scrutinize both the value and character of an applicant's assets, noting especially the probable stability of their value and their liquidity —their ability to be sold for money quickly and without loss of value. Other things being equal, an applicant whose assets have a high stability of value and a high degree of liquidity is more likely to obtain credit easily than one whose assets are less liquid and fluctuate more widely. Since a potential creditor is interested primarily in the applicant's *net capital position*, he investigates the applicant's other debts as well as his assets.

The size of an applicant's future income is another major determinant of his ability to obtain credit. We all know of cases in which credit was extended, even though the borrower lacked capital, on the basis of his expected income. Thus, a man with a steady job may buy on credit, a governmental unit borrows against expected revenue, or a business firm secures credit because of the lenders' faith in the ability of its management to make money. On the other hand, doubt as to an applicant's future income is likely to reduce his ability to obtain credit. A major part of credit is based on the expectation that the debt will be paid out of future income rather than from the sale of assets. This is partly because assets may have little value if they cannot be made to yield an income. For example, a factory or railroad that cannot be made to yield an income may have only a salvage value, whatever may have been its cost of construction.

In most cases an applicant's ability to obtain credit depends on his own credit worthiness as determined by factors such as those already noted. Sometimes, however, one may borrow on the basis of guarantees given by others. A friend endorses Joe's note, promising "to make it good" if Joe fails to pay. A giant corporation guarantees the bonds of its subsidiaries. A bank guarantees payment by one of its customers. The Federal Housing Administration guarantees payment of a home mortgage. We shall find later that there are many ways in which a debtor's friends or relatives, or his bank, or his business associates, or the government can bolster his ability to secure credit by lending their own credit worthiness.

Since debts are promises to pay at some future date, credit worthiness depends upon potential creditors' expectations as to future asset values and income levels. These expectations may fluctuate widely. When, as in a period of prosperity, lenders in general expect future asset values and income levels to remain high and perhaps to rise further, they may be willing to lend liberally. But when, as in depression periods, they become pessimistic and fear falling asset values and shrinking money incomes, they may become less willing to take new debts and may insist on repayment of some of those already outstanding. Such fluctuations in expectations relating to credit worthiness may aggravate fluctuations in income flows in our credit-debt economy, as we shall see later.

Types of Credit or Debt

Though credit or debt can be classified on many bases, we shall mention only four. (1) On the basis of the nature of the debtor. A broad classification on this basis would be: individual debt, business debt, and government debt.

A more detailed classification on this basis could be complex indeed, for almost every type of person and organization in our society incurs debt at one time or another. (2) On the basis of the nature of the creditor. Here, too, a more detailed classification is possible, but we shall mention only credit extended by (debts taken by) individuals, commercial banks, other financial institutions, nonfinancial businesses, and the government. (3) On the basis of the purpose for which the debt was created. *Consumption credit* (or *debt*) is that created in the acquisition of money, goods, or services for consumption purposes. *Production* or productive debt is that created in the acquisition of money, goods, or services to aid in the process of production: to meet payrolls, to purchase inventory, to cover costs of storage and transportation, or to purchase land, buildings, and equipment to be used in production. (4) On the basis of the length of time elapsing between the time the debt is created and the time it is to be retired. On this basis debts are: (a) long-term—over five years, (b) intermediate term—one to five years, (c) short-term—less than a year, or (d) payable on demand.

A cross-classification of debt on these various bases suggests how varied is our debt structure, how complex our creditor-debtor relationships, and how pervasive the use of debt in our society.

THE FUNCTIONS OF DEBT OR CREDIT

Debt does not, despite its widespread use, enjoy unqualified approval. Many people are sympathetic with, even though they do not heed, Shakespeare's admonition, "Neither a borrower nor a lender be." They speak lugubriously of "the burden of debt," refer in unflattering terms to those who "live on credit," and express fears that "the nation will borrow itself into serious trouble." Such attitudes are not solely reflections of puritanism or of opposition to "usury" in all its forms. Too many individuals, business firms, and governments have been guilty of unwise use of this powerful instrument. But instances of its unwise use should not be allowed to obscure the great benefits that debt can yield.

Even debt created for consumption purposes may benefit the debtor. For example, a person may go into debt to secure goods and services during periods of illness or unemployment or to meet urgent extraordinary needs, repaying later with dollars that have less utility to him. In more general terms, the use of consumption debt can enable a person to maximize the usefulness of his income through time. He may borrow to augment his consumption when additional consumption has a high utility to him and repay later when the dollars have less utility to him, either because his income becomes higher or his needs decrease. Or he may save and lend his savings to others when the marginal utility of consumption is low and later collect the debt and spend for consumption when the utility of consumption is higher, either because his income is lower or his needs greater. Personal debt may also be productive. For example, a person may increase both his own net income and his social productivity by borrowing to finance his education. This may raise his lifetime earnings by far more than the amount of the debt and the interest charges on it. The same is true of business borrowing for productive purposes. The borrowing firm is enabled to increase the volume of assets available for its use and may increase its earnings by more than the interest charges. In this way it may increase not only its own profits but also the productivity of the economy.

In later chapters we shall deal at length with the highly important roles of credit or debt in the process of capital formation and in determining the behavior of national money income. At this point we shall discuss these functions in only general terms. At high levels of employment we save large amounts of our national money income. Saving is simply that part of our income which we do not spend for consumption. Thus an act of saving—of not spending for consumption—taken by itself tends to be deflationary. This may be expressed in two ways: (1) It tends to decrease the flow of expenditures for output. The process of income creation and use is a circular flow process. Money received as income is spent back into the market for output, which creates money incomes for producers and their employees; this money income is respent for output, which creates money income for its recipients; and so on. An act of saving—of not spending for consumption—tends to shrink this circular flow. (2) Saving tends to hold down the demand for consumers' goods and to fail to employ in the consumers' goods industries some part of the supply of labor and other productive factors. These factors are freed for other uses, such as the production of capital goods. But saving merely frees factors for other uses; it does not assure that they will actually be used elsewhere. The released factors will be employed elsewhere only if attracted by a sufficient demand for their potential products.

Saving by some members of the community will actually shrink the flow of national money income unless the money saved is injected back into the spending stream by others: unless saving by some is offset by the deficit spending of others. This can occur in three principal ways: (1) By dissaving—by others consuming in excess of their current incomes. In effect, the savers transfer consuming power to those consuming beyond their current incomes. Such transfers frequently involve the creation of debt by the dissavers, though to get the necessary money they may transfer to others some of their existing assets, such as shares of stock or debt claims against others. (2) By government deficit spending—government spending in excess of its current income. This almost always involves a creation of government debt to get the required money. And (3) by spending by business firms to maintain or increase their stock of capital goods—to produce or buy plants, durable equipment, inventories, and so on.

Business firms have two principal ways of getting the money required for these expenditures: (1) By issuing ownership claims against themselves. Though many business expenditures are financed in this way, many savers are unwilling to assume the risks involved in becoming owners of business, even the part ownership involved in buying shares of corporate stock. (2) By creating and selling debt claims against themselves. They borrow the money to produce or buy the capital goods. Thus the creation of capital goods has as its necessary counterpart the creation of financial claims, and these are either ownership claims or debt claims.

We find, in short, that we can achieve and maintain a level of national money income consistent with practically full employment and relatively stable price levels only if the saving by some members of the community out of that level of income is offset by the deficit spending by other individuals, governmental units, and business firms. This requires the transfer of money savings from savers to spenders. Such transfers can be achieved through the creation of ownership claims or debt claims. Roughly speaking, debt should grow each year by an amount equal to the amount saved out of a full-employment-without-inflation level of national money income minus the amount of saving transferred through the creation of new ownership claims. If debt grows less rapidly than this, the flow of national money income will fall and the economy will be depressed. If it grows more rapidly, the flow of national money income will rise faster than real output and inflation will probably result.

This analysis will be elaborated and refined later, but what has already been said should suggest the varied and crucial roles of credit or debt in our economy.

CREDIT OR DEBT INSTRUMENTS

By a credit or debt instrument we mean a "thing" evidencing the existence and terms of a debt. It indicates the identity of the debtor, the amount of the debt it represents, and arrangements as to maturity, interest rates, and so on. More or less formal evidences of debt are highly useful even when the original creditor intends to hold the debt claim throughout its life and to collect it himself at its maturity. Such instruments can obviate controversy over the existence, amounts, and terms of a debt and serve as valuable evidence if legal action becomes necessary. These instruments greatly enhance the transferability or marketability of debt claims. Many lenders do not want to commit themselves to hold a debt claim throughout its life. They fear that in the meantime they will need money for their own use or they wish to be able to sell the particular claim and buy others as circumstances change. Debt claims may be hard to sell in the first place, or can be sold only at high interest rates, if they are not expected to be transferable quickly and at low cost. Even a short-term debt claim may have numerous holders during its life. Many types of debt instruments are so designed as to maximize their salability, and laws to facilitate this have been evolved.

Not all outstanding credit or debt is evidenced by a written contract. We have all been parties to "parole credit" transactions in which the agreement to pay was purely oral. Such arrangements have their disadvantages even when the sums are small and the principals are close friends or business associates. They are usually quite unsatisfactory in transactions involving large sums and less intimate relationships. A large volume of debt is evidenced only by "book accounts" or "book credits." Bank deposits fall in this category; the bank's debts to depositors are evidenced by entries on the bank's books, though depositors have such evidence as their deposit slips and canceled checks. Sellers of goods and services also use entries in their books as evidence of their debt claims. Thus, a college student's debt to his tailor is usually evidenced only by an entry in the tailor's ledger; the tailor's debt to his supplier of woolens is evidenced only by an entry in the supplier's books; and so on. Such debt claims are sometimes sold by creditors, but they are usually less salable than pieces of paper clearly evidencing the debtor's unconditional obligation to pay.

Credit instruments can be sold whether they are *nonnegotiable* or *negotiable*. Nonnegotiable credit instruments are those whose rights are governed by the general common and statute laws of contract, whereas negotiable instruments enjoy special advantages conferred by the negotiable instruments laws.[1]

Under the general common and statute laws of contract that govern nonnegotiable instruments, title is transferred from one owner to another by assignment only.

In assignment, only the assignor's title is transferred, so that the assignee gets only such title as his assignor possessed, and any defense existing at the time of the assignment, whether by reason of breach of warranty, set-off, recoupment, or fraud in the inducement, can still be used against the assignee.

At the present day, an assignee takes no better right or title than his assignor possessed; he is said "to stand in the shoes of his assignor" and is subject to all defenses which the obligor possessed against the assignor.[2]

For these reasons nonnegotiable paper should be purchased only with full knowledge of the various conditions surrounding its creation. Some of the dangers involved in purchasing nonnegotiable paper can be indicated by an example. Suppose that Smith buys a car from the Ajax Motors Company, giving in return his written but nonnegotiable promise to pay $1000 at the

---

[1] For a good discussion of this general subject, see C. N. Hulvey, *Commercial Law*, Macmillan, New York, 1930, chap. 9.

[2] *Ibid.*, pp. 173–174.

end of three months. Suppose also that this paper is transferred by assignment from the Ajax Motors Company to Reilly, who then transfers it by assignment to Johnson. As holder of the paper, Johnson runs several risks. In the first place, Smith may legally refuse to pay him, claiming that the car was not as warranted, that the Ajax Motors Company owed him $500 that should be offset against his debt, or that he was fraudulently induced to issue the promise to pay. In short, Smith may refuse to pay Johnson for any of the reasons that would have excused him from making full payment to the Ajax Motors Company. In the second place, Johnson runs the risk that Reilly had found or stolen the note, for Johnson gets no better title to it than Reilly had.

It was for reasons of this sort that, even as early as the Middle Ages, merchants, traders, financiers, and others dealing in credit found nonnegotiable paper inconvenient. To facilitate their operations they needed credit instruments that were unconditional obligations to pay and that could be freely bought and sold without the usual doubts concerning title. To satisfy this need for easy negotiability a new branch of law evolved; it culminated in the negotiable instruments laws. Credit instruments that meet the specifications of these negotiable instruments laws are known as negotiable instruments.

To be negotiable, an instrument must meet the following requirements:

1. It must be in writing.
2. It must be signed by the maker or drawer.
3. It must be an unconditional promise or order to pay a certain sum of money.
4. It must be payable on demand or at a fixed or determinable future date.
5. It must be payable to order or to bearer.

Most of these requirements are self-explanatory. Instruments that meet them are written and signed unconditional promises or orders to pay a fixed sum of money at a fixed or determinable future time. Special attention should be given to the terms "bearer" and "order," for paper failing to contain at least one of them is not negotiable. An instrument promising or ordering payment to "bearer" or to "John Smith or bearer" is payable to any "holder in due course." An instrument promising or ordering payment to "John Smith or order" or "to the order of John Smith" is payable either to John Smith or to anyone to whom he transfers title by endorsement. In fact, it becomes payable to bearer if John Smith endorses it in blank by signing his name.

A *holder in due course* of a negotiable instrument has a title to the instrument that is nearly perfect. Such a holder in due course is one who has taken the instrument under the following conditions:

1. The instrument is complete and regular upon its face.
2. He became the holder of it before it was overdue, and without notice that it had previously been dishonored, if such was the fact.

3. He took it in good faith and for value.
4. At the time it was negotiated to him he had no notice of any infirmity in the instrument or defect in the title of the person negotiating it.

A holder in due course not only has a nearly perfect title to the negotiable instrument, but is also free from all debtor's defenses mentioned above in connection with nonnegotiable instruments. The debtor retains only the defense that the instrument never had a legal existence because of such reasons as forgery, alteration, or infancy of the maker.

Title to negotiable instruments is transferred not by assignment but by *endorsement*. Such instruments payable to bearer require no endorsement for negotiability, though a buyer may, of course, ask for one. It is important to note that one who gives an unqualified endorsement to a negotiable instrument in effect warrants that:

1. The instrument is genuine and in all respects valid.
2. He has good title to it.
3. He has no knowledge of any fact that would impair the validity of the instrument or render it valueless.
4. If on due presentment it is dishonored by the debtor, the endorser will pay the holder or any subsequent endorser who may be compelled to pay it.[3]

There are three general classes of unqualified endorsements: (1) blank endorsement, (2) endorsement to a specified person or order, and (3) restrictive endorsement. To illustrate each, let us take the case of a promise or order to "pay to John Smith or order." If Smith endorses it in blank, merely signing "John Smith," the instrument is in effect made payable to bearer; it becomes freely negotiable without further endorsement. If he endorses it by writing "Pay to Sam Jones" or "Pay to Sam Jones or order" and signs his name, the instrument is not further negotiable without endorsement by Sam Jones. If he writes "Pay only to Sam Jones" and signs his name, the instrument at this point loses its negotiability.

Owing to the ease of transferring title by endorsement and the ample protection given their holders in due course, negotiable instruments are easily and widely bought, sold, and exchanged for each other.

Credit instruments are divided into two broad classes: (1) promissory notes, and (2) bills of exchange, or drafts. Both nonnegotiable and negotiable credit instruments fall into these two categories, but we shall discuss here only those that meet the requirements of the negotiable instruments laws.

Promissory Notes. A promissory note is an unconditional statement in writing made by one person to another and signed by the maker, promising

[3] We shall not discuss qualified endorsements here. On this subject, see *ibid.*, pp. 174–180.

to pay on demand, or at a fixed or determinable time in the future, a stated sum of money to order or to bearer. When a note is drawn to the maker's own order, it is not complete until endorsed by him. Several aspects of this definition should be noted carefully.

1. The promise to pay must be in writing.
2. The promise to pay must be unconditional.
3. The amount to be paid must be certain in terms of money.
4. The note must be payable on demand, at a fixed time, or at a determinable time.
5. The note must be payable to bearer or to the order of a specified person.

All these conditions must be met if the note is to be negotiable.

There are at least two parties to a promissory note: the *maker* or *payer*, and the *payee*. In some instances, the maker and the payee are the same person,

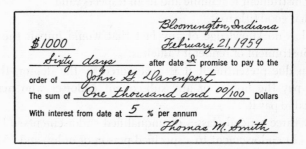

$1000   *Bloomington, Indiana*
                         February 21, 1959
Sixty days _____ after date *I* promise to pay to the
order of _____ *John G. Davenport* _____
The sum of _____ *One thousand and 00/100* _____ Dollars
With interest from date at *5* % per annum
                         Thomas M. Smith

FIG. 1.   A Simple Negotiable Promissory Note.

the maker promising to pay to himself or order and then endorsing the note so that it becomes negotiable. The payee may be "bearer" or a specified person. Subsequent purchasers of the note become involved as holders and often as endorsers. Fig. 1 shows the general form of a simple promissory note. Though all negotiable promissory notes contain these elements, they vary greatly in other respects. They differ as to the time elapsing before maturity; some mature only after a long period of years, some in a year, some in a few months or weeks, and some are payable on demand. Some are secured, others unsecured. Some are issued by corporations, some by governments, some by banks, and so on.

Bills of Exchange, or Drafts.   In contrast to promissory notes, which are promises to pay, bills of exchange or drafts (both are the same) are orders to pay. "A bill of exchange is an unconditional order in writing addressed by one person to another, signed by the person giving it, requiring the person to whom it is addressed to pay on demand or at a fixed or determinable future time a sum certain in money to order or to bearer."[4] There are

---

[4] Section 126 of the Negotiable Instruments Law.

three parties to a draft: the *drawer,* or the one who orders payment; the *drawee,* or the one who is ordered to pay; and the *payee,* or the one to whom payment is ordered to be made. In most cases the three parties are different persons; thus, Jones (the drawer) may order Smith (the drawee) to pay to the order of Thompson (the payee). In other cases only two persons are involved, the drawer and the payee being the same. Thus, Jones may order Smith to pay to the order of Jones. In a few cases drawer, drawee, and payee are the same person. Thus Jones may order himself to pay himself or order and then make the draft negotiable by endorsing it.

Drafts or bills of exchange are classified on several bases, of which we shall explore only a few of the most important. One basis for classifying drafts or bills is the type of drawee involved. Thus, an order on a bank to pay is a *bank draft* or *bank bill,* or a *banker's draft* or *banker's bill.* An order to any other type of drawee to pay is a *trade draft* or *trade bill.*

Drafts or bills are also classified on the basis of the amount of time elapsing before payment is to be made. A draft ordering payment "on demand" or

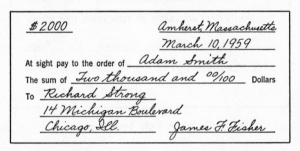

FIG. 2. A Simple Sight or Demand Trade Draft.

"at sight" is known as a *sight draft* or *sight bill,* or a *demand draft* or *demand bill.* A draft ordering payment after a lapse of time is known as a *time draft* or *time bill.* Time drafts fix the time of payment in three general ways. Some state a specific date of payment in the future. Others accomplish the same thing by requiring payment a stipulated number of days after the date of drawing the draft. Still others require payment a certain number of days "after sight," that is, after the bill is presented to the drawee. This last method is largely a legacy of the period when both land and water transportation were so irregular as to make forecasts of dates of arrival unreliable.

Before discussing time drafts let us look at the form and use of sight or demand drafts. In the sight trade draft shown in Fig. 2, the drawer (Fisher) ordered the drawee (Strong) to pay to the order of the payee (Smith) $2000 at sight. This draft may have had any one of several purposes. It may have been used to clear debts. If Fisher owed Smith $2000 and Strong owed Fisher the same amount, all the debts could be cleared by having Strong pay Smith or his order. The draft could have been to force Strong to pay for supplies before he received title to them. For example, Fisher may have shipped maple syrup to Strong by Smith's truck and ordered payment before delivery of title. Such a draft can also be used as a means of "putting pressure" on a slow-paying debtor. Suppose, for example, that Strong has bought $2000 worth of syrup from Fisher on book credit and has refused to pay or has blithely ignored numerous requests for payment. By drawing a draft on Strong and then routing it through Strong's bank for collection, Fisher can put Strong in the position of having to pay or of letting his bank discover his untrustworthiness. This use of trade bills for "dunning" purposes has reduced their popularity in this country.

The appearance and use of a sight bank draft (Fig. 3) should be familiar to everyone, for bank checks belong in this category.

The check shown in Fig. 3 is of the type that might be drawn upon a bank

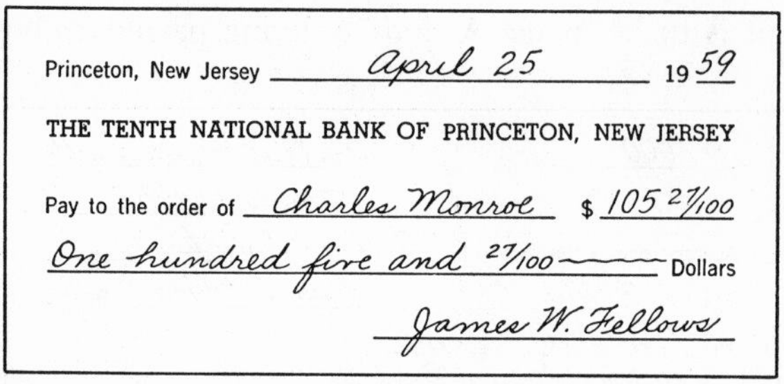

Princeton, New Jersey _____ *April 25* _____ 19*59*

THE TENTH NATIONAL BANK OF PRINCETON, NEW JERSEY

Pay to the order of _*Charles Monroe*_ $ *105 27/100*

One hundred five and *27/100* ———— Dollars

James W. Fellows

FIG. 3.   A Sight Bank Draft.

by one of its depositors. Such checks may be unacceptable in some cases because of doubt that the drawer has a deposit account at the bank or that he will have sufficient deposits to cover the check when it is presented. Other types of instruments have been developed to obviate these difficulties. One is the *certified check*. This works as follows: the depositor draws a check on his bank and presents it to an appropriate official of the bank for certification. When the official stamps "certified" on the check and signs his name he attests, in effect, that a sufficient amount of the depositor's account has been set aside to cover the check. About the same thing could be accomplished by the use of a *cashier's check*. In this case the depositor writes a check ordering the bank to pay a stipulated amount out of his account to the bank itself. The cashier or another authorized official of the bank then writes a draft ordering the bank to pay the payee. Thus the actual payment is made with an order by a banker on a bank rather than an order by a depositor on a bank. But the final results are the same: the payer loses a deposit claim and the payee gains one. Orders by bankers on banks are used to make a very large volume of payments. Thus an officer of a Dallas bank may order his own bank to pay, either to make payments for the bank's own account or to pay for the account of a customer. Or he may draw an order on a New York bank with which his bank has a deposit account. Or he may draw an order on a London bank with which his bank or his New York correspondent bank has a deposit account. Though these orders to pay are most commonly communicated by written orders similar to the ordinary check, they are sometimes transmitted by telegraph or cable.

Time drafts (or *bills*), those payable only after a lapse of time, are either *time trade drafts* (or *bills*), or *time bank drafts* (or *bills*), depending on the type of drawee involved.

It is important to note that a draft, as such, is only an order to pay; it is not

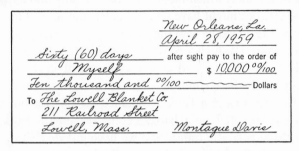

FIG. 4.   A Time Trade Draft or Bill.

an obligation of the drawee to pay. In fact, you can draw a draft on any person or firm, but the mere drawing of the draft does not obligate the drawee to pay. The order to pay can be converted into a binding unconditional obligation to pay through *acceptance* by the drawee. The drawee *accepts* the order to pay by writing on either the face or the back of the draft the word "accepted" and by affixing his signature and the date of acceptance. Thus, the drawee may accept the draft in Fig. 4 by writing on it:

> Accepted, May 4, 1959
> The Lowell Blanket Company
> By: Cabot L. Lawrence, Treasurer

By this act the drawee transforms the trade bill into a *trade acceptance*, which is his unconditional obligation to pay Davis or his order $10,000 60 days after the date of acceptance.

Acceptances are widely used in finance and trade though they are not as popular in the United States as in some foreign countries. To illustrate their use in financing trade, let us follow through a specific transaction. Our example will be simpler than many actual transactions. Suppose that the Lowell Blanket Company purchases $10,000 worth of wool from Montague Davis, a wool merchant in New Orleans. The buyer does not wish to pay until 60 days after receiving the wool. The seller does not wish to surrender title to the wool until he has received from the buyer a negotiable unconditional obligation to pay. The problem may be solved somewhat as follows. Davis draws on the Lowell Blanket Company the draft shown in Fig. 4, ordering it to pay to him or his order $10,000 60 days after sight. He also arranges that the Lowell Company shall not gain title to the wool until it accepts the draft. When the draft is accepted the Lowell Company gets the wool but does not have to pay until 60 days later. Davis has acquired an unconditional debt claim, which he can sell in the market for face value less interest at the prevailing rate for 60 days. Who pays this interest? It was probably taken into account in fixing the price of the wool. Credit to finance this transaction was provided by the holder of the acceptance, which might be a bank or any other type of lender. In fact, the acceptance might have several holders during its life, each supplying credit during the period he held the paper.

A trade acceptance is a highly convenient and negotiable instrument when the drawee is widely known and enjoys an excellent credit standing. It is less satisfactory when these conditions are not met. For such reasons buyers and sellers often try to use a bank acceptance, which is a bill of exchange drawn upon and accepted by a bank. Let us see how a bank acceptance could be used to finance the transaction we have just described. The Lowell Company may go to the National Shawmut Bank of Boston to secure a *letter of credit*. This letter of credit will contain the bank's promise to accept the draft drawn on it in accordance with an agreement concerning the amount

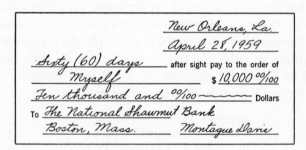

FIG. 5.   A Time Bank Draft.

of the draft, the time of shipping the wool, and so on. The bank will issue the letter of credit only if it is satisfied that the Lowell Company will place in its hands the required amount of money before the draft matures. The letter of credit will be sent to Davis. He will then draw against the National Shawmut Bank a draft similar to that in Fig. 5, and will arrange that the bank shall not get title to the wool until it accepts the draft. When the bank has accepted the draft and received title to the wool, it will turn the latter over to the Lowell Company. Davis now has an unconditional debt claim against a bank of impeccable credit standing, a claim that is readily salable in the market. It should be noted that the bank is obligated to pay whether or not the Lowell Company keeps its promise to provide the money before the acceptance matures.

It is interesting to note the role played by the National Shawmut Bank in this transaction. At no time did it lend money unless, of course, the Lowell Company failed to meet its obligation or the bank elected to buy and hold the claim against itself. Instead, it substituted its credit standing for that of the Lowell Company, thereby increasing the ability of the textile firm to secure credit from other lenders. For this it received a small *acceptance fee*.

In the following chapters we shall refer frequently to various points that have been brought out with respect to credit, debt, and credit or debt instruments. We shall pay special attention to: (1) those specific types of debts that we call money because they have come to be generally acceptable in payments, (2) demand drafts on banks, which are used to transfer deposit claims on banks from payers to payees, (3) the many types of debt instruments that are not themselves money but are bought and sold by our monetary institutions in the process of creating and destroying money, and (4) the role of debts in transferring money savings from savers to spenders, in facilitating the process of capital formation, and in influencing the level of national money income.

INTEREST

Debts that are themselves money usually do not yield interest. Most others do. Debtors are ordinarily required to pay not only the amount they received when they borrowed but also something in addition. In some cases interest rates are easy to state and compute. For example, if Jones borrows $100 and repays $106 a year later, we can say that the interest rate is 6 percent per year. The $6 of "something in addition" is 6 percent of the amount received by the borrower. The rate of interest is almost always stated on an annual basis. We shall see later that the computation of effective interest rates or yields can be highly complicated in some cases.

The Variety of Interest Rates

At various times we shall refer to "the" interest rate, which suggests that there is but one interest rate in a given market at a given time. This is a useful device making for simplicity and brevity of exposition. But we should always remember that this is an oversimplification, and one that can be dangerous for our analysis. The fact is that at any point of time there is not just one interest rate but a complex of rates in the market and that these can differ widely. Moreover, these various rates may not move in a parallel manner through time, though they usually move in the same direction.

How can such differences in rates persist? Why do not lenders shift their funds from debts with low yields to those with higher yields until all yield differentials have been wiped out? A part of the answer may be found in imperfections in the credit market, which inhibit the mobility of loan funds from one branch of the market to another. Some of the most important of these are lack of knowledge by lenders or borrowers, legal limitations on the types of loans that can be made by some financial institutions, differing degrees of monopoly power in the various branches of the market, and so on. The actual structure of rates cannot be fully understood without reference to such imperfections. But these do not by any means provide a full explanation of the variety of yields; yields would still differ even if the credit market were perfectly competitive with credit perfectly mobile. This is because the debts themselves have such differing characteristics.

Some of the most important factors that would cause yields to differ even in a perfectly competitive market are the following: (1) Differences in costs of administration per dollar of loan per year. Interest charges usually include costs of investigating the credit worthiness of the applicant, of holding the loan, and of collecting principal and interest. On some loans these costs are very low per dollar per year. For example, the administrative cost per dollar on a very large loan to a business firm whose credit standing need not be investigated may be almost negligible. On the other hand, such costs per dollar of loan per year may be very high on small installment loans to a consumer where the applicant's credit standing must be investigated and interest and principal collected in weekly or monthly installments. (2) Differences in risk. This risk is of two types. The first is the risk that the debtor will fail to pay principal and interest. Different debts of the same debtor may differ in degree of risk. One debt may have prior claim on assets and income or be amply secured by pledged collateral. Another may be only a general claim against the debtor's assets and income and may be payable only after other debt claims have been satisfied. Risks obviously vary widely among different debtors. A loan to the United States government is far less risky than one to a struggling business firm whose future is uncertain. The second type of risk is often called "the market risk"—the risk that the market value of the debt claim will change because of changes in the level of interest rates in the market. Even if there is no change in expectations relative to a debtor's willingness and ability to pay a debt, the market value of the obligation will fall if interest rates rise, or its market value will rise if interest rates fall. In general, debt obligations with a long maturity are subject to wider fluctuations in market value than are those that are short term, as we shall see later. (3) Differences in liquidity. Because of their own nature and the organization of the market, some debts can be sold quickly, at very small cost, and with little effect on price. Others are far less liquid. For example, a short-term obligation of the United States government can be sold almost instantaneously in the well-organized market, dealers' margins are small, and rather large amounts may be sold with little effect on price. But even the safest conventional home mortgages do not enjoy these advantages. (4) Differences in taxability. For example, the fact that income yielded by securities issued by states and municipalities is exempt from the federal income tax tends to enable these obligations to be sold at lower yield rates.

Because of such differences as these, we should expect to find a variety of yields on different debts in the market at any point of time. A calculating lender thoroughly familiar with all market opportunities would be willing to take lower gross yields on some debts than on others.

Yield Rates and Market Values

We return now to two points raised earlier: the calculation of effective interest rates or yields and the relationship between the rate of yield and the market value of a debt obligation.

We can best approach the problem of calculating effective interest rates by distinguishing three different types of "yield." The first is the *nominal yield*, which is simply the yield stated on the face of the obligation. Thus, a note promising to pay $100 at the end of a year with interest at 3 percent has a nominal yield of 3 percent. A bond promising to pay $1000 at the end of ten years and $30 at the end of each year also has a nominal yield of 3 percent. The nominal yield is of importance primarily in fixing the *dollar amount* of interest to be paid each year. The nominal yield and the effective rate of interest will be the same only if the market value of the debt is equal to its par or stated value, and this may not occur. In fact, the debt may not even have been sold initially at its par or stated value. For example, when the debtor originally issued his promise to pay $1000 at the end of ten years and $30 of interest at the end of each year, interest rates in the market on comparable obligations may have been below 3 percent so that the bond could be sold above par, say for $1050. Or interest rates on comparable obligations may have been well above 3 percent so that he had to sell the bond below par, say for $950. In any case, the market value after issue can deviate from par value.

Another type of yield is the *current yield*. This is simply the dollar amount of interest per year divided by the current market price of the obligation. If the bond described above has a market value of $950, its current yield is $\frac{$30}{$950}$, or 3.15 percent. If its market price is $1050, its current yield is $\frac{$30}{$1050}$, or 2.85 percent. Though current yield is more meaningful than nominal yield, it does not measure accurately the average *net* return per year to be gained if the obligation is purchased at its current market price and held to maturity. This is best reflected by *yield to maturity*, which takes into consideration current market value, annual interest receipts, and the relationship between current market value and the value at which the debt will be paid off at maturity. The general nature of this measure can be explained most easily by an example using simple interest rather than compound interest. Suppose that one buys the 10-year bond described above at $950. He will receive not only $30 a year in interest but also a capital appreciation of $50 over the 10-year period, or an average of $5 per year. Thus, his average return per year will be $35 and his average yield to maturity will be $\frac{\$35}{\$950}$, or 3.68 percent. Suppose, however, that the market price of the 10-year bond is $1050. In such a case the buyer must recognize that his average net return will not be $30 a year; from this he must deduct an average of $5 per year because he paid $1050 for the debt and will collect only $1000 at maturity. Thus his average net return per year will be only $25, and the average yield to maturity will be $\frac{\$25}{\$1050}$, or 2.38 percent. This is only approximate because we used simple interest; in practice buyers would use compound interest. We shall do this later.[5]

When we refer hereafter to yields, to effective interest rates, or simply to interest rates, we shall mean rates of yield to maturity because that is the best measure of the rate of return on debt obligations at any time.

We can now deal with the relationship at any point of time between yield rates and the capital value (market value) of a debt obligation or any other income-yielding asset. The present capital value of such an asset is arrived at by a process of *capitalization*, by which we mean discounting the expected flow of money receipts. Discounting means taking out interest in advance. A buyer who paid for an obligation the full amount of its future dollar returns would receive no net interest at all. He usually will not buy it unless the purchase price is such that the yield on the purchase price will be as great as that available to him on other comparable obligations. Of course, he would like to buy at a lower price but this is likely to be prevented by competition from other purchasers.

The discounting process is easiest to understand when only simple interest or discount is involved. Suppose that, when the market yield on this class of paper is 3 percent, buyers are offered a promise to pay $1030 one year later. Each buyer will reason as follows: this piece of paper is of value today only because it represents a claim against money receivable in the future. I will buy it only at such a price that I will receive the going rate of return on my money, and this "price" is that amount which, if put out at the prevailing yield rate, would be worth $1030 a year hence. There is some amount of

---

[5] This example assumes that the debtor does not have the option of paying off the debt before maturity. If the issuer has the option of "calling" it before maturity at some stated price, the buyer should also compute "yield to call date" to determine what his rate of net return will be if the security is called.

money (P) which, if put out at the current rate of yield (i) on this type of obligation, will be worth $1030 a year later. Thus

$$P(1 + i) = \$1030$$

or

$$P = \frac{\$1030}{1 + i}$$

If $i = .03$, the formula becomes

$$P = \frac{\$1030}{1.03} = \$1000$$

The present value of $1030 receivable a year hence will be lower if yield rates are higher, and higher if yield rates are lower. For example, if the yield rate is 4 percent the formula becomes

$$P = \frac{\$1030}{1.04} = \$990.38$$

If, however, the yield rate is 2 percent,

$$P = \frac{\$1030}{1.02} = \$1009.80$$

The general formula for simple discount is $P = \dfrac{A}{1 + i}$, where P is the present value, A is the dollar amount receivable at the end of the interest period, and i is the rate of interest for that period stated in hundredths, such as .02 or .04.[6]

The process of arriving at a present capital value for a longer-term obligation, such as the bond described above, is based on the same principle but is a bit more complicated, for two reasons. First, the obligation is to make a number of payments through time rather than a single payment; second, it involves compound interest or discount. Each prospective buyer will reason as follows: this obligation is of value only because it represents a claim against $30 at the end of each of the next ten years and $1000 at the end of the 10-year period. I will buy it only at such a price that I will receive the going rate of return on my money. The price (P) is the sum of the discounted values of all the individual payments expected in the future. For example, there is some amount of money (P_1) which, if put out at the prevailing yield rate, would be worth $30 a year hence. That is, $P_1(1 + i) = \$30$, or $P_1 = \dfrac{\$30}{1 + i}$. There is another smaller amount of money (P_2) which, if put out at compound interest at the prevailing rate, would be worth $30 at the end of 2 years. Compound interest is used because during the second year I would re-

[6] Here and later we shall assume that the interest period is one year and that the interest rate is the rate per year. We shall also assume that interest is compounded annually. In some cases the interest period is less than a year. For example, it may be six months. In such cases the i in our formula will be the interest rate for half a year and the number of interest periods will be twice as large as it would be if the interest period were one year.

ceive interest on the first year's interest. That is, $P_2(1 + i)^2 = \$30$, or $P_2 = \dfrac{\$30}{(1 + i)^2}$. Similarly, there is a yet smaller amount of money (P_3) which, if put out at compound interest, would be worth $30 at the end of 3 years. $P_3(1 + i)^3 = \$30$, or $P_3 = \dfrac{\$30}{(1 + i)^3}$. The present values of the other interest payments can be arrived at in the same way. There remains the $1000 of principal payable at the end of 10 years. Its present value is $\dfrac{\$1000}{(1 + i)^{10}}$. The present value of the bond is the sum of the present values of the various payments to be received on it.

The general formula for arriving at present capital value by discounting is:

$$P = \frac{A_1}{1 + i} + \frac{A_2}{(1 + i)^2} + \frac{A_3}{(1 + i)^3} + \cdots\cdots\cdots + \frac{A_n}{(1 + i)^n} + \frac{F}{(1 + i)^n}$$

where P is the present value, the A's are the dollar amounts receivable at the ends of the various interest periods, F is the amount of the principal repayment, i is the rate of discount, and n is the number of interest periods. For-

TABLE 5.   Discounting and Present Values

End of Year	Formula	Values of Col. 1 at Interest Rates of:			Present Values[a] of $30 at End of Indicated Years at Discount Rate of:		
		2%	3%	4%	2%	3%	4%
	(Col. 1)	(Col. 2)	(Col. 3)	(Col. 4)	(Col. 5)	(Col. 6)	(Col. 7)
1	$(1 + i)$	1.0200	1.0300	1.0400	$ 29.412	$ 29.126	$ 28.846
2	$(1 + i)^2$	1.0404	1.0609	1.0816	28.835	28.278	27.737
3	$(1 + i)^3$	1.0612	1.0927	1.1249	28.270	27.454	26.670
4	$(1 + i)^4$	1.0824	1.1255	1.1699	27.715	26.655	25.644
5	$(1 + i)^5$	1.1041	1.1593	1.2167	27.172	25.878	24.658
6	$(1 + i)^6$	1.1262	1.1941	1.2653	26.639	25.124	23.709
7	$(1 + i)^7$	1.1487	1.2299	1.3159	26.117	24.393	22.798
8	$(1 + i)^8$	1.1717	1.2668	1.3686	25.605	23.682	21.921
9	$(1 + i)^9$	1.1951	1.3048	1.4153	25.103	22.992	21.197
10	$(1 + i)^{10}$	1.2190	1.3439	1.4719	24.610	22.323	20.382
Subtotal					$ 269.48	$ 255.90	$243.56
Present value of $1000 receivable at the end of 10 years					820.35	744.10	679.38
Total					$1089.83	$1000.00	$922.94

[a] The values in Columns 5, 6, and 7 are arrived at by dividing $30 by the numbers shown in Columns 2, 3, and 4 respectively.

tunately, each potential buyer need not solve such equations for himself; bond tables, easily available, have done this for him.

Columns 5, 6, and 7 of Table 5 show the present value of the bond at discount rates of 2, 3, and 4 percent. It will be worth $1000.00 if the rate is 3 percent, only $922.94 if the rate is 4 percent, and $1089.83 if the rate is 2 percent.

One special case is worth noting because of its simplicity: the case of an obligation to pay fixed annual amounts in perpetuity. In this case the formula above becomes simply

$$P = \frac{A}{i}$$

Thus, the present value of the right to receive $30 a year in perpetuity becomes:

1. If the discount rate is 3 percent, $P = \dfrac{\$30}{.03} = \$1000$

2. If the discount rate is 2 percent, $P = \dfrac{\$30}{.02} = \$1500$

3. If the discount rate is 4 percent, $P = \dfrac{\$30}{.04} = \$750$

It is important to note that the longer the maturity of an obligation, the greater is the effect of any given change of market rates of interest on its present value. This is illustrated by the following examples.

	Present Value if Discounted at		
	3%	2%	4%
An obligation to pay $1030 at the end of 1 year	$1000.00	$1009.80	$990.38
An obligation to pay $30 annually for 10 years and $1000 at the end of 10 years	1000.00	1089.83	922.91
An obligation to pay $30 a year in perpetuity	1000.00	1500.00	750.00

CONCLUSIONS

Several of our findings with respect to yields and market prices of debt obligations will be useful to our later analysis.

1. The wide variety of debts in the market and differences in their yields pose policy problems to commercial banks and all other dealers in these obligations. Such investors must constantly weigh differences in yields against differences in such attributes as costs of administration, risks, liquidity, and taxability. To get higher yields they must usually take debts whose other characteristics are less desirable; to get claims whose other attributes are more favorable they must usually take lower yields.

2. As we discuss periods of "tight money" and "easy money" it will be useful to remember that rising interest rates are reflected in declining prices of outstanding debt obligations and that falling interest rates are reflected in rising prices of these obligations. As interest rates rise, newly issued obligations are likely to carry increased nominal yields. For example, the stated interest on new bonds may rise from 3½ to 4 percent. Outstanding obligations whose nominal yield is fixed by contract can become equally attractive only if their prices fall. The opposite occurs in periods of falling interest rates.

Nominal rates on new issues fall; outstanding obligations whose dollar returns are fixed by contract rise in price.

3. The fact that any given change in interest rates affects the prices of long-term obligations more than the prices of shorter-term obligations should be remembered for at least two reasons.

In the first place, it helps to explain why some lenders, such as commercial banks, who want to avoid decreases in the value of their assets, tend to confine their loans to short term. Though they may buy some long-term obligations, they tend to keep them to a small part of their total holdings, especially when they fear that interest rates may rise. In the second place, this fact helps to explain why yields on short-term debts tend to fluctuate more widely than yields on longer-term obligations, especially when the rise or fall of rates is expected to be only temporary. Consider the case in which there is a large excess supply of loan funds but this situation is not expected to be permanent. Lenders may make their funds available at very low rates on short-term loans. The commitment is for only a few months and any subsequent rise of rates would decrease but little the market values of these short obligations. But they would not lend at such low rates for long periods, such as 10 or 20 years. They would not want to be committed to such low rates for so long a period. Moreover, a subsequent rise of rates might lower the market prices of long-term obligations so much as to offset interest receipts for several years.

On the other hand, consider a case in which there is a large excess demand for loan funds relative to the supply but this condition is expected to be temporary. If lenders lend for short terms they will have the advantage of high rates for only so long as market yields are high. But if they lend long term they will have the advantage of high rates for all the years covered by the debt contract. This provides an opportunity for capital gains as interest rates decline later. For these reasons loanable funds are likely to be divided between short-term and long-term loans in such a way as to cause short-term rates to rise more than long-term rates in periods of credit tightness.

This analysis is applicable when the fall or rise of rates is expected to be short lived. It may not be valid if investors expect the initial decline or rise of rates to be followed by still further movements in the same direction.

SELECTED READINGS

Bigelow, M. M., *Law of Bills, Notes and Checks*, Little, Brown, Boston, 3d ed., 1928.

Dewing, A. S., *The Financial Policy of Corporations*, Ronald, New York, 5th ed., 1953.

Graham, B., and Dodd, D. L., *Security Analysis*, McGraw-Hill, New York, 3d ed., 1951.

Green, T. F., Jr., *Practical Summary of Negotiable Instruments*, Longmans, Green, New York, 1938.

CHAPTER 4
The Commercial Banking System

We return now to the central subject of this section of the book, our monetary institutions and the processes through which they create and destroy money. We shall first concentrate our attention on commercial banks, whose debts in the form of checking deposits make up about three quarters of our money supply and whose operations account directly for the major part of fluctuations of the money supply through time. However, we should remember that the functioning of commercial banks is closely intertwined with that of the other two sets of monetary institutions, the United States Treasury and the Federal Reserve System, and especially the latter. The nature of these interrelationships will become clear as we go along.

THE COMPOSITION OF THE AMERICAN COMMERCIAL BANKING SYSTEM

Our commercial banking system is made up of some 13,500 commercial banking corporations. These differ in many respects. In size they range all the way from the huge Bank of America with assets of more than $10 billion down to little banks with less than a million of assets. Some 11,600 are "unit" banks, each operating only a single banking office. About 1900 are "branch" banks, operating a total of 9900 banking offices. Some 4600 are called national banks because they operate under charters granted by the federal government. About 8900 operate under charters granted by the various states. All the national banks and about 1800 of the state-chartered banks are members of the Federal Reserve System. They hold about 85 percent of all commercial bank assets. The other 7100 state-chartered banks, usually called "nonmember banks," are not members of the Federal Reserve.[1] Banks also differ in the types and proportions of loans and securities held, and in many other ways.

[1] These numbers refer to the situation in mid-1958. Owing largely to a merger movement among commercial banks during recent years, the number of commercial banking corporations has been decreasing and the number of branch offices increasing.

Yet despite these differences, all commercial banks have enough in common to justify our dealing with them collectively as a "system." They all create and destroy money and do so in the same general ways.

In the remainder of this chapter we shall deal with the commercial banking system as a whole, largely ignoring relationships among the individual banks and concentrating on the relationships of the commercial banks as a whole with other members of the community. This is because we are here interested in what the commercial banks as a group do, not in which particular bank does it. As a result, we shall make a number of statements about the commercial banking system as a whole that may not be valid if applied to an individual bank. Interrelations among these banks will be discussed later.

SOME PROBLEMS OF NOMENCLATURE

Though these institutions have long been called "commercial" banks, the name is not accurately descriptive and may be misleading. In the first place, it does not indicate accurately the scope of their lending. The name was originally applied because of a belief that they should make only short-term "commercial" loans—loans of not more than a year to traders and merchants to finance the transportation of goods in domestic and international trade and to finance the holding of inventories during the relatively short periods required for their sale. As industry developed, this theory was modified to admit the propriety of short-term lending to producers to meet payrolls, finance inventory, and meet other needs for circulating capital. Commercial banks do indeed make such short-term commercial and industrial loans; in fact, they are by far the largest lenders in this market. But they never confined themselves to such loans, and today they make loans of almost every type: loans on real estate, loans to consumers, loans for purchasing and carrying securities, loans to governments, and many others. They even make some very long-term loans, though these are usually kept to a small part of their total portfolios.

In the second place, the name may obscure the fact that these institutions perform not just one but many types of functions. Most of them are department store banks, not specialty shops. They not only issue and transfer checking deposits but also operate savings departments, which issue time and savings deposits in competition with savings banks and other similar financial institutions. They also operate trust departments, act as agents for their customers in buying and selling securities, underwrite and sell new security issues for state and local governments, sell insurance, and so on.

In the third place, the name fails to bring out the one unique characteristic of these institutions. They are differentiated from other institutions not primarily by the types of loans they make but by the fact that among all private financial institutions they are the only ones whose debts circulate as money and that have the power to create and destroy money. In their early decades they issued money in the form of both bank notes—their debts evidenced by circulating pieces of paper—and checking deposits. Though they have lost the right of note issue, they still create and issue money in the form of checking deposits.

For such reasons we would much prefer to call these institutions checking deposit banks, money-creating banks, or some other name that would highlight their uniqueness among private financial institutions. However, we shall bow to popular usage and call them commercial banks. In the following pages we shall concentrate our attention on the checking deposit function, largely ignoring the other functions performed by these department store institutions.

BALANCE SHEET ACCOUNTING

A short discussion of some elementary principles of double-entry accounting will not only illuminate the processes through which commercial banks issue and withdraw their debts that serve as money but will also prove useful later when we discuss the operations of the Treasury, the Federal Reserve, and other institutions.

In drawing up financial statements for any unit, be it a business firm, a government, or any other organization, an accountant considers the unit to be an entity separate and distinct from its owners. The entity must, therefore, account to its owners as well as to other claimants against it. There are two principal types of financial statements. One is the *income statement* or *profit and loss statement*. Such statements summarize, for some stated period of time, all the gross income accruing to the entity and the claims against that gross income—claims of owners as well as others. We shall not use income statements at this point though we shall later refer back to them.

In contrast to income statements, which refer to flows over a stated period of time, the *balance sheet* refers to a stock at a point of time. One side of the balance sheet, the *asset* side, lists the types and values of everything owned by the entity. These things of value may be money itself, debt claims against others, shares of ownership in other firms, inventories, plant and equipment, and so on. The other side of the balance sheet, *liabilities and capital account*, lists the types and amounts of claims against the entity's assets. Since double-entry accounting requires that the entity account for the total value of its assets, no more and no less, the total value of claims against assets must be exactly equal to the value of its assets. Any value of assets in excess of other claims against them accrues to the owners. Liabilities are all claims against assets other than ownership claims. Under the law they have priority over ownership claims. They are mostly debt claims of some sort; they may be evidenced by formal documents such as promissory notes or bills of exchange, or they may be evidenced only by book entries. *Capital account* or *net worth* is simply the value of ownership claims against the entity. Since owners have only a residual claim, capital account or net worth is equal to the value of assets minus liabilities.

A highly simplified balance sheet might appear as follows:

Assets		Liabilities and Capital Account	
		Liabilities	$ 85,000
		Capital Account	15,000
Total	$100,000	Total	$100,000

This necessary equality of assets with the sum of liabilities and capital account permits us to write three simple equations that will be useful:

1. Assets = Liabilities + Capital account
2. Capital account = Assets − Liabilities
3. Liabilities = Assets − Capital account

People are sometimes amazed at the accuracy of accountants, noting that no matter how complex the situation or how great the amounts involved the accountant still manages to make the two sides balance. This becomes less remarkable when we realize how the value of net worth was arrived at.

For most of our purposes it will be sufficient to deal with capital account as a lump sum without further breakdown. However, it is perhaps worth noting that the $15,000 net worth in our example might have been broken down somewhat as follows:

Total net worth	$15,000
Capital (10,000 shares of stock at a par value of $1)	10,000
Surplus	5,000

Capital or *capital stock* is the value of ownership claims evidenced by the par or stated value of outstanding shares of stock. Surplus is simply the excess of total ownership claims over the par value of outstanding stock. Any other interpretation may be misleading. In some cases surplus is broken down still further. Thus the $5000 above might be shown as

Surplus	$3,000
Undivided profits	2,000

The latter suggests that owners have a claim for dividends which will be paid in the near future. This may not occur; firms often carry such an item in their balance sheets for years. Undivided profits are best viewed as but a part of ownership claims.

In analyzing the functioning of monetary institutions we shall emphasize one aspect of the necessary equality of assets and the sum of outstanding claims against assets in the form of liabilities and net worth: that an entity can acquire assets only by creating an equal value of claims against itself. Of course it may change the composition of its assets without affecting at all the other side of its balance sheet. For example, it may trade some of its cash assets for an equal value of inventory, or some of its inventory for an equal value of equipment, or some of its short-term claims against others for an equal value of long-term claims against others. Such exchanges of assets may not disturb either the total value or the composition of outstanding claims against the entity. But the entity can make net additions to its assets only by creating an equal value of additional claims against itself. And in the process of reducing its total assets it must withdraw an equal value of outstanding claims against itself.

Because we are interested in the volume of outstanding debts of monetary institutions, we shall pay special attention to Equation 3 above:

$$\text{Liabilities} = \text{Assets} - \text{Capital account}$$

Their outstanding liabilities at any time are equal to the total value of their assets minus the amounts paid for by the creation of ownership claims against themselves. Similarly, their outstanding liabilities must change between any two points of time by an amount equal to the change of their assets that is not offset by changes in the volume of ownership claims. Thus, to the extent that additional assets are not bought by creating ownership claims, they must be paid for by the creation of new liabilities. And to the extent that net decreases of asset holdings are not offset by reductions of ownership claims they must be matched by a net withdrawal of outstanding liabilities.

A BALANCE SHEET FOR THE COMMERCIAL BANKING SYSTEM

Table 6 is a simplified consolidated balance sheet for the commercial banking system. It is simplified in the sense that it eliminates or lumps together some minor items in order to concentrate attention on major variables. It is consolidated to eliminate claims of the various commercial banks against each other, leaving only the claims of the commercial banks as a whole against other members of the community, and the claims of other members of the community against commercial banks.

This balance sheet brings out several important points. One is that banks buy assets primarily by creating liabilities in the form of deposits. These deposits are simply debt claims against the assets of the banks. Banks do issue some other forms of liabilities and some ownership claims but these are equal to only a small percentage of assets. Banks might, of course, create deposits through the purchase of any kind of assets. However, a look at the asset side reveals that in practice they create most of their deposit debts to purchase cash, deposit claims against the Federal Reserve banks, and debt claims against others—mostly the last. Loans and discounts include the banks' holdings of short-term debts of their borrowers, these being evidenced by promissory notes or acceptances, mostly the former. The item "securities," sometimes called "investments," includes a small amount of stock, such as stock

TABLE 6.   Consolidated Balance Sheet for the Commercial
Banking System, December 31, 1957
(In billions of dollars)

ASSETS		LIABILITIES AND CAPITAL ACCOUNTS	
Cash in vault	$ 3.3	Demand deposits	$114.2
Deposits at Federal Reserve	19.0	Time and savings deposits	56.5
Loans	93.9	Other liabilities (net)	4.3
Securities	76.2	Capital accounts	17.4
Total	$192.4	Total	$192.4

SOURCE: *Federal Reserve Bulletin*, June, 1958, pp. 670–671.

in the Federal Reserve banks, but is made up largely of longer-term debt instruments purchased and held by the banks. It includes government obligations, corporation bonds, mortgages, and other similar items.

As we realize that banks create their own deposit debts primarily by purchasing debt claims against others, we begin to see why these institutions are often referred to as "monetizers of debt."

THE CREATION OF CHECKING DEPOSITS

To simplify our description of the processes through which the banking system creates money, we shall assume at first that the banks pay for all assets by the creation of checking or demand deposits. We shall deal with purchases of three types of assets: cash, loans, and securities.

Deposits for Cash

The first case to be considered is that in which banks issue deposits in exchange for a net inflow of cash into the banking system. We shall use the term "cash" to include both cash in vault and deposit claims against the Federal Reserve banks. This is justified because banks are free to exchange one of these assets for the other. Thus they may use a net inflow of coin and paper money from circulation to increase their cash in vault or they may send it along to the Federal Reserve banks to increase their deposits there. Moreover, they can ship cash from their vaults to increase their deposits at the Federal Reserve, and they can write checks on their deposits at the Federal Reserve to get coin and paper money to hold in their vaults. The amount of "cash," in this sense, in the commercial banking system is equal to all the "money" issued by the Treasury and the Federal Reserve minus that in circulation outside the banking system. Thus a net inflow of cash to the banking system can result either from new issues of money by the Treasury or the Federal Reserve, or from a net decrease of coin and paper money outside the banks.

Suppose there is a net cash inflow of $1 billion into the commercial banking system. The direct effect on the banks' balance sheets will be as follows:

ASSETS	LIABILITIES
Cash + $1 billion	Demand deposits + $1 billion

The banks have bought $1 billion of assets in the form of cash by creating their own debt of $1 billion in the form of demand deposits.

It was perhaps injudicious to begin with this case, for it may reinforce popular misconceptions. The reactions of some may be, "Just as I thought! Deposits are nothing but claims on deposited cash, they arise only from the 'deposit' of cash, and anyone leaving cash on deposit can get back that same cash on demand." Such conclusions would be quite wrong. (1) Only a small part of outstanding deposits was created to pay for net inflows of cash; most deposits were created to pay for other types of assets. (2) The cash holdings of banks are equal to only a small fraction of bank deposit liabilities. And (3) one who "deposits" cash with a bank gets no preferred claim; he gives up title to the cash and takes his place with all other depositors as creditors of the bank.

Though deposits created to pay for net cash inflows to the banking system become indistinguishable from all other deposits, two characteristics of the process of creating deposits to pay for net inflows of cash should be noted. (1) In this case, and this case only, the creation of deposits enables the banking system to increase its holdings of cash. Such deposits are often called *primary deposits*. Those created to pay for other assets are called *derivative deposits*. (2) When the commercial banks create checking deposits to pay for net cash flows to them, they do not themselves directly increase the total money supply. If the cash flows in from circulation, the increase of money in the form of checking deposits is offset by the decrease of coin and paper money in circulation. If the net cash flow to the bank results from new creations of money by the Treasury or the Federal Reserve it is these institutions, not the banks, which initially increase the money supply. However, we shall see that net flows of cash into the banks have the very important effect of enabling the banks to create more money by purchasing other assets.

Deposits for Debt Claims

By far the largest part of outstanding deposits was created to pay for assets in the form of debt claims against others. Suppose the banks increase their loans to customers by $10 billion, giving their customers checking deposits. The effects on the banks' balance sheets are as follows:

ASSETS	LIABILITIES
Loans + $10 billion	Demand deposits + $10 billion

The banks have created $10 billion of money that did not exist before, and have done so by purchasing debt claims. In effect, the banks traded debts with their customers, presumably to their mutual satisfaction. The banks acquired debts that were not themselves money but that yield income in the form of interest or discount. The borrowers acquired debt claims—deposits—that usually yield no income but have the advantage of being generally acceptable in payment for all kinds of goods and services. In short, the banks monetized debt.

Banks do not by any means confine their granting of credit to short-term loans to their customers. They also lend for longer terms to their customers and buy various sorts of securities in the open market from sellers they do not even know. Among these are such things as government securities, corporation bonds, and mortgages. We should not be surprised to find that banks create checking deposits in buying such assets. Suppose the banks purchase $10 billion of securities. The effects on their balance sheets will be:

ASSETS	LIABILITIES
Securities + $10 billion	Demand deposits + $10 billion

The banking system has created $10 billion of money that did not exist before and has done so by purchasing debt claims against others. Here again it has monetized debt.

Two points that are crucial to an understanding of commercial banking should be emphasized: (1) Most checking deposits are derivative deposits—deposits created in the process of bank purchases of debt claims against others. (2) Checking deposits created to pay for such assets are a net addition to the money supply; there is no offsetting decrease of coin and paper money in circulation.

THE DESTRUCTION OF CHECKING DEPOSITS

Checking deposits are extinguished by processes just the reverse of those that create deposits. They are destroyed as the banking system decreases its assets in the form of cash, loans, and securities.

Net Cash Drains

The banking system as a whole may suffer a net drain of its cash assets, either through net withdrawals of coin and paper money for circulation outside the banks or because of a net decrease in the amount of money provided by the Treasury and the Federal Reserve. In either case those withdrawing the cash will probably do so by drawing down their checking deposits at the banks.

Suppose the cash assets of the banking system are reduced by $500 million. The banks' balance sheets will be affected as follows:

Assets	Liabilities
Cash — $500 million	Demand deposits — $500 million

In the process of selling $500 million of cash assets the banks destroyed $500 million of their outstanding deposit liabilities.

Two aspects of this particular process of reducing the volume of checking deposits should be noted. First, when checking deposits are reduced by net outflows of cash from the banking system, the banks themselves do not directly decrease the total money supply. If the cash flows out into circulation, the decrease of money in the form of checking deposits is offset by the increase of coin and paper money in circulation. If the net cash loss by the banks resulted from a net withdrawal of money by the Treasury and the Federal Reserve, it is these institutions, not the banks, that initiated the decrease of the money supply. Second, the drain of cash from the banks may have very important repercussions, for it may force the banks to decrease the money supply by selling other assets.

Net Reductions in Bank Assets in the Form of Debt Claims

Most reductions in the volume of checking deposits are traceable to net reductions of bank assets in the form of debt claims against others. Suppose that the banking system reduces its outstanding loans by $5 billion. The former borrowers usually repay loans by drawing checks against their deposit accounts; bank liabilities are reduced accordingly. The effects on the banks' balance sheets are:

Assets	Liabilities
Loans — $5 billion	Demand deposits — $5 billion

In this process of reducing their outstanding loans the banks have destroyed $5 billion of money in the form of checking deposits. This is a net reduction of the money supply; there is no offsetting increase of coin and paper money in circulation.

Similar results flow from net reductions of bank holdings of securities. Suppose the banking system sells $3 billion of its security holdings, the buyers paying for them by relinquishing checking deposit claims against the banks; this will affect the banks' balance sheets as follows:

ASSETS	LIABILITIES
Securities − $3 billion	Demand deposits − $3 billion

Here again the banks have destroyed checking deposits and decreased the total money supply through net sales of their debt claims against others.

Summary

The preceding sections traced out the processes through which the commercial banking system creates checking deposits by purchasing various types of assets and destroys checking deposits by net sales of assets. During some periods the banks may make net purchases of some types of assets and net sales of others. It should be evident that the net change in the volume of checking deposits during any period will equal the net change in total bank assets—still assuming that the banks issue claims only in the form of checking deposits.

LIMITATION OF THE VOLUME OF DEPOSIT LIABILITIES

The primary purpose of a commercial bank from the point of view of its owners is to make profits. It is probably not too inaccurate to say that bankers strive to maximize their profits. We have seen that banks get a gross income from the process of creating checking deposits by purchasing debt claims against others, for the debts purchased yield interest income whereas the resulting checking deposits usually do not. Why, then, do not the banks buy up all the debt instruments existing in the economy and monetize them? Why should banks stop with monetizing all the debts that they could induce governments, business firms, and individuals to issue? Why should they not proceed to buy up great quantities of real goods and services which yield income, paying for them with newly created demand deposits?

In the absence of effective limitation and regulation, the banks might indeed operate in such a highly inflationary manner. Moreover, their money-creating and money-destroying policies might be such as to accentuate cyclical fluctuations in the economy. In boom periods, when optimism reigns and the demand for loans is high, banks might create very large amounts of new money, thereby "booming the boom." Then in depression periods, when the outlook is gloomy and risks increasing, the banks might seriously reduce the money supply, thereby worsening the depression. These dangers are so great that the creation of money by commercial banks is subject to limitation and regulation in practically every country. In the United States this is achieved primarily through regulating the dollar volume of *reserves* available to commercial banks and imposing *legal minimum reserve requirements*.

By *legal reserves* or simply *reserves* we mean those particular types of assets of commercial banks which the law permits them to count toward meeting legal reserve requirements. These assets should be of such a type that their dollar volume can be regulated by the monetary authority. For the commercial banks that are members of the Federal Reserve System—and these banks account for about 85 percent of all commercial bank deposit liabilities—there is only one type of asset that can be counted as a legal reserve: deposit claims against the Federal Reserve banks. One of the major functions of the Federal Reserve is to regulate the volume of its outstanding deposit liabilities to member banks, for these are legal reserves of member banks and are a major determinant of the volume of deposits that the banks can create. Legal minimum reserve requirements, which are defined by law or some administrative agency, require banks to hold reserves equal to *at least* some stated fraction of their deposit liabilities. For example, each bank might be required to hold legal reserves equal to at least one fifth of its deposit liabilities.

To fix a minimum ratio of reserves to deposit liabilities is the same as fixing a maximum ratio of deposit liabilities to reserves. For example, to say to a bank, "You must hold reserves equal to at least 20 percent of your deposit liabilities" is the same as saying, "Your deposit liabilities may not exceed five times the volume of your reserves." If the minimum reserve requirement is 10 percent, the volume of deposit liabilities may not exceed 10 times the volume of bank reserves. Thus we find that the maximum volume of commercial bank deposit liabilities that may be outstanding depends on (1) the dollar volume of reserves available to the banks, and (2) the size of the minimum legal ratio of reserves to deposit liabilities. Stated algebraically, this becomes:

$$D = A \times \frac{1}{R}, \text{ or } D = \frac{A}{R}$$

where D = the maximum dollar volume of deposits that the banks may have outstanding

A = the dollar volume of legal reserves available to the banks

R = the legal minimum ratio of reserves to deposits (e.g., .10 or .20)

$\frac{1}{R}$ = the maximum legal ratio of deposit liabilities to reserves

For example, suppose A is $20 billion.

If $R = .20$,

$$D = \frac{\$20 \text{ billion}}{.20} = \$100 \text{ billion}$$

If $R = .10$,

$$D = \frac{\$20 \text{ billion}}{.10} = \$200 \text{ billion}$$

We now see why dollars in bank reserves are often referred to as "high-powered" money; under a fractional reserve commercial banking system each dollar of legal reserves can "support" several dollars of checking deposits. And the lower the required reserve ratio, the higher-powered is each dollar of reserves.

We have now discovered the two principal ways in which the Federal Reserve can regulate the behavior of the money supply. Though it uses a number of instruments, they are all aimed at regulating either the dollar volume of reserves available to commercial banks or the height of the minimum legal ratio of reserves to deposit liabilities. These are, in the first instance, methods of regulating the volume of commercial bank deposit liabilities. But they also regulate indirectly the volume of bank loans and security holdings, for changes in these would affect the volume of deposits.

The combination of the dollar volume of bank reserves and the legal minimum reserve ratio determines only the *maximum* level of deposit liabilities; it does not force the banks to expand their holdings of loans and securities until this ceiling on their deposit liabilities is reached. The only pressure on banks to reach this maximum comes from the profit motive. Dollars of excess reserves yield no interest; loans and securities do. Usually, therefore, banks are impelled to expand their loans and security holdings to the maximum permitted by their reserve positions. However, there may be times—especially in depression periods—when bankers believe that risks of lending and buying securities are so high relative to prevailing interest rates that they prefer to hold some excess reserves and fail to expand their deposit liabilities to the maximum permitted by their reserve positions.

MULTIPLE EXPANSION OF DEPOSITS

What we have already said suggests that under a fractional reserve system the commercial banks as a group can expand their deposit liabilities by some multiple of any initial increase in the dollar volume of their reserves, and must reduce their deposit liabilities by some multiple of any initial decrease in the volume of their reserves. But the size of this multiple depends on a number of factors, which we shall now investigate.

Multiple Expansion with No Induced Cash Drain from the Banks

Let us begin with a case in which the banking system enjoys an initial increase of $1 billion in its reserves and the ensuing expansion of bank credit induces no net cash drain from the banking system. In other words, all the initial increase of reserves remains in the banks. Let us also assume that the reserve requirement is .20.

The formula indicating the maximum expansion permitted by this initial increase of reserves is

$$\Delta D = \Delta A \times \frac{1}{R}, \text{ or } \Delta D = \frac{\Delta A}{R}$$

where ΔD = the maximum expansion of deposit liabilities
   ΔA = the initial increase in the dollar volume of bank reserves
   R = the legal minimum reserve ratio

In our example,

$$\Delta D = \frac{\$1 \text{ billion}}{.20} = \$5 \text{ billion}$$

In other words, the multiple of expansion is $\frac{1}{R}$, or 5.

To show the effects on the banks' balance sheets we should distinguish two cases. The first case is one in which the increase of reserves occurred through a primary deposit in the banking system. The initial effect on the banks' balance sheets will be:

Assets	Liabilities
Reserves + $1 billion	Demand deposits + $1 billion

Addenda:
   Required reserves + $200 million
   Excess reserves + $800 million

The net inflow of cash increased both deposit liabilities and actual reserves by $1 billion. But required reserves were increased by only 20 percent of the rise of primary deposits, or $200 million. This left $800 million of excess reserves to serve as a basis for a further creation of deposits through increased loans and security holdings. If the banks expand to the maximum permitted by the increase of their reserves, the total effects on their balance sheets will be:

Assets	Liabilities
Reserves + $1 billion	
Loans and securities + $4 billion	Demand deposits + $5 billion

Demand deposits will have increased by $5 billion, of which $1 billion resulted from the primary deposit, and $4 billion from the expansion of loans and security holdings.

The second case is that in which the banks get a net increase in their reserves in some way other than an increase of primary deposits. For example, they might borrow $1 billion from the Federal Reserve banks. The immediate effect on their balance sheets would be:

Assets	Liabilities
Reserves + $1 billion	Borrowings from the Federal Reserve + $1 billion

In this case the entire increase of reserves is an addition to excess reserves and can serve as a basis for the creation of derivative deposits. If the banks expand to the maximum permitted by the increase of reserves, the total effects on their balance sheets will be:

ASSETS	LIABILITIES
Reserves + $1 billion	Demand deposits + $5 billion
Loans and securities + $5 billion	Borrowings from the Federal Reserve + $1 billion

The expansion of deposits was the same in the two cases. However, in the first case $1 billion of the deposit expansion resulted from the primary deposit and $4 billion from the expansion of loans and security holdings. In the second case, the entire $5 billion increase was in derivative deposits.

It should be evident that the size of the multiple of deposit expansion varies inversely with the minimum legal reserve ratio. Suppose, for example, that the reserve ratio is only .10 and the banks receive a $1 billion addition to their reserves. In such a case,

$$\Delta D = \frac{\$1 \text{ billion}}{.10} = \$10 \text{ billion}$$

The reader is invited to show how this would be reflected in the balance sheet of the commercial banking system.

Multiple Expansion with Induced Cash Drains

The case above assumed that all the initial increase of bank reserves remained in the banks—that the expansion of bank credit did not induce any cash drain from the banks. But we should recognize that an expansion of bank credit may, under some circumstances, induce a cash drain from the banking system, thereby draining off some of the initial increase of reserves. These drains may be of two types. (1) A domestic drain of coin and paper money into circulation. This is especially likely if the expansion of bank credit is large and is accompanied by increases of total payrolls, retail trade, and other payments for which coin and paper money are ordinarily used. (2) An external drain—a drain of gold or its equivalent to other countries. For example, a large expansion of bank credit in the United States might lead Americans to increase greatly their purchases abroad and hence lead to the necessity of shipping gold to other countries.

The multiple of expansion on the basis of an initial increase in bank reserves may be much reduced if the expansion of bank credit induces a drain of cash from the banking system, for every dollar of cash drain removes a dollar of reserves that would have been capable of supporting several dollars of deposits if it had remained in the banks.

The general formula for determining the maximum expansion of deposits on the basis of a given initial increase of reserves is

$$\Delta D = \frac{\Delta A}{R + C}$$

ΔD, ΔA, and R have the meanings already given to them. $C =$ the drain of cash from the banking system induced by the expansion of deposits, this being expressed as a fraction of the increase of deposits. Thus, the dollar drain of cash is $\Delta D \times C$.

This formula is derived in the following way. The banks will have expanded to the maximum only when all of the initial increase of reserves (ΔA) has been used to meet induced cash drains ($\Delta D \times C$) and as reserves for new deposits ($\Delta D \times R$). Thus,

$$\Delta A = \Delta D \times R + \Delta D \times C$$
or
$$\Delta A = \Delta D (R + C)$$
or
$$\frac{\Delta A}{R + C} = \Delta D$$

To show how an induced cash drain reduces the multiple of expansion, let us assume that $R = .20$ and $\Delta A = \$1$. If there is no cash drain—that is, if $C = 0$, $\Delta D = \dfrac{\$1}{.20 + 0} = \$5$. However, if $C = .10$, $\Delta D = \dfrac{\$1}{.20 + .10} = \dfrac{\$1}{.30} = \$3.33$. If $C = .20$, $\Delta D = \dfrac{\$1}{.20 + .20} = \$2.50$.

In trying to forecast the effects of its actions that increase the volume of bank reserves, the monetary authority must try to guess whether and how much an increase in the volume of bank credit will induce cash drains. This is sometimes difficult.

One further point is worth noting. When an expansion of derivative deposits induces no cash drain from the banking system, the increase of derivative deposits is the entire increase in the money supply. However, when there is an induced cash drain, the total increase in the money supply is equal to the rise of derivative deposits plus the drain ($\Delta D \times C$) of coin and currency into circulation. This can be clarified by an example. Suppose that banks get an initial increase of $1 billion in their reserves by borrowing from the Reserve banks. The initial effects on their balance sheets are:

ASSETS	LIABILITIES
Reserves + $1 billion	Borrowings from the Federal Reserve + $1 billion

Suppose further that $R = .20$ and $C = .20$. After the banks have expanded to the maximum the net effects on their balance sheets will be:

ASSETS	LIABILITIES
Reserves + $0.5 billion	Demand deposits + $2.5 billion
Loans and securities + $3.0 billion	Borrowings from the Federal Reserve + $1.0 billion

The increase in the total money supply is equal to the $3 billion expansion of bank loans and security holdings. Of this amount, $2.5 billion is in derivative deposits remaining in the banks and $0.5 billion in an induced outflow of coin and paper money. This $0.5 billion of induced cash outflow was provided by drawing down the initial increase of reserves.

MULTIPLE CONTRACTION OF DEPOSITS

As might be expected, an initial loss of reserves by a commercial banking system operating on fractional reserves necessitates a multiple contraction of deposits if the banks had no excess reserves to begin with. The reasoning here is completely symmetrical to that relating to multiple expansion on the basis of an initial increase of reserves.

The general formula for determining the minimum necessary contraction of the deposit liabilities of the banking system in response to an initial loss of legal reserves is

$$\Delta D = \frac{\Delta A}{R + C}$$

where ΔD = the minimum required contraction of deposits
ΔA = the initial loss of reserves
R = the legal minimum ratio of reserves to deposits
C = the inflow of cash to the banking system induced by the contraction of deposits, this being expressed as a percentage of the decrease of deposits

To illustrate the process involved we shall assume (1) that the initial loss of reserves is $1 billion, (2) that this loss results from an initial net withdrawal of cash from the banking system, and (3) that the minimum required ratio of reserves to deposits is .20.

Multiple Contraction with No Induced Cash Inflow

Let us begin with the case in which $C = 0$; that is, the contraction of deposits induces no inflow of cash to the banking system.

The immediate effects of the $1 billion cash withdrawal on the balance sheets of the commercial banks will be:

ASSETS	LIABILITIES
Reserves − $1 billion	Demand deposits − $1 billion
Addenda:	
Required reserves − $200 million	
Deficiency of reserves $800 million	

Since actual reserves were reduced by $1 billion while required reserves were reduced by only 20 percent of the decrease of deposits, or $200 million, the reserves of the banking system will be deficient by $800 million if the banks had no excess reserves to begin with. The system obviously must reduce its deposit liabilities further, and does so by reducing its loans and security holdings. It will have repaired its reserve position only when its balance sheet has been changed as follows:

ASSETS	LIABILITIES
Reserves — $1 billion	Demand deposits — $5 billion
Loans and securities — $4 billion	

Of the $5 billion decrease of deposits, $1 billion resulted from the initial cash withdrawal and $4 billion from the decrease of bank loans and security holdings.

Multiple Contraction with Induced Cash Inflows

In the example above, the banks were unable to induce a cash inflow by reducing their deposit liabilities. They therefore had to make the entire adjustment by decreasing deposits. In some cases, however, a reduction of deposits may induce cash to flow back into the banking system. This is most likely if the reduction of bank credit is accompanied by significant declines of payrolls, retail trade, and other types of payments for which coin and paper money are ordinarily used. To the extent that this occurs, the amount of contraction required in response to an initial loss of reserves will be lessened, for each dollar of induced cash inflow to bank reserves will enable the banks as a group to escape liquidating several dollars of deposits.

To illustrate this, let us assume that the initial loss of reserves is $1 billion, $R = .20$, and $C = .20$. Then

$$\Delta D = \frac{\$1 \text{ billion}}{.20 + .20} = \$2.5 \text{ billion}$$

The final effects on the banks' balance sheets will be:

ASSETS	LIABILITIES
Reserves — $0.5 billion	Deposits — $2.5 billion
Loans and securities — $2 billion	

In this case the necessary contraction of deposits was only $2.5 billion, rather than $5 billion as in the preceding case, because the induced cash inflow of $0.5 billion assisted the banking system in adjusting its reserve position.

OTHER CLAIMS AGAINST COMMERCIAL BANKS

In order to simplify our analysis of the basic principles of checking deposit banking we assumed in the preceding sections that commercial banks issue no claims against themselves other than demand deposit liabilities, and that all these are owned by the "public"—that is, by individuals, business firms, and state and local governments. We concentrated on these checking deposits because they are the only deposits we include in our definition of the money supply. However, we must now take into account the fact that commercial banks also issue other claims against themselves, as indicated in Table 7. The volume of ownership claims against banks is shown by capital

TABLE 7.   Assets of and Claims Against All Commercial Banks
in the United States, March 14, 1957[2]
(In billions)

ASSETS		LIABILITIES AND CAPITAL ACCOUNT	
Cash in vault	$ 2.9	Capital account	$ 16.5
Deposits at Federal Reserve	18.6	Misc. liabilities (net)	4.2
Loans	90.0	Time deposits	52.5
Securities	73.6	Demand deposits owed to:	
		U.S. government	2.0
		Foreigners	1.6
		"Public"	108.3
Total	$185.1	Total	$185.1

account. Time deposits—a term which for the sake of brevity we shall use to cover both time and savings deposits—are liabilities that the banks are not legally required to pay on demand, but only at some future date or some stipulated period of time after the depositor has given notice of his intention to withdraw. In practice banks usually waive these legal rights, but they ordinarily do not permit time deposits to be transferred to others in payment. Demand deposit liabilities to the United States government and to foreigners are like other checking deposits except for their ownership.

The volume of checking deposits owned by the public at any time is equal to total commercial bank assets minus the outstanding volume of other claims against the banks (see Table 8). We shall call these "nonmonetary claims" because we do not include them in the money supply. This relationship becomes understandable when we remember that banks can purchase assets by creating these other claims instead of checking deposit liabilities to the public. Moreover, members of the public may surrender checking deposits for other claims against the banks. For example, the public might surrender $3 billion of checking deposits to buy ownership claims against banks, to acquire time deposit claims, or to make net payments to the government or to foreigners.

It follows that the increase of the public's checking deposits during any period will be equal to the increase of total commercial bank assets minus any in-

[2] This is a consolidated balance sheet, omitting claims of commercial banks against each other. The item, miscellaneous liabilities (net), is a net figure reflecting other liabilities minus some minor asset items.

crease of nonmonetary claims against the banks or plus any decrease of non-monetary claims against the banks. Similarly, the public's checking deposits will be decreased during any period by an amount equal to the decrease of total commercial bank assets minus any decrease of outstanding nonmonetary claims against banks or plus any increase of nonmonetary claims against banks. For example, Table 8 shows that the public's checking deposits rose by $23.2 billion between the end of 1947 and the end of 1957. This was a resultant of

TABLE 8.   Changes in Assets of and Claims Against Commercial Banks
(In billions)

	Amount, Dec. 31, 1947	Amount, Dec. 31, 1957	Changes During the Period
ASSETS			
Cash in vault	$ 2.2	$ 3.3	+$ 1.1
Deposits at Federal Reserve	17.8	19.0	+ 1.2
Loans	38.1	93.9	+ 55.8
Securities	78.2	76.2	− 2.0
Total assets	$136.3	$192.4	+$56.1
Minus: NONMONETARY CLAIMS			
Capital account	10.1	17.4	+ 7.3
Miscellaneous liabilities	1.0	2.9	+ 1.9
Time deposits	35.4	56.1	+ 20.7
Demand deposits			
of U.S. government	1.3	3.9	+ 2.6
of foreigners	1.4	1.8	+ 0.4
Total nonmonetary claims	$ 49.2	$ 82.1	+$32.9
Equals: DEMAND DEPOSITS OF THE PUBLIC	$ 87.1	$110.3	+$23.2

the $56.1 billion rise of total commercial bank assets and the $32.9 billion in-crease of nonmonetary claims against the banks.

It should be noted that this type of analysis can be used even by those who do not accept our definition of the money supply and would like to accord the status of "money" to some other commercial bank liabilities, such as demand deposits owned by the United States government or time deposits. They need only move the liabilities they wish to regard as money from the status of non-monetary claims to the same status we have accorded to demand deposit liabilities to the public.

As we take into account other claims issued by commercial banks, we must also modify somewhat our earlier discussion of the relation between the volume of available bank reserves and the maximum volume of the public's checking deposits. Demand deposits owed to the government or to foreigners are usually subject to the same reserve requirements as other demand deposits. Time de-posits are also ordinarily subject to reserve requirements, but these are usually much lower than those for demand deposits. For example, Federal Reserve officials may fix reserve requirements against demand deposits at member banks at levels that average not less than 10 percent or more than 20 percent. But they may set reserve requirements against time deposits at these banks at not less than 3 percent or more than 6 percent. To the extent that banks must use a part of their available reserves to meet reserve requirements against other deposit liabilities they can have outstanding only a smaller volume of checking deposit liabilities to the public. However, to the extent that banks can induce others to hold time deposit claims against which reserve requirements are low rather than demand deposits against which reserve requirements are higher, they can have larger loans and security holdings. For example, suppose the public gives up $1 billion of demand deposits against which reserve requirements are 20 percent and takes in return an equal amount of time deposits against which reserve requirements are only 6 percent. This will give the banking system $140 million of excess reserves, for the decrease of demand deposits freed $200 million of reserves while the rise in time deposits required only $60 million of reserves. With excess reserves, the banks can expand their loans and security holdings. If all the proceeds become demand deposits the banks can expand their loans and security holdings by $\dfrac{\$140 \text{ million}}{.20}$, or $700 million.

Such factors as these make more complex the quantitative relationship between the dollar volume of bank reserves on the one hand and on the other hand such quantities as total bank liabilities and checking deposit liabilities to the public. But they do not invalidate the general principles developed in this chapter. It remains true that banks operating on the fractional reserve principle can have outstanding deposit liabilities equal to a multiple of their reserves, that a net increase of their reserves enables them to expand their deposit liabilities by some multiple, and that a net decrease of their reserves forces them to contract their deposit liabilities by some multiple if they did not have excess reserves to begin with.

CONCLUSIONS

Though all the points made in this chapter are important to an understanding of our monetary system, the following will be especially useful in our analysis.

1. Dollars in commercial bank reserves are "high-powered" dollars, for under a fractional reserve system each dollar of bank reserves can support several dollars of money in the form of checking deposits.

2. Net cash inflows to the commercial banking system and net cash outflows from the system can have important effects on the monetary situation, for inflows tend to increase and outflows to decrease the dollar volume of bank reserves.

3. Though the Federal Reserve uses several instruments in its general monetary management, practically all these are aimed at regulating either (a) the supply of reserves to the commercial banks, or (b) the height of the minimum legal ratio of reserves to deposits.

4. The fact that commercial banks create money primarily by purchasing loans and securities helps to explain why changes in the money supply are likely to have important effects in the credit markets. As the banks create new money by purchasing loans and securities, the money is injected into the credit market in the first instance. It may be looked upon as either a new supply of loan funds or a new demand for debt obligations. This tends to lower interest rates and raise prices of debt obligations. On the other hand, as the banks reduce the money supply by decreasing their loans and security holdings, the money is in the first instance removed from the credit markets. This may be viewed as either a reduction in the supply of loan funds or a decrease in the demand for debt obligations. It tends to raise interest rates and to lower the prices of debt obligations. However, commercial banks are not the only lenders and do not by themselves determine the behavior of interest rates. The latter depend on the demand for loan funds and the total supply of loan funds, including the quantities supplied by other lenders, as well as those from commercial banks.

SELECTED READINGS

Angell, J. W., and Ficek, K. F., "The Expansion of Bank Credit," *Journal of Political Economy*, 1933, pp. 1–32, 152–193.

Crick, W. F., "The Genesis of Bank Deposits," *Economica*, June, 1927.

Phillips, C. A., *Bank Credit*, Macmillan, New York, 1926.

Shaw, E. S., *Money, Income, and Monetary Policy*, Richard D. Irwin, Chicago, 1950.

CHAPTER 5

Individual Banks in the System

Up to this point our discussion of commercial banking has dealt largely with the system as a whole; almost nothing has been said about the thousands of individual banks in the system. This was done deliberately to emphasize the functioning of the banking system as a composite and is appropriate when we are interested in the relation of banking to the functioning of the economy as a whole. Now, however, we shift our attention to the functioning of individual banks and to the interrelationships of the individual banks that make up the system.

INTERBANK PAYMENTS

Each individual bank can gain or lose "cash"—we use this term to include both cash in vault and deposits at the Federal Reserve banks—in the same ways as the banking system as a whole. Like the system, it can gain cash through net inflows from the public, the Federal Reserve, or the Treasury. Also, like the system, it can lose cash through net outflows to the public, the Federal Reserve, or the Treasury. But each bank may also gain or lose cash in still another way: through net receipts from other banks in the system or net payments to them. Such transfers do not affect the total reserves, assets, and liabilities of the system, but they do redistribute these among the individual banks. Each bank gains funds from other banks by receiving "on deposit" many checks drawn on them. It loses funds to other banks as checks that are drawn on it are deposited with them. Sometimes these gains and losses balance out; sometimes they do not. When a bank enjoys a net gain from other banks it is ordinarily paid, at least in the first instance, by the transfer of an equal volume of reserves from the accounts of other banks to its own account, usually a deposit at the Federal Reserve. When it suffers net losses it usually pays by transferring to their accounts an equal volume of its reserves.

To illustrate these points, let us consider the position of the Excelsior State Bank. Its deposits and assets are increased when deposits are transferred to it from other banks. For example, suppose that you deposit with this bank a $1000 check drawn by John Adams on the First National Bank of Keokuk. The Excelsior State Bank will experience a $1000 increase in its deposits and the First National Bank of Keokuk an equivalent decrease in its deposits. The Keokuk Bank must pay $1000 to the Excelsior Bank, which it will probably do by transferring to it a deposit credit at a Federal Reserve bank. The effects of this entire transaction on the balance sheets of the two banks will be as follows:

EXCELSIOR BANK		KEOKUK BANK	
ASSETS	LIABILITIES	ASSETS	LIABILITIES
Increase deposits at Federal Reserve $1000	Increase deposits $1000	Decrease deposits at Federal Reserve $1000	Decrease deposits $1000

It will be noted that the total assets and deposits in the banking system as a whole remain unchanged, but that they are redistributed among the banks in the system. On the other hand, if you write a $500 check on your deposit at the Excelsior Bank and give it to someone who deposits it at the Hibernia National Bank of New Orleans, deposits at the Excelsior Bank will be decreased by $500, deposits at the Hibernia will be increased by $500, and the Excelsior Bank will have to transfer to the Hibernia Bank $500 of its deposits at the Federal Reserve.

These interbank transfers of funds must be borne in mind for at least three reasons. In the first place, they help to explain why banks seek to attract deposits away from other banks. A bank that succeeds can thereby draw reserves from other banks and increase its lending power. In the second place, they make the "liquidity problem" of an individual bank quite different from that of the commercial banking system as a whole. An individual bank must be able to meet not only its customers' demands for coin and currency but also its payments to other banks. And in the third place, because of these interbank transfers an individual bank that receives an initial addition to its reserves usually cannot expand its loans, investments, and deposits by a multiple amount.

EXPANSION AND CONTRACTION OF AN INDIVIDUAL BANK

We found earlier that upon receiving an initial addition to its legal reserves the commercial banking system as a whole can expand its earning assets and deposits by a multiple amount, the size of the multiple depending on the height of the legal reserve ratio and the size of any induced cash drain. Is the same true for an individual bank in the system? To answer this question let us consider an individual bank, which we shall call "the first bank," and make the following assumptions: (1) That the first bank receives a $10 million addition to its reserves through the deposit with it of a government check drawn on a Federal Reserve bank. This is an addition to the reserves of the banking system as a whole. (2) That all banks operate under 20 percent reserve requirements. And (3) that the ensuing expansion of bank credit induces no drain of cash from the banking system as a whole.

The initial effects on the balance sheet of the first bank are as follows:

ASSETS	LIABILITIES
Reserves + $10 million	Deposits + $10 million
Addenda:	
Required reserves + $2 million	
Excess reserves + $8 million	

Now that it has $8 million of excess reserves, can the first bank proceed to increase its loans and security holdings by $\dfrac{\$8 \text{ million}}{.20}$, or $40 million, thereby creating an equal amount of derivative deposits? The answer is "Yes" if, and only if, all these derivative deposits remain at the first bank and are not checked out to other banks. In this case all the initial increase of reserves will remain at the first bank, available to support its deposit liabilities. But this is most unlikely to occur in a system with more than 13,000 banks. It is much more likely that a large part of the derivative deposits will be checked out to other banks, thus requiring the first bank to transfer reserves to those banks and thereby reducing the first bank's ability to expand its own loans and security holdings.

Table 9 shows the expansion for individual banks and for the banking system as a whole, on the assumption that *all* the additional deposits created by the loans of one bank are checked out to other banks and that an equal amount of reserves must be paid over to the transferee banks.

After receiving the $10 million addition to its deposits and reserves, the first bank sets aside the necessary $2 million addition to its reserves and creates $8 million of new deposits by making new loans or purchasing additional securities. These loan-created deposits of $8 million are checked out to the second bank and an equal amount of reserves paid over to it. The second bank sets aside the necessary $1.6 million addition to its reserves and creates $6.4 million of new deposits by making loans and investments. These deposits and an equal amount of reserves are paid over to the third bank, which continues the expansion, as do other banks in their turn. Thus, the $50 million expansion of deposits in the system as a whole—$40 million of which was created by new loans and security purchases—represents increases at many banks.

This example indicates how it is possible to reconcile the economists' emphasis on multiple expansion for the banking system as a whole with the individual banker's insistence that "I can't expand my loans and investments by a multiple of any excess reserves I may have; I can expand them only by an amount equal to my excess reserves." It also helps to explain how a flow of new reserves into only one or a few banks can lead to an easing of credit throughout the banking system.

We found earlier that upon losing reserves the banking system as a whole may be forced to contract its earning assets by a multiple amount. Is the same true for an individual bank that loses reserves? To answer this question, let us reverse our earlier assumptions and assume that "the first bank," operating under a 20 percent reserve requirement, loses $10 million of deposits and re-

TABLE 9. Deposit Expansion on New Reserves by a Banking System

	Additional Deposits Received	Additional Reserves Retained Against Deposits Received (20%)	Additional Loans Made (80%) (The deposits created by these loans are all checked out to the next bank)
1st bank	$10,000,000	$ 2,000,000	$ 8,000,000
2nd bank	8,000,000	1,600,000	6,400,000
3rd bank	6,400,000	1,280,000	5,120,000
4th bank	5,120,000	1,024,000	4,096,000
5th bank	4,096,000	819,200	3,276,800
6th bank	3,276,800	655,360	2,621,440
7th bank	2,621,440	524,288	2,097,152
8th bank	2,097,152	419,430	1,677,722
9th bank	1,677,722	335,544	1,342,178
10th bank	1,342,178	268,436	1,073,742
Total, first ten banks	$44,631,292	$ 8,926,258	$35,705,034
Other banks in turn	5,368,708	1,073,742	4,294,966
Grand total	$50,000,000	$10,000,000	$40,000,000

SOURCE: This table is based on that in Board of Governors of the Federal Reserve System, *The Federal Reserve System—Its Purposes and Functions*, 1939, p. 73.

serves. The initial effect is to make its reserves deficient by $8 million, for it has lost $10 million of reserves while its required reserves have been reduced only $2 million. Must it proceed to reduce its earning assets and deposits by another $40 million to meet its reserve requirements? The answer is "Yes" if all the reduction of loans and sales of securities are paid with checks drawn on deposits at the first bank. In this case the process of contraction brings no new reserves to the first bank, so it must repair its reserve position solely by reducing its deposit liabilities. But this is unlikely in a system where there are many banks. It is much more likely that those who repay loans to the first bank or buy securities from it will pay with checks drawn upon other banks, thereby supplying reserves to the first bank at the expense of others.

Suppose that all the retirement of loans and sales of securities at each bank is paid for by transferring to that bank checks drawn on other banks. The process and the results can be shown by changing the headings of the three columns in Table 9. The heading of the first of these columns is changed to read "Decrease in deposits and reserves," the second to read "Decrease in required reserves because of loss of deposits; this is equal to 20 percent of the decrease of deposits." The third will read, "Decrease in loans; this is equal to 80 percent of deposits lost." The first bank, whose reserves are deficient by $8 million, calls loans and sells securities in that amount, thereby drawing deposits and reserves from the second bank. That bank, having lost reserves, reduces its loans and securities, thereby drawing reserves from the third bank. This process continues until no further contraction is required to restore the reserves of the system to their legally required ratio to deposits. Total deposits in the system will have been reduced by $50 million, of which $40 million was destroyed by the reduction of loans and security holdings, even though no individual bank reduced its earning assets by more than the amount of its reserve deficiency.

This example helps to explain how a net drain of reserves from one bank or a small group of banks can lead to a tightening of credit conditions throughout the banking system. Competitive attempts by banks to repair their reserve positions by reducing loans and selling securities can bring about crises or panics if there is no way to supply new reserves to the banking system. To avert such crises and panics by supplying new reserves is one, but only one, of the functions of a central bank.

CORRESPONDENT RELATIONSHIPS

No account of interbank relations would be complete without mention of "correspondent banking" in the United States: the arrangement under which some banks hold deposits with other banks and use these banks as agents in various types of transactions, such as check clearing and collection, purchases and sales of securities, purchases and sales of foreign exchange, and participations in large loans. This is our domestic counterpart of international correspondent banking, under which banks located in different countries hold deposits with each other and act as agents for each other in many types of transactions. Nations with only a small number of banks, each operating a nation-wide system of branches, have no need for such a highly developed domestic correspondent system. In such cases each bank has an office in the country's major financial center and can reach all parts of the country through its own branches. The importance of correspondent relationships in the United States derives from the structure of our banking system—the fact that most of our thousands of banks operate only one office, that no branch bank is permitted to have branches outside its home state, and that many of our banks are relatively small.

The center of American correspondent banking is New York City, the nation's great financial center with its foreign-exchange market, its short-term money market, and its long-term capital markets. Almost every important bank in the country maintains correspondent relations with at least one large bank in that city. Chicago is the next most important center. Each of its two largest banks has more than a thousand correspondents. In addition there are many regional centers, among them Boston, Philadelphia, Atlanta, New Orleans, Cleveland, St. Louis, Kansas City, Dallas, San Francisco, and Seattle. The network of correspondent relations is complex, for many banks hold deposits in more than one center, and correspondent banks in one center often have correspondent relations with banks in other centers. Thus, a bank in a small Missouri town may have deposits in a St. Louis bank and possibly in a Chicago or New York bank, and the St. Louis bank is almost certain to have deposits in Chicago or New York, or both.

These interbank deposits serve several functions. Among these are: (1) To serve as legal reserves. Though members of the Federal Reserve may count as legal reserves only their deposits at the Federal Reserve banks, nonmember banks have more leeway. The relevant state laws permit most nonmember banks to hold at least a part of their legal reserves, usually a large part, in the form of deposit claims against other commercial banks. (2) To facilitate check clearing and collection. Many banks have their correspondent banks pay at least some of the checks drawn on them and collect checks on other banks that are deposited with them. A New Jersey bank may have such an arrangement with the Chase Manhattan Bank of New York. If so, at least some checks drawn on the New Jersey bank and deposited with other banks will be routed to Chase Manhattan, which will deduct them from the New Jersey bank's deposit account. And checks drawn on other banks and deposited with the New Jersey bank will be sent to Chase Manhattan, which will credit the New Jersey bank's deposit account and send the checks along for collection. (3) To facilitate domestic and foreign payments. A customer of the New Jersey bank may want to make payments with a draft drawn on a New York bank or on some foreign bank. Holding deposits at Chase Manhattan, the New Jersey bank can draw drafts on that bank or on a foreign correspondent of that bank. (4) To facilitate agency operations. The New Jersey bank may use Chase Manhattan as an agent to buy or sell securities, to make loans for it on the Stock Exchange, or to accept or draw drafts. Interbank deposits that can be credited or debited to finance these transactions are helpful. (5) To increase the geographical mobility of credit. Banks with funds in excess of their current needs can increase their deposits at correspondent banks, thereby shifting reserves to them and increasing their lending power. On the other hand, banks that wish to increase their other assets or to meet withdrawals may withdraw some of their deposits from their correspondent banks. Geographical mobility of credit is also promoted, of course, when banks buy securities and other assets outside their own locality, or sell some of their securities and other assets to buyers outside their own locality.

ASSETS AND LIABILITIES OF COMMERCIAL BANKS

To bring out other aspects of banking, let us now study commercial bank assets and liabilities. Table 10 presents the combined balance sheets of the

TABLE 10.   Assets and Liabilities of All Insured Commercial Banks in the
United States, December 31, 1957

ASSETS

	Amount (In billions)	Percent of Total Assets	Amount (In billions)	Percent of Total Assets
Cash, balances with other banks, and cash collection items: Total			$ 48.2	21.8
Currency and coin	$ 3.3	1.3		
Reserve with Federal Reserve banks	19.0	8.6		
Demand deposits at banks in U.S.	12.1	5.5		
Other balances with banks in U.S.	—	—		
Balances at foreign banks	0.1	—		
Cash items in process of collection	13.7	6.2		
U.S. government obligations held: Total			57.7	26.0
Maturing in 5 years or less	45.2	20.4		
Maturing beyond 5 years	12.4	5.6		
Other securities: Total			17.6	7.9
Loans and discounts: Total			93.8	42.3
Commercial and industrial loans	40.5	18.3		
Loans to farmers (excluding loans on real estate)	4.0	1.8		
Loans on securities	4.1	1.8		
Real estate loans	23.1	10.4		
Other loans to individuals	20.2	9.1		
All other loans	2.8	1.3		
Bank premises, other real estate, etc.: Total			2.3	1.0
Miscellaneous assets: Total			1.9	0.9
Total assets			$221.5	100.0

13,142 insured commercial banks in the United States as of December 31, 1957. These banks comprised 97 percent of all commercial banks in the United States and held more than 99 percent of all commercial bank assets. This balance sheet differs in two major respects from that used in the preceding chapter: (1) It is a combined, rather than a consolidated, balance sheet. It is simply a summation of the balance sheets of the individual banks. It therefore includes claims of the banks against each other, the principal items being checks and other cash items in process of collection and interbank deposits, which are assets of some banks and liabilities of others. (2) Its classification of assets and liabilities is much more detailed.

Commercial Bank Assets

These data confirm our earlier finding that debt claims against others are the principal type of asset bought and sold by banks in the process of creating and destroying deposit liabilities. On this date loans and securities made up 76.2 percent of all commercial bank assets. Cash in vault was only 1.3 percent and deposits at the Federal Reserve only 8.6 percent of all their assets.

LIABILITIES AND CAPITAL ACCOUNTS

	Amount (In billions)	Percent of Total Assets	Amount (In billions)	Percent of Total Assets
Demand deposits: Total			$139.2	62.8
Individuals, partnerships and corporations	$109.2	49.3		
U.S. government	3.9	1.8		
States and subdivisions	10.6	4.8		
Foreign	1.7	0.8		
U.S. banks	13.8	6.2		
Time and savings deposits: Total			57.7	26.1
Individuals, partnerships, and corporations	53.3	24.0		
U.S. government	0.3	0.1		
States and subdivisions	2.8	1.3		
Foreign	1.2	0.5		
U.S. banks	—	—		
Certified and officer's checks, cash letters of credit, and traveler's checks outstanding, and amounts due Federal Reserve banks: Total			3.6	1.6
Miscellaneous liabilities			4.0	1.8
Capital accounts: Total			17.0	7.7
Total liabilities and capital accounts			$221.5	100.0

SOURCE: *Annual Report of the Federal Deposit Insurance Corporation, 1957.*

An analysis of commercial bank loans, discounts, and securities reveals their wide variety. Applying four common classifications of debt obligations held by commercial banks, we find: (1) On the basis of the nature of the debtor, there are debts of the United States government, of states and political subdivisions, of corporations, of unincorporated businesses, of individuals, and so on. (2) On the basis of maturity, debts range all the way from "call loans," which are payable on demand, to very long-term government bonds, corporation bonds, and real estate mortgages. (3) On the basis of the type of security pledged for satisfaction of the debt, some loans are "unsecured"; they have no specific assets pledged for their security, but rest on the general credit standing of the debtor. Others have claims on specific assets pledged for their security, such as real estate, stocks, bonds, or chattels. (4) On the basis of the "declared purpose" of the loan, the borrower may declare that he will use the proceeds of the loan to buy inventory and meet payrolls, to finance the storage or shipment of goods, to buy or carry securities, to purchase plant and equipment, to buy specified types of consumers' goods, and so on.

The summary in Table 11 indicates that the so-called "commercial banks"

TABLE 11.　Loans, Discounts, and Securities Held by All Insured Commercial Banks in the United States, December 31, 1957

	Amount (In billions)	Percent of Total
U.S. government obligations	$ 57.7	33.9
Other securities	17.6	10.4
Commercial and industrial loans	40.5	23.8
Loans to farmers (excluding loans on real estate)	4.0	2.4
Loans on securities	4.1	2.4
Real estate loans	23.1	13.6
Other loans to individuals	20.2	11.9
All other loans	2.8	1.6
Total	$170.0	100.0

SOURCE: Data from Table 10. The figures, except the total, are gross amounts before subtracting a valuation reserve.

are by no means institutions specializing in short-term commercial, industrial, and agricultural loans. At the end of 1957 these loans (excluding loans on farm real estate) made up less than 25 percent of the banks' total earning assets, and some of these had maturities of more than a year. United States government obligations were by far the most important single type of earning asset held by the banks, making up more than a third of the total. Some of these had maturities of less than a year, well over half had maturities within five years, and some were due to run for longer periods. Other securities, such as obligations of state and local governments and corporation bonds, accounted for nearly 11 percent of total earning assets, loans on real estate for more than 13 percent, loans on securities for 2.4 percent, and other loans to individuals—many of them consumer loans—for about 12 percent.

This great diversity in commercial bank earning assets—the variety of debtors whose obligations are purchased, the diversification of maturities, the many types of collateral behind the debt obligations, and the variety of declared purposes—is an important fact for our understanding of bank operations. In the first place, it means that banks monetize and demonetize not one narrowly defined type of debt but many kinds of debt that already exist or can be created in very large amounts. And in the second place, it means that banks inject or withdraw money, not in just one narrow branch of the market for loanable funds, but in many of its important branches. Moreover, the banks often withdraw money from one branch of the money market and transfer it to other branches where interest rates and other conditions appear more attractive. They therefore exert an important influence on the availability and cost of loanable funds in the entire money market.

Though commercial bank operations in the various branches of the market for debt obligations can have an important influence on the amounts of money available to purchase these various types of instruments and on their prices and yields, we must not assume that the types of obligations acquired by the banks indicate accurately who receives the newly created bank money, the specific purpose for which the money will be spent, or the behavior of the various streams of spending. Some persons seem to believe that by discovering the identity of the debtors whose obligations the banks purchase they will know with accuracy who is receiving the newly created money, that by looking at the type of collateral pledged and at the declared purpose of a loan they will know precisely for what purpose the new money will be spent, and that by controlling the types of loans made by banks it is possible to control accurately the various streams of spending.

This view is for several reasons oversimplified and may even be seriously misleading. (1) In purchasing the obligations of a given type of debtor the banks do not necessarily put money in the hands of that debtor. This is because the obligations may be purchased, not from the debtor himself, but from someone else who has held the obligations for some time and who will spend the new money for various purposes. Thus individuals, insurance companies, nonfinancial corporations, or others may sell to commercial banks some of the government securities they have been holding for some time and then lend or spend the money as they see fit. Or they may sell to the commercial banks some of their holdings of corporation bonds, real estate mortgages, or shorter maturity loans and then spend or lend the money in various ways.

(2) Even when a bank buys obligations directly from the issuer, the types of assets pledged to secure a loan are not necessarily an accurate indicator of the types of assets that the new money will be used to purchase. For example, a debtor may borrow on the basis of real estate to get money to be used to buy inventory or meet payrolls, to purchase securities, to purchase consumers' goods, or for other purposes. Or a person may pledge stocks or bonds as collateral for a loan and use none of the new money to buy securities. In short, the choice of collateral behind a loan can often be adjusted to the tastes of the lender and borrower and is not necessarily related to the use to which the borrowed money will be put.

(3) The borrower's "declared purpose" for borrowing is not necessarily an accurate indicator of the way his various types of spending will behave if he receives the loan. It is probably true that if a borrower is granted a loan for some specified declared purpose, such as the purchase of inventory or some consumers' good, he will spend at least that amount of money for the declared purpose. But this does not mean that because his loan application was granted he will spend for the declared purpose that much more than he would have spent if the loan had been denied, and that his other types of spending will be unaffected. For example, a borrower may get a $10,000 loan for the declared purpose of buying inventory and in fact spend at least that amount for the purpose. But if the loan had been denied he might still have spent the same amount for inventory and reduced his other types of spending. The result of being able to get the loan for the declared purpose of inventory accumulation may be to free some of the borrower's other money for other types of spending. Many borrowers who engage in various types of spending are in a position to adjust the declared purpose of their borrowings to suit the tastes of lenders without relinquishing their freedom to determine for themselves the pattern of their spendings.

(4) Even if the banks were able to control the expenditure patterns of their borrowers, they could not control subsequent spendings of the new money. Once the money has been spent by the borrower it goes off on "rounds of its own," free of control by the bank that issued it.

The facts brought out above will be useful when we come to discuss "selective credit controls"—the various attempts by the monetary authorities to control not only the total volume of credit and money but also the amounts used for specified purposes, such as the purchase of stocks, of durable consumers' goods, and of new residential construction.

Commercial Bank Liabilities

Only three of these liability items appear to require clarification. These are "certified and officer's checks, cash letters of credit, and traveler's checks outstanding, and amounts due Federal Reserve banks." The first two are closely related to the volume of deposits and should be included in the total money supply. Certified checks outstanding represent bank liabilities to pay the holders on demand. For example, suppose that you are to receive payment from Jones but doubt his willingness or ability to pay. You may require payment by certified check; Jones will write a check on his account and have the bank certify it. By such certification the bank guarantees that the signature is good, that the bank has in its possession sufficient funds of the drawer to pay the check, and that it will hold the funds for this purpose. The certifying bank immediately deducts the amount of the check from the drawer's deposit account and the certified check becomes the evidence of the bank's debt. The certified check disappears from bank liabilities when it is paid, and its amount is then added to deposits at the bank where it is deposited. Officer's checks outstanding serve a similar function. Suppose you insist that Jones pay you with a cashier's check. Jones will write a check on his deposit account and use it to purchase a check drawn by the cashier or some other officer on his own bank. Bank deposits are thereby decreased for the time being, and bank obligations in the form of officer's checks outstanding are increased. When the cashier's check is paid, its amount is again added to deposits. Traveler's checks outstanding are similar in purpose to cashier's checks. They are usually purchased with checks drawn on deposits; while outstanding they are obligations of banks to pay, and when paid they are retired and an equal amount is added to deposits.

Cash letters of credit outstanding are also demand liabilities of banks and are similar in function to traveler's checks. Suppose that you are going on a trip and want $2000 in a safe but easily negotiable form. You may write a check on your deposit and buy from the bank a traveler's cash letter of credit, which is the bank's promise to pay drafts drawn on it by other banks that provide you with money under the letter of credit. Thus, the letter of credit represents the bank's obligation to pay on demand. The item "amounts due Federal Reserve banks" is self-explanatory; it represents borrowings from the Federal Reserve and the value of other Federal Reserve claims against the banks that have not yet been paid.

The balance sheet shows that commercial banks acquire assets largely by issuing debt claims against themselves—liabilities to pay fixed amounts in dollars. At the end of 1957 these debts came to more than 92 percent of their total assets. The "cushion" of ownership claims was less than 8 percent of assets. Moreover, these liabilities to pay fixed dollar amounts were promises to pay either on demand or on very short notice. Demand deposits, which were equal to about 63 percent of assets, are promises to pay legal-tender money on demand, as are certified and officer's checks outstanding, cash letters of credit, and traveler's checks. Even time deposits, which amounted to nearly 26 percent of assets, are obligations to pay within a few months.

This combination of very large bank debts relative to assets and the short-term nature of these debts suggests two important problems for bank management and public policy: (1) the problem of maintaining bank solvency, and (2) the problem of maintaining bank liquidity. A bank is solvent when the value of its assets is at least great enough to cover all its liabilities except those to its owners; it is insolvent when the value of its assets is insufficient to cover all the nonowner claims against it. By the liquidity of a bank we mean its ability to exchange its assets for money fast enough to meet the demands on it for payment. Though the problems of solvency and liquidity are closely related, we can separate them for analytical purposes. For example, a bank may not be able to acquire cash quickly enough to meet demands on it for payment on short notice or without any notice at all, even though the value of its assets would be considerably greater than its liabilities to nonowners if it had ample time in which to sell the assets. On the other hand, an insolvent bank—one whose deposits and bank note liabilities exceed the value of its assets—may continue to operate for a long time if it is not subjected to heavy demands for payment.

BANK SOLVENCY

Although an insolvent bank may be able to function for some time, such insolvency is obviously undesirable for several reasons. In the first place, even an impairment of the owners' claims is injurious to the owners, and an insufficiency of assets to meet other liabilities endangers the creditors' claims. And in the second place, such a condition, if it becomes known or even suspected, is likely to lead to immediate demands on the bank for payment and therefore to losses by depositors and other creditors. Regulatory authorities and conscientious bank officials are faced with a difficult decision when a bank's assets fall below its liabilities. If they close the bank and liquidate its assets under "bankrupt sale" conditions, depositors and other creditors are almost certain to suffer losses, whereas the bank might recover if allowed to continue in operation. On the other hand, if they permit it to stay open despite its unsound condition, its assets may deteriorate even further and the soundest assets may have to be sold to pay those who first demand payment, leaving only the poorer assets to satisfy remaining claims. The position of the remaining depositors after a bank has suffered large drains is often far from enviable.

Regulation of Bank Assets

Many methods have been employed to protect creditors against losses from bank insolvency. The first is to see that banks acquire only those types of assets that are least likely to decline in price. In the early days of banking in this country, bank officials were allowed a high degree of freedom in determining the types and proportions of the assets they acquired. So extensive were the abuses of these powers and so great were the consequent losses to holders of deposits and bank notes that many legal restrictions have been placed on the types of assets that banks may acquire and hold. For example, they are usually forbidden to hold common stocks, except stock in Federal Reserve banks and limited amounts of other stocks acquired through the calling of loans. Bank holdings of real estate other than banking premises are ordinarily either forbidden or limited in quantity. These assets fluctuate too much in value to be considered appropriate assets for banks.

In the second place, the quality of bank assets in the form of debt obligations is to some extent regulated by law and by the administrative actions of supervisory authorities. Attempts are made, with varying degrees of success, to exclude speculative and unsafe bonds, inadequately secured mortgages, and even highly questionable short-term paper.

In the third place, an effort is made to assure diversification of a bank's assets. Limitations are placed on the proportion of assets that may be held in any one form—in the form of real estate mortgages, for example—and also on the amount that may be lent to any one borrower. The principal purpose of such limitations is to enhance the safety of banks by preventing them from putting too many eggs in one basket. Another purpose, however, is to curb favoritism in the granting of loans and to make bank lending facilities more widely available.

In the fourth place, limitations are placed on a bank's loans to its owners, officers, and employees. These loans are doubly suspect. There is danger that such applications for loans will not be scrutinized as critically as they should be and that the quality of bank assets will suffer. Moreover, it is generally felt that the owners, officers, and employees of banks ought not to enjoy more than their fair share of a bank's limited lending ability at the expense of loans to other qualified borrowers. The definition of a banker as "one who takes care of your money by lending it to his friends" has too often been more than a witticism. Where arm's-length bargaining does not exist, loans are likely to be of doubtful safety and discriminatory as among borrowers.

From the point of view of bank solvency, it is obviously desirable that banks should make only relatively safe loans and investments. But this objective may conflict with another objective—that of providing adequate loan funds to business. Risk is inevitable in business. If the banks insist on too much safety in lending, they may fail to facilitate production and trade as much as is desirable. This is especially evident during periods of distrust, when business activity should be bolstered as much as possible and when the banks are likely to emphasize safety in loans. We shall see later that this dilemma of bank safety versus availability of loans in adequate volume is now avoided to some extent by government guarantee of loans or government participation in the risk on loans. By socializing the loan risks, bank safety may be achieved without sacrificing the availability of loans. The success of such plans depends on the wisdom and efficiency of the guaranteeing agencies.

Bank Capital Requirements

Solvency of banks depends not only on the stability of value of their assets, but also on the size of their capital accounts. The securing of adequate bank capital relative to assets has been a difficult problem in American banking history. Many of the early banks engaged in highly dangerous practices. Some of them had only a very small capital, with the result that creditors were injured by even a small depreciation of bank assets. And, to worsen the situation, the banks often made highly risky loans. Other banks had a large nominal capital, the actual value of which was doubtful. For example, promoters would establish a bank with $100,000 of capital stock, but the stock would be paid for not with money or valuable property but with promissory notes of the owners. This practice would not have been objectionable if the stockholders' debts had been fully collectible, but the stockholders were too often merely adventurers whose credit standing was uncertain or worse. Even when the owners originally paid for their stock with good coin or currency, they sometimes borrowed it back as soon as the bank was established, giving promissory notes in return; hence the net result was the same as if they had originally paid for the bank stock with their debt instruments. In other cases bank capital was reduced by excessive dividend payments.

To eliminate or at least to reduce these abuses, banks are now subject to numerous legal capital requirements. The federal government and most of the states fix minimum capital requirements that banks must meet before they begin operation. In some cases these requirements set a minimum ratio of capital to assets or to noncapital liabilities. Stock must be paid for with money, and loans by banks to their owners are regulated to prevent deterioration of assets. The conditions under which dividends can be declared are also prescribed in order to prevent a reduction of capital through excessive payments to owners. At one time attempts were made to protect bank creditors by providing "double liability" on bank stock. That is, the owner of a share of stock could be assessed an amount equal to the par value of his stock to meet the claims of bank creditors; he could lose not only the amount of his original investment in the stock but also the amount of the assessment. This method of protecting depositors and other bank creditors has now been largely abandoned. In practice it offered only limited protection, for bank stocks often gravitated into the hands of people who could not pay the assessments levied on them, and the courts proved reluctant to force payment by unfortunate stockholders whose equities had already been eliminated. Moreover, the dangers inherent in double liability interfered, especially during depression periods, with the securing of adequate capital funds for banks.

The two general methods described above—enhancing the stability of the value of bank assets and increasing bank capital relative to bank assets—attempt to protect bank creditors by maintaining the solvency of banks. But bank failures have been numerous in this country despite these efforts. This has led to the introduction of many insurance schemes in which some outside agency, usually sponsored by the government, insures creditors against loss.

BANK LIQUIDITY

The acuteness of the problem of bank liquidity stems from three facts that we have already noted: (1) The great bulk of bank liabilities is payable in legal-tender money on demand or on short notice. (2) By far the larger part of bank assets is in the form of debts that are payable only after a period of time. (3) The banks' outstanding obligations to pay on demand or on short notice are usually far in excess of the amount of coin and currency existing in the country. Banks expect, of course, that they will not be asked to pay any large part of their obligations during any short period of time, but these hopes are sometimes disappointed and heavy demands for payment do occur. To understand the problems involved in meeting these demands, we must analyze separately the liquidity problem of an individual bank and of the banking system as a whole.

Liquidity of an Individual Bank

An individual bank must be liquid enough to meet two types of demands for payment: (1) demands by its customers for coin and currency, and (2) payments of adverse clearing balances to other banks in the system with which checks and other claims against the individual bank have been deposited. The first demand can be met only with legal-tender coin and currency; the second can usually be satisfied with coin or currency, checks on the Federal Reserve banks, or checks on other well-known commercial banks. To meet these payments, an individual bank may have recourse to the following sources of funds:

1. Coin and Currency in the Bank's Vault. Although a bank may use its cash holdings to meet demands for payment, it usually gets but little help from this source, for these holdings are ordinarily small—not much in excess of day-to-day working requirements. They rarely exceed 2 or 3 percent of a bank's liabilities.

2. Deposits at the Federal Reserve. Many people persist in believing that a bank may use its legally required reserve for liquidity purposes. This is true only for extremely short periods. The laws governing the reserve requirements of member banks stipulate that these banks must meet their reserve requirements on the average over a period of time, which is one week for banks in the largest cities and two weeks elsewhere. A bank may therefore have a deficiency in its reserves during a part of a reserve period if this deficiency is balanced by sufficient excess reserves during the remainder of the period. But the general rule is that a bank may not pay out reserves it is legally required to hold; only its excess reserves are available for this purpose. Moreover, we must remember that if a bank operating on a 20 percent reserve loses $100,000 of deposits its reserve requirements are lowered by only $20,000 and it must pay the other $80,000 out of other funds.

3. Deposits at Other Commercial Banks. Many banks look upon their deposit claims against other banks as an important source of liquidity. If payees will accept deposits in payment, the effect is merely to redistribute the ownership of deposits in the system. If, however, the payees demand coin or currency, an individual bank can meet demands on it only by draining cash from the other banks—if they can supply it.

4. Collection of Loans or Sale of Debt Instruments to Buyers Other Than Central Banks. To assist itself in meeting demands for payment, a bank usually holds some assets that it considers its "secondary reserves." These are debt instruments, which it believes it can sell quickly and without loss of value. They are made up of such things as call or demand loans on securities, bank acceptances, short-term government securities, and so on. In addition, a bank can sell its other creditor claims over longer periods but perhaps with greater losses. The liquidity of an individual bank depends to a great extent on the quick salability of its assets to other banks and other buyers. Such sales of assets may to some extent induce a flow of coin or currency into the bank without similar losses by other banks; individuals and corporations paying off loans or buying securities may reduce their net holdings of cash to make the necessary payments to the bank. But it must be emphasized that this occurs to only a limited extent. In most cases payment to the individual bank will be made by check, and these checks will be drawn on other banks. Thus, the individual bank secures funds at the expense of other banks.

5. Sale of Assets to and Borrowings from Federal Reserve Banks. A bank may secure funds to meet demands for payment by selling assets to the Federal Reserve banks or by borrowing from them.

The management of a bank faces difficult problems in determining the amount and sources of its liquidity. Not to be liquid enough may prove embarrassing, if not fatal, yet to forecast precisely the amount of liquidity needed is impossible. To be more liquid than necessary is to sacrifice earnings. Moreover, the cost of liquidity varies with the type of asset held for the purpose. Cash in vault, deposits at other banks, and excess reserves may be the most liquid of all assets but they yield no money income. Other assets of high but lesser liquidity yield income, though usually less than assets that are more illiquid. Bank managements therefore strive for some sort of optimum balance between liquidity and earnings and among the various sources of liquidity.

Liquidity of the Banking System as a Whole

As noted earlier, the liquidity problem of the banking system as a whole differs significantly from that of an individual bank in the system. In the first place, an individual bank is subject to "cash" drains to other banks in the system as well as drains to outsiders. The system as a whole need be prepared only against outside drains. But these drains, including net withdrawals of coin and currency, gold exports, and net drains by the Treasury and the Federal Reserve, may at times be large. In the second place, the banking system as a whole has fewer sources of liquidity. We have already noted the extent to which an individual bank attempts to maintain its own liquidity by drawing funds from other banks—by drawing on its deposits at other banks and by calling loans and selling securities in the hope of drawing payments from other banks. For the system as a whole to attempt to meet cash drains in this way may be both calamitous and ineffective. To illustrate this, let us suppose that the public has come to fear that banks in general are in a weak position and cannot meet their obligations to pay in full and on demand. Each depositor is therefore likely to try to withdraw cash before payments are suspended.

When not only one bank but all or most of the banks in the system simultaneously face demands for payment in coin or currency, there are only a few sources of cash with which to meet the drain.

1. Coin and Currency in Bank Vaults. This source, as we have seen, is not of much assistance.

2. Interbank Deposits. This source is of little or no assistance in meeting a general run on the banking system. One bank may try to meet its own problem by drawing on another, but if the latter is also facing demands from individual depositors and other depositor banks, it is likely to be in trouble itself.

3. Deposits of Cash by the Public. If the public has lost confidence in them, the banks can hardly expect net deposits of coin and currency.

4. Calling of Loans and Sale of Bank Assets to Buyers Other Than Federal Reserve Banks. These sources are likely to offer little assistance. When all or most of the banks face large demands for payment, they are hardly likely to be buyers of securities of any kind; virtually all of them will be on the selling side. Moreover, even sales of bank assets to individuals and corporations offer only limited help. Some may pay loans or buy securities from banks by reducing their net holdings of coin or currency, but most of them will do this by writing checks against their deposits. This will reduce the total of deposits outstanding, but it will not supply the banks with coin or currency to be used in meeting demands for payment. And, it must be emphasized, the effect of a widespread calling of loans and selling of assets by the banks is to reduce the money supply in the form of checking deposits, thereby aggravating any existing deflationary trend. By selling assets or calling loans an individual bank may draw cash from other banks. But the banking system as a whole may attract virtually no coin or currency by this means; the result may be merely a ruinous contraction of the total money supply.

5. Reserves at Federal Reserve Banks. The banks may demand cash at Federal Reserve banks in exchange for deposits there. But reserves are only a fraction of bank deposits, and the banks must continue to meet their reserve requirements. Thus, if the banking system suffers a cash drain of $1 billion and operates under 20 percent reserve requirements, the $1 billion reduction of deposits frees only $200 million of reserves; the remaining drain of $800 million must be met from other sources.

6. Borrowings from and Sales of Assets to Federal Reserve Banks. The banking system can get cash to meet demands that are made on it to the extent that the Federal Reserve banks (or other monetary authorities) are willing and able to create additional coin or currency by making loans to banks or buying assets from them. In some cases the Treasury may release idle cash that it holds in its vaults.

In summary, *the banking system as a whole* can obtain cash with which to meet net cash withdrawals only from the following principal sources: (1) From cash drawn from its reserve accounts in the central bank to the extent that its reserve requirements are reduced by the decrease of deposits with the banks. Relief from this source is equal to only a fraction of the reduction in deposits, the amount of the relief depending on the height of the ratio of reserves to deposits. (2) The issue of additional cash by the Federal Reserve System and the Treasury. We shall emphasize many times that in the last analysis the liquidity of the banking system as a whole—its ability to meet its obligations with coin or currency—depends on the extent to which the monetary authorities are able and willing to issue additional cash by buying assets or by lending.

SELECTED READINGS

Federal Deposit Insurance Corporation, *Annual Reports*, Washington.

Robinson, Roland I., *The Management of Bank Funds*, McGraw-Hill, New York, 1951.

CHAPTER 6

United States Banking History

No one can understand fully the present structure of the United States commercial banking system, banking practices and policies, and public attitudes toward banking without some knowledge of the nation's banking history. To bring out some of the major events in our banking history we shall divide it into three main periods: (1) from 1781 to the establishment of the National Banking System in 1863; (2) from 1863 to the establishment of the Federal Reserve System in 1914; and (3) since 1914. Each of these periods will be further subdivided for more detailed analysis.

BANKING FROM 1781 TO 1863

In banking, as in most other aspects of American life, this early period was one of rapid development and widespread controversy. Having gained its independence, the new nation was struggling to determine its social, political, economic, and financial patterns. On all these matters there were important differences of opinion. By far the largest part of the population lived on farms, most of which were largely self-sufficient, all except a few of the cities were small, manufacturing was still in its infancy, and trade occupied a far less important position than it does today. The nation had virtually no experience with banking of modern types, and there were wide disagreements concerning the contributions that banks could make. Some were perhaps too laudatory, overestimating the extent to which banks could stimulate capital formation and promote productivity and trade by providing credit and a more generous supply of money in the form of bank notes and deposits. Others denied that banks were productive at all; instead, they insisted that banks merely lowered the quality of the nation's money because issues of bank notes and deposits drove out, or kept out, an equal value of good metallic coins. Alexander Hamilton and others who shared his goal of developing an industrial and commercial type of economy were generally favorably disposed toward banking, believing that banks were an essential part of such an economy. Thomas

93

Jefferson and his sympathizers, who believed that the country should remain largely agricultural, were generally opposed to banks, at least partly because banking was closely related to industry and commerce. The Federalists and others who favored centralization of political power believed that the power to charter and supervise banks should be exclusively federal. They questioned the constitutionality of state activities in this field. On the other hand, the Anti-Federalists and their friends, who opposed centralization of political power and championed states' rights, insisted that only the states had the power to create and supervise banks and that such federal activities were unconstitutional. Much of the banking controversy of the period is understandable only as a part of the broader controversy over industrialization versus agrarianism and centralization of political power versus states' rights.

It is also important to remember that as a means of payment bank notes were more important than deposits until about the time of the Civil War. Checking deposits were used, especially in the cities, but they were not well suited to a predominantly agricultural country with few towns and slow travel and communication. In fact, during the colonial period the word "bank" meant "a batch of paper money." The first bank of a modern type in this country was the Bank of North America, which was established in Philadelphia in 1782 to aid in financing the Revolutionary War. The Bank of New York and the Bank of Massachusetts were established in 1784. These three were the only incorporated banks in the United States in 1790. There were, however, a few unincorporated or private banks, for under the common law everyone had a right to engage in banking as well as in other types of business. Only later, after 1800, did the states begin to limit banking by unincorporated firms.

The First Bank of the United States, 1791–1811

This bank, the first to be authorized by the federal government, received a twenty-year charter in 1791. It had a capital stock of $10 million, of which $2 million was subscribed by the federal government with funds borrowed from the bank; the remainder was subscribed by private individuals, some of them residents of foreign countries. By today's standards it was a small bank; in its day it was huge. It was not only by far the largest bank of its day but also the largest corporation in America. It established its head office in Philadelphia and branches in the other principal cities of the country: Boston, New York, Baltimore, Norfolk, Charleston, Savannah, and New Orleans. It was in fact a nation-wide bank. Thus, the first federally chartered bank was a nation-wide branch bank jointly owned by the federal government and private investors.

The bank made loans and purchased securities; issued both deposits and bank notes; transferred loan funds and payments from one end of the country to the other; and performed useful functions for the government in lending to it, acting as its depository, and transferring funds for it. It also performed some central banking functions, for it regulated the lending and note-issuing powers of state banks. As the largest bank in the system, its own lending policies greatly affected the reserves of the other banks. When it expanded its loans some of the proceeds flowed to other banks, thereby augmenting their reserves in the form of deposits at the First Bank, notes of the First Bank, or gold and silver specie. When the First Bank contracted its loans it drained reserves from the other banks and limited their lending ability. It could greatly affect their specie reserves and lending power by its disposal of their bank notes that came into its possession. By simply holding these notes or paying them out into circulation it could permit the banks to retain their specie reserves. But by presenting their notes to the issuing banks for redemption it could decrease their specie reserves. It was in the exercise of its central banking power, and especially in limiting the loans and note issues of state banks, that the First Bank made some of its bitterest enemies.

The First Bank seems to have functioned well, especially so when compared with other banks during the first half of the nineteenth century. Nevertheless, Congress refused to renew its charter when it expired in 1811. Several arguments against recharter were advanced. (1) Much of the bank stock was owned by foreigners. Some people feared that foreigners would exercise excessive control over our economy through the bank—though foreign stockholders had no vote—and they also argued that money was drained out of the country by the payment of dividends to foreign stockholders. (2) Only "hard money" was good money. A large part of the community was still opposed to paper money of any sort, whether issued by banks or by government. (3) The bank was unconstitutional. The Constitution contained no express provision for bank charters. The Anti-Federalists contended that no such power was even implied, hence the bank had been unconstitutional from the beginning. Moreover, they feared that it would tend to centralize power in the federal government at the expense of the states, as its foremost proponent, Alexander Hamilton, hoped it would. It was frequently charged, apparently with some justice, that the bank was dominated by Federalists and that it discriminated against Anti-Federalists in making loans. (4) The bank discouraged the growth of state banks. That it curbed the issue of state bank notes by presenting them regularly for redemption is clear. Some elements of the community, including the owners and officers of state banks as well as other proponents of "easy money," wanted to eliminate the curbing effects of the bank. But whatever the deciding motives of Congress in refusing its recharter, the First Bank of the United States expired in 1811.

State Banking, 1811–1816

Freed from the restraining influence of the First Bank and favored by the inflationary financing of the War of 1812, state banks went on a spree. They grew in number from 88 in 1811 to 246 in 1816, and their note issue rose from $45 million in 1812 to at least $100 million in 1817. Virtually all of them ceased redeeming their notes in gold or silver, and their notes depreciated by varying amounts; the notes of many banks became virtually worthless. All the banking abuses that we shall study later appeared during this period. It was largely because of these gross abuses of the banking privilege by state banks and because of the extreme disorder of the monetary system that the Second Bank of the United States was established in 1816.

The Second Bank of the United States, 1816–1836

The Second Bank of the United States received a twenty-year charter from the federal government in 1816. In many respects it resembled the First Bank, but it was much larger and some of its charter provisions were different. Its capital was fixed at $35 million, of which one fifth was to be subscribed by the federal government and paid for with its bonds. The remaining $28 million was subscribed by individuals, corporations, companies, and states, no one of whom was permitted to subscribe more than $300,000. At least one fourth of these private subscriptions had to be paid in gold or silver; the remaining three fourths could be paid in either specie or securities of the federal government. The bank was governed by a board of directors, of whom five were appointed by the President of the United States and twenty were elected by the private stockholders. The amount of property that the bank could hold was limited to $55 million, and its debts, excluding deposits but including bank notes, were limited to $35 million. These limitations did not prevent the bank from being a giant institution as compared with other firms of the period. It established 25 branches to serve all the settled parts of the country.

Like the First Bank, the Second Bank performed both commercial and central banking functions. As a commercial bank it lent to individuals, business firms, states, and the federal government; it accepted deposits from individuals and business firms as well as from governmental units; it issued bank notes; it transferred funds from one area to another; and it engaged in foreign-exchange operations. It also performed various functions that are usually entrusted to a central bank. It held government deposits, acted as fiscal agent of the government, and transferred funds from area to area for government account. Moreover, it acted as a regulator of state banks, presenting their notes for redemption, insisting that they redeem their obligations promptly in specie, and in general limiting the amount of credit they created. This was one of the principal purposes for which the Second Bank was created.

By 1833 the Second Bank had become so unpopular with President Andrew Jackson and many of the Jacksonian Democrats that federal deposits were withdrawn from it and placed with selected state banks, and its charter was not renewed on its expiration in 1836. The country was to see no more federally chartered banks until 1863 and was not to have another central banking system until 1914.

To evaluate the success of the Second Bank and the wisdom of Jackson's action in abolishing it is still a difficult task, for most of the contemporary discussions were rabidly partisan, and even some present-day writers are inclined to be apologists for either the bank or Jackson. We shall, however, note some of the reasons for the refusal to recharter the bank. No special attention will be given to charges that it was grossly mismanaged. It is true that mismanagement did appear in its early years and that later the bank performed some of its functions unwisely, or at least clumsily. But the principal objections to it came from deeper sources.

1. **Unconstitutionality.** Although the power of the strict constructionists had diminished greatly, critics of the bank again alleged that the federal government had no constitutional power to charter a bank. It is unlikely, however, that these people would have raised the question of constitutionality if they had not opposed the bank on other grounds.

2. **Opposition to Paper Money.** "Hard-money" men such as Senator Benton opposed paper money of any kind and favored the exclusive use of gold and silver coin. They denied that banks could increase the total quantity of money in a country or that they could "quicken trade" and insisted that bank money merely drove out of circulation an equivalent amount of gold and silver.

3. **Opposition by State Banks.** State banks, especially those that wanted to follow liberal lending and note-issue policies, were much opposed to the Second Bank. In the first place, the bank brought pressure on them to keep their notes redeemable in specie and to limit the quantity of their notes to the amount that they could redeem at par. This had the obvious effect of limiting state bank earnings. In the second place, the Second Bank competed with state banks in making loans. Not only did it take the business of lending away from state banks, but it also reduced interest rates in some areas, for its discount rate was limited to 6 percent. And in the third place, some state banks, especially those in New York, wanted the large volume of federal government deposits that the Second Bank enjoyed. This opposition by state banks was a potent factor in the Second Bank's undoing.

4. **Opposition by Others Who Favored Easy-Money Policies.** Realizing that the Second Bank tended to restrict the total amount of money created and the total volume of loans extended by banks, many businessmen, landowners, potential land speculators, and others who felt they would benefit by easier money worked for the abolition of the bank.

5. **Opposition to the Concentration of Financial and Economic Power.** We have already mentioned that the Second Bank was a giant institution during the period in which it operated. It held about a third of all the banking

assets of the country and was probably larger than any other business firm. Its critics insisted that a free people could ill afford to grant such power to any small group, for with this financial power went the ability to determine the life and death of banks and other business enterprises, the level of employment and prosperity, and even the political freedom of the people. Such critics repeatedly asserted that concentration of economic power in the hands of a few was incompatible with political democracy.

6. **Political Activity by the Bank.** Although some attempts were made to secure members of both political parties as directors and officers of the bank, it was well known that the large majority of those in control of it were opposed to Jackson and his party. Moreover, some of these men were aggressive in their political activities. It is difficult to discover the extent to which the bank's officers took the political initiative and to what extent their activities were merely defenses against earlier attacks on the bank. But it seems certain that the bank did enter the political arena and that at least some of its branch managers used their lending power to influence votes. The fate of the bank was sealed when its president, Nicholas Biddle, openly but vainly opposed Jackson's reëlection in 1832 and made the recharter of the bank one of the principal issues of the presidential campaign. A diplomatic president of the Second Bank might have been able to arrive at a satisfactory *modus vivendi* with the choleric President Jackson. But Biddle was not such a man. "Nicholas Biddle was a man of intense energy, autocratic in temper, and possessing supreme confidence in his own judgment. It was inevitable that he should rule and not merely reign, and the proofs that he did rule are observable everywhere."[1] The inevitable clash between Biddle and Jackson may have altered the entire course of our banking history.

Was President Jackson right in refusing to recharter the Second Bank in 1836? A full answer to this question would require far more space than we can devote to it. Two facts now seem clear, however. In the first place, it is questionable public policy to grant central banking powers to a corporation largely owned and controlled by private individuals and corporations, which is operated by its owners primarily for profit, and which as a profit-seeking enterprise has interests in conflict with those of the banks that it regulates. We now recognize that central banking is a governmental function that can be properly exercised only by institutions whose primary motive is not profits but financial and economic stabilization. A properly managed central bank must often follow policies that will decrease its profits. In the second place, however, it is quite clear that the abolition of the Second Bank without establishing another institution to take over its functions was a major blunder. It ushered in a generation of banking anarchy and monetary disorder.

[1] Davis R. Dewey, *The Second Bank of the United States*, Senate Document No. 571, Government Printing Office, Washington, 1912, p. 263.

State Banking, 1836–1863

From the lapse of the Second Bank's charter in 1836 until the establishment of the National Banking System in 1863, our banking system was made up exclusively of private (unincorporated) banks and of banks operating under corporate charters granted by the various states. We shall not discuss the unincorporated banks except to say that as a group they seem to have been neither significantly better nor significantly worse than the incorporated banks as a group. The incorporated banks, operating under widely diverse state laws, varied from good to very bad. Some performed their functions satisfactorily, especially toward the end of the period. At the other extreme, many engaged in practically all the banking abuses known to man.

Prior to 1837 a bank could secure a corporate charter from a state only by a special legislative act. This method of granting bank charters gradually fell into disfavor for several reasons. It injected banks into politics and politics into banks. Loyal members of the political party in power might receive a bank charter, whereas members of the minority party had little chance of success. The controversy over bank charters threatened to corrupt state governments. Legislators were offered large sums of money to grant new charters, and other large sums by existing banks to reject the applications of potential competitors. Furthermore, this method of granting charters often gave monopoly power to the favored banks. This was considered objectionable, both because of its alleged unfairness to those who wished to become bankers and because it was believed to restrict the total amount of credit granted, thereby impeding the economic expansion of the country.

To remedy this situation, Michigan in 1837 and New York in 1838 enacted "free banking laws." Most of the other states later enacted laws of the same general type. These laws ended the practice of granting charters by special legislative act and provided that anyone might secure a corporate charter and engage in banking by complying with the provisions of a general bank incorporation law. Banking was made "free" to all enterprisers who met the specified general requirements. The quality of state banks came to depend upon the appropriateness of these general requirements and upon the effectiveness with which they were enforced. In some states the requirements were strict; banks could issue notes only by depositing with a state official an equivalent amount of high-quality bonds and by meeting adequate capital and reserve requirements. But in more of the states the collateral requirements for notes were hopelessly inadequate, and capital and reserve requirements were virtually meaningless.

The relationships between banks and the states varied widely. At one extreme, the state banks merely received their charters from the state; they secured all their capital from private sources and made any loans that were permitted within the broad framework of the banking laws. At the other extreme, many banks were wholly owned and operated by states. There were all sorts of variations between these two extremes. Thus, some banks were owned jointly by a state and private investors. Others had to pay large sums to the state for the privilege of banking. And still others were permitted to act as banks only if they would lend stipulated amounts to canal companies, railroads, or other enterprises considered meritorious by the state legislature. In a period when "capital" was still scarce, states encouraged and even forced banks to lend large amounts for financing selected projects.

Abuses by the State-Chartered Banks Before the Civil War

Without inferring that all the banks were guilty, we shall now investigate the principal banking abuses during this period. These abuses were so wide-

TABLE 12.   State Banks, 1834–1861

Year	Number of State Banks	State Bank Notes Outstanding (In millions)	Deposits at State Banks (In millions)	Total State Bank Notes and Deposits (In millions)
1834	506	$ 95	$ 76	$171
1835	704	104	83	187
1836	713	140	115	255
1837	788	149	127	276
1838	829	116	85	201
1839	840	135	90	225
1840	901	107	76	183
1841	784	107	65	172
1842	692	84	62	146
1843	691	59	56	115
1844	696	75	85	160
1845	707	90	88	178
1846	707	106	97	203
1847	715	106	92	198
1848	751	129	103	232
1849	782	115	91	206
1850	824	131	110	241
1851	879	155	129	284
1852	815	161	137	298
1853	750	146	146	292
1854	1208	205	188	393
1855	1307	187	190	377
1856	1398	196	213	409
1857	1416	215	230	445
1858	1422	155	186	341
1859	1476	193	260	453
1860	1562	207	254	461
1861	1601	202	257	459

SOURCE: Board of Governors of the Federal Reserve System, *Banking Studies*, Washington, 1941, pp. 417–418.

spread that they greatly influenced both public attitudes toward banks and subsequent banking legislation. Some of the most serious banking abuses were the following:

1. **Violent Fluctuations in the Amount of Money Created by the Banks in the Form of Bank Notes and Checking Deposits.** With the transfer of federal deposits from the Second Bank to selected state banks and the removal of the moderating hand of the Second Bank, both the number of state banks and the volume of their credit increased. This is shown in Table 12.

This growth was far from steady, however. The banks would expand rapidly for a time and then undergo severe contraction. The principal expansions and contractions during this period are shown in Table 13, though the data are admittedly imperfect. Business activity and prices fluctuated widely as banks al-

TABLE 13. Principal Expansions and Contractions of State Bank Notes and Deposits, 1834–1860

Period	Percentage Expansion (+), or Contraction (−)		
	Bank Notes	Bank Deposits	Total Notes and Deposits
1834 to 1837	+56%	+67%	+61%
1837 to 1843	−60	−56	−58
1843 to 1848	+119	+84	+102
1848 to 1849	−11	−12	−11
1849 to 1854	+78	+107	+91
1854 to 1855	−9	+2	−4
1855 to 1857	+15	+21	+18
1857 to 1858	−28	−19	−24
1858 to 1860	+36	+37	+35

SOURCE: Derived from data in Table 12.

ternated inflationary periods of increased money supplies and liberal loans with periods of shrinking money supplies and reduced loans. The banks' policies were not the sole causes of these fluctuations, but they were unquestionably contributory.

2. **Inadequate Bank Capital.** Having used all of the devices described earlier, many banks failed to have large enough capital accounts to protect their creditors. Some made no pretense of having adequate capital. Others had a large enough nominal capital, but it was paid for with the promissory notes of the stockholders, many of whom were unable to meet their obligations. Even when bank stocks were initially paid for with gold or silver, stockholders often borrowed back the coin, giving in return their doubtful paper. Furthermore, bank capital was frequently dissipated by excessive dividend payments.

3. **Risky and Illiquid Loans.** Many of the banks made highly risky and highly speculative loans without regard for the safety of their creditors, and

some lent excessively to their own stockholders and officers. Moreover, many of the loans were highly illiquid. This was especially true of the banks' large loans on real estate, much of which was not in use but was being held for speculative purposes. This combination of inadequate bank capital and highly risky and illiquid loans could lead to but one result: numerous bank failures and serious losses to noteholders and other bank creditors.

4. Inadequate Reserves Against Notes and Deposits. In certain of the state banking laws reserve requirements were either wholly absent or very inadequate, and evasions of existing requirements were widespread. Many banks issued large quantities of notes and deposits with little or no regard for their reserve situation and with little ability to redeem their obligations on demand.

As a result of all these abuses—excessive issues of bank notes, inadequate bank capital, risky and illiquid bank assets, and highly inadequate reserves—bank notes had widely differing values. The notes of some banks were freely redeemed in gold and silver and circulated at their face value. Others circulated at small but varying discounts; still others circulated at only a small percentage of their face value; and many became completely worthless. A "know your money" campaign would have been an utter failure in this period.

State bank notes in this period may be divided into four main categories: (1) genuine notes of banks still in operation, (2) genuine notes of failed banks, (3) genuine notes whose denominations had been raised, and (4) counterfeits. The genuine notes of banks still in operation varied greatly in value, for around 1860 such notes were issued by nearly 1600 banks operating under the widely diverse laws of some 30 states. Even the banks in a given state varied widely in quality. Some, as we have seen, issued their notes in moderation and redeemed them freely in specie. Others issued notes in great quantity and with virtually no assets behind them and then employed ingenious devices to avoid redeeming them. For example, an enterpriser would secure a bank charter, pledge virtually worthless securities as collateral for a large volume of bank notes, set up a banking "office" in a remote swamp, put the notes into circulation, and use various ruses to keep his location secret. Only later would some innocent recipient of the bank's notes find that they were virtually worthless.

The period was a counterfeiter's paradise. Each of the hundreds of banks issued notes of its own design and in many denominations; the notes were made of many kinds of paper, mostly of low quality; the workmanship on the genuine notes was usually poor; and no one could be familiar with all the bank notes outstanding. Under these conditions it was easy to raise the denomination of genuine notes and to issue counterfeits on existent or even nonexistent banks. "Bicknall's Counterfeit Detector and Bank-Note List of January 1, 1839, contains the names of 54 banks that had failed at different times; of 20 fictitious banks, the pretended notes of which are in circulation; of 43 banks besides, for the notes of which there is no sale; of 254 banks, the notes of which have been counterfeited or altered; and 1,395 descriptions of counterfeited or altered notes then supposed to be in circulation, from one dollar to five hundred."[2] That these conditions had not been remedied by 1858 is indicated by the fact that Nicholas's Bank Note Reporter gave 5400 separate descriptions of counterfeit, altered, and spurious notes. There were 30 different counterfeit issues of the Bank of Delaware notes.[3]

The numerous "counterfeit detectors and bank note reporters" that attempted to warn against counterfeits and to indicate the current values of the various bank notes were of only limited assistance. Even with their supplements they were often out of date, they were beyond the reach of small tradesmen and individuals, and they could not remove the confusion in trade resulting from the fact that the price charged for an article depended on the type of bank note with which payment was to be made.

Though banking abuses during this period were widespread, we must not leave the impression that all state banks were unsound. Some states, notably New York, Massachusetts, and Louisiana, enacted highly protective banking laws and implemented them with bank supervision and examinations. In fact, some of these laws, especially those of New York, contributed much to the legislation establishing the national banking system.

THE NATIONAL BANKING SYSTEM, 1863–1914

In 1863, just 27 years after the expiration of the Second Bank of the United States, the federal government again entered the banking field by passing "An act to provide a national currency, secured by a pledge of United States Stocks, and to provide for the Circulation and Redemption thereof." The 1863 law, which contained a large number of imperfections, was replaced by a new law in 1864. This latter is usually referred to as the National Banking Act.

In providing for a new system of national (federally chartered) banks to be owned and operated by private individuals, Congress had two principal motives: (1) to replace the unsound and unsafe state banking system with new banks that would issue safe and uniform currency, and (2) to secure a new source of loans with which to finance the Civil War. Ever since the demise of the Second Bank there had been a widespread demand for banking reform, and many contended that a satisfactory system of note issue could be achieved only with centralized control and uniform notes. This demand was not successful, however, until reinforced by the exigencies of Civil War finance. Sec-

---

[2] Raguet, quoted by Horace White, *Money and Banking*, Ginn, Boston, 1896, pp. 403–404.
[3] *Ibid.*, p. 398.

retary Chase and others believed that they could create an additional market for government bonds by permitting the creation of new banks that could issue notes only on the basis of their holdings of these securities. Thus, the National Banking System owes its birth to the demand for safer types of bank money and to the financial embarrassment of the Treasury. But it proved more useful as a means of banking reform than as a source of Civil War funds.

Principal Provisions of the National Banking Act

We have already said that the National Banking Act owed much to earlier state banking laws, especially those of New York. The new law provided for "free banking." Anyone meeting the general requirements of the act was to receive a charter and permission to engage in banking. A new office, the Comptroller of the Currency, was created in the Treasury Department to grant charters and to administer all laws relating to national banks. Some of the principal provisions regulating the establishment and operation of national banks were the following:

1. **Capital.** To enhance bank safety, several capital requirements were imposed. Minimum capital requirements, which are the same today, were fixed as follows:

$ 50,000 in cities of not over 6000 inhabitants.
$100,000 in cities with from 6000 to 50,000 inhabitants.
$200,000 in cities with over 50,000 inhabitants.[4]

At least 50 percent of the subscribed capital had to be paid in before a bank could begin business, and the remainder had to be paid within five months. The stock was subject to double liability. In order to expand the market for government securities, each bank was required to deliver to the Treasury of the United States registered bonds amounting to not less than $30,000 or one third of its capital stock, whichever was larger.[5] These bonds could be used as collateral for issues of national bank notes.

2. **Regulation of Bank Loans.** In order to promote safety and liquidity, many restrictions were placed on bank assets. Each national bank was forbidden to lend on real estate or to lend to any one borrower an amount exceeding 10 percent of its capital stock.

3. **Supervision and Examination.** In order to insure compliance with both the letter and the spirit of the act, national banks were required to supply the Comptroller of the Currency with periodic reports on their financial condition and were made subject to examination by his representatives.

4. **Reserve Requirements Against Notes and Deposits.** In order to enhance

[4] From 1900 to 1933 the minimum capital requirement was only $25,000 in places with not more than 3000 inhabitants. This was reëstablished at $50,000 in 1933.

[5] This requirement that national banks buy government securities was modified toward the end of the century and dropped after 1900. The double-liability provision was repealed during the depression of the 1930's.

bank liquidity and limit the amount of bank money, minimum reserve requirements were specified for both circulating notes and deposits. Banks in reserve and central reserve cities were required to hold reserves of 25 percent and banks in other cities 15 percent, of their outstanding circulating note and deposits. In 1874 national banks were relieved of the necessity of carrying reserves against their note issues.

5. Protection to Noteholders. Remembering the sorry record of state bank notes, the framers of the National Banking Act were determined that national bank notes should be perfectly safe, that they would all circulate at parity with other types of money, and that they would always be freely redeemable. To this end the act provided that: (a) These notes could be issued only against United States government bonds deposited with the Comptroller of the Currency, the amount of notes not to exceed 90 percent of the par value of the bonds or 90 percent of the market value of the bonds, whichever was smaller. (b) The issuing bank should maintain a redemption fund with the Comptroller equal to 5 percent of its outstanding notes, though this could be counted as part of the bank's required reserve. (c) In case of refusal by a national bank to redeem its notes, the Comptroller might sell the pledged bonds and use the proceeds to pay noteholders, any remaining claims of noteholders to constitute a first claim against the assets of the bank. (d) No national bank might issue notes in amounts exceeding its capital stock. (e) The total circulation of national bank notes should not exceed $300 million (this limitation was later revised and was wholly removed after 1875). (f) Each national bank should accept the notes of every other national bank at par. Thus, every effort was made to insure the safety and parity of value of national bank notes. In these respects the act was successful.

State Banks

It was hoped that the authorization of national banks would induce state banks to take out federal charters and comply with the requirements of the National Banking Act. When it became evident that few state banks were going to do this, Congress decided to force the issue by levying a 10 percent tax on any bank or individual paying out or using state bank notes. The purpose was to end the issuance of circulating notes by state banks and to force all or most of these banks to become national banks or to cease doing a general banking business. As shown in Table 14, the act did succeed in reducing the number of state banks from 1089 in 1864 to 247 in 1868. After that time, however, state banks again began to expand, and by 1914 they outnumbered national banks by more than 2 to 1.

How were state banks able not only to survive but even to expand greatly in spite of the prohibitive tax on their notes? First and foremost is the fact that note issue had become of much less importance in banking. With the growth of cities and more rapid transportation and communication, people used checking deposits more and more as a means of payment. With the privilege of creating checking deposits a bank could now operate successfully without issuing notes. But why did many banks prefer to operate under state rather than federal charters when national banks also had the right to create circulating notes? The answer is to be found largely in the fact that many states imposed less rigid restrictions and granted more liberal powers than those contained in the National Banking Act. In general, state banking laws provided lower capital

TABLE 14. State and National Banks in the United States, 1864–1914

Year	State Banks	National Banks
1864	1,089	467
1868	247	1640
1870	325	1612
1880	650	2076
1890	2,250	3484
1900	5,007	3731
1910	14,348	7138
1914	17,498	7518

SOURCE: Board of Governors of the Federal Reserve System, *Banking Studies*, Washington, 1941, p. 418.

requirements, lower reserve requirements, less supervision by the government, more liberal powers to lend on real estate, greater ability to accept drafts drawn on a bank, and more power to engage in fiduciary activities, such as operating trust departments. This was especially true in the western and southern states, where many of the state banks were located.

Shortcomings of the National Banking System

Though the National Banking System unquestionably raised greatly the general quality of United States banking, it became subject to an increasing amount of criticism. Demands for further banking reform swelled during the late years of the nineteenth century and grew still more in the first years of the twentieth, finally ushering in the Federal Reserve System in 1914. Although many aspects of national banks were criticized, the greatest complaint was against their "inflexibility" or "inelasticity." The keynote of the National Banking Act was safety, especially safety of national bank notes. Less attention was paid to the safety of deposits. Critics now complained that the system was too inflexible and that it must be given a greater degree of "elasticity." The meaning of this term was often unclear, but we can discover its general content as we proceed.

Though national bank notes were safe, there was no provision for appropriate variations in their quantity over the long run, in response to seasonal variations in the need for them, and during crisis periods. We have already seen that these notes could be issued only on the basis of federal bonds, the amount of notes being limited to 90 percent of the par or market value— *whichever was lower*—of the bonds deposited with the Comptroller. Thus, the supply of national bank notes depended on the government bond market. The supply obviously could not exceed 90 percent of the eligible bonds outstanding. Within this limit the quantity of notes actually issued by banks depended on the profitability of issuing them. When government bonds could be purchased at or below par, a relatively large volume of national bank notes was issued, because a bank could issue notes equal to 90 percent of the purchase cost of the bonds. But the profitability of issuing notes was decreased and in some cases eliminated as the market price of bonds rose above their par value. It was for these reasons that the volume of national bank notes outstanding fell from $352 million in 1882 to $162 million in 1891, a reduction of 54 percent. But they had risen to $715 million by 1914. Critics maintained that a note system of this type based on the government bond market could never supply a properly "elastic" currency that would respond properly to the needs of business. The volume of these notes fluctuated, but not necessarily in ways that were appropriate to economic needs.

National bank notes were also criticized for their lack of seasonal elasticity. The demand for currency for hand-to-hand use showed marked seasonal variations, reaching peaks in the early autumn and around Christmas and dropping to lower levels during other seasons. But the volume of outstanding national bank notes remained relatively constant throughout the year; hence banks could meet the seasonal peak demands for currency only by draining funds from their reserves, and the inflow of currency to the banks during slack seasons increased their reserves. Critics complained that the seasonal inelasticity of national bank notes brought about seasonal credit stringencies by forcing banks to draw on their reserves to meet peak seasonal demands for cash, and then led to an undue easing of credit in other seasons as currency flowed back into bank reserves. They demanded the creation of a currency that would be seasonally elastic—that would increase and decrease with seasonal demands for coin and currency and would leave bank reserves unaffected.

Critics also complained of the inelasticity of national bank notes during banking crises. They pointed out that there was no existing way in which new currency could be created to satisfy general demands on the banks for cash, and that banks could not meet these demands out of the limited cash in their vaults. They proposed the authorization of a new type of currency whose quantity could be increased to meet crisis demands and then decreased again as demands for cash subsided. We shall see later that one of the principal purposes of the Federal Reserve Act of 1914 was to supply an elastic currency in the form of Federal Reserve notes.

The disturbing effects of an inelastic bank note system were intensified by a defective system of reserve requirements. We have already seen that national banks were required to maintain reserves against both notes and deposits—later against deposits only—equal to 25 percent in central reserve and reserve cities and 15 percent in other places. The banks in a few of the largest cities—New York, Chicago, and St. Louis—were designated as "central reserve city banks," those in 47 other cities as "reserve city banks," and those in other places as "country banks." That this general classification of banks for the purpose of fixing reserve requirements was carried over into the Federal Reserve Act will be made clear later. Though these reserve requirements appeared large, the form of reserves was defective, as is suggested by the following summary:

Type of Bank	Percentage Reserve Requirement	Composition of Required Reserves
Country banks	15	$\frac{2}{5}$ of reserve (or 6% of deposits) as cash in vault; remaining $\frac{3}{5}$ of reserve (9% of deposits) to be either cash in vault or deposits with reserve city or central reserve city banks.
Reserve city banks	25	$\frac{1}{2}$ of reserve (12.5% of deposits) as cash in vault; remaining $\frac{1}{2}$ of reserve (12.5% of deposits) as either cash in vault or deposits in central reserve city banks.
Central reserve city banks	25	All as cash in vault.

This reserve system had three principal weaknesses. In the first place, a large part of the nominal reserve was "fictitious," in the sense that it was not available for meeting actual cash drains from the banking system. This was because such a large part of the reserves was in the form of deposits with other banks, which in turn held only a small percentage of actual cash as a reserve against their deposit obligations. Suppose, for example, that customers of country banks should demand large amounts of coin or currency. Holding an actual cash reserve equal to only 6 percent of their deposits, the country banks would call on the reserve city banks to send them cash. But the reserve city banks held a reserve equal to only 25 percent of their total deposits, only half of the reserve being in actual cash. To meet the drain, they in turn would call upon central reserve city banks for cash; but these banks had reserves equal to only 25 percent of their deposits. Thus, the central reserve and the reserve city banks were in a precarious position; they were liable to drains not only by their own customers but by all the banks that held "reserves" in the form of deposits with them. The threat of general cash withdrawals by the public or of a suspension of cash payments by the banks in large cities could therefore bring on a banking panic, or at least a general tightening of credit, for it would lead country banks to withdraw their "reserves" from reserve city and central reserve city banks in order to hold their reserves in the form of cash in their own vaults, and the reserve city banks would make similar withdrawals from the central reserve city banks. It is no wonder that the National Banking System was susceptible to panics.

In the second place, reserve requirements were very inflexible. Each bank was ordered to meet its reserve requirements at all times; it could not legally make any new loans while its reserves were deficient. Thus, when banks had lent up to the limit permitted by their reserves, and especially when their reserves had decreased, new lending was brought to a sudden stop and a scramble to liquidate loans was likely to occur. There arose a general demand that reserve requirements be relaxed by being suspended in periods of crisis, or at least by banks' being allowed to meet these requirements on the average over a period of time, deficiencies at one time being balanced by overages at another. This latter method is employed for banks that are members of the Federal Reserve System.

In the third place, many criticized the "parcelation of reserves" resulting from the lack of any orderly way of pooling the reserves of individual banks to meet drains of cash from any segment of the banking system. Some compared existing reserve requirements with attempts to fight fires by placing a pail of water in each house; the greater effectiveness of pooling the water and providing a system of pipes to concentrate it at the point of need is obvious. Advocates of bank reform proposed the establishment of a similar system of pooling individual bank reserves so that they could be concentrated at the points of greatest need in time of emergency. This was another purpose of the Federal Reserve Act of 1914.

The inelasticity of national bank notes and the defects—or at least the inadequacy—of bank reserve requirements were dramatized by the recurrent banking panics that occurred under the National Banking System before 1914. There were full-fledged panics in 1873, in 1884, in 1893, and in 1907, and serious credit stringencies threatened at other times. Unable to meet their obligations to pay cash on demand, most banks suspended payments for periods of varying lengths; some of them never reopened, a mad scramble to call loans ensued, and business activity suffered. The panic of 1907 was the last straw; popular disgust with recurrent panics made the Federal Reserve Act politically possible, though it had objectives beyond that of panic prevention.

Summary

When the Federal Reserve Act was passed in 1913 it had been 121 years since the establishment of the first modern-type bank in the United States in 1792. This long period had been one of controversy and vacillation, but out of it emerged many aspects of banking structure and policy that are still observable. In the struggle for power to charter and regulate commercial banks, neither the advocates of federal jurisdiction nor the advocates of state jurisdiction had won a complete victory. The outcome was a compromise, with both the federal government and the 48 states remaining in the field. After two temporary successes with the First and Second Banks, the federal government entered the field permanently with the authorization of national banks in 1863. Through the device of taxing their notes it even succeeded in depriving state-chartered banks of the privilege of note issue. Yet state banks multiplied and by 1914 accounted for more than two thirds of all commercial banks in the United States. They had become so firmly established, both economically and politically, that it has been impossible to secure federal legislation to force them to join the Federal Reserve System or the Federal Deposit Insurance Corporation and subject themselves to the jurisdiction of those federal agencies. Their friends still successfully insist that they should have the privilege of joining if they wish to do so, but that they should not be subjected to legal compulsion. This so-called "dual banking system"—the co-existence of federal- and state-chartered banks without a clear centralization of responsibility for their creation and regulation—puzzles many foreign observers who are accustomed to centralized jurisdiction over banks.

By the early twentieth century the banking systems of most other countries had become highly concentrated. They had only a few banks, each operating many branches. In contrast, the United States had more than 25,000 commercial banking corporations in 1914. A great majority of these had only a single office; most of the branch banks that did exist operated only a few offices, and none was more than state-wide in scope. In short, the American system was predominantly one of "independent unit banking." This structure was encouraged by nineteenth-century policies that permitted ease of entry and discouraged the establishment of branches. "Free banking," first permitted in New York and Michigan in the 1830's but soon adopted in other states and in the National Banking Act, opened banking to all who could meet the requirements laid down in the general banking laws. Even the requirements in the National Banking Act were liberal enough to permit the establishment of many national banks. Most of the state requirements were even less onerous. While banking laws permitted ease of entry, they became increasingly restrictive against branch banking. As noted earlier, many of the early banks were branch systems. Both the First and Second Banks of the United States operated nation-wide systems of branches. Many of the state banks also had branches. Despite this early history, the National Banking Act made no specific mention of branches and this was construed as a prohibition. However, an amendment in 1865 permitted a state bank converting into a national bank to retain its existing branches. Many of the states also enacted restrictive laws. Some permitted no branches; others limited their geographical area or number. These restrictions on branch banking tended in at least two ways to encourage the establishment and continuation of a large number of independent unit banks. In the first place, by limiting the ability of existing banks to supply additional banking facilities through the establishment of branches, they encouraged the establishment of new independent unit banks. In the second place, they discouraged bank mergers by prohibiting, or at least restricting, the conversion of absorbed banks into branches.

We shall see later that the structure of our banking system is still a highly controversial issue. Neither public officials nor bankers can agree upon the relative merits and roles of independent unit banks and multiple office banking.

BANKING SINCE 1914

Though we shall later deal with many aspects of contemporary commercial banking, it will be useful at this point to look briefly at a few of the main events in our banking history since the establishment of the Federal Reserve System in 1914.

The Number of Banks

The number of banks grew rapidly during the late nineteenth and early twentieth centuries. In 1870 there were fewer than 2000 banks in the United States; by 1914 there were more than 25,000 and by 1921 nearly 30,000. But this was the peak, to be followed by a sharp decline. By the late 1950's, less than four decades later, the number of banks had declined by more than 50 percent—this despite a great growth of the nation's population and an even greater growth of its real income and wealth. Why did this reversal occur?

TABLE 15. Commercial Banks in the United
States, 1914–1957

Year	Total	State Banks	National Banks
1914	25,510	17,992	7,518
1921	29,788	21,638	8,150
1929	25,113	17,583	7,530
1941	14,305	9,175	5,130
1957	13,622	8,975	4,647

SOURCES: Board of Governors of the Federal Reserve System, *Banking and Monetary Statistics*, Washington, 1943, p. 16; *Federal Reserve Bulletin*, March, 1958, p. 317.

The decrease in the number of banks obviously reflects the fact that the number of banks discontinuing operations greatly exceeded the number of new banks created. But why did so many banks discontinue operations? Most of them failed; a smaller number were merged with other banks. Though not all the bank failures involved losses to depositors, a large proportion of them did.

Bank Failures

Even in the nineteenth and early twentieth centuries the United States enjoyed the dubious distinction of having one of the highest failure rates, if not the highest, to be found in any important commercial banking system. Nearly 3000 banks failed in the 1864–1920 period. But the worst was yet to come.

Another 5411 banks had suspended operations by 1929, and still another 8812 by the end of 1933. The mortality rate was especially high among smaller banks, but many large ones fell. Since the banking purge and reform of 1933, bank failures have been few.

TABLE 16.   Bank Suspensions in the United States

Period	National Banks	State Banks	Total
1864–1896	328	1,234	1,562
1897–1920	256	1,177	1,433
1921–1929	766	4,645	5,411
1930–1933	1947	6,865	8,812
1934–1950	72	343	415
Total	3369	14,264	17,633

SOURCES: For the period 1864–96, Cyril B. Upham and Edwin Lamke, *Closed and Distressed Banks*, Brookings Institution, Washington, 1934, p. 245. For 1897–1941, Board of Governors of the Federal Reserve System, *Banking and Monetary Statistics*, Washington, 1943, p. 283. For the period since 1941, *Annual Reports of the Federal Deposit Insurance Corporation*.

The figures are not strictly accurate or comparable for different periods, but they indicate the general situation faithfully enough for our present purposes.

To generalize about the reasons for bank failures or failures of any type of business enterprise is difficult, for the reasons vary from case to case and even in a particular case failure usually results not from a single cause but from a combination of conditions. Nevertheless, it is possible to isolate some of the most important factors making for high bank failure rates prior to 1934.

1. Inherent weaknesses in small independent unit banks. Whatever may be the relative merits of large independent unit banks and branch banking systems, it is clear that small independent unit banks are especially liable to failure. Many are too small to be efficient, their management is often not well trained, and a large percentage of their assets is likely to be in the form of loans to local agriculture, industry, or trade. Thus they are likely to be weak in the face of unfavorable economic developments, not only those in the economy at large, but also those limited to their own localities.

2. "Overbanking." Because it is difficult to specify the "proper" amount of banking for an area, it is difficult to say precisely when that area is "overbanked." Yet despite the ambiguity of the term it is clear that many places

were overbanked in the early 1920's when we had nearly 30,000 banks, and that this situation was remedied only slowly. Some places did not have excessive amounts of banking resources, but they had too many small banks to achieve efficiency and safety. It was not unusual for a village with 2000 inhabitants to have three or more banks; many small and medium-sized cities were similarly overbanked. Some banks in such situations would have failed even under favorable economic conditions; adverse economic developments assured disaster.

3. Shifts in the location of business. Thousands of banks were seriously weakened by the revolution in highway transportation during the 1920's and 1930's. Prior to the days of hard-surfaced roads, automobiles, and farm trucks, farmers took much of their business to nearby agricultural villages or small towns. Here they sold many of their products, bought supplies, and did their banking. But as new roads and motor vehicles increased the speed and reduced the cost of transportation the farmer took his business—including his deposits and borrowing—to the county seat or some other larger city. The smaller village or town was left to wither on the vine; its banks were fortunate if they escaped a less lingering death. Other shifts of business also helped bring about failures of individual banks: shifts of plants from one area to another, the replacement of small firms by larger ones that did their banking business elsewhere, and so on.

4. Deflation and depression. Bank failures and business depressions are mutually aggravating; a depression tends to break banks, and bank failures deepen a depression. Falling prices, incomes, sales, and employment lessen the abilities of debtors to meet their obligations and thereby threaten both the solvency and the liquidity of banks. Many banks were destroyed or seriously weakened during the sharp deflation starting in May, 1920. The failure of agriculture to recover fully during the 1920's injured banks heavily dependent on farming. Then came the great depression, which started in 1929 and lasted a decade. Thousands of banks failed to survive under its strains, and bank failures and threats of failure played an important role in deepening and prolonging the depression.

Bank failures injure the economy in numerous ways. Most obvious but not necessarily most important are the losses to bank owners and depositors, many of whom can ill afford to lose their money. Perhaps more serious are the effects on employment, output, and prices, especially when failures are numerous. Large volumes of deposits are frozen in failed banks and hence unavailable for purchasing the output of industry and agriculture. Failures of some banks may create lack of confidence in others, induce large withdrawals of coin and currency, reduce bank reserves, and force banks to contract their loans and security holdings. Even the threat of cash drains may lead banks to follow niggardly lending policies in vain attempts to protect and improve their liquidity. The result can only be a worsening of employment and production. Bank failures, and even the threat of such failures, interfere seriously with attempts of the central bank to maintain and improve the availability of credit and lower interest rates to combat depression and promote recovery.

These widespread bank failures between World War I and 1933 led to at least two important modifications in American public policy relative to banking. One was a modification of the policy of "free banking." In the earlier period, as already noted, the Comptroller of the Currency and most state banking authorities granted charters freely to all who could meet the requirements of the general banking laws. This policy has been modified because it was responsible for "overbanking." Now the Comptroller and most state banking authorities refuse to grant charters when they find that the place in which the proposed bank would be located already has "adequate banking facilities." They apply similar tests in judging applications for the establishment of new branches.

The widespread failure of banks also led to the establishment of the first federally sponsored plan for insuring bank deposits. Since this plan will be discussed more fully later, we shall note here only a few of its more important aspects. A temporary plan was established in 1933. In 1935 this was superseded by the permanent plan operated by the newly established Federal Deposit Insurance Corporation, hereafter referred to as the FDIC. The FDIC insures the first $10,000 of each deposit account in an insured bank, charging therefor a small annual premium based on the volume of deposits. When the plan was under consideration, many advocated that all commercial banks be required to join. But those who resisted federal compulsion on state banks were again at least partially victorious. The outcome was that only banks that were members of the Federal Reserve—all national banks and the state banks that had elected to join—were forced to join the FDIC. Nonmember state banks were permitted to join if they could meet entrance requirements. In fact, however, all except a handful of state banks have joined to get the benefits of deposit insurance.

The contribution of the FDIC goes far beyond that of protecting "small" depositors. It performs useful services in maintaining confidence in banks and preventing surges of cash withdrawals, thereby increasing the effectiveness of monetary policy, and in improving the quality of supervision and examination of state banks that are not members of the Federal Reserve and therefore not subject to supervision and regulation by Federal Reserve authorities. Nevertheless, we shall see later that for performing these functions the FDIC still has several shortcomings.

Independent Unit Banks and Multiple Office Banking

Recent decades have witnessed marked changes in the relative importance of independent unit banks and banks operating multiple offices. In 1900, when there were more than 8700 banks in the United States, only 87 banks had more than a single office and they operated a total of only 119 branches. Even as late as 1920 only 530 out of nearly 30,000 banks had branches, and the total number of branches was only 1281. Since that time branch banking has grown rapidly. By 1957, when the number of banks had shrunk to 13,566, there were 1893 branch banks with a total of 7968 branches. Branch banking systems held well over half of all commercial bank assets. Moreover, recent decades have witnessed a large growth of *group banking*—arrangements under which two or more separately incorporated banks are controlled by a corporate holding company.

In a later chapter we shall see that the structure of our commercial banking system, involving policies relative to chartering banks, establishing branches, and regulating branch and group banking, continues to be a highly controversial issue at both federal and state levels. What the outcome will be remains to be seen, but one can be sure that many of the points of conflict will not be new to one familiar with United States banking history: conflicts of federal and state jurisdictions over banks; the long history of bank failures; the desire for "free banking" and the fear of "overbanking"; the aversion of established banks to new competition and the desire of others to establish new banks or to expand the area served by their banks; and the advantages of bigness and the fear of concentration of financial power.

SELECTED READINGS

Board of Governors of the Federal Reserve System, *Banking Studies*, Washington, 1941.

Dewey, D. R., *Financial History of the United States*, Longmans, Green, New York, 11th ed., 1931.

Hammond, Bray, *Banks and Politics in America from the Revolution to the Civil War*, Princeton University Press, Princeton, 1957.

Sprague, O. M. W., *History of Crises Under the National Banking System*, Senate Document No. 538, Government Printing Office, Washington, 1910.

Taus, E. R., *Central Banking Function of the U.S. Treasury, 1789–1941*, Columbia University Press, New York, 1943.

CHAPTER 7

The Federal Reserve System

In passing the Federal Reserve Act in late 1913 and actually establishing the Federal Reserve banks in November, 1914, the United States was one of the last of the great economic powers to provide itself with a central bank. The Bank of Sweden was founded in 1656, the Bank of England in 1694, the Bank of France in 1800, the Netherlands Bank in 1814, and the Bank of Belgium in 1835; most of the other leading European countries established central banks well before the end of the nineteenth century. In general outline the functions of the Federal Reserve are similar to those of central banks in other countries. Like other central banks, its primary function is to regulate monetary and credit conditions. To this end it creates and destroys money and regulates the creation and destruction of money by commercial banks. Like them it also performs many other functions, including check clearing and collection, acting as fiscal agent for the government, engaging in operations in the foreign exchange market, and so on.

Despite these similarities there are also important differences in the structure, control, and functioning of the various central banks. For example, most countries have only one central bank with control clearly concentrated in a central authority. The United States has twelve separately incorporated Federal Reserve banks located in as many Federal Reserve districts, with control power divided among the twelve banks and the Board of Governors of the Federal Reserve System located in Washington. This arrangement seems sprawling indeed to those accustomed to a single central bank under centralized control.

Such differences arise from many sources, only a few of which can be mentioned here. (1) Differences in geographical area. In small countries without pronounced regional variations there was little reason to establish more than one central bank. But in the United States, with its large geographical area and differing economic and financial conditions in the various regions, it was at least plausible to argue in 1913 that each broad region should have its own central bank, which could adapt its policies to the peculiar conditions of the region. (2) Differences in allocations of jurisdiction over banking. In countries where the central government enjoyed exclusive jurisdiction over the chartering, supervision, and regulation of commercial banks there was little opposition to a single central bank. This was not true in the United States with its dual banking system. (3) Differences in commercial banking structures. In countries with only a few banks, each operating a nation-wide system of branches, it was clear that the banking system could best be regulated by a centralized management in the nation's financial center. This was not clear in the United States with its thousands of banks, most of them operating only a single office and none with branches outside its home state.

To understand the original structure and control of the Federal Reserve System and their evolution since 1914, it is helpful to bear in mind some aspects of American monetary history before 1913 and the objectives of those responsible for the passage of the Federal Reserve Act. The major point to be emphasized is that the purposes of the Federal Reserve System as conceived by its originators were far different from those of today. Almost everybody now believes that the primary purpose of the Federal Reserve is to manage money deliberately and continuously. We believe that "money will not manage itself; it must be managed." And we expect the Federal Reserve to use its powers continuously and positively to promote the achievement of selected objectives, such as high levels of employment, economic growth, and stable price levels. Such ideas were alien and unacceptable to those who conceived and established the Federal Reserve System. They did not want a "managed money"; they were well pleased with the international gold standard then in operation. After decades of controversy over bimetallism, greenbackism, and other "unsound" proposals, the nation had confirmed its loyalty to the international gold standard by adopting the Gold Standard Act of 1900. The following decade of rising gold production, rising price levels, and prosperity seemed to confirm the wisdom of the decision. There would almost certainly have been no Federal Reserve System if its advocates had heralded it as an instrument for continuous monetary management. This function of the Federal Reserve developed only several years later when the international gold standard had broken down and the nation had, for the first time in its history, accumulated a large volume of excess gold reserves.

Thus the original purpose of the Federal Reserve was not the ambitious one of introducing a high degree of monetary management but the much more limited one of remedying a number of shortcomings in the existing system of state and national banks. The Federal Reserve Act sought to replace the slow and expensive system of check-clearing and collection with one that would be faster and more efficient; to provide a more satisfactory fiscal agent for the federal government; to achieve a better coördination of state and national banks, and especially to secure more effective supervision of state banks; to promote the development of an acceptance market in the United States; and to provide for national banks more liberal powers, such as those of establishing trust departments and lending on real estate, to enable them to compete more effectively with state banks and trust companies, many of which enjoyed more freedom of action. These reforms were important, but they were secondary. The primary purpose of the new banking reform was to end recurrent banking panics and crises. The panic of 1907, following similar events in 1893, 1884, and 1873, and serious credit stringencies on several other occasions, was the last straw; banking reform became politically feasible. As Carter Glass told the House of Representatives:

> Financial textbook writers in Europe have characterized our banking as "barbarous," and eminent bankers of this country . . . have not hesitated to confess that the criticism is merited. . . . The failure of the system in acute exigencies has caused widespread business demoralization and almost universal distress. Five times within the last thirty years financial catastrophe has overtaken the country under this system; and it would be difficult to compute the enormous losses sustained by all classes of society—by the banks immediately involved; by the merchants whose credits were curtailed; by the industries whose shops were closed; by the railroads whose cars were stopped; by the farmers whose crops rotted in the fields; by the laborer who was deprived of his wage. The system literally has no reserve force. The currency based upon the nation's debt is absolutely unresponsive to the nation's business needs. The lack of coöperation and coördination among the more than 7300 national banks produces a curtailment of facilities at all periods of exceptional demand for credit. This peculiar defect renders disaster inevitable.[1]

Many other observers agreed with Glass that the primary problem was that the existing system had no "reserve force," no "elasticity" in time of strain. No existing institution was motivated to hold large excess reserves for use in time of strain, none had the power to create new bank reserves in such periods, and none was empowered to create additional currency in time of need. The remedy followed from the diagnosis; there should be created new institutions to provide a "reserve force," to provide "elasticity." Some part of the nation's gold reserve should be concentrated in the new institutions, which would be empowered to create new currency and new bank reserves "as needed." "Elasticity" was the central theme of the new "reserve system."

Even among those who favored banking reform, and many did not, there were widely differing opinions as to the proper control and structure of any new institutions that might be established. Some thought they should be regarded as coöperative or mutual aid societies formed by banks to enable banks to function more safely and effectively. To those holding this view it seemed only natural that banks should contribute the capital of the new institutions and exercise exclusive control over them. Others thought that the new

[1] *The Congressional Record.* September 10, 1913, p. 4642.

institutions should be regarded as regulators of banks and that to allow bankers to regulate themselves would be absurd. This was properly a function of the government or its appointees. Opinions as to the proper structure of the new system also differed. Some insisted that the United States, like most other countries, should have a single central bank with centralized control. Such a single institution could most effectively pool the nation's gold reserves, make its resources available at the points of greatest need, and effectuate a national credit policy. Others thought such centralization both unnecessary and undesirable. It would bring a dangerous concentration of financial power, invite domination of the entire country by Wall Street or Washington, and ignore regional differences in economic and financial conditions. They preferred a system of largely autonomous regional reserve banks that could amass sufficient resources and adapt their policies to regional conditions. One congressman thought that fifty such regional institutions would be about the right number.

The Federal Reserve Act represented a compromise among such conflicting views. The country was divided into a number of districts, each with its own Federal Reserve bank, and a central authority was established in Washington to supervise the various Reserve banks and to coördinate their policies while permitting some degree of regional autonomy.

STRUCTURE OF THE FEDERAL RESERVE SYSTEM

The 12 Federal Reserve Banks and Their Branches

The Federal Reserve Act provided that the continental United States, excluding Alaska, should be divided into not less than 8 or more than 12 Federal Reserve districts, each to have a Federal Reserve bank. The maximum number of districts and Reserve banks was established at the outset, so we have 12 Federal Reserve districts and 12 Federal Reserve banks. The boundaries of these districts are shown on the map in Fig. 6. Each Federal Reserve bank is named after the city in which it is located; thus there is the Federal Reserve Bank of Boston, the Federal Reserve Bank of New York, and so on. To facilitate their operations, some of the Federal Reserve banks have established branches in their districts. There are now 24 of these branches distributed unequally among the various Federal Reserve districts. The numbers of the Federal Reserve districts and the names and locations of the Federal Reserve banks and their branches are shown on page 121.

It is interesting to note, as is shown in Table 17, that the Federal Reserve banks differ greatly as to both their size and their influence on credit and monetary conditions. The Federal Reserve Bank of New York, which is by far the largest, holds more than a quarter of the total assets of all the Reserve banks.

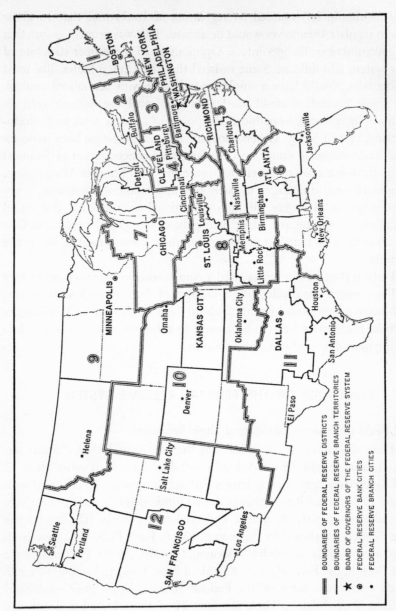

FIG. 6. Federal Reserve System. Boundaries of Federal Reserve Districts and Their Branch Territories. (Source: Board of Governors of the Federal Reserve System.)

FEDERAL RESERVE DISTRICTS, FEDERAL RESERVE BANKS, AND
BRANCHES OF THE FEDERAL RESERVE BANKS

Federal Reserve
District Number

1	Federal Reserve Bank of Boston
2	Federal Reserve Bank of New York
	Branch: Buffalo, New York
3	Federal Reserve Bank of Philadelphia
4	Federal Reserve Bank of Cleveland
	Branches: Cincinnati, Ohio
	Pittsburgh, Pennsylvania
5	Federal Reserve Bank of Richmond
	Branches: Baltimore, Maryland
	Charlotte, North Carolina
6	Federal Reserve Bank of Atlanta
	Branches: Birmingham, Alabama
	Jacksonville, Florida
	Nashville, Tennessee
	New Orleans, Louisiana
7	Federal Reserve Bank of Chicago
	Branch: Detroit, Michigan
8	Federal Reserve Bank of St. Louis
	Branches: Little Rock, Arkansas
	Louisville, Kentucky
	Memphis, Tennessee
9	Federal Reserve Bank of Minneapolis
	Branch: Helena, Montana
10	Federal Reserve Bank of Kansas City
	Branches: Denver, Colorado
	Oklahoma City, Oklahoma
	Omaha, Nebraska
11	Federal Reserve Bank of Dallas
	Branches: El Paso, Texas
	Houston, Texas
	San Antonio, Texas
12	Federal Reserve Bank of San Francisco
	Branches: Los Angeles, California
	Portland, Oregon
	Salt Lake City, Utah
	Seattle, Washington

The predominance of the New York Bank is even greater than these statistics imply, for it is the principal point of contact with foreign central banks, it has a direct influence on international financial transactions, it is located in the midst of the great New York money market, which draws funds from and dispatches funds to every part of the country, and its member banks, especially the giant banks in New York City, greatly influence banks in all parts of the nation through their correspondent relationships. At the other extreme, the

TABLE 17.   Relative Sizes of the 12 Federal
Reserve Banks, April 30, 1958

Federal Reserve Bank of	Assets (In Billions)	Percent of Total Federal Reserve Banks Assets
Boston	$ 2.8	5.5
New York	13.1	25.5
Philadelphia	2.9	5.7
Cleveland	4.5	8.8
Richmond	3.2	6.2
Atlanta	2.6	5.1
Chicago	9.0	17.5
St. Louis	2.1	4.1
Minneapolis	1.1	2.1
Kansas City	2.2	4.3
Dallas	2.0	3.9
San Francisco	5.8	11.3
Total	$51.3	100.0

SOURCE: *Federal Reserve Bulletin*, May, 1958, p. 560.

relatively small Federal Reserve Bank of Minneapolis holds less than 2.2 percent of all the assets of the Reserve banks, and its actions have much less influence on nation-wide credit and monetary conditions.

Member Banks in the Federal Reserve System

Each Federal Reserve bank has many "member banks," by which we mean
the commercial banks in the district that have met at least the minimum requirements and have been accepted for membership in the Federal Reserve
System.[2] As a member of the Federal Reserve, a commercial bank has both
obligations and privileges. It must continue to meet various requirements for
membership, submit to supervision and examination by Federal Reserve authorities, subscribe to stock in its Federal Reserve bank, and hold all its legal
reserves in the form of deposits at its Federal Reserve bank. On the other hand,
it enjoys the privilege of borrowing from its Federal Reserve bank and of
using the other facilities of the System.

Before the establishment of the Federal Reserve System, there were wide
differences of opinion as to what commercial banks should be required or permitted to become members. At one extreme, those who were opposed to further "regimentation" of banks would have made membership in the System
optional with each bank. At the other extreme, some would have forced every
commercial bank in the country to become a member or cease to perform commercial banking functions. Here again the issue was settled by compromise.

[2] Morris Plan banks and certain other incorporated banking institutions engaged in a
similar type of business may also petition for membership.

Every national bank must become and remain a member of its Federal Reserve bank or forfeit its federal charter. Each state bank may, at its option, become a member if it can meet the minimum requirements for membership.

Table 18 shows the number of members and nonmembers of the Federal Reserve System on various dates. In 1957 there were 6393 member banks, of which 4620 were national banks and 1773 were state banks. Thus slightly less

TABLE 18.   Member and Nonmember Commercial Banks

Data as of June 30	Total Number of Commercial Banks	Member Banks			Non-member State Banks	Number of Member Banks as a Percentage of All Commercial Banks	Deposits at Member Banks as a Percentage of Total Deposits
		Total	National	State			
1915	25,875	7,615	7,598	17	18,260	29.4	49.4
1925	27,858	9,538	8,066	1,472	18,320	34.2	72.8
1935	15,478	6,410	5,425	985	9,068	41.4	84.5
1945	14,003	6,840	5,015	1,825	7,163	48.8	86.6
1950[a]	14,121	6,873	4,958	1,915	7,248	48.7	85.7
1955[a]	13,719	6,543	4,692	1,851	7,176	47.7	85.2
1957[a]	13,571	6,393	4,620	1,773	7,178	47.1	84.7

[a] Data as of end of the year.

than half of all commercial banks, holding about 85 percent of total deposits in commercial banks, were members of the Federal Reserve. But 7178 state banks, or about 80 percent of all state-chartered banks, were nonmembers. However, most of these institutions are relatively small, as is indicated by the fact that though they comprise about 53 percent of the total number of commercial banks they account for only 15 percent of all commercial bank deposits.

There are several reasons why many state banks have failed to become members of the Federal Reserve System.[3] Many of them cannot qualify for membership because of their inability to meet its minimum capital requirements. For example, 2389 state banks had insufficient capital for membership at the end of 1939; more than half of these, 1614, had a capital of less than $25,000. But many state banks with sufficient capital for membership have for various reasons failed to join: (1) The Federal Reserve requirement of par clearance by its members. No member of the System may make "exchange charges" on checks forwarded to it for payment through the Reserve banks. That is, the member bank on which a check is drawn must pay the full face

[3] For an excellent discussion of this subject, see B. Magruder Wingfield, "Deterrents to Membership in the Federal Reserve System," in Board of Governors of the Federal Reserve System, *Banking Studies*, Washington, 1941, pp. 273–292.

amount of the check to the payee or to the agencies taking the check for clearance and collection; it may not deduct any amount to cover costs of making payment.[4] But many nonmember banks—1741 of them at the end of 1957—refuse to pay such checks at par, for they are unwilling to forgo this source of revenue in order to join the Federal Reserve. (2) Lower reserve requirements under state laws. The fact that reserve requirements for member banks are higher than those prescribed by some state laws makes some banks unwilling to join. (3) Unwillingness to comply with other regulations applicable to member banks. Many state banks operating under more lenient state banking laws are unwilling to comply with member bank regulations, such as the Clayton Anti-Trust Act prohibitions against interlocking bank officers, directors, and employees; restrictions on affiliates of member banks; limitations as to the types of assets acquired; limitations on a bank's loans to its executive officers; and reports required. (4) Availability of Federal Reserve services without membership. With certain limitations, nonmember banks may use the Federal Reserve clearing system, and various other Federal Reserve facilities. A less generous policy toward nonmembers would probably force more banks into the System.

OWNERSHIP OF THE FEDERAL RESERVE BANKS

Another controversial question prior to the passage of the Federal Reserve Act was, "Who shall provide the capital for the Federal Reserve banks?" Some wanted government ownership. Some others wanted the stock to be sold to the general public, and still others wanted all of it to be sold to member banks. The solution was a compromise. Each member bank is required to subscribe to the stock of its Federal Reserve bank in an amount equal to 6 percent of its own paid-up capital and surplus. It was provided, however, that stock would be offered to the public if insufficient capital was obtained from this source; and if subscriptions by the banks and the public were insufficient, stock would be sold to the federal government. In reality, no stock of the Federal Reserve banks has been sold to either the public or the government, and even the member banks have been required to pay in only half of their subscriptions. Thus, the Federal Reserve banks are owned wholly by their member banks, each member bank having paid in to its Federal Reserve bank an amount equal to 3 percent of its own paid-up capital and surplus.

It is important to note, however, that in this case ownership does not carry with it full control of the corporation and the enjoyment of all its earnings.

---

[4] It must be noted that these "exchange charges" differ somewhat from the service charges with which we are now familiar. A member of the Federal Reserve may still charge its customers for the services it performs for them, including charges for cashing checks that are drawn on other banks. But it may not remit less than the face amount of a check drawn on it and presented to it by a Federal Reserve bank for payment.

(The distribution of control is discussed in the next section.) Annual dividends to stockholders of the Reserve banks are limited to 6 percent of the paid-in capital stock. The remainder of Reserve bank earnings has been used to build up the surplus accounts of the Reserve banks and to provide revenue for the Treasury. Prior to 1933 each Reserve bank was required by law to pay the Treasury a franchise tax equal to 90 percent of its net earnings in excess of dividends after it had accumulated a surplus equal to its subscribed capital. By the end of 1932 the Reserve banks had accumulated surplus accounts amounting to $278 million and had paid $149 million in franchise taxes to the Treasury. The Banking Act of 1933 required the Reserve banks to pay half of their accumulated surplus, or $139 million, as a subscription to the capital stock of the Federal Deposit Insurance Corporation, and in return repealed the franchise tax in order to enable the Reserve banks to use all their earnings in excess of dividend requirements to replenish their surplus accounts. By the end of 1946 the Reserve banks had built their combined surplus accounts up to nearly $440 million. Partly because of this the Board of Governors in April, 1947, voluntarily put into operation a plan to channel into the Treasury most of the Reserve bank earnings in excess of their dividend requirements.[5] About 90 percent of these excess earnings go to the Treasury through an interest charge on outstanding Federal Reserve notes.

CONTROL OF THE FEDERAL RESERVE SYSTEM

Closely related to the heated controversies over the structure of the Federal Reserve System were those concerning its control. The most widely debated questions were: (1) Who should control the Federal Reserve? (2) Should control be centralized or decentralized? Three principal groups wanted a voice in control—the federal government, member banks, and businessmen who were customers of member banks. Some, arguing that central banking is essentially a governmental function and that one of its principal objectives is the regulation of member banks, demanded full government control. On the other hand, many bankers who looked upon the new Reserve banks as essentially coöperative institutions for member banks demanded that full control be placed in the hands of bankers, although small banks feared domination by their larger competitors. Others argued that businessmen as customers of banks should be given a voice. No less heated were the discussions concerning the degree of centralization of control. Some wanted almost complete centralization, whereas others demanded a large degree of regional autonomy.

Here, too, the issue was settled by compromise. All the competing groups were given representation, and control was divided between a central author-

---

[5] *Federal Reserve Bulletin*, May, 1947, pp. 518–519. The authority for this action by the Board is found in Section 16, paragraph 4, of the Federal Reserve Act.

ity in Washington and the regional Federal Reserve banks. In the following sections we shall describe the present system of control. It should be remembered, however, that the original division of authority proved unsatisfactory in many respects and that it has been changed in several ways during the period since 1914. In general, the evolution has been toward greater centralization of authority and a greater degree of control by the federal government.

The Board of Governors of the Federal Reserve System. The central controlling authority, which has its offices in Washington, is the Board of Governors of the Federal Reserve System. This Board is composed of seven members (each called a governor) appointed by the President of the United States with the advice and consent of the Senate. Each member devotes his full time to the Board, is appointed for a term of 14 years, and is ineligible for reappointment if he has served a full term.[6] No more than one member of the Board may be selected from any one Federal Reserve district, and in making appointments the President is to "have due regard to a fair representation of the financial, agricultural, industrial, and commercial interests, and geographical divisions of the country." The President designates one of the members as chairman of the Board and another as vice-chairman.

Though the actual location of control has in the past depended greatly on economic and political conditions and on the forcefulness of the various personalities involved, the Board of Governors is now clearly the most powerful controlling force in the entire Federal Reserve System. Among its most important powers are the following:

1. To exercise general supervision over the Federal Reserve banks, to examine their accounts and affairs, and to require reports by them.
2. To approve or disapprove appointments to the positions of president and first vice-president of each Federal Reserve bank and to suspend or remove any officer or director of any Federal Reserve bank.
3. To supervise the issue and retirement of Federal Reserve notes by each Federal Reserve bank.
4. To serve as a majority of the members of the Federal Open-Market Committee.
5. To permit one Reserve bank to lend to another, and by a vote of at least five members of the Board to require it to do so.
6. To suspend the reserve requirements applicable to the Reserve banks.
7. To determine, within the broad limits prescribed by law, the types of loans that the Reserve banks may make.
8. To approve or disapprove discount rates established by the Reserve banks.
9. To fix, within the limits established by law, member bank reserve requirements.
10. To regulate loans on securities.

---

[6] Prior to 1935 this body was known as the Federal Reserve Board. Both the Comptroller of the Currency and the Secretary of the Treasury were ex-officio members of the old Board. The Board was reconstituted in 1935, its members being given higher salaries and longer terms in order to strengthen it and centralize control to a greater degree.

Though this list is far from complete, it indicates the general scope of the Board's authority.

Federal Open-Market Committee. As we shall see later, one of the most powerful instruments of credit control in the hands of the Federal Reserve System is its power to buy and sell government securities, acceptances, and other obligations in the open market. The Reserve banks can create additional member bank reserves by purchasing obligations in the open market and can contract member bank reserves by selling securities. The original Federal Reserve Act was vague as to who should control this function, with the result that the individual Reserve banks sometimes followed conflicting policies and sharp controversies arose within the System. Attempts were made to solve the problem in the 1920's by creating an informal open-market committee made up of representatives of the Federal Reserve banks, but these efforts were only partially successful. Some Reserve banks complained that they were not adequately represented, others ignored the decisions of the informal committee, and the Board in Washington felt that it should have more control of this function.

The Federal Open-Market Committee was created by amendments to the Federal Reserve Act, to clarify the location of authority and to centralize the control of Federal Reserve Open-Market operations.[7] It is composed of 12 members; seven of these (a majority) are members of the Board of Governors of the Federal Reserve System and five are representatives of the Reserve banks. The latter are elected annually, must be either presidents or vice-presidents of Reserve banks, and are elected by the boards of directors of the various Reserve banks, each board having one vote. The distribution of the five Reserve bank representatives is as follows:

One from the Federal Reserve Bank of New York
One from the Federal Reserve Banks of Boston, Philadelphia, and Richmond
One from the Federal Reserve Banks of Cleveland and Chicago
One from the Federal Reserve Banks of Atlanta, Dallas, and St. Louis
One from the Federal Reserve Banks of Minneapolis, Kansas City, and San Francisco

Because of its key position the New York Bank is always represented on the Committee.

The Federal Reserve Bank of New York occupies a unique position with respect to the Federal Reserve System, the Treasury, and the banking system of the country. Its resources total approximately 40 percent of the aggregate of the twelve Federal Reserve Banks. It is located at the central money market and at the

---

[7] The first Federal Open-Market Committee was established by amendment to the Federal Reserve Act in 1933. The Committee was reconstituted by further amendments in 1935, and minor changes have been made since that time.

principal market for Government securities; its operations as fiscal agent of the United States and its transactions with foreign governments, foreign central banks and bankers, as well as its operations in foreign exchange, are in far greater volume than those of any other Federal Reserve Bank. It is clearly in the public interest that the Federal Open-Market Committee be given at all times the benefit of counsel of the Federal Reserve Bank which is in constant touch with the domestic and international money and capital markets and has had long experience in these fields.[8]

The Federal Open-Market Committee has full control of all open-market purchases and sales by the Reserve banks. No Reserve bank may engage or decline to engage in open-market operations except in accordance with the regulations adopted by the Committee.

Federal Advisory Council.   The Federal Advisory Council is composed of 12 members, one being selected by the board of directors of each Reserve bank. The sole function of this Council is to act in an advisory capacity to the Board of Governors. The only sources of its power are its eloquence and the prestige of its members, most of whom are prominent men.

Control of Individual Federal Reserve Banks.   The control of each of the 12 Federal Reserve banks is divided among the member banks in the district, businessmen in the district, and the Board of Governors of the Federal Reserve System. Each Reserve bank has a board of directors with nine members. Three of these are known as Class A directors, three as Class B directors, and three as Class C directors. The Class A directors represent the member banks of the district and are chosen by them. To prevent domination of the Reserve bank by any one banking group, the member banks of the district are divided into three groups based on size, and each group elects one Class A director. The Class B directors represent industry, commerce, and agriculture in the district and must be actively engaged in one of these pursuits at the time of their election. They may not be officers, directors, or employees of any bank. They are, however, elected by the member banks of the district in the same way as the Class A directors. All three of the Class C directors are appointed by the Board of Governors. One of these, who must be "a person of tested banking experience," is chairman of the board of directors and "Federal Reserve Agent" at the bank. As Federal Reserve Agent he acts as official representative of the Board of Governors in carrying out its legal functions. Another Class C director at each Reserve bank acts as deputy chairman of the board of directors.

The chief executive officer of each Reserve bank is its president, who is appointed by its board of directors with the approval of the Board of Governors. The first vice-president of each Reserve bank is appointed in the same way. Other Reserve bank officers and employees are appointed by the

[8] *Federal Reserve Bulletin*, August, 1942, pp. 740–741.

bank's board of directors, though they may, of course, be removed by the Board of Governors.

After a long period of doubt as to the proper location of authority in the Federal Reserve System, it is now clear that the Board of Governors occupies the dominant position. Some power still rests with the representatives chosen by member banks, but the Board of Governors has many sources of power. (1) Exclusive regulation of many Federal Reserve and commercial bank functions is in the hands of the Board. (2) Its members make up a majority of the members of the powerful Federal Open-Market Committee. (3) The Board appoints three members of the board of directors of each Reserve bank, one of its appointees at each bank being chairman of the board of directors and Federal Reserve Agent. (4) The Board may disapprove appointments of presidents and first vice-presidents of the Reserve banks and remove directors, officers, and employees.

SUMMARY OF THE PRESENT STRUCTURE OF THE
FEDERAL RESERVE SYSTEM

Board of Governors	Located in Washington, composed of 7 members appointed by the President.
Federal Open-Market Committee	12 members, including the Board of Governors and 5 representatives of the Reserve banks.
12 Federal Reserve Banks	Each separately incorporated, each located in an important city, each with a board of directors of 9 members, and each with its president and other officers.
24 Branches of the Federal Reserve Banks	To facilitate the functioning of the Federal Reserve banks of their districts.
Member Banks	Nearly 7000 banks (mostly commercial banks), of which about 5000 are national banks and nearly 2000 are state banks. These banks hold more than 85 percent of all commercial bank assets and by their magnitude can dominate commercial banking operations in this country. It is largely through its effects on member banks that the Federal Reserve can control the credit policies of nonmember commercial banks.

It would be rash indeed to assume that the evolutionary development of the Federal Reserve has now ended and that the System will continue unchanged for an indefinite period. There are still heated controversies over both the structure and the control of the System, and these tend to center around membership and control. Most Federal Reserve officials, and probably a majority of monetary economists, believe that all commercial banks should be required to become members of the Federal Reserve, or at least be required to hold reserves equal to those of comparable classes of member banks. They contend that monetary management is a responsibility of the federal government and that the freedom of state-chartered banks to abstain or withdraw from membership tends to weaken the Federal Reserve in performing the functions delegated to it by Congress. This is especially true when the Federal Reserve attempts to raise member bank reserve requirements considerably above those of nonmember banks, but it applies to some other Federal Reserve actions as well. Such actions tend to put member banks at a competitive disadvantage relative to nonmembers, to create discontent and threats of withdrawal among members, and to lessen the willingness of Federal Reserve officials to apply appropriate restrictive measures to members. For these reasons it has been proposed several times that, as a minimum, nonmembers should be required to hold reserves as high as those of member banks, and there is considerable support for legislation to require all commercial banks to join the Federal Reserve.

To these proposals there is strong opposition, especially from bankers and state bank commissioners. These opponents bolster their position with several arguments. (1) The Federal Reserve already has adequate credit control powers, since its members hold more than 85 percent of total commercial bank assets and deposits. Moreover, the presence of nonmembers is disadvantageous only when the Federal Reserve tries to increase reserve requirements of members to excessive levels, and this should not be done anyway. (2) Such an extension of federal power would violate states' rights, in this case the right of states to regulate the banks that they charter. (3) The ability of banks to abstain from Federal Reserve membership or to withdraw if already in the System is a desirable part of our governmental system of "checks and balances"; it acts as a check on the severity of Federal Reserve actions. (4) A requirement that all banks hold their reserves in the form of deposits at the Federal Reserve would cause some of the bigger banks to lose at least part of their profitable interbank deposits. The opposition to both universal membership and the extension of federally determined reserve requirements to all commercial banks is by no means confined to bankers whose institutions are now outside the System.

The location of control over Federal Reserve activities also continues to be a subject of intense controversy. Involved here are both the relation of the Federal Reserve to the executive branch of the government and the distribution of control within the System. The Federal Reserve is based on the principle of "independent central banking." It is, of course, responsible to Congress; it was created by Congress, must make reports to Congress, and Congress can at any time change its basic legislation, give it directives, or even abolish it. It is not, however, responsible to the executive branch. This "independence" from the executive branch is based on several considerations: (1) The administration in power is likely to have an easy-money inflationary bias, partly because easy money and mild inflation tend to be popular and to increase the ability of the incumbent political party to remain in power, and partly because the Treasury is likely to insist on easy money and low interest rates to keep down interest charges on the national debt and to facilitate its refunding and new borrowing operations. (2) Control of the central bank is likely to inject "politics" into that bank's operations—patronage, discrimination on the basis of party affiliation, and so on. (3) Successful monetary management requires greater continuity among top officials than would be likely to result from responsibility to the President, whose term may not last more than four years. (4) The existing arrangement elicits from the commercial banks more confidence and coöperation than they would give to a "politically dominated" institution.

On the other hand, several arguments are advanced for terminating the "independence" of the Federal Reserve and for making it responsible to the executive branch. (1) Monetary policy, like other governmental policies, should be controlled by people responsible to the electorate. (2) The present arrangement makes difficult the appropriate coördination of monetary policy with the other economic policies of the government. It is intolerable that the Federal Reserve should follow policies in conflict with those determined by the elected representatives of the people. (3) Especially serious are the overlapping of powers and the conflict of interest between the Federal Reserve and the Treasury during inflation periods. At such times the debt management policies of the Treasury, when it emphasizes low interest rates, are in conflict with the Federal Reserve objective of curbing inflation. Some people would resolve this conflict between institutions, if not between objectives, by making the Federal Reserve responsible either to the Treasury or to the President. Others, however, would secure coördination by instructing the Treasury to adjust its debt management policies to the monetary policies of the Federal Reserve.

It is still too early to forecast the outcome of this controversy over the relationship between the Federal Reserve and the executive branch. Some method of achieving better coördination of monetary, debt management, and other economic policies is clearly needed. But it is to be hoped that the tradition of an "independent" central bank will not be discarded without full consideration of the resultant dangers.

Less intense but nevertheless important are the continuing controversies over the location of control within the Federal Reserve System. Some who believe that centralization has gone too far would transfer some power back to the Reserve banks, or at least from the Board to the Federal Open-Market

Committee on which the Reserve banks are represented. Others would concentrate still more power in the Board.

FEDERAL RESERVE "CHORES"

Having examined the structure and control of the Federal Reserve System, we can now begin to study its functions. We shall look first at its service functions or "chores," leaving its credit control functions for later chapters. In performing these chores the Federal Reserve has improved the quality of banking and greatly increased the convenience derived by the public from banks.

Banking Supervision

The supervision and examination of banking in this country are not exclusively a Federal Reserve function, but are shared with several other authorities. The Comptroller of the Currency has jurisdiction over all national banks. State banking authorities have jurisdiction over state banks. And the Federal Deposit Insurance Corporation has jurisdiction over all banks with deposit insurance, which includes all members of the Federal Reserve System and most nonmembers. Though there are still many drawbacks to this system of overlapping jurisdiction, a considerable amount of coöperation among the regulatory authorities has been achieved. Each Reserve bank has its staff of bank examiners, and the member banks must make periodic reports as to their condition. In addition to requiring reports and examining member banks, the Federal Reserve exercises other important supervisory powers, among which are the powers to:

1. Fix maximum rates of interest that member banks may pay on time and savings deposits. The principal purpose of this limitation is to prevent banks from bidding these rates so high as to weaken their condition.[9]
2. Remove officers and directors of member banks for continued violation of banking laws or for continued unsafe or unsound banking practices.
3. Suspend a member bank's borrowing privileges at the Federal Reserve if it is found to be making undue use of bank credit for speculation in securities, real estate, or commodities.
4. Permit national banks, where appropriate, to exercise trust powers.
5. Permit holding companies, when it is not against the public interest, to vote the stocks of member banks controlled by them.
6. Permit member banks to establish branches in foreign countries.

Clearing and Collection of Checks

The Federal Reserve System has greatly enhanced the speed, convenience, and cheapness of clearing and collecting checks and other similar items. Be-

[9] Banks are not allowed to pay interest on demand deposits.

fore 1914 a check might spend two weeks or more in the process of being cleared and collected, especially if it had to move long distances. The maximum time now required is only a few days, and banks clearing checks through the Federal Reserve receive payment in two days or less. The whole process is completed with virtually no shipment of coin or currency. Deposit accounts at the Federal Reserve banks play a central role in this process. All member banks must hold deposit claims against their Federal Reserve banks to meet their legal reserve requirements. Many nonmember banks have deposits at the Federal Reserve for clearing purposes. This permits banks to make or receive net payments through the transfer of deposit credits on the books of the Federal Reserve.

To illustrate the high development of the clearance and collection system for checks and other similar instruments, let us look at the process in a few typical situations. The processes often vary in detail from those described below, but the principles involved are similar. Let us suppose that Smith deposits with the First Hartford Bank in Connecticut a check for $100 given him by Jones. If Jones's check is drawn on the First Hartford Bank, the process of clearance is simple; the bank merely adds $100 to Smith's deposit account and deducts $100 from Jones's account.

Suppose, however, that Jones has written the check on another bank in the same city—the Second Hartford Bank. After Smith has deposited the check with the First Hartford Bank, it may be cleared in either of two general ways. The two banks may informally exchange their claims against each other at the end of the day, the net debtor then paying the other bank with a check drawn on another bank—probably the Federal Reserve bank of the district. Final payment is thus made by transferring a deposit credit at the Federal Reserve from the account of the Second Hartford Bank to that of the First Hartford Bank. Or the banks may clear and collect checks through a local clearing house. Each bank in the area takes to the clearing house at an appointed time each day all the checks and other matured claims that it has against the other members of the clearing house. There the clearing house officials compare the total amounts of checks presented by each bank against all other banks with the total amount of checks presented by all other banks against it, and then pay it the net amount due it or collect the net amount owed by it. These net payments are usually made with checks, often with checks drawn on the Reserve bank of the district. Actual coin or currency is almost never used to pay net differences at a clearing house.

If the check Jones gives to Smith is drawn on a bank located in another city in the same Federal Reserve district, say in Springfield, Massachusetts, the clearance and collection procedure is somewhat as follows. Smith deposits the check with the First Hartford Bank, which credits his account and sends the check, along with others, to the Federal Reserve Bank of Boston for clearance and collection. The Boston Reserve bank then sends the check to Springfield, and the Springfield bank deducts the amount of the check from Jones's deposit account. After the lapse of sufficient time for notification if the check is not good, the Boston Reserve bank deducts the amount of the check from the Springfield bank's reserve account with it and adds the same amount to the Hartford bank's reserve account. Payment of the check has been achieved quickly and with no shipment of coin or currency.

The procedure is only slightly more complicated if Jones's check is drawn on a bank in another Federal Reserve district, say on the Los Angeles Commercial Bank. Smith deposits the check with the Hartford bank, which credits his deposit account and sends the check, along with others, to the Federal Reserve Bank of Boston. The latter then sends the check, along with others, via air mail to the Federal Reserve Bank of San Francisco, which then sends it to the Los Angeles Commercial Bank. If the San Francisco bank is not notified within an appointed time that the check is bad it deducts the amount of the check from the Los Angeles bank's reserve account with it. At or about the same time the Boston Reserve Bank adds the amount of the check to the Hartford bank's reserve account. At this point Smith has been paid, Jones has paid, Smith's bank has been paid, and Jones's bank has paid. But the San Francisco bank still owes the Boston bank the amount of the check if it has not been offset by counterclaims. How is a net balance paid between Reserve banks? This is accomplished without any shipment of coin or currency by the simple expedient of book entries in the Interdistrict Settlement Fund, which is maintained by the Board of Governors in Washington. Each Reserve bank establishes a credit in the Interdistrict Settlement Fund. Any net balance due a Federal Reserve bank at the end of a day is added to its account in the Fund, and any net claim of other Reserve banks against it is deducted from its account.

It is through arrangements of this type that payments can be made to all points within the country quickly and without the inconvenience and expense of shipping coin or currency. Federal Reserve facilities for clearing and collection are available without charge to all member banks and to all nonmembers who will remit the par value of checks drawn on them. The Federal Reserve will not, however, clear and collect checks drawn on nonmembers who refuse to pay the full face amounts of checks drawn on them. The "nonpar banks" are still an inconvenience in the banking system.

Wire Transfer of Funds

In addition to providing a rapid and efficient system for clearing and collecting checks and other similar paper, the Federal Reserve System operates highly useful facilities for the telegraphic transfer of funds. The government and bank customers as well as the banks themselves can transfer funds of any amount from one end of the country to the other almost instantaneously. Suppose, for example, that Jones in Los Angeles wishes to transfer by wire $1 million to Smith in Hartford. Jones gives his bank a check for that amount, and his bank telegraphs the Federal Reserve Bank of San Francisco, asking it to transfer the funds. The San Francisco Reserve bank deducts the amount from the reserve account of the Los Angeles bank and telegraphs the Federal Reserve Bank of Boston, telling it to transfer the funds to Smith at the First Hartford Bank. The Boston Reserve bank adds the amount of the check to the Hartford bank's reserve account and wires the Hartford bank to credit Smith's account. The whole process is completed within minutes. The Federal Reserve Bank of San Francisco settles with the Boston bank through a transfer on the books of the Interdistrict Settlement Fund.

Through its wire transfer system the Federal Reserve can also transfer federal government securities from one end of the country to the other within a few minutes. Suppose, for example, that a bank in Seattle wishes to transfer $10 million of Treasury obligations to a government security dealer in New York. The bank will take the securities to the Seattle branch of the Federal Reserve Bank of San Francisco. The Seattle branch will invalidate these securities and wire the Federal Reserve Bank of New York to issue and deliver to the government security dealer new Treasury obligations of the same issue and in the same amount. After the dealer has sold these securities he may pay the Seattle bank through the wire transfer system.

Fiscal Agency Functions

As noted earlier, one purpose of the Federal Reserve Act was to provide the Treasury with a more satisfactory fiscal agent. In acting as fiscal agent, the Federal Reserve banks do an enormous amount of work for the federal government and its various offices and corporations. Though not the sole depositories of federal government funds, they do hold Treasury deposits, assist in the collection of taxes, cash government checks, transfer great sums from one area to another for government account, solicit and receive applications for the purchase of federal securities, redeem federal securities as they fall due, pay interest coupons, and perform many other useful functions for the government. Government funds are now far safer and government fiscal operations are carried out much more efficiently and with far less disturbance to general monetary and financial conditions than at any time before 1914.

SELECTED READINGS

Bach, G. L., *Federal Reserve Policy Making*, Knopf, New York, 1950.
Board of Governors of the Federal Reserve System:

The Federal Reserve System, Its Purposes and Functions, Washington, 2d ed., 1947.

Banking Studies, Washington, 1941.

Banking and Monetary Statistics, Washington, 1943.

Federal Reserve Bulletins (monthly).

Annual Reports.

Burgess, W. R., *The Reserve Banks and the Money Market*, Harper, New York, 1946.

Chandler, L. V., *Benjamin Strong, Central Banker*, Brookings Institution, Washington, 1958.

Glass, Carter, *Adventure in Constructive Finance*, Doubleday, Doran, New York, 1927.

Goldenweiser, E. A., *American Monetary Policy*, McGraw-Hill, New York, 1951.

Hardy, C. O., *Credit Policies of the Federal Reserve System*, Brookings Institution, Washington, 1932.

Harris, S., *Twenty Years of Federal Reserve Policies*, Harvard University Press, Cambridge, 1933.

U.S. Congress, Joint Committee on the Economic Report:

Subcommittee on Monetary, Credit, and Fiscal Policies,

 Statements on Monetary, Credit, and Fiscal Policies, 1949.

 Hearings on Monetary, Credit, and Fiscal Policies, 1949.

 Report on Monetary, Credit, and Fiscal Policies, 1950.

Subcommittee on General Credit Control and Debt Management,

 Replies to Questions and Other Materials, 1952.

 Hearings, 1952.

 Report, 1952.

(All published by the Government Printing Office, Washington, D.C.)

CHAPTER 8

Federal Reserve Credit
and Bank Reserves

Though its service functions or "chores" are very useful, by far the most important function of the Federal Reserve is monetary management—that is, regulation of the quantity of money and of the supply and availability of loan funds for business, consumer, and government spending. Federal Reserve powers in these areas are inescapably great; the System cannot avoid exerting an important influence on the behavior of real output, employment, and price levels. If these powers are used in an appropriate manner the Federal Reserve can act as a powerful stabilizing factor, but if they are used in other ways the System can be a potent destabilizing force.

The monetary or credit management activities of the Federal Reserve are of two broad types: (1) general monetary or credit controls, and (2) selective credit controls. The immediate objective of the general controls is to regulate the total supply of money and credit, the general availability of loan funds, and the general level of interest rates. Their purpose is not to determine the allocation of the available supply of credit among the various types of borrowers or among its various possible uses. This allocative function is left to the private market. Selective credit controls may affect the total supply of money and credit, but their immediate purpose is to regulate the amount of credit used for specified purposes, such as credit extended to purchase consumption goods, to purchase or carry securities listed on the national exchanges, or for new residential construction. To the extent that the Federal Reserve employs such selective controls it does interfere with the allocative functions of the private credit market. Further discussion of these selective controls will be postponed to a later chapter; the remainder of this chapter will discuss general monetary and credit controls.

GENERAL CREDIT CONTROLS

In carrying out its general monetary and credit management functions—its regulation of the total supply of money and credit and the general level of interest rates—the Federal Reserve relies largely on two types of powers. (1) One is its power to alter the height of member bank reserve requirements. As we have already seen, the Federal Reserve Act not only provides that all the legal reserves of member banks must be in the form of deposits in the Reserve banks, but it also gives the Board of Governors power to alter, within limits, the percentages of reserves required against deposits in member banks. By raising the percentage reserve requirements for member banks, the Board can inhibit the creation of money by the banking system and exert an anti-expansionary or even a contractionary influence. And by lowering these requirements the Board can permit and even encourage an expansion of money and credit. (2) The other type of power arises out of its ability to create and destroy bank reserves, and to alter the terms on which reserves are made available to the commercial banking system. The Federal Reserve can create additional bank reserves by increasing its loans and security holdings. And it can destroy bank reserves by decreasing its loans and security holdings. Prior to the mid-1930's, when the Federal Reserve was first given the power to alter member bank reserve requirements, the System carried on its general monetary management function almost exclusively through its ability to regulate the dollar volume and cost of commercial bank reserves, and even now regulation of the volume and cost of bank reserves is the most frequently used method of general monetary management.

FEDERAL RESERVE BALANCE SHEETS

An analysis of the combined balance sheets of the twelve Federal Reserve banks will help us understand the processes through which the Federal Reserve increases or decreases the reserves of the commercial banking system. We start with the basic balance sheet equation that was developed earlier in Chapter 4:

$$\text{Assets} = \text{Liabilities} + \text{Capital accounts}$$

"Assets" include everything of value owned by the Federal Reserve banks at the stated point of time. "Liabilities" are debt claims against the Federal Reserve banks. "Capital accounts" are the ownership claims against the Federal Reserve banks. At any point of time the Federal Reserve banks must have outstanding a total of debt claims and ownership claims exactly equal to the value of their assets. They can increase their holdings of assets only by issuing an equal increase of debt or ownership claims against themselves.

And when they decrease their assets they must withdraw an equal value of outstanding debt and ownership claims against themselves.

An examination of the Federal Reserve balance sheet in Table 19 reveals that the Federal Reserve banks pay for only a very small fraction of their as-

TABLE 19.   Balance Sheet for the Federal Reserve Banks,
May 28, 1958
(In millions)

ASSETS		LIABILITIES AND CAPITAL ACCOUNTS	
Gold certificates	$21,055	Federal Reserve notes	$26,556
Cash	669	Deposits due:	
Discounts and advances	173	Member banks	18,036
Acceptances	41	U.S. Treasury	382
U.S. government		Foreign	277
securities	24,065	Other	400
Uncollected cash items	4,389	Deferred availability	
		cash items	3,745
Other assets	391	Other liabilities	21
		Capital accounts	1,366
Total assets	$50,783	Total liabilities and capital accounts	$50,783

Addendum:	
Uncollected cash items	$4,389
Minus: Deferred availability cash items	3,745
Equals: Float	$ 644

SOURCE: *Federal Reserve Bulletin*, June, 1958, p. 661.

sets by issuing capital account or net worth claims. Moreover, these net worth claims vary only slowly through time, reflecting net retained earnings by the Reserve banks and new stock subscriptions by member banks equal to about 3 percent of any increase in the paid-up capital and surplus of member banks. Thus the Reserve banks pay for their assets largely by issuing debt claims against themselves, and most of the changes in Federal Reserve assets are reflected in changes in their outstanding liabilities.

Federal Reserve liabilities are largely of two types: Federal Reserve notes and deposit liabilities. As indicated earlier, Federal Reserve notes make up the great bulk of paper money in the United States. Though impressively engraved and endowed by law with full legal-tender powers, they are nothing but debt claims against the Federal Reserve banks. Deposits at the Federal Reserve banks are also merely debts owed by the Federal Reserve. They are evidenced by book entries. Table 19 indicates that the Federal Reserve issues deposit claims against itself to only a few types of holders. It will not accept deposits from individuals, businesses, or state and local governments. Most of its deposit liabilities are to member banks. These serve both as legal reserves for member banks and as a medium for clearing and collection, as noted earlier. Smaller deposit liabilities are owed to the federal government, to non-member banks for check-clearing purposes, and to foreign central banks. It should be evident that member bank deposits at the Federal Reserve may be decreased as these deposits are shifted to the ownership of other depositors at the Federal Reserve and that member bank deposits at the Federal Reserve may be increased as other depositors at the Federal Reserve transfer these deposits to the ownership of member banks.

Changes in the volume of Federal Reserve notes outstanding reflect changes in the demand for paper money to be held in commercial bank vaults or to be used as currency in circulation, predominantly the latter. Whenever the public wants more currency, the commercial banks are the first to feel the impact. Customers write checks on their deposit accounts and withdraw cash. Their banks ask the Federal Reserve banks to send them the required amount of Federal Reserve notes or other cash and to deduct that amount from their deposit balances at the Reserve banks. Thus an increase in Federal Reserve notes outstanding is initially at the expense of bank deposits at the Federal Reserve. On the other hand, when the public wishes to hold less paper money it deposits the excess with commercial banks, which then send it along to the Federal Reserve. The latter retires the net inflow of Federal Reserve notes and adds an equal amount to its deposit liabilities to banks. This brings out several important points. (1) It indicates how the volume of Federal Reserve notes is made responsive to the public's demand for paper money. (2) It shows that increases in Federal Reserve notes outstanding initially tend to be at the expense of bank deposits at the Federal Reserve, and that decreases in Federal Reserve notes outstanding tend initially to increase the volume of bank deposits at the Federal Reserve. (3) It suggests why we are justified in assuming that when the Federal Reserve makes net purchases of assets it initially pays for them by creating deposit liabilities, and when it makes net sales of assets it initially collects by withdrawing an equal value of its deposit liabilities. For simplicity of exposition we shall assume in the following sections that when the Federal Reserve purchases assets it makes payment by adding to the reserves of commercial banks and that when it sells assets it collects by deducting from the reserve balances of commercial banks.

It should be emphasized that the Federal Reserve banks can create or destroy their own deposit liabilities by purchasing or selling any kind of asset whatsoever. Thus they can create deposit liabilities to pay for land, buildings, equipment, services, or any sort of claim against others. Or they can withdraw their deposit liabilities by making net sales of any kind of asset. This point should be borne in mind, for even now the Federal Reserve makes several kinds of purchases and sales and it might in the future broaden the categories of assets in which it deals.

It will be useful to distinguish between two types of Federal Reserve purchases and sales of assets. (1) Transactions with member banks. When the Federal Reserve purchases assets from a member bank, it pays that bank by adding to its reserve account. When it sells an asset to a member bank, it collects payment by reducing the bank's reserve account. (2) Transactions with the "public." When the Federal Reserve buys an asset from the "public"—from an individual, business firm, or state or local government—it usually pays with a check drawn on a Federal Reserve bank. The seller of the asset usually deposits the check at a commercial bank, receiving in return a deposit credit there, and the commercial bank then sends the check to its Federal Reserve bank, which adds the amount of the check to the commercial bank's reserve account. Thus, Federal Reserve purchases of assets from the "public" tend to increase directly both the public's money supply and commercial bank reserves. Federal Reserve sales of assets to the public have the reverse effects. When a member of the public buys an asset from the Federal Reserve, he usually pays with a check drawn on a commercial bank. The Federal Reserve deducts the amount of the check from the commercial bank's reserve account and sends the check to the commercial bank, which deducts its amount from its customer's deposit account. Thus a Federal Reserve sale of an asset to the public tends to reduce directly both the public's money supply and commercial bank reserves. The effect on commercial bank reserves is, of course, the more important, for each dollar of change in commercial bank reserves may induce, or even force, several dollars of change in the commercial banks' loans, investments, and deposit liabilities.

Though the Federal Reserve can create or destroy commercial bank reserves by buying or selling assets of any kind, Table 19 indicates that in practice Federal Reserve purchases and sales are largely confined to only a few types of assets. Because the asset item "gold certificates" will be discussed more fully at a later point we need make only a few comments about it here. These gold certificates are simply claims against the nation's monetary gold stock, all of which is owned by the United States Treasury. Only the Federal Reserve may hold these gold certificates, and their volume is approximately equal to the value of the nation's monetary gold stock. They constitute the legal reserves of the Federal Reserve banks. When the Federal Reserve buys these assets it usually pays for them by creating deposit liabilities; when it sells them it collects by decreasing its deposit liabilities. It should be noted that the Federal Reserve has no direct control over its holdings of gold certificates. Under the law it must purchase all of these offered to it by the Treasury and must surrender gold certificates when the monetary gold stock decreases. This point will be elaborated later.

Most other Federal Reserve assets are in the form of debt claims against others. These not only make up more than half of all Federal Reserve assets but they are also the only types of assets that the Federal Reserve deliberately buys and sells for monetary management purposes. "Discounts and advances" are simply outstanding Federal Reserve loans to borrowers, mostly member banks. They are, of course, assets to the Federal Reserve, for they are valuable claims against borrowers. When the Federal Reserve makes such discounts and advances for a member bank, it pays that bank by adding to its reserve account, thereby creating commercial bank reserves that did not exist before. When it reduces its outstanding discounts and advances—sells some of these debt claims against others—it collects by deducting from member bank reserve accounts, thereby destroying that volume of bank reserves.

When the Federal Reserve makes discounts and advances, it enters into a banker-customer relationship with its borrowers. It also buys and sells debt claims against others in "open-market operations" that do not involve such a customer-banker relationship. The Federal Reserve usually buys and sells these claims through dealers in an impersonal market, and the purchases and sales are often not with the ultimate debtor but with some intermediate holder. The principal debt claims purchased and sold by the Federal Reserve in the open market are acceptances and United States government securities, now predominantly the latter. By now it should be clear that when the Federal Reserve buys these assets it creates commercial bank reserves. When it sells these assets it collects by deducting from commercial bank reserve accounts.

In our later discussion of general monetary management, Federal Reserve assets in the form of discounts and advances, acceptances, and United States government obligations will play a central role. These are the only Federal Reserve assets over whose volume Federal Reserve authorities have direct control power, and it is through buying and selling these assets that the Federal Reserve seeks to regulate the dollar volume of commercial bank reserves.

Two other Federal Reserve balance sheet items should be noted. One is the asset "Uncollected cash items"; the other is the liability, "Deferred availability cash items." Both arise out of the Federal Reserve function of clearing and collecting checks and other such claims. Checks worth billions of dollars flow into the Federal Reserve banks every day and require some time to be cleared, paid to the reserve accounts of the banks that deposited them, and deducted from the reserve accounts of the banks on which they are drawn. As a result, at any point of time the Federal Reserve owns a great volume of checks which it has not yet collected and which it has not yet paid. The asset "Uncollected cash items" indicates the value of checks in its possession on which it has not yet collected by deducting from its deposit liabilities to banks. The liability "Deferred availability cash items" indicates the value of checks it has not yet paid by adding to its deposit liabilities to the banks that sent the checks to it. If the Federal Reserve paying and collection schedule worked out perfectly, these asset and liability items would balance out exactly, for the Federal Reserve attempts to pay banks depositing checks at the same time that it collects from the banks on which the checks are drawn. As checks flow into the Reserve banks they are classified as payable "today," "tomorrow," or "the day after tomorrow," the date depending on the estimated time required for the checks to reach the banks on which they are drawn. On the appointed day the amounts of the checks are credited to the reserve accounts of the depositing banks. Ideally, they would on the same day be deducted from the reserve accounts of the banks on which they are drawn. In this case "Deferred availability cash items" would be exactly equal to "Uncollected cash items"; the Federal Reserve would not have paid depositing banks before it collected from others. In the process of clearing and collection it would have neither created nor destroyed bank reserves but would only have shifted reserves from some banks to others. In practice, however, the Federal Reserve sometimes pays depositing banks before it collects from the banks on which checks are drawn. To this extent it contributes to total bank reserves. This source of bank reserves is called "Federal Reserve float." It is a net asset item arrived at by subtracting the liability "Deferred availability cash items" from the asset "Uncollected cash items." At any point of time, it measures the net amount the Federal Reserve has contributed to bank reserves because it has paid some banks before it collected from others.

Several factors account for the existence of Federal Reserve float. (1) Unrealistic collection schedules. In at least a few cases, checks could not within the appointed time reach the banks on which they are drawn even if their flow was unimpeded. For example, checks drawn on banks located in remote sections of Utah and Nevada and deposited at the Federal Reserve Bank of Boston are credited two days later to the reserve accounts of the banks that deposited them, even though the checks cannot within that time reach the banks on which they are drawn. (2) Delays in the transit departments of the Federal Reserve banks. The time of paying a check is determined at the time of its receipt at a Federal Reserve bank. If the process of clearing is delayed because of inadequate staff, or an unusually heavy flow of work, or for any other reason, the collection of checks may be delayed. And (3) delays in transportation. Anything that delays the transportation of checks after they have been received by a Reserve bank and their dates of payment have been determined can increase float. For example, a heavy fog over the eastern half of the United States could delay the air mail and the collection of checks from the banks on which they are drawn and increase Federal Reserve float and bank reserves by several hundred million dollars.

Once the Federal Reserve has determined its time schedules for clearing and collection, it has no direct control over the volume of float. It must passively pay and collect checks in accordance with its announced schedules.

Unfortunately, Federal Reserve float fluctuates widely over short periods. Sometimes it rises by several hundred million dollars, owing to such things as delays or large increases in the value of checks in transit. This, of course, tends to increase bank reserves and to ease credit conditions. Float falls by several hundred millions at other times, owing to such things as a reduction in the value of checks in transit or a reduction in the backlog of uncollected checks. This tends to reduce bank reserves and to tighten credit conditions. We shall see later that one function of the Federal Reserve is to prevent fluctuations in the volume of float and in other things capable of altering the reserve positions of banks from exerting unwanted influences on monetary and credit conditions.

Limitations on Federal Reserve Liabilities and Assets

What, if anything, limits the volume of Federal Reserve notes and deposit liabilities that the Federal Reserve may create by purchasing assets? One limit is provided by the legal reserve requirements of these banks. The Federal Reserve Act requires the Reserve banks to maintain gold certificate reserves equal to at least 25 percent of their outstanding Federal Reserve note and deposit liabilities. This is just another way of saying that the sum of outstanding Federal Reserve notes and deposits shall not be more than four times the gold certificate reserves held by the Reserve banks. In an indirect way this reserve requirement sets an upper limit on Federal Reserve acquisitions of loans and securities, for these lending and investing operations create Federal Reserve note or deposit liabilities.

It would, however, be a mistake to assume either that these reserve requirements set an inflexible upper limit to the volume of Federal Reserve liabilities or that they are often the operative limitation. In the first place, the Board of Governors is empowered to suspend the reserve requirements of the Reserve banks for a period not exceeding 30 days and to renew the suspension an indefinite number of times, each renewal not to exceed 15 days. The only legal penalty is a graduated but not prohibitive tax on the amount of a Reserve bank's reserve deficiency and a requirement that the Reserve banks raise the interest rates on their loans by the amount of the tax. The Board would be reluctant to use this power, but it remains available. In the second place, Congress can lower these reserve requirements and might do so if existing requirements threatened to limit the ability of the Federal Reserve to achieve ends that Congress believed to be desirable. This has already occurred once. Prior to 1945 the Federal Reserve Act required the Reserve banks to hold reserves equal to at least 35 percent of their deposit liabilities and 40 percent of their Federal Reserve notes outstanding. By the middle of 1945 the actual ratio of reserves to Federal Reserve note and deposit liabilities had fallen below 45 percent and it was feared that the Reserve banks would soon have to choose between suspending their reserve requirements and ceasing to expand their loans and security holdings to facilitate war finance. Congress, wanting a continuance of easy-money policies, lowered the reserve requirements to 25 percent. That further reductions will occur in the future is by no means impossible.

TABLE 20.   Ratios of Reserve Bank Reserves to Their
Deposits and Outstanding Federal Reserve Notes

Year (Average for June)	Percentage of Reserves to Deposits and Outstanding Federal Reserve Notes	Year (Average for June)	Percentage of Reserves to Deposits and Outstanding Federal Reserve Notes
1917	70.9	1938	82.5
1918	57.4	1939	85.4
1919	50.6	1940	88.5
1920	41.3	1941	91.1
1921	65.2	1942	89.3
1922	77.8	1943	73.8
1923	76.7	1944	56.3
1924	82.5	1945	44.9
1925	76.3	1946	42.7
1926	75.4	1947	47.7
1927	77.8	1948	51.2
1928	68.0	1949	54.2
1929	74.5	1950	56.3
1930	82.4	1951	46.6
1931	84.3	1952	48.1
1932	58.4	1953	45.6
1933	68.3	1954	45.5
1934	69.5	1955	46.1
1935	73.8	1956	45.9
1936	78.8	1957	47.2
1937	79.6	1958	45.3

SOURCE: *Federal Reserve Bulletins.*

Most important, however, is the fact that only rarely have legal reserve requirements limited the freedom of the Reserve banks to expand their credit. The actual reserve ratios of the Reserve banks have approached the legal minimum on only three occasions—in 1920, 1931, and 1945. During the rest of the period since 1914 the Reserve banks have usually had very large excess reserves; they have expanded their loans and security holdings far less than would have been permitted by their reserve positions. We found earlier that profit-motivated commercial banks tend to expand their loans and security holdings to the maximum permitted by their reserves unless they are deterred by fear of risk. But the primary purpose of the Reserve banks is not to make profits; it is to regulate the supply of money and credit in the social interest. During most of the Federal Reserve's history it has not been socially desirable for the Reserve banks to create as large a volume of Federal Reserve notes and deposits as would have been permitted by their actual reserves and their legal reserve requirements. Many students of monetary management believe that all legal reserve requirements for the Reserve banks should be repealed. These requirements are usually inoperative and if they do become operative it is likely to be in a period of stress or crisis when their effects are undesirable. Repeal of these requirements would both give the Federal Reserve somewhat more freedom to deal with crisis situations and highlight the fact that the most effective and desirable limitation on Federal Reserve credit must be supplied by the monetary managers.

DETERMINANTS OF MEMBER BANK RESERVES

While pointing out that the Federal Reserve can create or destroy member bank reserves by purchasing or selling assets of any sort, we stressed the fact that it has direct control over only two types of its asset holdings: its loans in the form of discounts and advances and its holdings of acceptances and United States government securities acquired in the open market. These assets it can buy or sell at its discretion. It has no direct control over the volume of its holdings of other assets, notably gold certificates and float, though these affect the volume of member bank reserves. There are also several other factors that have important effects on the volume of member bank reserves and over which the Federal Reserve has no direct control. To understand fully either the operation of the monetary and banking system or several aspects of Federal Reserve policy, one must have a thorough understanding of all these major determinants of the volume of member bank reserves.

To aid our understanding and to facilitate its own operations, the Federal Reserve has developed an excellent statistical series entitled "Member Bank Reserves and Related Items." These statistics, which are issued weekly by the Board of Governors, are carried in the major Thursday afternoon and Friday morning newspapers, in the monthly *Federal Reserve Bulletin,* and in several other periodicals. Table 21 presents such a statement for the week ending May 21, 1958.[1] All these items are derived from the balance sheets of

---

[1] For back figures and an excellent description of this series and of the method of deriving it, see Board of Governors of the Federal Reserve System, *Banking and Monetary Statistics,* Washington, 1943, pp. 360 ff., or *Federal Reserve Bulletin,* July, 1935.

the United States Treasury and the Federal Reserve banks. The column on the left, labeled "Sources," includes all the sources of funds that are capable of being used as member bank reserves. If there were no competing uses for these funds the volume of member bank reserves at any time would be equal

TABLE 21. Member Bank Reserves and Related
Items for the Week Ending May 21, 1958
(Figures are in millions of dollars and are
a weekly average of daily figures)

Sources		Uses	
U.S. government		Money in circulation	$30,822
securities	$23,876	Treasury cash holdings	732
Discounts and advances	104	Treasury deposits with	
Other	42	Federal Reserve banks	459
Float	994	Foreign deposits with	
Total Federal Reserve		Federal Reserve banks	309
credit	$25,016	Other deposits with	
Monetary gold stock	21,779	Federal Reserve banks	381
Treasury currency	5,200	Other Federal Reserve	
		accounts (net)	1,043
		Member bank reserves	18,248
Total, all sources	$51,995	Total, all uses	$51,995

to the sum of these sources. We have already discussed the first principal source, total Federal Reserve credit. This is simply the volume of funds that has been created by the Federal Reserve in the process of acquiring and holding assets in the form of United States government securities, acceptances, discounts and advances, and float. This source accounted for nearly half of all these funds. The second major source is the monetary gold stock of the United States, sometimes referred to simply as "the gold stock." This is the volume of funds that has been supplied as the Treasury bought and held gold. The third source, Treasury currency, indicates the volume of funds supplied by the volume of outstanding coin and paper money issued by the Treasury.

The right-hand column, labeled "Uses," shows the various uses to which the total funds provided by the sources are put and the amounts absorbed in each use. It is immediately apparent that large amounts of the funds supplied by the sources are not available for use as member bank reserves because they are absorbed by competing uses. The volume of member bank reserves at any time is equal to the total volume of funds supplied by the sources in the left column minus the amounts of these funds absorbed in other uses, shown in the column on the right. This can be put in the form of an equation:

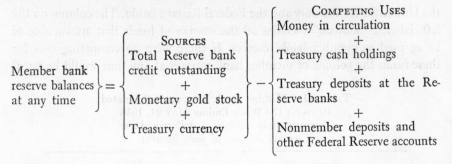

$$\text{Member bank reserve balances at any time} = \left\{ \begin{array}{c} \textsc{Sources} \\ \text{Total Reserve bank credit outstanding} \\ + \\ \text{Monetary gold stock} \\ + \\ \text{Treasury currency} \end{array} \right\} - \left\{ \begin{array}{c} \textsc{Competing Uses} \\ \text{Money in circulation} \\ + \\ \text{Treasury cash holdings} \\ + \\ \text{Treasury deposits at the Reserve banks} \\ + \\ \text{Nonmember deposits and other Federal Reserve accounts} \end{array} \right\}$$

For example, Table 22 shows an average of $18,248 million of member bank reserve balances for the week ending May 21, 1958; these were equal to the $51,995 million supplied at that time by the various sources minus the $33,-747 million absorbed in competing uses.

The discussion above related to the factors determining the size of member bank reserves *as of a given date.* Changes in these factors over any stated period of time determine the change in the volume of member bank reserves during that period. Increases or decreases in the source items tend to increase or decrease member bank reserves. On the other hand, increases in the amounts of funds absorbed in competing uses tend to reduce bank reserves, and decreases in the amounts of funds employed in competing uses tend to increase bank reserves. This is illustrated in Table 22, which compares member bank reserves and related items during the week ending May 21, 1958, with the situation a year earlier. During that period of a year member bank reserve balances tended to be increased by increases in Federal Reserve holdings of government securities and acceptances and in Treasury currency outstanding, and by decreases in the competing use items Treasury cash holdings, Treasury deposits at the Federal Reserve, foreign deposits at the Federal Reserve, and other Federal Reserve accounts (net). On the other hand, member bank reserves tended to be decreased by declines in Federal Reserve discounts, advances and float, by a decrease in the gold stock, and also by increases in the competing use items money in circulation and other deposits at the Federal Reserve. Member bank reserves fell by $570 million because the factors tending to decrease them were that much larger than the factors tending to increase them.

Both to clarify further the nature of all the items directly affecting the volume of member bank reserves and to describe their interrelationships, we shall now analyze them one by one. In order to simplify our exposition, we shall in each case assume that the effects of changes in an item are directly reflected in member bank reserve accounts. It will be convenient to begin with the monetary gold stock.

TABLE 22. Member Bank Reserves and Related Items, Week
Ending May 22, 1957, and Week Ending May 21, 1958
(Weekly averages of daily figures. Amounts in millions
of dollars)

	May 22, 1957	May 21, 1958	Changes in Items During the Year[a]	
			Changes Tending to Increase Bank Reserves	Changes Tending to Decrease Bank Reserves
SOURCES				
U.S. government securities	$22,915	$23,876	$+961	
Acceptances	20	41	+ 21	
Discounts and advances	793	104		$−689
Float	1,341	994		−347
Total F. R. credit	$25,070	$25,016		
Gold	22,320	21,779		−541
Treasury currency	5,098	5,200	+102	
Total sources	$52,488	$51,995		
Minus: COMPETING USES				
Money in circulation	30,645	30,822		+177
Treasury cash holdings	790	732	− 58	
Treasury deposits with F. R. banks	525	459	− 66	
Foreign deposits with F R. banks	362	309	− 53	
Other deposits with F. R. banks	273	381		+108
Other F. R. accounts	1,074	1,043	− 31	
Total competing uses	$33,669	$33,747		
Equals: MEMBER BANK RESERVE BALANCES	$18,818	$18,248		
Total changes tending to increase member bank reserves			$1,292	
Total changes tending to decrease member bank reserves				$1,862
Net decrease in member bank reserves				$ 570

[a] + indicates rise in item; − indicates decline in item.

Monetary Gold Stock

Since the effective date of the Gold Reserve Act of 1934 the United States has been on a type of monetary standard called "a limited gold bullion standard." Several aspects of this arrangement are relevant to our purpose here. (1) No one in the United States other than the Treasury may hold or deal in gold without a license, and even those who are licensed must abide by Treasury regulations. Generally speaking, the Treasury permits Americans to hold only such gold as is needed for industrial, scientific, and artistic purposes.

They may not hold gold as money or for speculation. In short, all the nation's monetary gold is held as an asset of the Treasury. (2) No one except a Federal Reserve bank may hold gold certificates. These are simply claims issued by the Treasury against its holdings of monetary gold, and the amount of them outstanding at any time is approximately equal to the value of the Treasury's gold holdings. Some of these "gold certificates" are pieces of paper evidencing a claim against the Treasury. However, most of them are simply an entry called "gold certificate account" on the liability side of the Treasury's balance sheet. Federal Reserve claims against this account are, of course, assets for the Reserve banks. We shall see later that when the Treasury purchases gold it usually issues an equal amount of gold certificates to the Federal Reserve banks; when it sells gold it usually withdraws from the Reserve banks an equal amount of gold certificates. (3) The Treasury stands ready to buy at approximately $35 an ounce all gold offered to it.[2]

To illustrate the Treasury's usual method of paying for gold, let us assume that it purchases $100 million of gold. On receipt of the gold it will issue $100 million of gold certificates to the Reserve banks, receiving in return a $100 million deposit there. It will then pay the gold seller with a check drawn on the Federal Reserve. Suppose that the gold seller is some American other than a commercial bank. On receiving the $100 million check he will deposit it at his bank, which will credit that amount to his deposit account, thereby creating money that did not exist before. The bank will send the check to the Federal Reserve, which will deduct it from the Treasury's deposit account and add it to the member bank's reserve account. These are the usual direct effects of net gold purchases by the Treasury: equal increases in the gold certificate reserves of the Reserve banks, in member bank reserves, and in the public's money supply. Suppose, however, that the gold seller is not a member of the public but an American commercial bank. The Treasury will draw a $100 million check on its deposit at the Federal Reserve and send it to the commercial bank. The latter will then send the check to its Reserve bank, which will deduct the check from the Treasury's account and add it to the member bank's reserve account. The results are the same as in the preceding case except that there may be no direct effect on the public's money supply. But it is quite possible and even probable that the commercial bank which sold the gold had already created money for some customer from whom it bought the gold or the foreign exchange that it used to buy the gold.

Finally, let us suppose that the gold seller is a foreign central bank that maintains a deposit account at the Federal Reserve. When the foreign bank deposits the check at the Federal Reserve, the latter will deduct it from the Treasury's account and add it to foreign bank deposits. If the foreign bank

---

[2] More precisely, the Treasury's buying price is $35 an ounce less ¼ of 1 percent service charge, and its selling price is $35 an ounce plus ¼ of 1 percent service charge.

then checks out the $100 million to the public, the direct effects will be to increase both the public's money supply and member bank reserves by that amount, for the public will deposit the check at a commercial bank, which will then forward it to the Federal Reserve for deposit. If the foreign bank checks out the $100 million to a commercial bank, the effect will be to increase member bank reserves. Only if the foreign bank continues to hold its new deposit at the Federal Reserve will the Treasury's purchase of gold fail to affect the volume of bank reserves. In this case the funds created by the Treasury's purchase of gold would be absorbed in the competing use, foreign deposits at the Federal Reserve. We are fully justified in saying that increases in the monetary gold stock will, unless offset by changes in other factors, tend to increase the gold certificate reserves of the Reserve banks, member bank reserves, and the public's money supply.

(4) The Treasury stands ready to sell at a price of approximately $35 an ounce all the gold demanded from it for legal purposes. As noted earlier, it will not sell gold for domestic hoarding or monetary use but it does sell gold for export and for domestic industrial, scientific, and artistic uses. Net sales of gold by the Treasury have monetary effects that are just the reverse of those resulting from gold purchases by the Treasury. To illustrate these briefly, let us assume that the Treasury sells $100 million of gold to some member of the American public, who pays for the gold with a check drawn on his bank. The Treasury will make the gold available and send the check that it has received to the Federal Reserve to retire $100 million of outstanding gold certificates. The Federal Reserve will deduct the $100 million check from the reserve account of the bank on which it is drawn, and send the check to the bank, which will deduct it from the customer's deposit account. These are the usual direct effects of a decrease of the monetary gold stock: equal decreases in Federal Reserve reserves in the form of gold certificates, in member bank reserves, and in the public's money supply.

Thus we find that the size of our monetary gold stock is an important determinant of the volume of member bank reserves. Some people, knowing that a large part of this gold is buried at Fort Knox, seem to feel that it is idle and without influence on monetary conditions. Whether we need so much gold for monetary purposes, whether it could be put to better uses domestically, and whether it should be exported in exchange for things that would be more useful are questions we cannot discuss here. But the gold certainly has some effect on our monetary system. When the Treasury bought the gold it had to pay for it, and in doing so it tended to create both member bank reserves and money for the public. Moreover, as suggested by Table 23, fluctuations in our monetary gold stock have often been very large and an important source of changes in the volume of member bank reserves.

It should be noted that neither the Federal Reserve nor the Treasury has

TABLE 23.   Monetary Gold Stock of the United States on
Selected Dates
(In millions of dollars)

Date	Monetary Gold Stock	Change from Preceding Date
August, 1917	$ 2,896	
November, 1924	4,230	$+1,334
August, 1928	3,831	−399
September, 1931	4,688	+857
January, 1934	4,036	−652
November, 1941	22,786	+18,750
December, 1945	20,065	−2,721
October, 1949	24,584	+4,519
May, 1951	21,755	−2,829
October, 1952	23,340	+1,585
November, 1955	21,686	−1,654
January, 1958	22,784	+1,098
June, 1958	21,356	−1,428

any direct control over the size of the monetary gold stock, for the Treasury
must passively buy at a fixed price all gold offered to it and must passively
sell all gold demanded from it for purposes permitted by law and by Treasury
regulations. Such influences on the size of the gold stock as the Treasury
and the Federal Reserve have are largely indirect and operate through credit
and fiscal policies and their effects on the balance of international payments.

Treasury Currency Outstanding

Outstanding Treasury currency is another source of funds for member
bank reserves and competing uses. This includes all the types of coin and
paper money for which the Treasury is primarily responsible—silver dollars
and silver certificates, other coin, United States notes (greenbacks), Federal
Reserve bank notes, and national bank notes. We must avoid the common
mistake of believing that an increase in these types of money outstanding
leads to a corresponding rise in the total amount of coin and currency in circulation. Such an increase in Treasury currency usually has the effect of increasing member bank reserves. Suppose, for example, that the Treasury issues an additional $100 million of money in the form of greenbacks, silver
certificates, or coin. It usually issues the money by depositing it with the Reserve banks, taking in payment a deposit account. When it writes checks on
this Reserve bank deposit, the funds are transferred to member bank reserve
accounts. The Reserve banks may, and usually do, pay the new currency into
circulation and retire an equal amount of Federal Reserve notes, but the
total amount of coin and currency in circulation is not directly affected by
the new Treasury issue; the effect is to increase bank reserves. In the absence

of an increased demand for coin and currency in circulation, the effect would be the same if the Treasury paid the new currency into circulation; the extra currency would flow back into the banks and would be sent by them to the Federal Reserve banks to be added to reserve balances. We should remember, whenever it is proposed that outstanding Treasury currency be increased, that the effect of such an increase would be to add to commercial bank reserves and to permit, though not necessitate, a multiple expansion of checking deposits. On the other hand, a reduction of Treasury currency outstanding would tend to decrease the volume of funds available for member bank reserves and competing purposes.

As shown in Table 22, Treasury currency outstanding in 1958 amounted to about $5,200 million. Thus it was the smallest of the three principal sources of funds for member bank reserves and competing uses. Moreover, in recent years it has changed only slowly, largely reflecting new Treasury issues of about $35 million of silver certificates each year and some additional subsidiary and minor coins. The Federal Reserve has no control over the volume of Treasury currency, and the Treasury's discretionary power is limited. The latter is required by law to purchase at 90.5 cents an ounce all the newly mined domestic silver offered to it. Fortunately the rate of domestic silver production is only about 40 million ounces a year.

Money in Circulation

We come now to the first of the competing uses for the funds supplied by the three sources. "Money in circulation" as used here refers to all paper money and coin outside the Treasury and the Federal Reserve. It therefore includes not only paper money and coin outside the commercial banks but also cash held in the vaults of commercial banks. The latter, however, is by far the smaller part of the total and fluctuates only narrowly. Changes in the volume of money in circulation reflect largely changes in the amounts of coin and paper money demanded by the public. Table 22 shows that in 1958 about $31 billion of the funds supplied by the sources was absorbed in this use and therefore not available for use as bank reserves.

Increases in the volume of money in circulation tend to decrease member bank reserves. For example, suppose that members of the public wish to increase their holdings of coin and paper money by $1 billion. They will do so by withdrawing this cash from their banks, giving up an equal amount of their deposit claims. Their banks usually have to get the cash from the Federal Reserve, paying for it by drawing down their reserve accounts. On the other hand, decreases in the volume of money in circulation tend to increase member bank reserves. Suppose that members of the public decrease their demand for coin and paper money by $1 billion. They will take the extra cash to the banks and exchange it for additions to their deposits. In turn, the banks will send the cash to the Federal Reserve to be added to their reserve accounts.

The Federal Reserve has no direct control over the volume of coin and paper money in circulation. This is determined largely by the public as it chooses between holding deposits and hand-to-hand cash. The Federal Reserve does, however, attempt to vary the volume of its earning assets in such a way as to offset fluctuations in the volume of money in circulation and to prevent their having unwanted effects on the reserve position of member banks.

Treasury Cash Holdings and Treasury Deposits at the Reserve Banks

Because they are so closely related and because their fluctuations have the same effects on the general monetary and credit situation, we shall consider together Treasury cash holdings and Treasury deposits at the Federal Reserve banks. Both compete with member bank reserves for funds supplied by the sources. Increases in both tend to decrease bank reserves, and decreases in both tend to add to bank reserves.

The Treasury can alter both the size of its money balance and the form in which it is held. It holds its money balance in three principal forms: (1) as cash in its own vaults, (2) as deposits at the Reserve banks, and (3) as deposits with commercial banks. The last are usually called "tax and loan accounts," for the Treasury usually acquires these deposits by depositing with the banks on which they are drawn checks that it receives in payment of taxes or for issues of Treasury securities. To illustrate the process through which increases in Treasury cash holdings or in Treasury deposits at the Federal Reserve tend to reduce member bank reserves, let us consider two cases. (1) The Treasury deposits at the Federal Reserve $100 million of checks it has received from the public. These checks might represent payments of taxes or for securities bought by the public. On receiving the checks, the Federal Reserve will add $100 million to Treasury deposits and deduct the same amount from the reserve accounts of the banks on which they are drawn. The checks will then go to the banks on which they are drawn, which will deduct them from the public's deposit accounts. Thus the effects are to decrease by $100 million both the public's money supply and member bank reserves. (2) The Treasury increases its deposits at the Federal Reserve by withdrawing $100 million of deposits from commercial banks. On receiving the checks, the Federal Reserve will add them to Treasury deposits and subtract them from member bank reserves.

In drawing down its cash in vault or its deposits at the Federal Reserve, the Treasury has the reverse effects. (1) Suppose the Treasury pays to the public $100 million of checks drawn on the Federal Reserve. The public will deposit the checks at commercial banks and the latter will send them to the Federal Reserve, which will deduct them from Treasury deposits and add them to member bank reserve balances. Thus the effects are to increase by $100 million both the public's money supply and member bank reserves. (2) Suppose the Treasury pays out to commercial banks $100 million of checks drawn on the Federal Reserve banks. When the commercial banks return the checks to the Federal Reserve, the latter will deduct them from Treasury deposits and add them to bank reserves.

We shall see later that fluctuations in the size of Treasury holdings of cash and deposits at the Federal Reserve often tend to have important effects on the reserve positions of commercial banks, especially in periods of large net receipts or net payments by the Treasury, and that the Federal Reserve often takes action to prevent their having undesired effects on the general credit situation. We shall also see that the Treasury itself may engage in monetary management by regulating the size and location of its cash and deposit holdings.

Foreign Deposits at the Federal Reserve

These are largely deposits owed by the Federal Reserve to foreign central banks. Like Treasury deposits at the Federal Reserve, they compete with member bank reserves for funds supplied by the sources. Increases in this item tend to decrease member bank reserves, and decreases in it tend to add to member bank reserves. Suppose, for example, that foreign central banks pay out to the United States public $100 million of checks drawn on the Reserve banks. This will tend to increase by $100 million both the public's money supply and member bank reserves, for the public will deposit the checks at commercial banks, which will send them to the Federal Reserve to be added to their reserve accounts. If foreign central banks deposit at the Federal Reserve $100 million of checks received from the United States public the effects will be just the reverse: decreases in both the public's money supply and member bank reserves.

Other Deposits at the Federal Reserve

These are largely deposits that nonmember banks maintain at the Federal Reserve to facilitate check clearing and collection. They are usually relatively small and fluctuate narrowly. Nevertheless, they are competitive with member bank reserves for funds supplied by the sources. Increases in this item tend to reduce member bank reserves, largely because they reflect net losses of reserves by member banks to nonmembers. On the other hand, decreases in this item, usually reflecting gains of reserves by members from nonmembers, tend to increase member bank reserves.

Other Federal Reserve Accounts (Net)

This item is made up largely of Federal Reserve net worth or capital account with adjustments for minor asset and liability items not taken into account elsewhere. It competes with member bank reserves for funds supplied by the sources. To the extent that the Federal Reserve acquires assets by issuing ownership claims, it does not have to issue liability claims. This item usually fluctuates only narrowly over short periods.

Summary

In carrying out its monetary policy, and especially its open-market operations in acceptances and government securities, the Federal Reserve relies heavily upon the type of analysis developed above. As Robert V. Roosa has pointed out, Federal Reserve open-market purchases and sales are of two principal types: dynamic and defensive. Dynamic purchases or sales are those undertaken to effect net increases or net decreases in member bank reserves. Defensive purchases or sales are those undertaken to prevent other factors from bringing about unwanted changes in bank reserves. In effect they are offsetting operations. These defensive operations can be in the right direction and in the right magnitude only to the extent that the Federal Reserve can forecast the behavior of the various determinants of member bank reserves. The manager of the open-market account, therefore, seeks not only to detect changes as they occur but also to forecast future changes.

For this purpose he has several sources of information. To help him forecast the behavior of Federal Reserve float, he has elaborate studies of its seasonal behavior in the past and reports from the various Reserve banks concerning any unusual conditions that might cause it to rise or fall. The behavior of float has proved difficult to forecast with accuracy. With respect to current and prospective changes in the monetary gold stock he has several sources of information. The Reserve banks themselves, and especially the Federal Reserve Bank of New York, report purchases or sales of gold for Treasury account. The Treasury also reports its own transactions. Moreover, foreign central banks sometimes report several days in advance any plans they may have for buying or selling gold in the United States market. The Treasury reports any significant changes that it plans in the volume of its outstanding currency and in the size and location of its money balance. Studies of past seasonal patterns are used in predicting the volume of money in circulation. Instructions from foreign central banks assist in forecasting the behavior of foreign deposits at the Federal Reserve. The Reserve banks also report changes in their deposit liabilities to nonmember banks and any large transactions that would affect significantly the size of other Federal Reserve accounts.

In short, an understanding of the nature and behavior of the various determinants of member bank reserves is essential for both the student and the practitioner of monetary management.

FEDERAL RESERVE CREDIT

We shall now look more closely at the only two sources of bank reserves over which the Federal Reserve has direct control, and which it regulates not only to effect net changes in commercial bank reserves but also to prevent changes in other factors from having undesired effects on the banks' reserve positions. These are the Federal Reserve credit items: discounts, advances, and holdings of acceptances and United States government securities.

Both the theory and form of Federal Reserve credit have changed markedly since the inception of the Federal Reserve System. The framers of the Federal Reserve Act seem to have assumed that the new Reserve banks would be guided by two principles in extending their credit. (1) They would provide credit largely, if not exclusively, by lending to member banks. They would act as "bankers' banks," lending to their members much as commercial banks lend to their own customers. They might occasionally buy or sell securities in the open market, but these operations would be limited and of minor importance. (2) They would extend their credit largely on the basis of private debt obligations. In lending to members they would either discount paper acquired by banks in lending to their own customers or would make advances to banks on the basis of collateral consisting of these private debt obligations. They were to provide credit to only a limited extent, if at all, on the basis of the debt of the federal government. All of this is now reversed. The Reserve banks still lend to member banks, but most of their credit is provided by purchasing securities in the open market. Moreover, most of their credit is based not on private debt but on the debt of the federal government. The debts that they buy and sell in the open market are largely federal debt obligations, and even their loans to member banks are largely collateraled by Treasury obligations.

Of the many factors accounting for this reversal two should be emphasized: (1) Changes in the composition of outstanding debt. Most of the debt outstanding just prior to World War I was private debt. The federal debt had shrunk to less than a billion dollars and nearly three quarters of it was pledged at the Treasury as collateral for national bank notes. Banks had few free government securities that they could pledge as collateral for loans, and the volume of "floating" government securities in the market was far too small to permit large Federal Reserve purchases and sales even if the System had wished to make them. Two world wars and a great depression changed all this. By the end of World War I the federal debt had grown to $26 billion. After falling about $9 billion during the 1920's it grew to more than $55 billion during the great depression. After the end of World War II, federal debt outside the Treasury amounted to more than $200 billion and was widely held by banks and almost all other types of investors. As banks increased their holdings of federal securities, they tended to pledge them as collateral for loans from the Federal Reserve. Even in the 1920's more than half of all member bank borrowings at the Reserve banks were collateraled by Treasury obligations; since the mid-1930's almost all their borrowings have been of this type. Moreover, the very large growth of the federal debt and its wide ownership have made possible large Federal Reserve open-market operations in these securities.

(2) Changes in concepts of Federal Reserve responsibilities. The original theory of the Federal Reserve was one of "passive accommodation." The theory was that the Reserve banks should "accommodate commerce, industry, and agriculture" by assuring that their "legitimate" needs for credit were met. So long as this theory prevailed it was plausible, if not valid, to argue that the volume of Federal Reserve credit should be made passively responsive to the member banks' demands for loans, for these demands would reflect faithfully increases and decreases in the economy's "needs" for credit. Gradually, however, it became apparent that such a policy of passive accommodation could seriously destabilize the economy. A policy of passively supplying rising demands for credit during periods of high prosperity could "boom the boom," and a policy of passively accepting repayment of outstanding Federal Reserve loans in periods of declining business activity could "depress the depression." The Federal Reserve therefore shifted from a philosophy of passive accommodation to one of positive control. The new policy called for resistance to undesirable changes in the supply of money and credit and for efforts to achieve selected objectives. This shift of philosophy encouraged a substitution of Federal Reserve open-market operations for Federal Reserve lending, for by undertaking open-market operations on its own initiative the Federal Reserve could control more accurately the volume of bank reserves. It no longer had to depend on member banks to take the initiative in increasing or decreasing their demands for Federal Reserve credit.

Federal Reserve Discounts and Advances

Though by far the largest part of its loans is to member banks, the Federal Reserve sometimes makes small direct loans to the Treasury, nonmember banks, foreign central banks, and business. Congress so fears that the Treasury might abuse its power to borrow directly from the Reserve banks that it extends the enabling legislation only one year at a time and provides that at no time shall the Reserve banks hold more than $5 billion of securities acquired directly from the Treasury. Only rarely does the Treasury borrow directly from the Federal Reserve. Federal Reserve loans to nonmember banks are largely limited to periods of war and national crisis. It is felt that in more normal times these banks should not have the privilege of borrowing if they will not assume the obligations involved in becoming members of the Federal Reserve. Loans to foreign central banks are usually small but extremely useful when these banks need additional gold and foreign exchange reserves. The Reserve banks never lent directly to business firms until the mid-1930's. However, complaints that worthy borrowers were unable to secure credit led to an amendment to the Federal Reserve Act providing that the Reserve banks might lend directly to a business firm if that firm could prove both that it was credit-worthy and that it could not secure credit from its normal sources at reasonable rates. Federal Reserve loans of this type were never large even during the great depression and they have since become even less important. This power of the Reserve banks to lend to business was repealed by Congress in 1958.

Though the distinction has little economic significance, Federal Reserve loans to member banks are of two principal types: discounts (sometimes called rediscounts) and advances. When a bank secures Federal Reserve credit by discounting or rediscounting, it simply endorses some of its customers' paper and sends it to a Reserve bank for "discount." In effect, the Federal Reserve subtracts interest at its prevailing discount rate and credits the remainder to the borrowing bank's reserve account. Advances are simply loans to a bank on its own promissory note, though some sort of acceptable collateral is required. In recent years most Federal Reserve loans have been in the form of advances.

What types of paper should be eligible for discount or as collateral for Federal Reserve advances to member banks? This was long a controversial subject. The original Federal Reserve Act was based on the theory that the Reserve banks should take only "short-term self-liquidating agricultural, industrial, or commercial paper which was originally created for the purpose of providing funds for producing, purchasing, carrying or marketing of goods." They should not take paper whose proceeds were "used to finance fixed investments of any kind; or any investments of a purely speculative character; or for carrying or trading in stocks and bonds except obligations of the United States; or to finance relending operations except relending by coöperative marketing associations and factors." The theory that this short-term, self-liquidating paper should be given preferential status still survives in the provision that the Reserve banks may discount (or rediscount) only paper of this type, but this provision is now of only limited importance, for most Reserve bank loans take the form of advances, and other types of bank assets may be used as collateral for these advances.

The so-called "commercial loan theory of banking" on which the lending provisions of the original Federal Reserve Act were based has lost most of its adherents since 1914 and has virtually ceased to serve as a guide to Reserve bank lending. There are several reasons for this. (1) The mechanical difficulties of discounting customers' paper or of using it as collateral for advances to commercial banks. Reserve bank advances to banks with government securities as collateral are much simpler. (2) Inadequacy of member bank holdings of eligible commercial paper. Because of changes in the business structure and in commercial bank lending practices after World War I, bank holdings of high-quality commercial paper declined markedly. The decline was especially great during the depression following 1929. As a result, it was necessary to make other types of bank assets eligible as a basis for borrowing if the Reserve banks were to be of maximum usefulness to their members. (3) The basic fallaciousness of the commercial loan theory. With the passage of time it became increasingly evident that the restriction of commercial bank and Reserve bank loans to "commercial paper" could not attain any of the objectives claimed for it. It could not automatically adjust the volume of credit to the amount that is socially desirable, for harmful inflations and deflations of the volume of credit can occur even if both commercial banks and Reserve banks make only "commercial loans." Moreover, it has become increasingly clear that "commercial paper" is often less liquid than some other types of assets, especially call loans on securities and short-term government obligations. An individual commercial bank can achieve "liquidity" more easily by selling highly marketable securities than by calling its commercial loans. The "liquidity" of any asset for the commercial banking system as a whole depends on the ability and willingness of the Reserve banks to buy it or lend on it and to issue currency or bank reserves in exchange. Thus, the liquidity of the commercial banking system as a whole is enhanced by broadening the Reserve banks' lending powers, not by limiting the types of paper on which they can lend. It is hard to see how any asset can be "illiquid" for the Reserve banks if it can be used as a basis for issuing Federal Reserve notes, which have full legal-tender powers.[3]

Because of the factors indicated above, the types of assets on which the Reserve banks may lend have been greatly broadened. The present powers of the Federal Reserve to lend to member banks may be summarized as follows: (1) The Reserve banks may discount (or rediscount) for member banks only short-term commercial paper of the type described above. Only infrequently, however, do banks borrow in this way. (2) By far the greater part of Reserve bank loans take the form of advances to banks, with collateral in the form of eligible short-term commercial paper or United States government securities. Most of these advances have government securities rather than commercial paper as collateral. (3) Though virtually all Reserve bank loans to banks take the above forms, the Banking Act of 1935 provides that a Reserve bank can also make advances to a member bank on its note "secured to the satisfaction

[3] For a good short criticism of the commercial loan theory as applied to Reserve banks, see W. R. Burgess, *The Reserve Banks and the Money Market*, Harper, New York, 1936, pp. 41–67.

of the Federal Reserve bank" and complying with rules and regulations prescribed by the Board of Governors. The effect of this provision is to give the Federal Reserve System almost complete freedom to determine the types of collateral it will accept. But loans made under this provision must bear interest at a rate not less than ½ of 1 percent above the highest rate applicable to loans of the types under (1) and (2) above. As a result, banks will not borrow under this section as long as they have an adequate supply of eligible commercial paper and government obligations.

In short, the trend has been toward greater freedom for the Federal Reserve to determine the type of loans it will make. It is difficult to see why this trend should not be extended by eliminating from the Federal Reserve Act all its complex eligibility requirements and stating simply that the Federal Reserve may lend to member banks on any assets it deems acceptable. This would not only enable the Reserve banks to be of maximum help in time of strain but would also end forever the implication that there is any necessary relationship between the type of paper offered to the Reserve banks for discount or as collateral and the type of use to which the borrowed funds will be put.

Acceptances

Acceptances were not widely used in the United States before the passage of the original Federal Reserve Act. National banks were not permitted to accept time drafts drawn on them for the benefit of their customers, and there was no well-developed acceptance market. Critics found many faults with this situation. They complained that banks were deprived of legitimate business, that America's growth as an international financial center was inhibited, that industry was deprived of a convenient and cheap method of short-term finance, and that temporarily available short-term funds tended to be diverted into security speculation rather than channeled into the financing of commerce and industry. To remedy this situation, the Federal Reserve Act empowered national banks to accept drafts drawn on them, thereby promoting a supply of acceptances, and provided that the Reserve banks might purchase acceptances in the open market, thereby helping create a market for them.

The importance of Federal Reserve open-market operations in acceptances has varied widely. During the period prior to the great depression, Federal Reserve holdings of this paper were often large, sometimes larger than its holdings of governments. The volume of outstanding acceptances declined sharply during the great depression and remained very low until after the end of World War II. Federal Reserve operations in acceptances were negligible during this period. More recently, however, the volume of acceptances has again begun to grow and the Federal Reserve has resumed its purchases and sales of them. These operations are still very small but they could grow in the future.

United States Government Obligations

As already noted, one of the striking developments in Federal Reserve policy has been the rise of open-market operations in government securities as a means of creating Federal Reserve credit and as an instrument of monetary management. The great increase in Federal Reserve holdings of these securities, both in absolute size and as a fraction of total Federal Reserve credit, is indicated in Table 24. We shall later discuss variations in these holdings,

TABLE 24.   Average Federal Reserve Credit Outstanding in
Selected Periods
(Averages of daily figures in millions of dollars)

Period	Discounts and Advances	Acceptances	U.S. Gov't Securities	All Other	Total
1915	$ 24	$ 10	$ 8	$ 17	$ 60
1920	2,523	385	324	158	3,390
1925	490	287	359	59	1,195
1930	272	213	564	38	1,087
1935	7	5	2,431	32	2,475
1940	4	—	2,417	67	2,487
1945	376	—	21,351	472	22,199
1950	129	—	18,405	521	19,055
1955	665	13	23,889	901	25,468
1958 (March)	139	41	23,486	893	24,559

SOURCES: Board of Governors of the Federal Reserve System, *Banking and Monetary Statistics*, Washington, 1943, p. 368, and *Federal Reserve Bulletins*.

reflecting net purchases and sales by the Federal Reserve for dynamic and defensive purposes.

SELECTED READINGS

Board of Governors of the Federal Reserve System:
     "Supply and Use of Member Bank Reserve Funds," *Federal Reserve Bulletin*, July, 1935.
     Banking and Monetary Statistics, Washington, 1943, pp. 360–402.
     Banking Studies, Washington, 1941.
     Federal Reserve Bulletins.
     Annual Reports.
Goldenweiser, E. A., *American Monetary Policy*, McGraw-Hill, New York, 1951.

CHAPTER 9

Instruments of Monetary Management

The purpose of this chapter is to analyze the various instruments of monetary management in the hands of the Federal Reserve and the Treasury. We shall first discuss what were earlier referred to as "general" monetary or credit controls—those directed toward regulating the total supply of money or credit without necessarily regulating the allocation of credit among its various possible borrowers or uses. These controls are of two principal types: (1) Federal Reserve controls of member bank reserve requirements, and (2) various measures affecting the volume and cost of member bank reserves. Selective controls—those used to influence or regulate the allocation of credit—will be discussed later.

MEMBER BANK RESERVE REQUIREMENTS

Prior to 1935, member bank reserve requirements were rigidly set by the Federal Reserve Act and could not be altered by Federal Reserve officials. This legislation provided that nothing other than deposits at Reserve banks would count as legal reserves. Minimum reserve requirements against time and savings deposits were set at 3 percent for all member banks.[1] In fixing reserve requirements against demand deposits at member banks, the Federal Reserve Act carried over the classifications used in the National Banking Act. Central Reserve city banks are those located in New York and Chicago, reserve city banks are those located in about sixty other specified large cities; country banks are those located elsewhere.[2] The minimum percentages of reserves required against demand deposits were fixed at 13 percent for central

[1] This discussion relates to the legislation in effect from June, 1917, to 1935. We shall not discuss here the earlier arrangements.
[2] In some cases banks in the outlying areas of large cities are placed in a category with lower reserve requirements. Thus a bank located in an outlying area of New York or Chicago may be classified as a reserve city bank or even as a country bank.

reserve city banks, 10 percent for reserve city banks, and 7 percent for country banks.

The Banking Act of 1935 empowered the Board of Governors to alter the reserve requirements of any class or of all classes of member banks. However, it placed limits on these alterations, providing that the percentages required should not be fixed below those already prevailing or more than twice those already prevailing. Thus the Board of Governors may vary member bank reserve requirements within the following limits:

	Lowest Level at Which Requirements May Be Set	Highest Level at Which Requirements May Be Set
On net demand deposits		
At central reserve city banks	13%	26%
At reserve city banks	10	20
At country banks	7	14
On time deposits		
At all member banks	3	6

As shown in Table 25, the Board first used this power in 1936 and has since employed it many times. Sometimes it raised reserve requirements to eliminate some or all excess member bank reserves and even to create a deficiency of bank reserves. At other times it reduced these requirements, thereby tending to create excess reserves for member banks. Table 25 reveals two other things worth noting. First, since the late 1930's member bank reserve requirements have been fixed closer to the top of the permitted range than to the bottom. Second, in recent years the Board has lowered reserve requirements much more often than it has raised them.

Changes in member bank reserve requirements are a powerful instrument for monetary management. Even a change of one percentage point can have a marked effect on monetary and credit conditions. To illustrate this let us start with a situation in which member banks have neither excess reserves nor a deficiency of reserves, their deposits subject to reserve requirements total $150 billion, their average reserve requirement is 14 percent, and their actual reserve balances are $21 billion. Suppose now that the Board of Governors lowers average reserve requirements to 13 percent. This reduction of one percentage point decreases required reserves by $1.5 billion, thereby creating an equal amount of excess reserves. If the average percentage reserve requirement remains at this new lower level of 13 percent and the banking system suffers no net cash drain in the process of expansion, this $1.5 billion of excess reserves would enable the banks to expand both their earning assets and their deposits by $\frac{\$1.5 \text{ billion}}{.13}$, or about $11.5 billion. This would surely tend to increase the availability of credit and to lower market rates of interest.

Suppose, on the other hand, that the Board of Governors raises the average reserve requirements of member banks from 14 percent to 15 percent. This rise of one percentage point will increase required reserves by $1.5 billion,

TABLE 25. Member Bank Reserve Requirements
(Percent of Deposits)

| Period in Effect | Net Demand Deposits[a] | | | Time Deposits (All Member Banks) |
	Central Reserve City Banks	Reserve City Banks	Country Banks	
June 21, 1917—Aug. 15, 1936	13	10	7	3
Aug. 16, 1936—Feb. 28, 1937	19½	15	10½	4½
Mar. 1, 1937—Apr. 30, 1937	22¾	17½	12¼	5¼
May 1, 1937—Apr. 15, 1938	26	20	14	6
Apr. 16, 1938—Oct. 31, 1941	22¾	17½	12	5
Nov. 1, 1941—Aug. 19, 1942	26	20	14	6
Aug. 20, 1942—Sept. 13, 1942	24	20	14	6
Sept. 14, 1942—Oct. 2, 1942	22	20	14	6
Oct. 3, 1942—Feb. 28, 1948	20	20	14	6
Feb. 28, 1948—June 11, 1948	22	20	14	6
June 11, 1948—Sept. 16, 1948	24	20	14	6
Sept. 16, 1948—Sept. 24, 1948	24	20	16	7½
Sept. 24, 1948—May 1, 1949	26	22	16	7½
Sept., 1949—Jan. 11, 1951[b]	22	18	12	6
Jan. 11, 1951—Jan. 16, 1951	23	19	12	6
Jan. 16, 1951—Jan. 25, 1951	23	19	13	6
Jan. 25, 1951—Feb. 1, 1951	24	20	13	6
Feb. 1, 1951—July 1, 1953	24	20	14	6
July 1, 1953—July 9, 1953	24	20	13	6
July 9, 1953—June 16, 1954	22	19	13	6
June 16, 1954—June 24, 1954	22	19	13	5
June 24, 1954—July 29, 1954	21	19	13	5
July 29, 1954—Aug. 1, 1954	20	18	13	5
Aug. 1, 1954—Feb. 27, 1958	20	18	12	5
Feb. 27, 1958—Mar. 1, 1958	19½	17½	12	5
Mar. 1, 1958—Mar. 20, 1958	19½	17½	11½	5
Mar. 20, 1958—Apr. 1, 1958	19	17	11½	5
Apr. 1, 1958—Apr. 17, 1958	19	17	11	5
Apr. 17, 1958—Apr. 24, 1958	18½	17	11	5
Apr. 24, 1958 and after	18	16½	11	5

[a] Demand deposits subject to reserve requirements, i.e., demand deposits other than war loan deposits, minus cash items in process of collection and demand balances due from domestic banks.

[b] The reductions between May and September, 1949, were made in several steps.

thereby creating a reserve deficiency of that amount. If average reserve requirements remain at the new higher level, if member banks are unable to secure new reserves, and if the process of contraction induces no net inflow of cash, the banks will be forced to contract both their earning assets and their deposits by $\dfrac{\$1.5 \text{ billion}}{.15}$, or \$10 billion. This would produce decreases in the availability of credit and higher market rates of interest.

This instrument is well adapted to two purposes. The first is to absorb large excess reserves or to offset large losses of reserves by the banking system. For example, in the late 1930's, owing largely to huge gold inflows, member banks accumulated several billions of excess reserves—far more than the Federal Reserve could have eliminated by selling all its government securities and other earning assets. Large increases in member bank reserve requirements served a useful purpose in absorbing most of these excess reserves and in reducing the potential expansion of bank credit on the basis of the excess reserves that remained. Reductions of reserve requirements might be similarly useful if the banks should at some time suffer large losses of reserves. A second purpose for which this instrument is well adapted is for announcing important policy decisions to both the public and the banks. Changes in reserve requirements are overt and well-publicized actions that the public can understand and that immediately affect the reserve positions of thousands of banks. They are, therefore, an effective way in which the Board of Governors can in effect say, "This is the direction our policy is taking and we really mean it!"

In general, this instrument is employed only infrequently and to bring about relatively large changes in the reserve positions of banks; it is not used for day-to-day or week-to-week adjustments. In part this is because it has acquired the reputation of being "more like an ax than a scalpel." This reputation, which dates largely from the late 1930's when requirements were changed several percentage points at a time, is not wholly justified. More delicate adjustments can be made if the changes are smaller, announced well in advance, and made effective in steps. Nevertheless, Federal Reserve officials prefer to rely largely on open-market operations and discount policy for their finer and day-to-day adjustments.

Of all the restrictive measures available to the Federal Reserve, increases in member bank reserve requirements are by far the most unpopular with member bankers, especially when these requirements are already toward the top of the permitted range. Bankers view required reserves as sterile assets that yield no return and they resent any requirement that a larger percentage of their assets be held in this form. The resentment of member bankers is increased by their feeling that their higher reserve requirements place them at a competitive disadvantage. Generally speaking, nonmember banks operate under much lower reserve requirements than member banks. So do mutual savings banks, savings and loan associations, and other financial institutions with which member banks compete for savings accounts. In making their decisions Federal Reserve officials are probably influenced somewhat by these attitudes of member bankers and also by the possibility that further increases in reserve requirements might influence some member banks to withdraw from the System or some nonmembers to refrain from joining. Congressional action forcing all commercial banks to become members of the Federal Reserve or at least to hold reserves as large as those required of member banks might change the situation markedly.

There is general, if not unanimous, agreement that both legal reserve requirements and the power of the Federal Reserve to alter these requirements are useful instruments of monetary management. Nevertheless, the particular set of arrangements described above has been widely criticized on several grounds.

1. The classification of demand deposits for reserve requirement purposes is illogical. As noted earlier, this classification was carried over from the National Banking Act and was apparently based on the theory that the purpose of required reserves is to assure the liquidity of banks. Banks in larger cities were assumed to need greater liquidity because most of them held deposits of other banks and were, therefore, subject to drains by both their customers and their depositor banks. This reasoning is now unacceptable for at least two reasons. In the first place, the purpose of required reserves is not to provide liquidity but to serve as an instrument for regulating the supply of money. In the second place, if the purpose was to require higher reserves against interbank deposits, the law should have said precisely that. Many of the banks in central reserve and reserve cities do not hold deposits of other banks, whereas some "country" banks do. Under the present arrangement, a mere shift of demand deposits from one class of member bank to another can alter average reserve requirements and affect monetary conditions. For example, a shift of deposits from banks with lower reserve requirements to banks with higher requirements can raise average reserve requirements and restrict credit. Moreover, banks located in the areas of highest reserve requirements complain that they bear an unduly large share of the burden of monetary management because they must hold such a large percentage of their total assets in nonearning form.

2. Not only deposits at Federal Reserve banks but also cash in vault should count as legal reserves for member banks. This change could be made without decreasing the effectiveness of monetary management, for the Federal Reserve could control the sum of member bank deposits at the Federal Reserve and cash in member bank vaults as accurately as the former alone. Such a change would also reduce considerably the cost of shipping coin and currency, for when these do not count as legal reserves, banks ship excess supplies to the Federal Reserve for deposit and then withdraw them again when they are needed for circulation.

3. The general level of reserve requirements is too high. To force banks

to hold such a large percentage of their assets in sterile form decreases their profits, lessens their ability to compete with more profitable industries for capital funds, and puts them in an unfavorable competitive position relative to financial institutions that hold a larger percentage of their assets in earning forms.

Criticisms of these types are so widespread that some sort of reform of member bank reserve requirements seems probable within the next few years. The most likely directions are toward counting cash in vault as legal reserves; toward uniform requirements against demand deposits regardless of the location of the member bank, or at least toward narrower differentials; and perhaps toward lower average percentage requirements.

OPEN-MARKET OPERATIONS

We turn now to the instruments used by the Federal Reserve to regulate the cost and dollar volume of member bank reserves. The most important of these are open-market purchases and sales of acceptances and government securities, largely the latter. We shall discuss in detail only operations in government securities; the same principles apply to Federal Reserve purchases and sales of acceptances.

As noted earlier, Federal Reserve open-market operations are controlled by the Federal Open-Market Committee (hereafter referred to as the FOMC), which is composed of the seven members of the Board of Governors, the president of the Federal Reserve Bank of New York, and four other presidents of Reserve banks. The FOMC meets in Washington at least once every three weeks, and its members communicate with each other much more frequently, often daily, by telephone. This body determines open-market policy, setting its objectives and prescribing in a general way the nature and magnitude of the actions to be taken. Actual purchases and sales are made by the manager of the open-market account, who is a vice-president of the Federal Reserve Bank of New York but is accountable to the FOMC. Because New York is the nation's great financial center, all transactions occur there. In buying and selling, the manager deals with about seventeen government security dealers. These dealers are at the center of a national and even international market for United States government obligations. They purchase these securities from, and sell them to, all sorts of institutions and people located in all parts of the United States and in foreign countries—the United States Treasury, foreign sellers and buyers, the Federal Reserve, commercial banks, insurance companies, savings banks, savings and loan associations, pension funds, nonfinancial business firms, individuals, and others.

When the manager of the open-market account purchases government securities from a dealer, he pays the dealer with a check on the Federal Reserve

Bank of New York. The dealer must, of course, pay these funds to the seller of the securities. If the seller is a commercial bank, the immediate effect is to increase the volume of bank reserves. If the seller is someone other than a bank, the effect will be to increase directly both the public's money supply and the dollar volume of bank reserves, for the seller will deposit the check with his bank, which will deposit it at a Reserve bank. Sales of government securities by the manager of the open-market account have the opposite effect. The dealer who sells the securities to the Federal Reserve pays for them, in effect, with funds that he receives from the buyer to whom he sells the securities. If the buyer is a commercial bank, the effect is to reduce bank reserves. If the buyer is someone other than a bank, the effect is to reduce directly both bank reserves and the public's money supply. In effect, the dealer pays the Federal Reserve with a check received from a customer of some bank, the Federal Reserve deducts the check from the bank's reserve account and sends the check to the bank, which deducts it from the customer's deposit account.

Two aspects of open-market operations should be emphasized. (1) Though these transactions occur in New York City, their effects are by no means confined to that area. Those who sell the government securities purchased by the Federal Reserve and thereby gain Federal Reserve funds may be located all over the country. So may those who buy the government securities from the Federal Reserve and thereby lose Federal Reserve funds. (2) The most powerful effects of Federal Reserve purchases and sales are achieved through their impact on the reserves and lending power of banks, whether these operations are with banks or others. But Federal Reserve purchases from and sales to others than banks may also have other important influences on the availability of money for investment and other purposes. For example, Federal Reserve purchases of government securities from insurance companies or other nonbank financial institutions directly provide those institutions with money that they can lend for other purposes. On the other hand, Federal Reserve sales of securities to such investors absorb money that they might otherwise have lent to others.

Federal Reserve open-market operations are of two principal types: "outright" purchases and sales, and acquisitions under "repurchase agreements." Outright purchases and sales, which make up by far the larger part of the total, are ordinary transactions in which neither the buyer nor the seller commits himself to resell or rebuy. The transaction is final. In some cases, however, the Federal Reserve buys securities from a dealer with an agreement that the dealer will repurchase the securities within a stipulated period, which never exceeds 15 days. This is much like a short-term loan to the dealer. A sort of interest charge is made, approximately equal to the discount rate at the Federal Reserve Bank of New York, by paying the dealer a price below that at which he is obliged to repurchase the security. Federal Reserve officials regard money created in this way as "dollars with strings on them," for the very purchases that involve the issue of the dollars make provision for return of the dollars on a stipulated date. Acquisitions under repurchase agreements are a useful instrument for at least two purposes. For one thing, they are a convenient way of supplying funds to meet a temporary need and of withdrawing funds when the need has passed. For example, the Federal Reserve may acquire securities under repurchase agreements during the week before Christmas when currency is being drained from the banks, arranging for dealers to repurchase the securities just after Christmas when large amounts of currency flow back into the banking system. This device is also useful for avoiding disorderly changes in the market prices of government securities. Dealers in these securities ordinarily hold inventories far larger than they could finance with their own capital funds. They rely heavily on borrowed money. If at some time they could not borrow sufficient funds, or could do so only at very high rates of interest, they might dump large amounts of their inventory on the market, thereby disturbing seriously not only government security prices but also money market conditions in general. Judicious Federal Reserve acquisitions under repurchase agreements can help avoid such occurrences.

Federal Reserve outright open-market operations are either "regular way" or "cash." Purchases or sales "regular way" call for payment and delivery of the securities on the day following the transaction. Such purchases or sales thus involve a one-day delay in putting money into the market or taking it out of the market. However, in purchases or sales for "cash" the securities are delivered and payment is made or received on the day of the transaction. Open-market operations are a highly timely and flexible instrument of monetary management. The manager of the open-market account and his lieutenants are at their trading desks during all hours when the government securities market is open and can operate at any time. Though they must conform to the general policy prescribed by the FOMC, they have considerable freedom to adapt the timing and rates of their purchases and sales to actual and prospective changes in economic and financial conditions. They can adjust their actions from day to day and even from hour to hour, and their actions may be either defensive or dynamic in nature, or any combination of the two.

We have already emphasized that open-market operations achieve their most powerful effects through their impact on the reserve positions of commercial banks, for each one-dollar change in these reserves may encourage or force a change of several dollars in the banks' holdings of loans and securities. But Federal Reserve purchases or sales of government securities may directly tend to raise or lower the market prices of these securities. Prior to 1937 the Federal Reserve tended to ignore the direct effects of its purchases and sales on the prices and yields of government securities, concentrating instead on their effects on the reserve positions of banks. But since that time it has frequently paid much more attention to the direct effects of its actions on the prices and yields of Treasury obligations. From 1942 to 1951 it even went so far as to "peg" these prices and yields within narrow limits. It purchased at the selected level of prices all the securities that others did not want to hold at those prices, thereby preventing their prices from falling. On the other hand, it sometimes sold a sufficient amount of these securities to prevent their prices from rising above selected levels.

We shall later deal more fully with these issues, but two points should be emphasized here. (1) The System must choose between accurate control of the volume of its holdings of government securities on the one hand and stabilization of interest rates on the other. If it is to control accurately the volume of its holdings, it must allow the prices and yields of government securities to fluctuate in response to changes in the supply of and demand for these obligations. If it is to stabilize their prices and yields, it must abandon accurate control of the volume of its holdings and passively buy or sell all the securities offered to it or demanded from it at the selected level of prices and yields. In this case the initiative is with other investors, for it is they who determine the volume of securities offered to or demanded from the Federal Reserve. This means, of course, that they also determine the volume of bank reserves. (2) So long as investors can shift freely between government securities and other obligations, the Federal Reserve can dominate the entire structure of interest rates by regulating yields on the federal debt. This debt now makes up about a third of all the outstanding interest-bearing debt of the country, and is equal to many times the annual increase in total debt. If the Federal Reserve buys and sells these securities freely in such a way as to maintain a certain structure of yields on them, it also establishes, within narrow limits, the structure of yields on other debts. The reason for this is that private investors are free to arbitrage among the various branches of the debt market—to sell in one and buy in another until they see no further advantage in shifting their funds. This applies not only to banks but to other investors as well. In short, Federal Reserve operations in the government security market can dominate the entire money market. However, we shall see later that if this power is used to stabilize interest rates, the effect may be to destabilize the rest of the economy.

DISCOUNT RATES AND DISCOUNT POLICY

Member banks may, of course, increase the volume of their reserves by borrowing from the Reserve banks, and they may decrease their reserves by reducing their debts to the Federal Reserve. One instrument for regulating the volume and cost of bank reserves acquired from this source is the Federal Reserve discount rate. This is simply the interest rate charged by the Reserve banks on their loans. Increases in discount rates increase the cost of acquiring reserves by borrowing, whereas decreases in discount rates make it cheaper for banks to acquire reserves in this way.

Discount rate changes are ordinarily initiated by the boards of directors of the twelve Federal Reserve banks but are subject to the approval of the Board of Governors. Each Reserve bank must submit its rate for approval at least once every fourteen days, and oftener if required by the Board of Governors. The Board could, if it wished, disapprove all rates except the one it wished to see established. Discount rates at the various Reserve banks can differ, and they sometimes do. But they are usually the same, and the occasional differences are ordinarily small and short-lived.

Under certain conditions a central bank's discount rate could regulate with accuracy the level of market rates of interest, or at least of short-term interest rates. Suppose, for example, that two conditions obtain: (1) The central bank stands ready to lend freely at its established discount rate; it uses no other rationing methods and relies on the discount rate alone to regulate the volume of its loans. (2) Commercial banks have no inhibitions against borrowing from the central bank. Intent on maximizing their profits, they borrow from the central bank and lend whenever market rates of interest exceed the discount rate by an amount sufficient to cover the cost of risk-bearing and loan administration. They also withdraw loans from the market and repay their borrowings at the central bank whenever market rates of interest are not sufficiently higher than the discount rate. Under such conditions the central bank discount rate could dominate market rates of interest. Increases and decreases in the discount rate would almost automatically raise or lower market rates of interest. Moreover, discount rates would be the central bank's sole method of regulating the volume of bank reserves that it created by lending.

These are not the conditions in American banking, and the Federal Reserve discount rate does not play exactly this role. Member banks do have inhibitions against large and continuous borrowings from their Reserve banks. Even before the establishment of the Federal Reserve there was a "tradition against continuous borrowing"—a feeling that it was "unsound" for a bank to borrow continuously to extend its own lending power. Federal Reserve officials have maintained and strengthened this tradition. They have stated repeatedly that borrowing is a privilege and not a right, that a member bank should not borrow simply because it is profitable to do so, that a bank should not borrow large amounts for long periods, and that generally speaking a bank should borrow only to meet drains that it could not foresee, and even then for only short periods. A recent statement of these principles was included in a foreword to regulations issued by the Board of Governors concerning member bank borrowing.

Federal Reserve credit is generally extended on a short-term basis to a member bank in order to enable it to adjust its asset position when necessary because of developments such as a sudden withdrawal of deposits or seasonal requirements for credit beyond those which can reasonably be met by use of the bank's own resources. Federal Reserve credit is also available for longer periods when necessary in order to assist member banks in meeting unusual situations, such as may result from national, regional or local difficulties or from exceptional circumstances involving only particular member banks. Under ordinary conditions, the continuous use of Federal Reserve credit by a member bank over a considerable period of time is not regarded as appropriate.

In considering a request for credit accommodation, each Federal Reserve bank gives due regard to the purpose of the credit and to its probable effects upon the maintenance of sound credit conditions, both as to the individual institution and the economy generally. It keeps informed of and takes into account the general character and amount of the loans and investments of the member bank. It considers whether the bank is borrowing principally for the purpose of obtaining a tax advantage or profiting from rate differentials and whether the bank is extending an undue amount of credit for the speculative carrying of or trading in securities, real estate, or commodities, or otherwise.

A Reserve bank rarely refuses to lend to a member bank facing an actual or prospective deficiency in its reserves. But after making a short-term loan to a bank it studies the situation carefully. If it finds that the bank has borrowed too often, too continuously, too much, or for improper reasons, it may advise the bank to contract its loans or sell securities in order to reduce or retire its borrowings. It may even go as far as to refuse to renew the loan, and in extreme cases it may suspend the bank's borrowing privilege.

Federal Reserve officials could, of course, attempt to regulate the volume of member bank borrowing by varying their own attitudes toward lending, being very strict at some times and more liberal at others. Though this is done to some extent, it is not a very flexible or effective instrument.

This combination of member bank inhibitions against large and continuous borrowing from the Federal Reserve and the latter's unwillingness to make such loans to a member helps explain several things about monetary policy in the United States. (1) When member bank borrowings from the Federal Reserve are large, credit is usually "tight" and there is some pressure against further expansion and even toward contraction. Credit is, of course, less tight than it would have been if the banks had not been able to borrow and secure reserves, but it is tighter than it would have been if the banks had had the same volume of reserves without borrowing. Banks in debt to the Federal Reserve are under pressure not to extend their credit further and even to contract their outstanding loans and security holdings. (2) The role of discount rates in regulating the volume of bank reserves is reduced in importance. The Federal

Reserve does not rely solely or even largely on increased discount rates to limit member bank borrowing. And decreases in discount rates are not likely to be very effective in inducing larger member bank borrowings.

Nevertheless, it would be a mistake to dismiss changes in discount rates as ineffective and useless. They influence the economy in several ways.

1. They do have some effect on the volume of member bank borrowings from the Federal Reserve. A member bank with an actual or prospective deficiency in its reserves can repair its reserve position in either of two general ways: by borrowing or by selling some of its earning assets, such as short-term government obligations. It is tempted, despite the tradition against continuous borrowing, to repair its reserves in the cheapest way. If the Federal Reserve discount rate is lower than the yield it would have to sacrifice if it sold some of its earning assets, a member bank may elect to borrow from the Federal Reserve and may be in no hurry to repay its borrowings. This is especially true of banks that have not been borrowing continuously and therefore fear no early chastisement by Federal Reserve officials. The result can be a significant increase in member bank borrowings and reserves and a minimum of pressure toward credit restriction. However, if the discount rate is higher than the yields on assets that the banks might sell to repair their reserve positions, many banks will not borrow or will repay their borrowings quickly. They will attempt to repair their reserve positions by calling loans or selling securities. The result may be to decrease member bank borrowings and to enhance restrictive pressures.

2. Changes in discount rates are an effective way of announcing to both the banks and the public the direction of Federal Reserve policy. Open-market operations are not well suited to this purpose, partly because they are not widely understood and partly because dynamic operations are often obscured for some time by defensive operations. On the other hand, changes in discount rates are widely publicized as soon as they occur and are generally believed to be important. In fact, many exaggerate their importance. An increase in discount rates is generally interpreted as meaning that the Federal Reserve is moving toward tighter credit and higher interest rates. This may lead some lenders to restrict their loans, hoping for higher interest rates in the future. A reduction of discount rates, presaging an easier monetary policy and lower interest rates, may induce some lenders to increase immediately their willingness to lend. Of course, there is the possibility that changes in discount rates will have perverse announcement effects. For example, if an increase in discount rates is interpreted to mean that Federal Reserve officials believe inflation is coming, such an action might encourage people to borrow and spend, thereby increasing the danger of inflation. If a decrease in discount rates is taken as a forecast of business recession, it could encourage a reduction of

spending and hasten a business decline. However, such perverse announcement effects are likely to occur only if changes in discount rates create expectations about the trend of business that the public would not have had anyway, and if the public believes the Federal Reserve will not be able to achieve its objectives. The public has so many other sources of information that it would usually know about dangers of inflation or recession even if the Federal Reserve did nothing to announce its intention of combating such disturbances.

3. Changes in discount rates affect market rates of interest in various ways. We have already noted that increases or decreases in this rate may affect lenders' expectations about future rates and immediately cause them to lend less liberally or more liberally. There are other effects as well. A few, but only a few, long-term debt contracts escalate their interest rates with the Federal Reserve discount rate. The other principal effects are less direct but nevertheless important. For example, an increase in the discount rate increases the bargaining power of lenders relative to borrowers. A banker can argue, "I have to charge you more because I have to pay more when I borrow." Nonbank lenders may insist that "even the Federal Reserve recognizes that credit is scarcer and interest rates should go up." Reductions in discount rates generally increase the bargaining power of borrowers and tend to bring down "sticky" rates of interest, such as those on loans by banks to their large and medium-sized customers. They are less effective in reducing rates to small borrowers.

MORAL SUASION

In many countries with only a handful of commercial banks, the central bank relies heavily on moral suasion to accomplish its objectives. It can confer informally with responsible officials of the five or ten important commercial banks and persuade them to follow policies that it considers appropriate. For example, it may get them to agree to limit their borrowing from the central bank, to refrain from expanding their loans or even to contract them, or to lend less liberally for some purposes than for others. Such techniques of monetary management are not well adapted to the American system with its thousands of widely scattered banks, more than half of which are not members of the Federal Reserve. Nevertheless, Federal Reserve officials often use moral suasion to supplement their other policies. At times they use publicity, interviews, and other devices to persuade banks to borrow less and tighten their credit policies. On a few occasions, as in 1947 and in 1951, they have encouraged banks and other lenders to follow "voluntary credit restraint programs" to curtail "nonessential credit." At other times they attempt to persuade banks to follow more liberal lending policies.

Opinions as to the efficacy of moral suasion differ widely. There would, however, be general agreement that it is a useful device for gaining support for Federal Reserve policies.

COÖRDINATION OF THE INSTRUMENTS OF GENERAL MONETARY MANAGEMENT

We have now discussed the three major Federal Reserve instruments of general monetary management—changes in member bank reserve requirements, open-market operations, and discount policy. We turn now to a consideration of the interrelationships of these instruments and the coördination of their use.

If one looks only at the legal provisions of the Federal Reserve Act, he may fear that these instruments will not be used in a coördinated way, for authority over them is not fully centralized. Member bank reserve requirements are set by the Board of Governors alone. Open-market operations are controlled by the FOMC. Discount rate changes are usually initiated by the twelve Federal Reserve banks, subject to approval by the Board of Governors. Loan officers at the twelve Reserve banks decide whether or not to make specific loans to member banks, though they operate under general regulations prescribed by the Board of Governors. There is far more coördination than this dispersion of legal authority might suggest, and it is achieved in many ways, both formal and informal. In this process the Board of Governors plays a central role. With full authority over member bank reserve requirements, a majority of the members of the FOMC, power to approve or disapprove discount rates, and the authority to prescribe regulations for lending to member banks, its legal powers are formidable. It is also in a position to persuade other Federal Reserve officials to coöperate. Officials of the various Reserve banks also confer frequently among themselves and with the Board, exchanging information and points of view.

In this process the meetings of the FOMC, held in Washington at least once every three weeks, are very important. These meetings are attended not only by the members of the FOMC but also by the seven presidents of Reserve banks not currently members of the FOMC, the principal economists on the Board's staff, and an economist from each of the Reserve banks. The presidents who are not members of the FOMC are free to discuss but not to vote. For two days those assembled analyze current and prospective financial and economic conditions and discuss various policy alternatives. By the end of the meeting they all know what the open-market policy will be, probably also the Board's intentions with respect to member bank reserve requirements, the Board's attitude toward discount rates, and even the intentions of the various presidents with respect to the discount rates they will recommend to their boards of directors. In these and various other ways a high degree of centralization is desirable.

The three principal instruments may be used singly or in various combinations. Open-market operations are often used alone, especially for defensive purposes or where only small dynamic effects are desired. For larger operations they are ordinarily combined with changes in discount rates. In some cases, and especially when much easier monetary conditions are desired, both will be combined with changes in member bank reserve requirements. Though there is no invariable sequence in its use of these instruments, the Federal Reserve usually "leads off" with open-market operations and then adjusts its discount rate as market conditions are changed.

To illustrate this, let us assume that the Federal Reserve, which has been following a tight money policy, decides to reverse that policy and pursue one of monetary ease. It may lead off by purchasing government securities, say $400 million of them. The immediate effect is, of course, to add that amount to bank reserves. Some of these new reserves will go to banks that were not borrowing from the Federal Reserve and will become excess reserves. These banks can now lend more liberally. Another part of the newly injected reserves may go to banks that were in debt to their Reserve banks, and at least some of these new funds may be used to repay borrowings at the Federal Reserve. These banks will at least be under less pressure to contract their credit even if they do not actually feel impelled to expand their loans and security holdings. Thus both the increase in excess reserves and the reduction of member bank borrowings tend to increase the supply of credit in the market and to lower interest rates. As market rates of interest fall, the Federal Reserve will adjust its discount rate downward. Only infrequently will it lower discount rates before market rates have been reduced. This process may be aided by a reduction of member bank reserve requirements. Suppose required reserves are reduced by $500 million. The immediate effect is to increase excess reserves by that amount, though some of these may be used by banks that are borrowing from the Federal Reserve to reduce their indebtedness. But both the increase of excess reserves and the ability of member banks to reduce their debts to the Federal Reserve without reducing their loans and security holdings will tend to liberalize credit and lower interest rates.

Suppose, on the other hand, that the Federal Reserve reverses its policy of monetary ease and moves toward credit restriction. It might lead off by selling government securities, perhaps $300 million. The immediate effect is to decrease bank reserves. Some banks that formerly had excess reserves now have fewer of these or none at all and some find themselves with deficient reserves. Some of the latter may repair their reserve positions, at least temporarily, by borrowing at the Federal Reserve, but they will lend less liberally. The results will be a lesser availability of credit and a rise of interest rates. As interest rates rise in the market the Federal Reserve usually adjusts its discount rate upwards. An increase of member bank reserve requirements could be used to achieve results similar to those of open-market sales.

In the examples above, the Federal Reserve took the initiative in changing monetary and credit conditions. Sometimes it "lets the market tighten itself" by refusing to take defensive actions to offset changes emanating from other factors. Suppose, for example, that the banks lose several hundred millions of reserves because of gold outflows or drains of currency into circulation, and that the Federal Reserve welcomes a tightening of credit at that time. Instead of buying securities to offset these drains, it may stand by as banks lose excess reserves and have to borrow to repair their reserve positions. Then as the availability of credit declines and interest rates rise in the market, it may raise its discount rate.

TREASURY INSTRUMENTS OF MONETARY MANAGEMENT

The Treasury influences monetary and credit conditions in many ways—through its revenue and expenditure policies, its debt management policies, its policies relative to the size and location of its money balance, and so on. At this point we shall deal only with its policies relative to the size of its money balance and the distribution of this balance among its three possible forms—Treasury cash in vault, Treasury deposits at the Federal Reserve, and Treasury deposits at commercial banks. Owing to the magnitude of Treasury operations, these policies can have marked effects on monetary and credit conditions, especially over short periods. Ordinarily, the Treasury does not use these powers for deliberate and continuous monetary management; this is the primary responsibility of the Federal Reserve. However, it does try to manage them in such a way as to avoid creating serious problems for the Federal Reserve and on occasion it uses them deliberately to supplement Federal Reserve policies.

We shall build here upon some of our findings in the preceding chapter: that, generally speaking, increases or decreases in the size of the Treasury's money balance tend directly to restrict or liberalize the supply of money and credit to the public. Moreover, shifts of the Treasury balance from deposits at commercial banks to Treasury cash in vault or Treasury deposits at the Federal Reserve tend to reduce member bank reserves, and shifts in the opposite direction tend to increase member bank reserves. We shall now see how these actions can be used for restrictive or liberalizing purposes.

Restrictive Actions

Let us deal here with three major cases. (1) The Treasury increases its money balance $1 billion by taxing the public or selling securities to the public.

When the Treasury cashes the checks, the public will lose $1 billion of its deposits. If the Treasury holds these deposits at commercial banks, this is the extent of the effects; the reserve positions of the banks are unaffected. But if the Treasury uses the $1 billion to build up its cash in vault or its deposit at the Federal Reserve, member bank reserves will be reduced by $1 billion.[3] (2) The Treasury increases its balance $1 billion by borrowing from commercial banks. In this case there is no direct effect on the public's money supply. If the Treasury continues to hold the balance at commercial banks, there is no change in the dollar volume of bank reserves; nevertheless credit conditions tend to be tightened because the banks must hold reserves against the Treasury deposit and therefore have fewer reserves to support deposits owed to the public. If the Treasury transfers the deposit to the Federal Reserve or converts it to cash in vault, member bank reserves will be reduced. (3) The Treasury builds up its money balance by borrowing from the Federal Reserve banks. This action cannot restrict credit. If it holds the increased balance in the form of cash in vault or deposits at the Federal Reserve, there is no effect on either the public's money supply or bank reserves. But if it transfers the funds into a deposit at a commercial bank the effect is actually to increase member bank reserves and to ease credit conditions.

In short, we find that an increase in the Treasury's money balance tends to be restrictive unless the Treasury acquires the extra money by borrowing from the Federal Reserve. If it acquires the money balance by taxing the public or selling securities to it, the public's money supply is directly decreased. If it acquires the money by selling securities to commercial banks the public's money supply is not directly decreased, but the ability of the banks to create deposits for the public is reduced because they must use some of their reserves to support the Treasury deposit. However, given the size of any increase in the Treasury's balance, the degree of restrictiveness depends on the form in which it is held. The effects are least restrictive if the balance is held in the form of deposits at commercial banks and most restrictive if it is held as cash in vault or deposits at the Federal Reserve.

Liberalizing Actions

The Treasury can ease monetary conditions by taking actions that are just the reverse of those described above—by decreasing its money balance and by shifting it from the forms of cash in vault or deposits at the Federal Reserve into deposits at commercial banks.

The most liberalizing action that it can take is to draw down its balance in the form of cash in vault or deposits at the Federal Reserve to make payments to the public or to retire debt held by the commercial banks. If it uses these

---

[3] We are here neglecting the income effects of tax collections.

funds to make payments to the public, it increases directly both the public's money supply and commercial bank reserves. The banks can then expand their loans and security holdings by a multiple of the additional reserves not required to support the initial increase of the public's deposits. If the Treasury uses the funds to retire debt held by commercial banks, the effect is to increase by that amount both the actual and excess reserves of commercial banks.

Less powerful liberalizing actions are those of using Treasury deposits at commercial banks to make payments to the public or to retire Treasury debt held by the commercial banks. If these deposits are transferred to the public, the effect is to increase the public's money supply without changing the banks' reserve positions. If they are used to retire Treasury debt held by the commercial banks, there is no direct effect on either the public's money supply or the dollar volume of bank reserves. However, the reduction of Treasury deposits reduces required reserves and enables the banks to create new deposits by lending or buying securities. If the Treasury uses some of its deposits at commercial banks to retire debt held by the Federal Reserve, the effect is to reduce the dollar volume of bank reserves.

Summary

The Treasury sometimes uses these powers in a positive way to restrict or ease credit to supplement Federal Reserve actions. More often, however, it uses them to avoid creating conditions that would make the job of the Federal Reserve more difficult. For example, it avoids large shifts of its balance among the categories of cash in vault, deposits at the Federal Reserve, and deposits at commercial banks unless the Federal Reserve would welcome the resulting tendency toward ease or restriction. When it has large net tax receipts, it often seeks to minimize restrictive effects by using the funds to retire debt held by the public or the commercial banks rather than to increase its money balance. And if it does increase its money balance, it holds the extra funds at commercial banks.

SELECTIVE CREDIT CONTROLS

We have emphasized that the purpose of general monetary management is to regulate the total supply of credit and the general level of interest rates; it is not to determine the allocation of this supply among its many possible users and uses. This allocative or rationing function is left to the private market. The monetary managers do not become involved in the complex and controversial question of "who gets how much for what purposes?" Those who believe in a free-market economy generally favor primary reliance on general monetary management because the allocation of credit helps allocate real resources and they believe these should be allocated by competition in the market place. However, many persons, including some of those who favor primary reliance on general measures, believe that these should be supplemented by "selective controls"—by measures that would influence the allocation of credit, at least to the point of decreasing the volume of credit used for selected purposes without the necessity of decreasing the supply and raising the cost of credit for all purposes.

Selective controls may take various forms. However, we shall discuss here only the one selective control now wielded by the Federal Reserve and two others that the System has used in the past.

Margin Requirements on Security Loans

This selective control arose out of the Federal Reserve's unhappy experience with stock market speculation in the late 1920's, and especially in 1928 and 1929. There was at that time nothing in the basic economic situation that called for a policy of very tight money. Employment was not over-full, commodity prices were steady, and the objective of promoting recovery and prosperity abroad called for easy money. But the stock market was booming; the rapid rise of prices was supported in part by large increases of loans on stocks. Federal Reserve officials were convinced that this was unsound and that less credit should be available for stock purchases. However, they then had only two methods of dealing with the situation—moral suasion and general credit restriction. They attempted to use moral suasion, exhorting banks not to make loans on stocks while borrowing at the Federal Reserve. This did not work, partly because most of the banks were not in debt to the Federal Reserve, and partly because of the huge and rising volume of nonbank loans on stock. They also invoked general credit restriction, which seemed to dampen business activity more than stock speculation. The outcome is now famous; stock speculation climbed until the great crash in October, 1929, and the Federal Reserve's policy of general credit restriction came to be blamed in part for the ensuing great depression.

It was largely because of this experience that Congress in 1934 gave the Board of Governors power to fix, and to alter at its discretion, the height of minimum margin requirements on loans for purchasing or carrying securities listed on the national exchanges. Minimum margin requirements are, in effect, minimum required down payments stated as a percentage of the market value of the security; they are the percentage of the value of the security that may not be borrowed or lent upon. To set a minimum margin requirement is an indirect way of setting a maximum loan value. The latter, in percentage terms, is equal to 100 percent minus the minimum margin requirement. As shown in Table 26, the Board of Governors has changed these requirements many times, sometimes lowering loan values to discourage borrowing and lending for these purposes, at other times raising loan values to reduce the degree of restriction. On one occasion, in 1946, it raised margin requirements to 100 percent, thereby preventing any loans for these purposes.

TABLE 26.   Margin Requirements and Maximum Loan Values

Period	Margin Requirement	Maximum Loan Value
Oct. 1, 1934—Jan. 31, 1936	25–45%[a]	55–75%[a]
Feb. 1, 1936—Mar. 31, 1936	25–55[a]	45–75[a]
Apr. 1, 1936—Oct. 31, 1937	55	45
Nov. 1, 1937—Feb. 4, 1945	40[b]	60
Feb. 5, 1945—July 4, 1945	50	50
July 5, 1945—Jan. 20, 1946	75	25
Jan. 21, 1946—Jan. 31, 1947	100	0
Feb. 1, 1947—Mar. 29, 1949	75	25
Mar. 30, 1949—Jan. 16, 1951	50	50
Jan. 17, 1951—Feb. 19, 1953	75	25
Feb. 20, 1953—Jan. 4, 1955	50	50
Jan. 5, 1955—Apr. 22, 1955	60	40
Apr. 23, 1955—Jan. 15, 1958	70	30
Jan. 16, 1958—Aug. 4, 1958	50	50
Effective Aug. 5, 1958	70	30

[a] Maximum loan value was either 75 percent of current market value or 100 percent of lowest price since July 1, 1933, whichever was smaller, but it could always be at least 55 percent of current market value (45 percent after Feb. 1, 1936.)

[b] Fifty percent for short sales.

SOURCE: *Federal Reserve Bulletins.*

Several aspects of this selective control are worth noting. (1) It applies to borrowers as well as lenders. It is just as illegal for a borrower to borrow in excess of the maximum loan value as it is for a lender to make such loans. Thus this control limits the demand for such credit as well as limiting the supply for this purpose. (2) It applies not only to member banks but to lenders of every type. Thus for this purpose it extended the jurisdiction of the Board of Governors. This precedent was followed in later selective controls. (3) It not only enables the Federal Reserve to restrict the volume of credit used for this purpose without restricting the supply or raising the cost of credit for other purposes but it may actually ease credit for other purposes. To the extent that less credit is demanded or supplied for this purpose, more tends to be made available for other uses.

Consumer Credit Controls

Selective controls of consumer credit, which were administered under Federal Reserve Regulation W, have had a checkered career. They were first instituted in the autumn of 1941, under an Executive Order, and remained in effect until 1947, when they were withdrawn. They were reinstated in September, 1948, under a temporary authorization by Congress which expired in June, 1949. After the outbreak in Korea they were imposed again but were withdrawn in 1952. Since that time the Federal Reserve has not been empowered to use this type of control.

This selective control employed two devices—minimum down payments and maximum periods of repayment. Both applied to consumer loans on listed articles. Raising the required down payment—which is, of course, the same as lowering the maximum loan value—tended to reduce the demand for credit for this purpose as well as to reduce the amount that could be legally supplied for it. Shortening the maximum period of repayment, which increased required monthly payments, also tended to reduce the demand for such loans. Only the latter device applied to consumer loans for unlisted purposes.

Real Estate Credit Controls

From 1950 until 1952, as a part of the anti-inflation program initiated after the outbreak in Korea, Congress authorized the Board of Governors to exercise selective control over credit extended to finance new residential construction. This it did under Regulation X. It utilized the same devices as Regulation W—minimum down payments and maximum periods of repayment. Also, like Regulation W, its terms were not uniform for all loans of this general type. Instead, they were designed to favor low-cost housing and housing for veterans. They therefore required higher down payments and shorter periods of repayment for higher-cost housing and on loans to nonveterans.

Conclusions

Attitudes of economists toward selective credit controls vary widely. Few object to their use in time of war or rapid military mobilization when the government will in any case intervene heavily to determine the allocation of resources and output. At such times selective credit controls may serve a useful purpose both in diverting resources away from nonessential uses and in inhibiting inflation. But their use in noncrisis peacetime periods is another matter. As might be expected, they are often opposed by those whose business may be reduced by them. Thus some stock exchange members and officers are not friendly toward margin requirements on security loans, automobile manufacturers and dealers have criticized consumer credit regulations, and the construction industry and real estate dealers opposed restrictions on credit for residential purposes. Many economists have opposed them on various grounds: (1) that they may interfere unduly with the freedom of borrowers and lenders, (2) that they prevent an allocation of resources and output in line with buyers' wishes, (3) that they are unnecessary because general monetary management and fiscal policies are sufficient, (4) that they may come to be looked upon as a substitute for more general and more widely effective measures, and (5) that they are likely to prove unenforceable. This last argument applies primarily to regulations of consumer and real estate credit where the precise value of the asset used as collateral is hard to determine and the number of entities to be regulated is very large.

SELECTED READINGS

Fousek, Peter G., *Foreign Central Banking: The Instruments of Monetary Policy,* Federal Reserve Bank of New York, 1957.

Roosa, R. V., *Federal Reserve Operations in the Money and Government Securities Markets,* Federal Reserve Bank of New York, 1956.

CHAPTER 10

The Monetary System:
An Overall View

INTRODUCTION

The purpose of this brief chapter is not to present new materials but to summarize some of our most important findings up to this point, to bring them into focus, and to enable us to visualize more clearly the functioning of the United States monetary system as a whole. More specifically, it will analyze the *direct* determinants of the money supply at any point in time and of its fluctuations through time. Its central interest will be in those types of transactions that directly increase or decrease the public's money supply, but it will give some attention to effects on the reserves of the commercial banking system.

Several of our earlier findings are essential to this analysis. (1) By the money supply we mean the amount of coin, paper money, and checking deposits owned by the United States "public"—that is, by all individuals and entities of the United States other than the federal government, the Federal Reserve, and the commercial banks. (2) All these types of money are debt money; they are debt claims against their issuers. They may also be called the "monetary liabilities" of the issuing institutions. (3) Only three types of institutions have the power to create debts that serve as money: the Treasury, the Federal Reserve, and the commercial banks. (4) In general, these institutions create and issue monetary liabilities in the process of purchasing assets, and they withdraw and destroy monetary liabilities when they decrease their assets.

THE MONETARY EQUATION

Our analysis will be based upon a consolidated balance sheet for the commercial banks, the Federal Reserve banks, and the monetary operations of the Treasury. Two points should be emphasized: (1) The balance sheet will not include all the many aspects of Treasury operations; it will include only those related to the money supply function, which we shall call the monetary operations of the Treasury. (2) The balance sheet is not simply a summation of the three separate sets of balance sheets; it is a partially consolidated balance sheet. Because we are interested primarily in the relation of these institutions to others we eliminate many of their claims against each other.[1]

We start with the following fundamental balance sheet equation:

(1)   Assets = Liabilities + Capital accounts

The asset side of the balance sheet for a stated point of time shows the total value of assets that have been acquired and that are owned by the entities at that time, while the other side shows the types and amounts of claims that have been issued to acquire those assets. "Liabilities" represent the value of outstanding debt claims; "capital accounts" or "net worth" represents the value of ownership claims. The two together must be exactly equal to the value of assets. Moreover, these monetary institutions can acquire an increased value of assets during any period only by creating and issuing an equal increase of debt and ownership claims. If they decrease their assets they must reduce by an equal amount the value of outstanding debt and ownership claims against themselves.

For our purposes it is necessary to divide total liabilities into two categories: nonmonetary liabilities and monetary liabilities. In nonmonetary liabilities we include all the types of debt liabilities issued by these institutions that are not money. Thus we may rewrite our fundamental equation as follows:

(2)   Assets = Monetary liabilities + Nonmonetary liabilities + Capital accounts

This is the same as Equation 1 except that it makes the distinction, essential for our purposes, between debt liabilities that serve as money and those that do not.

Transposing in the above equation, we get the following:

$$(3) \quad \text{Monetary liabilities} = \text{Assets} - \left\{ \begin{array}{c} \text{Nonmonetary liabilities} \\ + \\ \text{Capital accounts} \end{array} \right.$$

This equation shows that the value of the money supply (monetary liabilities) at any time is equal to the total value of assets held by these institutions minus the value of their outstanding nonmonetary liabilities and capital or net worth accounts. And through time the size of the money supply varies directly with

[1] Though it differs from them in several respects, the analysis in this chapter borrows very heavily from both of the following: Morris A. Copeland and Daniel H. Brill, "Banking Assets and the Money Supply Since 1929," *Federal Reserve Bulletin*, January, 1948, pp. 24–32 (statistical tables based on this formulation appear monthly in the *Federal Reserve Bulletin*); Edward S. Shaw, *Money, Income, and Monetary Policy*, Richard D. Irwin, Chicago, 1950, chaps. 2 and 3.

the value of these assets and inversely with the value of nonmonetary liabilities and capital accounts.

By listing in Equation 3 the principal types of assets actually held by these institutions and the types of nonmonetary liabilities issued by them we get Equation 4, which we shall use in the remainder of this chapter.

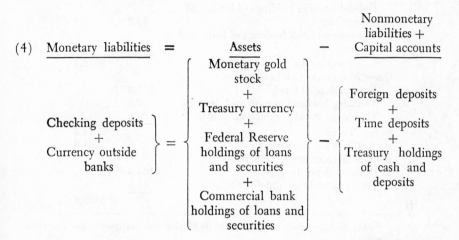

(4) Monetary liabilities = Assets − Nonmonetary liabilities + Capital accounts

Checking deposits + Currency outside banks = { Monetary gold stock + Treasury currency + Federal Reserve holdings of loans and securities + Commercial bank holdings of loans and securities } − { Foreign deposits + Time deposits + Treasury holdings of cash and deposits }

Table 27 applies this analysis to the situation on May 28, 1958. It shows that the money supply of $133.6 billion on that date resulted from the acquisition and holding of $226.4 billion of assets by these monetary institutions less the $92.8 billion of outstanding claims against them in the form of nonmonetary liabilities and capital accounts.

ASSETS

To isolate the effects of purchases and sales of assets by these institutions, we shall assume that when they buy assets they pay for them by issuing coin, paper money, or checking deposits to the public, and that when they sell assets they withdraw an equal amount of money from the public. The cases in which nonmonetary debts and capital accounts are involved will be considered later.

Monetary Gold Stock

This is an asset of the Treasury. As we found earlier, the Treasury buys gold at $35 an ounce. It usually pays for gold by creating for the Federal Reserve banks an equal amount of gold certificates, receiving in return a deposit credit, and then pays the seller of gold with a check drawn on the Federal Reserve. The seller deposits the check with his bank, which sends it to the Federal Reserve to be added to its reserve account and deducted from the Treasury's deposit account. Thus the effects of a Treasury purchase of gold are to increase

TABLE 27.   Direct Determinants of the Money Supply,
May 28, 1958
(In billions of dollars)

ASSETS

Monetary gold stock	$ 21.6	
Treasury currency	5.2	
Federal Reserve holdings of loans and securities	24.2	
Commercial bank holdings of loans and securities	175.4	
Total assets		$226.4
Less: NONMONETARY LIABILITIES		
Foreign deposits, net	$ 4.0	
Treasury holdings of cash and deposits	6.8	
Time deposits at commercial banks	60.7	
Total		71.5
Less: CAPITAL ACCOUNTS[a]		21.3
Equals: MONETARY LIABILITIES		
Demand deposits	$105.8	
Currency and coin outside banks	27.8	
Total		$133.6

[a] Also contains some miscellaneous liabilities and statistical discrepancy.

SOURCE: Derived from data in Federal Reserve Bulletin, July, 1958, pp. 805, 814, 815. As used here, the item "capital accounts" is a balancing item. It is simply total assets minus the sum of nonmonetary liabilities and monetary liabilities as shown. This was done to escape the laborious job of accounting for a number of minor items in the balance sheets of the Treasury, the Federal Reserve, and the commercial banks.

by equal amounts the public's money supply, member bank reserves, and the gold certificate reserves of the Federal Reserve banks.

Net sales of gold by the Treasury have the opposite effects. Gold buyers usually pay the Treasury with checks on their banks, thereby giving up deposits. The Treasury retires an equal amount of gold certificates and the Federal Reserve deducts an equal amount from the reserves of the bank on which the check is drawn.

Treasury Currency Outstanding

This source of money includes all coins in the United States and paper money issued by the Treasury. Increases of this item tend to increase not only the public's money supply but also the volume of member bank reserves. Consider two cases: (1) The Treasury issues additional currency to the public when there is no increase in the demand for currency in circulation. The public will return the excess currency to its banks in exchange for increased deposits, and its banks will ship the redundant currency to the Federal Reserve in exchange for increased reserve balances. (2) The Treasury issues additional currency equal to an increase in the public's demand for currency. In this case the public has an increase in its money supply in the form of currency, and the banking system is spared the loss of reserves it would have suffered in the absence of the increased Treasury issue.

Federal Reserve Holdings of Loans and Securities

These are obviously assets of the Federal Reserve banks. In general, Federal Reserve purchases of assets tend to increase both the public's money supply and member bank reserves, and its net sales of assets have the opposite effect. But two cases need to be distinguished. (1) It lends to the public or buys assets from the public. In this case it pays with checks on itself, the public deposits the checks at banks, and the banks send them along to be added to their reserve accounts. (2) It lends to banks or buys assets from them. In this case the banks receive additional reserves, but there is no direct addition to the public's money supply. However, the increase of Federal Reserve assets has prevented the public's money supply from being decreased by the decrease of commercial bank assets or by the rise of commercial bank nonmonetary liabilities in the form of debt to the Federal Reserve.

Net sales of assets by the Federal Reserve tend to have the opposite effects, but here again the two cases need to be distinguished. Net sales to the public tend to decrease both the public's money supply and bank reserves. But net sales of assets to commercial banks or net decreases of loans to commercial banks decrease bank reserves without directly decreasing the public's money supply. However, these decreases in Federal Reserve assets offset the increase of commercial bank assets or the decrease of commercial bank monmonetary liabilities in the form of debt to the Federal Reserve and prevent them from being reflected in an increase of the public's money supply.

Commercial Bank Holdings of Loans and Securities

When commercial banks buy assets in these forms, they pay for them by creating deposit credits or by paying out coin and currency, usually the former. When they sell these assets, they decrease their deposit liabilities or withdraw coin and currency from the public, mostly the former.

Summary

We find that the assets in the consolidated balance sheets of the three sets of monetary institutions are of four types: (1) monetary gold stock, (2) Treasury currency, (3) Federal Reserve holdings of loans and securities, and (4) commercial bank holdings of loans and securities. In purchasing these assets, the monetary institutions tend to issue debt money to the public, and in selling these assets they tend to withdraw and destroy money formerly held by the public. Increases or decreases in the first three also tend to increase or decrease the dollar volume of member bank reserves.

NONMONETARY LIABILITIES AND CAPITAL ACCOUNTS

The size of the money supply depends not only on the total volume of assets of the monetary institutions but also on the volume of their nonmonetary liabilities and capital accounts. The nonmonetary liabilities are foreign deposit claims against the Federal Reserve and commercial banks, Treasury holdings of cash and of deposit claims against the Federal Reserve and commercial banks, and time deposit claims against commercial banks. The item, capital accounts, is the value of ownership claims against the Federal Reserve and commercial banks. All these claims have the following points in common: (1) They are not a part of the money supply as we have defined it; (2) they are alternatives to and compete with monetary liabilities as claims against assets; and (3) when considered by themselves, increases or decreases in these claims tend to produce opposite variations in the money supply.

The monetary institutions can acquire assets by issuing nonmonetary liabilities or ownership claims. For example, they may acquire assets by issuing claims to the Treasury, to foreign depositors, to time depositors, or to their owners. In this way they can secure assets without increasing the supply of money. On the other hand, they may reduce their assets without decreasing the money supply to the extent that they reduce their other liabilities and ownership claims against themselves.

Moreover, the money supply can be decreased or increased by an exchange of monetary liabilities for other claims, or vice versa. Thus, the public's holdings of money can be reduced as it relinquishes money in exchange for time deposits at commercial banks or to make net payments to the accounts of foreigners or the Treasury. Its holdings of money can be increased if it converts its time deposit claims against commercial banks into monetary claims or receives net payments out of foreign deposits or out of Treasury holdings of cash and deposits.

SUMMARY

The various types of developments that tend directly to increase or decrease the money supply are summarized in the following list:

FACTORS TENDING TO EXPAND THE MONEY SUPPLY	FACTORS TENDING TO CONTRACT THE MONEY SUPPLY
Increases of Assets	*Decreases of Assets*
1. Increase of the monetary gold stock	1. Decrease of the monetary gold stock
2. Increase of Treasury currency outstanding	2. Decrease of Treasury currency outstanding
3. Increase of Federal Reserve holdings of loans and securities	3. Decrease of Federal Reserve holdings of loans and securities

Increases of Assets (cont.)

4. Increase of commercial bank holdings of loans and securities

Decreases of Nonmonetary Liabilities

5. Decrease of foreign deposits
6. Decrease of Treasury holdings of
cash and deposits
7. Decrease of time deposits

Decrease of Capital Accounts

Decreases of Assets (cont.)

4. Decrease of commercial bank holdings of loans and securities

Increases of Nonmonetary Liabilities

5. Increase of foreign deposits
6. Increase of Treasury holdings of
cash and deposits
7. Increase of time deposits

Increase of Capital Accounts

It is important to remember that the first three items also appeared in our analysis of "member bank reserves and related items" as determinants of the dollar volume of member bank reserves.

BEHAVIOR OF THE MONEY SUPPLY

Table 28 shows the size of the money supply and of its various direct determinants on selected dates beginning with 1929. One is immediately struck by the wide fluctuations of the money supply during this period.

TABLE 28.   Direct Determinants of the Money Supply
(In billions of dollars)

	June 29, 1929	June 30, 1933	Dec. 30, 1939	Dec. 31, 1945	May 28, 1958
ASSETS					
Monetary gold stock	$ 4.0	$ 4.0	$17.6	$ 20.1	$ 21.6
Treasury currency	2.0	2.3	3.0	4.3	5.2
Federal Reserve holdings of loans and securities	1.3	2.2	2.5	24.4	24.2
Commercial bank holdings of loans and securities	49.2	30.4	40.7	124.0	175.4
Total	$56.5	$38.9	$63.8	$172.8	$226.4
Less: NONMONETARY LIABILITIES					
Foreign deposits, net	0.4	0.1	1.2	2.1	4.0
Treasury holdings of cash and deposits	0.6	1.1	3.9	27.9	6.8
Time deposits at commercial banks	19.6	10.8	15.3	30.1	60.7
Total	$20.6	$12.0	$20.4	$60.1	$71.5
Less: CAPITAL ACCOUNTS	9.8	7.7	7.2	10.3	21.3
Equals: MONETARY LIABILITIES					
Demand deposits	22.5	14.4	29.8	75.9	105.8
Currency and coin outside banks	3.6	4.8	6.4	26.5	27.8
Total	$26.1	$19.2	$36.2	$102.4	$133.6

SOURCE: Computed from data in *Federal Reserve Bulletins.*

From mid-1929 to the low point of the depression in mid-1933, the money supply declined from $26.1 billion to $19.2 billion, for a drop of 26 percent. From that time to the end of 1939 it rose 89 percent. During the defense and war period from the end of 1939 to the end of 1945, it rose $66.2 billion, or 183 percent. From that time to the end of May, 1958, it rose another $31.2 billion, or 30.4 percent. Thus at the end of May, 1958, the money supply was 3.7 times as large as at the end of 1939, 6.9 times its level at the bottom of the depression, and 5.1 times its level in mid-1929.

The table also indicates the relative importance of the various direct determinants. By far the most important single direct determinant of the money supply, both in total size and in breadth of fluctuations, has been commercial bank holdings of loans and securities. These did not comprise less than 63.8 percent of the total assets in the consolidated balance sheet on any of the dates shown in Table 29 and on most dates they accounted for an even

TABLE 29.   Commercial Bank Loans and Security Holdings and the Total Assets of the Monetary System

Date	Total Assets in Consolidated Statement (In billions)	Commercial Bank Holding of Loans and Securities (In billions)	Commercial Bank Holdings of Loans and Securities as Percentage of Total Assets
June 29, 1929	$ 56.5	$ 49.2	87.1
June 30, 1933	38.9	30.4	78.1
December 30, 1939	63.8	40.7	63.8
December 31, 1945	172.8	124.0	71.8
May 28, 1958	226.4	175.4	77.5

larger part of the total. Moreover, as shown in Table 30, fluctuations of this item accounted for a major share of the fluctuations in both the total assets and the supply of money during these periods, which were not unusual in this respect.

However, the other direct determinants should not be neglected. The volume of Treasury currency outstanding has grown slowly and rather steadily in recent years, largely reflecting additional issues of minor and fractional coin and silver certificates issued to pay for purchases of newly mined domestic silver. The capital accounts of the Federal Reserve and commercial banks have also risen rather steadily. Most of the other direct determinants have moved less steadily. Increases and decreases in the monetary gold stock and in Federal Reserve holdings of loans and securities have often accounted for several billion dollars of increase or decrease in the money supply. Increases and decreases of foreign deposits have on several occasions decreased or increased

TABLE 30.   Changes in Commercial Bank Holdings of Loans and Securities, in Total
Assets in the Consolidated Statement, and in the Total Money Supply
During Selected Periods

Period	Bank Loans and Security Holdings (In billions)	Change in Total Assets in Consolidated Statement (In billions)	Change in Money Supply (In billions)	Change in Commercial Bank Loans and Security Holdings as a Percentage of Change in Total Assets	Change in Commercial Bank Loans and Security Holdings as a Percentage of Change in Money Supply
June, 1929—					
June, 1933	$−18.8	$ −17.6	$− 6.9	106.8	272.4
June, 1933—					
Dec. 1939	+10.3	+24.9	+17.0	41.4	60.6
Dec. 1939—					
Dec. 1945	+83.3	+109.0	+66.2	76.4	125.8
Dec. 1945—					
May, 1958	+51.4	+53.6	+31.2	95.1	162.6

the public's money supply by two or three billion dollars. The Treasury often
tends to add several billions to the public's money supply by drawing down
its own holdings of cash and deposits; just as frequently it tends to reduce
the money supply by adding to its cash and deposit balances. The other
nonmonetary liability, time deposits at commercial banks, shows an upward
trend, but its growth is by no means steady.

CONCLUSIONS

The purpose of this chapter has been to summarize all the principal types
of transactions that affect directly the size of the money supply. This analysis
is important to anyone who wishes to explain the size of the money supply
at a point of time and its changes through time. It needs, however, to be
supplemented by an analysis of the factors that determine the ability of the
monetary institutions to acquire assets and to issue monetary liabilities. For
this purpose our earlier study of "member bank reserves and related items" is
highly useful.

SELECTED READINGS

Copeland, Morris A., and Brill, Daniel J., "Banking Assets and the Money Supply
Since 1929," Federal Reserve Bulletin, January, 1948, pp. 24–32.
Shaw, Edward S., Money, Income, and Monetary Policy, Richard D. Irwin, Chi-
cago, 1950.

CHAPTER 11

An Introduction to Monetary Theory

Up to this point we have centered our discussion on money and the monetary mechanism themselves, paying but little attention to interrelationships between them and other aspects of the economic system. More specifically, we have discussed the nature and functions of money, the composition of the United States money supply, the processes through which the stock of money is increased or decreased, and the powers of the monetary authorities, and especially the Federal Reserve, to regulate the supply of money and credit. These things may be worthy of study simply because some people make a living operating monetary institutions or because they are interesting examples of man's ingenuity. But they derive most of their economic significance from the fact that money and monetary policy affect the behavior of such basically important economic phenomena as real income or output, the state of employment and unemployment of labor and other productive factors, price levels, and the distribution of income and wealth. To analyze such interrelationships is the central function of monetary theory.

Monetary theory, like other branches of economic theory, is worthy of study for several reasons. As an intellectual exercise it helps develop abilities for orderly and logical analysis. It is cultural in the sense of helping us understand the world in which we live. It is also "practical" for those who make or evaluate monetary policies. By sheer coincidence or rare good luck a policy-maker might do the thing most conducive to the achievement of his chosen objectives even though his actions were not guided by valid theory. In practice, however, policies that are not based on theory are likely to be whimsical or worse. Policy-makers need theory to help them not only to analyze the nature of the effects of their various possible actions but also to realize something of the magnitude of these effects and the length of time that will be required to achieve them. In short, rational policy-making involves at least two steps. The first is to select the objectives to be promoted. The second is to take actions to promote those objectives. Without a theory as to the probable effects of his various possible actions, the policy-maker is in no position to decide rationally on the actions to be taken.

The Scope of Monetary Theory

Monetary theory does not limit itself to analyzing the economic effects of influences "originating on the side of" money and monetary policy. This is, of course, one of its functions. It can help the policy-maker answer such questions as these: "What will be the economic effects of my actions, or of my failure to act? In what ways and to what extent will the behavior of the economy differ if I do this instead of doing that?" But all valid monetary theories recognize that money and monetary policy are not the only important determinants of the behavior of the economy and that many changes originate in nonmonetary factors, such as decisions of the public to consume more and save less or vice versa, and changes in businessmen's expectations as to the profitability of new investment. The policy-maker needs to understand these relationships in order to adjust his policies appropriately.

As noted earlier, monetary theory may be used to analyze many different types of interrelationships, and its emphasis has shifted from time to time. During most of the nineteenth century and the early part of the twentieth, monetary theory concerned itself largely with the determination of the value of money, or the general level of prices. The central interest of economics was then on "long-run equilibrium," and this equilibrium was usually assumed to be one with full employment of productive resources. It should be noted that this type of analysis was essentially timeless; it dealt with the nature of the "equilibrium" conditions that would obtain after all adjustments had been made but paid little attention either to the length of time that would be required for the adjustments to occur or to effects during the period of adjustment. John Stuart Mill was speaking primarily of long-run equilibrium when he stated, "The relations of commodities to one another remain unaltered by money; the only new relation introduced is their relation to money itself; how much or how little money they will exchange for; in other words how the Exchange Value of money itself is determined."[1]

Monetary theorists are still interested in the relationship of money to the conditions of long-run equilibrium and to the long-run behavior of price levels. Over the years, however, their emphasis has shifted markedly. They have, as noted earlier, come to deal not only with price levels but also with such other economic phenomena as the relationship of actual output to the productive capacity of the economy, the state of employment and unemployment, the behavior of market rates of interest, and so on. Moreover, they now give

[1] See pp. 11–13.

more attention to economic disequilibrium, business cycle fluctuations, and transitions from one state of equilibrium toward another. This marked shift of emphasis has resulted from several closely related forces.

1. A recognition that money is often "out of order." John Stuart Mill and others who minimized the importance of money as a causative factor in the economy, especially in the long run, tacitly assumed that money worked so perfectly that it was only a "veil"—that it was "neutral" and enabled the economy to function just as it would if it operated under a highly efficient and economical system of barter. But Mill noted that money "exerts a distinct and independent influence of its own when it gets out of order." Most economists now believe that money is, or may be, "out of order" a large part of the time, though in different ways and in varying degrees. In this respect monetary theory has at least two functions. One is to identify the various types of "monetary disorders" and to define the conditions of "monetary order." Another, closely related, is to analyze the effects of the various classes of monetary disorder.

2. A recognition that conditions of long-run, full-employment equilibrium fail to obtain much of the time. Even if there is a tendency toward full-employment equilibrium, the movement is often slow and protracted. Some even contend that the equilibrium that tends to be established need not be one with full employment of labor and other productive resources—that the equilibrium may be one of underemployment, with millions of workers totally unemployed or working shorter hours than they would like. In any case, we know from experience that economic conditions differ frequently, markedly, and sometimes for long periods from those that would obtain in full-employment equilibrium. Widespread and prolonged unemployment not only lowers actual output below the economy's capacity levels but also brings important shifts in the distribution of wealth and income. Sharp or prolonged inflation may also bring large and persisting changes in wealth and income distribution, whether or not it affects the rate of real output. A type of monetary theory that concentrates on long-run, full-employment equilibrium is obviously not very helpful for analyzing such disequilibrium situations.

3. Changes in public attitudes and public policies. During recent decades people have become increasingly less tolerant of economic disequilibrium and fluctuations—of depression and deflation on the one hand and of sharp and persistent inflation on the other. They demand that the monetary authorities and the government "do something" to prevent these or at least to lessen their breadth and duration. Monetary theory has been responsive to these demands, attempting to provide some assistance to policy-makers by analyzing the causes of such fluctuations and by indicating the various types of actions that might be taken to prevent or ameliorate them.

The type of monetary theory that we shall present is eclectic. It will deal with short-run and disequilibrium conditions as well as long-run equilibrium. Moreover, it will deal with various other relationships as well as those between money and price levels. Our central interest will be in the relationships between money and various aspects of national income or output: the rate of real output or production, the price level of output, and the state of employment and unemployment of labor and other productive factors. At some points we shall also discuss the behavior of interest rates and their relations to money and other economic phenomena.

On the assumption that "the long way round may be the surest way home," we shall not proceed immediately to discuss the relationships of money to the phenomena indicated above. Instead, we shall first deal with some background materials that will facilitate our understanding of these relationships.

MONEY STOCKS AND MONEY FLOWS

As noted earlier, the money supply is a *stock*; it is the quantity of money in existence at a point of time.[2] Yet our primary interest is in money *flows*, for it is the rate of flow of money expenditures that is of prime importance to the behavior of the economy. For example, we may be interested in the question of whether the rate of flow of expenditures for output is at a rate of $450 billion a year, or $600 billion a year, or some other rate. As a first step toward understanding the relationship between the size of the supply or stock of money and the annual rate of money expenditures for output, we may note that the latter is equal to the dollar value of the stock of money multiplied by the average number of times each dollar of the money supply is spent for output each year. The latter is usually called "the income velocity of money." This can be greater than one because money is a durable good that can be spent over and over again by its successive recipients. Suppose the stock of money is $150 billion. If each dollar is spent for output an average of four times a year, this stock of money will support a flow of expenditures for output of $600 billion a year. If each dollar is spent for output at an average rate of only three times a year, the stock will support expenditures of only $450 billion a year. In short, the flow of expenditures for output tends to vary directly with the size of the stock of money and with the average income velocity of each dollar of the stock of money.

Generally speaking, the monetary authority has no direct control over the income velocity of money. It may control the supply of money and attempt to manipulate it in such a way as to offset the effects of fluctuations in velocity, but it cannot directly control velocity itself. The behavior of the latter is de-

---

[2] See pp. 14–15 above. We shall deal later with the case in which the money supply at any point of time is not an absolute quantity but a supply schedule or function.

termined by the collective decisions of the various recipients of money as they decide whether to hold small or large amounts of money relative to their expenditures. If they elect to hold only very small money balances relative to their expenditures, the flow of expenditures will obviously be large relative to the money supply. If they elect to hold large money balances relative to their expenditures, the flow of expenditures will obviously be small relative to the money supply.

We shall later discuss at length the determinants of the income velocity of money and its reciprocal, the quantity of money balances demanded by the public in relation to its expenditures for output. However, the general relationship will be indicated briefly and in an oversimplified way at this point. We may assume that each individual and business firm adjusts the size of his money balance and his rate of expenditures in such a way as to maximize his own net advantage, taking into consideration both the benefits and costs of holding money. Holding money, which is safe, liquid, and generally acceptable in paying debts and purchasing goods and services, obviously has its advantages. But it is also costly, for money itself yields no income and its holder forgoes, during the period that he holds the money, the pleasure of consumption or the income that he could get by retiring his own debt or buying income-yielding assets. Each person or business firm balances these benefits and costs, at least in a rough way, and arrives at decisions with respect to the size of his money balance. Suppose that at some time the community as a whole finds that its actual holdings of money are larger than it desires in relation to its current rate of expenditures. How will it try to get rid of the excess of its actual supply of money over its demand for money balances? The answer is, it will increase its rate of expenditures. Suppose it finds that its actual holdings of money are smaller than it desires in relation to its expenditures. It will try to increase its balances by decreasing its rate of expenditure. But if the monetary authority adamantly holds the supply of money constant, the community cannot adjust its actual money-to-expenditure relationship to the desired level by altering the total of its money balance; it can do so only by adjusting its rate of expenditures.

This point can be illustrated by a numerical example. Suppose that the monetary authority firmly fixes the total supply of money at $150 billion. This is the amount of money that must be held by someone. Suppose also that the community demands to hold money balances equal to exactly one third of its rate of annual expenditures for output. Larger balances it would consider "excessive," smaller ones "deficient." All these things are indicated in Fig. 7. On the OM axis we measure the size of the money supply and the quantities of money balances demanded for holding. On the OY axis we measure the annual rate of expenditures for output, which we shall denote by Y. The line MM represents the supply of money, which we assume is held constant by

the monetary authority at \$150 billion. The *LL* line represents the quantities
of money that the community demands to hold at the various possible levels
of *Y*. These, we assume, are equal to ⅓*Y*. Fig. 7 tells us that as long as the
money supply is *MM* and the demand for money balances is *LL*, the only
equilibrium level of expenditures for output is \$450 billion per year. That is,

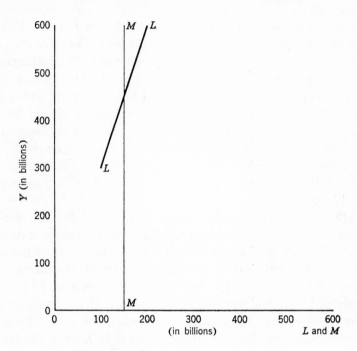

FIG. 7.   Supply of and Demand for Money.

if the money supply is \$150 billion and the community demands to hold
money balances equal to ⅓ of its annual rate of expenditures, the demand for
money can be made equal to the supply of money only if *Y* is at \$450 billion
per year. And *Y* is determined at that level at which the demand for money
balances is exactly equal to the supply of money. To establish this point, we
shall resort to the economist's favorite device of showing that any level of
Y either below or above \$450 billion would be one of disequilibrium and could
not persist. Suppose, for example, that *Y* is below \$450 billion, say at \$300
billion. At this level of *Y* the community's demand for money balances would
be only \$100 billion, while its actual holdings are \$150 billion. It would try
to "get rid of" the \$50 billion excess supply of money by increasing its ex-
penditures. This process will continue until the rise of *Y* has brought the demand for money balances up to the level of the money supply. It is important
to note that the community "gets rid of" its excess supply of money by increasing its rate of expenditures. Suppose, on the other hand, that *Y* is above

$450 billion, say at $600 billion. At this level of Y the community would demand $200 billion of money balances while the money supply is only $150 billion. It would try to repair the $50 billion deficiency in its actual holdings of money by reducing its expenditures. This process would continue until Y had fallen sufficiently to lower the demand for money to the level of the available supply.

The reader may find it instructive to solve these problems. (1) Suppose that the money supply is held constant at $150 billion and that the community demands money balances equal to ¼ rather than ⅓ of its annual rate of expenditures for output. What will be the equilibrium level of Y? Why cannot Y remain either higher or lower than this? What will be the income velocity of money? (2) Suppose that the community's demand for money balances continues at ⅓ of its annual rate of expenditures for output but that the monetary authority increases the supply of money from $150 billion to $200 billion. What will be the new equilibrium level of Y? Why can it be neither higher nor lower than this level? Through what process will the new level be established?

Several of our findings deserve emphasis. The rate of flow of expenditures for output is determined at that level which equates the supply of money and the community's demand for money balances. If the supply of money is in excess of the community's demand for money balances, the community will try to get rid of the excess supply of money by increasing its flow of expenditures. If its demand for money balances exceeds the supply of money, the community tries to satisfy its excess demand for money by reducing its flow of expenditures for other things. Thus it is through adjustments in the flow of expenditures that the demand for money balances is brought into equality with the supply of money.

We shall later discuss in more detail and in a less simplified way the relations between the stock of money and the flow of money expenditures for output. In the meantime we shall concentrate our attention largely on the flow of expenditures.

DEMAND AND SUPPLY

As a further step toward understanding the relationships between money and such other economic phenomena as price levels, the rate of real output, and employment it will be useful to recall some aspects of general economic theory relating to the output, sales, and prices of a particular commodity, such as copper. Theory tells us that these are all determined simultaneously by demand and supply conditions. Suppose, for example, that the demand and supply conditions for this commodity are represented by the DD and SS curves in Fig. 8. Price (designated by P) is measured along the vertical axis.

The quantities demanded and supplied per period of time, such as per year, are measured along the horizontal axis and designated by Q. We find that as long as demand and supply conditions continue to be those represented by the DD and SS curves, the market for this commodity can be in equilibrium only if the quantities actually supplied and demanded are at Q_0 and

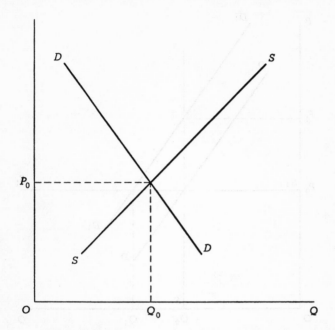

FIG. 8. Demand for and Supply of a Commodity.

the price is P_0. Only this combination of P and Q will exactly clear the market, leaving no excess supply or demand.

This example illustrates at least two principles that will be useful for our later analysis. First, the market equilibrium is not determined by demand conditions alone or supply conditions alone but by both together. Second, both price and the actual rate of output and sales are determined simultaneously. Thus demand and supply conditions determine price, rate of real output and sales, and the money value of output and sales, $P_0 Q_0$. If we knew more about production conditions in the industry, we could also determine the amount of productive factors employed in producing the commodity, for the amount of these resources required depends on the actual rate of output.

We have already noted that price will remain at P_0 and actual real sales at Q_0 as long as demand and supply conditions continue to be those represented by the DD and SS curves. How can the market situation be changed? It can be altered only by a shift in demand conditions, or supply conditions, or both. Suppose the demand for the commodity rises. That is, the community demands more of the commodity at each price or will pay a higher price for each quantity. This is indicated in Fig. 9 by a shift of demand from DD to D_1D_1. This increase of demand will tend to raise the price, to increase the quantities actually supplied and purchased, or some combination of the

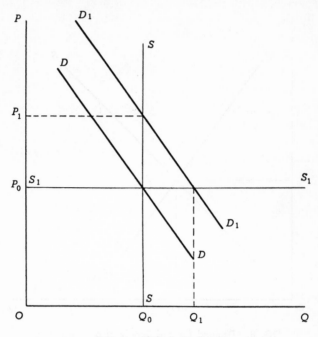

FIG. 9.   Shifts in Demand.

two. The actual effects of any given increase of demand will depend on supply conditions, and more specifically on the responsiveness of the quantities supplied to changes in price. Suppose supply is completely unresponsive or inelastic to price, as indicated by the supply curve SS. In this case, because the quantity supplied remains constant, the entire effect of the increase of demand appears in the rise of price from P_0 to P_1. Suppose, to go to the other extreme, that supply is completely elastic or responsive to price, as indicated by S_1S_1. That is, the suppliers stand ready to supply unlimited amounts at the price P_0 but none at any lower price. In this case the increase of demand will raise actual output and sales from Q_0 to Q_1 without any effect on price. Most actual cases will fall between these two extremes, with supply being neither completely unresponsive nor completely responsive to price. The more responsive supply is to price, the more will a given increase of demand show up in increased output and sales and the less in increased price.

The reader may find it useful to trace out the effects of a decrease in demand, such as a shift from D_1D_1 to DD, noting the relevance of the responsiveness of supply to the effects on price and output. He may also wish to trace through the effect of a decrease in supply, by which we mean a willingness to supply any given amount at a higher price only, and of an increase in supply, by which we mean a willingness to offer for sale each given amount at a lower price.

In the remainder of this chapter we shall adapt this type of analysis, which was originally developed to explain the prices and output of individual commodities, to the economy as a whole. More specifically, we shall apply a demand and supply analysis to the real output of the economy as a whole, the price level of output, and the state of employment of labor and productive factors. We shall argue that these are all determined simultaneously by demand and supply conditions, and that they can be changed only by shifts of demand, or supply, or both. Moreover, the effects of any given shift of the demand for output will depend on the responsiveness of supply. The reader is forewarned that this analysis, though helpful, is only a first approximation, is based on oversimplified assumptions, and ignores some complex interrelationships between demand and supply. Some of these deficiencies will be remedied later.

SHIFTS OF DEMAND WITH OUTPUT COMPLETELY UNRESPONSIVE

It will be convenient to begin our analysis of real output, prices, and employment with the relatively simple case in which the rate of output is completely unresponsive to price. That is, the same output is produced and offered for sale regardless of the market price. We shall assume further that this output is one at which the economy is operating at full capacity with all productive factors employed. In the upper graph in Fig. 10 we measure the rate of real output (O) on the horizontal axis. Real output is measured at annual rates; it is the rate of production of real goods and services per year.[3]

---

[3] In what unit is this real output measured? The usual physical measures, such as pounds, tons, gallons, barrels, dozens, or units, are unacceptable for aggregating diverse types of output such as coal, petroleum, and eggs. For one thing, the choice of units is quite arbitrary; we could measure coal in pounds or bushels as meaningfully as in tons. Moreover, physical measurements of different commodities have little or no economic meaning. For example, a ton of gravel is usually not considered economically equivalent to a ton of rubies. For such reasons our unit for measuring real output is that amount of each commodity which sold for $1 in some selected base period. For example, if the price of coal in the base period was $20 a ton, our unit of measurement is $1/20$ of a ton of coal. If the price of wheat was $3 a bushel, our unit is $1/3$ of a bushel of wheat, and so on. Our reason for using this unit is that quantities of the various commodities which in the base period sold for the same price must in some sense have been considered economically equivalent to each other, at least in that period. These quantities change, of course, as the relative prices of the commodities change. Since we measure real output in units of one dollar's worth in the base period, P, the average price per unit of output at any given time is the average number of dollars required to buy the quantity of output that $1 bought in the base period.

The rate of output O_F is assumed to be full capacity; higher rates are unachievable with the available technology and supplies of productive factors. P is the average price per unit of output. SS is the supply curve of output, which we assume to be at the full capacity of the economy and completely unresponsive or inelastic to P. DD is the demand schedule for output, show-

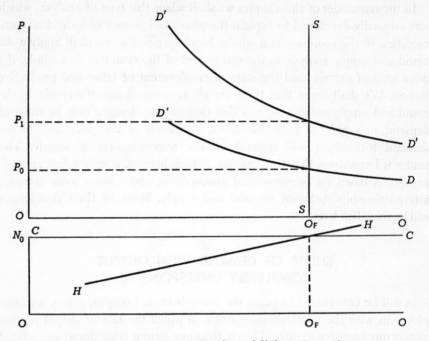

FIG. 10.   Unresponsive Supply, and Shifts in Demand.

ing the amounts that would be demanded at the various possible levels of P. The lower graph relates to the supply of labor and the demand for labor in relation to the rate of real output. On the vertical axis we measure the quantity of labor supplied and demanded, this being measured in man-hours and denoted by N. The curve CC represents the supply of labor available for hire. The curve HH represents the demand for labor for use in production, this demand being assumed to depend on the rate of output. Since labor is hired for production, the amount demanded depends on the rate of output.[4] Full employment exists only at that level of output at which

---

[4] The quantity of labor demanded, as measured in man-hours, is equal to the rate of output (O) divided by the average output per man-hour worked. It will be recognized that our analysis of the relationship of the demand for labor to the rate of output is oversimplified. For example, the quantity of labor used per unit of output may change with changes in the price of labor relative to the prices of other productive factors. Moreover, there may not be a straight-line relationship between output and the employment of labor because of economies or diseconomies of scale. In the stage of increasing returns, output increases more than in proportion to the labor used; in the stage of decreasing returns the quantity of labor used rises more than in proportion to output.

the demand for labor is equal to the available supply—at the intersection of the CC and HH curves. The amount of unemployment at each lower level of output is measured by the vertical distance between the CC and HH curves at that level of output.

Under the conditions shown in Fig. 10, O will be at capacity levels and full employment will prevail. If demand conditions are those represented by DD, the average price of output will be P_0. The aggregate money value of output, or national money income, will be equal to real output multiplied by its average price per unit, or P_0O_F.

Increase in Demand for Output

Suppose now that, because of an increase in the money supply or for some other reason, the demand for output doubles in the sense that the community becomes willing to pay twice as much for each rate of output. This is indicated by the shift of the demand curve from DD to $D'D'$. If the quantity of output available for purchase remains constant, the effect must be to double the price level of output, raising it from P_0 to P_1. The total money value of output must also double, rising from P_0O_F to P_1O_F.

We may be sure that such a rise in the demand for output and such an increase in the price of output will lead to an increase in money wage rates and in the prices paid for the use of other productive factors, for the demand for these factors is based on the money value of their output. The rise of money wages may occur quickly or slowly, but it will occur as employers, enjoying a marked increase in the prices of their output, bid against each other for labor and other productive factors. If these rises occur very rapidly and parallel closely the rise in the prices of output, the community may engage in bitter arguments as to whether the increase in prices caused the rise of costs, or vice versa. In this case both resulted from the rise of demand, which might have been induced by an increase in the supply of money.

This phenomenon of rising prices with no change in real output or real income we shall call "pure price inflation." Such an inflation cannot harm everybody in the community, for the total real income or output available for sharing remains unchanged and the stock of real wealth in the form of land, buildings, equipment, and other improvements is not diminished. But pure price inflation can bring about important shifts in the distribution of real income and wealth. When the price level doubles, all those whose money incomes fail to double suffer a decrease in their real purchasing power over income goods. Those whose money incomes remain constant lose half of their real incomes. Many types of money income are of this type: interest on debt holdings, building or land rentals fixed by long-term contracts, and pensions and annuities. Some other types of money income may rise, but less than in proportion to the rise of prices. Among these are likely to be salaries of government employees, teachers, and employees of religious and charitable institutions. On the other hand, those whose money incomes rise more than in proportion to price increases gain real income. Among these are likely to be recipients of business profits and highly volatile types of wages.

It is difficult to generalize about the behavior of money wage rates in periods of pure price inflation. In some periods they have lagged seriously behind the rise of prices so that real wages fell during the period of the lag. More recently, however, labor has found ways of reducing or eliminating the lag; it has used escalator clauses and other devices to increase wages as fast as prices rise. Nevertheless, some types of wages and salaries still lag.

Pure price inflation also redistributes real wealth. Those types of assets whose prices rise less than in proportion to the general level of prices lose real purchasing power. Those whose prices remain constant lose half their purchasing power when the price level doubles. Among these are money itself; savings accounts; mortgages, bonds, and other debt obligations; and accrued values of annuities and life insurance policies. Huge amounts of wealth are held in these forms and are subject to erosion by inflation. On the other hand, some assets enjoy price increases more than in proportion to the increase in the price level and thereby increase in real purchasing power. Among these are likely to be ownership claims against real estate, commodities, and business firms.

Price inflation is a potent means of transferring real wealth from creditors to debtors. For example, suppose that at some point in time Riley buys a house for $20,000, paying for it with $10,000 of his own money and an equal amount borrowed from McGrath on a mortgage. Suppose now that the price level doubles and that the money value of the house rises to $40,000. McGrath still has his $10,000 mortgage claim, but it will buy only as much as $5000 would have bought at the time the loan was made. Riley, on the other hand, now has an equity claim against the house of $30,000, which will buy as much as $15,000 would have bought when he purchased the house. In effect, inflation transferred from McGrath to Riley an amount of purchasing power equal to $5000 at the time of the loan. It is no cause for wonder that creditors and debtors have different attitudes toward inflation.

Large and persistent price inflation that gives rise to expectations of still further price increases may seriously reduce real output. Farmers may refuse to sell their products for money. Business firms may find it more profitable to hoard inventories than to process materials and sell them. The community may refuse to save or to make its savings available in exchange for debt obligations. Production may be interrupted by bitter labor strife.

Hyperinflation, such as that in Germany after World War I, may endanger the very survival of the existing social and economic system. It may virtually eliminate the economic power of those with fixed money incomes and fixed money wealth, create widespread feelings of injustice and discontent, and pave the way for extremist radical groups, such as fascists or communists.

Decrease in Demand for Output

Let us now consider the opposite case in which, because of a decrease in the money supply or for some other reason, the demand for output decreases while the supply of output is completely unresponsive and unchanged. More specifically, let us assume that demand falls by half, in the sense that the community will pay only half as high a price for each amount of output. This may be represented in Fig. 10 by a shift of the demand curve from $D'D'$ to DD. The price level of output will fall by half, declining from P_1 to P_0. So will the money value of output or national money income; it will fall from $P_1 O_F$ to $P_0 O_F$.

These are the necessary results of a decrease of the demand for output when the supply of output is completely unresponsive to price. But is it realistic to assume that the supply of output is completely unresponsive to price? It clearly is not if either money wage rates and the prices of other productive factors or the prices of output are "sticky" and not freely flexible downward—if workers accept unemployment rather than take decreased wage rates or if producers reduce output rather than lower their prices enough to sell a capacity level of output. But it may be realistic if both the prices of productive factors and the prices of output are freely flexible downward. Suppose, for example, that at the first threat of unemployment workers accept lower wage rates rather than run the risk of losing their jobs. This lowers the cost schedules of producers and enables them to lower their prices without squeezing their profit margins. Suppose that they lower their prices to the extent necessary to sell their output at capacity levels. In such a case the effect of a decrease in the demand for output might be to lower the prices of output without lowering real output or employment. This is a case of "pure price deflation." We do not claim that in actuality the prices of productive factors and output are freely flexible downward or that the supply of output is completely unresponsive to declines in its price. Rather we cite this case to emphasize the importance of supply responses in determining the economic effects of any given decrease in the demand for output.

Pure price deflation cannot harm all members of the community, for by definition it does not decrease the total real output to be shared or the total stock of real wealth. However, it can effect important shifts in the distribution of real income and wealth. In general, these are the reverse of those resulting from pure price inflation. The reader may find it useful to note which types of income and assets gain real purchasing power and which types lose.

SHIFTS OF DEMAND WITH OUTPUT RESPONSIVE

Let us now contrast the economic effects of shifts in the demand for output when the supply of output is not completely unresponsive to price but rises somewhat as prices rise. It must, of course, become unresponsive when ca-

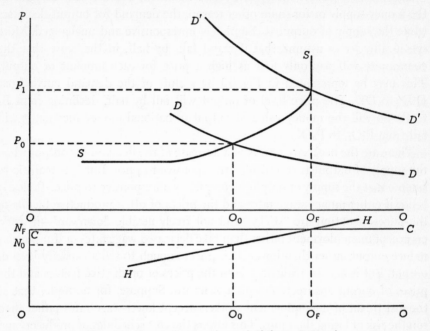

FIG. 11. Responsive Supply, and Shifts in Demand.

pacity-level output is reached. The curve SS in Fig. 11 represents such a price-responsive supply curve of output. It is essentially a relatively short-run supply function, assuming that the state of technology and the supply of productive factors change little, if at all. We also assume that the level of wage rates and the prices of other productive factors have been determined by past events. Initially, we shall assume that these are not changed by shifts in the demand for output.

Suppose that while the supply conditions for output are those represented by SS, the demand for output is DD. The rate of output will be O_0, the price level of output P_0, and the money value of output or national money income P_0O_0. The economy is producing far below its capacity level; O_0 is far short of O_F. The amount of unemployed labor is indicated by the vertical distance between the CC curve, the supply of labor, and the HH curve, the demand for labor, at the rate of output O_0. We may safely assume that when so much labor is unemployed there is also large excess capacity in mines, factories, and merchandizing establishments.

Increase of Demand for Output

Suppose now that the demand for output rises from DD to $D'D'$. The effects will be to raise real output from O_0 to O_F, the price level of output from P_0 to P_1, the money value of output from P_0O_0 to P_1O_F, and the amount of employment from N_0 to N_F. It will be noted that in this case the rise of demand elicited large increases in real output and employment. This it is reasonable to expect when the rise of demand starts from a situation of widespread excess capacity and unemployment. The existence of large numbers of unemployed laborers inhibits wage increases that would raise the cost structures of producers. With large excess capacity, producers are usually able to increase output without encountering seriously increasing marginal costs. In any case, the existence of large amounts of unused capacity discourages price increases for output. In such situations, producers may respond to increases of demand largely by offering more employment and by expanding output and to only a small extent by raising the prices of their output. But further increases of demand as capacity levels of output are approached may be reflected less and less in increased output and employment and more and more in price increases. One industry after another becomes a "bottleneck" and encounters sharply increasing costs per unit of output, more and more firms come to operate in the range of sharply rising marginal costs, and in general the bargaining power of sellers rises relative to that of buyers. Further rises of demand after full employment is reached bring the economy into a state of pure price inflation.

This case presents important lessons for monetary and fiscal policy-makers. Increases in the money demand for output that are reflected in pure price inflation with no increase in output may be highly undesirable because of their effects on the distribution of wealth and income. But increases of demand at times of unemployment and underutilization of productive capacity may elicit large increases in the nation's real output. And some increase in the prices of output may be necessary to achieve these increases in output. In trying to manipulate demand to achieve "maximum employment without inflation," monetary and fiscal authorities face the difficult task of forecasting the effects of any given change in demand on output and prices, and of determining the degree of responsiveness of output to price changes.

Decrease of Demand for Output

Let us now consider the reverse case in which the demand for output falls and the supply of output is responsive to price. This may be represented as in Fig. 11 by the decline of demand from $D'D'$ to DD. We see that the effects are to lower real output, employment, the price level of output, and the money value of output. In some cases decreases in demand are reflected largely in declines in output and employment and to only a small extent in reduced prices. This may be expected when cost and price structures are inflexible downward. Workers or their bargaining agents may successfully resist decreases in their money wage rates even if several million are unemployed. This prevents, or at least inhibits, downward shifts in producers' cost schedules.[5] Because of the rigidity of their costs or for other reasons producers may respond to decreases in the demand for their products by reducing their output as well as their prices, or even by reducing output while keeping prices unchanged. In highly competitive industries where no one seller has any significant control of the price of his product, a relatively small decline of the market price may lead producers to abandon large amounts of output whose marginal costs come to be in excess of the lowered market price. Relatively small declines may lower the market prices of a product below the lowest point on the average cost curves of some producers and lead them to close their plants entirely. Producers in industries characterized by monopoly power often believe that the demand for their product is so unresponsive or inelastic to price decreases that they will be better off if they maintain their prices and allow the decrease of demand to be reflected in reduced sales. It has often been observed that in administered price industries decreases in demand are reflected much more in decreased output than in reduced prices. But prices actually paid usually decline more than published or list prices; some "price chiseling" is likely to break out under such conditions.

We noted earlier that a decrease of the demand for output that is reflected in pure price deflation with no change in real output or employment may be highly undesirable because of its effects on the distribution of income and wealth. But a decrease of demand that markedly lowers real output (or income) and employment may be much worse. Such price declines as occur tend to shift income and wealth because of the changed purchasing power of the dollar. Much worse is the decrease in the total of real income to be distributed. Many people may be hurt, not so much because their percentage share of the national income is reduced as because the size of the income pie available for sharing has shrunk so much. A man may lose his house or his business, not so much because each dollar of his debt now represents more purchasing power as because his money income has shrunk so much. We need not dwell on the plight of those, such as the unemployed or businessmen who are making losses instead of profits, who receive a shrunken share, or no share at all, of a shrunken national income.

It is for reasons such as these that most people fear price deflation less for

[5] Note that we do not say that in practice employment and output would be sustained if wage rates were reduced. For one thing, a reduction of wage rates may, by lowering the money incomes of workers, decrease the demand for output still more. Moreover, an initial decline of wage rates and prices may create expectations of still further decreases in the future and lead purchasers to postpone their buying.

itself than for its usual companions, reduced real income and underutilization of productive resources.

CHANGES IN DEMAND THAT SHIFT THE SUPPLY CURVE OF OUTPUT

In the preceding section we assumed that shifts in the demand for output
left the supply curve unchanged. This may be a fairly realistic assumption,
especially when wage rates and the prices of other productive factors are rigid
and the economy is operating considerably below full employment levels both
before and after the shift of demand. Let us now consider the case in which a
shift of demand for output shifts the supply curve of output.

In Fig. 12 the initial demand for output is represented by DD and the
initial supply curve of output by SS. Output and employment are at virtually
full-employment levels. Suppose now that the demand for output doubles, as
indicated by the upward shift of demand from DD to $D'D'$. Since output

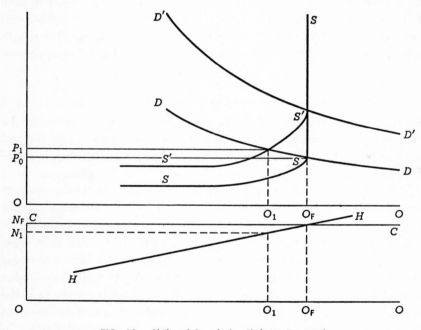

FIG. 12.   Shifts of Supply by Shifts in Demand.

cannot be increased, the price level of output will also double. Starting from
a full-employment situation, such a rise of demand and prices will almost
certainly tend to raise money wage rates and the prices of other productive factors. Let us suppose that they also double, thereby raising producers' cost
schedules. But though wage rates and the prices of other productive factors are

flexible upward, they may not be flexible downward. They may remain at the new high levels even in the face of widespread unemployment. If so, producers' cost schedules will remain high and the new higher supply curve $S'S'$ will be established. This curve shows that suppliers will produce and offer only at a higher price any given rate of output.

Suppose now that the demand for output falls back to its initial position, DD. Originally this demand produced full employment and a price level P_0. Now, however, after the rise of cost schedules, it produces a higher price level, P_1, and a rate of output considerably below full-employment levels.

This example contains an important lesson for policy-makers in periods following price and cost inflation. They may regret that the inflation occurred and be tempted to lower the prices of output to some earlier, lower level. But they can do so only by lowering the demand for output. If wage and cost structures are inflexible downward, such decreases of demand may not succeed in lowering prices significantly, or may do so only after a long period of unemployment and underproduction. In nations devoted to goals of continuously high levels of output and employment, prices are likely to have an upward "ratchet effect." Prices may rise at times but they are not allowed to slip back to their earlier lower position because the community is not willing to pay the necessary price in terms of unemployment and loss of output.

SHIFTS OF THE SUPPLY CURVE OF OUTPUT

Shifts in the supply curve of output may also bring about changes in the rate of output, the prices of output, and the state of employment and unemployment. Instead of dealing with these in detail, we shall mention only a few cases.

1. The supply curve shifts to the right but is not lowered. This may result from anything that increases the productive capacity of the economy without lowering costs per unit of output—for example, a growth of the labor supply without any change in output per man-hour or any change in money wage rates. If the demand curve remains unchanged, the effect will be a decrease in prices or a failure of the economy to expand its output to the new higher potential level. If wage rates and other costs are inflexible downward the latter may result. This suggests that in an economy with a rising supply of productive factors the demand for output should be increased roughly in proportion to the rise in productive capacity.

2. The supply curve shifts downward. That is, producers become willing to offer each amount of output at a lower price. This might result from technological advances that increase output per man-hour without an offsetting rise of wage rates, so that cost per unit is lowered. If the demand for output remains unchanged the effect will be to lower prices, to raise output, or both.

Price declines matched by decreases in costs need not be depressing to the economy, for they do not lower the profitability of production.

3. The supply curve shifts upward. That is, producers become willing to offer each amount of output only at a higher price. This might result from irresistible demands by labor for wage increases more than in proportion to increases in output per man-hour, thereby raising producers' cost schedules. If the demand curve for output remains unchanged, the effect will be to raise the prices of output, to lower output and employment, or some combination of these. This is often called the "cost push" type of inflation. Such upward shifts of cost and supply curves may pose serious problems for the fiscal and monetary authorities. If they reduce the demand for output to prevent price increases from occurring, or even if they refuse to increase the demand for output enough to maintain the level of output and employment, they will be criticized for condoning unemployment and underproduction. They may even be blamed for it. But if they raise the demand for output enough to prevent any decline of output and employment they facilitate price increases. Moreover, if employers and employees are allowed to become confident that such a policy will always be followed, the effect may be to encourage a wage-price spiral. Employees, confident that they will not lose their jobs, will be encouraged to demand excessive increases in their wage rates. Employers, confident that demand will be increased enough to allow them to pass through all cost increases in the form of price increases without losing sales, may have little incentive to put up a strong resistance to wage demands. This is especially true if they know that their competitors will grant the same wage increases and raise their prices.

CONCLUSIONS

This chapter has had the limited objective of presenting some background materials that will facilitate our understanding of the relationships between money and monetary policy and such economic phenomena as the rate of real output, the price level of output, the money value of output, and the state of employment and unemployment. We have dealt with some of these materials in an incomplete and oversimplified way. Perhaps the most outstanding instance was our incomplete treatment of the interrelationships of demand and supply—how shifts of the demand schedule for output may shift the supply schedule, and vice versa. We shall return to this point later.

Nevertheless, several of our findings will be useful.

1. The rate of real output, the price level of output, the money value of output, and the state of employment are all determined simultaneously by supply and demand conditions. They usually are not determined singly and independently of each other.

2. Since all these things are determined by demand and supply conditions and can be changed only by changes in demand or supply, or both, money and monetary policy can affect them only by affecting the demand for output or the supply of output. We should be suspicious of any form of monetary theory that does not indicate the process through which money achieves its effects. Generally speaking, money and monetary policy affect other economic variables primarily through their effects on the actual and prospective demand for output, though by changing the level of demand they may shift the supply curve of output. For example, an expansionary monetary policy that raises the demand for output may induce a rise in wage rates and the prices of other productive factors, thereby raising producers' cost schedules and shifting upward their supply curves. One of the major tasks of monetary theory is to analyze the relationship between the size of the money supply and the behavior of the demand for output.

3. The effects of any given change in the demand for output, whether induced by monetary policy or other forces, depend on the response of the supply of output. For example, a rise of demand when the economy is already operating at capacity levels may be reflected wholly in pure price inflation, with no change in either output or employment. But the same rise of demand starting from a situation of widespread unemployment and excess capacity may be reflected largely in expanded output and employment. A decrease of demand in a community in which costs and prices are freely flexible downward may be manifested largely in pure price deflation. But the same decrease of demand in a community characterized by cost and price structures that adjust downward slowly, if at all, may be reflected largely in shrunken output and employment.

It follows that a monetary theory that would explain the relations between monetary policy and these other economic phenomena must concern itself not only with effects on the demand for output but also with the responsiveness of supply. Thus it is led into such matters as the degree of utilization of productive resources, the upward and downward adjustability of wage rates, and producers' output and price policies. These may differ significantly from one country to another and even from one period to another in a given country.

SELECTED READINGS

American Economic Association, *Readings in Monetary Theory*, Blakiston Co., Philadelphia, 1951. This source includes a valuable classified bibliography.

CHAPTER 12

Gross National Product or Expenditures

In this chapter we shall continue our study of the flow of expenditures for output. More specifically, we shall consider one of the most commonly used measures of these expenditures: the gross national product, the various types of expenditures making up this total, some interrelations among them, the relations between expenditures for output and the money incomes received by the public, the circular flow of expenditures for output into money incomes and back again into the market for output, and the roles of saving and investment in the circular flow process.

THE NATURE OF GNP

Gross national product or expenditure, popularly known as GNP, is the market value of the output of goods and services produced by a nation's economy during a stated period of time before deduction of depreciation charges and other allowances for business and institutional consumption of durable capital goods.[1] It is usually stated at an annual rate. It avoids double-counting and includes the nation's entire output once and only once. Thus, it does not add together the values of autos produced and sold by the manufacturer to the dealer and by the dealer to consumers; it includes only their value at the point of final sale. It does not add together the values of the flour and other components of the bread produced and the values of bread sold by the baker to the merchant and by the merchant to the final buyer; it includes only the value of the bread at its point of final sale. Thus

---

[1] For excellent descriptions of GNP and other income concepts as well as a wealth of statistical materials relating to the behavior of GNP and its components since 1929, see U.S. Department of Commerce, *National Income*, Government Printing Office, Washington, 1954. For later data see the *Survey of Current Business* for July of each year.

GNP includes the value of all output at its point of final sale, and this value includes all the values added at earlier stages of processing and handling.

It is important to note that GNP may be viewed and measured in at least two principal ways: (1) as the market value of output or expenditures for output during a stated period, and (2) as the sum of the shares of gross income accruing to the members of the nation during the period. We shall emphasize that the total of the gross income shares accruing to the members of the community during any period must be exactly equal to the market value of output or expenditures for output during that period.

Since GNP is the market value of output, its behavior reflects changes in

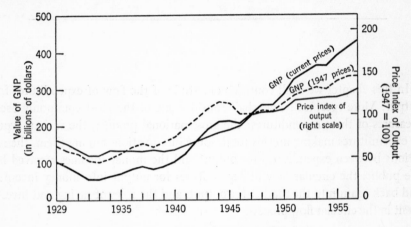

FIG. 13.   Gross National Product, 1929–1957.

the prices of output as well as in real output. This is illustrated in Fig. 13. The line "GNP (current prices)" reflects the value of output in each year at the average prices of output prevailing during that year. The line "GNP (1947 prices)" attempts to show the behavior of real output by valuing output in every year at the average prices prevailing in 1947. The line "Price index of output" shows the price levels of output in the various years as percentages of the prices prevailing in 1947. A study of Fig. 13 reveals how important it is to distinguish between real output and the market value of output. For example, owing to a fall of demand between 1929 and 1933, the market value of output fell 46 percent. This reflected decreases of 31 percent in real output and 23 percent in the prices of output. Between 1933 and 1945 the market value of output rose 281 percent, reflecting increases of 153 percent in real output and 50 percent in the prices of output. The 107 percent rise in the market value of output between 1946 and 1957 reflected increases of 43 percent in real output and 45 percent in the price level of output.

GNP AS EXPENDITURES FOR OUTPUT

GNP is composed of four main categories of expenditures for output: (1) personal consumption expenditures, (2) gross private domestic investment, (3) net foreign investment, and (4) government purchases of goods and services. GNP for any given period is, therefore, equal to the sum of these

TABLE 31.   Gross National Product as Expenditures for Output, 1929–1957
(In billions of dollars)

Year	GNP	Personal Consumption	Gross Private Domestic Investment	Net Foreign Investment	Government Purchases of Goods and Services
1929	$104.4	$ 79.0	$16.2	$0.8	$ 8.5
1930	91.1	71.0	10.3	0.7	9.2
1931	76.3	61.3	5.5	0.2	9.2
1932	58.5	49.3	0.9	0.2	8.1
1933	56.0	46.4	1.4	0.2	8.0
1934	65.0	51.9	2.9	0.4	9.8
1935	72.5	56.3	6.3	—	10.0
1936	82.7	62.6	8.4	—	11.8
1937	90.8	67.3	11.7	—	11.7
1938	85.2	64.6	6.7	1.1	12.8
1939	91.1	67.6	9.3	0.9	13.3
1940	100.6	71.9	13.2	1.5	14.1
1941	125.8	81.9	18.1	1.1	24.8
1942	159.1	89.7	9.9	−0.2	59.7
1943	192.5	100.5	5.6	−2.2	88.6
1944	211.4	109.8	7.1	−2.1	96.5
1945	213.6	121.7	10.4	−1.4	82.9
1946	210.7	147.1	28.1	4.6	30.8
1947	234.3	165.4	31.5	8.9	28.5
1948	259.4	178.3	43.1	1.9	36.1
1949	258.0	181.2	33.0	0.5	43.4
1950	284.6	195.0	50.0	−2.2	41.8
1951	329.0	209.8	56.3	0.2	62.6
1952	347.0	219.8	49.9	−0.2	77.5
1953	365.4	232.6	50.3	−2.0	84.4
1954	363.1	238.0	48.9	−0.4	76.6
1955	397.5	256.9	63.8	−0.4	77.1
1956	419.2	269.4	68.2	1.4	80.3
1957	440.3	284.4	65.3	3.5	87.1

SOURCE: *Survey of Current Business*, July, 1958, pp. 4–5, Table 1.

four types of expenditures and it varies with their total. This is shown in Table 31.

Personal Consumption

Personal consumption expenditures include all purchases of current output by consumers. These include durable consumers' goods, nondurable consumers' goods, and consumers' services. The durables include such things as new automobiles, TV sets, refrigerators, and furniture. The nondurables include food, beverages, clothing, tobacco, and so on. Consumers' services embrace a wide variety of services such as shelter, medical care, barber and beauty services, domestic service, and admissions to theaters and professional sporting events. All these are, of course, valued at their market prices.

Gross Private Domestic Investment

Every word in this title is important. The term "investment" as used here has nothing directly to do with buying stocks, bonds, or any other type of financial instrument. We use it here and in the following sections to mean simply expenditures for the current output of goods and services for the purpose of maintaining and increasing the stock of capital goods. The term "domestic" indicates that we include here only expenditures for the purpose of maintaining or increasing the stock of capital goods at home, not those for maintaining or building up capital abroad. "Private" means that only private expenditures for these purposes are included, not those by the government. The term "gross" indicates that we include expenditures for output to offset the depreciation of capital goods as well as to make net additions to the stock. If we deduct from gross private domestic investment for any period the depreciation or "using up" of capital during the period we arrive at net private domestic investment—the net increase in the stock of these goods during the period.

Gross private domestic investment is made up of three broad classes of expenditures for output: (1) New construction, both residential and nonresidential. Residential construction is the value of output of new dwelling units during the stated period, both single units and multiple units. Nonresidential construction embraces the output of such things as new farm, industrial, commercial, public utility, and private college buildings and new dams by privately owned public utilities. (2) Producers' durable equipment. This includes the output of such things as farm machinery, manufacturing equipment, scientific instruments, railroad rolling stock, accounting machines, and store fixtures. And (3) net changes in the size of business inventories. This item requires further clarification.

Business inventories in existence at any point of time are, of course, a part of the community's stock of capital goods; they are raw materials, goods in process, and finished goods held by business firms to facilitate their operations. Some of these are held by the firms that produced them; others are held by firms in later stages of the production-distribution process, such as fabricators of raw materials, wholesalers, or retailers, who purchased them from their producers. A net increase in business inventories during a given period is "investment" because it is an addition to the stock of capital goods. A net decrease of business inventories during a period is negative investment, or disinvestment, for it represents a decrease in the stock of capital goods. The net change of business inventories during any period is equal to total output minus final sales, for output tends to increase inventories, and sales to reduce them.

Changes in the volume of output used to increase or decrease inventories are an important source of fluctuations in GNP and employment, especially over short periods. To illustrate this point, let us assume that the rate of final sales remains constant but that the rate of change of inventories varies. Suppose that in the first period business is increasing its inventories at an annual rate of $4 billion. GNP will be equal to final sales plus the $4 billion of output used to effect the net increase of business inventories. This rise of inventories represents expenditures for output, either expenditures by firms that bought the output from other firms or production expenditures by firms that produced the goods and held them. It also provided employment. Suppose that in the next period business firms reduce their output enough to decrease their inventories at an annual rate of $4 billion. GNP will be equal to final sales minus $4 billion. Thus the shift by business from increasing its inventories at a rate of $4 billion a year to decreasing its inventories at a rate of $4 billion a year tends directly to lower GNP by $8 billion and also to lower employment. By reducing the incomes of producers and workers it may induce still further declines of GNP by decreasing consumption expenditures.

In the example above, where final sales were assumed to continue at a constant rate, fluctuations in the rate of change of inventories were a source of fluctuations of GNP. But this item can be a stabilizing force, at least in the short run, if it moves counter to changes in the rate of final sales. Suppose, for example, that the rate of final sales falls by $5 billion. GNP may remain constant, at least temporarily, if business maintains its rate of output and increases its rate of inventory accumulation. However, if this increase of inventory is "unwanted," business may later reduce output sharply to draw down its inventories. The adjustment of output to the decline of final sales is delayed but it may be magnified. Suppose, on the other hand, that the rate of final sales rises by $5 billion. This need not be reflected in the current rate of output if business offsets it by allowing its inventories to be drawn down. But when inventories fall below desired levels business may try to step up output sharply to replenish them.

Net Foreign Investment

Net foreign investment is the value of the nation's output used to change its net claims against foreigners during a stated period. It is the excess of the nation's exports of goods and services over its imports of goods and services and its net gifts and grants to foreigners.[2] This may be stated in the form of an equation:

Exports of goods and services *minus* Imports of goods and services *minus* Net gifts and grants to foreigners = Net foreign investment

This can be clarified by a numerical example. Suppose that during some year

Exports   = $20 billion
Imports   = $16 billion
Net gifts and grants   = $3 billion
Net foreign investment   = $1 billion

By exporting $20 billion of its output the nation received an equal amount of proceeds from abroad. It used $16 billion of these to buy imports; these obviously were not available to increase its net claims against foreigners. By making gifts and grants it gave away $3 billion of its exports; these too could not be used to increase its net claims against foreigners. But the remaining $1 billion of the value of its exports could. It could be used in three principal ways. (1) To retire foreign claims against the nation. For example, to buy back from foreigners ownership and debt claims formerly held by foreigners against the nation's government, business firms, or people. (2) To buy ownership or debt claims against foreigners, and (3) to buy gold from foreigners, this gold being considered a general claim against other countries.

It should be evident that net foreign investment can be negative, reflecting an excess of the nation's imports and net gifts and grants to the rest of the world over the value of its exports.

We can see that net foreign investment is properly called "investment" by looking at it from two points of view. In the first place, it is a way of adding to the nation's net wealth, in this case by using some part of its output to retire foreign claims against the nation's wealth or to acquire valuable claims against the rest of the world. In the second place, it is an offset to saving—a method of injecting savings back into the flow of expenditures for output. It is the value of exports purchased by foreigners with dollars made available to them by the nation's repurchase of claims against it that were formerly owned abroad, by its purchase of ownership and debt claims against the rest of the world, and by its purchases of gold. The simplest example is that in which Americans use a part of their savings to buy foreign securities

---

[2] Private gifts and grants to foreigners are included in personal consumption expenditures, government gifts and grants under government purchases of goods and services. It is assumed that the donor purchased the goods and services and gave them away.

and foreigners use the dollar proceeds to buy United States exports. It is this aspect of net foreign investment—as an offset to saving—that we shall stress later.

Government Purchases of Goods and Services

This item includes the expenditures of the federal, state, and local governments for the current output of goods and services. These are of two major types: (1) Direct expenditures for the services of productive factors, primarily for labor. In this category are the services of both military and civilian government personnel. These services are valued at the prices paid for them by the government. (2) Expenditures for the output of business firms. These are large and diverse; they include government expenditures for construction materials and services, military equipment and supplies, red tape, and the tens of thousands of other items purchased by government from private producers. Business firms provide employment and produce in response to government demand much as they would if the demand emanated from private sources.

Summary

We find, then, that GNP for any period is the sum of expenditures for output in the form of personal consumption, gross private domestic investment, net foreign investment, and government purchases of goods and services. It therefore fluctuates with the sum of these four types of expenditures.

For convenience we shall denote these expenditures by the following symbols:

C = personal consumption
I = total gross investment; it is the sum of gross private investment and net foreign investment
G = government purchases of goods and services
Y = GNP or gross national product

Thus for any period

$$Y = C + I + G$$

The reader will find it instructive to study carefully Table 31 on page 217, noting the size and variability of GNP, the relative sizes of its various components, and their variability.

GNP AS GROSS NATIONAL INCOME

We noted earlier that GNP may be viewed not only as the value of output or expenditures for output but also as the sum of gross national income shares accruing to the members of the community, including the government. We also noted that the sum of these shares accruing to the community during any period must be exactly equal to the value of output or expenditures. On reflection this becomes almost obvious. Value created must accrue to someone; it cannot disappear in thin air. Nor can the community as a whole receive values that are not created. To put the same thing another way, expenditures made must be received by someone, but no one can receive expenditures that are not made.

This is shown in Table 32. For any period the sum of the distributive shares of gross national income indicated by the column heads is determined by and equal to total expenditures for output. A part of these expenditures accrues to the government as income in the form of indirect business taxes, by which

TABLE 32. Gross National Product as the Sum of Gross Income Shares, 1929–1957
(In billions of dollars)

Year	Total Gross National Income	Indirect Business Taxes	Business Capital Consumption Allowances	Compensation of Employees	Rental Income of Persons	Net Interest Income	Earnings of Unincorporated Business[a]	Corporate Profits[a]
1929	$104.4	$ 7.0	$ 8.6	$ 51.1	$ 5.4	$ 6.4	$14.8	$10.1
1930	91.1	7.2	8.5	46.8	4.8	6.0	11.5	6.6
1931	76.3	6.9	8.2	39.7	3.8	5.8	8.7	1.6
1932	58.5	6.8	7.6	31.0	2.7	5.4	5.3	−2.0
1933	56.0	7.1	7.2	29.5	2.0	5.0	5.6	−2.0
1934	65.0	7.8	7.1	34.3	1.7	4.9	7.0	1.1
1935	72.5	8.2	7.2	37.3	1.7	4.8	10.4	2.9
1936	82.7	8.7	7.5	42.9	1.8	4.7	10.5	5.0
1937	90.8	9.2	7.8	47.9	2.1	4.7	12.7	6.2
1938	85.2	9.2	7.8	45.0	2.6	4.6	11.1	4.3
1939	91.1	9.4	7.8	48.1	2.7	4.6	11.6	5.7
1940	100.6	10.0	8.2	52.1	2.9	4.5	13.0	9.1
1941	125.8	11.3	9.0	64.8	3.5	4.5	17.4	14.5
1942	159.1	11.8	10.2	85.3	4.5	4.3	23.9	19.7
1943	192.5	12.7	10.9	109.6	5.1	3.7	28.2	23.8
1944	211.4	14.1	12.0	121.3	5.4	3.3	29.6	23.0
1945	213.6	15.5	12.6	123.2	5.6	3.2	30.8	18.4
1946	210.7	17.3	10.7	117.7	6.2	3.1	36.6	17.3
1947	234.3	18.6	13.0	128.8	6.5	3.8	35.5	23.6
1948	259.4	20.4	15.5	141.0	7.3	4.2	40.2	30.8
1949	258.0	21.6	17.3	140.8	8.3	4.8	35.6	28.2
1950	284.6	23.7	19.1	154.2	9.0	5.5	37.5	35.7
1951	329.0	25.6	22.0	180.3	9.4	6.3	42.3	41.0
1952	347.0	28.1	24.0	195.0	10.2	7.1	42.2	37.7
1953	365.4	30.2	26.5	208.8	10.5	8.2	40.7	37.3
1954	363.1	30.2	28.8	207.6	10.9	9.2	40.4	33.7
1955	397.5	32.9	32.0	223.8	10.7	10.4	42.2	43.1
1956	419.2	35.6	34.7	241.8	10.9	11.3	42.4	42.9
1957	440.3	37.6	37.7	254.6	11.8	12.6	43.0	41.9

[a] After inventory valuation adjustment.

SOURCE: *Survey of Current Business*, July, 1958, pp. 4–6, Tables 1 and 4. For some years the components do not give exactly the totals shown. This is due partly to rounding, partly to statistical discrepancies in the original data, and partly to the elimination of minor items under the headings of "government subsidies minus current surplus of government enterprises" and "business transfer payments."

we mean all business taxes except those on corporate net income. These include taxes on production and sales by business, license fees of business, taxes on business property, and so on. The remainder of GNP accrues to private business and individuals as gross money income before any taxes except indirect business taxes. One part accrues to business in the form of depreciation and other capital consumption allowances. This is not net income but it is a part of the expenditures for output received by business and at its disposal. Another part accrues as compensation of employees, in the form of wages, salaries, commissions, and so on. Another part accrues as rental incomes of persons, and another in the form of interest. All the remainder accrues as profits of business enterprises—as earnings of unincorporated enterprises and as corporate profits. This is a residual claim; all the value of business output not claimed by others accrues to the owners of business.

These relations between expenditures for output and income receipts suggest both the interrelatedness of the various sectors of the economy and the nature of the circular flow of income. Suppose we divide the economy into three major sectors: consumer households, business, and government. The interrelationships are so numerous and complex that we can mention only a few. The government receives income in the form of taxes from both households and business. It creates income for both by purchasing goods and services. Its expenditures for labor directly create income for households; its expenditures for the output of business create income for both business and households. Households pay tax income to the government and create income for business by their expenditures; in turn they receive income from both the government and business. Business, too, both receives income from and pays income to the other sectors.

As already noted, the flow of income is a circular flow. Expenditures for output become income receipts, these income receipts are spent for output, these spendings create income receipts, and so on. If this circular flow continued at a constant rate GNP would, of course, remain at a constant level. But we know that the circular flow sometimes slows down and lowers GNP and at other times speeds up and raises GNP. This raises several important questions. Through what processes do these rises and falls occur? How are they related to the ways that income recipients dispose of their incomes? Which types of income disposal tend to maintain or increase expenditures for output, which types to lower expenditures? As a first step toward answering these questions, we shall analyze the disposal of income receipts.

DISPOSAL OF INCOME AND THE CIRCULAR FLOW

For the purpose of analyzing the disposal of income receipts the classification of income shares used in Table 32 is inadequate. In the first place, it shows income shares by functional type rather than by type of recipient. In the second place, it shows income shares before any taxes except indirect business taxes, and also before transfer payments. For our analysis of income disposal we shall divide income recipients into three classes—government, business, and persons or households—and consider their "disposable incomes," by which we mean the amounts of money income left at their disposal after all taxes and all transfer payments.

As indicated in Table 33, the total disposable gross national income for any period must be exactly equal to GNP for that period, and it must fluctuate with GNP. It is equal to the sum of disposable government income, disposable business income, and disposable personal income. Let us look at each of these in turn.

Disposable Government Income

Disposable government income during a period is the amount of money income remaining at the disposal of the government after all taxes and transfer payments. We shall denote it by T_n, for it is in effect the government's net tax collections in excess of its transfers. It is total government revenues, which for the sake of simplicity we shall call taxes, minus government transfer payments to business and persons. By transfer payments we mean all government expenditures for which the government does not receive any goods and services in return. Their principal components are social security benefits, relief payments, bonuses and other benefits to veterans and their dependents, interest on the federal debt, and subsidies. These transfer payments become, of course, a part of the disposable incomes of their recipients. Table 34 shows government revenues, transfer payments, and disposable income for the various years since 1929.

How does the government dispose of its disposable income? One way is to spend for goods and services (G). If G is exactly equal to T_n, the government tends to maintain the circular flow constant, for its spendings create money income equal to the net income it received from others. But G may be less than T_n, leaving the government with a tax surplus. Such a surplus, reflecting a failure to spend for output all of its net tax collections, tends to reduce the level of GNP. On the other hand, G may exceed T_n, in which case the government is said to run a deficit. Such expenditures in excess of the government's disposable income tend to raise the level of GNP.

In our later analysis the relationship $(T_n - G)$ will play an important role. An excess of T_n over G, the government surplus, we shall call government saving and denote by S_g. We do this because a government surplus is similar to private saving in both nature and effects. Private saving is simply that part of disposable private income that is not returned to the market as expenditures for consumers' goods and services. A government surplus is that amount of its disposable income that it does not spend for goods and serv-

TABLE 33. Disposable Gross National Income, 1929–1957
(In billions of dollars)

Year	Total Gross Disposable Income (=GNP)	Disposable Income of Government	Disposable Business Income	Disposable Personal Income	Total Disposable Private Income (3) + (4)	Statistical Discrepancy
1929	$104.4	$ 9.6	$11.5	$ 83.1	$ 94.6	$0.3
1930	91.1	9.0	8.8	74.4	83.2	−1.0
1931	76.3	6.4	5.2	63.8	69.0	0.8
1932	58.5	6.4	2.7	48.7	51.4	0.8
1933	56.0	6.6	2.6	45.7	48.3	0.9
1934	65.0	7.5	4.9	52.0	56.9	0.7
1935	72.5	8.1	6.3	58.3	64.5	−0.2
1936	82.7	8.9	6.5	66.2	72.8	1.1
1937	90.8	12.3	7.8	71.0	78.7	−0.2
1938	85.2	11.2	7.8	65.7	73.5	0.5
1939	91.1	11.2	8.3	70.4	78.7	1.2
1940	100.6	13.3	10.4	76.1	86.4	0.8
1941	125.8	21.0	11.5	93.0	104.5	0.4
1942	159.1	28.3	14.2	117.5	131.6	−0.8
1943	192.5	44.4	16.3	133.5	149.6	−1.7
1944	211.4	44.6	17.2	146.8	164.2	2.8
1945	213.6	43.2	15.6	150.4	165.9	4.5
1946	210.7	34.8	13.1	160.6	173.7	2.1
1947	234.3	41.8	18.8	170.1	188.9	3.5
1948	259.4	44.4	26.6	189.3	215.9	−0.8
1949	258.0	40.3	27.7	189.7	217.4	0.5
1950	284.6	50.0	27.7	207.7	235.4	−0.7
1951	329.0	68.6	31.5	227.5	259.0	1.2
1952	347.0	73.8	33.3	238.7	272.0	1.4
1953	365.4	77.2	34.4	252.5	286.9	1.3
1954	363.1	69.8	35.5	256.9	292.4	0.9
1955	397.5	80.0	42.1	274.4	316.5	1.0
1956	419.2	86.6	43.1	290.5	333.5	−0.9
1957	440.3	88.7	45.6	305.1	350.7	0.7

SOURCE: Computed from various tables in *Survey of Current Business*, July, 1958. The components were calculated as follows: (1) Data on disposable personal income were taken directly from the national income accounts. (2) Disposable business income was secured by adding capital consumption allowances and undistributed corporate profits after inventory valuation adjustments. (3) Disposable government income was computed by deducting from total government receipts all government expenditures except government purchases of goods and services. These government transfer payments were computed by deducting government purchases of goods and services from total government expenditures.

ices. Both private saving and government saving, taken by themselves, tend to lower the level of GNP. Moreover, government saving, like private saving, is a potential source of funds to finance investment expenditures. Suppose, for example, that during some period the government has a net tax surplus

TABLE 34. Disposable Government Income, 1929–1957
(In billions of dollars)

Year	Total Government Receipts	Transfer Payments	Disposable Government Income	Government Purchases of Goods and Services	Government Surplus or Deficit (−)
1929	$ 11.3	$ 1.7	$ 9.6	$ 8.5	$ 1.0
1930	10.8	1.8	9.0	9.2	−0.3
1931	9.5	3.1	6.4	9.2	−2.8
1932	8.9	2.5	6.4	8.1	−1.7
1933	9.3	2.7	6.6	8.0	−1.4
1934	10.5	3.0	7.5	9.8	−2.4
1935	11.4	3.3	8.1	10.0	−2.0
1936	13.0	4.1	8.9	11.8	−3.0
1937	15.4	3.1	12.3	11.7	0.6
1938	15.0	3.8	11.2	12.8	−1.6
1939	15.4	4.2	11.2	13.3	−2.1
1940	17.7	4.4	13.3	14.1	−0.7
1941	25.0	4.0	21.0	24.8	−3.8
1942	32.6	4.3	28.3	59.7	−31.8
1943	49.2	4.8	44.4	88.6	−44.2
1944	51.2	6.6	44.6	96.5	−51.9
1945	53.2	10.0	43.2	82.9	−39.7
1946	51.1	16.3	34.8	30.8	4.1
1947	57.1	15.3	41.8	28.5	13.3
1948	59.2	14.8	44.4	36.1	8.2
1949	56.4	16.1	40.3	43.4	−3.1
1950	69.3	19.3	50.0	41.8	8.2
1951	85.4	16.8	68.6	62.6	6.1
1952	90.6	16.8	73.8	77.5	−3.8
1953	94.9	17.7	77.2	84.4	−7.1
1954	90.0	20.2	69.8	76.6	−6.7
1955	101.4	21.4	80.0	77.1	2.9
1956	110.4	23.8	86.6	80.3	6.3
1957	116.1	27.4	88.7	87.1	1.7

SOURCE: *Survey of Current Business*, July, 1958. Total government receipts were found by summing (1) corporate profits tax liability, (2) personal tax and nontax payments, (3) indirect business taxes, and (4) contributions for social insurance. Transfer payments are the total of (1) subsidies less current surplus of government enterprises, (2) government transfer payments, (3) net interest paid by government.

of $5 billion and uses that part of its disposable income to retire debt held by insurance companies or other investors. The recipients of the money may lend it to others to finance their investment expenditures. The government may, of course, fail to make its savings available for use or they may for other reasons fail to find their way into investment spendings, but the same is true of private savings.

We shall also see that a government deficit, measuring the excess of G over T_n, has effects similar to those of private investment expenditures, for it too is an offset to saving—a way of converting savings into expenditures for output. The simplest example is that in which the government borrows current private savings and uses them to finance its deficit spendings.

Disposable Business Income

Disposable business income is the amount of gross money income left at the disposal of business after all taxes and transfer payments. As shown in Table 35, disposable business income is made up of two parts: (1) Capital consumption allowances. As indicated earlier, a part of expenditures for output accrues to business firms as depreciation and other allowances for the decline in value of capital goods during a period. This is not net income but it is a part of gross national income that remains at the disposal of business firms. (2) Undistributed corporate profits, or the part of corporate net profits after taxes that is retained by corporations and not paid out to stockholders. As shown in Table 35, undistributed corporate profits fluctuate widely. During periods of unusually high profits, corporations often retain a large fraction of their net earnings after taxes. But in periods of low profits or losses they often pay out more than their current net earnings; their undistributed profits are negative.

How does business dispose of its disposable income? All of it is "saved," none of it is spent for consumption. To emphasize this aspect of disposable business income, we shall refer to it also as gross business saving and denote it by the symbol S_b. A business firm may, of course, use some of its own S_b to finance its own current expenditures for output to maintain or increase its stock of capital goods. But this need not occur; the firm may use such savings in ways that do not directly contribute to expenditures for output—to add to money balances, to retire debt or other claims against itself, to buy securities, and so on. Even if these savings are transferred to others they, like personal savings, may fail to find their way into expenditures for output.

Disposable Personal Income

Disposable personal income during a stated period is the money income remaining at the disposal of persons (or households) after all taxes and transfer payments. We can arrive at personal disposable income in either of two ways. (1) As shown in Table 36, we can compute it by adding the components of personal income and subtracting personal taxes. Thus it is equal to the sum of wages, salaries, and other income received for labor, net incomes of proprietors of unincorporated business enterprises, personal rental incomes, dividends, personal interest income, and transfer payments received from government and business, minus personal taxes. (2) We can also com-

TABLE 35. Disposable Business Income, 1929–1957
(In billions of dollars)

Year	Total Disposable Business Income	Capital Consumption Allowances	Undistributed Corporate Profits[a]
1929	$11.5	$ 8.6	$ 2.9
1930	8.8	8.5	0.2
1931	5.2	8.2	−3.0
1932	2.7	7.6	−4.9
1933	2.6	7.2	−4.6
1934	4.9	7.1	−2.2
1935	6.3	7.2	−1.0
1936	6.5	7.5	−1.0
1937	7.8	7.8	—
1938	7.8	7.8	—
1939	8.3	7.8	0.5
1940	10.4	8.2	2.2
1941	11.5	9.0	2.4
1942	14.2	10.2	4.0
1943	16.3	10.9	5.2
1944	17.2	12.0	5.4
1945	15.6	12.6	3.0
1946	13.1	10.7	2.4
1947	18.8	13.0	5.8
1948	26.6	15.5	11.1
1949	27.7	17.3	10.4
1950	27.7	19.1	8.6
1951	31.5	22.0	9.5
1952	33.3	24.0	9.3
1953	34.4	26.5	7.9
1954	35.5	28.8	6.7
1955	42.1	32.0	10.1
1956	43.1	34.7	8.4
1957	45.6	37.7	7.9

[a] After inventory valuation adjustment.
SOURCE: *Survey of Current Business*, July, 1958.

pute it by subtracting the disposable incomes of government and business from total gross national income. We shall have many occasions to emphasize the fact that by no means all gross national income accrues to persons or households as disposable personal income; some of it remains at the disposal of government and business. Business may increase disposable personal income at any given level of GNP by retaining less disposable income and disbursing it to households, and it may lower disposable personal income by retaining more itself. The government may also raise disposable personal income at any given level of GNP by reducing its collections of personal taxes, or by increasing its transfer payments to households, or by some combination

TABLE 36.   Personal Income and Disposable Personal
Income, 1957
(In billions of dollars)

Wage and salary receipts and other labor income	$247.0
Proprietors and rental income	54.8
Dividends	12.4
Personal interest income	18.7
Transfer income	21.5
Equals: PERSONAL INCOME	$354.4
Less: PERSONAL TAXES	49.3
Equals: DISPOSABLE PERSONAL INCOME	$305.1

SOURCE: *Federal Reserve Bulletin*, July, 1958, pp. 856–857.

of the two that lowers T_n. Or it may lower disposable personal income at any given level of GNP by raising personal tax collections or lowering its transfer payments to households.

Disposable personal income is disposed of in two ways. (1) As personal consumption expenditures, which we denote by the symbol C. This is the same C that we used in the equation showing GNP as the sum of expenditures for output. This method of disposing of disposable personal income clearly tends to maintain the circular flow of spendings for output. (2) As personal saving, which we shall denote by the symbol S_p. Personal saving is simply that part of disposable personal income that is not spent for consumption. Such an act obviously does not itself create expenditures for output; it is simply "not spending" for consumption.

In later sections we shall find it convenient to deal with total disposable private income. This may be looked upon in two principal ways. (1) As total GNP minus T_n. This view emphasizes the fact that at any given level of GNP the government may increase disposable private income by reducing T_n, either by lowering its tax collections or raising its transfer payments. Or it may lower total disposable private income by increasing T_n, either by raising its tax collections or by reducing its transfer payments. (2) As the

TABLE 37. Disposable Private Income and Its Disposal, 1929–1957
(In billions of dollars)

Year	Disposable Private Income	Disposable Personal Income	Personal Consumption	Personal Saving	Gross Business Saving (Disposable Business Income)	Total Private Gross Saving
1929	$ 94.6	$ 83.1	$ 79.0	$ 4.2	$11.5	$15.7
1930	83.2	74.4	71.0	3.4	8.8	12.2
1931	69.0	63.8	61.3	2.5	5.2	7.7
1932	51.4	48.7	49.3	−0.6	2.7	2.0
1933	48.3	45.7	46.4	−0.6	2.6	1.9
1934	56.9	52.0	51.9	—	4.9	5.0
1935	64.5	58.3	56.3	2.0	6.3	8.4
1936	72.8	66.2	62.6	3.6	6.5	10.1
1937	78.7	71.0	67.3	3.7	7.8	11.5
1938	73.5	65.7	64.6	1.0	7.8	8.9
1939	78.7	70.4	67.6	2.9	8.3	11.2
1940	86.4	76.1	71.9	4.2	10.4	14.6
1941	105.4	93.0	81.9	11.1	11.5	22.6
1942	131.6	117.5	89.7	27.8	14.2	41.9
1943	149.6	133.5	100.5	33.0	16.3	49.3
1944	164.2	146.8	109.8	36.9	17.2	54.2
1945	165.9	150.4	121.7	28.7	15.6	44.3
1946	173.7	160.6	147.1	13.5	13.1	26.6
1947	188.9	170.1	165.4	4.7	18.8	23.5
1948	215.9	189.3	178.3	11.0	26.6	37.6
1949	217.4	189.7	181.2	8.5	27.7	36.2
1950	235.4	207.7	195.0	12.6	27.7	40.3
1951	259.0	227.5	209.8	17.7	31.5	49.2
1952	272.0	238.7	219.8	18.9	33.3	52.2
1953	286.9	252.5	232.6	19.8	34.4	54.2
1954	292.4	256.9	238.0	18.9	35.5	54.4
1955	316.5	274.4	256.9	17.5	42.1	59.6
1956	333.6	290.5	269.4	21.1	43.1	64.2
1957	350.7	305.1	284.4	20.7	45.6	66.3

SOURCE: *Survey of Current Business*, July, 1958.

sum of disposable business income (S_b) and disposable personal income $(C + S_p)$.

Summary

We find, then, that for any period total disposable income must be exactly equal to GNP, which we denote by the symbol Y. It is also equal to the sum of its components, disposable government income (T_n), disposable business income (S_b), and disposable personal income $(C + S_p)$. Thus,

$$Y = C + S_p + S_b + T_n$$

SAVING AND INVESTMENT

By now we should begin to suspect that the processes of saving and investment play central roles in the circular flow of income and in determining the level of Y. Personal consumption, as a form of expenditure for output, clearly tends to maintain the circular flow and support GNP. But private saving, S_b and S_p, is a part of total disposable income not spent for C; this "not spending" can hardly tend to maintain the circular flow or support GNP. Neither can the government saving (S_g), which results when the government's expenditures for output are less than its disposable income. How can the "not spending" represented by private and government saving be offset? How can it be returned to the market as spending for output? The answer is, only as investment expenditures for output—gross private domestic investment plus net foreign investment—and government deficit spending.

To establish these facts, let us recall two equations developed earlier. We have just found that, looking at GNP or Y as the sum of disposable incomes,

$$Y = C + S_p + S_b + T_n$$

Earlier, when looking at Y as the sum of expenditures for output, we found that

$$Y = C + I + G$$

where C = personal consumption expenditures
  I = investment expenditures, or the sum of gross private domestic investment and net foreign investment
  G = government purchases of goods and services

It follows, therefore, that for any period,

$$C + I + G = C + S_p + S_b + T_n$$

The C on each side of the equation is, of course, the same thing. Since we know that C is a way of maintaining the flow of expenditures for output, let us subtract it from both sides of the equation. We find that

$$I + G = S_p + S_b + T_n$$

One further rearrangement of our equation will be useful, for we found earlier that the relationship $(G - T_n)$ is very important. Let us introduce this into our equation by subtracting T_n from both sides. We find that for any period

$$I + (G - T_n) = S_p + S_b$$

TABLE 38. Sources and Uses of Gross Saving, 1929–1957
(In billions of dollars)

Year	Personal Saving	Capital Consumption Allowances	Undistributed Corporate Profits[a]	Statistical Discrepancy	Total $S = I +$ Government Deficit	Gross Private Domestic Investment	Net Foreign Investment	Government Deficit
1929	$ 4.2	$ 8.6	$ 2.9	$0.3	$16.0	$16.2	$0.8	$ –1.0
1930	3.4	8.5	0.2	–1.0	11.3	10.3	0.7	0.3
1931	2.5	8.2	–3.0	0.8	8.5	5.5	0.2	2.8
1932	–0.6	7.6	–4.9	0.8	2.8	0.9	0.2	1.7
1933	–0.6	7.2	–4.6	0.9	3.0	1.4	0.2	1.4
1934	—	7.1	–2.2	0.7	5.6	2.9	0.4	2.4
1935	2.0	7.2	–1.0	–0.2	8.2	6.3	—	2.0
1936	3.6	7.5	–1.0	1.1	11.3	8.4	—	3.0
1937	3.7	7.8	—	0.2	11.2	11.7	—	–0.6
1938	1.0	7.8	—	0.5	8.4	6.7	1.1	1.6
1939	2.9	7.8	0.5	1.2	12.3	9.3	0.9	2.1
1940	4.2	8.2	2.2	0.8	15.4	13.2	1.5	0.7
1941	11.1	9.0	2.4	0.4	23.0	18.1	1.1	3.8
1942	27.8	10.2	4.0	–0.8	41.1	9.9	–0.2	31.4
1943	33.0	10.9	5.2	–1.7	47.6	5.6	–2.2	44.2
1944	36.9	12.0	5.4	2.8	56.9	7.1	–2.1	51.9
1945	28.7	12.6	3.0	4.5	48.7	10.4	–1.4	39.7
1946	13.5	10.7	2.4	2.1	28.7	28.1	4.6	–4.1
1947	4.7	13.0	5.8	3.5	27.0	31.5	8.9	–13.3
1948	11.0	15.5	11.1	–0.8	36.8	43.1	1.9	–8.2
1949	8.5	17.3	10.4	0.5	36.7	33.0	0.5	3.1
1950	12.6	19.1	8.6	–0.7	39.6	50.0	–2.2	–8.2
1951	17.7	22.0	9.5	1.2	50.4	56.3	0.2	–6.1
1952	18.9	24.0	9.3	1.4	53.6	49.9	–0.2	3.9
1953	19.8	26.5	7.9	1.3	55.5	50.3	–2.0	7.1
1954	18.9	28.8	6.7	0.9	55.3	48.9	–0.4	6.7
1955	17.5	32.0	10.1	1.0	60.6	63.8	–0.4	–2.9
1956	21.1	34.7	8.4	–0.9	63.3	68.2	1.4	–6.3
1957	20.7	37.7	7.9	0.7	67.0	65.3	3.5	–1.7

[a] After inventory valuation adjustment.
SOURCE: *Survey of Current Business*, July, 1958, Table 5, p. 6.

In other words, total private saving for any period is exactly equal to investment expenditures for output plus any government deficit or minus any government surplus. Consider three cases. (1) $G = T_n$; the government has neither a surplus nor a deficit. In this case $S_p + S_b = I$. (2) T_n is greater than G. This surplus, representing that part of the government's disposable income that it fails to spend for goods and services, we earlier called government saving and denoted by S_g. In this case, $S_p + S_b = I - S_g$, or $S_p + S_b + S_g = I$. In other words, the total of private and government saving is equal to investment expenditures. (3) G is greater than T_n; the government is engaging in deficit spending, which we denote by D. In this case, $S_p + S_b = I + D$.

Were it not for some unfortunate statistical discrepancies in the original data, Table 38 would confirm our finding that for every period $S_p + S_b = I + (G - T_n)$. That is, total private gross saving in the form of personal saving, capital consumption allowances, and undistributed corporate profits equals the sum of investment expenditures plus the government deficit or minus the government surplus. This equality obtained year in and year out, in years of prosperity and years of depression, in years of peace and years of war. It could not be a mere coincidence.

Why does this equality hold for any period? From an accounting point of view it must. As we saw earlier, the total disposable income of the nation for any period $(C + S_p + S_b + T_n)$ is created by and is equal to total expenditures for output $(C + I + G)$. But the private sectors do not save the income represented by their consumption expenditures, nor do they save income taken by the government as T_n. Deducting these from both equations, we find that

$$S_p + S_b = I + (G - T_n)$$

In other words, the community cannot in any period succeed in saving more or less than the amount of expenditures represented by $I + (G - T_n)$ in that period. The remainder of expenditures for output are absorbed by C and T_n.

The economic meaning and significance of this equality will be discussed fully in the following chapter. Here we shall only note that Y will be determined at such a level that $S_p + S_b = I + (G - T_n)$. Y cannot remain at a level where total saving would exceed current expenditures for investment and $(G - T_n)$, for some part of saving would fail to flow back into the market as expenditure for output, thereby lowering Y. Nor can Y remain at a level at which expenditures in the form of $I + (G - T_n)$ exceed total saving, for these excess expenditures would tend to raise the level of Y. It should be noted that it is through adjustments in the level of Y that saving and $(I + G - T_n)$ are brought into equality of each other.

For our later analysis it will be useful to look at saving in two different ways. For simplicity let us assume that the government has a surplus so that total saving (S) is equal to $S_p + S_b + S_g$. (1) As that part of total disposable income that is not spent for consumption or for government purchases and is therefore potentially available to finance investment expenditures by the savers themselves or by others. The mere fact that the private sectors are willing to save such and such an amount out of a given level of Y does not necessarily mean, of course, that precisely that amount, no more and no less, will find its way into investment expenditures for output. (2) As that part of the total value of output that is not purchased as C or G—the amount left over after consumer and government purchases. Since the value of output is equal to the sum of disposable income shares, the value of output left over after C and G purchases must be equal to total saving at that level of Y—that is, to $S_p + S_b + S_g$. How can this "leftover" output be taken off the market, if at all? The answer is, only by purchases for investment purposes. Or to make the case more general to allow for government deficits, it can be taken off the market only by investment expenditures and government deficit spending. In the next chapter we shall employ this concept, viewing saving at each level of Y as that value of output left over after consumption and government purchases.

SUMMARY AND CONCLUSIONS

This chapter has concerned itself largely with what is usually called "national income accounting," showing the nature of national income, in this case GNP, the components of GNP, and some of their relationships to the total and to each other. It has dealt little with "national income analysis," by which we mean the determination of the level of national income at any time and of its fluctuations through time. For example, it did not consider such questions as these: "Why was Y, at a particular time, where it was rather than higher or lower? Why and through what processes did it change from one level to another?" Such questions will be discussed in the next chapter.

Nevertheless we have made many useful discoveries.

1. Expenditures for output, and only expenditures for output, create money income for the nation. Money income must, therefore, vary with the level of expenditures.
2. The income flow is a circular flow involving flows of expenditures into the market for output, into income receipts, back again into the market for output, and so on.
3. In this process saving and investment play crucial roles. Saving can be re-injected as spending for output only through investment spending and government deficit spending.
4. During any period the nation as a whole can succeed in saving only an amount just equal to expenditures for output in the form of $I + (G - T_n)$.
5. The government can directly affect the flow of incomes by altering its rate of expenditures for output, the amount of its tax collection at each level of Y, and its rate of transfer payments.

SELECTED READINGS

Hansen, A. H., *Business Cycles and National Income*, Norton, New York, 1951.
Ruggles, R., and Ruggles, N. D., *National Income Accounts and Income Analysis*, McGraw-Hill, New York, 1956.

CHAPTER 13

Saving, Investment, and National Income

We now turn our attention to national income analysis, attempting to answer such questions as these: What determines the level of GNP (or Y) at any time? Why and through what processes does it change? How, in what way, and how much does a given change in one element of national output or income change the other elements and the total?

Our analysis will be essentially a demand and supply analysis. We shall argue that Y is determined at that level at which the demand for output is exactly equal to the supply of output, and that Y changes only in response to changes in the demand for it, or the supply of it, or both. In this case we measure Y, the demand for output, and the supply of output in terms of their money values. However, in order to escape certain complexities we shall in this chapter assume that the average prices of output remain at a constant level.

More specifically, we shall deal with investment demand for output and the supply of output represented by the nation's supply of saving, and shall show that a necessary condition for an equilibrium level of Y is that investment demand be exactly equal to the supply of saving. If investment demand is less than the supply of saving, Y must fall. If investment demand is greater than the supply of saving, Y must rise. Let us start our analysis with investment demand.

INVESTMENT DEMAND FOR OUTPUT

By the investment demand for output, which we shall denote by the symbol I, we mean a schedule or curve showing the values of output demanded for investment purposes, or the values of expenditures for output for these purposes, at the various possible rates of interest, which we shall denote by r. This may also be called an investment demand function showing investment demand as a function of interest rates. I includes all demands for output for gross private domestic investment and net foreign investment. It therefore includes, in addition to net foreign investment, expenditures for new construction, both residential and nonresidential, producers' durable equipment, and desired net changes in business inventories. Note that because we are interested in determining an equilibrium level of Y we include in investment demand only "wanted" or desired changes in business inventories. An "unwanted" actual increase of inventory would be followed by a decrease of Y as business tried to get rid of its excess inventory. On the other hand, an "unwanted" decrease of inventory would be followed by an increase of Y as business stepped up its output to restore inventories to the desired level.

Most of the components of I are demands by business for output with which to maintain or increase stocks of capital goods. These demanders are presumably motivated by a desire for profits, perhaps a desire to maximize their profits. For this purpose they compare the expected returns from new investment with the costs involved. However, some of the investment demand, notably expenditures by homeowners for new residential construction, may not be profit-motivated. But even these demanders presumably arrive at decisions by balancing expected benefits and costs. And, other conditions being constant, they will presumably buy less when the cost to them is higher. Interest costs are an important part of the carrying charges of a house.

An investment demand schedule or curve, such as that shown in Fig. 14, is a typical demand curve showing the relation of quantity demanded to price. In this case the price of loan funds, or the interest rate on investable funds, is measured along the horizontal axis. The values of output demanded for investment, or investment expenditures, are measured along the vertical axis. The II curve depicts the size of investment demand at the various possible levels of r. From the point of view of the spender for investment, r is a cost. If he gets the money to finance investment by borrowing from others, r is the annual interest rate he must pay to lenders. If he finances his investment spending by using his own money, r is his opportunity cost; it is the interest rate he sacrifices by using the money himself rather than lending it to someone else. It is therefore plausible to assume that, other things remaining the same, a rise of interest rates will decrease the actual investment demand for output and a fall of interest rates will stimulate it.

We are engaging in oversimplification in assuming a single interest rate in the market. There are, of course, many rates. Moreover, other terms of lending and borrowing may change: the length of time for which lenders will make funds available, the risks that they will take at any given interest rate, the amount of security demanded for loans, and so on. Nevertheless, it will be convenient to let r represent the height of the structure of interest rates and the annual cost per dollar of borrowed funds.

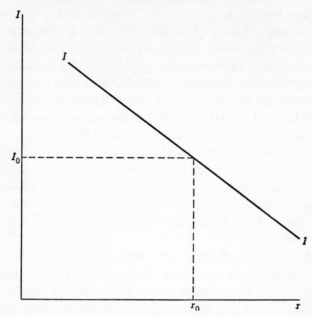

FIG. 14. An Investment Demand Function.

In drawing any demand curve showing quantities demanded at various levels of price, thereby isolating the effects of price on quantities taken, we have to assume that all other conditions affecting demand are given and unchanged. This we did in drawing the II curve in Fig. 14. But it is important to know what determines the position of the demand curve. We need to answer questions such as these: Why is the demand curve neither higher nor lower at each level of interest rates? For example, why at the interest rate r_0 is the demand for investment at I_0 rather than much higher or much lower? What forces can shift I upward at each rate of interest? What forces can shift the curve downward? To answer such questions, we need to know the motivations of those who spend for investment and the nature of the benefits they balance against interest costs in arriving at decisions as to whether to spend for investment and at what rate of expenditure.

The Marginal Efficiency of Capital

The great bulk of investment expenditures are made by business firms intent on making net profits. Hence, in determining whether or not to make a capital expenditure they ask, "Will the acquisition of this capital good add at least as much to my revenues as it adds to my costs?" This applies to purchases for replacement as well as to net additions to capital. Decisions as to the amount of new investment, therefore, depend on a comparison of interest costs and the expected annual rate of return on new investment. The latter has been given many names, including "marginal revenue product of capital" and "marginal efficiency of capital." We shall use the latter term and define it as the annual amount, stated as a percentage of the cost of the capital, that the acquisition of the new capital good is expected to add to the enterprise's net revenues after deduction of all additional costs of operation except the interest costs on the money used. For our purposes we shall view the marginal efficiency of capital as a schedule or function showing the various amounts of new investment that are expected to yield at least various rates of return. The demand for investment is derived from the marginal efficiency of capital schedule. Enterprisers intent on maximizing their profits tend to buy those types and amounts of capital that they expect to yield a rate of return in excess of the interest cost of the money used to purchase them. Presumably they will not buy capital whose expected rate of return is below the interest rate.

Note that we have emphasized the central role of "expected" average annual rates of return on new investment. Enterprisers must base their decisions on their expectations as to average annual yields—on the best forecasts they can make. They cannot be certain as to these returns, for many types of capital yield their returns only over a long period and much can change in the meantime. But they must make decisions even if they recognize the fallibility of their forecasts.

The schedule of the marginal efficiency of capital depends on many things, of which the following are among the most important. (1) The size and composition of the existing stock of capital goods, especially its adequacy relative to the current demand for output. If the existing stock of capital goods is largely obsolete and too small to produce most economically the rate of output currently demanded, large amounts of new investment may be expected to yield high rates of return. But if the existing stock of capital goods is very large relative to the current demand for output and if it includes the most efficient types of capital that man knows how to make and utilize, only small amounts of new investment will be profitable. If there is already excess capacity, business firms may refrain from replacing some of their equipment when it wears out. (2) The rate of innovation. If the rate of innovation is high, it may be profitable to undertake much new investment in order to produce the new types of products or to use new and more economical processes of production. If the rate of innovation is low, the profitability of new investment goods for this purpose may be smaller. (3) The expected future behavior of demands for output. If demands for output are expected to rise rapidly, much new investment may be expected to yield high profits. If demands for output are expected to remain at existing levels and the present stock of capital goods is adequate, the demand for new capital goods may be largely a replacement demand. And if demands for output are expected to decline, many potential spenders for investment may not replace their capital equipment when it wears out. (4) Expectations as to future wages, other costs, taxes, and government policies. Estimates of the profitability of new investment may be greatly affected by expectations regarding the future course of these factors. (5) The state of "business psychology." In view of the scarcity and vagueness of our knowledge about the future and the precariousness of any forecast based on that knowledge, it is not at all surprising that expectations concerning the future should be greatly affected by prevailing conditions and the trends of the immediate past. As the late J. M. Keynes put it,

> It would be foolish, in forming our expectations, to attach great weight to matters which are very uncertain. It is reasonable, therefore, to be guided to a considerable degree by the facts about which we feel somewhat confident, even though they may be less decisively relevant to the issue than other facts about which our knowledge is vague and scanty. For this reason the facts of the existing situation enter, in a sense disproportionately, into the formation of our long-term expectation; our usual practice being to take the existing situation and to project it into the future, modified only to the extent that we have more or less definite reasons for expecting a change.[1]

This convention of projecting into the future the present situation, and particularly the trend of the immediate past, is an aggravating factor in the business cycle. In the period of upswing, an original increase in the profitability of production is likely to give birth to expectations of still greater profits, whereas in the downswing an original decline is likely to breed expectations of continued contraction.

Partly because of the paucity and uncertainty of our knowledge concerning future economic events, expectations are inordinately influenced by waves of excessive optimism and pessimism. Realizing the untrustworthiness of his own opinions with respect to the future, each person relies heavily upon those of others, which may be as undependable as his own. By a process that only a social psychologist can explain, the public temperament fluctuates from exultation to melancholia. At one time it exhibits the exuberance and optimism of a New Era. Then it lapses into dark discouragement and despair. In these alternating periods of overoptimism and overpessimism, enterprisers are prone to overestimate and underestimate the returns to be realized from new investment.

> . . . It is an essential characteristic of the boom that investments which will in fact yield, say, 2 per cent in conditions of full employment are made in the expectation of a yield of, say, 6 per cent, and are valued accordingly. When disillusion comes, this expectation is replaced by a contrary "error of pessimism," with the result that the investments, which would in fact yield 2 per cent in conditions of full employment, are expected to yield less than nothing; and the resulting col-

[1] *The General Theory of Employment, Interest, and Money,* Harcourt, Brace, New York, 1936, p. 148.

lapse of new investment then leads to a state of unemployment in which the investments, which would have yielded 2 per cent in conditions of full employment, in fact yield less than nothing.[2]

It is difficult to assess the relative importance of the state of "business psychology" as a determinant of the marginal efficiency of capital. It can easily be overstressed as a determinant of expectations. We should be quite suspicious of explanations based solely on mob psychology and ignoring such basic factors as the supply of capital goods relative to other factors of production, the state of technology and its rate of advance, the rate of growth of population, and so on. On the other hand, explanations based solely on these basic factors and their rate of change cannot deal adequately with short-run and cyclical shifts of the marginal efficiency of capital.

In any case, the schedule of the marginal efficiency of capital is capable of wide shifts. This should be borne in mind for two reasons. (1) When we draw an investment demand schedule to show the effects of interest rates on investment demand, we are assuming that the schedule of the marginal efficiency of capital is given and constant. (2) We shall later want to deal with upward and downward shifts of the investment demand schedule and their effects on Y. An upward shift of the II curve, an increase of investment demand at each interest rate, may be brought about by any force that raises the marginal efficiency of capital schedule. The II curve may be shifted downward at each level of interest rates by anything that lowers the marginal efficiency of capital schedule.

THE MARGINAL RESPONSIVENESS OF INVESTMENT DEMAND TO INTEREST RATES

Let us now return to the investment demand curve that is drawn on the assumption that the marginal efficiency of capital is given and constant, and which therefore enables us to consider the effects of interest rates on the size of the investment demand for output. In determining the equilibrium level of Y it is sometimes sufficient to know that I tends to be larger when r is lower, and lower when r is higher. For some purposes, however, it is useful to try to quantify this relationship, to ask how much a given change of interest rates would alter the size of the investment demand. We shall call this the "marginal responsiveness of investment to interest rates." By this we shall mean the dollar change in the annual rate of investment expenditure for output in response to a change of 1 percentage point in the interest rate. This can be denoted by $\frac{\Delta I}{\Delta r}$, where ΔI is the change in the investment demand for output and Δr is a change of 1 percentage point in the interest rate. In Fig. 15 $\frac{\Delta I}{\Delta r}$ is clearly larger on the I_0I_0 investment demand curve than

[2] *Ibid.*, p. 322.

it is on the I_1I_1 curve.[3] The change of investment in response to any given change in interest rates (Δr) while the investment demand schedule remains unchanged will depend on the marginal responsiveness of investment and the size or r. Suppose, for example, that investment demand declines $2 billion for every percentage point rise in interest rates, and that interest rates rise by 2 percentage points. The effect will be, of course, to lower investment

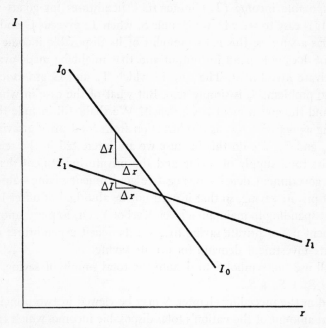

FIG. 15.   The Marginal Responsiveness of Investment to the
Interest Rate.

spendings by $4 billion. But the decline of investment spendings would have been smaller if the marginal responsiveness of investment had been less. We shall find later that differences of opinion with respect to the marginal responsiveness of investment to interest rates underlie much of the controversy concerning the efficacy of monetary policy in regulating the rate of investment.

THE SUPPLY OF SAVING

By the supply of saving we mean a schedule or curve showing the various amounts of saving that would occur in the nation at the various possible levels of GNP, or Y. This is sometimes called a "saving function," showing saving as a function of Y.

[3] An investment demand curve need not, of course, be a straight line, and the value of $\frac{\Delta I}{\Delta r}$ may be different at different ranges of interest rates.

As we found in the preceding chapter, the nation's saving in any period is composed of three parts. (1) Personal saving, or S_p. This is simply that part of disposable personal income that is not spent for consumption. (2) Business gross saving, or S_b. This includes all disposable business income and is composed of capital consumption allowances and undistributed corporate net profits. (3) Government saving, or S_g. This is equal to the government's disposable income (T_n) minus its expenditures for goods and services (G). It is easy to see why we include S_g when T_n exceeds G and the government has a surplus; this is the amount of its disposable income that the government does not spend for output and that might be made available to finance private investment. The case in which T_n and G are exactly equal presents no problem; S_g is simply zero. But what of the case in which G exceeds T_n and the government has a deficit? We shall still include this under total saving as negative S_g—as a subtraction from total private saving in the form of S_p and S_b. We do this because we are interested in the relationship between the total supply of saving and the private investment demand for output. A government deficit—or negative government saving—absorbs that amount of private saving, so that it need not be absorbed or offset by private investment spending to maintain a given level of Y. Or, to put it another way, a government use of private saving to cover its deficit expenditures competes with private investment demand for private saving.

We shall use the symbol S to denote the total supply of saving, which is the sum of $S_p + S_b + S_g$.

As noted in the preceding chapter, S may be viewed in two principal ways. (1) As that amount of the nation's total disposable income, which is equal to expenditures for output, which is not spent for personal consumption or for government purchases of goods and services and is therefore potentially available to finance private investment. Of course, the mere fact that the nation would elect to save some given amount out of some given level of Y does not assure that the saving would be made available to investment spenders or that investment spenders would demand just that quantity of investable funds and spend them for output. We shall later investigate the relationship between the supply of saving and the market supply of investable funds and their relevance to the behavior of interest rates. (2) As that value of the nation's output, at each level of output, that remains after personal consumption and government expenditures. It is this "leftover" supply of output that is available to satisfy investment demand. It is this view of the supply of saving that we shall emphasize in our analysis of the determination of the level of Y. We shall argue that the level of output or gross national income is determined at a level at which the supply of saving (S) is just equal to I, the investment demand for output.

It should be noted that in concentrating our attention on S and I we are not ignoring the other two components of the demand for output, C and G. S is that value of output not taken as C and G; $S = Y - C - G$. Thus when we say that S is $60 billion when Y is $450 billion we are saying that expenditures for output in the form of C and G are $390 billion. It will be useful to remember that when we say that S increases by a certain amount at a given level of Y, this is the same as saying that expenditures in the form of $C + G$ decline by that amount at that level of Y. And when we say that S decreases by a certain amount at a given level of Y, this is equivalent to saying that the effective demand for output in the form of $C + G$ rose by that amount at that level of Y.

As indicated at the beginning of this section, we define the supply of saving as a schedule, curve, or function showing the various amounts of saving that would occur in the nation at the various possible levels of Y. Such a supply curve or function is depicted in **Fig. 16**. The supply of saving is measured

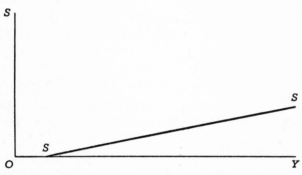

FIG. 16.   A Saving Supply Function.

along the vertical axis, the level of Y along the horizontal axis. This is much like the ordinary supply curve except that it relates quantities supplied to the level of output or income rather than to price. As usual, we are interested in two aspects of supply. (1) In isolating the effect of changes in the level of income on the quantities of saving supplied. In order to do this we must assume that all other conditions affecting supply are given and constant. The supply curve SS in Fig. 16 is drawn on this assumption. (2) In the quantity of saving supplied at each level of Y. For example, why at each level of Y is the supply of saving neither higher nor lower? What forces can shift SS upward, indicating a greater supply of saving at each level of Y? What forces can shift it downward, indicating a smaller supply of saving at each level of Y? Let us consider some of these questions.

Determinants of the Supply of Saving at a Given Level of Y

Since the total supply of saving is the sum of government saving, gross business saving, and personal saving we shall begin by looking at some of the forces determining the quantities of saving supplied by each of these types of savers at a given level of Y.

1. Government saving. Since this is equal to $(T_n - G)$ it reflects government policies relative to taxation, transfer payments, and expenditures for goods and services. Depending on the nature of these policies, $(T_n - G)$ at any given level of Y may be positive and large, zero, or negative. To explain the government's actual policies, one would have to delve into all the forces brought to bear on the government, and into the response of the government to them. The government can increase its saving at any given level of Y by increasing its tax collections at that level of Y, by lowering its transfer payments, by decreasing its expenditures for output, or by any combination of these that increases $(T_n - G)$. However, a given increase in the government's saving may not raise total saving by the same amount, for by lowering disposable private income the government may reduce private saving somewhat.

2. Gross business saving. This, as we have seen, is composed of capital consumption allowances and undistributed net profits. The size of capital consumption allowances varies with the size of the stock of business capital subject to depreciation and business policies relative to depreciation. Gross saving in this form may be small if business depreciates its capital only over a very long period, writing off only a small fraction of its value each year. But it may be large if business follows very "conservative" policies, writing off a large fraction each year. Gross saving in this form is very large in the United States, partly because of the huge stock of business capital and partly because of the generally conservative depreciation policies of business. The volume of business saving at any given level of Y in the form of undistributed net profits after taxes depends on the amount of these net profits at that level of Y and also on the policies of corporations pertaining to the retention and distribution of profits. Thus, the volume of gross business saving at any given level of Y can be shifted by anything that changes the stock of depreciable business capital, business depreciation policies, business net profits after taxes, or corporate policies relative to the retention and distribution of net profits.

3. Personal saving. The supply of personal saving at any level of Y depends on the size of personal disposable income at that level of Y and on the choices of households in dividing their disposable income between consumption and saving. Since disposable personal income at any level of Y is equal to Y minus T_n and S_b, it can be shifted downward at any level of Y by anything that increases $T_n + S_b$, or shifted upward by decreases of $T_n + S_b$. How households divide a given level of disposable income between consumption and saving depends on a host of economic and social conditions: on such things as attitudes toward present consumption as against provisions for the future, on their responsiveness to advertisements for consumers' goods as against admoni-

tions to save and grow rich, on the distribution of income among households that have higher and lower propensities to save, and so on. How much they will save out of a given level of Y may depend in part on the value of assets they have already accumulated. If their assets are already very large they may save less than they would if their accumulated assets were smaller. Thus a great rise in stock market prices, raising the values of outstanding claims to wealth, might increase consumption and lower saving at a given level of Y, and a sharp fall of stock prices might have the opposite effect.

How does the level of interest rates affect the supply of saving out of any given level of Y? Some economists argue that since interest is a reward for saving, if the resulting savings are put to work, a rise of interest rates will increase the supply of saving at any level of Y, and a decline of interest rates will decrease saving and raise consumption at each level of Y. Others deny that the supply of saving is responsive to interest rates, or at least minimize the degree of responsiveness. Some even go so far as to claim that the relationship may be the reverse; that at higher interest rates people will save less out of a given level of Y than they would if interest rates were lower. The reason for this, they argue, is that the higher are interest rates the less need one save in order to achieve any given level of future income. We shall not here take any position on these issues. However, in the analysis that follows we shall assume the supply of saving at each level of Y is not responsive to interest rates. We do this largely to avoid certain complexities that would otherwise result. But if the reader is willing to risk increased complexity, he may introduce any assumptions that he considers reasonable concerning the responsiveness of the supply of saving to interest rates.

In summary, we have considered in this section some of the conditions determining the supply of saving at any level of Y. These are the types of conditions that we must assume to be given and constant when we draw a supply curve of saving, such as the SS curve in Fig. 16, which isolates the effect of changes in the level of Y on the quantities of saving supplied. Shifts in conditions such as these can bring about upward and downward shifts of the SS curve at each level of Y.

The Marginal Propensity to Save

Let us return now to the SS curve, or saving function, in Fig. 16. This, as we have already seen, isolates the effects of changes in the level of Y on the quantities of saving supplied. For the purpose of analyzing static equilibrium, it is usually sufficient to know that the SS curve slopes upward to the right—that the higher the level of Y the greater will be S. But for analyzing changes in Y we need to quantify the responsiveness of S to Y—to ask how much S will change in response to any given change in Y. Using a term coined and popularized by the late J. M. Keynes, we shall call this the "marginal propensity to save." The marginal propensity to save, sometimes called the MPS, is defined as the change in saving (ΔS), in response to a change in the level of Y, (ΔY), this being stated as a fraction. Thus, MPS = $\frac{\Delta S}{\Delta Y}$. For example, suppose that the supply of saving changes $.25 for every $1 change in Y. Then MPS = $\frac{.25}{1} = \frac{1}{4}$. We shall refer to MPS or $\frac{\Delta S}{\Delta Y}$ repeatedly, for it plays a central role in determining the response of Y to changes in such things as I and G and upward and downward shifts of the SS curve.

Since the total supply of saving (S) is the sum of $S_g + S_b + S_p$, a change in S, (ΔS), is the sum of the changes of these components. Thus,

$$\Delta S = \Delta S_g + \Delta S_b + \Delta S_p$$

Other conditions remaining constant, a rise of Y tends to increase all these components, and a fall of Y to reduce all of them.

With a given tax and expenditure program, government saving ($T_n - G$) tends to rise and fall with Y, though not by the same amount. T_n is especially responsive to Y, as suggested in Fig. 17. This is largely because actual tax

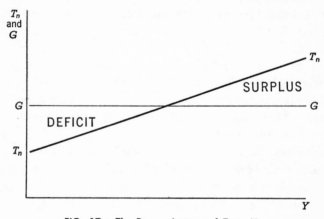

FIG. 17.   The Responsiveness of T_n to Y.

collections are responsive to Y, but partly because certain types of transfer payments tend to vary inversely with the level of Y. Actual tax yields are responsive to Y because of the nature of our most important taxes. These are not fixed in absolute amounts; rather, the tax laws define the tax base, or the types of things subject to tax, and prescribe tax rates to apply to the tax base. For example, they include in the tax base personal incomes, corporate net profits, the production, sale, or purchase of commodities and services, and so on. They also prescribe tax rates to apply to these bases. Some of these are percentages of money value; others are stated as amounts per physical unit, such as per gallon of distilled spirits, per 20 cigarettes, and so on. Thus with no changes in the tax laws, a rise of Y increases the value of the tax base and raises total tax collections. At the effective tax rates prevailing in the late

1950's, it is probable that a \$1 change in Y would automatically change government revenues by at least 25 cents and probably more. The responsiveness of T_n to Y is also enhanced by the nature of some of the government's transfer payment programs. If a decline of Y is reflected in lessened employment, there will be increased transfer payments in the form of unemployment compensation, relief, and social security payments to the aged who may remain at work if employment opportunities are ample but who retire and claim their benefits if they lose their jobs.

Thus we see that even if G remains constant, the high responsiveness of T_n to the level of Y makes government saving $(T_n - G)$ rise as Y rises and fall as Y falls. With an unchanged tax and expenditure program, the government may exactly balance its budget at some level of Y, have surpluses (or positive saving) at higher levels of Y, and deficits (or negative saving) at lower levels of Y. This "automatic flexibility" of T_n—the automatic responsiveness of tax collections and transfer payments to changes in Y without any changes in government policy—is a source of bitter unhappiness to those who would like to see the government's budget balanced at all times. But it is a source of satisfaction to those who want government fiscal policy to contribute to economic stability, or at least to lessen the degree of instability. The automatic decrease of tax collections and increase of transfer payments as Y falls prevents the decline of Y from being reflected fully in decreased private disposable incomes, thereby helping to sustain private demands for output. On the other hand, the automatic increase of tax collections and decline of transfer payments as Y rises prevents the rise of Y from being reflected fully in increased disposable private incomes, thereby damping the rise of private demand for output. This can be very useful in times of inflationary pressure.

Gross business saving also tends to vary with the level of Y. Business net profits usually rise with Y and business usually retains some part of the increase. On the other hand, when business profits fall with declines of Y, business usually decreases its saving in the form of undistributed profits. Capital consumption allowances are ordinarily less responsive to changes in Y.

Changes in the level of Y are reflected to a large extent in changes in disposable personal incomes, and households ordinarily use a change in their disposable incomes to change both their rate of consumption and their rate of saving. They use a large part of any increase in their disposable incomes to increase their rate of consumption expenditures, but a small part to increase their rate of saving. Similarly, a decline in their disposable incomes is usually reflected largely in decreased consumption spendings but some of it is reflected in a decreased rate of saving.

Later, as we use the MPS, or $\frac{\Delta S}{\Delta Y}$, in our analysis, it will be useful to remember that this reflects not only the responsiveness of personal saving to changes in Y but also the responsiveness of government and business saving.

INVESTMENT DEMAND AND THE SUPPLY OF SAVING

Having investigated both the investment demand for output and the supply of saving, we can now see how these two curves or functions enter into the determination of the equilibrium level of Y. In this section we shall assume that both functions are given and constant. We assume that the investment demand function, the II curve, is constant, being based on a constant marginal efficiency of capital schedule. We also assume that all other conditions affecting the supply of saving are constant so that the supply of saving depends solely on the level of Y. At this point it will be useful to emphasize the view of the supply of saving as that value of output, at each level of Y, that is "left over" after C and G expenditures. It is the amount that would remain unsold if not absorbed by investment demand.

The first point to be made is essential to all our later analysis: Y *can be at an equilibrium level only when the investment demand for output is exactly equal to the supply of saving.* Note that we say only that this is a *necessary* condition for an equilibrium level of Y; we do not say that it is always a *sufficient* condition to establish a unique equilibrium level for Y. However, for the sake of simplicity let us start with a case in which the condition $I = S$ is not only necessary but also sufficient to establish a unique equilibrium level for Y. In Fig. 18 both I and S are measured on the vertical axis; the level of Y on the horizontal axis. For the sake of simplicity we assume that invest-

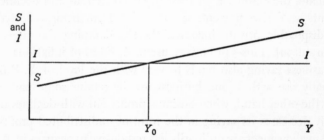

FIG. 18. The Equality of Investment Demand and the Supply of Saving.

ment is some fixed quantity measured by the vertical distance from the horizontal axis to the II curve.

Given the II and SS functions, the only equilibrium level of Y is Y_0. Only at this level of Y is the investment demand for output exactly equal to the supply of output represented by the supply of saving, that is, to the supply of output in excess of the amount taken off the market by C and G. Only at this level of Y is the market just cleared of output, with neither excess demand nor excess supply. Any level of Y greater than Y_0 would be one of disequilibrium, for the supply of output represented by saving would exceed investment demand; some part of the supply would not be cleared from the market. If such a situation occurred, producers might immediately respond by reducing their rate of output, thus lowering Y. If they do not respond quickly enough, some of their output will pile up in "unwanted" inventories, which will lead them to cut production later to get rid of their excess stocks. In this process they may temporarily reduce their output below Y_0 until their excess inventories have been sold off.

Any level of output below Y_0 would be one of disequilibrium, for at lower levels of Y the investment demand for output would exceed the supply of output represented by saving. Faced by such a situation of excess demand, producers might immediately increase their rate of output, thereby raising the level of Y. If they do not step up output fast enough, they will experience an "unwanted" depletion of their inventories, which will lead them to step up production later to rebuild their stocks. In this process they may temporarily raise their rate of output above Y_0 until their inventories have been replenished.

In the case above the condition $I = S$ was a sufficient as well as a necessary condition to determine a unique level of Y only because investment demand was assumed to be one fixed quantity. Let us return now to a more realistic case in which investment demand is not a fixed quantity, but depends on the rate of interest (r), tending to be greater at lower rates of interest. We shall find that in this case $I = S$ is still a necessary condition for an equilibrium level of Y; the latter cannot be in equilibrium if I and S are not equal. But this condition alone is not sufficient to determine a unique equilibrium level of Y. Since the size of I depends on the level of interest rates, there may be many levels of Y at which the $I = S$ condition is satisfied.

This is illustrated in Fig. 19. The vertical scales in Parts A and B of Fig. 19 are the same, so that the same vertical heights indicate equal amounts of S and I. Even a casual inspection of the two upper graphs reveals that there are various combinations of interest rates and income levels that will produce the condition $I = S$. For example, $S = I$ at the low vertical level $I_0 S_0$ if r is at the high level r_0, thereby holding I to a low level, and if Y is at the low level Y_0, thereby generating only a low supply of S. $I = S$ at the somewhat higher level $I_1 S_1$ if the rate of interest is at the lower level r_1, thereby stimulating I, and if Y is at the higher level Y_1, thereby generating a larger supply of saving. $I = S$ at the very high level $I_2 S_2$ if the rate of interest is at the very low level r_2 and income is at the high level Y_2. We might thus note all the possible combinations of interest rate levels and income levels that would produce the condition $I = S$.

This has been done in Part C of Fig. 19. The line $I = S$ plots out all those combinations of r, measured on the vertical axis, and Y, measured on the horizontal axis, at which S and I would be equal. The $I = S$ line slopes downward to the right because the supply of S would be larger at higher levels of income, and with a given investment demand function I can be made correspondingly larger only by a fall of r.

No point representing a combination of r and Y that is off the I = S line can represent equilibrium conditions. For example, consider any point A that lies above the I = S line. At any such point I would be less than S. We know this because at the same level of Y there is some lower rate of interest directly below A on the I = S line at which I is exactly equal to S. If by some chance

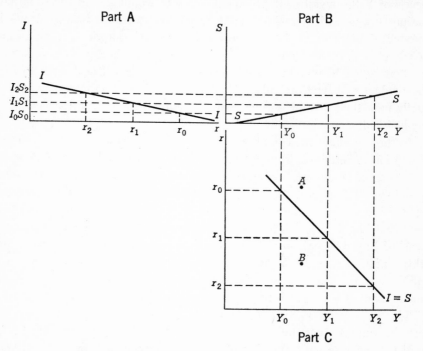

FIG. 19.   Investment Demand and the Supply of Saving.

the combination of r and Y represented by point A should occur, the excess of S over I could be remedied only by a fall of interest rates to stimulate I, a decline of Y to reduce S, or some combination of changes of r and Y to a point on the I = S line. On the other hand, at any point, such as B, below the I = S line, I would be greater than S. We know this because at the same level of Y there is some higher rate of interest directly above B on the I = S line at which I is exactly equal to S. A disequilibrium combination such as B could be remedied only by a rise of r to reduce I, an increase of Y to increase S, or a combination of changes of r and Y to a point on the I = S line.

In summary, we find that Y can be in equilibrium only if I and S are exactly equal. This is always a necessary condition. But it is not sufficient to determine a unique equilibrium level for Y if S is at all responsive to Y and I is at all responsive to r. There are as many possible equilibrium levels of Y as there are rates of I, and I depends on the rate of interest. We must therefore know what the market rate of interest is before we can know what the level of income will be. This we cannot determine from our analysis up to this point. What is missing? What must we introduce into our analysis to complete it? The answer is, an analysis of the supply of and demand for money. Only when these are added will we be able to determine the market rate of interest and a unique equilibrium level of Y. We also need to introduce the supply of money and the demand for money for another reason. Throughout this chapter we have assumed a given and constant average level of prices for output. In effect, our analysis of S, I, and Y was in real terms. Only after we have analyzed the supply of money and the demand for money can we know what price level of output is consistent with equilibrium.

The following chapter will analyze the supply of money and the demand for money and their roles in determining the levels of interest rates and of national money income. We shall then combine these with our analysis of investment demand and the supply of saving. When we have completed our analysis, we will have found that the level of Y and the level of r are determined simultaneously by four functions or schedules: (1) the investment demand function, (2) the supply of saving function, (3) the supply of money function, and (4) the demand for money function. Moreover, r and Y will be in equilibrium when, and only when, two conditions are met—investment demand and the supply of saving are exactly equal, and the demand for money is exactly equal to the supply of money.

THE MULTIPLIER

Before beginning our study of the supply of money and the demand for money, it will be useful to investigate some of the relationships between the level of r and the level of Y when the II and SS functions are given and constant. For this purpose reference to Fig. 19 will be helpful. Part C in that figure indicates that increases in r are associated with lower levels of Y, and decreases of r with higher levels of Y. This raises several questions: "Why and through what processes will a fall or rise of r tend to increase or decrease Y? How much will Y change in response to a given change of r? What factors determine the amount of the response of Y to a given change in r?" To answer these questions let us assume some given decrease in r. The same increase of r would have the opposite effects.

The first effect of the decrease in r is, of course, to increase the investment demand for output. This directly increases Y by the same amount, for I is a component of Y. The size of this increase depends on the marginal responsiveness of investment demand to interest rates, which we defined earlier as $\frac{\Delta I}{\Delta r}$, or the dollar change in the annual rate of investment expenditures in response to a change of 1 percentage point in interest rates. The actual change in I will be equal to the change in interest rates (Δr) times $\frac{\Delta I}{\Delta r}$. Suppose, for example, that interest rates fall by 2 percentage points and that I rises by $2 billion for each percentage point decline in r. In this case I would rise $4 billion. But the same decline of r would raise I by $8 billion if I responded by rising $4 billion for each percentage point decline in r. Let us assume that the latter is the actual case and that the given decline of r raises I by $8 billion. This raises Y by the same amount. But is this the end of the story? An inspection of Fig. 19 suggests that it is not, for a rise of I induced by a fall of r seems to raise Y by some multiple amount. In other words $\frac{\Delta Y}{\Delta I}$ is greater than 1. This must occur because Y can be in equilibrium only if $S = I$, and with an increase of I by the amount ΔI, S must increase the same amount to produce a new equilibrium level of Y. With a fixed SS function, S can be increased only by an increase of Y. How much must Y increase in order to increase S by $1? This depends on the size of our old friend, the marginal propensity to save, $\frac{\Delta S}{\Delta Y}$. If the nation changes S only $.25 for each $1 change of Y, a $4 change in Y is required to change S by $1. But if it changes S by $.50 for each $1 change in Y, only a $2 change in Y is required to change S by $1. Stated more generally, the change in Y required to change S by $1 is equal to $\frac{1}{\Delta S/\Delta Y}$. This is 5 if $\frac{\Delta S}{\Delta Y} = \frac{1}{5}$, 4 if $\frac{\Delta S}{\Delta Y} = \frac{1}{4}$, 2 if $\frac{\Delta S}{\Delta Y} = \frac{1}{2}$ and so on. This is usually called "the multiplier." It is equal to $\frac{\Delta Y}{\Delta I}$ and reflects the *multiple* of ΔI that Y must change in order to change S by an amount equal to ΔI. This may be written as

$$\Delta Y = \Delta I \times \frac{1}{\Delta S/\Delta Y}$$

For example, suppose that ΔI is an increase of $8 billion. If the multiplier is 4 the equilibrium level of Y will be increased by $32 billion. With an MPS of ¼ this rise of Y is required to raise S enough to match the $8 billion rise of I. If the multiplier is 2 the equilibrium level of Y will be increased by only $16 billion. With a higher MPS of ½ only this smaller rise of Y is required to raise S by $8 billion. In the case below we shall assume that MPS = ¼ and the multiplier is 4.

In the example above we found that a rise of investment expenditures of $8 billion raised the equilibrium level of Y by $32 billion. Where did the other $24 billion rise of expenditures for output come from? It came from an induced rise of consumption expenditures.[4] We assumed that the

---

[4] We assume here that government expenditures for output (G) remain constant so that the only changes in expenditures for output are in I and C.

nation used $\frac{1}{4}$ of each increase of Y to increase S in the form of government saving, gross business saving, and personal saving. The remainder of each increase of Y, or $\frac{3}{4}$, is used to increase its rate of consumption expenditures. This change of C in response to a change of Y, stated as a fraction, $\frac{\Delta C}{\Delta Y}$, is called "the marginal propensity to consume." It is sometimes abbreviated as MPC. Since a nation can use a change of its income only to change S and C, MPC + MPS = 1. For example, if MPS = $\frac{1}{4}$, MPC must = $\frac{3}{4}$. Since MPS = 1 − MPC, we can also express the multiplier, earlier written as $\frac{1}{\Delta S/\Delta Y}$, as $\frac{1}{1 - \Delta C/\Delta Y}$. Both must have the same value.

The multiplier process can best be illustrated by tracing out the consequences if I rises by $8 billion and MPC = $\frac{3}{4}$. The rise of I increases by $8 billion the incomes of those employed in the capital goods industries. These people use $\frac{3}{4}$ of this rise of income to increase their consumption expenditures by $6 billion, thereby raising the incomes of the recipients. They, in turn, raise their consumption expenditures by $\frac{3}{4}$ of $6 billion, or 4\frac{1}{2}$ billion, thereby increasing the incomes of the recipients. These recipients increase their consumption by $\frac{3}{4}$ of 4\frac{1}{2}$ billion, or 3\frac{1}{3}$ billion. And so on. If we followed the whole process through until a new equilibrium level of Y was reached, we would find that the initial rise of I had brought about a $32 billion rise of Y, of which $8 billion represented the rise of I and $24 billion the induced rise of C. The reader is invited to compare the results if MPC were $\frac{1}{2}$ instead of $\frac{3}{4}$.

It should be evident that the multiplier may operate in the downward direction as well as the upward. For example, an $8 billion decline of I would lower the equilibrium level of Y $32 billion if MPC = $\frac{3}{4}$ and MPS = $\frac{1}{4}$.

The multiplier is not brought into play solely by changes in I induced by changes in r. It also operates in response to shifts of I reflecting shifts in the marginal efficiency of capital, to upward and downward shifts of G, and to upward and downward shifts of the SS function. Such shifts will play prominent roles in our later analysis. The multiplier serves a highly useful purpose by highlighting the fact that changes in one type of expenditures may induce changes in others, and the latter may be large relative to the initial change.

SUMMARY

Some of our most important findings in this chapter are the following:
1. The investment demand function or schedule for output stated as a function of interest rates assumes that other conditions affecting investment demand are given and constant. It therefore isolates the effects of

changes in interest rates on the rate of expenditures for investment. We called this "the marginal responsiveness of investment demand to interest rates." But we are also interested in the amount of investment demand at each level of interest rates. We therefore studied the marginal efficiency of capital and some of the principal factors that determine the level of investment demand at each interest rate at a point of time, and that are capable of shifting the investment demand function upward and downward through time.

2. The supply of saving function or schedule, stated as a function of the level of income or output, assumes that other conditions affecting S are given and constant. It therefore isolates the effects of changes in the level of Y on the size of S. We called this responsiveness of S to Y "the marginal propensity to save," or $\frac{\Delta S}{\Delta Y}$. Assuming G to be constant, this is equal to 1 minus the "marginal propensity to consume," or $\frac{\Delta C}{\Delta Y}$, meaning by the latter the fraction of any change of Y that is used to change C. Thus

$$\frac{\Delta C}{\Delta Y} + \frac{\Delta S}{\Delta Y} = 1$$

However, we also discussed some of the principal forces that determine the amount of S at each given level of Y, and that can shift the SS curve upward and downward.

3. Y can be in equilibrium only if $I = S$. An excess of S over I would mean that some part of the output "left over" after consumption and government purchases would not be taken off the market by investment demand and would remain unsold. This excess supply of output, or deficient demand for output, would induce a decrease of Y. On the other hand, an excess of I over S would mean that the demand for output would be in excess of the supply "left over" after consumption and government purchases. This excess demand, or deficient supply, would induce producers to try to expand their output, thus raising Y. But if the economy is already operating at capacity levels, the effect may be only to raise the price level of output.

4. The condition, $I = S$, is always a necessary condition for an equilibrium level of Y. But it is also a sufficient condition to determine a unique equilibrium level of Y only if I is a fixed quantity. Where I is responsive to r, there is a different equilibrium level of Y for every level of r and its accompanying level of I. Only when we know the level of r can we determine what Y will be. To do this we must bring in the supply of money and the demand for money.

5. An increase or decrease of interest rates, with given II and SS functions, can decrease or increase the level of Y not only by changing I but also by inducing changes in C. The size of the effect of any given change in r

depends on the size of the change in interest rates (Δr), the marginal responsiveness of investment to interest rates $\frac{\Delta I}{\Delta r}$, and the size of the multiplier $\frac{1}{\Delta S/\Delta Y}$, or $\frac{1}{1 - \Delta C/\Delta Y}$. We may express this as

$$\Delta Y = \Delta r \times \frac{\Delta I}{\Delta r} \times \frac{1}{\Delta S/\Delta Y}$$

The multiplier operates downward as well as upward.

6. Multiplier effects may follow not only changes in I induced by changes in r; they may also follow changes in I reflecting shifts in the marginal efficiency of capital, shifts of G, and upward and downward shifts of the SS function.

SELECTED READINGS

Hicks, J. R., "Mr. Keynes and the 'Classics,' a Suggested Interpretation," *Econometrica*, 1937, Vol. V, pp. 147–159.

Keynes, J. M., *The General Theory of Employment, Interest, and Money*, Harcourt, Brace, New York, 1936.

CHAPTER 14

The Supply of Money and the Demand for Money

In the preceding chapter we found that we could not determine the price level of output, and usually not the rate of real output or the level of interest rates, by dealing only with the investment demand function and the supply of saving function. We also need to consider the supply of money and the demand for money. We shall find that equilibrium requires not only that $I = S$ but also that the demand for money be equal to the supply of money available for holding.

THE SUPPLY OF MONEY

Having discussed this at length in earlier sections, we can deal with it summarily here. It will be sufficient to note that the supply of money is the stock of things generally accepted as a medium of exchange, and that we assume in this section that the monetary authority adamantly keeps this stock at a fixed quantity. It successfully prevents the supply of money from rising or falling in response to increases or decreases in the demand for it. Other types of money supply functions and shifts in the supply of money will be discussed later.

One consequence of this assumption of a rigidly fixed money supply should be noted. If the quantity of money available for holding (M) does not change, the demand for money must be brought into equality with the supply through adjustments in the quantities demanded. Excesses of the supply of money over the demand for it must be eradicated by increases in the quantity of money demanded. And excesses in the quantity demanded over the available supply of money must be corrected by some sort of development lowering the quantity demanded.

THE DEMAND FOR MONEY

The demand for money has already been discussed briefly. By it we mean the quantities of money balances that the members of the nation demand to hold. If their actual balances, which are determined by the money supply, are in excess of the demanded balances, they try to get rid of the excess by increasing their rate of expenditures for other things. If their actual balances are below the demanded level, they try to repair the deficiency by decreasing their rate of expenditures. We shall now broaden and deepen this analysis, investigating the motives for holding and not holding money and looking at some of the factors determining the quantities of money balances demanded.

The demand for money clearly is not just one fixed quantity; its size varies with some other things. Like other types of demand, it must be stated as some sort of schedule, curve, or function. We shall state it as a function of both the level of national money income (Y) and the level of interest rates (r). As in other cases, we shall also investigate the forces that determine the quantities of money demanded at each level of Y and r and that are therefore capable of shifting these demand functions.

As a first step we shall divide the total demand for money, which we shall denote by L, into two parts. One part is the transactions demand for money, which we shall call L_1. This is the demand for money to be used as a means of payments—to purchase goods and services, and so on. These are sometimes called "active balances" because they flit from payer to payee. The other part may be called the store of value demand, for it is the demand for money not for the purpose of making payments but as a form of holding wealth or assets. We shall call this the L_2 demand for money. These are sometimes called "idle" or "inactive" balances. This does not mean they are performing no function; they are meeting the community's demand for assets in the form of money. But the dollars in these balances are "inactive" in the sense that they are not serving as a means of payment; they are not being spent. The total demand for money is the sum of the L_1 and L_2 demands. That is,

$$L = L_1 + L_2$$

Let us look at these in turn.

The Transactions Demand for Money

The transactions demand for money is not made up solely of balances held for the purpose of spending for output at its final stage of sale in the form of C, I, and G. It includes balances held to make payments for things that do not enter into Y at all: for such things as land, existing buildings and second-hand goods, payments in the various intermediate stages of production and distribution, payments in the form of wages, interest, dividends, and so on. This does not, however, prevent our relating the transactions demand for money to the level of Y. We take account of these other payments by noting that their existence leads the demand for money at any given level of Y to be higher than it would be in their absence. Moreover, a rise or fall of these transactions can increase or decrease the demand for transactions balances at each level of Y. In general, however, these other payments tend to move parallel with Y.

The quantities of money balances demanded for transactions purposes varies with: (1) The money value of Y. Note that Y is real output times the average price of output. It will be useful to remember that a rise or fall of prices tends, by raising or lowering the money value of transactions payments, to increase or decrease the quantity of money demanded. That the community's demand for money balances tends to vary with the money value of its income transactions is plausible. For example, a household is likely to want to hold larger money balances when its expenditures for output are at an annual rate of $5000 than when these expenditures are lower. So with business firms; their demanded money balances are likely to vary with the size of their payrolls, their rate of expenditures for raw materials, components, fuels, new capital goods, and so on. (2) The quantity of money balances demanded for transactions purposes at any given level of Y, this quantity being stated as a fraction of Y. We shall call this fraction j; it is $\frac{L_1}{Y}$. For example, it might be $\frac{1}{5}$, indicating that at each point of time the members of the community in the aggregate demand transactions balances equal to $\frac{1}{5}$ of their annual rate of expenditures for output. The quantities of these balances actually demanded (L_1) is therefore $L_1 = Y \times \frac{L_1}{Y}$, or $L_1 = j \times Y$. For example, if $Y = \$450$ billion and $\frac{L_1}{Y} = \frac{1}{5}$, $L_1 = \$90$ billion. When we state the transactions demand for money as a function of the level of Y, we must assume that other conditions affecting this demand for money are given and constant so that we can isolate the effects of changes of Y on the quantities of money demanded. Let us now investigate some of the principal factors that determine the size of j, or $\frac{L_1}{Y}$, at any time and that are capable of increasing or decreasing it.

Determinants of the Size of j, or L_1/Y

We may assume that both households and business firms arrive at their decisions concerning the size of their money balances for transactions purposes by balancing, in at least a rough way, the benefits and costs of holding the various possible amounts of money relative to their rate of expenditures. The benefits are those of a medium of payments—the possession of something that remains fixed in terms of the monetary unit in which most contracts are stated and that will be accepted by almost everyone at face value in payment of debts and in the purchase of goods and services. But holding money costs something—the forgone pleasure of consuming immediately the goods or services that the money balances could be used to buy, or interest on outstanding debt that the money balance might be used to retire, or the forgone income on earning assets that could be purchased by getting rid of the money. Though the calculus lacks precision in many cases, each money-holding unit seeks to avoid holding money whose benefits are less than the costs involved, and it seeks to add to its balances when the addition is expected to yield greater benefits than costs.

Households and business firms hold money balances for transactions purposes because they think they will, or may, want to make expenditures before they enjoy a sufficient inflow of money receipts. They might hold little or no money if they were assured that money would flow to them in sufficient volume just a moment before they wanted to spend. But they usually have no such assurance. They therefore elect to hold some money to cover the excess of their expenditures over their receipts during some period. This is true even if they can forecast perfectly and confidently both the amounts and timing of their expenditures and receipts. For example, a household may know exactly what it is going to spend during the remainder of the month but also that it will receive no further income until the end of the month. Or a business firm may forecast perfectly both its flow of cash receipts and its flow of expenditures but know that for some time its expenditures will exceed its receipts. But forecasts of cash receipts and expenditures can rarely be made with such precision and confidence. Expected receipts may fail to materialize, or highly important expenditures may be earlier or larger than anticipated, or unusually attractive bargains may become available. Some money balances are held against such contingencies.

What factors determine the size of the $\frac{L_1}{Y}$ that the members of the community consider to be most advantageous, considering both benefits and costs? Some of the most important of these are suggested in Table 39.

TABLE 39.   Some Determinants of $\frac{L_1}{Y}$, or j [1]

I. The system of payments in the community.
   1. The frequency of receipts and payments.
   2. The regularity of money receipts and disbursements.
   3. The ease and certainty of securing credit.
   4. The extent of barter.
II. The number of times that currently produced goods and services are sold for money in the processes of production and distribution.
III. The value of transactions in goods other than those included in current output.
IV. The rapidity of transportation of money.
V. The state of the community's expectations.
   1. As to the future money incomes.
   2. As to the future prices of commodities and services.
VI. The height of interest rates.

In general, j tends to be smaller as the length of the period between in-

[1] For many of these points, see Irving Fisher, *The Purchasing Power of Money*, Macmillan, New York, 1926, pp. 79–89. Professor Fisher's analysis aimed at explaining the velocity of money.

come receipts is shortened. To illustrate this, let us consider a family that holds both its money income receipts and its expenditures at a constant rate of $7200 a year, and spends its income at a constant rate of $20 a day. (We neglect here the other five days of the year; they would complicate our arithmetic.) (1) Suppose it receives all its income at the beginning of the year, that its money balance is $7200 just after it receives its income, and that its balance is zero at the end of the year. Its average transactions balance during the year is $3600 and its j is $\frac{3600}{7200}$, or $\frac{1}{2}$. (2) Suppose it receives $600 each month and spends all this during the month. Its average balance will be $300 and its j will be $\frac{300}{7200}$, or $\frac{1}{24}$. Shortening the income period to a week would reduce j still further. We find, then, that one important determinant of the size of j is the length of the average income period in the community.

Another is the regularity of receipts and disbursements. If people and business firms receive predictably stable amounts of money at regular intervals, they are likely to feel free to spend most of it before the next date they are to receive money. But if receipts are highly unstable and unpredictable, they are likely to feel a need to hold more money to tide them over lean periods.

The size of j also depends in part on the ease and certainty of securing credit. If credit were unavailable, or were available only uncertainly and on onerous terms, both households and business firms would find it advantageous to hold large money balances relative to their expenditures. But if financial institutions and the use of credit are highly developed, the community may hold smaller transactions balances relative to their expenditures. Consumers need not accumulate large balances to pay for an expensive item, such as a car or TV set; they buy it "on credit" and pay so much each payday. They need not hold balances to cover their expenditures between paydays; they "charge it" and pay when they receive income. So with business; it need not hold as much money relative to its expenditures if it is assured of credit to meet excesses of expenditures over receipts.

A widespread use of barter tends to decrease the quantity of transactions balances demanded relative to the value of output. When goods and services are bartered directly for each other, less money is needed. But as barter declines and the economy becomes more and more a "money economy," the transactions need for money tends to rise relative to the value of output. Changes in this factor are usually small in the short run, but may be important over longer periods of economic development.

The greater the number of times that currently produced goods and services are sold for money in the process of production and distribution, the larger is j likely to be. Suppose, for example, that in producing a certain product all the processes of producing the raw material, fabricating, jobbing, wholesaling, and retailing are carried out by different firms, and that all payments among them are made with money. The transactions demand for money relative to the final value of output is likely to be large. But j is likely to be smaller if all these processes are combined within vertically integrated firms with no money payments among the departments of each firm.

The same principle applies to the value of transactions in goods other than those included in current output—in such things as securities, land, existing stocks of building and equipment, and so on. The larger these are, relative to Y, the larger is j likely to be.

The more rapid the transportation of money, the lower does j tend to be. For example, j may be large if money does not reach its receiver until two weeks after it left the spender; in the meantime it is not available for respending. But j may be much smaller if money is received within a day or so and is available quickly for respending.

The size of j is also affected by the community's expectations as to the certainty and size of its future income receipts. Suppose, for example, that at some time the community comes to fear that its future income receipts will be less certain and may decline seriously. Its members may try to build up their money balances to tide them over the feared or expected lean period. But if they come to believe that the flow of income receipts will rise markedly in the future they may decrease their money holdings relative to their current rate of expenditure; that is, they may increase their current rate of expenditures relative to their money balances.

Expectations concerning the future behavior of prices are also relevant to the size of j. If the members of the community believe that the prices of the things they intend to buy will remain stable, that a dollar will buy in the future just what it will buy today, they may elect to hold one quantity of money relative to their expenditures. They are likely to increase j if they expect prices to fall. Both business and consumers may postpone purchases and hold larger balances relative to expenditures. They may elect to hold money, which they expect to increase in purchasing power, rather than inventories of goods that they expect to depreciate relative to money. They try to do this by decreasing their expenditures. Expectations of higher prices have the reverse effects; the members of the community are likely to try to hold smaller balances relative to their expenditures. They try to buy before prices rise. In hyperinflations, such as that in Germany after World War I, j falls to very low levels. When members of the community come to fear that each monetary unit will lose half or more of its purchasing power in a day or two, they try to avoid holding money. They refuse to accept money for their goods and services, resorting to barter instead, or if they sell for money they race to get rid of it immediately.

We noted earlier that interest is a cost of holding money, for the holder could use it to retire outstanding debt, thereby lowering his interest costs, or to buy earning assets, thereby earning interest income. Thus a rise of interest rates may induce some to reduce their money balances relative to their expenditures, and a fall of interest rates may have the reverse effect. It will be convenient to include the interest effect on the demand for transactions balances along with the interest effects on the demand for store of value or L_2 balances. These will be discussed later.

In summary, we have noted in this section some of the most important conditions affecting the size of $\frac{L_1}{Y}$, or j. These are the conditions that we must assume to be given and constant when we state the transactions demand for money as a function of the level of Y in order to isolate the effects of changes in Y on the size of L_1. They are also the types of conditions whose shifts can shift j upward and downward. It will be noted that some of these conditions reflect institutional, structural, and customary conditions that usually change only slowly. Among these are the customary length of income periods, the state of development of lending institutions and sources of credit, the extent of barter, the structure of production and distribution and the average number of times each unit of output is sold for money in the production-distribution process, and the rapidity of transportation of money. The relative stability of these factors in the short run tends to make j stable. But some of the conditions—such as expectations with respect to future incomes and prices—may be unstable in the short run and can shift j upward and downward over short periods.

In the process of analyzing the determination of the size of j, we have also analyzed the determination of the income velocity of transactions balances —the average number of times each dollar of these active balances is spent for Y each year. The income velocity of these active balances is simply the reciprocal of j. Whereas $j = \frac{L_1}{Y}$, the income velocity of the balances represented by L_1 is $\frac{Y}{L_1}$. Some economists prefer to analyze $\frac{L_1}{Y}$, noting the way in which the community adjusts its rate of expenditures to achieve the desired ratio. Others prefer to analyze the same problem by using the reciprocal ratio, $\frac{Y}{L_1}$. Both are, of course, essentially the same theory, paying attention to the same sets of conditions, and using essentially the same line of reasoning. In our later analysis it will be useful to remember that the income velocity of transactions balances is the reciprocal of j. Thus if $j = \frac{1}{5}$, it is 5. If $j = \frac{1}{3}$, it is 3.

The Store of Value Demand for Money, L_2

We now turn our attention to money balances demanded not for purposes of spending in the regular course of business or household operations but as a store of value—as a form for holding wealth or assets. Money is not, of course, the only form in which assets can be held. Assets of many forms are available: ownership claims against real estate, durable equipment, and all other forms of physical goods; shares of stock in corporations; debt claims against governmental units, business firms, and individuals; claims against savings banks and savings and loan associations; and so on. The members of the community presumably determine how much money they will hold as a store of value by comparing the benefits and costs of holding money as compared with other assets. As an asset money has certain advantages that other assets lack in some degree. It is perfectly safe in the sense that it remains at face value and does not depreciate in terms of the monetary unit. It is perfectly liquid; it is the only asset that is itself generally acceptable at face value in payment of debt or in the purchase of goods and services without the inconvenience and cost of first being sold for money. But holding money costs something, for money itself ordinarily yields no income other than the convenience, safety, and liquidity that it bears. The cost of holding a money balance is the income, and at some times the probable capital gain, that might be acquired by giving up the money for other assets. Households and business firms presumably balance these types of benefits and costs in determining what part of their total assets to hold in the form of money and what part in other forms.

We shall state the store of value or L_2 demand for money as a function of interest rates (r) in order to isolate the effects of interest rates on the quantities of money demanded for this purpose.[2] First, however, we shall look at some of the factors that determine at any given time the size of L_2 at each given rate of interest and that are capable of increasing or decreasing L_2 at each rate of interest. Some of the most important of these are suggested in Table 40.

TABLE 40.   Some Determinants of the Size of L_2 at
Each Rate of Interest

I. The money value of the nation's total wealth or assets
II. The characteristics and variety of other assets
III. Expectations as to the future prices of other assets

Other things being equal, the richer a nation is in terms of the total money value of its wealth or assets, the higher is likely to be the amount of money that it will elect to hold as an asset. This is not to say that as it is richer it will hold a larger part of its assets in money, only that it will tend to demand a larger absolute amount of money for holding as an asset.

The size of L_2 also depends in part on the variety and characteristics of the other assets available for holding. Imagine, for example, a community with

[2] Note that we also include here the effect of interest rates on the transactions demand for money.

no available assets other than money except ownership claims against physical wealth, and with no specialized means for selling and exchanging these assets, so that they are highly illiquid and the net prices at which they can be sold are highly uncertain. Under such conditions, the L_2 demand at each interest rate would be large indeed. Suppose now that the community develops highly efficient securities markets to permit these claims to be sold quickly and at low cost; that it creates a wide variety of securities ranging from those that are relatively illiquid and risky but offer prospects of high returns to those that are highly safe and liquid but offer lower but still positive returns; and that it develops and popularizes new types of institutions, such as savings banks and savings and loan associations, which create claims against themselves that offer a degree of safety and liquidity approaching that of money itself. Such developments clearly tend to decrease L_2 at each level of interest rates. We shall later see how the development of financial institutions other than commercial banks can decrease L_2, or at least prevent the demand for money as a store of value from rising in proportion to the rise in total wealth, both by increasing the safety and liquidity of existing types of assets and by creating new types of claims with greater safety and liquidity.

Expectations with respect to the future prices of other assets affect the size of L_2 by affecting the benefits and costs of holding money. Expectations of a decline in the prices of other assets increase the expected benefits from holding money; the holder of money escapes an expected decline in the money value of his assets. On the other hand, expectations of a rise in the prices of other assets increase the cost of holding money; holding money involves the sacrifice of an expected gain in the money value of other assets.

For analytical purposes it will be useful to distinguish three different types of expectations as to changes in the future prices of other assets. Other types and combinations of these could occur.

1. Expectations as to changes in the general level of the prices of goods and ownership claims. If the community in general comes to believe that these prices will rise, it will tend to shift its preference toward holding these things and away from holding money and debt obligations whose prices are relatively fixed in terms of money. If it comes to feel that these things are likely to fall in price, it will shift its preferences away from them and toward money and debt obligations.

2. Expectations of changes in the prices of other assets because of changes in expectations regarding the receipt of income on them or of principal repayments. For example, suppose the community comes to feel that dividends on stock will be less than formerly expected and that debtors are less likely to make their promised payments of interest and repayments of principal. Such a development would lead the community to shift its preference away from both ownership shares and debt obligations and toward the holding of money

as an asset. A shift of expectations in the opposite direction would, of course, have the opposite effect. Such shifts can be important during a business cycle even though the general price level of output changes but little.

3. Expectations of changes in the prices of other assets because of changes in the level of interest rates. If the members of the community expect that interest rates will continue at the same level into the future, their L_2 demand may be at one level. But suppose they come to believe that interest rates will rise markedly and that this will be reflected in decreased prices of obligations yielding a fixed money income. This change of expectations may increase significantly the community's demand for L_2 balances at a given level of interest rates. On the other hand, new expectations of a fall of interest rates, which would be reflected in rising prices of debt obligations, would tend to reduce the L_2 demand for money at a given interest rate. Such changes in expectations may have very important short-term effects. They may even be manipulated in a useful way by the monetary authority. For example, a dramatic rise of discount rates that is interpreted as a sign of tighter money and higher interest rates in the future may immediately lead lenders to reduce the availability of loan funds and to hold larger money balances until interest rates have risen. On the other hand, a dramatic decrease of discount rates that is interpreted as a first step toward easier money and lower interest rates may immediately induce lenders to draw down their L_2 balances and increase the supply of loan funds.

These, then, are the types of conditions that determine the size of L_2 at any given level of r. They are the things we must assume to be given and constant when we state L_2 as a function of r in order to isolate the effects of changes in r. They are also the things whose changes may increase or decrease L_2 at any given level of r.

We assume that, other relevant conditions being given, the size of L_2 is smaller at higher interest rates and larger at lower interest rates. In Fig. 20, where the level of r is measured on the vertical axis and L_2 on the horizontal axis, the L_2L_2 curve slopes downward to the right. For some analytical purposes it is not enough to know that L_2 is greater at lower rates of interest; we need to ask, "How responsive is L_2 to r?" For this purpose we shall use the concept, "the marginal responsiveness of L_2 to r," denoting this by $\frac{\Delta L_2}{\Delta r}$. This is the dollar change in the demand for money as a store of value induced by each change of 1 percentage point in r. The value of $\frac{\Delta L_2}{\Delta r}$ need not be the same at all levels of interest rates. For example, at high levels of interest rates $\frac{\Delta L_2}{\Delta r}$ may be very small; that is, L_2 may be almost entirely unresponsive to small changes in r. But at a very low level of interest rates $\frac{\Delta L_2}{\Delta r}$ may be very large. Even a very small decline of r from that level might induce a huge increase of L_2, and only a very small rise of r might reduce L_2 very greatly. We shall return to this important point later.

Why should L_2 be smaller at higher levels of r than at lower levels of r? We have already given one answer, noting that r is the cost of holding assets in the form of money because it is the income that is forgone if one holds money rather than spends it for other assets that would yield a rate of return equal to r. But it may be useful to look at r as the reward for holding other assets and incurring the "costs" involved therein. These "costs" are of two types:

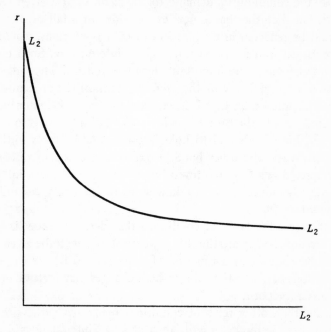

FIG. 20.   An L_2 Demand for Money Balances.

(1) The inconvenience and out-of-pocket costs of buying, holding, servicing, and selling earning assets. The holder incurs some inconvenience and expense in acquiring the assets, in providing safekeeping for them, in collecting income and protecting his position as claimant, and in disposing of the assets if he wishes to spend. (2) Bearing the risk that the assets may decline in price. Even if these "costs" remain constant, the members of the community are likely to hold less of their assets in these other forms and more in the form of money as r falls. At lower levels of r more people are likely to feel that the return is not sufficient to overbalance the costs, including the risk, involved in acquiring and holding other assets.

The late J. M. Keynes emphasized another reason why people are likely to prefer to hold a larger part of their assets in the form of L_2 as r falls, and especially at relatively low levels of r. His point was that the lower r is, the higher will be the estimated risk that the prices of other assets will decline because of a future rise in the rate of interest. This is especially true of long-term fixed-income assets whose prices are greatly affected by changes in interest rates. His argument ran somewhat as follows: at any given time the community may have become accustomed to some level of long-term interest rates. If this level of rates has persisted for some time it may come to be regarded as "natural" or "normal" in the sense that any deviation from it will be followed by a return to it. Thus, any tendency for r to fall below this level may make the community unwilling to hold other assets because they feel that any income that they receive will be more than offset by their capital losses when interest rates rise. At some levels of interest rates above zero they may prefer to add indefinitely to their L_2 holdings rather than hold other assets at a lower level of r. In Fig. 20 this can be depicted as a perfectly horizontal section of the L_2L_2 curve at some rate of interest that is low by historical standards but still above zero. Such a curve would represent a situation in which the value of $\frac{\Delta L_2}{\Delta r}$ approached infinity; L_2 would be almost completely responsive to r. Keynes called this "the liquidity trap," for money would be trapped in the L_2 demand and could not lower interest rates below this level.

Such a situation, if it existed, would have serious implications for the efficacy of monetary policy. Suppose that in time of depression the monetary authority increases the money supply in an attempt to lower interest rates and stimulate investment demand for output. If the L_2L_2 curve is completely horizontal at the existing level of interest rates—if L_2 is completely responsive to r—the increase in the money supply will not lower r at all; the community will simply add all the additional supply of money to its idle L_2 balances at the existing rate of interest. On the other hand, suppose that at some time the monetary authority decides to decrease the money supply in order to raise interest rates and discourage the investment demand for output, but the community is then holding very large L_2 balances that are completely responsive to r at that level of r. The decrease of the money supply may not either decrease the supply of loanable funds or raise the rate of interest at all; people will simply disgorge money from their L_2 balances to meet loan demands at the prevailing rate of interest.

Many economists now believe that the point originally made by Keynes has been exaggerated by some of his followers, if not by him. In the first place, it relates largely to market rates of interest on long-term obligations. Since the prices of short-term securities are but little affected by changes in the level of interest rates, the monetary authority can force short-term rates to very low levels, though not down to zero. It can even reduce significantly the rates on medium-term securities—those with maturities up to five years or so, especially if the easy-money policy is expected to last for some time. In the second place, it is probably an exaggeration to suppose that even long-term rates cannot be reduced at all from a level closely approximating that previously prevailing. If the community comes to believe that the demand for long-term loans will for some time be small relative to the supply of loanable funds, it will revise downward its concept of a "normal" long-term rate of interest and will make loans available at lower rates. Moreover, by skillful use of moral suasion, discount rates, and open-market operations, the monetary authority may convince the community that interest rates will fall and that the wise investor will do well to lend before the rates fall further.

But however much Keynes's point may have been exaggerated, it should not be dismissed as of no importance. The marginal responsiveness of L_2 to r does pose a problem for the monetary authority. It means that a larger increase in the money supply is required to achieve any given decrease in r, if that decrease can be achieved at all. To convince the community that long-term rates will go down and stay there for some time is often a long and laborious process. In the other direction, the disgorging of money from L_2 balances in response to increases in r reduces somewhat the restrictive effects of a given decrease in the money supply. This may, however, be less serious, for unless it is inhibited from doing so the monetary authority may offset this by appropriating larger decreases in the money supply.

$$L = L_1 + L_2$$

Having investigated the nature and determinants of both the L_1 and L_2 demands for money balances, we can now analyze the total demand for money (L), which is the sum of these two components, and its relations to the total supply of money. We shall assume that the supply of money (M) is rigidly fixed at some absolute amount. Assuming all other relevant conditions to be constant, we shall state L_1 as a function of the level of Y. Thus, $L_1 = j \times Y$. This is illustrated by the L_1L_1 curve in Part A of Fig. 21. Let us suppose that $j = \frac{1}{5}$. With this value for j, L_1 would be $40 billion if Y were $200 billion, $60 billion if Y were $300 billion, $90 billion if Y were $450 billion, and so on. Also assuming other relevant conditions to be constant, L_2 is stated as a function of r, as exemplified by the L_2L_2 curve in Part B of Fig. 21.

We shall now add together the L_1 and L_2 demands to get the total demand for money. But a question immediately arises: How can we do this when L_1 and L_2 are not fixed amounts but vary with Y and r? Fig. 22 supplies the answer. We do it by drawing a different L curve for each possible level of Y. From the origin rightward on the horizontal axis we measure the L_1 demand at some given level of Y and to the right of that we measure the L_2 demand as a function of the level of interest rates. Thus the LL_{Y_0} curve is the demand for money when the L_1 demand for money is small because Y is at a low level. The LL_{Y_1} curve is the demand for money when the L_1 demand is somewhat larger because Y is higher. And so on. (Remember that $L_1 =$

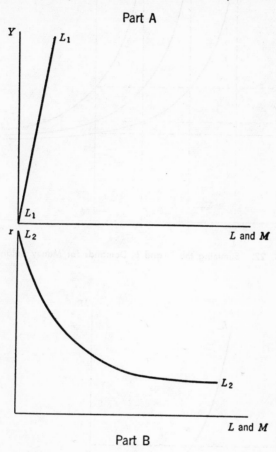

Part A

Part B

FIG. 21.   The Total Demand for Money Balances.

$j \times Y$.) Thus we could draw as many LL curves as there are possible levels of Y. We shall soon return to this point.

At several earlier points we stated that Y and r can be in equilibrium only if the demand for money (L) is exactly equal to the supply of money (M). This statement raises several questions. Why is the condition $L = M$ necessary for equilibrium? Through what processes is L equated to M? How is any excess or deficiency of L relative to M remedied? To answer these questions, let us assume that we start with Y equal to Y_0, so that the total demand for money is LL_{Y_0}. The supply of money is fixed at MM. As shown in Fig. 23, the only equilibrium level of r when Y is at Y_0 is r_0. Only at that level of r is

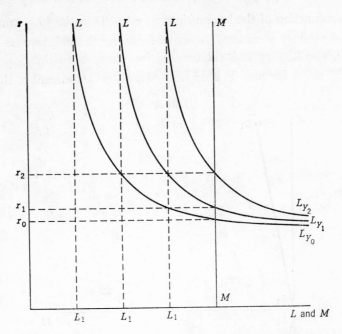

FIG. 22. Summing the L_1 and L_2 Demands for Money Balances.

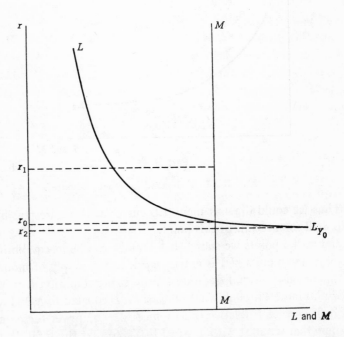

FIG. 23. Equality of L and M.

the quantity of money demanded exactly equal to the supply, leaving no excess of L over M or of M over L. To demonstrate this we shall show that under the assumed conditions all other levels of r represent conditions of disequilibrium. For example, assume that r is at some higher level r_1. At this higher interest rate, the quantity of money demanded would be smaller than the actual supply; the community would feel that its actual balances were excessive and would try to get rid of the excess. It can do this in either or both of two principal ways. (1) It can use its excess supply of money to increase its expenditures for output. This tends, of course, to raise Y, and since L_1 varies with Y it tends to shift the LL curve to the right. Thus the excess supply of money may be eliminated at least in part by increases of Y that increase the L_1 demand. (2) It can use its excess supply of money to retire debt claims against itself or to buy earning assets in the form of stocks, debt obligations, and so on. Some may feel that at the higher interest rate some part of their money balances are too expensive to hold and therefore use them to retire debt. This use of money to retire debt increases the supply of loan funds to others and tends to lower interest rates. Others may use their excess supply of money to make loans to others and to buy securities. This, too, tends to lower interest rates. Thus the use of an excess supply of money to retire debt and purchase securities tends to lower interest rates. Since L_2 is responsive to interest rates, this tends in itself to increase the quantity of money demanded and thereby to eliminate the excess supply of money. But this is not the end of the story. To the extent that investment demand is responsive to interest rates, the decline of r stimulates I and tends to raise the level of Y both directly and through induced multiplier effects. In sum, an excess supply of money can be eliminated only by a rise of Y, a fall of r, or some combination of the two. And the very attempt of the community to rid itself of excess money balances tends to bring about these results.

Suppose, on the other hand, that while Y is at Y_0 interest rates should come to be at some level below r_0, say at r_2. At r_2, L would exceed M. The members of the community would feel that their actual balances were deficient and would attempt to increase them. This they would try to do in one or both of two ways. (1) By decreasing their expenditures for output. This tends, of course, to lower the level of Y. Since L_1 varies with Y, this tends to shift the LL curve to the left. Thus at least some part of the excess demand for money may be eradicated by a decrease in Y that decreases L_1. (2) By increasing their borrowing or decreasing their lending. With interest costs lower, some may borrow more to build up their money balances. This tends to decrease the supply of loans for others. Others may seek to build up their balances by decreasing their new loans to others, or even by selling some of the securities they were already holding. All this tends to reduce the supply of investable funds and to raise the level of r. With the L_2 demand responsive to r, it tends to eliminate at least some part of the excess demand for money by decreasing L_2. Again, however, this is not the end of the story. The rise of r tends to discourage the investment demand for output, and the decline of I tends to reduce the level of Y both directly and through its multiplier effects. In sum, an excess demand for money can be eradicated only by a fall of Y, an increase of r, or some combination of the two. And the very attempt of the community to repair the deficiency in its money balances tends to produce these results.

A few of these findings are essential to our later analysis. (1) When the supply of money is in excess of the demand for it, the community tries to get

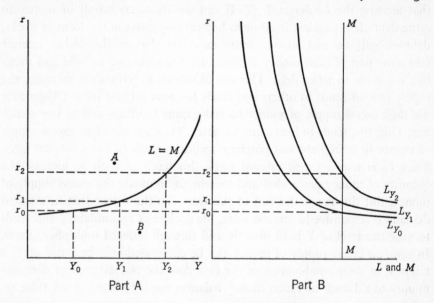

FIG. 24.   Derivation of an $L = M$ Line.

rid of the excess supply by increasing its expenditures for output, by increasing the supply of investable funds, or by some combination of the two. (2) When the demand for money balances is in excess of the supply of money, the community attempts to satisfy its excess demand for money by decreasing its expenditures for output, by borrowing more to add to its money balances, or by decreasing the supply of loan funds. The quantity of money demanded can be brought down to the level of the available supply only by a decrease of Y, a rise of r, or some combination of the two. The effects of changes of r on the investment demand for output should always be kept in mind.

Part B of Fig. 24 indicates that, with a given money supply and given L_1 and L_2 functions, there are various combinations of r and Y at which $L = M$. For example, $L = M$ when Y is at the low level Y_0, so that L_1 is small, and when r is at the low level r_0, so that L_2 is large. $L = M$ when Y is at the higher level Y_1, so that L_1 is larger, and when r is at the higher level r_1, so that L_2 is smaller. Thus we could trace out all those combinations of r and Y at which $L = M$. This is done in Part A of Fig. 24. The $L = M$ line includes every combination of r and Y that will equate the demand for money to the available supply. In general, it slopes upward to the right, for increases of r release money from L_2 balances to satisfy the increased demand for L_1 balances associated with higher levels of Y.

It should be noted that any combination of r and Y that lies off the $L = M$ line is one of disequilibrium. For example, consider any point, such as point A, which is above the $L = M$ line. At any such point M will exceed L. We know this because there is some point immediately below A on the $L = M$ line, at the same level of Y but at a lower r, at which M is exactly equal to L. Therefore at the same Y and a higher r there must be an excess of M over L. This can be eliminated only by a fall of r, a rise of Y, or changes in both Y and r. We have already noted the processes through which these changes would be induced. On the other hand, any point below the $L = M$ line, such as point B, would be a combination of r and Y at which L would exceed M. This excess demand for money could be eliminated only by a fall of Y, a rise of r, or changes in both Y and r.

At an earlier point we noted in passing that in general the $L = M$ curve slopes upward to the right. But for much of our later analysis this broad generalization will be inadequate. We need to ask such questions as these: on the $L = M$ curve, how much of a change of Y (which we shall denote by ΔY) will be associated with a given change of r, which we shall denote by Δr? In other words, how large is $\dfrac{\Delta Y}{\Delta r}$ on the $L = M$ curve? What factors determine the size of this $\dfrac{\Delta Y}{\Delta r}$?

To answer these questions let us assume a rise of r in an amount Δr. In general the same fall of r would have the reverse effects. We saw earlier that a rise of interest rates enables L to be equal to M at a higher level of Y because the rise of interest rates reduces the demand for L_2 balances and frees money to meet the larger L_1 demand associated with a higher level of Y. Thus one determinant of $\dfrac{\Delta Y}{\Delta r}$ on the $L = M$ curve is the amount of money freed from L_2 balances by the given rise of interest rates, Δr. This in turn depends on the marginal responsiveness of the demand for money to r, which we denoted by $\dfrac{\Delta L}{\Delta r}$ and defined as the dollar change in the demand for money in response to each change of 1 percentage point in r. Let us consider two extreme values for $\dfrac{\Delta L}{\Delta r}$. (1) $\dfrac{\Delta L}{\Delta r} = 0$. In other words, the rise of interest rates frees no money from L_2 balances, so that none is made available to meet the increased L_1 demand that would accompany a higher level of Y. In this case

Y cannot rise even though r has risen without making the demand for money greater than the supply. Here $\frac{\Delta Y}{\Delta r} = 0$. In Part A of Fig. 24 this would appear as a vertical $L = M$ curve, at some level of Y. (2) The value of $\frac{\Delta L}{\Delta r}$ approaches infinity. That is, the marginal responsiveness of the demand for money to r is nearly complete, so that even a tiny rise of r would free huge amounts of money from L_2 balances and permit great increases of Y without causing L to exceed M. In this case the value of $\frac{\Delta Y}{\Delta r}$ would approach infinity. This would appear in Part A of Fig. 24 as a virtually horizontal section of the $L = M$ curve. When $\frac{\Delta L}{\Delta r}$ has any value between zero and infinity, the value of $\frac{\Delta Y}{\Delta r}$ also depends on the marginal responsiveness of L_1 to Y. By this we mean the dollar change in L_1 (or ΔL_1) resulting from a $1 change in the level of Y. This may be written as $\frac{\Delta L_1}{\Delta Y}$. The rise of Y permitted by any given increase in the supply of money available to satisfy L_1 demands varies reciprocally with $\frac{\Delta L_1}{\Delta Y}$. For example, suppose that a given rise of interest rates frees from the L_2 demand $1 billion dollars and makes this amount available to meet the L_1 demand. If each $1 rise in Y raises L_1 by only $.10, Y will have to increase by $10 billion to raise L_1 enough to absorb the $1 billion released from L_2 balances. Another way of putting it is this: the greater the income velocity of the dollars transferred from idle balances to active balances, the greater will be the increase of Y that can be financed by such a transfer of any given number of dollars.

It should be noted that the marginal responsiveness of L_2 to r may be different at different ranges of interest rates at higher levels of r, the value of $\frac{\Delta L_2}{\Delta r}$ may approach zero, so that $\frac{\Delta Y}{\Delta r}$ also approaches zero, and the $L = M$ curve is practically vertical. But at very low levels of r, for reasons such as those noted by Keynes, the value of $\frac{\Delta L_2}{\Delta r}$ may be very high, so that the value of $\frac{\Delta Y}{\Delta r}$ is also very high and the $L = M$ curve is nearly horizontal. We have already noted the importance of the value of $\frac{\Delta L_2}{\Delta r}$ for the efficacy of monetary policy.

Equilibrium When $\Delta L/\Delta r$ Is Zero

We have found that Y and r can be in equilibrium only when the demand for money is exactly equal to the supply of money. This is always a necessary condition, but it is not necessarily a sufficient condition, for equilibrium also requires equality of investment demand and the supply of saving. However there is one interesting case in which the condition $L = M$ is sufficient to establish a unique equilibrium level of Y, the money value of output. This is the case in which the demand for money is completely unresponsive to interest rates, so that the L_2 demand may be represented by one fixed quan-

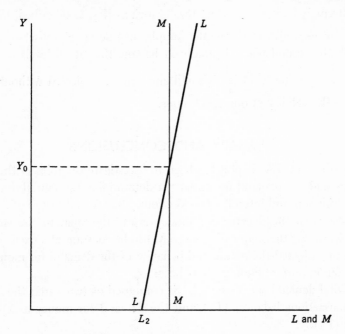

FIG. 25.   Demand for Money When $\Delta L/\Delta r$ Is 0.

tity. This is shown in Fig. 25. The total demand for money is composed of the L_2 demand, which is a fixed quantity, plus the L_1 demand, which is a function of the level of Y, such that $L_1 = j \times Y$. Thus $L = L_2 + j \times Y$. With the money supply MM and this LL function, the only equilibrium level of Y is Y_0. At any higher level of Y the demand for money would exceed the available supply; at any lower level M would exceed L.

This case has a long history in monetary theory. Assuming that the demand for money was completely unresponsive to the level of interest rates, or was so little responsive that the effects could safely be neglected, economists contended that the level of money income was determined by the demand for money and the supply of money. Investment demand and the supply of saving entered into their analysis not as determinants of the level of Y but as determinants of the rate of interest and of the relative shares of Y devoted to investment and consumption.

We must admit that the case in which the condition $L = M$ is both necessary and sufficient to determine a unique equilibrium level of Y lacks generality. Nevertheless, it is an important one to keep in mind. In the first place, it highlights the importance of the responsiveness of the demand for money to interest rates. If $\frac{\Delta L}{\Delta r}$ is zero, or even very small, we get results approximately those reached by a long line of monetary theorists. If $\frac{\Delta L}{\Delta r}$ is extremely large, we may get results such as Keynes described. Effects of increases or decreases in the money supply may be largely offset by changes in L_2. In the second place, it may well be true that at all levels of interest rates above very low ones $\frac{\Delta L}{\Delta r}$ is small and can be neglected without serious effects on the validity of our conclusions.

SUMMARY AND CONCLUSIONS

The purpose of this chapter has been to investigate the roles of the supply of money and the demand for money in determining the equilibrium levels of money income and interest rates. We found that Y and r can be in equilibrium only when the demand for money is exactly equal to the supply of money. Assuming the supply of money (M) to be constant at a fixed quantity, we then investigated the nature and behavior of the demand for money (L). Some of our important findings were these:

1. The total demand for money (L) is composed of two parts: the demand for transactions balances (L_1) and the demand for money as a store of value (L_2).

2. The size of balances demanded for L_1 purposes varies with the level of money income or output (Y) and the fraction $\frac{L_1}{Y}$, or j. We can state L_1 as a function of Y, thereby isolating the effects of changes of Y on L_1, only if we assume the conditions affecting the size of j to be given and constant. We noted some of the principal factors that determine the size of j at any time and that change it through time.

3. The L_2 demand for money was stated as a function of r, in order to relate the size of L_2 to the height of r. This requires, of course, the assumption that other relevant conditions are given and constant. Here again we noted some of the principal conditions that determine the size of L_2 at each interest rate at a given time and whose changes can increase or decrease L_2 at each interest rate.

4. Both Y and r can be in equilibrium only if $L = M$. If L is less than M, the community will try to get rid of its excess money balances in either or both of two ways: (a) By increasing its expenditures for output, thereby raising the level of Y, which will raise L_1. (b) By repaying loans or offering a

larger supply of loans, thereby raising the supply of investable funds and lowering r. This will increase the quantity of money demanded both by raising the L_2 demand and by stimulating investment demand and raising Y. On the other hand, if L is greater than M, the community will try to build its balances to the desired level in either or both of two ways: by decreasing its expenditures for output, thereby lowering Y and L_1, or by increasing its borrowings to build up its balances and decreasing the supply of loan funds to others. This would lower the supply of investable funds and raise r, which would both decrease L_2 and discourage investment, thereby lowering Y. These processes of equating L to M should be borne clearly in mind, for an understanding of them is essential to all later analysis.

5. The shape of the $L = M$ curve—the curve showing the various combinations of r and Y that would equate L and M with a given money supply and given L_1 and L_2 functions—depends on the marginal responsiveness of L_2 to interest rates $\left(\dfrac{\Delta L_2}{\Delta r}\right)$ and the marginal responsiveness of L_1 to Y, or $\left(\dfrac{\Delta L_1}{\Delta Y}\right)$. To illustrate this we shall consider three cases and assume a rise of r.

a. $\dfrac{\Delta L_2}{\Delta r} = 0$. In this case the rise of interest rates frees no dollars from L_2 balances to be used for L_1 purpose, so Y cannot rise at all without causing the demand for money to exceed the available supply. The $L = M$ curve would be vertical—completely unresponsive to r, at some level of Y. This case is interesting because in it the condition $L = M$ is sufficient to determine a unique equilibrium level of money income.

b. The value of $\dfrac{\Delta L_2}{\Delta r}$ approaches infinity. The $L = M$ curve would approach a horizontal position, indicating equilibrium at that interest rate for all levels of Y. Even a tiny rise of r would free enough dollars from L_2 balances to finance an indefinite expansion of Y. Even a tiny fall of r would have the reverse effect.

c. The value of $\dfrac{\Delta L_2}{\Delta r}$ is between zero and infinity. In this case the size of the increase of Y that can occur without causing L to exceed M depends not only on the number of dollars freed from L_2 balances by the given rise in r but also on the size of the marginal responsiveness of L_1 to Y. For example, a transfer of \$1 can finance a \$10 rise of Y if $\dfrac{\Delta L_1}{\Delta Y} = \dfrac{1}{10}$, but only a \$5 rise of Y if $\dfrac{\Delta L_1}{\Delta Y} = \dfrac{1}{5}$. It is usually assumed that the value of $\dfrac{\Delta L_2}{\Delta r}$ is lower at higher ranges of r than at lower ranges of r.

SELECTED READINGS

American Economic Association, *Readings in Monetary Theory*, Blakiston, Philadelphia, 1951.

Hicks, J. R., "A Suggestion for Simplifying the Theory of Money," *Economica*, 1935 (also reprinted in AEA, *Readings in Monetary Theory*).

Patinkin, D., *Money, Interest and Prices*, Row Peterson, Evanston, 1956.

CHAPTER 15

Equilibrium

Having investigated the investment demand for output, the supply of saving, the supply of money, and the demand for money, we can now see how these four functions combine to determine the level of the money value of national output or income and the level of interest rates. First we shall see how these four given functions determine an equilibrium. Then we shall shift these functions one by one and trace out the effects.

EQUILIBRIUM CONDITIONS

We begin by assuming that conditions are such that the four functions have the values shown in Fig. 26. (1) The investment demand function, II, is drawn on the assumption that the marginal efficiency of capital schedule is given and constant. It shows that the lower r is, the greater will be I. (2) The supply of saving function, SS, assumes other relevant conditions to be given and constant, so that S varies with the level of Y. (3) The supply of money is assumed to be fixed at a given quantity. (4) Assuming other relevant conditions to be given and constant, the demand for money function, LL, shows the relation between demand for money and the levels of Y and r. We assume this function is such that increases and decreases of Y tend to increase and decrease L, whereas decreases of r tend to raise L and increases of r to decrease L.

The I = S line in Part D of Fig. 26 shows all those combinations of r and Y at which investment demand and the supply of saving would be exactly equal; at all other combinations of r and Y, S and I would be unequal. At any point above the I = S line S would exceed I; at any point below the line I would exceed S. We know that the equilibrium combination of Y and r must lie somewhere on this line, for an equality of I and S is a necessary condition for equilibrium.[1] Similarly, the L = M line shows all those combinations of r

[1] We are deliberately postponing consideration of a troublesome problem. The II and SS functions that we developed earlier were essentially in real terms, for we assumed a certain price level of output and that this price level remained constant. We cannot be sure that

and Y at which the demand for money is exactly equal to the available supply; at all other combinations of r and Y, L would not be equal to M. At any point above the $L = M$ line, L would be less than M; at any point below the line L would exceed M. We find that there is only one combination of Y and r—Y_e, r_e—that simultaneously meets both of the necessary conditions, $I = S$ and $L = M$. We shall see that, given the values of the four functions, this

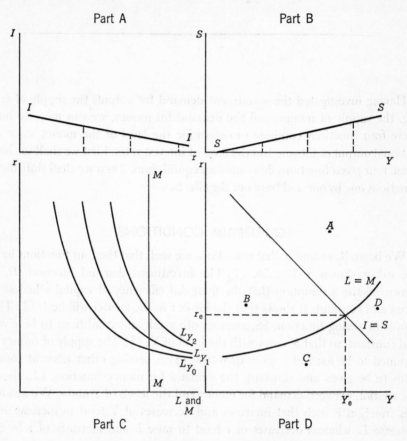

FIG. 26.   Equilibrium with Constant Functions.

is the only possible equilibrium combination. First, however, it will be helpful to make some comments about the SS function.

We noted earlier that the SS function may be viewed in two main ways: (1) As a function or schedule showing the values of output at the various possible levels of Y that are "left over" after C and G demands for output. It is therefore a schedule of the values of output at various levels of Y available to

any price level assumed is necessarily consistent with the supply of money and demand for money situation. At this point we shall assume that it is. We shall deal later with price level changes.

meet the investment demand for output, and that will remain unsold if not taken by investment demand. If this supply of output represented by saving is greater than investment demand, some part of output will remain unsold and producers will be induced to decrease output. If, on the other hand, I exceeds S, the total demand for output will exceed the supply at that level of Y and producers will be induced to try to increase their output. (2) As a function or schedule showing the amounts of the nation's disposable income at various levels of Y that it does not spend for C and G and that might, therefore, be made available to finance private investment spending. It is this aspect of the supply of saving—saving as a source of supply of investable funds—that we shall emphasize as we discuss the determination of the level of interest rates.

Just what is the relationship between the supply of saving at each level of Y and the supply of investable funds at the same level of Y? Let us denote the supply of investable funds by F. F will be the same as S at any level of Y if all S flows into F and F is not augmented from any other source. But they may differ. In general, their relationship may be expressed as $F = S + (M - L)$. Suppose we start with a situation in which the supply of money exceeds the demand for money, and the community tries to get rid of its excess balances by using them to retire debt, thereby making the money available to meet investment demand, and to increase its supply of loans. In this case F is equal to the supply of S at that level of Y plus the excess supply of money over the demand for money. On the other hand, consider the case in which L exceeds M and the community tries to satisfy its excess demand for money by borrowing funds to add to its idle balances or by offering fewer loan funds in the market. In this case F is less than S; some part of saving is offset by or absorbed by the use of funds to satisfy excess demands for money balances. Only when $L = M$ is the supply of investable funds (F) equal to S. And it is F, together with investment demand, that is relevant to the determination of interest rates.

The following sections will rely heavily on the idea that an excess of M over L tends to augment the supply of investable funds and lower interest rates, while an excess of L over M tends to make the supply of investable funds less than the supply of S at a given level of Y, thereby tending to raise interest rates.

Let us now see why, given the values of the four functions, Y_e, r_e is the only equilibrium combination, and how any deviation from this point would tend to be corrected. Consider first any r, Y combination, such as point A, which lies above both the $I = S$ and $L = M$ lines. At any such point S would exceed I. This excess of S over I could be corrected only by a decrease of r to stimulate investment demand, a reduction of Y to lower S, or some combination of changes in r and Y. The excess of S over I would tend to lower Y. Also, to the extent that the excess of S was offered in the market as a supply of loanable funds it would tend to lower r. This downward pressure on r would be accentuated by attempts of the community to get rid of its excess money balances, for at any such point M would exceed L. The community would try to get rid of its excess balances by increasing its expenditures for output, thereby tending to raise Y, or by increasing the supply of loan funds (F), thereby tending to lower interest rates. This pressure toward lower interest rates and higher income levels would end only when r and Y were back at some point on the $L = M$ line. But no point on the $L = M$ line above the $I = S$ line would be one of equilibrium, for each would be one at which S would exceed I, requiring a decline of r, a fall of Y, or some combination of both. On the other hand, at all points on the $I = S$ line above the $L = M$ line, the supply of money would exceed the demand for money, thereby exerting pressure toward lower levels of r and higher levels of Y.

Consider next any combination of r and Y, such as point B, which lies below the $I = S$ line but above the $L = M$ line. At any such point I would exceed S, and this excess demand for output would tend to raise Y. Also, at any such point the supply of money would exceed the demand for money. There would be a downward pressure on r and an upward pressure on Y as the members of their community sought to get rid of their excess balances. The expansionary pressures of the excess of I over S and the excess of M over L would end only when the point Y_e, r_e had been reached.

Let point C represent any combination of Y and r lying below both the $I = S$ and $L = M$ curves. At any such point I would exceed S. This excess demand for the investable funds represented by S would tend to raise interest rates. This upward pressure on interest rates would be accentuated by the excess of L over M as the community tried to build up its balances to the desired levels by offering fewer investable funds. The upward pressure on interest rates would end only when Y_e, r_e had been reached.

Lastly, let us consider any Y, r combination, such as point D, lying above the $I = S$ line but below the $L = M$ line. At any such point S would exceed I; this excess supply of output would lead producers to cut their rate of production, thereby lowering Y. But at any such point the demand for money would exceed the supply of money; Y would tend to be lowered and r to be raised as the community sought to build up its balances to the desired level. The contractionary pressures on Y would end only when Y_e, r_e was achieved.

In summary, we have seen how these four functions combine to determine equilibrium levels of Y and r, and the processes through which deviations from these levels would be corrected. Note that the levels of Y and r are not determined by the values of any one or two of the functions alone; they depend on the values of all four functions. We shall now investigate the effects of shifts of these functions. Our method will be to shift one at a time, assuming the other functions to remain constant. We shall start with an increase in the money supply function. In the first case it will be assumed that the price level of output remains constant.

INCREASE OF THE MONEY SUPPLY

In Fig. 27 we assume that the II, SS, and LL functions remain constant but that the supply of money is increased from MM to M_1M_1. How will this affect the levels of Y and r, which were in equilibrium at Y_e, r_e? One thing is clear: with the same demand for money schedules and a greater supply of

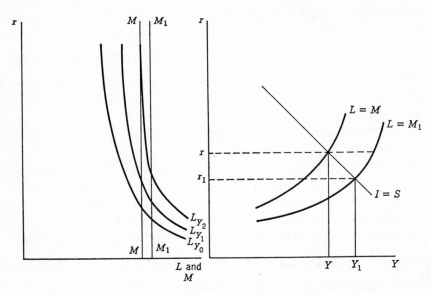

FIG. 27.   An Increase in the Money Supply.

money available for holding, the demand for money cannot be exactly equal to the new larger supply at the old combinations of Y and r. With an increased supply of money there will now be an excess of M over L at each of the r, Y combinations that formerly equated L to M. The quantities demanded can be equated to the larger supply only by a rise of Y, which increases the L_1 demand, a fall of r, which raises the L_2 demand, or a combination of both. In Fig. 27 this is shown as a shift of the $L = M$ line to the right and downward. This raises two questions: with any given increase of the money supply (ΔM), how much must r be decreased at each level of Y to raise the quantity of money demanded up to the new higher level of the money supply? In other words, how much will a given ΔM shift the $L = M$ line downward at each level of Y? Also, how much must Y be increased at each level of r to bring the demand for money up to the new higher supply?

In other words, how much will a given ΔM shift the $L = M$ line rightward at each level of r?

The size of the downward shift is extremely important, for it indicates the maximum amount by which the increase in the money supply could lower interest rates. It depends on both the size of the increase in the money supply and the marginal responsiveness of L to changes in r. This was earlier denoted by $\dfrac{\Delta L}{\Delta r}$ and defined as the dollar change in the quantity of money demanded in response to each change of one percentage point in r. Suppose the value of $\dfrac{\Delta L}{\Delta r}$ is very low. In this case the downward shift of the $L = M$ line would be very large; the increase in the money supply would make possible a large decrease of r because the quantity of money demanded is unresponsive to decreases in r. But suppose the value of $\dfrac{\Delta L}{\Delta r}$ is extremely large, approaching infinity. In this case, because even an infinitesimal fall of r would increase L_2 by a huge amount, the rise in the money supply may lower r not at all, or at most by only an infinitesimal amount. The new money has disappeared into Keynes's "liquidity trap," succeeding neither in lowering r nor in raising Y.

The size of the rightward shift of Y at each level of r—the amount by which Y can increase without causing L to exceed the increased money supply—is extremely important because it indicates the maximum amount by which the increase in the money supply can raise Y. It depends on the size of the increase in the money supply, ΔM, and on the marginal responsiveness of L_1 to Y. By this we mean $\dfrac{\Delta L_1}{\Delta Y}$, the amount that a \$1 change in Y will change the demand for transactions balances. For example, a \$1 increase in the money supply will finance a \$10 rise of Y if $\dfrac{\Delta L_1}{\Delta Y} = \dfrac{1}{10}$, but only a \$5 rise of Y if $\dfrac{\Delta L_1}{\Delta Y} = \dfrac{1}{5}$.

In summary, the increase of M will shift the $L = M$ curve downward and to the right. We know that a new equilibrium combination of r and Y must lie somewhere on this curve, which includes all the combinations of r and Y at which L will be equal to the enlarged money supply.

Let us now look at the processes through which the additional money may be injected into the stream of expenditures for output. We have already noted that whereas L was formerly exactly equal to the money supply at Y_e, r_e, M is now greater than L. The community may try to get rid of these excess balances by increasing its expenditures for output, thereby tending to raise Y, or by increasing the supply of investable funds, thereby tending to lower r.

But what is its initial response likely to be? Will it initially expand its purchases of output, or will it initially enlarge the supply of investable funds? This may depend in part on how the new money was created. Let us consider two cases.

1. The new money is received by people in transactions that represent an increase in their disposable incomes. For example, the new money may have been issued in exchange for gold that was imported to pay for increased American exports. When new money is initially created as a part of an income-creating transaction, the recipients may inject it into the spending stream as increased expenditures for consumption without any initial effect on the supply of investable funds or on r. However, if they use some part of the increased income and money to increase saving, the supply of investable funds may be increased, thereby tending to lower r.

2. The new money is created in transactions that do not directly create income or even increase the net wealth or net assets of the community. For example, it may have resulted as the Federal Reserve bought government securities from the public and the commercial banks, thereby creating bank reserves and enabling the banks to increase their earning assets by purchasing securities or increasing their loans. Such transactions need not increase the net wealth or net assets of the public, for although the latter now has more money, it has given up an equal value of securities or has increased its debts to the banks by an equal amount. It is therefore unlikely that the initial response of the public will be to increase its rate of consumption expenditures. But such an addition to the money supply does contribute an increase in the supply of investable funds, and this rise of F tends to lower interest rates. For example, suppose that the money supply is increased when Y and r are at the old equilibrium level of Y_e, r_e. The initial response may be to lower r. But the fall of r will stimulate the investment demand for output, which will raise the level of Y and disposable incomes. The new money injected into the spending stream as increased investment expenditures is then received by people who regard it as income, and they may use it to increase their consumption expenditures. The extent to which they do this depends, of course, on the size of our old friend, the marginal propensity to consume, or $\dfrac{\Delta C}{\Delta Y}$.

We have already seen that the size of the downward shift of the $L = M$ curve determines the maximum extent to which a given increase of M can lower interest rates, and the rightward shift determines the maximum extent to which it can increase the level of Y. But within these limits, what determines what the outcome will be when the new equilibrium is reached? Will it be reflected almost completely in a decline of r? A rise of Y? What combination of the two? An inspection of Fig. 27 indicates that this depends on the shape of the $I = S$ curve to the right of the old equilibrium, and more specifically on the $\dfrac{\Delta Y}{\Delta r}$ on that curve. If the $I = S$ curve were completely horizontal, the effect would be solely an increase of Y with no fall of r. If it were completely vertical, the effect would be solely a decline of r with no rise of Y. We found earlier that $\dfrac{\Delta Y}{\Delta r}$ on the $I = S$ curve varies directly with the marginal responsiveness of investment demand to interest rates and with the size of the multiplier. That is,

$$\frac{\Delta Y}{\Delta r} = \frac{\Delta I}{\Delta r} \times \frac{1}{\Delta S/\Delta Y}$$

If investment demand is completely unresponsive to r, an increase in the money supply may not increase Y at all even though it succeeds in lowering interest rates. But a higher degree of responsiveness of I to r tends to increase Y by greater amounts. So does a greater size of the multiplier, reflecting higher marginal propensities to consume and lower marginal propensities to save.

We find, then, that to analyze the effects of a given increase of the money supply on the level of Y when the other three functions are constant we need to ask four questions: (1) How much can it lower r? This depends on the responsiveness of the demand for money to interest rates. A low value of $\dfrac{\Delta L}{\Delta r}$ permits a relatively large decline of interest rates. A high value of $\dfrac{\Delta L}{\Delta r}$ permits only a smaller decline of r. (2) How much will it permit Y to expand without causing the demand for money to exceed the new higher money supply? This depends, of course, on the marginal responsiveness of the demand for money to changes in Y. That is, it depends on the size of $\dfrac{\Delta L}{\Delta Y}$. (3) How responsive is investment demand to interest rates? That is, how large is $\dfrac{\Delta I}{\Delta r}$? (4) How large is the multiplier, $\dfrac{1}{\Delta S/\Delta Y}$? That is, how small is the marginal propensity to save? Many of the controversies concerning the probable effects of a given increase in the money supply arise out of differences in the answers given to such questions.

The Case of Increased Prices of Output

Up to this point we have assumed that the price level of output remained stable so that changes in Y, I, and S represented changes in real output and income. This may not be unrealistic if the original level of Y, which was Y_e, was one reflecting underutilization of labor and other resources and if even the new higher level, Y_1, is still at a less-than-full-employment level. However, it is clear that the rise of demand for output may be reflected to at least some extent in a rise in the price level of output, and that it must be reflected completely in price levels if real output cannot be expanded.

To illustrate this case, let us assume that the original equilibrium situation, Y_e, r_e was one of full employment and that the money supply is now doubled. We shall start with the simple case in which the new equilibrium position will be one in which the rate of real output is unchanged but both the price level of output and the money value of output are doubled.

The initial effect of doubling the money supply is, of course, to create an excess supply of money over the demand for money at Y_e, r_e, an excess supply that can be eliminated only by an increase of Y, a fall of r, or some combination of the two. Let us suppose that the L_2 demand for money at each interest rate is a demand for a fixed amount of real purchasing power in the form of money, so that the number of dollars demanded for this purpose varies directly with the price level. Thus, a doubling of the price level would double the demand for L_2 balances at each level of r. Suppose also that the L_1 demand is some constant function of the money value of Y, such that $L_1 = j \times Y$. In this case, the total demand for money can be brought up to the level of the doubled money supply only by a doubling of Y at each level of r. In Fig. 28 this is reflected in the $L_a = M_a$ line whose Y value at each level of r is twice that on the old $L = M$ curve.

What about the investment demand for output? The initial fall of r will tend to increase investment spending for output, but since the economy is already operating at capacity, the effect may be only to drive up the prices of new capital goods. Will this rise in the prices of capital goods tend to reduce the rate of real investment by lowering expected rates of return? It need not, for the potential spenders for capital goods may expect that their annual net returns in dollars will rise just as much as the dollar cost of the capital goods. For example, they may expect that a capital good that cost $100 and was expected to yield annual net returns of $10 before the rise of prices will now cost $200 and yield net returns of $20. The expected rate of return remains unchanged at 10 percent. The rate of real investment may remain constant at each level of r, but the value of money expenditures for investment may vary directly with the level of prices. Thus, if prices double, the money value of expenditures for output may double at each level of r. In Fig. 28 this is shown by the upward shift from II to I_aI_a.

The supply function of saving may also be in real terms. That is, the rate of real saving may depend on real income. With a rise of prices, the community would have to save more money income to represent the same amount of real saving, but it may be willing to do so only at proportionately higher levels of money income representing the same real income. For example, if prices doubled the nation would have to save twice as much in money terms to represent the same rate of real saving, but it may do so only if its money income is also doubled. The supply of saving curve SS reflects such an assumption.

In short, a doubling of the price level of output might double investment expenditures at each level of r, but the nation may be willing to save twice as much in money terms only at twice as high levels of money income. Such shifts will be reflected in a rightward shift of the $I = S$ line. We see in Fig.

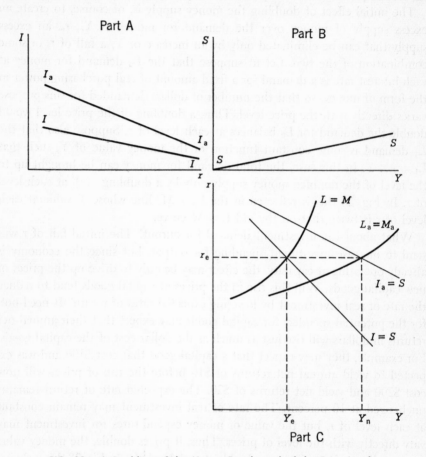

FIG. 28. A Doubling of the Money Supply and of the Price Levels.

28 that at each level of r the condition $I = S$ can be satisfied only at a level of Y twice that on the old $I = S$ curve. When we look at the point of intersection of the $I_a = S$ and the $L_a = M_a$ curves to find the new equilibrium combination of Y and r we discover, perhaps not surprisingly, that the new equilibrium level of Y, measured in money terms, is twice the old equilibrium level. This reflects a doubling of the price level of output. But we also dis-

cover that a doubling of the money supply has not permanently lowered the rate of interest; at the new equilibrium level the interest rate is unchanged from its old level, r_e.

This is an important discovery. When the economy is operating at less than capacity levels, an increase of the money supply may indeed lower interest rates and these may remain at a lower level. In fact, some decline of interest rates to stimulate investment demand may be necessary to raise the level of real output and keep it at a higher level. But a decline of interest rates when the economy is already operating at capacity levels may only lead to price inflation, and interest rates may have to be allowed to rise again if the inflation is to be terminated. For example, suppose that at some time a nation's marginal efficiency of capital and its propensities to consume and save are such that S and I would be equal at a full-employment but noninflationary level of Y with interest rates at 5 percent. Suppose, however, that the monetary authority is determined to maintain interest rates at some lower level, such as 3 percent, and to this end stands ready to provide the banking system with whatever additional lending power it may require to maintain the 3 percent rate. The decline of interest rates will stimulate investment spending, but since the economy is already operating at full-capacity levels, the effect may be only to raise the prices of capital goods. This may not deter purchasers of new capital, for they may expect every rise in the cost of capital goods to be offset by increases in their net dollar profits. And so it may go; every rise in the prices of capital goods will evoke larger investment expenditures, which will both add directly to the money demand for output and also create larger money incomes for recipients. And the latter may use a large part of every increase in their money incomes to increase their rate of expenditures for consumption, thereby producing large multiplier effects. The inflationary spiral may therefore continue until such time as interest rates are again allowed to rise.

The inflationary spiral may be even more dramatic if the induced rise of prices raises the expected profitability of new investment. And it may do so. Businessmen may come to expect that their dollar returns will increase much more than in proportion to the cost of capital goods because their selling prices for output will rise much faster than their operating costs. Capital goods that were expected to yield 5 percent with stable price levels may come to be expected to yield 10 percent or more with rising prices. The great gap between the low level of interest rates and the much greater expected rates of returns on new investment may increase investment expenditures much more than in proportion to the rise of price levels. And it may well turn out that though the inflationary spiral was started by a monetary policy of lowering interest rates from 5 percent to 3 percent, it can be halted only if interest rates are raised considerably above 5 percent. But once expectations of further price increases are eliminated, the interest rate may have to be decreased to 5 percent or even lower to prevent a deflationary spiral from developing.

DECREASE OF THE MONEY SUPPLY

Suppose that, starting from an equilibrium situation with given *II*, *SS*, *LL*, and *MM* functions, we leave the other functions constant and reduce the money supply. In Fig. 27 this might be represented by a decrease in the money supply from M_1M_1 to *MM*. We need not trace out in detail either the effects or the processes, for they may be inferred from our discussion of the effects of increases in the money supply. A few comments may be helpful, however.

With a decrease in the supply of money available for holding, the immediate effect will be that the supply of money will be deficient relative to the demand for it at each *Y*, *r* combination, including Y_e, r_e, which formerly equated *L* to *M*. The community will try to repair its money balances by decreasing its expenditures, by lowering the supply of investable funds, or both. Its initial response may depend in part on the way the money supply was reduced. If the money supply was reduced as a part of a transaction that also lowered money incomes, such as an export of gold to pay for increased imports, the public may immediately lower its consumption expenditures. But this is unlikely to be the initial response if the money supply is decreased in transactions that do not decrease directly either the incomes or the net wealth of the community. Suppose, for example, that it resulted from open-market sales by the Federal Reserve or from increases in member bank reserve requirements that force the commercial banks to sell securities or reduce their outstanding loans. The net wealth position of the public is not directly altered; the public now has smaller money balances, but it holds more securities or owes less debt to the banks. However, the supply of investable funds is decreased, which tends to raise the level of interest rates, discourage investment expenditures, lower disposable incomes, and induce a decline of consumption expenditures.

We have already noted that with a decreased money supply the demand for money can be brought into equality with it only by a rise of *r*, a fall of *Y*, or some combination of the two. This raises two important questions: (1) How much must *r* be raised at each level of *Y* to reduce *L* to the new lower level of *M*? This depends, of course, on $\dfrac{\Delta L}{\Delta r}$, the marginal responsiveness of *L* to *r*. If the demand for money is highly unresponsive to a rise of *r*, a given decrease in the money supply may require a very large rise of *r* to bring *L* down to the level of *M*. But if $\dfrac{\Delta L}{\Delta r}$ is very large, the required rise of *r* may be extremely small. This is an important point for monetary managers. They should realize that if the situation is such that a small rise of r would release very large amounts of money from inactive L_2 balances, the restrictive effects of any given decrease in the money supply may be largely negated. (2) How much must Y be decreased at any given level of r to reduce L to the new lower level of the money supply? This depends on the size of $\frac{\Delta L}{\Delta Y}$, the marginal responsiveness of L to Y.

We find, then, that the decrease of the money supply cannot raise r more than the upward shift of the $L = M$ curve or lower Y more than the leftward shift of the $L = M$ curve. But within these limits, will the actual results be largely a rise of r or largely a decrease of Y? What combination of the two? This depends, of course, on the shape of the $I = S$ curve to the left of the old equilibrium level. If this curve is nearly vertical, the effect will be largely to raise interest rates. But the flatter the $I = S$ curve, the greater will be the decrease of Y and the smaller the actual increase of r. Both a greater responsiveness of investment demand to interest rates and a larger multiplier, reflecting a smaller marginal propensity to save, contribute to the flatness of the $I = S$ curve.

In summary, we find that in order to analyze the extent to which a given decrease in the money supply will lower Y if the other functions remain constant we need to ask these questions: (1) How much can it raise interest rates? This depends on $\frac{\Delta L}{\Delta r}$. (2) How much must Y decrease at each level of interest rates to lower L to equality with the decreased money supply? This depends on $\frac{\Delta L}{\Delta Y}$. (3) How responsive is investment demand to interest rates? (4) How large is the multiplier; that is, how small is the marginal propensity to save?

It is important to note that we have been considering the decrease in Y which would result if the money supply were decreased while all the other functions remained constant. If price and cost structures are inflexible downward the decline in the money value of Y may reflect largely a decrease in real output and employment. This decline in real output was initiated by the rise of interest rates that discouraged real investment and through multiplier effects that reduced real consumption. The final outcome of an initial reduction in the money supply may, however, be more complex. Let us consider two cases. The first is one in which price and cost structures are inflexible downward and the decline of Y lowers the marginal efficiency of capital. This is possible, for the initial declines of Y are likely to decrease the rate of utilization of existing capital and to lower expected net returns on investment in new capital. Thus actual investment expenditures may fall for two reasons: the initial rise of interest rates and the induced downward shift of the investment demand schedule reflecting lower expected returns. The result is likely to be a greater fall of Y. The net change in interest rates is hard to predict, for although the decrease in the supply of investable funds reflecting the decrease in the money supply tends to raise interest rates, the induced decline of investment demand tends to lower interest rates.

The second case is that in which price and cost structures are completely flexible downward. Suppose we start from some original equilibrium position and decrease the money supply. The initial effects will be to raise interest rates, decrease investment expenditures, and induce a decline of consumption expenditures. But suppose the response is not to lessen output and employment but to lower cost and price levels. Workers and the owners of other productive factors lower their prices rather than accept unemployment, and producers reflect their lower costs in lower prices of output. Spenders for capital goods may not reduce their real investment at each level of interest rates because their expected rate of return remains unchanged. The decrease in their expected dollar returns may be offset by a decrease in the prices of capital goods. But what of the initial rise of interest rates? Will it not persist and decrease the rate of real investment? It may not. The decrease in the money value of Y, reflecting the falling price level of output, decreases the transactions demand for money. Moreover, the L_2 demand for money may fall as the price level falls because each dollar now represents a larger amount of real purchasing power. Thus the decrease in the demand for money as prices fall may remedy the deficiency of money balances caused by the initial reduction in the money supply and allow interest rates to fall back to their old level.[2] The outcome could be that the level of interest rates, real output, real investment, and real consumption all remain unchanged but the money value of Y is lower, reflecting lower price levels.

This case has often been dealt with by monetary theorists. They have argued that if cost and price structures for output were completely flexible downward, an initial decline in money expenditures for output that lowered price levels would create an excess supply of money by lowering the quantities of money demanded at each level of real output or income. As the community tried to get rid of these excess money balances by spending them for output or by increasing their lending, they would end the deflationary price spiral. In short, the very process of price declines would increase the "real" supply of money, eliminate any excess demand for money, tend to lower interest rates, and end the fall of prices. Why, then, do we not rely on price declines to increase the real supply of money in such circumstances? Why do we ask the monetary authority to do approximately the same thing by creating new money? A part of the answer is that we believe cost and price structures are not that flex-

---

[2] Some argue that the excess supply of money arises out of the automatic increase in the "real" supply of money as prices fall.

ible downward. They fall only slowly and after a lag; in the meantime real
output and employment suffer. But even if costs and prices adjusted downward very rapidly we might not like the redistributions of wealth and income
that would accompany pure price deflation.

SHIFTS OF THE DEMAND FOR MONEY

Holding constant the other functions, including the supply of money, we
shall now trace out the effects of shifts in the community's demand function
for money balances. By shifts of this function we shall mean increases or decreases in the quantity of money demanded at each level of interest rates. We
shall find that a decrease in the quantity of money demanded at each interest
rate has about the same effects as would an equal increase in the supply of
money, for it creates an excess supply of money over the demand for it. On
the other hand, an increase in the quantity of money demanded at each interest rate has much the same effects as would an equal decrease in the supply, for it creates an excess of the demand for money over the available supply.

Decrease in the Demand for Money

A decrease in the quantity of money demanded at each level of interest
rates could reflect a decrease of L_1 at each level of Y, a decrease of L_2 at each
level of r, or some combination of the two. A decrease of L_1 at each level of
Y would, of course, reflect a decrease in the size of the fraction, j. For example, it may reflect a decrease of j from $\frac{1}{4}$ to $\frac{1}{6}$, so that L_1 would now equal
$\frac{1}{6}Y$ rather than $\frac{1}{4}Y$. Such a decrease in j might be brought about by changes
in any of the conditions that determine its size. As examples, it could be
reduced by a shortening of the average length of the income period, a greater
use of credit facilities to economize on money balances, the development of
refined barter techniques, faster transportation of money, new expectations
that future income receipts will be larger and more certain, or expectations
that the prices of other things are less likely to fall and more likely to rise.
A decrease of L_2 at each level of interest rates could result from changes in
any of the conditions determining the size of L_2 at each interest rate. For
example, it could reflect a decrease in the cost of acquiring, holding, and
disposing of other types of assets; the development or popularizing of more
attractive types of earning assets with greater safety and liquidity; or new
expectations that the prices of earning assets are less likely to fall and more
likely to rise.

Such a decrease in the demand for money at each interest rate while the
supply of money remained constant would create what the members of the
community would regard as excess money balances. They would seek to get

rid of the excess money by increasing their expenditures, offering a larger supply of investable funds, or some combination of the two. The excess supply of money could be eliminated only by a rise of Y, a fall of r, or some combination of the two. In Fig. 27 this would appear as a rightward shift of the $L = M$ line, indicating the demand for money could be equated to the available supply only by a higher level of Y at each level of r, or a lower level of r at each level of Y.

In general we have no reason to suppose that the response of the economy to attempts to get rid of excess money balances resulting from a reduction of the demand for money will differ from its response to attempts to get rid of excess money resulting from an increase in the money supply.

Increase in the Demand for Money

The results of an increase in the demand for money balances are in general the reverse of those of a decrease in the demand for money. We need only comment, therefore, that such an increase, with the money supply remaining constant, will create an excess demand for money, which will lead the members of the community to try to repair their balances by decreasing their expenditures, by decreasing the supply of investable funds, or some combination of the two. The consequences are in general the same as those of an equal reduction in the money supply.

SUMMARY AND CONCLUSIONS

This chapter has attempted to do three principal things: to show how the four functions combine to determine the levels of national money income and interest rates, to trace out the effects of increases and decreases in the supply of money, and to show briefly the effects of increases and decreases in the demand for money balances.

Several of our findings are important for making and understanding monetary policy.

1. If the money supply is increased or decreased as a part of a transaction that also increases or decreases the money income of the community, it may initially be injected into the spending stream for output or withdrawn from that stream by increases or decreases in consumption expenditures. But this initial reaction is unlikely if the money supply is changed in a way that does not initially change either the money income or the net worth position of the community. In such cases the initial impact is likely to be on the supply of investable funds and the level of interest rates.

2. The extent to which a given increase or decrease in the money supply can increase or decrease the total supply of investable funds and lower or raise interest rates depends on the responsiveness of the demand for money to

interest rates. If the demand for money balances is quite unresponsive to interest rates, a given change in the money supply will be largely reflected in a change in the total supply of investable funds and a large change in the level of interest rates is possible. But if the demand for money balances is extremely sensitive to interest rates, an increase or decrease in the supply of money may be largely offset by increases or decreases in the idle L_2 balances, so that there can be little net effect on the total supply of investable funds or on the level of interest rates.

3. The response of the economy depends not only on the extent to which the total supply of investable funds can be changed but also on the marginal responsiveness of investment demand to interest rates and on the size of the multiplier.

SELECTED READINGS

See references at the end of Chapters 13 and 14.

CHAPTER 16

Shifts of Investment and Saving

We shall now trace out the effects of shifts of the two remaining functions —the investment demand function and the supply of saving function. As in the preceding chapter, we shall assume that when one function is shifted all the others remain constant.

SHIFTS OF THE INVESTMENT DEMAND FUNCTION

By increases or decreases in the investment demand function we mean increases or decreases in investment expenditures for output at each level of interest rates. These can also be viewed as increases or decreases in the demand for investable funds at each level of interest rates. Such changes reflect shifts in the marginal efficiency of capital schedule.

Increase of Investment Demand

Investment demand can be increased at each level of interest rates by anything giving rise to expectations of higher rates of return on new investment. For example, it could result from new technological breakthroughs that increase opportunities for profitable investment, from more optimistic expectations concerning future demands for output, from the election of a popular new president who is expected to create a favorable environment for business, from a rise of optimism in general, and so on. Such a rise of investment demand is illustrated in Fig. 29 by the upward shift from I_0I_0 to I_1I_1. Let us assume that the increase of I at each level of r is $5 billion. The original equilibrium position was with Y at Y_e and r at r_e, for only at that combination were both of the necessary conditions, $L = M$ and $I_0 = S_0$, satisfied. But this is no longer an equilibrium situation when I would be $5 billion larger at each level of interest rates. I and S can now be brought into equality at any given level of interest rates only by a rise of Y sufficient to increase S by an amount equal to the rise of I. How large must this increase in Y be? Here again the answer depends on the size of our old friend, the multiplier, or $\frac{1}{\Delta S/\Delta Y}$. If $\frac{\Delta S}{\Delta Y}$ is $\frac{1}{5}$ the multiplier is 5 and Y will have to rise by \$25 billion to raise S by \$5 billion. But if $\frac{\Delta S}{\Delta Y}$ is $\frac{1}{2}$, Y will have to rise only \$10 billion to increase S by \$5 billion. In general, the necessary rise of Y at each level of r may be stated as $\Delta Y = \Delta I \times \frac{1}{\Delta S/\Delta Y}$, where ΔI is the dollar increase in invest-ment demand at each interest rate. In Fig. 29 the curve $I_1 = S$ shows all the

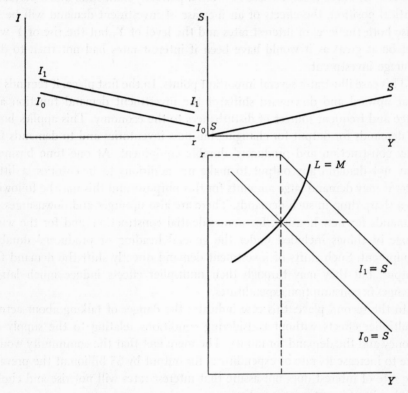

FIG. 29. Shifts in Investment Demand.

new combinations of r and Y at which I and S will be equal. It is to the right of the old $I_0 = S$ curve at each level of r by an amount equal to $\Delta I \times \frac{1}{\Delta S/\Delta Y}$.

Will Y actually increase by the full amount $\Delta I \times \frac{1}{\Delta S/\Delta Y}$, as some users of the multiplier seem to imply? Not necessarily. It will if interest rates do not rise at all but remain at r_e. Suppose that the L_2 demand for money is completely responsive to interest rates at the level r_e; this would appear as a horizontal section of the $L = M$ curve at that level. Even an infinitesimal rise of r

would free enough money from inactive L_2 balances to finance the rise of I and Y, so that the rise of investment spending would not be inhibited by any rise of interest rates. But let us consider a quite different possibility. Suppose that above the level of interest rates r_e the $L = M$ curve is completely unresponsive to interest rates. Further increases in interest rates release no money from idle L_2 balances. In this case there can be no actual rise of Y or of investment expenditures. The only effect is to raise the level of interest rates sufficiently to hold investment expenditures down to the old level. If the $L = M$ curve is somewhere between a perfectly horizontal and a perfectly vertical position, the effects of an increase of investment demand will be to raise both the level of interest rates and the level of Y, but the rise of Y will not be as great as it would have been if interest rates had not risen to discourage investment.

This case illustrates several important points. In the first place, it reminds us that upward and downward shifts of the investment demand function are large and frequent sources of disturbances to the economy. This applies both to demands for output for changing business inventories and to demands for new construction and producers' durable equipment. At one time business may not demand any output to make net additions to inventories; a little later it may demand large amounts for this purpose; and this may be followed by a sharp drop in such demands. There are also upsurges and downsurges in demands for new housing, for nonresidential construction, and for the wide range of things included under the general heading of producers' durable equipment. Such shifts of investment demand directly shift the demand for output, but they may through their multiplier effects induce much larger changes in consumption expenditures.

In the second place, this case indicates the danger of talking about actual multiplier effects without considering conditions relating to the supply of money and the demand for money. The mere fact that the community would like to increase its rate of expenditures for output by $5 billion at the prevailing rate of interest does not assure that interest rates will not rise and choke off the rise of investment spending.

In the third place, this case has important implications for monetary policy. Many, if not a majority, of the actions of the monetary authority are "defensive" in nature; they are designed to prevent such things as shifts of investment demand or of the supply of saving from having undesired effects on the economy. An increase of investment demand such as we assumed might well create strong inflationary pressures. Let us suppose that it does—that the old level Y_e was one of full employment and that any further increase in the demand for output would necessarily be reflected in increased prices. In dealing with a rise of investment demand under such conditions, the monetary authority should keep the following points in mind. (1) A purely defensive policy of preventing any rise in the supply of money will be inadequate if the demand for money is at all responsive to interest rates. As the rise of investment demand tends to raise interest rates, each rise of r will release money from inactive L_2 balances to finance the rise of investment expenditures and to provide money to satisfy the larger L_1 demand as Y rises. Thus, to prevent any such rise from occurring, the monetary authority would have to reduce the money supply enough to absorb or offset the money released from L_2 balances. (2) With a given supply of saving function, the appropriate level of market rates of interest depends on the height of the investment demand function. For example, when the investment demand function was I_0I_0 the interest rate r_e may have been appropriate for maintaining expenditures for output at the full-employment-without-inflation level Y_e. But after investment demand has risen to I_1I_1, reflecting expectations of much higher returns or new investment, the level of interest rates would have to rise to r_1 to prevent expenditures for output from rising above Y_e. Any lower level of r would now be inflationary. Suppose, for example, that despite the rise of investment demand the monetary authority tries to maintain interest rates at the old level r_e, doing so by keeping the banks well supplied with increased reserves and lending power. The community would spend more for investment, but with the economy already operating at capacity levels the effect may be largely to bid up the prices of capital goods. Such price increases may not deter at all the purchasers of capital goods, for they may expect their dollar net returns to rise at least in proportion. These increased expenditures enhance disposable incomes and increase consumption expenditures. And so on. As indicated earlier, an inflationary spiral may ensue, ending only when interest rates are increased sufficiently or when the marginal efficiency of capital declines.

Decrease of Investment Demand

A decrease of investment demand can be illustrated in Fig. 29 by a downward shift from I_1I_1 to I_0I_0. Such a decrease of investment demand at each level of interest rates could result from anything that decreases the expected profitability of new investment—from such things as a temporary shortage of profitable investment opportunities when new opportunities fail to develop as fast as old ones are used up, from a deterioration of expectations concerning future demands for output, and so on. Let us suppose that for such reasons investment demand at each level of interest rates falls by $5 billion.

It is clear that each Y, r combination that formerly equalized I and S will no longer do so. With I reduced by $5 billion at each level of r, S would have to fall by the same amount to become equal to I. But S could be reduced only by a decline of Y. The size of the reduction of Y required to reduce S by \$5 billion depends, of course, on the size of the multiplier. For example, if $\frac{\Delta S}{\Delta Y} = \frac{1}{5}$, the multiplier is 5 and Y would have to fall by \$25 billion to reduce S by \$5 billion. All the new possible combinations of Y and r at which S would be equal to the new lower level of I are on the line $I_0 = S$, which lies to the left of the old $I_1 S_1$ line at each level of interest rates by the amount

$$\Delta Y = \Delta I \times \frac{1}{\Delta S / \Delta Y}.$$

Will Y actually fall by an amount equal to the \$5 billion decrease in investment demand times the multiplier? It will if interest rates do not fall at all so that I actually declines \$5 billion. Suppose, for example, that at the old level of r the demand for money is completely responsive to interest rates. That is, the $L = M$ curve is horizontal at that level of r. In this case the community would not lend at all at any lower rate, the interest rate could not fall, and the decline of the investment demand function could not be offset at all by a cheapening of investable funds. But the downward shift of the investment demand schedule may induce some decrease of interest rates, which by encouraging investment may offset at least in part the downward shift of the investment function. (Note what happens to the value of I on the $I_0 I_0$ curve as r falls.) Let us take the extreme case in which the $L = M$ curve is completely vertical; that is, the demand for money is completely unresponsive to interest rates. In this case interest rates may fall markedly, thereby helping to sustain the actual rate of investment spending.

Economists have pointed out, as noted earlier, that a decline of the money value of Y will itself tend to lower interest rates if the money supply remains constant. With declines in Y, the transactions demand for money will decline, thereby increasing the supply available for L_2 purposes. As its L_2 balances rise, the community will try to get rid of the excess by increasing the supply of investable funds, thereby lowering interest rates. Some economists have argued that this "automatic" effect may lower interest rates sufficiently so that expansionary policies by the monetary authority will be unnecessary. For several reasons most economists now doubt this. (1) It may operate too slowly. In the meantime the economy suffers from underemployment. (2) Because the demand for money may be highly responsive to interest rates, especially at low levels of interest rates, most of the money freed from L_1 balances by the decline of Y may not appear in the market as a supply of investable funds but may be added to inactive L_2 balances. (3) Investment may be relatively unresponsive to such decreases of interest rates as do occur. For such reasons, most economists now believe that the "automatic" effects should be strongly supplemented by an expansionary monetary policy.

The appropriate policy under such conditions is, of course, to increase the money supply in order to create an excess of the supply of money over the demand for money, so that the community will try to get rid of the excess supply by increasing its expenditures, by enhancing the supply of investable funds, or by some combination of the two. If the money supply is increased in ways that do not directly raise money incomes or increase the net wealth position of the community—for example, through open-market operations or decreases in member bank reserve requirements—the initial impact is likely to be that of increasing the supply of investable funds and lowering interest rates. But can we be assured that such an easy-money policy will succeed in preventing any decline of investment expenditures? We cannot. Let us consider two adverse cases. (1) The investment demand function has declined so much that the old rate of investment expenditures could be maintained only if interest rates were at or below zero. But when the community can hold money balances at no out-of-pocket cost it is obviously impossible to drive interest rates down to zero, to say nothing of negative levels. (2) Investment expenditures could be maintained at their old level at some interest rate above zero, but that rate is below the minimum rate at which the banks and the community will lend. At some higher rate all new money will simply be added to L_2 balances; it will disappear into the liquidity trap. In such cases an expansionary monetary policy cannot alone prevent a decline of investment expenditures. For this purpose it will require the assistance of government fiscal policy.

It would, however, be too pessimistic to conclude that easy-money policies are useless in the face of a decline of the investment demand function. (1) As a minimum such policies can lessen pressures by banks for repayment of outstanding loans and discourage refusals to meet requests for loans. Some recessions and depressions have been deepened and prolonged by the unwillingness of banks to satisfy the loan demands that they received. This was due in part to fears of loss, in part to inadequate bank liquidity. A policy of flooding the banks with excess reserves can make them more receptive to such loan demands as they receive. (2) Such policies may succeed in lowering interest rates markedly. This is especially true when rates were formerly high by historical standards. Under such conditions it may not be difficult to convince the community that rates will be even lower in the future. (3) If the decline of the investment demand function is not severe, an easy-money policy alone may be sufficient to prevent a decline of investment spending. The investment demand function may still be high enough and responsive enough to a decline of interest rates to enable investment expenditures to be maintained at their old level at an interest rate that is still high enough to prevent all the new money from being added to L_2 balances. (4) Even if it does not succeed in preventing a decline of investment spending, an easy-money policy may reduce the extent of the decline. (5) If deficit spending by the government is invoked to combat the decline, an easy-money policy can perform a useful function in assuring that the government's borrowing does not decrease the supply or increase the cost of investable funds for private use. Some other effects of easy-money policies will be discussed later.

SHIFTS OF THE SAVING SUPPLY FUNCTION

Let us now trace out the effects of shifts of the saving supply function, assuming the other three functions to remain constant. By an increase of this function we mean an increase in the supply of saving at each level of Y, and by a decrease we mean a decrease of saving at each level of Y.

Before starting our analysis it will be useful to recall two ways of viewing the supply of saving. (1) At any level of Y it is the sum of personal saving (S_p), gross business saving (S_b), and government saving $(S_g$, or $T_n - G)$. This view emphasizes the supply of saving as a potential source of funds to finance private investment. It is the total of private saving plus any government surplus, but minus any government deficit, the last being a competing use of funds. (2) It is the total value of output minus that value of output demanded for personal consumption (C) and by the government (G). It is this view that we shall find most useful here, though the first should also be kept in mind. That is, $S = Y - (C + G)$. This view makes it clear that a decrease of S at each level of Y reflects an equal increase of the demand for output at that level of Y in the form of $C + G$. It is the same thing as saying that consumption and government demands are higher at that level of Y. On the other hand, a rise of S at each level of Y reflects an equal decrease in the demand for output at that level of Y in the form of $C + G$.

When we look at S in this way, it seems reasonable to expect that a given dollar decrease of the saving function would have about the same effect on Y as an equal dollar increase of investment demand. The latter has both a direct and a multiplier effect on Y. So does a downward shift of S, reflecting an upward shift of $C + G$ at each level of Y. It is also reasonable to expect that a given dollar increase in the saving function, reflecting a downward shift of $C + G$ demands, would have both direct and multiplier effects on the level of Y similar to those that would result from an equal dollar decline of investment demand. Because of these similarities we can deal more briefly with shifts of the saving function.

Decrease of the Supply of Saving

Let us suppose in Fig. 30 that in the initial situation the supply of saving is S_0S_0 and the equilibrium combination of Y and r is $Y_e r_e$. Now suppose that, reflecting an increase of $C + G$ demands for output, the supply of S falls by $5 billion at each level of Y. I and S are no longer equal at the old combinations of Y and r that formerly equalized them. Now that S has fallen by $5 billion at each level of Y, they can again be equalized only by a rise of interest rates to reduce I, a rise of Y to increase S, or some combination of the two. How much would Y have to rise at each level of r to increase S by $5 billion? Again, this depends on the size of the multiplier, $\dfrac{1}{\Delta S/\Delta Y}$. The new curve, $I = S_1$, shows all the new combinations of Y and r that would equalize S

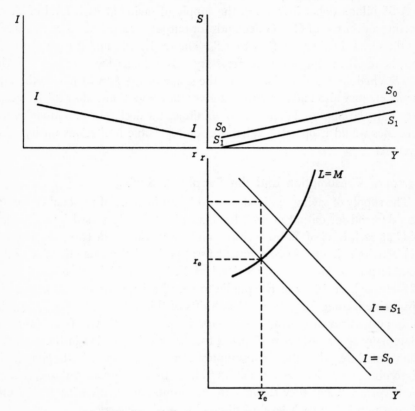

FIG. 30.   Shifts in the Supply of Saving.

and I. At each level of interest rates it is to the right of the old $I = S_0$ curve by an amount equal to the $5 billion decrease of the supply of saving times the multiplier.

Will Y actually rise this much? It will if the interest rate remains unchanged at r_e so that none of the adjustment can occur through a reduction of I. But suppose the $L = M$ curve is perfectly vertical at the income level Y_e. In this case the rise of interest rates frees no money from L_2 balances and there is no rise of Y. The net effect is to raise the level of interest rates and thereby to decrease actual investment by an amount equal to the rise of $C + G$. If the shape of the $L = M$ line is between the horizontal and the vertical, the decrease in the supply of saving will raise both interest rates and the level of Y, but the rise of Y will not be as large as it would have been if interest rates had not risen. Again we see how dangerous it is to talk about actual multiplier effects without considering conditions relating to the supply of money and the demand for money.

Increase of the Supply of Saving

A $5 billion dollar increase in the supply of saving at each level of Y, reflecting a decrease of $C + G$ demands for output, can be illustrated in Fig. 30 by the upward shift from S_1S_1 to S_0S_0. The reader will find it useful to trace out the results, noting both the necessary leftward and downward shift of the $I = S$ schedule and the relevance of the shape of the $L = M$ line to the outcome. He may also find it useful to answer these questions: How might monetary policy be employed to prevent or minimize the decline of Y? Through what processes would it operate? What are some possible limitations on its effectiveness?

Personal Consumption and the Supply of Saving

The supply of saving can be decreased by an increase of personal consumption demand for output at each level, and it can be increased by a decrease of C at each level of Y. Such shifts might come about in two general ways. (1) Through changes in government fiscal policy that change the size of disposable private income at each level of Y. These will be considered later. (2) Through decisions of the public to spend a larger or smaller part of its disposable income for consumption. Shifts of this latter type clearly could be an important source of economic fluctuations. But are they in fact? For some time many economists were disposed to answer this question in the negative. They noted that the rate of consumption was highly responsive to changes in disposable private income emanating from changes in investment and government spending, but they thought the consumption function itself—the rate of consumption at each level of disposable private income—remained rather stable over the short run. More recently, however, the belief has grown that the consumption function is less stable than was formerly thought. In a few cases the shift has been dramatic. For example, the fear of wartime shortages and higher prices shifted consumption sharply upward at the outbreak of the Korean conflict. Less dramatically, people may shift their consumption functions because of changed expectations concerning their future employment and incomes, the future behavior of prices, or because of changes in their asset and debt positions. For example, if large sections of the public come to feel that their asset holdings have become too small and they are too heavily in debt, they may use a larger part of their current incomes for saving and a smaller part for consumption. But if they have built up their assets and reduced their debts they may feel free to spend a larger part of their current incomes for consumption and to save a smaller part.

GOVERNMENT FISCAL POLICY

The government's fiscal policy is made up of three principal parts: its policy relative to its purchases of goods and services, its tax policy, and its policy relative to transfer payments. Partly because of the huge volume of its economic operations, the government's fiscal policies inevitably affect greatly the functioning of the economy. They may initiate or at least aggravate inflation or deflation. But they may also be used to stabilize the economy, to offset shifts of private investment demand or private consumption functions. We shall now investigate the effects of each of these policies, starting with those relative to government purchases of goods and services.

Changes in G

Let us start from the situation indicated in Fig. 30 in which Y is at the level Y_e. Now, while all the other functions remain constant, including the government's policies relative to taxes and transfer payments, the government raises its demand for output at each level of Y by $5 billion. This $5 billion rise of G will be reflected in a decline of S by $5 billion at each level of Y, this representing the decline of government saving $(T_n - G)$. This $5 rise of G clearly raises Y by that amount. But is this the end of the story? It is not, for with the $5 billion decline of S at each level of Y, S will no longer be equal to I at each of the Y, r combinations that formerly equalized them. I will now exceed S, and they can again be equalized only by a rise of Y to increase S, a rise of r to lower I, or some combination of the two. How much must Y increase at each level of r to increase S by $5 billion? This again depends on the size of $\frac{\Delta S}{\Delta Y}$ and the multiplier. For example, if the multiplier is 5, Y will have to rise $25 billion to raise S by $5 billion. All the new Y, r combinations at which $I = S$ are on the $I = S_1$ line, which lies to the right of the old $I = S_0$ curve at each level of r by an amount,

$$\Delta Y = \$5 \text{ billion} \times \frac{1}{\Delta S/\Delta Y}$$

This may be viewed in another way. The $5 billion increase in the government's expenditures not only added that amount to the total demand for output, but also increased disposable incomes by that amount. The recipients of these increased incomes may be expected to increase their consumption expenditures, the amount depending on their marginal propensity to consume, $\frac{\Delta C}{\Delta Y}$. This increases the incomes of the producers of consumers' goods, who increase their consumption, and so on. These facts are very important for fiscal policy. Government officials should realize that the expansionary or contractionary effects following increases or decreases of G will not be limited to the direct effects of Y; they will also include the effects of induced increases or decreases of consumption demand. Government spending, as well as private investment spending, has its multiplier effects.

But will Y actually rise by an amount equal to the $5 billion rise of $G \times \dfrac{1}{\Delta S/\Delta Y}$? It will if the other functions remain constant and the interest rate does not rise and decrease private investment spending. But the very rise of G and the accompanying decline of government saving may tend to raise interest rates and lower private investment. Again we shall see how dangerous it is to talk about actual multiplier effects without considering conditions relating to the supply of money and the demand for money. Let us consider three cases.

1. The monetary authority adamantly holds the money supply constant, so that the $L = M$ curve remains unchanged. The $5 billion decline of government saving at the level of income Y_e tends to reduce the supply of investable funds for private investment and to raise interest rates. For example, suppose the government formerly had a tax surplus at a rate of $5 billion a year, that this was being used to retire government debt, and that the recipients were relending it to business. This source of funds for private investment now disappears. Or suppose that the government formerly had an exactly balanced budget, so that it now has a negative saving, or a deficit, of $5 billion a year. This new government borrowing in competition with the private sectors will tend to raise interest rates. The supply of investable funds might, of course, be maintained and interest rates prevented from rising if the community were holding very large L_2 balances that were completely responsive to r at its old level. In this case the disgorging of money from idle balances would permit the full multiplier effects to be achieved. The entire rise of Y could be financed by activating what were formerly idle money balances. But if L_2 is less than completely responsive to interest rates, the latter must rise. In the extreme case in which L_2 is completely unresponsive to interest rates and the $L = M$ curve is completely vertical at Y_e, interest rates must rise enough to decrease I by the amount that G has risen. There is no source of investable funds to replace those removed by the decrease of government saving.

2. The monetary authority expands the money supply just enough to prevent any rise of interest rates, but not enough to reduce interest rates. In this case interest rates obviously do not change at all, I is unaffected, and the full multiplier effects of the rise of G are achieved.

3. The monetary authority buys government securities at an annual rate of $5 billion to match the rise of G. This, of course, creates reserves for the com-

mercial banks. If the latter operate on 20 percent reserves, they may be enabled to increase the money supply by $25 billion a year. Such a huge increase of the money supply would increase the supply of investable funds much more than the decline of government saving tended to reduce it, would lower interest rates, and would induce a rise of private investment spending. This induced rise of I, as well as the rise of G, would induce increases in consumption expenditures. Such continuing increases in the money supply would, of course, be reflected in a continuing shift of the $L = M$ curve to the right and downward. The potentially explosive inflationary results should be apparent. This case indicates one reason why it is dangerous for governments to borrow from their central banks.

Several points are illustrated by this example. (1) The actual effects of any given change in government demand for output and in government saving depend in part on monetary conditions. On some occasions the presence of very large inactive L_2 balances that are highly responsive to interest rates may prevent or at least minimize the rise of interest rates. But a decrease in government saving is likely, in the absence of an increase in the money supply, to raise interest rates. (2) If the government wishes to minimize the expansionary effects of any given increase in its expenditures, it should borrow in ways that do not involve an increase in the money supply. If it wishes to maximize expansionary effects it should borrow in ways that do increase the money supply. Most expansive of all is the financing of expenditures by creating and issuing fiat money or by borrowing from the central bank, both of which tend to increase bank reserves and to permit a multiple increase in the money supply.

The effects of a $5 billion decrease in the government's demand for output at each level of Y, which would be reflected as a $5 billion rise in the supply of saving at each level of Y, are in general just the reverse of those described above. The decline of G would both decrease directly the total demand for output and reduce disposable incomes, thereby inducing downward multiplier effects through decreased consumption spending. After this rise of S at each level of Y, S would exceed I at each of the Y, r combinations that formerly equalized them. They can be brought into equality again only by a fall of r to increase I, a fall of Y to decrease S, or some combination of the two. All the new combinations of Y, r that will equalize them will be on a new $I = S$ curve that lies to the left of the old $I = S$ curve at each level of r by an amount equal to $5 billion $\times \dfrac{1}{\Delta S/\Delta Y}$.

The level of income will actually fall by this full amount if interest rates and private investment spending remain unchanged. This may happen. For example, the L_2 demand for money may be completely responsive to interest rates at the old level of r, so that none of the increase in government saving appears in the market as an increased supply of investable funds and there is no downward pressure on interest rates. But if the L_2 demand for money is less than completely responsive to interest rates and the money supply remains constant, at least some part of the increase in government saving will appear in the market as an increased supply of investable funds, which will tend to lower interest rates and stimulate private investment spending. An expansionary monetary policy could, of course, increase the downward pressure on interest rates.

In the preceding discussion we have assumed that the investment demand function remained constant in the face of increases or decreases of government demand for output. This may be realistic if the shifts of G are not large or dramatic. But we should recognize that shifts of G may shift the investment demand function. Suppose, for example, that the government increases markedly its demand for output and that the community expects that both the rise of G and the induced rise of C will bring large increases in demands for the output of industry. The marginal efficiency of capital may rise, and with it the investment demand function. In such a case the total rise of expenditures for output will consist of the initial rise of G and the induced rise of I and the induced rise of C resulting from both the rise of G and the rise of I. But in this case, as in the others discussed earlier, the actual behavior of I will depend in part on monetary conditions and the behavior of interest rates. After all, I cannot rise if additional investable funds are not available.

Similarly, an initial decrease of G may, by lowering expectations concerning total demands for output, lower the investment demand function. Any induced fall of I, as well as the initial decline of G, will tend to reduce consumption demand. Here again the actual behavior of I will depend in part on monetary conditions and the behavior of interest rates.

Changes in T_n

Let us now consider changes in the government's tax policy while all the other functions, including the government's purchases of goods and services and its transfer payments, remain constant. We shall start with an increase of taxes, assuming that the government increases its tax collections at each level of Y by \$5 billion. In our analysis this will appear as a \$5 billion rise of government saving.

How can this rise of taxes affect the demand for output? It does not directly constitute either an addition to or a reduction of spendings for output. But it does lower disposable private incomes, and this initial decline of disposable private incomes is likely to decrease consumption demand at each level of Y. How much will it lower C at each level of Y? Will it lower C by the full \$5 billion at each level of Y? Probably not; with lower disposable incomes the community is likely to decrease its saving as well as its consumption. Let us suppose that for every \$1 decrease of its disposable income the community reduces its consumption spending $0.80 and its saving $0.20. In this case the $5 billion decrease of disposable private income would initially reduce C by $4 billion. But this is not the end of the story. The initial $4 billion decrease of C would reduce the incomes of those employed in the consumers' goods industries, the latter would in turn decrease their consumption, and so on. Thus the initial $4 billion reduction of C induced by the $5 billion tax increase would have its downward multiplier effects. In our diagrams this would appear as a leftward shift of the $I = S$ curve. The new $I = S$ curve would lie to the left of the old by an amount equal to the initial $4 billion decrease of $C \times \dfrac{1}{\Delta S/\Delta Y}$.

Several important points are brought out by this example. (1) By increasing its tax collections at each level of Y the government can lower disposable private incomes at each level of Y. (2) This is likely to lower consumption demand at each level of Y. However, the initial decrease of C is not likely to be as large as the rise of government tax collections, for some of the taxes may be paid with income that would otherwise have been saved. (3) Any initial decline of C that does occur will have downward multiplier effects.

Here, as in other similar cases, we cannot be sure that Y will actually fall by an amount equal to the initial $4 billion decline of $C \times \dfrac{1}{\Delta S/\Delta Y}$. It will if interest rates and investment spending remain unchanged. But the very increase of government saving and the decline of the demand for money as Y falls may tend to lower interest rates and stimulate private investment. On the other hand, the decline of consumption demand can have the further effect of lowering the investment demand function. The outcome may differ from case to case. But of one thing we can be fairly certain: the total effects on Y will not be only those of the initial decline of consumption.

The effects flowing from a $5 billion decrease of tax collections at each level of Y are just the reverse of those described above. Such a tax reduction would raise disposable private income at each level of Y; this would tend to increase consumption demand at each level of Y, and upward multiplier effects would follow. Thus tax reductions may be a powerful instrument for raising expenditures for output, especially if the public uses a very large part of every increase in its disposable income to increase its rate of consumption.

We now come to the government's transfer payments. These, as noted earlier, are not themselves a government demand for output, but they are a part of disposable private income. The government can therefore increase or decrease disposable private incomes at each level of Y by increasing or decreasing the amounts of its transfer payments. In general, an increase of transfer payments has effects similar to those of a decrease of taxes; both serve to raise disposable private incomes at each level of Y. Also, a decrease of transfer payments has effects similar to those of an increase of taxes; both serve to lower disposable private incomes at each level of Y. And both may be used to influence the level of demand for output.

Conclusions

We find, then, that the government has three principal instruments of fiscal policy: its demand for output, its tax policy, and its transfer payments policy. It can exert an expansionary influence on the economy by increasing its demand for output, by raising its transfer payments, or by lowering taxes. It can exert a restrictive influence by decreasing its demand for output, by decreasing its transfer payments, or by raising taxes. These instruments may be used in various combinations. Used unwisely or clumsily, they can initiate or aggravate economic fluctuations. Employed wisely and skillfully, they may be effective in stabilizing the economy by offsetting shifts in private investment demand and private consumption functions. In all cases both direct and multiplier effects should be considered. And in all cases current monetary conditions and monetary policy will affect the outcome. For example, the expansionary effects of increased government expenditures or decreased taxes may be at least partially offset if the supply of funds for private investment is allowed to decline. This emphasizes the usefulness of a proper coördination of monetary and fiscal policies.

SUMMARY AND CONCLUSIONS

There are, of course, literally thousands of things that enter into the determination of the level of real and money income and the height of the interest rate structure. But all these can be grouped under four main headings: the investment demand function, the supply of saving function, the supply of money function, and the demand for money function. Our first task was to show that the level of income and the level of interest rates are not determined independently of each other but are determined simultaneously, and that they are determined not by one or two functions alone but by all four functions in combination. Then we proceeded to show how a shift of each function would alter results, and how the final results would depend on the responsiveness of the other functions.

Though our central interest in this book is in money and its effects on the functioning of the economy, we have tried to avoid overemphasizing the role of money and monetary policy. No one can explain fully the behavior of income and interest rates by considering money and monetary policy alone. For this purpose we must include all those things behind the marginal efficiency of capital schedule and the investment demand function; all the determinants of the nation's supply of saving at each level of income; and all the conditions affecting the amounts of money the community would elect to hold in relationship to its level of income and in relationship to the level of interest rates. Moreover, monetary managers need to take all such things into consideration in formulating monetary policy. They are unlikely to know what to do if they do not understand the effects of changes in these things or how these things will respond to the various possible types of monetary policy. But while dealing with these various other determinants, we have also insisted on including the money supply as a determinant. There is still room for much intelligent disagreement on such matters as the extent of the effects of any given change of the money supply or the degree to which manipulations of the money supply can effectively offset changes in the investment demand function or the supply of saving function. But to contend that the size of the money supply is irrelevant to the outcome would be absurd.

Our technique of shifting one function at a time, assuming the others to remain constant, is one commonly used in economics. It is the economist's closest approach to the laboratory method of the physical scientist in which all other conditions are kept constant so that the effects of changes in one variable can be isolated. This method may be realistic in many cases; it may indeed be possible to shift one function without in the process shifting the others. But we should frankly recognize that this is not always true, and is not likely to be when the shifts of a function are large or dramatic. For example, a dramatic rise of government expenditures, such as might occur at the beginning of a war that is expected to be long and expensive, may raise markedly the investment demand function and also the consumption function. A sharp rise of investment demand may, especially if it portends inflation, create expectations of increased money incomes and raise the consumption function and perhaps also lower the demand for money at each level of income and interest rates. Changes of the money supply, and even expectations of future changes of it, may shift the demand for money. The most dramatic examples are those of hyperinflation in which increases of prices initiated by increases in the money supply have generated fears of still further rises in the future and have virtually eliminated the demand for money balances. In some cases success in stopping the creation of new money has been enough to eliminate expectations of further price increases and to raise markedly the demand for money. Increases and decreases in the money supply, or even expectations that they will occur, may raise or lower investment demand by affecting expectations concerning future demands for output.

When shifts of one function do shift other functions, the analysis becomes more complex and the results are, of course, changed. The analysis developed here should enable the reader to infer the directions in which a shift of one function may shift others and the nature of the effects of such induced shifts.

Largely to avoid increased complexity, we have used some oversimplified assumptions. One of these is that the supply of saving is not responsive to the level of interest rates. Many economists believe that this involves no serious error. But they may be wrong. A rise of interest rates, especially a large one, may shift the supply of saving upward and the consumption function downward, and a fall of interest rates may have the opposite effect. If so, this is another way that restrictive or expansionary monetary policies may affect the demand for output. We also oversimplified when we assumed a single interest rate in the market and that changes in this rate reflected the tightness or ease of credit conditions. This assumption tends to obscure the fact that some interest rates move only sluggishly, and that changes in interest rates are not the only method of equating the demand for investable funds to the available supply. In markets where interest rates are sluggish—especially on bank loans to their medium-sized and small borrowers—lenders often employ various types of nonprice rationing. For example, suppose banks find that their lending power is smaller than the demand for loans. Instead of raising interest rates enough to reduce demand to the level of their lending power, they may refuse to meet some loan requests, scale others down, or raise collateral requirements or credit standards enough to eliminate the excess demand. On the other hand, when their lending power is larger relative to demand they may not expand their loans solely by lowering interest rates, but also by relaxing their nonprice rationing and lending more generously to applicants. To assume that the full effects of more restrictive or easier monetary policies are reflected in the accompanying rise or fall of interest rates would be a serious mistake.

SELECTED READINGS
See references at the end of Chapters 13 and 14.

Appendix to Chapter 16: Quantity Theories

The preceding chapters have presented an eclectic type of theory combining national income analysis and a variant of a type of monetary theory often referred to as "the cash-balance approach." The purpose of this appendix is to outline briefly the logic and essential content of two types of quantity theory that have had long and distinguished careers in the history of monetary theory.

THE CASH BALANCE APPROACH

The general logic of this approach is that which we used in our analysis of the supply of money and the demand for money and the process of equilibrating them. It deals with the supply of a stock of money and the demand by the community for a stock of money to hold. Nevertheless, most versions of the cash balance approach differ from our earlier treatment in at least two respects: (1) They assume that the demand for money (L) is not at all elastic to interest rates, or is so inelastic that effects on it of changes in interest rates can be ignored with little loss of accuracy. (2) Their central interest is not in explaining the level of interest rates, employment, or income, but in explaining the behavior of price levels. Let us now consider two variants of this approach.

The Income Variant

We shall denote the supply or stock of money by (M). This is assumed to be fixed by the monetary authority. The demand for money balances (L) is assumed to be related to the level of national money income in such a way that

$$L = kOp$$

where O = the rate of real output or income stated at an annual rate
  p = the average price level of output
  Op = the level of national money income, the latter stated at an annual rate
  k = the fraction of national money income, the latter stated at an annual rate, over which the community demands to hold purchasing power in the form of money balances

Those who employ this theory analyze the determinants of k in much the same way that we earlier analyzed the determinants of j. The community arrives at what it considers to be the most advantageous size of k by weighing both advantages and costs of holding money balances. If $k = \frac{1}{3}$, the community's demand for money balances will be equal to one third of its annual rate of national money income.[1] By assuming the rate of real output or income (O) to be constant, we can state the demand for money as a function of p. This is reflected in the LL curve in Fig. 31.

This figure shows that with the given money supply and demand for money functions, the only equilibrium price level for output is p_0, for this is the only price level that equates the demand for money to the supply of money. At any lower price level the demand for money would be less than the supply of money, the members of the community would increase their rate of expenditures in efforts to rid themselves of their excess money balances, and the increased expenditures with a constant rate of real output would raise the price level of output. At any level of prices above p_0 the reverse would occur. The demand for money would exceed the supply of money, the community would reduce its expenditures in an attempt to repair the deficiency of its money balances, and prices would fall.

[1] In some variants $L = b + kOp$, where b is some absolute amount of money demanded as "hoards" or for store of value purposes.

The price level can be shifted by shifts of *MM, LL,* or both. Suppose that while the demand for money function remains constant the supply of money is shifted to the right. This will create an excess of the supply of money over the demand for money at the old equilibrium level of prices, and prices will be bid up as the community increases its expenditures in an effort to rid itself of ex-

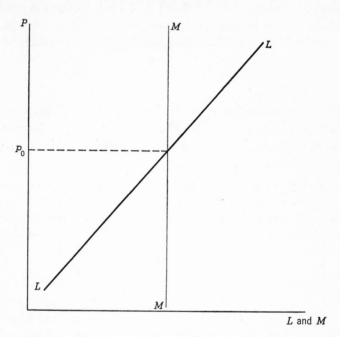

FIG. 31. The Price Level of Output with Given MM and LL Functions.

cess balances. A leftward shift of the money supply would have the opposite effect.

The price level can also be shifted by rightward or leftward shifts of the *LL* curve, and these can result from changes in either *O* or *k*. Suppose, however, that while both *O* and the money supply remain constant, *k* rises from $\frac{1}{3}$ to $\frac{1}{2}$. This will shift *LL* to the right at each level of *p*. The demand for money will now exceed the supply of money at the old equilibrium level of prices, the community will try to repair the deficiency of its balances by reducing its rate of expenditures, and the reduction of expenditures will lower the price level. A reduction of *k*, say from $\frac{1}{3}$ to $\frac{1}{4}$, would reduce the demand for money at each level of prices, create an excess of the supply of money over the demand for it at the old equilibrium level of prices, and evoke a rise of expenditures and prices.

This type of analysis becomes more complicated if we assume that the rate of real output is responsive to the rate of money expenditures. In this case a rise of expenditures, whether evoked by an increase in the supply of money or an initial decrease of k, would tend to raise real output, shift the LL curve to the right, and produce a smaller rise of prices than would otherwise occur. Similarly, a decrease of expenditures resulting from either a decrease of M or an initial rise of k would lower the rate of real output, shift the LL curve to the left, and produce a smaller fall of prices than would otherwise occur.

In equilibrium the demand for money must be exactly equal to the supply of money; that is, $L = M$. We can therefore state that in equilibrium

$$M = kOp$$

This formulation will be useful later.

The Total Expenditures Variant

The type of cash balance approach outlined above concentrates its attention on the flow of expenditures for current output or income, the price level of current output, and the demand for money as a function of the money value of output. Another variant, using exactly the same logic, deals with the total flow of expenditures for everything entering into trade, with the price level of those things, and with the demand for money relative to the value of all these transactions.

In this version T represents the physical volume of trade, stated at an annual rate. T includes not only all current real output at its final stage of sale but also all intermediate transactions in the process of production and distribution, as well as all second-hand goods involved in transactions during the period. T is therefore very much larger than O during any period. P is the average price of each unit of T. The value of all these transactions, stated at an annual rate, is PT.

The demand for money is assumed to be related to value of these transactions in such a way that $L = KPT$, where K is the fraction of PT, the latter being stated at an annual rate, over which the community demands to hold purchasing power in the form of money balances. Since L is in both cases the total demand for money balances and PT is much larger than Op, the size of K is much smaller than k. For example, when $k = \frac{1}{3}$, we might expect K to be $\frac{1}{10}$ or even smaller. K is assumed to be determined by the choices of the community as it weighs the costs and advantages of holding larger or smaller money balances relative to its rate of expenditures.

Since $L = KPT$, we can relate the demand for money to the height of P if we assume K and T to be constant. The quantity of money demanded will increase and decrease with P. Thus a given money supply and a constant demand for money function will determine a unique equilibrium level of P. At any higher price level the demand for money would exceed the available supply, the community would reduce its expenditures in an attempt to repair its money balances, and the price level would fall. At any price level below the equilibrium level, the demand for money would be less than the money supply and prices would be driven up as the community increased its rate of expenditures in attempts to rid itself of its excess money balances.

Here again the price level can be shifted by shifts of the money supply and of the demand for money function. An increase of the money supply while the demand for money function remains constant would create an excess supply of money at the old equilibrium level of P and evoke increases of expenditures and prices. A reduction of the money supply would have the opposite effect.

The demand for money function can be shifted by changes in K and T. Suppose that while T remains constant K increases from $\frac{1}{10}$ to $\frac{1}{8}$. The increase of the demand for money at each level of P will create an excess demand for money at the old equilibrium level of P and evoke a decrease of expenditures and prices. A decrease of K, which would decrease the quantity of money demanded at each level of P, would have the opposite effect, creating an excess supply of money, increased expenditures, and a rise of prices. The demand for money function can also be shifted by changes in the physical volume of trade, T. Thus a rise of T would increase the quantity of money demanded at each level of P, create an excess demand for money at the old equilibrium level of P, and induce a fall of prices. A decline of T, which would reduce the demand for money at each level of P, would have the reverse effect.

The analysis becomes more complex if T is responsive to changes in the rate of expenditures. In such cases an increase of expenditures, whether because of an increase in the money supply or an initial decrease of K, would increase T, shift the demand curve for money to the right, and result in a smaller rise of P than would otherwise occur. Also a decline of expenditures would decrease T, shift the LL curve to the left, and lessen the decrease of P.

Since equilibrium requires that the demand for money be exactly equal to the supply of money we may state that in equilibrium

$$M = KPT$$

VELOCITY APPROACHES

Another type of quantity theory that has been widely used was developed by Professor Irving Fisher and others. Its logic is essentially the same as that of the cash balance approach. The only difference is that it uses the concept of velocity or rapidity of circulation of money instead of the demand for money balances. But this is a difference of terminology rather than substance, as we shall see.

The Income Variant

In our earlier discussion of the income variant of the cash balance approach, we found that in equilibrium the demand for money must be exactly equal to the supply of money, so that we can write the equation,

$$M = kOp$$

Thus, if $k = \frac{1}{3}$, the money supply is equal to $\frac{1}{3}$ of Op, the annual rate of expenditures for output. But for at least two reasons we may be more interested in the size of Op relative to M. In the first place, if the size of M and k is given, it is through adjustments of Op that the demand for money is adjusted to the supply of money. In the second place, we may want to show how the size of M and k affects the size of Op. We can show these relationships by dividing both sides of the equation by k. Thus, we get $\frac{M}{k} = Op$, or $M\frac{1}{k} = Op$. This tells us, for example, that if $k = \frac{1}{3}$, equilibrium conditions will exist only if Op, the annual rate of expenditures for output, is three times the money supply. If Op were greater than this, the community's money balances would be less than a third of its rate of expenditures for output and the community would try to repair the deficiency of its money balances by decreasing its rate of expenditures. On the other hand, if Op were less than three times the money supply, actual money balances would be greater than a third of the annual rate of expenditures for output and the community would try to get rid of its excess money balances by increasing its rate of expenditures.

In essence, the income variant of the velocity approach uses the equation

$$M\frac{1}{k} = Op$$

But instead of using the symbol $\frac{1}{k}$ it uses V_i, the income velocity of money. This is the average number of times each dollar of the money supply is spent, at an annual rate, for output. Whereas $k = \frac{M}{Op}$, $V_i = \frac{Op}{M}$. Thus, $V_i = \frac{1}{k}$. If $k = \frac{1}{3}$, $V_i = 3$.

Though it is important to note that mathematically $V_i = \frac{1}{k}$, it is more important to recognize that they are determined by the same factors and the same decisions by the community. The cash balance approach notes that the members of the community weigh the various advantages and costs of holding money balances in determining the size of their demand for balances relative to their rate of expenditures, or $\dfrac{M}{Op}$. But this process can just as well be

viewed as one of adjusting the ratio $\dfrac{Op}{M}$ to the level considered most advantageous by the community. Thus the sizes of V_i and k at any time are determined by the same factors and they are changed by changes in the same
factors.

The equation $MV_i = Op$ suggests several things, among them: (1) The
flow of expenditures for output varies directly with the money supply and
with the income velocity of money. (2) If V_i remains constant, a change in
the money supply will be reflected in a proportional change in the rate of
expenditures for output. (3) Changes in V_i can bring proportional changes
in the rate of expenditures for output. (4) Whether and to what extent a
change in the rate of expenditures for output will be reflected in changes of p
depends on the responsiveness of O to changes in the rate of expenditures
for output. The equation is sometimes written in the form

$$p = \frac{MV_i}{O}$$

The Total Expenditures Variant

Employing exactly the same logic, we can translate the total expenditures
variant of the cash balance approach to its equivalent in the velocity approach.

We found that in equilibrium the demand for money must be exactly
equal to the supply of money. We can therefore state that $M = KPT$. Thus
if $K = \frac{1}{10}$, the money supply is equal to $\frac{1}{10}$ of the annual rate of expenditures for everything entering into trade. But for various purposes we are interested in the relationship of PT to M. To bring out this relationship, let
us divide both sides of the equation by K. This shows that $\dfrac{M}{K} = PT$,

or $M\dfrac{1}{K} = PT$. If, for example, $K = \frac{1}{10}$, equilibrium can exist only if the annual rate of expenditures (PT) is equal to ten times the money supply. If
PT were lower than this, actual money balances would be above the demanded level of $\frac{1}{10}$ of PT and the community would attempt to rid itself
of the excess money by increasing its rate of expenditures. If PT were more
than ten times the money supply, the community's actual balances would be
less than $\frac{1}{10}$ of PT and it would reduce its expenditures in order to repair
its balances.

In effect, those employing the velocity approach use the equation
$M\dfrac{1}{K} = PT$. But for $\dfrac{1}{K}$ they substitute the symbol V. This is the velocity of
money, the average number of times each dollar of the money supply is spent,

on an annual basis, for everything included in T. The equation of exchange, $MV = PT$, was made famous by Professor Fisher.

In one sense the equation of exchange is only a truism. It states that the value of the flow of money expenditures (MV) is equal to the market value of the things bought with those expenditures (PT). But it does highlight some significant facts and it becomes analytically useful as one analyzes the determinants of the values of M, V, T, and P. For example, it indicates that: (1) The flow of expenditures varies directly with M and V. (2) A given change in the value of MV must be reflected in changes of P, or T, or both. The actual results will depend upon the relative responsiveness of T and P. (3) The price level varies directly with M and V and inversely with T. This is often written as $P = \dfrac{MV}{T}$.

SUMMARY

This appendix outlined the logical frameworks of two principal types of quantity theories. It did not analyze the determinants of the behavior of the variables employed by these theories. However, earlier chapters have supplied most of the materials necessary for this purpose. For example, they analyzed at length the determinants of the money supply. They discussed the determinants of the demand for money balances, which also determine the behavior of velocity. And they dealt at some length with the factors determining the relative responsiveness of output and price levels to changes in the rate of expenditures.

SELECTED READINGS

Fisher, I., *The Purchasing Power of Money*, Macmillan, New York, 1926.

Hansen, A. H., *Monetary Theory and Fiscal Policy*, McGraw-Hill, New York, 1949.

Robertson, D. H., *Money*, Harcourt, Brace, New York, 1929.

CHAPTER 17

The Functions of Financial Institutions

We have already discussed in some detail three types of financial institutions—the Treasury, the Federal Reserve, and the commercial banks. These institutions deal in debt obligations and to a limited extent in other financial instruments, but their unique quality is their ability to create and destroy money. But we also find in the market an almost bewildering array of financial institutions that do not have the ability to create or destroy money—such institutions as securities exchanges, over-the-counter markets, dealers and brokers in securities, investment advisers, investment banks, commercial paper houses, savings banks, savings and loan associations, insurance companies, mortgage banks, investment trusts, farm credit institutions, and many others. What do such institutions do? What functions do they perform? How, if at all, do they contribute to the nation's real productivity or to the nation's enjoyment of its output or income? To consider such questions as these is the central purpose of this chapter.

THE SAVING-INVESTMENT PROCESS

The general purpose of these institutions is to facilitate the flow of money saving into investment. Ultimately, of course, the purpose is to build up the stock of real capital goods, and this real investment is a process of devoting some part of the nation's productive resources and output to capital accumulation rather than current consumption. This can occur in the absence of money and financial institutions. Thus a man may spend only a part of his time producing for current consumption and use the remainder of his working time building a house, a wagon, or some other capital good; or some members of a community may produce consumers' goods and barter part of them to workers who spend their time constructing capital goods. But as soon as a community comes to employ money as a medium of payments, the processes of saving and investment tend to become monetary processes. People save by failing to spend for consumption some part of their current money incomes. This tends to disemploy productive factors in the consumers' goods industries. Those who wish to accumulate capital spend money for new capital goods, thereby attracting productive factors into the production of such goods. In some cases an entity both saves and spends for investment in the same period. Thus a household may during some year save $1000 and spend it for new capital goods in the form of a new garage, a tractor, or carpenter's equipment. Or a corporation may during some period use all its gross saving to buy new construction, durable equipment, or additions to its inventories. In such cases, money-saving can become investment expenditures without previously being transferred from the saver to others. But the great bulk of saving is not of this type. The saver often has no intention of spending the money for investment in capital goods in the same period. This is true, for example, of many doctors, lawyers, corporations, and governmental units. Such savings can become investment expenditures only if transferred to some entity that will spend them.

Thus the saving-investment process in modern society usually involves three parts: (1) an act of saving, (2) a process of transferring money savings from the saver to the spender, and (3) an act of spending for output to maintain or increase the stock of capital goods. If any of these three parts is missing, it can interrupt investment. At this point we are interested primarily in the transfer process—the intermediation between the saver and the spender for investment purposes. This involves the creation of "securities" of some sort. The spender for investment must issue either ownership claims or debt claims to get the money he wants. Thus, there must be some sort of "money market" or "securities market." Both are, in effect, the same thing. The term "money market" emphasizes the offering of money for use by others. The term "securities market" emphasizes the offer of ownership or debt claims in exchange for money. Private spenders for investment purposes are not, of course, the only ones who enter the money market to acquire money for spending and who offer securities in exchange. So do consumers whose current expenditures for consumption exceed their current disposable incomes. To get the necessary money, they sell some of their claims against others or offer claims against themselves. Governmental units engaging in deficit spending do the same thing. These activities of consumers and governmental units in the money and securities markets should be kept in mind. In the following pages, however, we shall concentrate our attention on demands for investable funds by private spenders for investment.

A saver may, of course, offer his money savings in exchange for securities and put his money directly at the disposal of an investment spender without the use of any intermediary. Thus a saver may lend directly to one of his friends, he may buy ownership or debt claims directly from a local corporation, or he may lend directly to a local governmental unit. However, such direct transfers alone are likely to be inconvenient, expensive, risky, and 'ineffective as a means of promoting the flow of saving into investment. Specialized financial institutions can greatly improve the market process of bringing together the supply of saving and the demand for investable funds.

When we speak of "improving" the market process, we must have in mind some criteria of performance. What do we expect of such a market? What results do we want from it? One desired result has already been discussed at length; we want this market to contribute as much as it can to the achievement of what we may loosely call the promotion of continuous full employment without inflation. To this end it should provide savers with types of assets and rewards that will induce them to part with their money savings, and at the same time make funds available to investment spenders on such terms that they will spend at rates consistent with the full-employment-without-inflation objective. But this macroeconomic objective, important as it is, is not the only one. We could keep all our productive factors fully employed by using them wastefully. We also want maximum efficiency and productivity. To this end we want financial markets to ration the limited supply of savings, which carries the power to command capital goods, in such a way as to put them to the uses in which they will produce most. They should be put in the hands of those users who can make them add most to the value of the nation's output and denied to those who can use them less productively. In other words, savings should be made mobile; regardless of the area in which they originate, their supply should be capable of flowing to those areas where they can be used most productively.

Such a mobility of savings requires several processes. (1) The accumulation and dissemination of knowledge. Funds obviously cannot flow into their most productive uses if those dealing in the market are ignorant concerning available alternatives. To function satisfactorily, therefore, a financial market must somehow gather information concerning alternative opportunities, disseminate this information to decision-makers, and put the information to effective use. To some extent this requires a dissemination of the relevant information to ultimate savers. But many savers do not have the training, inclination, or time to use such information effectively. Greater economy and efficiency can be achieved if they transfer their savings to financial intermediaries whose very size enables them to accumulate more information and to use it more effectively. (2) The development of facilities for transferring savings and securities over wide geographical areas. An adequate mobility of savings could not be achieved if the nation were divided into many little regional markets with no interconnections. What is needed is some sort of nation-wide or even international market to which supplies of savings can be attracted from all areas, there to meet demands from all areas. This does not mean that all savings should flow through one central market. There is still room for local and regional financial markets. But there is need for a great central market in which excess supplies from some areas can meet excess demands from others. This requires the existence of at least some financial institutions with connections in the various areas.

Maximum efficiency and economy are other desirable characteristics of financial markets. We want the necessary functions performed as cheaply as possible. This is partly to economize on the use of productive resources, partly because high costs would discourage investment. We also expect such a market to deal fairly with savers and those who acquire funds for investment spending. We do not want dishonest dealing, exploitation of savers by those who acquire funds for investment spending or vice versa, or exploitation of either by intermediate institutions. This is partly because dishonesty and exploitation offend our sense of justice, partly because such conduct would in the long run undermine the effectiveness of the market itself.

Financial markets include many types of institutions. In our later discussion we shall divide them into three principal groups, depending on the types of functions they perform. The reader should be warned, however, that many individual institutions perform functions of more than one type. (1) Secondary securities markets. Some of the principal institutions in these markets are the stock exchanges, over-the-counter markets, and the brokers and dealers who transact business in these markets. These are called "secondary markets" because their major business is not that of selling new security issues; rather it is to facilitate trading in securities that are already outstanding. The market in which new issues are initially sold is called the "primary market." (2) Securities merchants. We apply this term to institutions that sell new securities created by others. Investment banks are an outstanding example. These merchants, like jobbers, wholesalers, and retailers in commodities, take new issues by corporations and governmental units and sell them to buyers over wide areas. Note that they sell to others the same securities that they buy. (3) Financial intermediaries. This term is applied to a wide variety of institutions that collect savings from others, issuing in return claims against themselves, and use the funds thus acquired to purchase ownership or debt claims. Outstanding examples are savings banks, savings and loan associations, insurance companies, and investment trusts. An outstanding feature of these institutions is that they issue to savers claims whose characteristics may be quite different from those that the institutions buy and hold. They do not merely intermediate; in the process they can also create higher degrees of safety and liquidity.

GENERAL FUNCTIONS OF FINANCIAL INSTITUTIONS

Financial institutions can facilitate the saving-investment process by performing one or more of the following general functions: (1) gathering, disseminating, and using information; (2) purchasing, holding, and selling securities; (3) providing diversification and insurance against risk; and (4) increasing liquidity.

Information

As noted earlier, savings cannot be directed into their most profitable uses if decision-makers do not have and use adequate information concerning alternatives. This is true not only from a social point of view but also from the saver's own point of view; without adequate information he cannot rationally decide what alternative is most attractive, taking into consideration expected returns, risk, and liquidity. Many types of information are relevant: information concerning past performance insofar as it bears on the future; the honesty, ability, and enterprise of the management and the nature of its plans for the future; future demands for the output of the firm and of the industry of which it is a part; and so on.

Much of the work of gathering and disseminating information is done by government agencies, Better Business Bureaus, specialists in market analysis, financial publications, economic advisory services, and investment counselors. But financial institutions that perform other services as well are involved in at least two ways. In the first place, they do much research and analysis themselves. In the second place, they can utilize more effectively the information that they get from others or collect themselves. An individual saver, even one well trained in such matters, would usually find it too inconvenient and expensive to gather and use existing information, to say nothing of engaging in original research. But a large financial institution with specialized facilities can economically collect more data and use them more effectively.

The Purchase, Holding, and Sale of Securities

In the absence of financial institutions, each owner of investable funds would have to perform for himself the routine and technical jobs of seeking out securities, insuring that they were valid, purchasing them, providing safekeeping for them, protecting his interests against the issuer, collecting income and principal payments, and selling the securities. Financial institutions aid in many ways. Investment banks, stock exchanges, and brokers and dealers simplify greatly the processes of buying and selling securities. Financial intermediaries that collect and use the funds of others perform all these functions for savers. In performing these functions they have the advantages of scale; they can employ specialists and achieve economies available only on large-scale operations. Moreover, they need not sell a security every time a saver withdraws funds; such withdrawals are usually at least partially offset by inflows of funds from others.

Diversification and Insurance Against Risk

We are all aware of the risk of putting all one's eggs in a single basket—one mishap, and all is lost. The same principle applies to holding all one's wealth in a single security. Yet only a few of the very wealthy own enough funds to secure wide diversification without assistance. Financial institutions that collect and use the funds of many savers can meet this need. For example, a savings bank may receive savings from 20,000 people and use them to purchase many kinds of securities issued by a large number of firms operating in several industries located in various geographical areas. The deposit claims issued to savers are less risky than the individual claims purchased by the savings bank, for the very process of diversification has lessened the overall risk. A decrease in the value of one security will have only a small effect on the value of the combined holdings, and a decline in one may be at least partially offset by a rise in others.

In addition to reducing the total amount of risk by increasing diversification, financial institutions can distribute the remaining risk unequally among those who provide the funds, thereby distributing risks in accordance with the willingness of savers to bear them. For example, those who buy ownership claims against a financial institution accept the position of residual claimants, thereby bearing a larger share of the risk and providing greater safety for those who supply funds by taking debt claims against the institution. An investment trust may acquire funds by issuing several different types of claims with varying degrees of priority of claim. Through such unequal distributions of risk a financial institution can secure funds from different groups of people who vary greatly as to their willingness to assume risk.

Some institutions specialize in insuring against loss. Thus, there are institutions that insure the safety of deposit claims against mutual savings banks. The Federal Housing Administration insures mortgages on residential properties. The Federal Savings and Loan Insurance Corporation insures the safety of funds left with savings and loan associations.

Increase of Liquidity

In earlier chapters we found that the illiquidity of securities is one of the reasons why savers are reluctant to hold them and may prefer to hold money balances instead. Financial institutions serve in several ways to provide a higher degree of liquidity to those who part with money and hold other claims. In the first place, a highly organized secondary securities market, including dealers, brokers, speculators, and stock exchanges, greatly increases the speed and economy of selling securities when one wishes to exchange them for money. They cannot, of course, provide perfect liquidity, for they cannot assure that security prices will be stable. They permit an individual seller to dispose of his securities quickly and without serious loss when others are in a buying mood, but not when there is a surge of mass selling. The various classes of securities still differ markedly in their degree of marketability. For some there is a highly organized market; among these are the federal debt, the obligations of many states and larger municipalities, securities of well-known corporations, and bankers' acceptances. But the marketability of consumer debts, uninsured mortgages, and the securities of small and little-known business firms is in many cases relatively low.

In the second place, financial institutions increase the liquidity of securities by standing ready to lend on them. The security holder can borrow money for use while he seeks a favorable market in which to sell.

In the third place, financial intermediaries manufacture liquidity for savers by creating and issuing to them claims that are more liquid than the securities that are acquired and held by the intermediary. For example, mutual savings banks acquire funds largely by issuing to depositors claims that are legally payable on short notice, but in fact are usually paid on demand, even though the banks themselves hold largely long-term mortgages and bonds. Savings and loan associations issue shares payable on short notice—but in practice usually paid on demand—even though most of their own holdings are of long-term mortgages. Why can they do this? A fundamental reason is that they do not expect any large net withdrawal of savings over any short period; they operate on the expectation that withdrawals by some savers will be offset, in large part at least, by receipts from others. To meet withdrawals such institutions rely on such sources as the following: (1) Current inflows of money. In part these are current inflows of savings from those who take in exchange new claims against the institution. In part they are payments of interest and repayments of principal, often on an installment basis, by borrowers. Some institutions have inflows of funds so much in excess of withdrawals that they hold almost no liquid assets. (2) Small money balances to meet possible excesses of withdrawals over receipts. (3) Small holdings of highly liquid earning assets, such as short-term government securities. And (4) an ability to borrow from other financial institutions.

Thus financial intermediaries manufacture liquidity. They make money available to spenders by taking in return securities that are long term and relatively illiquid. At the same time, they create and issue to savers claims that the latter consider to be almost, but not quite, as safe and liquid as money itself. This clearly promotes the flow of saving into investment. The availability of a wide variety of such liquid claims also tends to reduce the store of value (L_2) demand for money.

There are also specialized institutions that increase the liquidity of other financial institutions. None except the Federal Reserve has the power to create the money that it makes available, but several have the power to borrow money and make it available to these institutions to meet drains or extraordinary demands for loanable funds. Thus, the Federal Home Loan Banks lend to savings and loan associations and other similar institutions; the Federal Intermediate Credit Banks lend to institutions on various types of agricultural paper; and the Federal National Mortgage Association provides a continuous market for certain classes of insured mortgages. Other similar cases could be cited. All arrangements that permit a financial institution to secure money from others in time of need enable it to issue more liquid claims to savers, thereby encouraging them to make their money available for use at lower rates of return.

Summary

We found earlier that the reluctance of savers to part with money and to hold other claims is traceable to the fact that these claims involve the disadvantages of (1) the inconvenience and cost of purchasing, holding, servicing, and disposing of the claims, (2) the risk of loss of principal value, and (3) the illiquidity of the claims. To the extent that financial institutions reduce these disadvantages, they increase the amounts of money offered for use and reduce the cost of investable funds to their users.

Having outlined the general functions of financial institutions, we can now study some of the principal types of these institutions.

SECONDARY SECURITIES MARKETS

Of the many institutions that provide a continuous market for outstanding shares of stock and for debt obligations, we can deal with only two: securities exchanges and the over-the-counter market.

Securities exchanges are usually called stock exchanges, though they also provide some trading facilities for bonds. The United States has about 37 of these exchanges. The New York Stock Exchange is by far the largest, accounting for well over half of all transactions on the nation's exchanges. The American Stock Exchange, also located in New York, is next. Between them they account for more than three quarters of all the nation's trading on stock exchanges. A stock exchange does not itself deal in securities. Rather it is an entity, established and operated by its member brokers and dealers, which provides a trading floor or auction hall, supplies reporting services and other facilities, and establishes and enforces rules of conduct for its members. All transactions on the floor of the exchange are carried out by the members of the exchange, who are brokers and dealers of various types. As a dealer, a member of the exchange buys and sells for his own account. As a broker, he acts as agent for others who wish to buy or sell. These brokers and dealers receive orders to buy and sell securities from individuals, nonfinancial business firms, and financial institutions located all over the United States and in foreign countries. Many of these orders come in through a widespread network of branch offices of the brokerage firms that are members of the exchanges. Others are relayed to the member firms through local securities dealers and banks. But through one route or another, purchase and sale orders from all types of buyers and sellers located all over the country and in foreign countries as well come to the trading floor of a stock exchange. A stock exchange thus provides a great daily auction market with millions of potential participants.

Another important branch of the secondary market is the over-the-counter market. Though about 6000 of the most important securities in the country are listed on the various stock exchanges, more than ten times that number have not been admitted to trading on any exchange floor. These include the issues of many smaller industrial and commercial corporations, most bank and insurance company stocks, and most government bonds. Many of these are traded in the over-the-counter market. This "market" has no one location; it is instead a term applied to the aggregate of brokers and dealers located all over the country. It has often been characterized as a nation-wide network of telephone and telegraph wires because brokers and dealers use these methods of communication to secure information as to the supply of and demand for specific securities and to make purchases and sales for their own and their customers' accounts. This market is neither as highly organized nor as highly centralized as the markets provided by stock exchanges, but the brokers and dealers who operate in it serve a useful function in enhancing the marketability of securities that are not admitted to trading on the organized exchanges.

How may these secondary markets, which are not directly involved in the sale of new security issues, promote the saving-investment process? They can do it primarily by maintaining a continuous market in which securities can be sold quickly, at low cost, and at "fair" prices, thereby enhancing the safety and liquidity of securities. Many investors would not buy securities in the first place if such trading facilities did not exist. A highly efficient secondary market can also enhance the mobility of investable funds. For example, some savers are not willing to buy new issues; they want "seasoned" securities that have been outstanding for some time. The existence of secondary markets facilitates the flow of new saving into such securities, so that the sellers of these securities can use the funds to buy new issues.

Speculation in the secondary securities markets can serve a useful social purpose to the extent that it contributes to the maintenance of continuous markets and reduces price instability. Thus, speculative purchases that prevent undue declines of security prices protect those who sell at such times, and speculative sales that prevent undue rises protect buyers. Unfortunately, however, some types of speculation tend to promote price instability rather than price stability. Among these are the activities of those who try in various ways to "rig" prices. Also included are the speculative activities of those who know little or nothing about the prospective future earning powers of securities, who act on "hot tips" and "hunches," and who regard the exchanges more as gambling casinos than as important parts of the saving-investment process. A serious continuing problem in public policy is that of eliminating abuses in securities markets without impairing useful speculative activities. The objective is not merely to protect individual investors against unnecessary losses; it is also to maintain faith in the integrity and efficiency of these markets so that they can perform their important economic functions.

SECURITIES MERCHANTS

A business firm or governmental entity wishing to sell a new issue of securities, either shares of stock or debt obligations, could, of course, try to peddle the securities itself without using any intermediary. Thus when U.S. Steel offers a new $300 million bond or stock issue, it might have its employees try to sell the new securities door-to-door or visit thousands of financial intermediaries. This has obvious disadvantages. It is likely to be expensive, and it may fail. Securities merchants, institutions that aid in the sale of new issues, reduce these disadvantages. Investment banks are among the most important of these institutions. An investment bank is an institution whose primary purpose is to market new issues of long-term securities, either ownership shares or debt obligations, for corporations and governmental units. In this process investment banks perform three principal functions: (1) investigation and purchase; (2) underwriting; and (3) selling.

The first step is to investigate the worth of the new security. This involves a study of the industry, of the company's position in the industry, of the assets and probable income of the issuer, and of the rights carried by the new securities. A reputable investment bank will refuse to sell a new issue if its investigation indicates that the security is unlikely to be a "good buy." Several investment banks may investigate the issue simultaneously to see if they wish to bid for it. New issues are often awarded to an investment bank as a result of direct negotiation, without competitive bidding. Whether or not competitive bidding should be required is one of the most controversial issues in this field. The investment bank that is awarded the issue is usually called "the originating house."

The next step is underwriting, by which we mean a guarantee that by a specified date the issuer will receive the purchase price of the securities whether or not they have all been sold to ultimate investors. This relieves the issuing firm of the risk that the sale of the securities may be delayed and that the sale price may be less than anticipated. If the issue is small relative to the assets of

the originating house, that investment bank may alone bear the entire underwriting risk. But if the issue is large, an underwriting syndicate may be formed.
For example, a new $300 million bond issue by the U.S. Steel Corporation in
1958 was underwritten by a syndicate composed of 36 investment banks. Syn-
dicates are sometimes even larger than this. By such reciprocal sharing of new
issues, investment banks spread the risk and secure a more stable employment
of their facilities.

The final step is selling the new issue. In some cases the members of the
underwriting syndicate sell all the new issue through their own head offices
and branches. In others they form a sellers' syndicate, bringing in other investment banks and securities dealers all over the country.

Similar functions are performed for short-term obligations by commercial
paper houses and bill brokers and dealers. Suppose, for example, that Sears
Roebuck wishes to borrow $50 million on its six-month promissory notes. It
may draw up this value of short-term paper in denominations of $10,000 each
and sell all of them to a commercial paper house, which in turn will market
them to buyers all over the country. Commercial paper houses also stand
ready to deal in such paper after its original issue, thereby enhancing its safety
and liquidity. Bill brokers and dealers perform similar functions for acceptances, primarily for bankers' acceptances.

Thus securities merchants greatly enhance the ease of selling new securities
and increase the geographical mobility of investable funds. In effect, new securities from all parts of the country, and even from foreign countries, are
brought into a central market. Securities merchants sell them in all parts of the
country and in foreign countries to purchasers of all kinds—not only to individuals and nonfinancial business firms, but also to many types of financial
intermediaries. The latter, in turn, often purchase the securities with funds
they have drawn from wide areas.

Though securities merchants now provide generally adequate facilities for
most governmental units and medium-sized and large corporations, they
probably do not do so for small business firms that want to sell stock or long-
term debt obligations but are not well known. Because of the relatively small
amounts involved, the relatively high costs of investigation, and the relatively
high risk of underwriting, few securities merchants have taken this type of business.

FINANCIAL INTERMEDIARIES

One of the most striking developments in finance in the United States during recent decades has been what is loosely called an increasing "institutionalization of saving." This term is applied to at least two types of saving. The first
is that in which the individual or household does not directly make the saving

decision and does not directly dispose of the funds saved. Rather, some institution makes the saving decision and determines the use to which the saving will be put. Of this there are many cases, among which are: (1) Corporate gross saving. When a corporation sets aside capital consumption allowances and retains net profits it is in a sense saving for its owners. But the individual owners do not make the decision or determine the use to which the retained funds will be put. (2) Government social security and pension programs. Many of these are either compulsory or at least are made so attractive that millions join them. They are usually financed by taxes or compulsory contributions from the individual, his employer, or both. Such saving is for the benefit of the individual, but he does not directly make the decision or determine the use of the funds. (3) Private pension and insurance programs. These include, for example, retirement, pension, annuity, and insurance programs provided by private employers for their employees and financed by contributions from the employer, the employee, or both. They also include similar programs administered jointly by employers and labor unions, and various types of union welfare programs. In most cases the individual does not himself make the saving decision and does not determine the use of the funds.

Taken in the aggregate, saving in these forms is very large and growing. If an individual does not like the rate of saving that is being done for him he can, of course, try to offset it by adjusting his own saving decisions. For example, he may elect to decrease his own saving because so much is being saved for him in programs operated by his government, employer, or labor union. Nevertheless, the increasing institutionalization of saving in this sense of the term has important economic implications. For one thing, it probably increases the total supply of saving. Some who are compelled to save in these ways would not themselves decide to save, or would save less. Also, the resulting savings are probably used in different ways when they are pooled and disposed of by government, employers, and labor unions. Some of these funds are used directly to purchase business and government securities. Others are channeled into trust departments of banks, annuity companies, and insurance companies.

The term, "increased institutionalization of saving," is also applied to the situation in which the saver does make his own saving decision but places his money savings at the disposal of some financial intermediary that determines the ultimate uses to which the funds may be put. The saver does this in two principal ways. (1) By taking in exchange claims against the financial institution. These are in many forms: ownership claims against it, long-term debt claims, insurance policies, annuity contracts, time or savings deposit claims, and so on. (2) By repaying his outstanding debt to these institutions.

We cannot deal here with all the many types of financial intermediaries that pool the funds of others and dispose of them in the money and securities markets. Instead, we shall concentrate on three of the most important: life insurance companies, mutual savings banks, and savings and loan associations. Table 41 shows that by early 1958 these three types of institutions had amassed

TABLE 41.   Assets of Life Insurance Companies, Mutual
Savings Banks, and Savings and Loan Associations
(In billions)

End of Period	Life Insurance Companies	Mutual Savings Banks	Savings and Loan Associations	Total
1941	$ 32.7	$10.4	$ 6.0	$ 49.1
1945	44.8	16.2	8.7	69.7
1947	51.7	18.6	11.7	82.0
1955	90.4	29.9	37.7	158.0
1956	96.0	31.9	43.9	171.8
1957	101.0	33.8	48.3	183.1
April, 1958	102.7	34.7	50.1	187.5

SOURCE: *Federal Reserve Bulletin*, June, 1958, pp. 667, 669, and 677.

total assets of more than $187 billion, largely by issuing to others claims against themselves. This amounted to more than $1000 for every man, woman, and child in the country. Moreover, the assets of these institutions continue to grow year by year.

Life Insurance Companies

Life insurance companies engage in two principal types of business; they insure lives and sell annuities. Both of these functions occasion the collection of huge sums of money from millions of people, and much of this money is used by insurance companies to buy securities of various kinds. In insuring lives, the companies typically do not charge an annual premium just sufficient to cover operating expenses and insurance outpayments during that year. If they did, each policyholder would pay premiums that increased in amount as he grew older and as the probability of his death during the year increased. Most policies involve large elements of saving during their early years; that is, the premium payments by the policyholder are considerably larger than would be required to cover the probability of his death in those years. It is largely because of the prevalence of policies of this type that the performance of the life insurance function involves the accumulation of such a huge volume of investable funds.

Annuities are relatively simple in principle although complex in detail. The company collects funds, either in lump sums or in installments, invests these funds in income-earning assets, and then after a date selected by the annuitant pays him an annual income based on (1) the amount of funds accumulated in his account, and (2) his average life expectancy. Companies engaged in the annuity business control a very large volume of investable funds. Table 42 shows that by early 1958 the total assets of life insurance companies

TABLE 42. Assets of Life Insurance Companies
(In billions)

End of Year	Total Assets	Mort- gages	Business Securities	Govern- ment Securities	Real Estate	Policy Loans	Other
1941	$ 32.7	$ 6.4	$10.2	$ 9.5	$1.9	$2.9	$1.8
1945	44.8	6.6	11.1	22.5	0.9	2.0	1.7
1950	64.0	16.1	25.4	16.1	1.4	2.4	2.6
1955	90.4	29.4	39.5	11.8	2.6	3.3	3.7
1956	96.0	33.0	41.5	11.1	2.8	3.5	4.1
1957	101.0	35.2	43.6	10.6	3.1	3.9	4.6
April, 1958	102.7	35.8	44.5	10.8	3.2	4.0	4.4

SOURCE: *Federal Reserve Bulletin*, June, 1958, p. 677.

had grown to $102 billion and that they had recently been rising by about $5 billion a year. Two aspects of life insurance companies make them a rich source of long-term funds. (1) The nature of their liabilities. They get funds primarily by selling life insurance policies and annuity contracts, so that their liability to pay depends on the deaths of insured people and on annuity out-payments. These can be determined with a high degree of accuracy by consulting mortality tables and the ages of the insured and the purchasers of annuities. (2) The large excess of their cash receipts over their cash payments of insurance benefits and annuities. To meet such payments they need not sell securities; they can merely use for this purpose some part of their current cash receipts. For these reasons the life insurance companies feel free to hold a large part of their earning assets in long-term securities, many of which are relatively illiquid. Table 42 shows that these companies hold large amounts of mortgages, both residential and nonresidential, corporation bonds, and bonds of the federal, state, and local governments. Some of the companies also own and lease out real estate developments, such as apartment houses and office buildings. They have not as yet invested heavily in common stocks, though the long period of inflation after 1940 has convinced many people that they should, and that they should also sell insurance policies and annuities whose money values are not fixed but vary with the price level.

Fire, marine, and casualty insurance companies also accumulate funds and use them to buy securities, but their total assets are far less than those of life insurance companies.

Mutual Savings Banks

Mutual savings banks are coöperative banks; they issue no stock and in effect are owned by their depositors. Each is governed by its board of trustees, which is usually self-perpetuating. They were originally founded to promote thrift among small savers and to provide safety for them. Most of them accept deposits only from individuals, not from corporations, and they usually place an upper limit on the amount of deposits they will hold for each individual. This is ordinarily in the range of $2500 to $5000, exclusive of accumulated interest. Most of these banks are located on the Atlantic seaboard and in New England.

Table 43 shows that by early 1958 the total assets of mutual savings banks

TABLE 43.   Assets of Mutual Savings Banks
(In billions)

End of Year	Total Assets	Mortgage Loans	Other Loans	U.S. Government Obligations	Other Securities	Cash Assets
1941	$11.2	$ 4.8	$0.1	$ 3.7	$1.8	$0.8
1945	16.9	4.2	0.1	10.7	1.3	0.6
1950	22.5	8.3	0.2	10.9	2.3	0.8
1955	31.0	17.5	0.1	8.4	4.0	1.0
1956	35.0	19.7	2.2	8.0	4.2	0.9
1957	36.2	21.2	1.5	7.6	5.0	0.9
April, 1958	35.7	21.6	0.2	7.5	5.5	0.9

SOURCE: *Federal Reserve Bulletin*, June, 1958, pp. 667, 669, and 687.

had grown to nearly $36 billion. Most of these funds had been invested in long-term securities. About two thirds of their assets were in mortgages, and many others were in long-term government and corporation bonds. These institutions have long been an important source of real estate credit.

In this connection it should be recalled that the so-called commercial banks also perform the savings bank function. They, too, gather funds by creating and issuing to others time and savings deposit claims. At the end of 1957 more than $56 billion of these were outstanding.

Savings and Loan Associations

These institutions, formerly known popularly as building and loan associations, collect savings and use them primarily to make loans on urban residential real estate. Before 1933 all these associations operated under state charters, but a law of that year authorized the establishment of federal savings and loan associations that operate under charters granted by the Federal Home Loan Bank Administration. We shall later discuss the assistance given by the government to these and other institutions that lend on real estate.

Most of these institutions secure funds largely by issuing shares to savers. However, they usually stand ready to redeem them on demand or at very short notice at their face value. Many savers do not even know that they are taking ownership claims rather than deposit claims. Some of the associations gather funds by issuing both shares and deposit claims. On occasion they acquire further funds by borrowing from the Federal Home Loan Banks or others.

Table 44 indicates the phenomenal growth of these institutions in recent

TABLE 44. Assets of Savings and Loan Associations
(In billions)

End of Period	Total Assets	Mortgages	U.S. Government Obligations	Cash	Other
1941	$ 6.0	$ 4.6	$0.1	$0.3	$0.9
1945	8.7	5.4	2.4	0.5	0.4
1950	16.9	13.7	1.5	0.9	0.7
1955	37.7	31.5	2.3	2.1	1.8
1956	42.9	35.7	2.8	2.1	2.2
1957	48.3	40.1	3.2	2.1	2.8
April, 1958	50.1	41.4	3.2	2.5	2.9

SOURCE: *Federal Reserve Bulletin*, June, 1958, p. 677.

years. At the end of World War II their total assets were less than $9 billion; a little over twelve years later they were above $50 billion. About five sixths of these were in mortgages, mostly on residences. Almost no other type of institution concentrates so heavily on residential mortgages.

SUMMARY AND CONCLUSIONS

In this chapter we have not been able to deal fully with all the functions, processes, and institutions involved in the money and securities markets. At least a full volume would be required to do justice to these subjects. However, the materials that have been presented should suggest the great importance of the money and securities markets in the process of transferring savings from savers to those who ultimately spend them for private investment, for personal consumption in excess of current disposable income, and to cover government deficits.

A few of the most important results of highly developed money and securities markets are these: (1) An increase of the safety and liquidity of the earning assets available to savers. This is achieved in part through the quick and economical marketability of the securities issued by governmental units, business firms, and individuals. In part it is achieved through financial intermediaries that create and issue to savers claims that are in many cases far safer and far more liquid than the securities that the intermediaries acquire. (2) A great increase in the mobility of investable funds. This applies to mobility among geographical areas, among industries, and among firms. Securities merchants, such as investment banks, commercial paper houses, and bill brokers and dealers buy securities throughout this country and in some other countries and sell the securities to buyers of all sorts located in many areas. Members of the secondary securities markets, such as stock exchanges, brokers, dealers, and the over-the-counter market gather outstanding securities from all areas and sell them in all areas. Financial intermediaries also gather savings from many areas and use them to purchase securities originating in many areas. For example, the huge Metropolitan Life Insurance Company can gather savings from every state in the nation and employ them in the areas in which funds are in greatest demand.

Because of our interest in the processes through which monetary policy affects general credit conditions, it will be useful to sketch briefly some of the relationships between the Federal Reserve and commercial banks on the one hand and the money and security markets on the other.

In buying and selling government securities the Federal Reserve employs one branch of the over-the-counter market, the government securities dealers. When it buys and sells acceptances, it usually deals with bill brokers and dealers. Moreover, it puts money into the hands of many types of financial institutions or takes money out of their hands by purchasing acceptances or government securities that they formerly held, or by selling such assets to them.

The commercial banks are interlinked in many ways with other financial institutions and the money and securities markets. A few examples are these: (1) All these other institutions hold deposit accounts at commercial banks and use them in making payments. (2) In acquiring or selling open-market assets, commercial banks often act through securities merchants. For example, they buy new issues of bonds from investment banks, new issues of commercial paper from commercial paper houses, and new acceptances from bill brokers and dealers. (3) Commercial banks often buy and sell open-market assets through the secondary securities markets. Thus they patronize brokers, government securities dealers, and other dealers in debt obligations. (4) Commercial banks often buy assets from or sell assets to financial intermediaries. For example, they buy mortgages from insurance companies and sell mortgages to them. (5) Commercial banks lend to other financial institutions. For example, they lend to brokers to permit them or their customers to buy securities on margin, they lend to investment bankers to help them carry inventories of new issues until they can be sold, they lend to dealers in government securities for inventory purposes, and so on.

These few examples should suggest some of the ways that restrictive or liberalizing monetary policies can permeate the money and securities markets.

SELECTED READINGS

Goldsmith, R. W., *Financial Intermediaries in the American Economy Since 1900*, Princeton University Press, Princeton, 1957.

Leffler, G. L., *The Stock Market*, Ronald, New York, 2d ed., 1957.

Macrae, N., *The London Capital Market*, Staples, London, 1955.

Nadler, M., Heller, S., and Shipman, S. S., *The Money Market and Its Institutions*, Ronald, New York, 1955.

Securities and Exchange Commission, *Annual Reports*, Government Printing Office, Washington.

CHAPTER 18

The Federal Government and the Money Markets

Despite the great economic functions that they perform, or perhaps because of the importance of these functions, the institutions that make up the money and securities markets have not escaped criticism and regulation. Complaints against them have been of many kinds: that they have failed to provide adequate services to some parts of the economy; that some of them have acted unsoundly and even dishonestly; and that in the quest of institutional or personal gain some have perverted their purposes and have been used as instruments for exploitation. For reasons such as these both the federal and state governments have intervened in these markets, sometimes as regulators or supervisors, sometimes as promoters and principals. The central purpose of this chapter is to survey the principal types of government intervention and the public policy problems that they raise. We shall deal largely with the policies of the federal government.

We have already discussed many government policies that directly or indirectly affect the functioning of the money and securities markets. Among these are: general monetary management and selective controls by the Federal Reserve; Treasury actions affecting bank reserves and credit supplies; debt management by the Treasury; tax and expenditure policies; policies relating to the chartering of banks, the establishment of branches, and the formation of bank holding companies; policies relative to the regulation, supervision, and examination of banks; and policies relating to insurance of bank deposit liabilities. In the aggregate these policies give the federal government a very great influence over both the structure and the functioning of the money and securities markets. But the government also influences these markets in many other ways, as we shall now see.

REGULATION OF FINANCIAL INSTITUTIONS AND PRACTICES

The federal government regulates private financial institutions and practices through many agencies, of which one of the most important is the Securities and Exchange Commission, which was established in 1934 as an independent quasi-judicial body of five commissioners appointed for five-year terms by the President with the advice and consent of the Senate. Both the SEC and the legislation that it administers were responses to financial abuses and manipulations that were prevalent during the 1920's. The SEC administers seven important laws relating to transactions in securities. Five of these will be discussed here.[1]

The Securities Act of 1933 is designed to protect buyers against worthless, fraudulent, and misrepresented security issues. The problem is not new; Americans have lost billions in buying securities that were worth far less than their sellers claimed. Protective laws in effect prior to 1933 proved inadequate. Federal laws against use of the mails to defraud could be circumvented by using other methods of communication; moreover, it was often difficult to establish the fact that failure to provide buyers with complete and accurate information constituted fraud. State "blue-sky laws"—so called because some salesmen would sell patches of blue sky if they could find sufficiently gullible buyers—were generally ineffective. They did not reach interstate sales, they lacked uniformity, they were usually administered in a lax way, and embarrassed victims often failed to inform authorities of fraud. It became evident that only federal legislation, aggressively administered, could cope with the problem.

The Securities Act of 1933 is often called "the truth-in-securities act," and this name is an accurate indicator of its purpose. The Act does not prohibit the sale of risky securities or place its stamp of approval on those that are relatively safe. Instead, it compels disclosure of accurate and adequate pertinent information concerning securities publicly offered and sold in interstate commerce or through the mails, so that investors will be in a position to make informed judgments. Offerers of securities subject to the Act must file registration statements with the SEC a stipulated period of time before the securities go on sale, and must also supply a comparable amount of information in prospectuses made available to buyers. The SEC may require amendments to registration statements and postpone sales if it finds that the information filed is materially misleading, inaccurate, or incomplete. Persons responsible for filing false information subject themselves to risk of fine and imprisonment. Offerers may also be sued for damages by purchasers if, when the registration

---

[1] Because they are of less direct interest to our discussion of money markets, we shall not deal here with the Public Utility Holding Company Act of 1935 and Chapter X of the Bankruptcy Act.

statement became effective, it contained untrue statements of material fact or omitted required information.

The Securities Exchange Act of 1934 regulates practices on the securities exchanges and in over-the-counter markets. Abuses in these markets had been of many types, including misrepresentation, wash sales, other rigging and manipulating activities, and unfair use of "inside information" by corporation officers and brokers and dealers in securities. This Act specifically prohibits some practices, authorizes the SEC to regulate others, and provides for registration with the SEC of national securities exchanges, members of these exchanges, companies whose securities are listed on these exchanges, brokers and dealers who operate in the over-the-counter markets, and national associations of these brokers and dealers. Anyone violating the rules or failing to supply complete and accurate information is subject to punishment and may have his trading privileges suspended. The Act also gives the Board of Governors of the Federal Reserve System full power to determine margin requirements. Trading in the over-the-counter market is regulated both by the SEC itself and to some extent by a trade association, the National Association of Security Dealers, Inc., which is under the surveillance of the SEC.

The Investment Company Act of 1940 regulates practices of investment companies, or investment trusts as they are often called. These institutions grew rapidly both in number and in total assets during the latter half of the 1920's. They were supposed to provide greater safety and liquidity for savers by creating and selling their own securities and using the proceeds to buy a diversified list of claims against others. In fact, however, some were guilty of various types of unwise practices and abuses, including the riskiest types of stock speculation and the use of "other people's money" primarily to benefit their promoters, who were often investment banks with securities to sell or brokers who wanted the commissions to be earned on the trusts' purchases and sales. Excessive promotion and management fees were far from unknown. This Act is designed to prevent such evils. It requires investment companies to register with the SEC. The latter is empowered to apply for court orders enjoining an investment trust's plans for reorganization, merger, or consolidation that would be grossly unfair to any class of security holders, and for similar orders to restrain other acts involving gross misconduct or abuse of trust by the management of such a company.

The Trust Indenture Act of 1939 sets minimum standards for indentures. An indenture is, in effect, a contract between an issuing corporation and the holders of a particular security issue; it sets forth the rights of a holder of the security and contains provisions for protecting his claims. Indentures for bond and other debt issues are usually deposited with a trustee who is supposed to act for the security holders and protect their interests. These arrangements have not worked satisfactorily in all cases. Some indentures have been loosely drawn and have failed to provide adequate protection. Moreover, trustees have sometimes failed to enforce fully the protective features of an indenture. They have been passive in their attitude, related too closely to the issuing corporation to press the claims of its creditors, or involved as trustee for two or more security issues with conflicting interests. This Act provides that issues of bonds, notes, debentures and other similar debt securities exceeding $1 million in principal amount may be offered for sale to the public only if they are issued under a trust indenture that conforms to specific statutory standards. It also sets up standards for trustees under indentures with a view to insuring that they will be competent, independent, and free of interests that conflict with those of the particular class of security holders in whose behalf they are supposed to be acting.

The Investment Advisers Act of 1940 regulates those who act as investment advisers and counselors. It makes unlawful all practices that constitute fraud or deceit, requires registration of advisers who receive compensation for their services, and provides that advisers must disclose to their clients any interests they may have in transactions executed for clients. Those who violate the Act are subject to punishment and to revocation of their right to engage in this type of business.

Through these various activities the SEC has done much to make adequate and accurate information available to investors, to prevent the exploitation of purchasers and sellers of securities, and in these ways to reduce risk, raise the net incomes of security holders, and restore and maintain public confidence in the honesty of issuers and dealers in securities.

THE GOVERNMENT AS PROMOTER

In addition to regulating the policies and practices of private institutions, the government has also intervened in the money and securities markets on a large scale as a promoter. It has sought to fill in "gaps" of various sorts: to provide new or larger institutions where adequate facilities seemed to be lacking, and to promote the performance of functions that the existing financial system was not performing or was performing in a seemingly unsatisfactory manner. In some cases it has tried to achieve these results by permitting and encouraging the establishment of privately owned and privately operated institutions and by encouraging them to assume new functions. In others it has established federal financial institutions. In still others it has used both methods. Federal intervention of these types has been greatest in the fields of agricultural credit and residential credit, but it is by no means absent elsewhere. Let us look at a few of the outstanding examples.

Postal Savings Banks

The federal government established the Postal Savings banks in 1910. These are, in effect, departments of post offices that operate as branch offices for a board of trustees consisting of the Postmaster General, the Secretary of the Treasury, and the Attorney General. For more than forty years many had complained that there was a serious gap in available facilities for savers. Partly because banks were prone to failure, existing facilities were unsafe and inadequate, especially in the South and West. It was contended that the new institutions would render useful services by providing adequate and safe facilities for savings, stimulating thrift, and preventing hoarding. The Postal Savings banks accepted funds only from individuals, limited the account of each depositor to $2500 exclusive of interest, and paid 2 percent interest on deposits. Most of their funds were invested in United States government securities.

The Postal Savings banks served a useful purpose, especially during periods of widespread bank failures and loss of confidence in other financial institutions. At the end of World War II they were operating more than 8000 offices, had more than 4 million depositors, and held nearly $3.5 billion of deposits. However, since that time they have been less useful and have dwindled in importance. This is partly because of the low 2 percent rate, but perhaps more because of the increased availability of attractive other assets, especially United States savings bonds and insured accounts at commercial banks, mutual savings banks, and savings and loan associations.

Agricultural Credit

The federal government entered the field of agricultural credit with the passage of the Federal Farm Loan Act in 1916. Groups of farmers, especially those in the South and West, had for many years been critical of existing farm mortgage credit facilities. They complained: (1) that private individuals and institutions would not lend for more than five or ten years, a period too short to enable a farmer to pay for his land; (2) that existing institutions provided insufficient mobility of credit from the large cities, especially from the eastern seaboard, to the rural credit-deficit areas, thereby retarding the development of farm areas; and (3) that interest rates on farm mortgages were too high. These complaints were not without justification.

The Federal Farm Loan Act, which was much influenced by the example of European farm credit coöperatives, sought to remedy the situation by establishing two new types of institutions, Federal Land banks and national farm loan associations. The nation was divided into twelve districts, each with its Federal Land bank. These twelve banks provide the money to be lent. The federal government originally bought all their stock, but they acquire most of their money by selling their debt obligations through the central securities markets, thereby tapping credit supplies in all areas. These loan funds are actually distributed to individual farmers through a large number of national farm loan associations, which are local farm credit coöperatives made up of farmers who wish to get mortgage money. Each borrower is required to subscribe to stock in his Federal Land bank. All the government's stock in these banks has now been retired, so that the system is coöperatively owned through the national farm loan associations.

The federal government played several roles in establishing and developing the Federal Land bank system. (1) It took the initiative in establishing the Land banks and in promoting the formation of national farm loan associations. (2) By purchasing the stock of the Land banks it not only provided funds for lending but also enhanced the safety of the debt obligations that the system sold to others. (3) It regulated, supervised, and examined these institutions.

The Land bank system has unquestionably increased the mobility of funds into agricultural areas, helped to lessen interest rate differentials, and served to lengthen the maturities of farm mortgages.

In 1923 the federal government established 12 Federal Intermediate Credit banks. Farmers had complained for some years that short-term and intermediate-term credit facilities were inadequate. This was partly because of the credit restriction and bank failures that began in 1920, partly because many banks were reluctant to supply the intermediate-term credit needed by farmers for such purposes as purchasing machinery and raising livestock. The Federal Intermediate Credit banks do not make loans directly to farmers; rather, they attempt to increase the availability of short-term and intermediate-term credit by standing ready to make loans to or to discount paper for institutions that do lend to farmers. They get their money from two sources: partly from the government's subscription to their capital stock, but largely from the sale of their own debt obligations through the central money markets.

The great depression of the 1930's and the distress it brought to agriculture led to the establishment of a number of new federal agricultural credit institutions, some temporary and some more permanent. In the temporary category was the Federal Farm Mortgage Corporation. It was a "bailing-out" institution to bail out both farmers whose mortgages were in default and lenders who owned the distressed mortgages. For these purposes it used money acquired by the sale of its stock to the government and by the sale of its debt obligations, which carried the full guarantee of the government. Thus it relieved distressed farmers and increased the safety and liquidity of lenders by supplying them with claims far superior to the mortgages that they had held. The authority of the FFMC to make new loans expired in 1947.

Most of the new federal agricultural credit institutions established in the

1930's still exist. Among these are a large number of production credit associations. It had been hoped that the establishment of discount facilities at the Federal Intermediate Credit banks would induce private lenders to supply sufficient short-term and intermediate-term credit to farmers. During the depression, however, farmers complained that banks and other private lenders would not lend adequately even though they had access to the facilities of the Intermediate Credit banks. Production credit associations were authorized to fill this gap. These are much like the national farm loan associations, but their purpose is to facilitate the flow of short-term and intermediate-term credit. They lend for such purposes as the production, harvesting, and marketing of crops; the breeding, fattening, and marketing of livestock; poultry-raising; and other short-term and intermediate-term projects. They get most of their money by borrowing from the Federal Intermediate Credit banks.

The federal government also established a new credit system for farmers' coöperatives. This system includes the Central Bank for Coöperatives, which is located in Washington, and 12 district banks, one in each of the farm credit districts. In general, the Central Bank for Coöperatives makes loans to co-operatives that operate in more than one farm credit district, as well as handling loans that are too large for a district bank. The district banks make the smaller loans. This system provides complete credit facilities for coöperatives: loans on commodities, loans for operating capital, and loans to finance long-term facilities. It secures its funds from two sources: from its sale of stock to the federal government and to coöperatives, the latter subscribing in an amount equal to 5 percent of their borrowings, and from loans by the Federal Intermediate Credit banks.

The Farmers Home Administration provides credit only for farmers who are unable to obtain loans at prevailing rates from banks, coöperative lending agencies, and other normal sources in their communities. Its emphasis is on rehabilitation and assistance for smaller farmers. It makes both long-term and short-term loans, using for these purposes funds provided by Congress.

The Rural Electrification Administration, also established in the 1930's, makes self-liquidating loans covering 100 percent of the cost of constructing electrical facilities to serve rural people. These loans are not made directly to individual farmers, but to coöperatives and other firms engaged in rural electrification programs. The REA secured most of its funds by borrowing from the federal government.

The principal purpose of the Commodity Credit Corporation, which was established in 1933, is to make loans to farmers, or to guarantee private loans to farmers, as a means of supporting the prices of farm products. The loans it makes are nonrecourse loans. For example, if a farmer borrows $2.00 a bushel on his wheat, he has the option of paying the loan and claiming the wheat or of allowing the Corporation to keep the wheat. In this way, the Corporation prevents the prices realized by the farmer from falling below the amount it will lend on eligible products. The Commodity Credit Corporation secures all its funds from the federal government. At some times the volume of private loans guaranteed by the CCC exceeds the volume of its own loans.

Table 45 shows the volume of outstanding loans at the end of 1957 by the

TABLE 45. Outstanding Loans by Federal Agencies for Agricultural Purposes, December 31, 1957

(In millions of dollars)

Banks for Coöperatives	$ 454
Federal Intermediate Credit banks	935
Farmers Home Administration	832
Rural Electrification Administration	2,688
Commodity Credit Corporation	1,778
Total	6,687
Add: Federal Land banks	1,919
	$8,606

SOURCE: *Federal Reserve Bulletin*, June, 1958, p. 678; *Survey of Current Business*, April, 1958, p. S-16.

principal agricultural credit institutions in which the federal government has, or has had, a financial investment. Though the volume of these loans is substantial, it probably understates the economic significance of these institutions in the aggregate, for it cannot indicate how much the presence of these institutions has influenced the policies of private lenders.

Residential Credit

Not until the 1930's, during the great depression, did the federal government enter the field of urban mortgage finance. The housing situation was desperate; new construction and even repair work were at a virtual standstill, real estate prices were falling rapidly, hundreds of thousands of home mortgages were in default and many other defaults were imminent, foreclosure sales were numerous, and financial institutions were in dire straits, many of them already bankrupt and others in danger of becoming so. It was felt that federal financial assistance would serve the multiple purpose of preventing home owners from losing their homes, assisting financial institutions that were heavily laden with illiquid mortgages of low quality, reviving the flow of funds to finance new construction, encouraging business recovery by increasing employment in the construction industry, and providing decent housing for the "ill-housed third of a nation." It was against this background and for these purposes that the federal government established a number of housing credit agencies that have practically revolutionized residential credit practices.

A few of these new institutions were temporary; most of them still operate. The principal temporary institution was the Home Owners Loan Corporation, which was established in 1933 and ceased making loans in 1936. It acquired all its funds by issuing stock to the federal government and selling bonds with the government's full guarantee. In three years it disbursed $3.1 billion, most of it in exchange for defaulted mortgages held by financial institutions and other lenders on homes. There can be little doubt that the HOLC helped many home owners escape serious injury from the drastic deflation, restored the solvency and liquidity of many financial institutions, and helped revive the flow of new urban mortgage loans. The HOLC was expected to suffer heavy losses, but it finally wound up its affairs with a small profit, thanks largely to the war and postwar inflation of real estate prices.

The principal new permanent institutions that were established in this field during the 1930's or later include the Federal Housing Administration, the Veterans Administration, federal savings and loan associations, the Federal Savings and Loan Insurance Corporation, the Federal Home Loan banks, the Federal National Mortgage Association, and the Public Housing Administration.

The Federal Housing Administration, founded in 1934 by the federal government with federal money, does not itself make any loans; its function is to insure private lending institutions against loss on urban residential loans. It insures several types of loans: loans secured by mortgages on one- to four-family dwellings, mortgage loans on large-scale rental housing projects, and loans for property repair and improvement. At the end of World War II the Veterans Administration also entered this field, insuring housing loans to veterans. Charging an annual premium for this service, both the FHA and the VA insure long-term amortized mortgages on which no more than a small down payment is required. The terms have varied from time to time, but the maturities of insured mortgages have been as long as thirty years and required down payments have at times been zero.

The FHA and the VA have practically revolutionized home financing. In the first place, they have greatly altered the terms on home mortgages. Prior to 1934, most home mortgages were written for only short terms, usually no more than ten years; first mortgages were usually limited to 50 percent of the value of the real estate, so that borrowers wanting larger loans had to resort to expensive second and even third mortgages; and in many cases no provision was made for orderly repayment. The willingness of the FHA and the VA to insure very long-term amortized first mortgages equal to 90 percent or more of the value of houses has changed all this. People can now put down small payments and borrow to buy homes, making monthly payments that are in some cases less than the rent they would have to pay. In the second place, with the FHA or VA insurance and no longer dependent exclusively on the credit worthiness of an unknown borrower, mortgages originating in one area are much more easily sold in other areas to more classes of buyers.

The government also sought to increase the supply of housing credit by rehabilitating savings and loan institutions. Prior to 1933, all these had operated under state charters and state supervision. Though some of these institutions were sound in 1933, the industry was in general in a bad way. Hundreds had failed, others were illiquid if not insolvent, and thousands found it difficult to command enough public confidence to attract savings. The federal government took several steps to remedy the situation. One was to authorize the establishment of federal savings and loan associations that would operate under federal charters and federal supervision. These institutions have multiplied rapidly and now hold well over half of all the assets of savings and loan associations. Another step was to establish in 1934 the Federal Savings and Loan Insurance Corporation to protect savings entrusted to savings and loan associations in much the same way that the FDIC insures depositor claims against banks. All federal savings and loan associations are required to join, and state-chartered associations may join if they make application and are found acceptable. The FSLIC insures the first $10,000 of each account at an insured association. For this purpose it has several sources of funds: the government's stock subscription, admission fees and annual insurance premiums, earnings on its accumulated assets, and its power to borrow from the Treasury up to $750 million at any time.

Another step to assist savings and loan associations, and other lenders on housing as well, was the establishment of the 11 Federal Home Loan banks, one in each of the Federal Home Loan districts. All federal savings and loan associations are required to join and state-chartered associations are permitted to join if they meet entrance requirements and submit to supervision by the district bank. A few mutual savings banks and insurance companies have also joined the system. The 11 Federal Home Loan banks are designed to perform for their members some of the same functions that the Federal Reserve performs for its member banks; they increase the liquidity of these institutions and make available to them funds to meet withdrawals and abnormal loan demands. They do not, of course, create the money that they lend. Rather, they get it from four principal sources: by selling stock to the government and to their member institutions; by accepting deposits from member institutions; by selling consolidated Federal Home Loan bank obligations in the open market; and by borrowing up to $1 billion from the Treasury.

The original purpose of the Federal National Mortgage Association, established in 1938, was to enhance the marketability and geographical mobility of mortgages insured by the FHA and the VA. It was to stand ready to buy such mortgages originating in one area and then sell them to other buyers. Thus it was to act as a securities merchant and a dealer in the secondary market. In fact, however, it has often continued to hold large amounts of these mortgages, especially those insured by the VA, thereby supplying funds to the institutions originating these mortgages and to their borrowers. Prior to 1954, the FNMA secured all of its funds by borrowing from the Treasury. Since that time it has issued some stock to other financial institutions and has sold some of its own debt obligations in the market.

The principal purpose of the Public Housing Administration is now to make loans and pay subsidies to state and local governments to promote slum clearance and low-rent housing.

Table 46 shows the status of selected federal credit agencies in the housing

TABLE 46.   The Status of Selected Federal Programs in Housing, December 31, 1957
(Amounts in millions)

Mortgages insured by the Federal Housing Administration	$16,500
Mortgages insured by the Veterans Administration	30,700
Loans by Federal Home Loan banks	1,265
Loans and mortgage holdings of the Federal National Mortgage Association	3,998
Loans by the Public Housing Administration	104
Total	$52,567

SOURCE: *Federal Reserve Bulletin*, June, 1958, pp. 678, 679.

field as of the end of 1957. Such data cannot, however, indicate accurately the overall impact of federal activities in this area. For example, they cannot describe the extent to which FSLIC insurance has attracted savings to institutions that lend for housing purposes; the extent to which the existence of the FHA and VA has changed the length and terms of noninsured mortgages; and the extent to which low down payments and long-term amortized mortgages have altered the whole pattern of home ownership in America.

Other Federal Credit Agencies

Though the government has been most active in the fields of agricultural and housing credit, it has entered other fields as well. One of these is credit for small business. From 1932 until well after World War II such credit was supplied by the Reconstruction Finance Corporation. More recently the Small Business Administration, operating with government funds, has served this purpose. It lends to small business firms and insures private loans to such firms when a firm is credit-worthy and cannot secure funds from its normal sources at reasonable rates.

The Export-Import Bank, established in 1934 and reconstituted and enlarged in 1945, facilitates both short-term and long-term lending to assist the foreign trade of the United States. It does this both by making loans itself and by guaranteeing those funds from the Treasury.

Other credit activities of the federal government include insurance of loans to producers for government account, primarily producers of military supplies and equipment, and insurance by the Maritime Administration of mortgages on various types of shipping.

Summary

Table 47 shows the amount of credit being supplied by selected federal credit institutions at the end of 1957. Note that the $15.3 billion refers only to

TABLE 47.   Outstanding Loans of Selected Federal Credit Institutions, December 31, 1957

(In millions)

Federal Intermediate Credit banks	$ 935
Banks for Coöperatives	454
Farmers Home Administration	832
Rural Electrification Administration	2,688
Commodity Credit Corporation	1,778
Federal National Mortgage Association	3,998
Public Housing Administration	104
Federal Home Loan banks	1,265
Export-Import Bank	3,040
Small Business Administration	194
Total	$15,288

SOURCE: *Federal Reserve Bulletin*, June, 1958, pp. 678–679.

credit supplied by these institutions. It does not include the insurance of $47.2 billion of home mortgages by the FHA and the VA, the insurance of billions upon billions of claims against financial institutions by the FDIC and the FSLIC, and many other activities.

SUMMARY AND CONCLUSIONS

This chapter has not undertaken to describe in detail all the activities and policies of the federal government that impinge upon the structure and functioning of the money and securities markets and influence the saving-investment process. Rather, it has been intended to sketch in a general way and put in perspective the multiplicity of the government's activities in these areas and the broad pervasiveness of its influence. Some of the most important of these activities are summarized in Table 48.

We find that the government's influence on the money markets is by no means limited to Federal Reserve monetary policy, the government's tax and expenditure policies, and its debt management policy. In its various roles as regulator and as promoter and principal, the government can affect the number and location of financial institutions in the various branches of the market, the functions performed by these institutions, the volume of funds available to them for use, the safety and liquidity of securities available to them

TABLE 48. Some Important Federal Activities That Directly Affect the Structure and Behavior of Money Markets

Activity	Principal Federal Agencies
A. Monetary and debt management	
1. General monetary and debt management	Federal Reserve, Treasury
2. Selective credit controls	
a. Over margin requirements on security loans	Federal Reserve
b. Over residential real estate credit	Veterans Administration, Federal Housing Administration
B. Federal tax and expenditure policies	Congress, various others
C. Chartering of financial institutions	
1. National banks	Comptroller of the Currency
2. National farm loan associations	Farm Credit Administration
3. Production credit associations	Farm Credit Administration
4. Federal savings and loan associations	Home Loan Bank Board
5. Federal credit unions	Federal Security Agency
D. Supervision and examination of financial institutions and practices	
1. Of commercial banks	Comptroller of the Currency, Federal Reserve, Federal Deposit Insurance Corporation
2. Of various agricultural credit institutions	Farm Credit Administration
3. Of various lenders on residential real estate	Home Loan Bank Board, Federal Savings and Loan Insurance Corporation, Federal Housing Administration
4. Of federal credit unions	Federal Security Agency
5. Of stock exchange practices, investment trusts, investment advisers, etc.	Securities and Exchange Commission
E. Provision of money to private financial institutions through purchase of stock, loans, and purchase of securities	
1. Loans to commercial banks	Federal Reserve, Federal Deposit Insurance Corporation
2. Purchase of government securities from banks and other investors	Federal Reserve, Treasury
3. Loans to and purchases of assets from institutions making agricultural loans	Federal Reserve, Federal Intermediate Credit banks
4. Loans to and purchase of assets from institutions lending on residential real estate	Federal National Mortgage Association, Federal Home Loan banks, Federal Savings and Loan Insurance Corporation
5. Purchase of stock in private lending institutions	Treasury, others
F. Provision of loans to borrowers other than financial institutions, and insurance of private loans to such borrowers	
1. Loans and insurance of loans to many classes of such borrowers	Small Business Administration

TABLE 48 (*Continued*).

Activity	Principal Federal Agencies
2. Insurance of loans to producers for defense purposes	Various federal procurement agencies
3. Insurance of loans on urban residential real estate	Federal Housing Administration, Veterans Administration
4. Loans and insurance of loans to small farmers	Farmers Home Administration
5. Loans and insurance of loans on farm products	Commodity Credit Corporation
6. Loans for rural electrification and rural telephones	Rural Electrification Administration
7. Loans to farm coöperatives	Banks for Coöperatives
8. Loans, insurance of loans, and subsidies for slum clearance and low-rent housing	Public Housing Administration
9. Loans and insurance of loans on ships and other maritime craft	Maritime Administration
10. Loans and insurance of loans to promote American imports and exports	Export-Import Bank
G. Insurance of savings in private financial institutions	
1. Insurance of deposits in commercial and mutual savings	Federal Deposit Insurance Corporation
2. Insurance of claims against savings and loan associations	Federal Savings and Loan Insurance Corporation

for purchase, and the safety and liquidity of the claims that they issue to savers. In these ways it influences not only the behavior of the general availability and cost of investable funds during the various phases of the business cycle, but also the geographical mobility of funds and the allocation of funds among their various possible users and uses.

If employed wisely, these instruments can be highly useful in promoting a nation's economic objectives. For example, the government may promote economic stability by using in a flexible manner its power to insure the safety of savings entrusted to various institutions or to specified uses, its power to lend, and its power to insure loans made by others. Thus it may bear greater risks and lend and insure loans more liberally in times of actual or threatened unemployment, and then either discontinue these activities or act in a more restrictive manner in times of prosperity. However, the government's activities in these fields present many problems and dangers.

1. The allocation of credit and capital among their various possible users and uses that is promoted by government activities need not be superior to that which would result in the absence of the government's activities. The private market does not always ration supplies in a socially optimum manner.

This may be either because of imperfections in the market or because the distribution of supplies that is most profitable to private buyers and sellers is not considered most beneficial to society as a whole. For example, it might be desirable to spend large amounts for slum clearance even though this would be unprofitable for private enterprise. But the government, too, may allocate investable funds and, therefore, resources badly. Responding to partisan political considerations or to powerful special-interest groups, it may use its power to lend and insure loans in ways that do not maximize the nation's productivity in any meaningful sense of the term. There is always a danger that the government will use these powers to give unjustified subsidies to certain groups, either by maintaining artificially low interest rates for such uses or by bearing unduly large amounts of risk.

2. Such government activities may endanger the functioning and even the survival of private financial institutions. The government's supply of services in this field need not be a net addition to the total supply, for it may inhibit the growth of private supplies or cause an actual withdrawal of private supplies. This need not happen if the government merely fills gaps that others are unwilling to fill. In fact, many of the government's activities promote the establishment and growth of private institutions. But there is a real danger that liberal lending policies by the government, and especially lending at low rates that do not reflect any high risks that may be involved, may jeopardize supplies from private sources.

3. Policies in these areas may not be coördinated with monetary policy, especially not when conditions are such as to require credit restriction. The government may continue to lend and guarantee loans in a highly liberal manner even in the face of full employment and inflationary pressures. This has occurred in the fields of credit to small business, agriculture, and housing. The argument advanced is that these substantive programs are so important that they should be promoted at all times and under all conditions. A restrictive general monetary policy may succeed even though these other policies are not coördinated with it. Nevertheless, such conflicting policies jeopardize restrictive monetary policies in at least two ways. In the first place, they narrow the areas of the economy on which restrictive credit policies can operate. And in the second place, they tend to create unfavorable attitudes toward restrictive monetary policies. Private lenders are likely to be uncoöperative when they see the government continue to lend freely, perhaps to some of their own customers.

SELECTED READINGS

Saulnier, R. J., Halcrow, H. G., and Jacoby, W. H., *Federal Lending and Loan Insurance*, Princeton University Press, Princeton, 1958.

CHAPTER 19

Monetary Standards

With this chapter we begin a lengthy discussion of monetary policy, with special emphasis on United States monetary policy. The formulation and execution of monetary policy involve at least three elements: (1) selection of objectives—a choice of goals or purposes to be promoted, (2) development and use of monetary institutions and instruments to promote the objectives chosen, and (3) the use, at least implicitly, of some theory as to the economic effects of the various possible monetary actions. We have already discussed at some length the second and third elements. We dealt first with the various types of monetary institutions, the processes through which they create and destroy money, and some of the principal instruments used to regulate monetary and credit conditions. We then considered monetary theory, noting that a policy-maker could not rationally decide what to do if he had no theory as to the nature and extent of the economic effects that would flow from his various possible actions. Up to this point, however, we have paid little attention to the third essential element in policy-making, the selection of objectives.

OBJECTIVES OF MONETARY POLICY

The nature and extent of the monetary actions to be taken depend, of course, on the nature of the selected goals or objectives. For example, with the same set of monetary institutions and instruments and the same monetary theory, the monetary authority should do one thing if its goal is to induce inflation to wipe out the economic power of rentiers, quite another if its objective is a stable price level. It should take one set of actions if it wants continuously stable interest rates, quite another if it wants stable employment. Thus a selection of goals or objectives is a crucial element in policy-making. Several aspects of this process should be noted. (1) Policy usually has more than one goal or objective. We might, of course, sacrifice everything else to the extent necessary to achieve a single objective, but we usually want many things at the same time, and we insist that monetary policies keep all these in view. When these things conflict, as they often do, we have to sacrifice in part some objectives in order to achieve more of others. (2) These goals or objectives are often on different levels. For example, our ultimate objective may be to have a virtuous, happy, healthy people. But an intermediate objective is to have a prosperous people. A more immediate objective, which we hope will promote our ultimate goals, may be to maintain stable price levels. Still more immediate objectives may be to maintain a stable price of gold and stable exchange rates. But there may be conflicts between objectives at different levels and even at the same level.

The choice of a monetary standard often involves such problems. For example, when a nation instructs its monetary authority to maintain a stable price for gold, it selects an immediate objective. To achieve this objective the monetary authority must buy and sell gold in such a way as to prevent its price from fluctuating. The promotion of this objective may indeed promote the achievement of more ultimate objectives, but it may not. In the following pages we shall discuss monetary standards as immediate objectives of monetary policy and also as mechanisms influencing the achievability of other objectives.

THE NATURE OF A MONETARY STANDARD

The terms "standard money" and "monetary standard" were originally developed to apply to situations in which a nation's monetary unit was kept at a constant value in terms of some commodity (or commodities). The names of these standards are taken from the commodities in terms of which the monetary unit is stabilized. Thus, if a nation's monetary unit is stabilized in terms of gold, we say it is on a gold standard. If its monetary unit is stabilized in terms of silver, we say it is on a silver standard. If it is stabilized in gold and in silver, we say it is on a bimetallic standard. If its monetary unit is not kept at a constant value in terms of any metal, we say it is on an inconvertible standard.

We noted above that to be on a metallic standard a nation must keep its monetary unit at a constant value in terms of the selected metal. It must also keep its various types of money "convertible" in some sense into the selected metal at constant values. For example, all paper money and checking deposits must be kept at constant values in terms of the monetary unit, which in turn is kept at a constant value in terms of the metal. This difficult problem will be discussed later.

Some of the terminology in this field may lead to confusion, if not to erroneous conclusions. For example, the statement that under a gold standard a nation's monetary unit is kept at a constant value in terms of gold leads some to the conclusions that the monetary unit derives its purchasing power from gold, that its purchasing power can be changed only by changes in the purchasing power of gold, and that the purchasing power of gold is constant. None of these things is true. The only results that necessarily follow from the successful maintenance of a gold standard are that the price of gold in terms of the monetary unit will be stable, and that the amount of gold that one monetary unit will buy will also be stable. For instance, in the United States the gold value of the dollar has been kept constant since 1934 at $\frac{1}{35}$ of an ounce of gold, and the price of gold has been stabilized at $35 an ounce. This is achieved through a price support program for gold. The government stands ready to buy at $35 an ounce all the gold offered to it. Without such buying support the price of gold could fall, and the value of the dollar in terms of gold could rise.[1] The government also stands ready to sell at a price of $35 an ounce all the gold demanded from it for legal purposes. In the absence of this the price of gold could rise; the value of the dollar in terms of gold could fall.

Several points are worth noting. (1) Gold does not derive all its purchasing power over other things from the demand for it for nonmonetary purposes; the demand for it for monetary purposes also contributes to its purchasing power. We noted above that its price could fall in the absence of unlimited purchases of it by the government. (2) The purchasing power of any given quantity of gold, such as an ounce, varies with this fraction:

$$\frac{\text{Price of gold}}{\text{Prices of other things}}$$

Suppose, for example, that the price of gold is kept constant at $35 an ounce. Its purchasing power can be increased by anything that lowers the prices of other things, and it can be decreased by anything that raises the prices of other things. Changes in the prices of other things may result from changes in the supply of monetary gold. Thus, a big increase in gold production or a flow of gold out of nonmonetary uses into the monetary gold stock may swell the money supply and induce a rise in the price level. But the purchasing power of gold may also be altered by changes in the supply of other types of money, by changes in the demand for money, and so on. For example, a big increase in the supply of paper money and checking deposits or a decrease in the demand for money that raises price levels will decrease the purchasing power of gold if the price of gold is kept constant. (3) To stabilize a monetary unit in terms of gold does not assure that its purchasing power over other things will remain constant; it merely assures that the purchasing power of the monetary unit will vary with that of gold.

GOLD STANDARDS

The term "gold standard" is a generic term applied to a broad category of monetary systems that have one common characteristic: their monetary units are in some sense kept at a constant value in terms of gold. But this common characteristic should not be allowed to obscure the numerous and highly im-

[1] We neglect here the small $\frac{1}{4}$ of 1 percent handling charge.

portant differences among the many systems that have been called gold standards. The nature and significance of these differences will become clear as we go along. Several possible monetary roles of gold should be kept in mind as we study the various types of gold standards. These are: (1) as a component of the actual circulating medium; (2) as a medium for redeeming other types of money domestically; (3) as a determinant of the size and behavior of the money supply; and (4) as an international reserve, or a store of value for making international payments. With these possible roles in mind, let us look now at gold-coin, gold-bullion, and gold-exchange standards.

Gold-Coin Standards

Gold-coin standards are often called "the old type of gold standard," because most of the early gold standards were of this sort. They are also called "the gold circulation system," for gold coins were freely issued and actually available for circulation.

The maintenance of a gold-coin standard requires the following things to be done:

1. Define the monetary unit in terms of gold.
2. Provide for the unlimited coinage of gold at virtually no cost to the suppliers of the metal.
3. Permit the free and unlimited melting of gold coin.
4. Provide for the free interconvertibility of gold money and all other types of money at parity.
5. Allow free import and free export of gold.[2]

The purpose of each of these steps will be indicated by using as an example the gold-coin standard maintained in the United States from 1879 to 1933. (1) The dollar was defined as 23.22 grains of fine gold. This amounted to setting a buying price for gold at $20.67 an ounce, for each ounce—480 grains—could be coined into 20.67 dollars of 23.22 grains each. (2) Unlimited coinage of gold at virtually no cost to the supplier assured that the price of gold could not fall below $20.67 an ounce. (3) Free and unlimited melting of gold coins provided, in effect, a supply of gold from monetary uses to be used for other purposes and prevented the market price of gold from rising above $20.67 an ounce. The market price of gold for all purposes—hoarding, industrial uses, export, and so on—could not rise as long as gold could be acquired by melting down full-bodied gold coins.[3] (4) All other types of money were redeemable

---

[2] Some writers list a sixth requirement, that gold be given unlimited legal-tender powers. Though this provision was found in most gold-coin systems, it is easy to see how gold may become generally acceptable in payment of debts because of convenience and custom rather than compulsion.

[3] The market price of gold could, of course, rise above this level if the gold coins available for melting became of less than full weight because of clipping, sweating, or normal abrasion without replacement.

at par in terms of gold coins, and gold coins were redeemable at par in other types of money. This assured that all moneys would circulate at parity with each other as long as sufficient gold was available to meet demands for redemption. (5) The permission of free imports of gold prevented the domestic price of gold from rising above that abroad, and the permission of free exports prevented the domestic price of gold from falling below that abroad.

Several aspects of this "old type of gold circulation standard" are worth emphasis. In the first place, some part of the monetary gold stock actually circulated. And it was the people that determined how much gold they would use as a medium of payments, for they were free to demand gold in exchange for other types of money and to surrender gold for other types of money. In the second place, there was no official limitation on the redemption of other moneys in gold or on the uses of gold. Anyone with enough money to buy the smallest full-bodied gold coin could buy it and use the gold for any purpose. There were no limitations on the nonmonetary demand for gold. In the third place, the total supply of money was, even in this period, much larger than the nation's monetary gold stock. For example, at the end of 1930 when this country was on a full gold-coin standard and people were free to demand gold for circulation, hoarding, or any other purpose, our total monetary gold stock was only $4.3 billion while our total supply of money, all of which was redeemable in gold on demand, was $24.6 billion. This helps to explain why there could be recurrent "gold runs" and "gold crises." Promises to redeem all money in gold simply could not be met if many demanded gold simultaneously.

Gold-Bullion Standards

Gold-coin standards all but disappeared after World War I. The United States was the only major country that maintained a gold-coin standard in the 1920's, and even it shifted to a type of gold-bullion standard in 1934. We shall now examine this type of standard, looking first at what may be called a "full gold-bullion standard."

The principal differences between this and a gold-coin standard are the following: (1) The coinage of gold is discontinued and gold coins no longer circulate. Gold is still purchased by the government or central bank in unlimited amounts and at a fixed price, thereby preventing the price of gold from falling; but it is held in government or central bank vaults and payment to the sellers of gold is made in other types of money, such as government or central bank notes, deposit credits at the central bank, or deposits at other banks. (2) Other types of money are no longer convertible into gold or gold coin at the option of their holders in any amount requested; gold is sold only in the form of bars of a certain minimum weight. For example, the smallest bar that could be bought from the government under Great Britain's gold-bullion standard of the 1920's was worth about $7585. French peasants bitterly christened their own gold standard of this type "the rich man's standard." These gold bars were usually sold freely, however, whether they were to be used for hoarding, industry, or export.

Gold-bullion standards were usually adopted to "economize" gold. The countries wanted some sort of gold standard, but feared that the circulation of gold coins or the unlimited redeemability of money in gold would lead to such a drain of the metal from the government and the central bank as to endanger their ability to provide gold for foreign payments, or would reduce their reserves so seriously as to bring about undesired reductions in the total money supply.

Even the "full gold-bullion standards" embodied marked changes from the gold-coin standards. The circulation no longer included gold coins; the closest that gold came to circulation was as "backing," often in a vague sense, for money. Other moneys were convertible into gold no longer in small amounts, but only in large amounts; and even in these cases the gold received was not in the form of money. But perhaps most important of all, the concentration of gold in the hands of central banks and governments, together with the reduced responsibility for redeeming other types of money in gold, gave monetary authorities much more leeway in monetary management. The gold holdings of the monetary authorities were increased, the discontinuance of coinage and the increase of the minimum amount of gold that would be sold reduced somewhat the danger of gold withdrawals, and the need for gold relative to the total money supply was decreased.

From the "full gold-bullion standards" discussed above it was but a short step to what we may call "limited gold-bullion standards." Under the "full gold-bullion standard" the monetary authorities sold the large gold bars for all purposes. But this often led to unwanted results. People would buy gold for hoarding or for export, hoping to reap a speculative gain, or at least avoid a loss, if the nation's money depreciated in terms of gold. This permitted undesired drains of gold from government and central bank reserves, and tended to force decreases in the money supply and in the availability of credit. To escape these results, the monetary authorities placed still further limitations upon the purposes for which gold would be sold, and even went so far as to forbid anyone to buy or hold gold for any but "legitimate" purposes. For example, in the United States, and in most other countries as well, no one may legally deal in gold or hold gold except in accordance with government regulations, and these prohibit gold hoarding.

Such limitations on the redeemability of money in gold can cause a gold standard to operate in a manner quite different from that under a gold-coin standard. (1) Since gold can be purchased from the government at the official price only for "legitimate purposes," often strictly defined, black markets can arise in which people whose demands for gold are not met by the government may pay prices that are above the official price. (2) The increased concentration of gold in government and central bank reserves, as well as the reduced responsibility for redeeming money in gold, has the effect both of increasing the amount of money that can be supported by a given gold supply and of giving the monetary authorities still more leeway in their monetary management.

Countries have also placed limitations on their sale of gold for export. When this is carried so far as to permit the nation's money to depreciate in terms of gold held abroad and in terms of foreign gold moneys, it is doubtful that the system should be called a gold standard.

Gold-Exchange Standards

The term "gold-exchange standard" covers a wide variety of monetary arrangements. In general, however, it refers to a system in which a country does not redeem its money directly in gold, but redeems it in a foreign currency that in turn is in some sense redeemable in gold. Moreover, the country's "gold reserve" is not in the form of gold itself but in the form of claims against foreign moneys that have fixed gold values, at least in foreign payments. For example, the monetary unit of the Philippines has been the peso, and the actual circulating media are silver coins, paper money, and checking deposits. These are not redeemable directly in gold, but the government redeems them in United States dollars. For this purpose it holds not gold but claims against dollars. It then stabilizes the exchange rate between dollars and pesos by selling dollars for pesos whenever the peso price of the dollar tends to rise and by purchasing dollars with pesos whenever the peso price of dollars tends to fall. Essentially this is a method of redeeming a money in gold or its equivalent for purposes of international payments but not for domestic purposes. Several members of the British Commonwealth, and certain other countries as well, have a similar system in relation to the British pound sterling. Countries whose money is held by other countries for such purposes are usually called "center countries," for they are international reserve centers and centers of the international payments system. The United States and Great Britain are the world's two greatest center countries. New York and London are the most important center cities.

We shall apply the term "pure gold-exchange standard" to the situations in which a nation itself holds no gold but relies solely on its holdings of claims against foreign money to redeem its currency for international purposes. Most of the countries using this arrangement are relatively small. Much more important today are what may be called "mixed gold-exchange standards." By this we mean arrangements under which a nation holds some gold and also some claims against foreign money to redeem its own money for international purposes. Such standards are now used very widely. To illustrate their operation let us look at the mixed gold-exchange standards that use dollars and for which the United States is the center country.

Even though it may not redeem its own money in gold for domestic purposes, each country needs to hold an "international reserve," something that will be acceptable in payments to other countries. Like an individual or a business firm within a country, it needs to hold something that it could use to cover future excesses of its payments over its receipts. Foreigners may be willing to accept these excess payments in the form of the nation's own money and then continue to hold larger amounts of that money. But they may not; they may insist that it be redeemed in gold or in something else that they wish to hold. The nation therefore needs to hold something that will be acceptable to foreigners in payment, and that it can use to redeem its own money and keep it from depreciating in terms of foreign moneys. Under an international gold standard with virtually all important countries standing ready to buy at a fixed price in terms of their own moneys all the gold offered to them, gold is an excellent international reserve. A country holding gold can command any foreign money that it wants. But for a country to hold all its international reserve at home in the form of gold has at least two disadvantages. In the first place, shipping the gold abroad to make payments may be both slow and expensive. In the second place, gold holdings yield no money income. A nation may overcome the first disadvantage by holding at least a part of its gold in "earmark" in some great international center where it can be sold quickly and cheaply to buy other national moneys in the foreign-exchange market. In early 1958 foreign countries held $7.3 billion of earmarked gold in the United States. This is not a part of the United States monetary gold stock; it belongs to foreign countries and is only warehoused here in rented vaults at the Federal Reserve banks. But earmarked gold yields no money income to its owner. A nation's monetary authority is therefore likely to ask, "Isn't there something that will be just as acceptable as gold in international payments, that can be transferred in payment quickly and cheaply, and that will yield a money income?"

Claims against dollars meet these tests. Partly because of the huge gold reserves of the United States and the willingness of the Treasury to permit unlimited redemption of dollars in gold for international payments, the dollar is widely considered to be at least as "good as gold." Dollars, or more specifically deposit claims against United States banks, are acceptable in practically all international payments. For reasons such as these, many countries have come to hold a large part of their international reserves in the form of claims against dollars. These claims are of three principal types: (1) Deposits at the Federal Reserve banks. Most of these are at the Federal Reserve Bank of New York, but the other Reserve banks participate in this account. (2) Deposits at commercial banks. Some of these are demand deposits, many are interest-yielding time deposits. (3) Short-term investments. These are primarily in short-term Treasury obligations and acceptances, both of which can be sold quickly and at little cost.

In early 1958 foreign holdings of short-term claims against dollars amounted to $13.6 billion. Of these about $5.7 billion were owned by private foreign holders and $7.9 billion by foreign central banks and governments. This was at a time when the gold holdings, including the earmarked gold, of foreign central banks and governments amounted to $15.3 billion. Thus claims against dollars made up a very important part of the international reserves of other countries.

We cannot discuss in detail the somewhat similar role of the British pound sterling. We can only note that Britain is a highly important international center and that many countries hold large amounts of their international reserves in the form of claims against sterling—in the form of deposit claims against British banks and in short-term investments in the London money markets. There are also several other lesser centers that perform similar functions.

Several aspects of gold-exchange standards are worth comment. (1) With the growth of such arrangements there arise other assets that share with gold the function of acting as an international reserve. (2) Looked at from the point of view of the world as a whole, they are a means of "economizing gold." That is, they enable a given world monetary gold stock to support a larger money supply. This results from what is known as "gold pyramiding." The country that holds the actual gold counts it as "gold reserves," and the countries holding claims against it count these claims as "gold reserves" or their full equivalent. (3) Gold-exchange standards pose dangers for the countries that hold balances in another country, for the countries in which the balances are held, and for the world at large. This is especially true in the absence of thoroughgoing international coöperation. For the country owning the foreign balance, the danger is that the center country will be unable to redeem its money in gold or for various reasons will refuse to do so. Those owning the balances may suffer losses in the gold values of their international reserves or may be prevented from using them. For the center country the danger is that other countries will follow policies that will disturb its money market and its economy. For example, we found that other countries can get dollars for gold whenever they want, and they can get gold on demand in exchange for their dollar claims. They may shift their holdings among the categories of gold, deposits at the Federal Reserve, deposits at commercial banks, and holdings of short-term dollar securities. Such shifts can have important effects on United States markets. Suppose, for example, that foreign countries sell large amounts of gold to the Treasury and acquire deposits at commercial banks or short-term investments. This will increase bank reserves and tend to ease monetary conditions, which may or may not be desired by our monetary authorities. Suppose, on the other hand, that foreign countries sell their short-term investments or withdraw deposits from commercial banks and use the proceeds to build up their deposits at the Federal Reserve or to buy gold. This tends to reduce bank reserves and tighten credit, which may or may not please the Federal Reserve. In extreme cases such gold withdrawals could be highly deflationary and even force the center country to suspend gold payments. Such developments could also affect the whole world. In the first place, they could exert world-wide deflationary pressures, for the center country loses reserves but the withdrawing country has no net gain in reserves. It has merely elected to hold a given reserve in the form of gold rather than in the form of claims against the center country. In the second place, such withdrawals could derange the international payments mechanism by forcing center countries to abandon gold payments. The usefulness of international monetary coöperation under such conditions should be apparent.

THE MONETARY ROLES OF GOLD

Having surveyed the principal types of gold standards—gold-coin standards, gold-bullion standards, and gold-exchange standards—we shall now consider the various monetary roles of gold. We shall deal with these in perspective, attempting to indicate how these roles have changed through time and how they vary in different countries.

As a Component of the Actual Circulating Medium

Gold has lost most of its importance as a direct component of the circulating medium. At one time gold coin and gold certificates made up a large part of the supply of hand-to-hand currency and even of the total money supply. Now they are not used at all in most countries. Most nations have discontinued the coinage of gold and the issue of gold certificates to the public, have recalled those already in existence, and have forbidden their use. But gold's role in actual circulation began to dwindle long before governments restricted its availability and use for this purpose. This resulted as the public shifted its preference to other types of money. The public simply elected to hold and use more of other types of money, such as paper money and checking deposits, allowing more gold to be held by commercial banks, central banks, and governments.

This decline of gold as a component of the circulating medium has several important consequences. In the first place, it has made more tenuous the relationship between the size of the gold supply and the size of the money supply. Changes in the gold stock now affect the total money supply only insofar as they are allowed to affect the supply of nongold moneys. In the second place, it has served to "economize gold" in the sense of permitting the total supply of money to be larger relative to the size of the monetary gold stock. One dollar of gold in actual circulation "supports" only one dollar of money supply. But the one dollar of gold transferred into a fractional reserve banking system will "support" several dollars of money. In the third place, the promise to redeem all money in gold on demand became more and more difficult to keep as the money supply became a larger and larger multiple of the available gold supply. A growing recognition of this was one reason for limiting the redemption of money in gold.

As a Medium for the Domestic Redemption of Money

Gold's role as a medium for the domestic redemption of other types of money has also dwindled markedly. When all moneys were redeemable in gold without restriction, a country needed monetary gold for two purposes other than as a component of its actual circulating medium: (1) as an international reserve with which to make foreign payments in excess of its receipts and to prevent the exchange rate on its money from falling, and (2) as a reserve to meet domestic demands for the redemption of its other money in gold. In many cases this second need for gold was very large. Now it has almost disappeared as countries have ceased to redeem their money in gold domestically. When a nation refuses to sell gold for purposes other than export or for commercial, industrial, and artistic purposes, it has no need for a gold reserve for domestic purposes.

With this development, all a nation's gold becomes available to serve as an international reserve. This means, of course, that the nation can have a larger money supply relative to its gold stock. Many countries have symbolized this important change by repealing gold reserve requirements for their central banks and by removing all gold from their central banks, concentrating it in exchange stabilization funds that use it solely to make foreign payments and to regulate the prices of the nation's moneys in foreign-exchange markets.

As a Determinant of the Money Supply

Some have argued that one of the major functions of gold in a gold standard system is to regulate the total supply of money—to act as a discipline for monetary policy. They contended that a nation should increase its money supply in response to an increase in its monetary gold stock, and should decrease its money supply in response to a decrease in its stock of monetary gold. These ideas were elaborated by economists and central bankers into "rules of the international gold standard game." These rules were meant to apply to a situation in which the principal nations were on gold standards, each maintaining a fixed gold value for its monetary unit. One result of this arrangement would be virtually stable exchange rates among the various gold currencies. Moreover, it was argued, all the countries would be able to maintain their gold standards, and price levels in terms of gold would be in equilibrium in all the countries if the countries observed the rules of the game. If they violated these rules, disaster would follow.

They elaborated this argument by showing how an initial disequilibrium in a nation's international payments and receipts would be corrected by international gold flows if nations followed the rules of the game. Suppose, for example, that for some reason the price level in Country A rises relative to those in other gold standard countries. Country A will now be an expensive market in which to buy and an attractive market in which to sell. Its imports will exceed its exports, and it will have to export gold to cover its excess payments. But this gold flow will restore equilibrium if the countries follow the rules. Country A should allow its loss of gold to reduce its money supply and lower its price level. The other countries should allow their imports of gold to increase their money supplies and raise their price levels. Both the induced price decline in Country A and the induced price rise elsewhere tend to make Country A a somewhat more attractive market in which to buy and a less attractive market in which to sell, thereby bringing its international receipts and payments into equilibrium without further gold flows. Thus, following the rules of the game would terminate international gold flows, bring price levels in terms of gold into equilibrium throughout the gold-standard world, and equilibrate each nation's international receipts and payments.

What will happen if all the countries refuse to abide by the rules of the game? What if Country A refuses to allow its loss of gold to lower its money supply and its price level and if other countries refuse to allow their gold imports to increase their money supply and their price levels? Country A will be forced off the gold standard. With its price level remaining above those elsewhere, it will continue to import more than it exports, its international payments will continue to exceed its receipts, and the continuing drain of gold will eventually force it to abandon the gold standard. What of the other countries that gained the gold? They will have amassed gold less useful to them than the extra goods and services they might have imported and they will share the blame for Country A's abandonment of the gold standard and for the fluctuations of exchange rates that will follow.

In short, it was argued that each nation's monetary policy should be disciplined by its gold supply, that it should allow increases or decreases in its gold supply to increase or decrease its money supply, and that only by following such rules could gold standards be maintained and exchange rates stabilized. But even if these general rules were followed, the monetary effects of any given change in a nation's monetary gold stock would depend upon its monetary arrangements. To clarify this point let us consider a few type cases.

1. **The country has no money other than gold coins and gold certificates.** In

this case an increase in its monetary gold would automatically increase its total money supply both in proportion and by the same absolute amount.

2. The country's money supply is composed of gold coins and of checking deposits issued by banks operating on fractional reserves, say 20 percent reserves. In this case a given increase or decrease in the monetary gold stock may almost automatically bring about a multiple increase or decrease of the total money supply. For example, a $10 million gold inflow may induce a $50 million increase in checking deposits. Under the United States National Banking System in the latter part of the nineteenth century and up to the establishment of the Federal Reserve in 1914, gold imports and exports almost automatically eased and tightened monetary conditions. No existing institution had an incentive to hold large excess reserves, and none had the power to create new reserves to replace any that might be drained from the system under these conditions. Gold imports that increased bank reserves almost automatically eased monetary and credit conditions. And gold exports necessitated a multiple contraction of money and credit.

3. The country has both a commercial banking system operating on fractional reserves and a central bank operating on fractional reserves. Suppose that gold flows in through the commercial banks and into the central bank. As we found earlier, the direct effect is to increase both central bank reserves and commercial bank reserves. If the central bank takes no action, the commercial banks can expand their deposit liabilities by some multiple. Suppose that gold flows out of the country. We saw earlier that the loss of gold will directly decrease both central bank reserves and commercial bank reserves. In the absence of central bank action, the commercial banks will have to contract their deposit liabilities by some multiple of this initial loss of reserves.

How should the central bank respond to such increases or decreases in gold reserves? The rules of the international gold standard game, which were once very persuasive, indicated that the central bank should reinforce, not offset, the initial "automatic" expansive or restrictive effects. It should determine some "safe" ratio of its reserves to its liabilities. When its actual reserve ratio fell below this level, it should reduce its loans and security holdings to tighten monetary conditions. Whenever its actual reserves rose above the "safe" level, it should expand its loans and security holdings and ease monetary conditions. Suppose, for example, that a nation lost gold and that its central bank became worried about its reserve position. By raising its discount rate, lending less liberally, or selling securities, the central bank should tighten monetary and credit conditions. This would serve to end and even to reverse the gold outflow and protect the central bank's reserve position. It would do this in either or both of two ways. In the first place, the ensuing rise of interest rates at home would tend to discourage any outflow of loan funds and perhaps even attract an inflow from abroad. In the second place, the restrictive monetary policy would tend to lower price levels at home and to increase the nation's exports relative to its imports. Thus a restrictive central bank policy on top of the "automatic" restrictive effects of a gold outflow would reinforce the equilibrating process of bringing the nation's international payments and receipts into balance, ending gold outflows, and preserving its ability to maintain gold payments.

On the other hand, suppose that gold inflows raised the central bank's actual reserve ratio above the "safe" level. The old rules indicated that the central bank should reinforce the initial "automatic" expansionary effects by lowering its discount rate, lending more liberally, or purchasing securities. This would serve in two principal ways to end the gold inflow. For one thing, the decline of interest rates at home would tend to discourage inflows of loan funds and perhaps to encourage an export of loan funds. Moreover, the expansionary monetary policy would tend to raise price levels at home and to decrease exports relative to imports. Again, the central bank's policy would reinforce the process of equilibrating international payments and receipts and safeguarding the stability of exchange rates.

In summary, many nations once welcomed, or at least acquiesced in, the discipline of gold over their monetary policies. They allowed their monetary policies to be ruled by their international balance of payments position, adopting expansionary policies when they gained gold and restrictive policies when they lost gold. They considered such policies necessary to preserve the redeemability of their moneys in gold and to prevent their moneys from depreciating in terms of gold and foreign gold currencies. But in recent decades, and especially since World War I, nations have become increasingly restive under the discipline of gold and have in many cases rebelled against it. This is in large part because they feel that the old rules of the international gold standard game inhibit their achievement of important objectives. A nation that is already experiencing inflation and that wants a stable price level may not be willing to allow gold imports to expand its money supply, to say nothing of its attitude toward a reinforcing expansion of credit by its central bank. A country intent on "maximizing employment and promoting the highest sustainable rate of economic growth" is likely to be reluctant to allow gold exports to restrict its money supply, not to speak of its attitude toward a reinforcing restrictive policy by its central bank. Monetary restriction that results in pure price deflation is unpopular enough; restriction reflected largely in unemployment and lack of growth is even less acceptable.

For reasons such as these, monetary authorities often follow policies diametrically opposed to the old rules of the international gold standard game and try to "offset" or "sterilize" the monetary effects of gold inflows and outflows. For example, they offset the effects of gold imports by raising the reserve requirements of commercial banks, by central bank sales of securities in the open market, and so on. On the other hand, they offset the monetary effects of gold exports by such devices as lowering commercial bank reserve requirements, purchases of securities in the open market by central banks, and increased central bank loans. In such cases the role of gold as a regulator of monetary policy dwindles.

But to what extent can a nation that maintains a gold standard succeed in offsetting the effects of gold inflows and outflows? To what extent can it violate the old rules and still maintain enough gold to meet its foreign payments and maintain the value of its money in terms of gold and foreign currencies? A nation may use various ingenious devices to "sterilize" gold inflows and prevent their having inflationary effects, though many have failed to do so. But if one nation or a group of nations amasses great amounts of gold and prevents their having inflationary effects at home, they make it more difficult for other countries to keep enough gold to maintain gold payments. The ability of countries to continue to sterilize or offset the effects of gold outflows depends in large part on the adequacy of their holdings of gold and other international reserves. The United States, with its huge gold supplies, could continue to follow easy-money policies in the face of gold losses for a long time before a shortage of gold would limit its freedom of action. But most countries are not as generously supplied with international reserves and have no such leeway. Their ability to violate the rules of the gold standard game and still maintain a gold standard is much more limited. When they reach this limit they may, as we shall see later, follow any of several courses of action. They may bow to the old rules and follow a restrictive monetary and fiscal policy, distasteful as it may be. They may stay on a gold standard but reduce the gold value of their money. They may abandon gold entirely and adopt an inconvertible standard, or they may resort to all sorts of direct controls over international capital movements, trade, and payments in order to equilibrate their international receipts and payments.

The major point to be made here is that gold has lost much of its popularity as a determinant of the money supply and monetary policy. Gold standards are now managed standards with many objectives other than that of maintaining stable exchange rates.

As an International Reserve

As we have already seen, the role of gold as a component of the actual circulating medium has dwindled to very small proportions. So has its role as a medium for redeeming money domestically. Its role as a determinant of domestic monetary policy is also far smaller than it once was. Its most important remaining role is as a form of international reserve—as something that is generally acceptable in international payments and as a medium for stabilizing exchange rates. And it shares this role with such things as claims against dollars and the British pound sterling. We shall later explore the possibility of other substitutes for gold in this role.

Summary

The preceding pages have indicated some of the reasons why we said earlier that gold standards should not be looked upon as homogeneous and unvarying. Like most other institutions, they change through time and are adapted to changing conditions and objectives. A modern mixed gold-exchange standard that is highly managed has little more than a faint family resemblance to a gold-coin standard of the early nineteenth century.

BIMETALLIC STANDARDS

The United States was on a bimetallic standard for nearly 70 years, from 1792 to 1861. A bimetallic or double standard is one in which the monetary unit and all types of a nation's money are kept at a constant value in terms of gold and also in terms of silver. It is, in effect, the simultaneous maintenance of both a gold and a silver standard. The steps necessary for the maintenance of such a standard are the same as those for a monometallic standard, except that the provisions for unlimited purchase, sale, and redeemability apply to both metals. For example, in 1834 our dollar was defined as 371.25 grains of fine silver or 23.22 grains of fine gold. This in effect set the mint purchase and sale prices at $1.29 an ounce for silver $\left(\frac{480}{371.25} = 1.29\right)$ and $20.67 an ounce for gold $\left(\frac{480}{23.22} = 20.67\right)$. The ratio of the values of gold and silver at the mint is called "the mint ratio." In this case it was approximately 16 to 1 because the monetary unit contained 16 times as much silver as gold, or to put the same thing another way, the mint price of gold was set at 16 times that of silver. As long as the mint purchased both gold and silver freely at these prices and as long as both gold and silver full-bodied coins were available for melting, the market prices of the metals were fixed.

Several advantages were claimed for bimetallic standards as compared with either gold or silver monometallic standards. The first was that bimetallism provided convenient full-bodied coins for both large and small transactions. The prejudice in favor of full-bodied coins was strong during the period of bimetallism; credit money was widely suspect. Proponents of bimetallism pointed out that it provided portable gold money for large transactions and convenient silver money for smaller payments, arguments that lost their force as credit money was developed and became more acceptable. A second advantage claimed for bimetallism was its ability to stabilize exchange rates of all national currencies on bimetallic, gold, and silver standards. As long as gold and silver were stabilized in terms of each other, all national currencies with fixed values in gold or in silver would exchange for each other at nearly constant rates. Their exchange rates could not fluctuate by more than the cost of shipping an equivalent value of one of the metals. Thus, the effective use of bimetallism by any group of countries would link together all bimetallic and monometallic gold and silver currencies in an international network of stable exchange rates.

The third advantage claimed for bimetallism was that it provided a standard money whose purchasing power would be more stable than one based on a single metal. This would result because its purchasing power would be determined by supply and demand conditions for two metals, not just for one. Fluctuations of the two metals would tend to "average out." [4]

Critics of bimetallism alleged that in fact it was not a double standard but an alternating gold and silver standard, for one of the metals would disappear from circulation. They claimed that as supply conditions and nonmonetary demand conditions for the two metals changed, the market price of one would rise above the mint price, no more of this metal would be offered for coinage, and existing full-bodied coins of the metal would be melted down. This need not happen if all countries use the same mint ratio, and if this ratio is set at any reasonable level. With large amounts of both metals in monetary systems it seems unlikely that all the supply of one of them would be used for nonmonetary purposes. But a nation certainly can lose all its supply of one of the metals if its mint ratio differs from that in other countries. Our own monetary history shows this clearly.

The first monetary law enacted under the Constitution, the Coinage Act of 1792, put the United States on a bimetallic standard. The dollar was defined both as 371.25 grains of pure silver and as 24.75 grains of pure gold. Thus the mint ratio was $\frac{371.25}{24.75}$, or 15 to 1. But the French mint ratio at that time was 15.5 to 1. In other words, the French valued gold more highly relative to silver than we did. The natural result was that we lost all our gold and were left with only silver standard money. Arbitrageurs could profit by exporting gold and importing silver. They could exchange 15,000 ounces of silver here for 1000 ounces of gold, trade the gold in France for 15,500 ounces of silver, and thereby gain 500 ounces of silver to cover their costs and yield a profit. The outcome would have been about the same if the disparity had not been great enough to cover the shipping costs and risks involved in such "endless chain" operations. This is because Americans having to make payments in France found it cheaper to pay in gold, whereas Frenchmen found it cheaper to pay Americans in silver.

---

[4] For an excellent brief discussion of this point, see W. S. Jevons, *Money and the Mechanism of Exchange*, Appleton, New York, 1892, pp. 137–140.

In 1834 Congress attempted to remedy this situation by making the mint ratio more favorable to gold. It did this by reducing the gold content of the dollar from 24.75 to 23.22 grains while leaving its silver content unchanged at 371.25 grains. In effect, it raised the mint price of gold from $19.31 to $20.67 an ounce. The new mint ratio was approximately 16 to 1. Congress went too far, for the French mint ratio remained at 15.5 to 1. It now became profitable to reverse the old process and to export silver and import gold. The inevitable result was that little silver was offered for coinage, and existing silver coins disappeared. During the 25-year period 1836–1860, gold coinage amounted to nearly $446 million; during the same period only 3 million silver dollars were struck. Even fractional silver coins, which had previously been full-bodied, disappeared so that the nation had to resort to "shinplasters" (fractional money issued by banks) and other substitutes in small transactions. Fractional silver coins reappeared only after 1853 when Congress reduced their silver content and made them token money.

This mistake by Congress in 1834 may have altered the course of United States monetary history. Congress apparently had no intention of putting the country on a monometallic gold standard at that time; yet the de facto results were that during most of the 27 years immediately preceding the Civil War full-bodied silver coins were unavailable, and the country's only available standard money was gold. Then came the long Civil War and post-Civil War period, 1861–1879, during which the country was on an inconvertible standard with the dollar depreciated in terms of both gold and silver. Neither gold nor silver was offered for coinage during this period. In 1873, when Congress was making plans for the restoration of some sort of metallic standard, it had been nearly 40 years since significant amounts of silver had been offered to the mint for coinage. Thus, the elimination from this legislation of any provision for the free coinage of silver was merely the elimination of a privilege that had not been used to any considerable extent for about 40 years. With this action the era of bimetallism in the United States ended, and the period of the monometallic gold standard began. Though the government thereafter bought silver for monetary purposes on many occasions, it did so in only limited amounts and never restored free and unlimited coinage of silver. The "Crime of '73" was not soon forgotten by the advocates of silver. Nor have we yet seen the end of the "do-something-for-silver" demands.

INCONVERTIBLE STANDARDS

Systems in which monetary units are not kept at a constant value in terms of a metal are usually called inconvertible standards. Under systems of this type the various kinds of money in circulation within a country are usually maintained at parity with each other, but they are not kept constant in their relation to a metal. We cannot emphasize too much the broad scope of this category; the systems included under it vary greatly as to both form and functioning. Under some, the monetary authority continues to purchase a metal at a fixed price, thereby preventing the monetary unit from appreciating relative to the metal, but it does not sell the metal at a fixed price. Under others, no metal is either purchased or sold at a fixed price. Under some, the monetary authority carefully manages the money supply to achieve economic stabilization. Under others, money is issued prodigally for revenue purposes. To lump all these widely varying systems into one group and brand them "good" or "bad" is to misread monetary history and to ignore the principles of money.

Inconvertible moneys have been held in low regard in the past largely because they were usually associated with periods of widespread economic disturbance. The continental currency of the American Revolution, the assignats of the French Revolution, the greenbacks of the Civil War, the inflations of World Wars I and II, the inconvertible moneys of the great depression—these and many others are often cited to prove that inconvertible standards are always inferior to metallic standards and should be scrupulously avoided. These conclusions do not necessarily follow. During the periods from which these examples are taken, people in general believed in "metallism"; they wanted metallic standards as long as these could be maintained without great sacrifice of other objectives, and they used inconvertible standards only when their metallic standards had already broken down. They did not deliberately "adopt" these standards; they reluctantly sought refuge in them when war, panic, depression, or other serious economic disturbances made it impossible for them to keep their money convertible in metal, or made them unwilling to tolerate the limitations imposed on their policies by the maintenance of convertibility. Those who proclaim that "history proves that inconvertible standards are less satisfactory than metallic standards" might better say, "History shows that paper standards used in periods of extreme economic disturbance function less well than metallic standards during less troubled periods." And perhaps they should add that metallic standards have a habit of breaking down during periods of war, panic, and depression, leaving inconvertible standards to do their work.

All monetary standards, metallic as well as inconvertible, are now highly managed, and their success depends largely on the quality of their management. There are still wide differences of opinion among economists as to whether some sort of metallic standard or some sort of inconvertible standard is likely to be more conducive to wise and efficient monetary management.

SELECTED READINGS

Carothers, N., *Fractional Money*, Wiley, New York, 1930.
Dewey, D. R., *Financial History of the United States*, Longmans, Green, New York, 9th ed., 1924.

Jevons, W. S., *Money and the Mechanism of Exchange*, Appleton, New York, 1892.

Murad, A., *The Paradox of a Metal Standard: A Case History of Silver*, Graphic Arts Press, Washington, 1939.

CHAPTER 20

United States Monetary
Policies, 1914–1929

PROLOGUE

When Congress passed and President Wilson signed the Federal Reserve Act in late 1913, the international gold standard was in its heyday. Gold had achieved its status as a truly international monometallic standard only in the latter part of the nineteenth century. Few economically important countries other than Great Britain were on gold standards before 1870; most of them were on silver or bimetallic standards. But the last thirty years of the nineteenth century and the first few years of the twentieth saw gold triumph (see Table 49). The United States put its new gold standard into effect in 1879.

The first years of the new gold standard were stormy ones, especially in the

TABLE 49. Dates of Adopting Gold Standards[a]

Great Britain	1816	Holland	1875
Germany	1871	Uruguay	1876
Sweden		United States	1879
Norway	1873	Austria	1892
Denmark		Chile	1895
France		Japan	1897
Belgium		Russia	1898
Switzerland	1874	Dominican Republic	1901
Italy		Panama	1904
Greece		Mexico	1905

[a] The dates are approximate only, for some of the countries made the change from bimetallism or silver monometallism to gold in several steps.

United States. This was primarily because they were years of deflation. The United States had followed highly inflationary monetary and fiscal policies during the Civil War; these were reflected in a doubling of the price level and in a fall of about 50 percent in the gold value of the inconvertible paper dollar. It was decided that prices would have to fall so that the dollar could again be given its old prewar gold value of 23.22 grains. When the latter was done in 1879 the price level had already fallen more than 50 percent below its Civil War peak. But the price decline did not end at that point; it continued into the 1890's. Those who opposed falling prices joined forces with those who were infuriated by "The Crime of '73" and wanted to "do something for silver" in condemning the gold standard and in demanding more money of almost any sort: more greenbacks, more silver money, and more of anything that would bring the price decline to an end and help silver. Then, almost abruptly, the clamor subsided at the end of the century and the brief "golden age of gold standards" began. This was due in part to an upsurge in the growth of banking but more to an upsurge in gold production, following the invention of the cyanide process of amalgamation and new gold discoveries in the Rand district of the Transvaal and in the Klondike-Yukon area. The world's rate of gold production during the early years of the twentieth century was more than three times that in the period preceding 1896. The total money supply in the United States (coins, paper money, and checking deposits) tripled between 1896 and 1914, and wholesale prices rose more than 40 percent. Occasional complaints against the rising cost of living were lost amidst the praises of prosperity.

Those responsible for enacting the new Federal Reserve legislation had no intention of modifying basically the existing monetary standard. They implicitly assumed that the new system would operate within an international gold standard framework and probably that it would follow the old rules of the international gold standard game. What they could not know was that before a year was out, and even before the new Federal Reserve banks could be organized and opened for business, the old type of international gold standard would be a thing of the past. World War I broke out at the beginning of August, 1914, and carried almost all countries into inflation and off gold standards. Until 1925 only the United States and a very few other countries were on gold. During this period of more than ten years, the old rules of the international gold standard game were irrelevant, for there was no such standard. And the new standards that were established in the latter half of the 1920's were far different from those of the prewar period. In the meantime, the Federal Reserve had faced the task of helping finance a major war.

THE PERIOD OF UNITED STATES NEUTRALITY, 1914–1917

The war had already broken out in August before the Federal Reserve banks first opened for business in November, 1914. One of the first effects of the outbreak was to create crises in almost all financial markets, including those in the United States. Several forces combined to produce crisis conditions here:

the necessity of repaying large short-term debts to London, the unavailability of new credits from Europe, large foreign sales of securities on the New York Stock Exchange, German threats to ocean shipping and interruption of United States exports, domestic cash withdrawals from banks, and withdrawals by banks in the interior of some of their deposits with their city correspondents. At times it was feared that a full-fledged banking panic would occur and that gold payments would have to be suspended. The worst had passed, however, when the Federal Reserve banks opened in November. By the late spring of 1915, the United States was enjoying an export boom. Demands for its products were becoming almost insatiable as neutrals turned to it for products formerly purchased in Europe and as the Allied Powers bought heavily to meet their essential civilian needs and to promote their war efforts. Between August 1, 1914, and the entry of the United States into the war in April, 1917, United States exports totaled $11,585 million while its imports were only $5531 million, leaving an export surplus of $6054 million. Foreign buyers paid for these huge net purchases in three principal ways; they resold here $2000 million of their holdings of United States securities, borrowed $2375 million, and shipped $1100 million of gold. Since the United States gold stock had been only $1572 million at the beginning of the war, these imports increased it by nearly 70 percent. No one had ever anticipated such gold inflows. Both the great increase in the foreign demand for United States exports and the flow of gold into bank reserves created strong inflationary pressures.

During the period between the opening of the Reserve banks in late 1914 and the entrance of the United States into the war in April, 1917, Federal Reserve officials had no opportunity either to develop meaningful objectives or to use their instruments of control effectively. It was obvious to them that they should not, in response to the gold inflow, follow expansionary policies and enhance inflationary pressures. Yet they could do nothing to offset or sterilize the expansionary effects of gold inflows. They had almost no assets to sell and they had no power to raise member bank reserve requirements. They had to stand by while the money supply rose from $11.6 billion in mid-1914 to $15.8 billion in mid-1917. Wholesale prices had already risen more than 50 percent when the United States entered the war.

THE WAR PERIOD, 1917–1919

With this country's entrance into the war, the Federal Reserve entered a new phase. The system that had been created to "accommodate commerce and industry" now became one to "accommodate the Treasury"; its dominant objective became that of assuring that the prosecution of the war would not be hindered by any lack of money, regardless of inflationary consequences. The government's fiscal policy was the one common to periods of major war—

large deficits representing increases of expenditures far in excess of increases in tax collections. Federal expenditures rose from less than $750 million in 1916 to $18,515 million in fiscal 1919, nearly a 24-fold increase. For the three years ending June 30, 1919, they aggregated $33,190 million, a huge sum for those days. This great rise in the government's demand for output, occurring when the economy was already operating at near-capacity levels, enhanced inflationary pressures both directly and through its stimulus to private consumption and investment demands. Despite the imposition of many new taxes and in-

TABLE 50. Federal Receipts and Expenditures, 1916–1920
(In millions)

Fiscal Year Ending June 30	Expenditures	Receipts	Surplus (+) or Deficit (−)	Change in Treasury General Fund Balance	Change in Gross Federal Debt
1916	$ 734	$ 783	$ +48	$ +82	$ +34
1917	1,978	1,124	−853	+897	+1,750
1918	12,697	3,665	−9,032	+447	+9,480
1919	18,515	5,152	−13,363	−333	+13,029
1920	6,403	6,695	+291	−894	−1,185
Summary:					
1. Total for two fiscal years					
1918–1919	31,212	8,817	−22,395	+114	+22,509
2. Total for three fiscal years					
1917–1919	33,190	9,941	−23,248	+1,011	+24,259

creases in old ones, total tax collections in the three years ending in June, 1919, were only $9941 million, leaving a deficit of $23,248 million to be covered by new borrowing.

The Treasury tried to borrow as much as it could in ways that would not involve an increase in the money supply. Employing a nation-wide organization, high-pressure Liberty Loan campaigns, and various types of propaganda, it called upon the American people and business firms to "Save and buy bonds!" However, its receipts from these sales were far too small to cover its needs, so it turned to types of borrowing that did require increases in the money supply. These were of two principal sorts. (1) Sales of Treasury securities, primarily shorter-term issues, to the commercial banks. This obviously involved an increase in the money supply but the Treasury hoped, largely in vain, that it could later retire this money with borrowings from the public. (2) Sales of securities, largely of the longer-term varieties, to members of the public who would pay for them with money borrowed from the commercial banks. This, too, obviously involved an increase of the money supply, but the Treasury hoped that this new money would gradually be retired as banks brought pressure on their customers to save and repay their borrowings.

The Federal Reserve played a central role in this process by meeting the greatly increased demand for currency in circulation and by supplying the banking system with sufficient reserves to enable it to buy Treasury obligations, to lend to others for the purchase of Treasury securities, and to meet essential private demands for productive purposes. In sharp contrast to its policies during World War II, it did this to only a very small extent by purchasing government securities itself. It supplied the funds largely by lending to commercial banks. It did this in the following way. It set up "preferential discount rates" on Federal Reserve loans collateraled by Treasury obligations. These were preferential in the sense that they were below the discount rates applicable to loans secured by commercial paper. They were also below, usually about ¼ of 1 percent below, the coupon rates on the various types of Treasury obligations to which they applied. Thus, a bank could make a small profit by borrowing from the Federal Reserve and buying government securities, and also by borrowing to lend to customers at an interest rate equal to the coupon rate on the security bought and pledged by the customer.

Three aspects of this policy are important: (1) In effect, it enabled the Treasury to determine Federal Reserve preferential discount rates, for it was the Treasury that determined the coupon rates on its obligations. (2) The preferential rates became the effective discount rates at the Federal Reserve banks. With great and growing holdings of Treasury obligations eligible for the lower preferential rates, banks would have been foolish to borrow at the higher rates applicable to commercial paper. (3) The Federal Reserve could not restrict the supply of credit for other uses while maintaining such ample credit supplies for the Treasury. Banks could secure reserves by borrowing on government securities and then lend as they saw fit.

The government's highly expansionary fiscal policy and the Federal Reserve's "accommodating" monetary policy were accompanied by inflation and monetary expansion. By mid-1919, when the government's deficit spending came to an end, both Federal Reserve and commercial bank credit had expanded greatly. In March, 1917, just before this country's entrance into the war, total Federal Reserve credit outstanding was less than $300 million. In June, 1919, it was more than $2500 million, of which $1800 million represented bank borrowings. The nation's total money supply, which had been $11.6 billion in mid-1914 and $15.8 billion three years later, had risen to $21.2 billion by mid-1919. The wholesale price level was 25 percent higher than it was just before the entrance of the United States into the war and 95 percent above its level at the outbreak of the war.

Federal Reserve officials did not object to the domination of their policy by the Treasury's needs during the war itself or even during the period of continuing government deficits up to mid-1919. They, too, wanted to do everything they could to help win the war and they recognized that the inadequate tax policy of the period necessitated borrowing from the banks and Federal Reserve support. But in the last three months of 1919 they grew restive and finally rebelled against Treasury domination. The Treasury's needs were now less urgent, for it was enjoying a small tax surplus. Moreover, inflation was again well under way. After some hesitation in late 1918 and early 1919 as the government's demand for output fell, the economy was again under strong inflationary pressures from rising export and private domestic demands. Speculation in both securities and commodities was widespread, both Federal Reserve and commercial bank credit were expanding, and prices and wages were rising rapidly. This was no speculative bubble on the surface of the economy; it was a strong inflation that pushed up not only the prices of output but also wages and other elements of the cost structure. Under these conditions, Federal Reserve officials wanted to increase discount rates. The Treasury objected. Though it no longer had to borrow new money to cover current deficits, it insisted that its refunding operations should not be hampered by increases in Federal Reserve discount rates. Moreover, it wanted to avoid any further declines in the prices of outstanding Liberty Bonds. The controversy became prolonged and bitter. Gradually, however, the Treasury acquiesced and permitted a series of discount rate increases, the first of which occurred in November, 1919. In several cases its acquiescence was delayed and reluctant. By the end of May, 1920, discount rates at the various Reserve banks had been raised from their range of 4 to 4½ percent in the preceding October to a range of 6 to 7 percent.

The war and postwar inflation came to an abrupt halt in May, 1920. By then, however, price levels had risen markedly and both commercial bank and Federal Reserve credit were greatly expanded. Wholesale prices were 140 percent above their prewar level. Total commercial bank loans and investments had increased from $16.9 billion in mid-1914 to $36.3 billion, a rise of $19.4 billion or 115 percent. Only 23 percent of this increase was in bank holdings of Treasury obligations; the rest represented increased bank loans and holdings of private securities. Total Federal Reserve credit had risen to $3.4 billion, of which more than $2.5 billion was in the form of loans to banks. Thus member banks entered the postwar depression owing the Federal Reserve banks more than $2.5 billion, and on these borrowings they were paying discount rates of 6 and 7 percent.

POSTWAR DEPRESSION, 1920–1921

The end of the war and postwar inflation in the United States was signaled in May, 1920, by a world-wide break in the prices of such basic commodities as silk, tea, coffee, and most agricultural products. The ensuing depression, which ran into early 1922, was relatively short but sharp and painful. Wholesale prices in general fell 45 percent and the prices of farm products 50 percent. Millions lost their jobs, and thousands of business firms were injured by decreased demands for their products and by declines in the values of their high-priced inventories. Farmers were hard hit. Many who had bought high-priced land on credit or who had accumulated high-cost livestock and grain inventories became insolvent or nearly so. Thus both the solvency and the liquidity of the economy were seriously weakened. And the commercial banks, owing the Federal Reserve about $2.5 billion on which they were paying interest rates of 6 and 7 percent, were in no position to offer easier credit.

It was April, 1921, about a year after the depression started, before the Federal Reserve took a single action to ease monetary and credit conditions. The Reserve banks did refrain from putting pressure on member banks to repay their borrowings; they wanted the liquidation to be orderly rather than abrupt and panicky. But they did not buy either government securities or acceptances to provide the banks with reserves and enable them to reduce their borrowings, and they did not reduce a discount rate until April, 1921. Such a policy now seems incomprehensible to those who accept the view that the major objectives of the Federal Reserve should be to promote price stability, maximum employment, and the highest sustainable rate of economic growth. Why did the Federal Reserve follow the policies it did in the depression of 1920–1921?

The answer has many parts, but a basic point to be made is that the Federal Reserve had not yet come to believe that it had the responsibility of using its powers aggressively to promote economic stability. This concept of its function developed during the next few years. But the Federal Reserve had several reasons for wanting some liquidation of credit. The most important of these was to protect and improve its gold reserve position. In large part its policy was the traditional one of a central bank facing a threat to its reserve position and to its ability to maintain the redeemability of the nation's money in gold. The country's monetary gold stock had grown from $1.5 billion in 1914 to $2.9 billion in 1919. Moreover, a wartime campaign had succeeded in concentrating about three quarters of the nation's gold in the Federal Reserve banks. A wartime embargo on gold exports prevented gold from flowing out until the embargo was lifted in the spring of 1919. Yet by late 1919 and early 1920 the actual gold reserve ratios of the Federal Reserve banks as a group were very close to the legal minimum. The New York Federal Reserve Bank actually had deficient reserves on several occasions and had to pay penalties on the deficiencies. Several of the other Reserve banks would have been in even worse reserve positions if they had not borrowed from the other Reserve banks. This sharp decline in the reserve ratios of the Federal Reserve banks was brought about largely by the great rise of Federal Reserve note and deposit liabilities during the period of expansion and inflation. But it was aggravated by small gold outflows following the lifting of the gold embargo early in 1919.

This episode is interesting in part because it was one of the two occasions in Federal Reserve history when a shortage of gold led it to restrict credit. The only other was in the fall of 1931. It is significant that the Federal Reserve did not lower its discount rates in 1921 until its reserve position had improved markedly.

There were also other reasons why the Federal Reserve did not earlier remove downward pressures on credit. One was the belief that banks should not permanently hold large amounts of government securities. They should, instead, sell these securities and concentrate on commercial loans. Still another was the belief that member banks should not remain continuously in debt to their Reserve banks. Also important was the fact that the Federal Reserve had not yet learned how to use open-market operations for general monetary management purposes.

The 1920–1921 episode was extremely painful for the country and the Federal Reserve. Within a few years the Federal Reserve had so changed its objectives and its methods of operations that it would not have dreamed of repeating its policies of 1920–1921. Armed with ample gold reserves—and even threatened by a plethora of gold—it became an agency for economic stabilization.

THE POSTWAR WORLD

It was late 1921 or early 1922, when the Federal Reserve System was already more than seven years old, before Federal Reserve officials had an opportunity to develop anything like "normal" peacetime objectives and peacetime methods of monetary management. During their first two and a half years they had been powerless to prevent the flood of gold imports from feeding the inflation. From this country's entrance into the war until near the end of 1919 they had been chained to the objective of facilitating Treasury finance regardless of inflationary consequences. Then in 1920 and early 1921 their gold reserve positions were so tight that they felt they had little freedom of action. Only now were they rid of the problem of financing a war, free of Treasury domination, and possessed of enough excess gold reserves and enough earning assets to enable them to regulate monetary conditions. But as the Federal Reserve officials sought to formulate peacetime objectives and to develop peacetime methods of operation they did so under conditions that were never contemplated by the authors of the Federal Reserve Act and made most of the prewar rules of central banking obsolete. The postwar world was far different from that of 1913. The Federal Reserve Act contemplated that the new system would extend its credit almost exclusively on the basis of private debt obligations. The Reserve banks would create funds primarily by lending to member banks on the basis of commercial paper, and even their open-market operations would be largely confined to acceptances. This was partly because of the theory that the supply of credit would be best adjusted to the needs of trade if based on short-term, self-liquidating loans for production and distribution purposes. But it was also partly because the supply of federal debt was so small; for some time this debt had been less than $1 billion and three quarters of it was held as backing for national bank notes. All this was changed at the end of the war. The federal debt had grown to $25 billion and was widely held by all types of individuals and financial institutions. This altered the situation in many ways. In the first place, it increased the regional mobility of investable funds. These funds could now be shifted through interregional sales of government securities. In the second place, it enabled member banks to borrow on paper collateraled by Treasury obligations rather than commercial paper. In the third place, it provided the Federal Reserve with an excellent medium for open-market operations and facilitated the development and use of this powerful instrument.

Far more important, however, were the great changes in the world economy and in the relative position of the United States in that economy. The authors of the Federal Reserve Act implicitly assumed that the new system would operate within an international gold standard framework and would in general abide by the old rules of the international gold standard game. They had no reason to expect that the United States would become a major regulator of the world's monetary system, for the United States was in fact a minor financial center in the prewar period. She was still a net debtor to the rest of the world, she had few facilities for international lending, and her supply of knowledge and expertness in international monetary and financial matters was very limited. London was the almost undisputed monetary and financial center of the world. Britain was the world's greatest trading country and the world's greatest net creditor. And London was the world's center for international loans, both short term and long term, and for international payments. In effect, the Bank of England managed the international gold standard. It is but little exaggeration to say that gold was on the sterling standard.

All this was changed at the end of the war. The United States emerged more powerful than ever. Both by repurchasing American securities from abroad and by foreign lending she had become a net creditor to the rest of the world. Her industries, unscathed by the war, were more productive than ever. Her national income was probably greater than that of all Europe, and she was the principal potential source of savings for international lending. Almost alone, she remained on a gold standard. Within a few years she held more than 40 percent of all the world's monetary gold and stood in danger of receiving more

Europe, the old center of economic and financial power, was in economic and political distress. Her productive power was seriously reduced. This was partly because of physical destruction through military action, unrepaired wear and tear of productive facilities, lack of fertilizers, and malnutrition of workers. But at least as devastating were social, political, and economic disorders. Many governments were unstable, revolutionary movements were widespread, and international disputes were common. Inflation was rampant and financial disorders the rule. All countries had abandoned gold standards and few managed to reëstablish them before 1925. Great Britain's position was seriously undermined. In addition to her heavy loss of manpower in the war, she had lost much of her shipping, had sold large amounts of her assets abroad, and had borrowed more to help finance her war efforts and those of her allies. She had been forced to abandon the gold standard and did not return to it until April, 1925. In the meantime sterling exchange rates fluctuated widely. London was certainly in no position to play the role of manager of any sort of international gold standard.

Thus the inexperienced Federal Reserve officials found themselves at the head of the world's most powerful monetary system with an inescapable power to influence not only the purchasing power of gold throughout the world but also its distribution. By 1923 it was quite clear that in the absence of an international gold standard they could not follow the old rules of the game. By that time the nation's monetary gold stock had reached $3.7 billion and had increased $1 billion in the preceding 24 months. During the next two years it rose another $500 million. Even if the Federal Reserve merely allowed the "automatic" effects of gold imports to occur, an unwanted inflation might result. To reinforce these automatic effects by an expansion of Federal Reserve credit would compound the folly. The system therefore began a policy of "offsetting" or "sterilizing" the effects of gold flows except when, by coincidence, the effects of gold flows were consistent with the promotion of the System's objectives. But merely to reject the old rules of the gold standard game—to ignore reserve ratios in determining policy—was not enough. Federal Reserve officials had to evolve new objectives and guides to take their place.

OBJECTIVES OF FEDERAL RESERVE POLICY

During the relatively short period 1922–1924 Federal Reserve officials developed three main objectives or considerations that guided their policies during the remainder of the 1920's. These were: (1) promotion of price level stability and high and stable levels of business activity, (2) prevention of an excessive use of credit for speculative purposes, especially in the stock market, and (3) promotion of the restoration and maintenance of gold standards abroad. None of these objectives could be promoted by a Federal Reserve policy of passive accommodation; all required positive policies of regulation or control. It should be clear that no one of these objectives dominated Federal Reserve actions. When they came into conflict, as they sometimes did, Federal Reserve officials faced difficult problems of balancing and compromising.

PROMOTION OF PRICE AND BUSINESS STABILITY

Starting in about 1922 at the end of the postwar depression, the objective of promoting price level stability and high and stable levels of business activity became one of the most powerful determinants of Federal Reserve policy actions. Federal Reserve officials insisted that monetary policy alone could not assure the achievement of either of these objectives, for monetary policy regulated only the supply and cost of credit, and the behavior of prices and business activity was affected by many factors other than credit. Yet they insisted that the supply of money and credit should be so regulated that it would not be a source of disturbance to the economy and would contribute as much as it could to economic stability. This supply should be neither so small as to reduce prices, lower business activity, and hamper economic growth, nor so large as to induce price inflation.

On several occasions during the 1920's, Congress considered bills that would order the Federal Reserve to stabilize the general level of prices. All these were strongly opposed by Federal Reserve officials. They gave several reasons for this opposition. (1) The vagueness and technical defects of the proposals. They criticized the ambiguity of the term, "the general level of prices," and noted the diverse behavior of the various price indexes. Mr. Charles Hamlin, a member of the Federal Reserve Board, observed in 1928: "For example, in the period from 1925 to 1927 the Bureau of Labor wholesale indexes show a price decline of about 12 per cent; but if you take the curve of the cost of living, the decline was barely 2 per cent. If you take a composite index like Mr. Snyder's, there was hardly any decline at all."[1] But Federal Reserve officials had more basic objections to the proposed legislation. (2) Not all price declines are undesirable. Though admitting that price declines are usually harmful, they insisted that those resulting from general increases in efficiency may be beneficial. Price declines accompanied by proportional decreases in costs need not decrease the profitability of production or lower the incentive to employ labor. (3) Price changes are but tardy indicators of more basic difficulties. Federal Reserve officials contended that changes in price levels may be poor guides to policy because they tend to appear only after basic maladjustments have been under way for some time. "Credit administration must be cognizant of what is under way or in process in the movement of business before it is regis-

[1] *Hearings on H.R. 11806*, 1928, p. 393.

tered in the price index. The price index records an accomplished fact."[2] (4) Concentration on the behavior of prices might prevent the Federal Reserve from achieving other important objectives, such as the promotion of high and stable levels of business activity.

Though Federal Reserve officials opposed legislative mandates to stabilize price levels, they insisted that in fact their credit policies were designed to promote this objective as much as possible without an undue sacrifice of other objectives.

Fig. 32 shows the extent to which the Federal Reserve related its policies to

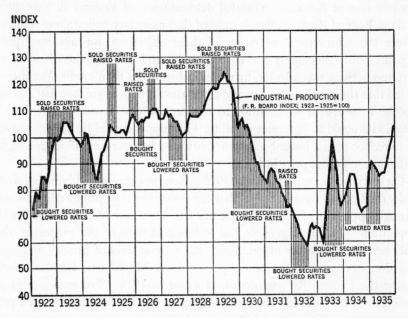

FIG. 32.   Timing of Federal Reserve Open-Market Operations and Discount Rate Changes Compared with Changes in the Volume of Industrial Production. (Source: Reproduced from W. R. Burgess, *Reserve Banks and the Money Market*, copyright, 1927, 1936, 1946, by Harper & Brothers.)

the behavior of industrial production, tightening credit when business activity was rising rapidly, and easing it when business was declining.

Restraint of Security Speculation

As indicated earlier, it was 1934 before the Federal Reserve acquired the power to regulate margins on loans for the purpose of purchasing and carrying securities. In the 1920's it could curb the use of credit for security speculation only through general credit restraint or clumsy attempts at direct controls over the lending policies of member banks that were in debt to their Reserve

[2] Federal Reserve Board, *Annual Report*, 1923, p. 32.

banks. We shall see later how Federal Reserve attempts to curb stock speculation in 1928 and 1929 conflicted with other objectives and prevented their attainment.

Restoration and Maintenance of Gold Standards Abroad

As noted earlier and as indicated in Fig. 33, almost all countries abandoned gold standards during World War I and few returned within the first six years after the end of the war. At the beginning of 1924, only the United States and a handful of small countries were on gold. A few others returned to gold during that year, but it was 1925 before a truly international gold standard began to reappear. In the meantime monetary and financial disorders were widespread. Great Britain and some other countries succeeded in stopping inflation in 1920; in others inflation continued until after the mid-1920's. In some, price levels merely doubled, in some they rose eightfold, and in some extreme cases they rose by the billionfold. All sorts of domestic difficulties promoted monetary disorder: extraordinary expenditures for reconstruction and reparations payments, political instability, unbalanced budgets, easy-money policies to help finance ministers manage their huge floating debts, and so on. The international exchange market performed erratically. Exchange rates on the various national currencies fluctuated widely, reflecting not only changes in the domestic purchasing powers of those currencies but also erratic and speculative international shifts of funds induced by such things as expectations of further inflation, domestic and international political disturbances, and uncertainties arising out of the great complex of reparations and war debt obligations.

These countries wanted to return to gold standards. More, they wanted to end inflation and deflation at home, restore more stable fiscal and monetary policies, and achieve stability of their currencies in exchange markets. Still more fundamentally, they wanted to restore their productive power and achieve social and political stability. For this purpose many of them needed loans or grants from abroad. In this whole process of stabilization and recovery the United States could be most helpful. But the United States government of that day would not provide the necessary funds or even enter officially into cooperative international programs for such purposes. It might provide small grants in the early postwar period to prevent actual starvation and deal generously with its debt claims against its former allies, but it would not go further. This was partly because of United States isolationism, partly because of the current philosophy that government should limit the scope of its activity. If United States funds were to be supplied for foreign reconstruction and stabilization purposes, they would have to come from the Federal Reserve and private sources.

It was under these conditions that the Federal Reserve System, under the

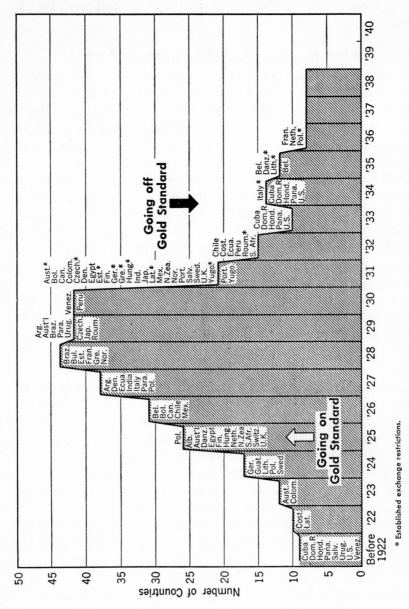

* Established exchange restrictions.

FIG. 33. Countries on the Gold Standard, 1921–1938. (Source: U.S. Treasury.)

leadership of Governor Benjamin Strong of the Federal Reserve Bank of New York, sought to assist both in the reëstablishment of gold standards abroad and in making them function in an acceptable manner. The Federal Reserve had several reasons for desiring the reëstablishment of an international gold standard. One was purely altruistic; Strong was deeply sympathetic with those who had suffered during the war and postwar disturbances and wanted to see them prosper again. But he also believed that stabilization abroad was in the interest of the United States. For one thing, it was necessary to end gold flows to the United States. Time and again he warned that the only way to stop these inflows and to avoid the danger of gold inflation at home was to help put other countries back on gold standards. Moreover, foreign trade of the United States would benefit. This was partly because stabilization within foreign countries would raise their real incomes and their demands for imports, partly because stability of exchange rates would promote trade.

Federal Reserve assistance in the restoration and maintenance of gold standards abroad was of several types. For one thing, the Federal Reserve extended stabilization credits to foreign central banks. When a nation had formulated an overall stabilization program that appeared to be appropriate, the Federal Reserve would extend a credit—a commitment to lend gold or dollars—to its

TABLE 51. Credits Extended to Foreign Central Banks by
Federal Reserve Banks[3]

Date	Bank Receiving Credit	Amount
1925	Bank of England	$200,000,000
1925	Banking Office of the Ministry of Finance of Czech-oslovakia (approx.)	5,000,000
1925	Bank of Poland	10,000,000
1925	National Bank of Belgium	10,000,000
1927	Bank of Poland	5,250,000
1927	Bank of Italy	15,000,000
1929	Bank of Roumania	4,500,000
1929	National Bank of Hungary	2,000,000
1931	National Bank of Austria	1,083,000
1931	National Bank of Hungary	5,000,000
1931	German Reichsbank	25,000,000
1931	Bank of England	125,000,000

central bank. The Federal Reserve acted alone in extending a $200 million line of credit to the Bank of England when Great Britain returned to gold in April, 1925. In most of the later stabilizations it acted in coöperation with other central banks, sometimes as many as twelve or thirteen of them. These central bank credits often served useful purposes even when they were not drawn

[3] For a comprehensive study of these credits, see A. Goldstein, "Federal Reserve Aid to Foreign Central Banks," *Review of Economic Studies*, February, 1935, pp. 79–98.

upon. For one thing, they created confidence in the ability of the central bank to maintain gold payments, thereby discouraging speculative withdrawals from the country and in some cases even inducing an inflow of funds. These credits also assisted countries in securing foreign loans. In most of the stabilizations, foreign central bank credits to the nation's central bank were supplemented by private loans to the nation's government. These private loans might not have been made available in the absence of the central bank credits and the implied approval of the nation's stabilization program by foreign central bankers. Federal Reserve officials and other central bankers, especially Governor Montagu Norman of the Bank of England, often performed useful services in helping countries formulate and gain acceptance of stabilization programs.

On some occasions the Federal Reserve also made funds available to countries after they had returned to gold. It did this by making outright loans or by purchasing claims against the nation's currency in the foreign-exchange market.

Of more interest to us at this point is the extent to which the objective of promoting the restoration and maintenance of gold standards abroad influenced the general monetary policies of the Federal Reserve. In the 1920's, and especially after 1923, this objective made for easier, or at least for less restrictive, general credit policies. Easier credit policies in the United States could in two principal ways help other countries to gain or retain gold and international reserves and to follow more liberal or less restrictive policies at home. (1) By raising United States national money income and price levels. This would increase United States imports and payments of gold and dollars to other countries while discouraging foreign purchases in the United States. (2) By discouraging flows of capital funds to the United States and encouraging capital flows out of the United States. This applies to both short-term and long-term funds. We shall see later that, after the restoration of gold standards, there was a great volume of short-term funds that proved to be highly sensitive to differentials between interest rates in the principal international financial centers, and especially between New York and London. When London was having difficulty in attracting and holding enough gold to maintain gold payments without an excessively restrictive monetary policy at home, Governor Strong and Governor Norman agreed that to the extent possible without undue sacrifice of other objectives they should try to keep interest rates in New York below those in London. This would have a double effect, they hoped. In the first place, it would shunt short-term international funds away from New York and toward London. In the second place, it would divert some part of the world's long-term borrowing away from London and toward New York. This would militate against a further concentration of gold in New York, lessen payments from Great Britain, and give the rest of the world access to a larger supply of gold and dollars.

The objective of helping other countries undoubtedly made for an easier monetary policy in the United States, especially after 1923. One outstanding case was in 1924, when an aggressive easy-money policy, the first in the history of the Federal Reserve, was undertaken both to combat recession at home and to stimulate capital outflows. Another was in 1927 when the System again initiated an aggressive easy-money policy to combat recession, stimulate foreign lending, and repel short-term funds from New York. On still other occasions Federal Reserve policies were probably easier or less restrictive than they would have been in the absence of this objective. Yet Governor Strong and other Federal Reserve officials insisted that they would not sacrifice their domestic objectives to promote international coöperation. For example, Strong rejected summarily a foreign suggestion that the Federal Reserve should deliberately induce price inflation in the United States in order to expel gold, increase the international reserves of other countries, and enable them to follow more liberal monetary policies. He would not, he asserted, sacrifice his objective of promoting stable price levels at home. He also warned his colleagues abroad that the Federal Reserve would tighten credit, despite the unfortunate international effects of such a policy, if faced at home by commodity price inflation or excessive stock market speculation. The latter did occur in 1928 and 1929 and led to a restrictive Federal Reserve policy that injured other countries both by attracting large volumes of short-term funds to New York and by decreasing long-term lending of the United States abroad.

By 1927 the process of restoring gold standards was largely completed, though a few stragglers joined during the next two years. But the new gold standards differed in both form and functioning from those of the prewar period. For one thing, gold-coin standards had largely disappeared except in the United States. Most of the major countries adopted gold-bullion standards to economize gold. Also, gold-exchange standards became far more important than they had been before the war. A large number of the smaller countries adopted pure gold-exchange standards. Several of the larger countries also went on some type of mixed gold-exchange standard, holding a part of their international reserves in gold and a part in the form of claims against some other nation's money. For example, the Bank of France held both gold and very large claims against New York and London. This great growth of gold-exchange standards and of the practice of holding international reserves in the form of claims against foreign financial centers was a major reason for the presence of a huge volume of short-term international funds highly sensitive to interest rate differentials. Moreover, the world now had two important center countries. Before the war London was the one great monetary and financial center, and so was not likely to suffer large net withdrawals of funds. Now it had to share the position with New York.

These developments increased the vulnerability of center countries. The countries that held great volumes of claims against these centers might demand payment in gold, thereby putting the center countries under deflationary pressure and even forcing them to suspend gold payments. Also, the presence of more than one important monetary center made possible large shifts of funds that could embarrass the country losing the funds and perhaps also the country receiving them. For example, a highly restrictive policy in the United States might raise interest rates in New York and attract a large inflow of funds from London, thereby putting Britain under deflationary pressure and also defeating, at least in part, the efforts of the Federal Reserve to reduce the total supply of credit.

The new standards were more highly managed than the old ones. After years of freedom from the discipline of gold, central banks were less willing to follow the old rules of the gold standard game and to initiate more restrictive policies when they lost gold and more expansionary policies when they gained gold. "Offsetting" and "sterilizing" actions became far more common than they had been before the war. This meant, of course, that the process of equilibrating international receipts and payments was inhibited, as was also the redistribution of gold. For example, the refusal of France to allow her money supply to increase in response to very large gold imports permitted gold inflows to continue at the expense of other countries. Also, the reluctance of countries to permit gold exports to restrict their supply of money and credit made ineffective or at least sluggish the process of terminating gold outflows and protecting their supply of international reserves.

The new international gold standard system was also characterized by disequilibrium relationships among the various national price levels as stated in terms of gold. In the prewar period these price level relationships were pretty well equilibrated. But many of the countries returned to gold on terms that either "undervalued" or "overvalued" their currencies in relation to those of other countries. For example, France almost certainly undervalued the franc in foreign-exchange markets when she stabilized it in 1926. She gave it a gold value equivalent to 3.92 cents, as against 19.3 cents in the prewar period. But this low exchange rate on the franc together with the price level within France made that country a cheap country in which to buy and an unattractive one in which to sell, so that her receipts exceeded her international payments on trade account. Her refusal to allow her gains of international reserves to raise her domestic price level permitted this excess of receipts to continue. On the other hand, Great Britain almost certainly returned to gold on terms that made her domestic price level in terms of gold "too high." The pound sterling was given its prewar gold content, so that the exchange rate on the pound hovered around $4.8665. But the British domestic price and cost levels had not been reduced enough to make Britain an attractive market in which to buy when each pound cost about $4.8665. As a result, British export industries did not thrive.

A reduction of British wage rates and other costs of production would have stimulated her export industries, but her cost structure had become inflexible downward. The functioning of the new gold standards suffered from these disequilibrium relationships among national price levels.

We shall see later that several of these aspects of the new gold standards contributed to their breakdown in the 1930's: the widespread use of gold-exchange standards, the large volume of international short-term funds highly sensitive to interest rate differentials and to shifts of confidence in foreign currencies, disequilibrium relationships among the various national price levels, and the reluctance of countries to follow the old rules of the gold standard game to equilibrate their balances of payments.

Summary

By 1922 Federal Reserve officials realized that the old rules of the gold standard game were obsolete and that new objectives and guides would have to be developed. Within the next two years they had developed three principal sets of considerations that guided their policies during the next decade: promotion of price level stability and high and stable levels of business activity, prevention of an excessive use of credit for speculation, and promotion of the restoration and maintenance of gold standards abroad.

DEVELOPMENT OF FEDERAL RESERVE INSTRUMENTS

While the Federal Reserve was developing new policy objectives and guides in the 1922–1924 period, it was also making remarkable progress in developing its instruments of control. The outstanding event of the period was the discovery and development of open-market operations in United States government securities. Never before 1922 had the Federal Reserve bought or sold these securities for monetary management purposes. The relatively small purchases and sales that had occurred were for such purposes as to provide earnings for the Reserve banks, to retire some national bank notes, and to assist the Treasury. Moreover, they were made by the individual Reserve banks without any sort of centralized coördination. Two very important events occurred in 1922 and 1923. In the first place, the Federal Reserve discovered how these operations might be used for monetary management purposes. In the second place, the execution of these operations was centralized in a System committee. After the discovery and development of this device, the Federal Reserve had three principal instruments: discount rates, open-market operations in acceptances, and open-market operations in United States government securities.

Within a short time the Federal Reserve was using open-market operations in government securities for both defensive and dynamic purposes. This was an excellent defensive weapon with which to offset or sterilize the effects of gold inflows and outflows. It was also used to offset net cash inflows or outflows domestically and large net Treasury receipts or expenditures. For dynamic purposes it proved to be extremely useful, for the Federal Reserve could itself determine both the timing and amount of its purchases and sales. The following pattern of dynamic operations soon developed. If the Federal Reserve wished to restrict credit it led off with sales of government securities. This reduced the volume of any excess reserves that previously existed and forced banks to borrow more heavily to repair their reserve positions. This in itself restricted credit somewhat and raised market rates of interest. The Federal Reserve would then decide whether and to what extent it would intensify restrictive pressures by raising its discount rates and its buying rate on acceptances. When it wished to initiate easier credit conditions it usually led off by purchasing government securities, which gave some banks excess reserves and enabled others to repay some of their borrowings at the Reserve banks. This directly eased credit somewhat and reduced market rates of interest. If the System wished to intensify the ease, it then reduced its discount rates and acceptance buying rates.

FEDERAL RESERVE POLICIES, 1923–1929

Having discussed both its objectives and its development of instruments for regulation, let us now look briefly at some of the principal episodes in Federal Reserve policy after the end of the postwar depression.

By 1923 the economy was well on its way to recovery and prices were rising slowly. The Federal Reserve therefore initiated a mildly restrictive policy. It sold more than enough government securities to offset the $250 million net increase of the monetary gold stock, thereby forcing member banks to increase their borrowing somewhat. Market rates of interest rose slightly and the Federal Reserve raised its discount rates, the New York rate going from 4 to 4½ percent.

Easy Money, 1924

In 1924 the Federal Reserve initiated its first peacetime aggressive easy-money policy. In the early months of the year it moved cautiously to lessen the degree of restraint that had existed in late 1923 when member banks had owed the Federal Reserve about $800 million. In May it began to act more vigorously. In all, it raised its holdings of government securities from $118 million to $488 million, or a net increase of $370 million. These purchases, together with continued gold inflows, enabled member banks to reduce their borrowings to less than $300 million. As market rates of interest fell, the Reserve banks lowered their discount rates. The New York Bank reduced its rate from 4½ to 4, then to 3½, and finally to 3 percent. Money market conditions became the easiest they had been at any time since the war.

This easy-money policy was initiated for both domestic and international reasons. A recession seemed to be starting; agriculture was still depressed in many areas, industrial production showed a downward drift, and wholesale prices declined about 3 percent during the first half of the year. If the recession was not serious enough to require an aggressive easy-money policy, it at least seemed to permit such a policy to be followed without adverse effects. The other major objective of the policy was to promote United States lending abroad and to create conditions that would hasten the restoration of gold standards and end the unwanted flow of gold to the United States. Governor Strong welcomed this opportunity to bring interest rates in New York below those in London. He had reason to think that conditions had now become such that his international objectives might soon be achieved. For one thing, the Dawes Plan for the temporary settlement of the controversial reparations question had created a more favorable atmosphere for international lending. For another, it appeared that England might soon return to gold if favorable conditions could be created.

The easy-money policy probably contributed to the rapid recovery of business activity during the latter half of 1924. It certainly increased United States lending abroad. Aided both by easy-money conditions and the improvement of international conditions, United States loans to other countries in the latter half of 1924 were far above their level in previous years. The larger outflow of United States dollars, and perhaps also the diversion of international borrowing away from London, tended to raise the exchange rate on sterling. At the beginning of the year it had been $4.25; by the end of the year it was $4.70, only 3 percent below its prewar parity. Soon thereafter Britain began to make plans for her return to gold. It is also significant that the flow of gold to the United States was stopped in 1924 and was not resumed until three years later. This easy-money policy may also have contributed, as some of its critics allege, to the subsequent growth of stock market speculation.

Relative Calm, 1925–1926

The objective of promoting the restoration and maintenance of gold standards abroad counseled a relatively easy-money policy during this period. Several countries had returned to gold standards with Britain; others soon followed. Continued large United States lending and avoidance of flows of funds to New York were desirable not only to help additional countries return to gold but also to enable countries that had already returned to maintain their international reserves without excessively restrictive monetary policies. Nor did the objective of preventing commodity price increases call for very restrictive policies. After recovering in late 1924 and the first few months of 1925, whole-sale prices drifted slightly downward during the rest of the decade. But stock speculation began to threaten. Recovery from the 1924 recession and rising stock market activity evoked a more restrictive policy in early 1925. The System sold about $250 million of government securities and raised its discount rates, the New York rate going from 3 to 3½ percent. As speculation continued to grow, the New York Bank raised its rate to 4 percent at the beginning of 1926. This rate was reduced to 3½ percent in April, 1926, as speculative ac-tivity subsided, but was restored to 4 percent in August when stock market activity again surged upward. Speculation had already become a problem, but the worst was yet to come.

Easy Money Again, 1927

The Federal Reserve's second aggressive easy-money policy also had both domestic and international objectives. A recession in domestic economic ac-tivity again threatened and wholesale prices began to fall slowly early in 1927. At least as important to the policy-makers, several foreign countries were losing international reserves, or could maintain them only by adopting more restrictive monetary policies. The rise of interest rates in New York accom-panying the more restrictive Federal Reserve policy in the latter part of 1926 was tending to attract funds from abroad and to restrict United States foreign lending. Gold inflows, which had been virtually halted since 1924, were re-suming. Federal Reserve officials feared that these developments would not only injure other countries, and especially Britain, but would also renew the flow of gold to the United States and reduce the foreign demand for United States exports, especially for agricultural products. The situation was further complicated by conflicts between the Bank of France and the Bank of Eng-land. France finally succeeded in achieving a de facto stabilization of the franc in late 1926. This was accompanied by a rapid repatriation of funds that pri-vate French holders had formerly held abroad, and especially in the form of claims against London. When the Bank of France bought these claims, it ac-quired the power to drain very large amounts of gold from London. In the midst of a controversy with the Bank of England, it withdrew some gold and threatened to withdraw more if the Old Lady of Threadneedle Street did not conform its policies to the wishes of the Bank of France. It was to discuss these and other matters relating to international conditions that Governor Strong invited representatives of the Bank of England, the Bank of France, and the German Reichsbank to meet with him in early July, 1927.

The easy-money policy of 1927 was initiated late in July after this meeting, though not solely because of it or of the issues discussed there. The Federal Re-serve purchased about $300 million of government securities and lowered dis-count rates from 4 to 3½ percent. These actions were accompanied by an easing of money market conditions. This easy-money policy probably contributed to the recovery of business activity in the latter half of 1927 and it clearly was effective for international purposes. The inflow of foreign funds was decreased and American foreign lending maintained. The inflow of gold was reversed; within the next year about $500 million of gold flowed out. Most European central banks were able to get through the year without adopting more restrictive policies. Again, however, the easy-money policy may have encouraged stock speculation.

The Stock Market, 1928–1929

From the beginning of 1928 until after the great crash in October, 1929, the objective of preventing an undue use of credit for stock market speculation virtually dominated Federal Reserve policy. The objective of promoting stability of prices and business activity justified the first move toward credit restriction in early 1928. But neither this objective nor that of promoting the maintenance of viable conditions abroad was responsible for the degree of restriction achieved by 1929. Between the end of 1927 and mid-1929 the Federal Reserve sold about $450 million of government securities. On the latter date it had left only $147 million. To maintain their reserve positions during the latter part of 1928 and the first nine months of 1929, member banks had to go into debt to the Federal Reserve by about $1 billion. This was by far the largest volume of member bank borrowings since 1921. All the Reserve banks raised their discount rates several times. Starting at 3½ in 1927, the New York Bank rate was raised to 4 percent in February, 1928, to 4½ percent in May, to 5 percent in July, and then a year later to 6 percent in August, 1929. Market rates of interest, both short term and long term, rose markedly. The rate applicable to call loans on the stock exchange was especially volatile. In late 1928 it was often above 8 percent, sometimes considerably above this level. In 1929 it ranged even higher. This rate became very important, partly because it was the rate to which short-term international funds responded.

Federal Reserve officials faced many perplexing questions as they tried to evaluate the behavior of the stock market and formulate their policies relative to it. One of these cannot yet be answered satisfactorily: "What would constitute a reasonable level of stock prices, assuming continued prosperity and continuing economic growth?" It has since become fashionable to laugh at those who defended as reasonable the highest levels reached in 1929. But no less silly were those who began to predict a crash as soon as stock prices began to rise above their depressed levels in 1921—levels that were below those of the prewar period. Even now we cannot be sure that the levels reached by June, 1928, would have proved unreasonable if prosperity had continued. It is important to note that between mid-1928 and Septem-

TABLE 52. Indexes of Common Stock Prices
1935–1939 = 100

Period	Total	Industrial	Railroad	Public Utility
1913	71	40	240	90
1921	58	47	164	68
1924	77	63	204	92
1925	95	80	238	111
1926	106	90	265	117
June, 1927	122	103	316	135
December, 1927	141	122	336	149
June, 1928	153	134	336	173
September, 1929	238	195	446	375
First half of 1930	175	141	364	276
June, 1932	36	30	38	64

SOURCE: Board of Governors of the Federal Reserve System, *Banking and Monetary Statistics*, 1943, pp. 479–481. These indexes are those of Standard and Poor's Corporation.

ber, 1929, stock prices rose more than they had during the preceding four years. Moreover, after the crash they quickly regained half their losses and during the first half of 1930 averaged above their mid-1928 level. Only as the country slid into depression and despair did stock prices fall so low as to make those of mid-1928 look absurdly high. But these were absurdly low, assuming any chance of business recovery.

Federal Reserve officials always insisted that their chief concern was not with the level of stock prices but with the use of credit for speculative purposes. They therefore faced the perplexing question of determining the boundary line between "reasonable" and "unreasonable" amounts for this purpose. The volume of credit used to purchase and carry stocks certainly increased markedly during this period. Much of this credit was not borrowed through brokers. But Table 53 shows that loans to brokers nearly quadrupled after 1924, rising to $8.5 billion on the eve of the crash. The sources of these loans should be noted. Taken as a group, commercial banks did not increase their loans of this type. Other lenders accounted for all the increase; on the eve of the crash they were supplying two thirds of all these loans. These other lenders, attracted by very high call loan rates, were of many types. They included not only individuals and financial intermediaries but also nonfinancial corporations and foreign lenders. The flow of funds from foreign centers was very embarrassing to several central banks.

Federal Reserve officials were perplexed as to how to limit the supply of credit for stock speculation. They did not then have the legal power to impose margin requirements—the power that has since proved effective in limiting the volume of credit used for this purpose without curtailing the supply and raising the cost of credit for other purposes. Nevertheless, the Federal

Reserve Board tried, early in 1929, to achieve this result by applying "direct action" to banks that were in debt to their Federal Reserve banks. Through its own pronouncements and through the various Reserve banks it informed members that they should not make loans on stocks for speculative purposes while borrowing at the Federal Reserve. This device failed to get a fair trial

TABLE 53. Loans to Brokers
(Amounts in millions)

Date	Total	By New York City Banks	By Outside Banks	By Others
Dec. 31, 1924	$2,230	$1,150	$ 530	$ 550
Dec. 31, 1925	3,550	1,450	1,050	1,050
Dec. 31, 1926	3,290	1,160	830	1,300
Dec. 31, 1927	4,430	1,550	1,050	1,830
June 30, 1928	4,900	1,080	960	2,860
Dec. 31, 1928	6,440	1,640	915	3,885
Oct. 4, 1929	8,525	1,095	790	6,640
Dec. 31, 1929	4,110	1,200	460	2,450

SOURCE: Board of Governors of the Federal Reserve System, *Banking and Monetary Statistics*, 1943, p. 494.

because several of the Reserve banks did not favor its use, at least not in the absence of further increases in discount rates. Nevertheless, it is highly unlikely that this type of direct action could have succeeded in curtailing loans on stocks without at the same time curtailing the supply and raising the cost of credit for other uses. It applied only to banks that were currently in debt to the Federal Reserve. These banks probably accounted for only a small part of this type of credit, and some of them would have curtailed their loans for other purposes in order to repay the Federal Reserve rather than call their highly lucrative stock market loans. It did not reach nonborrowing banks and certainly not the various types of other lenders who rushed in to lend more, probably at the expense of other types of lending or spending, as call loan rates rose.

Lacking any effective type of selective control, the Federal Reserve tried to regulate the situation through general credit restriction. It hoped that restrictive policies could kill the speculative fever and reduce the demand for speculative loans quickly, so that easier policies could then be instituted. Unfortunately, "legitimate business" and the international situation proved to be more vulnerable than the stock market.

These restrictive credit policies had almost no adverse effect on the international situation during the first half of 1928. United States foreign lending continued at a high level and gold continued to flow out of the country. But the tide began to turn in the latter part of 1928 as credit conditions became tighter. The rate of foreign flotations in the United States market in the latter half of 1928 and the first half of 1929 was only 65 percent of that in 1927; in the latter half of 1929 it was less than a third of that in 1927. Moreover, large amounts of funds flowed from abroad to New York, some to buy stock, more to take advantage of the high interest rates attainable there. These developments forced several European central banks to sell large amounts of their foreign-exchange holdings and ship gold to support their currencies. More than $260 million of gold flowed to the United States between mid-1928 and October, 1929. Many foreign central banks were impelled to raise their discount rates and adopt generally more restrictive policies in order to protect their reserve positions.

By mid-1929 the domestic business situation had begun to deteriorate. This was perhaps in part because the marginal efficiency of capital had been shifted downward by the large net accumulations of capital during the protracted investment boom. But it was at least aggravated, if not initiated, by the high cost of loanable funds, both short term and long term.

The rest of this story is now well-known history. After several weeks of vacillation the stock market crashed in October, 1929. With it crashed the "new era." The problems of the next decade were not to be those of excessive bullishness.

SELECTED READINGS

Brown, W. A., Jr., *The International Gold Standard Reinterpreted, 1914–1934,* National Bureau of Economic Research, New York, 1940, 2 vols.

Burgess, W. R., *Reserve Banks and the Money Market,* Harper, New York, rev. ed., 1946.

Chandler, L. V., *Benjamin Strong, Central Banker,* Brookings Institution, Washington, 1958.

Goldenweiser, E. A., *American Monetary Policy,* McGraw-Hill, New York, 1951.

Nurkse, R., *International Currency Experience, Lessons of the Inter-War Period,* League of Nations, Geneva, 1944.

CHAPTER 21

Monetary Policy in the Depression, 1930–1941

At the time of the stock market crash and even in 1930 no one could foresee that the depression into which the world was sliding would be the most devastating in its entire history and would be a major contribution to political and economic upheavals and even to the outbreak of a second world war. This depression lasted more than a decade and came to an end only in World War II. At its depth in the United States, national money income had fallen 50 percent and real output and income 25 percent. One worker out of four was without a job and many others were working only part time. Business firms failed by the tens of thousands, farmers lost their farms, and families their homes. Amidst falling incomes and price levels the monetary and financial system virtually collapsed. The gold standard system that had been so laboriously reconstructed in the latter half of the 1920's had largely disappeared by 1932. The United States banking system, weakened earlier, collapsed in 1933. Many other financial institutions closed their doors or at least ceased to function effectively in the saving-investment process. International lending came to a standstill. The whole complex of war debt and reparations obligations, which had been such disturbing issues in the 1920's, was largely repudiated. It is hardly surprising that under such circumstances monetary policies became unorthodox.

United States Monetary Policies, 1930–1931

There was little that was novel in United States monetary policies from the time of the crash in October, 1929, until the autumn of 1931. The government did not enter the field, and Federal Reserve policies followed the general patterns of 1924 and 1927. The Federal Reserve began to relax its restrictive policy and to ease credit almost immediately after the crash. By the end of the year it had increased its holdings of government securities about $300 million and reduced its discount rates. The New York rate was first reduced from 6 to 5 and then to 4½ percent.

Policies during 1930 and the first eight months of 1931 followed the same pattern. The system gradually added another $250 million to its holdings of government securities. By August, 1931, these stood at about $700 million, or $550 million above their level at the time of the crash. Largely because of these purchases and a net gold inflow of about $600 million, member banks were enabled to reduce their borrowings from about $1 billion to about $200 million while maintaining approximately constant the dollar volume of their reserves. Discount rates were reduced several times. In six steps the New York bank lowered its rate from 4½ percent at the beginning of 1930 to 1½ percent in May, 1931. Rate reductions at the other Reserve banks were smaller.

Federal Reserve policies during this early period have been criticized as too slow and too timid. Critics point out that even as late as August, 1931, member banks still owed the Federal Reserve about $200 million and had excess reserves of only about $120 million. They believe that the Federal Reserve should have purchased a much larger volume of government securities and acceptances to enable member banks to repay all their borrowings and to accumulate several hundred millions of excess reserves. This criticism is probably justified. At the same time, however, it should be noted that by August, 1931, credit conditions had been eased rather markedly.

Starting about September, 1931, the Federal Reserve allowed credit conditions to tighten significantly, and these tighter credit conditions persisted for several months. Two major developments were responsible for this. One was an upsurge of bank failures that damaged confidence in banks and induced large withdrawals of cash from the banking system. These began in 1930. Prior to that time cash had been flowing into the banking system, reflecting decreased needs for currency in circulation as payrolls and retail trade declined. By October, 1931, the volume of coin and currency outside the banking system was about $1 billion larger than it had been in mid-1930. Still more cash drains occurred in early 1933.

The other major event leading to tighter monetary conditions in the United States in the latter part of 1931 was the breakdown of the international gold standard.

THE BREAKDOWN OF GOLD STANDARDS

Four South American countries had suspended gold payments by the end of 1930. Twenty-three others, including Great Britain, abandoned gold in 1931. By the end of 1936 practically all countries had either left gold or had modified their old gold standards in fundamental respects.

What brought about this world-wide breakdown of gold standards? One basic factor was the devastating decline of real incomes and price levels, which decreased demands for exports and lowered the foreign-exchange earnings of exporting countries. Especially hard hit were countries that relied heavily on exports of raw materials whose prices dropped sharply. With great decreases in their export earnings, they found it difficult to reduce their international payments correspondingly and to protect their gold and other international reserves.

A second basic factor was the virtual cessation of international lending. During the latter part of the 1920's, many countries had come to rely heavily on foreign borrowings to meet their international payments and protect their international reserves. United States net lending abroad was over $700 million in 1926, over $1000 million in 1927, and about $850 million in 1928. In 1929, largely because of tight money conditions, these loans shrank below $300 million. Such lending practically disappeared as the depression deepened, the prospects of repayment darkened, and some foreign debtors began to default on their outstanding obligations. During 1931–1932 repayments to the United States actually exceeded her new foreign lending by nearly $500 million. Many countries could not bear the strain of losing their receipts from foreign borrowings and of making net payments of interest and principal at a time when their receipts for exports were falling.

A third factor was the presence of a huge volume of short-term international debt. We have already seen that the widespread use of gold-exchange standards involved very large foreign holdings of claims against financial centers, such as London and New York. Moreover, many countries, such as Austria, had borrowed heavily abroad on short term. All of these debts were payable on demand or on short notice. And foreign creditors were likely to demand payment the moment they came to fear that the debtors could not pay or that the debtor's currency would depreciate in terms of gold. In its first manifestation the international panic was an international banking panic.

The international panic began in May, 1931, with the failure of the Credit-Anstalt, the largest bank in Austria. This raised doubts as to the ability of any Austrian bank to meet its obligations, and not only foreigners but many Austrians as well withdrew large amounts of funds from the country. So great was the flood of withdrawals that it exhausted large loans from the Bank of England and the Bank for International Settlements as well as Austrian holdings of gold and foreign money; consequently Austria was forced to terminate the convertibility of her money in gold. Many creditors found their remaining credits frozen and depreciating in terms of gold.

The panic was now on. Fearful creditors, remembering losses in Austria, began to withdraw their credits from Berlin, and frightened Germans joined the run. Within a few weeks and despite sizable loans from the Bank of England, the Bank of France, the Bank for International Settlements, and the

Federal Reserve Bank of New York, Germany suspended gold payments in July, 1931, and placed strict limitations on international payments of all sorts. Millions of dollars' worth of short-term foreign credits were frozen in Germany.

Reinforced, the panic swept on to London, from which credits were rapidly withdrawn. An increase in its discount rate by the Bank of England, which was supposed to attract and retain foreign funds, seemed rather to publicize the fact that England was in financial difficulties and thereby hastened withdrawals. Even a $250 million joint credit from the Federal Reserve Bank of New York and the Bank of France was insufficient to stop the run or to cover withdrawals, which amounted to $975 million from July to late September. England departed from gold on September 21, 1931. The retreat from gold now became a rout. By April of 1932, gold standards had become inoperative in the following countries:[1]

Argentina	Estonia	Nicaragua
Australia	Finland	Norway
Austria	Germany	Paraguay
Bolivia	Greece	Portugal
Brazil	Honduras	Rhodesia
Bulgaria	Hungary	Russia
Canada	India	Salvador
Chile	Iraq	Spain
Colombia	Irish Free State	Sweden
Costa Rica	Japan	Turkey
Czechoslovakia	Jugoslavia	United Kingdom and
Denmark	Latvia	dependencies
Ecuador	Newfoundland	Uruguay
Egypt	New Zealand	Venezuela

This dramatic breakdown of the international gold standard affected monetary and economic conditions in the United States in at least two ways. In the first place, as we shall see later, it evoked large gold withdrawals from this country. In the second place, it tended to decrease the demand for United States exports and to lower their dollar prices. Most foreign currencies depreciated in terms of gold and in terms of dollars after their countries left gold standards. As shown in Table 54, most foreign currencies had depreciated at least 30 percent in terms of the dollar by early 1933. As foreign buyers saw it, the dollar had become much more expensive in terms of their own currencies. They would therefore buy fewer United States products unless the dollar prices of these products fell enough to offset the rise in the price of the dollar in the foreign-exchange market. Thus the depreciation of foreign currencies tended to depress United States export industries, including agriculture. Also, by making foreign products cheaper in terms of dollars, it tended to stimulate

[1] H. V. Hodson, *Slump and Recovery, 1929–1937*, Oxford, London, 1938, p. 92.

United States imports, which did not please some of those in import-competing industries. Many observed that this was what the world needed to bring international balances of payments into equilibrium and end the excess of United States exports over her imports. But such international objectives were

TABLE 54. Decline of Selected Foreign-Exchange Rates, 1929–February, 1933[2]

Money	Average Price in Dollars in 1929	Average Price in Dollars in February, 1933	Percentage Decline of Money in Terms of Dollars
British pound	$4.857	$3.422	30
Canadian dollar	0.992	0.835	16
Argentine peso	0.951	0.586	38
Brazilian milreis	0.118	0.076	35
Indian rupee	0.362	0.258	29
Chilean peso	0.121	0.060	50
Danish krone	0.267	0.153	43
Norwegian krone	0.267	0.175	34
Swedish krona	0.268	0.183	32
Portuguese escudo	0.045	0.031	31
Australian pound	4.81	2.72	45

not prized highly by a nation in the midst of depression. One of the major objectives of the United States policy of lowering the gold content of the dollar in 1933–1934 was to lower the exchange rate on the dollar, thereby tending to increase United States exports and to raise their dollar prices, and also to discourage imports and help import-competing industries.

UNITED STATES MONETARY POLICY, SEPTEMBER, 1931–MARCH, 1933

Let us now return to United States monetary policies during the period from Britain's suspension of her gold standard to the breakdown of the United States banking system in March, 1933.

Tighter Money, September, 1931–February, 1932

Almost as soon as Britain suspended gold payments, foreign demands for gold shifted to the United States. Gold losses were $250 million in September and $450 in October. The restrictive effects of these gold outflows were reinforced by an upsurge of cash withdrawals from the banking system. Between

---

[2] This table deliberately omits money which was inconvertible in terms of gold and which was artificially pegged, at least in official markets, at high prices. Most of these moneys were depreciated in unofficial or black markets.

August, 1931, and February, 1932, these net drains were almost $700 million. The Federal Reserve did not buy securities to offset these external and internal drains. As a result, member banks had to increase their borrowings by more than $600 million and suffered a $440 million net reduction in their reserves. Most of the Reserve banks raised their discount rates. The New York rate rose from 1½ to 2½ and then to 3½ percent. Market rates of interest rose and credit became less available.

Why did Federal Reserve officials refuse to buy securities in the open market to offset these drains and why did it actually raise discount rates in the face of a continuing and even accelerating decline of business and employment? Perhaps one reason was their fear that gold drains would become larger and prolonged. Another was that their gold position was precarious. The problem was not with the ratio of their gold reserves to their Federal Reserve note and deposit liabilities. This was comfortably above its legal minimum. Rather, their problem was created by a provision in the Federal Reserve Act requiring that Federal Reserve notes be collateraled dollar for dollar, and that the only assets eligible to serve as collateral were gold and commercial paper discounted by borrowing member banks. As member bank borrowings declined and reduced Federal Reserve holdings of commercial paper, more gold had to be used as collateral. To the extent that Federal Reserve purchases of government securities enabled member banks to reduce their borrowings the problem was intensified. At one time the volume of "free gold" was only $500 million. This impasse was finally broken in February, 1932, when Congress passed the Glass-Steagall Act permitting the Federal Reserve banks to use government securities as collateral for Federal Reserve notes. The Federal Reserve began almost immediately thereafter to purchase government securities.

Easy Money, March, 1932–Early 1933

Early in March, 1932, the Federal Reserve embarked upon a program of purchasing government securities that was by far the largest in its history up to that time. At the end of February its holdings of these securities were $740 million; at the end of the year they were $1855 million, an increase of $1115 million. These purchases permitted member banks to reduce their borrowings by about $600 million and to increase their reserve balances by $500 million. At the end of the year they had more than $550 million of excess reserves. The New York Bank reduced its discount rate from 3½ to 3 and then to 2½ percent. Most of the others left their rates unchanged at 3½ percent throughout the year. Market rates of interest declined again, but many banks were by this time in no shape to increase the availability of credit.

The Banking Panic of 1933

At the end of 1932 there was some reason to hope that monetary and financial conditions in the United States had been improved and would continue to improve. The banks had over half a billion of excess reserves, gold outflows appeared to have ended, and cash withdrawals from the banking system had recently slowed down. But the solvency and liquidity of individuals, business, and financial institutions had been seriously undermined by the prolonged and serious declines of real incomes and of the prices of output and assets. Many borrowers were in no position to pay their debts promptly, if at all. Thousands of banks were therefore illiquid if not insolvent. Any sharp jar to confidence could topple the entire structure. The storm broke in Detroit with the failure of the Union Guardian Trust Company, which was one of the largest banks in Michigan and was also closely connected with many other banks. So great was the blow to public confidence and so panicky were withdrawals from other banks that the governor of Michigan on February 14, 1933, declared an eight-day banking holiday. The panic quickly spread to other states. By March 4 every state in the Union had declared bank holidays and bank deposits were no longer redeemable in cash. President Roosevelt's decree of a four-day nation-wide banking holiday beginning on March 6 merely recognized the existing situation.

The panic period was characterized by gold and currency withdrawals. The country's monetary gold stock declined about $250 million. Net cash withdrawals from the banking system were nearly $2 billion and would, of course, have been larger if banks had not closed their doors so soon. These drains forced member banks to increase their borrowings at the Federal Reserve by $1.2 billion and reduced member bank reserves by more than $800 million.

From the closing of the banking system in March, 1933, until the end of the decade the relative role of the Federal Reserve in United States monetary policy was less than it had been earlier. The government now entered the field and acted vigorously and sweepingly, if not always wisely. Moreover, as a consequence of its policies and of developments abroad, the banking system was within a few years so amply supplied with excess reserves as to be largely beyond control by the Federal Reserve.

THE NEW DEAL AND MONETARY POLICY

One of the first projects of President Roosevelt and his administration after they assumed office on March 4, 1933, was that of reactivating a closed banking system. But their actions went far beyond this. Within a short time they had suspended the gold standard, depreciated the dollar in gold, established a new and quite different type of gold standard, provided for the monetization of great amounts of silver, and established many new financial institutions.

Reopening the Banks

The objective was not only to reopen the banks but to do so in such a way as to restore confidence in their solvency and liquidity, to prevent further cash withdrawals, to encourage cash to flow back into the system, and to enable the banks to resume their lending function. The first step was to discover the condition of the banks. All supervisory authorities quickly surveyed the banks and divided them into three classes. Those that were in good condition were permitted to reopen quickly. Those that were in hopeless condition were closed permanently. The middle group of banks that were not sound enough to open immediately but were capable of being saved were given help and allowed to open when their condition had been repaired. Most of this help came from the Reconstruction Finance Corporation, a government credit agency that had been established in 1932. A temporary deposit insurance program was instituted to restore confidence in the safety of deposits.

The public responded remarkably well. By the end of March $1.2 billion of cash had been redeposited with banks; another $700 million flowed back before the end of the summer. In the latter part of the year the Federal Reserve provided banks with additional funds by purchasing $600 million of government securities. Largely because of these developments, member banks were able to reduce their debt to the Federal Reserve from $1.4 billion at the time of the panic to only about $100 million late in the year and at the same time add $900 million to their reserve balances. Their excess reserves rose to about $800 million. From this level excess reserves continued to rise, largely because of the surge of gold imports that began in 1934.

Gold Policies

One of President Roosevelt's first official acts was to suspend the gold standard. Gold exports were prohibited, banks and other financial institutions were forbidden to pay out gold domestically, and everyone was ordered to surrender to the Treasury all his holdings of gold and gold certificates. Many thought at first that these were merely temporary measures that would be rescinded as soon as confidence was restored. But the old gold-coin standard and the old gold dollar were gone forever.

The prolonged depression and the severe decline of price levels had generated many schools of monetary expansionists similar to those during the long deflation following the Civil War. Some would settle for more money of any kind, others wanted more of a particular type of money. Some of the more conservative urged a greater expansion of Federal Reserve credit. Vocal groups in the South and West, remembering the battle cries of the late nineteenth century, demanded free coinage of silver at the old 16 to 1 ratio. Others, looking at the current use of "scrip," "prosperity checks," "corn money," and "cotton money" in a number of states, demanded national issues of scrip. Some wanted large issues of greenbacks of the Civil War type Technocrats wanted a whole new monetary system using the erg as the unit of account. Still others demanded an increase in the price of gold.

These influences were reflected in legislation enacted in May, 1933, which gave the President unprecedented discretionary powers to expand the money supply in many ways.[3] The President himself, or the Secretary of the Treasury acting under presidential direction, was empowered:

1. To enter into agreements with the Federal Reserve Board and the Federal Reserve banks for the latter to buy directly from the Treasury, and to hold, up to $3 billion of federal government securities in addition to those already in their portfolios.
2. To issue United States notes (greenbacks) in amounts not to exceed $3 billion. These were to be legal tender for all debts.
3. To fix the gold value of the dollar by proclamation, with the limitation that it should not be reduced more than 50 percent.
4. To fix the silver value of the dollar and to provide for the unlimited coinage of both gold and silver at fixed ratios. The President could reestablish a bimetallic standard in this country alone or he could enter into agreements with other countries to establish international bimetallism.
5. To accept silver at a price not to exceed 50 cents an ounce in payment of debts from foreign governments, the total accepted in this form not to exceed $200 million. Any silver acquired in this way was to be coined into silver dollars and held as backing for additional silver certificates.

The President did not use his discretionary powers to sell government securities directly to the Federal Reserve or to issue greenbacks. He did, however, take massive action with respect to gold and silver.

The dollar began to depreciate in terms of both gold and foreign currencies as soon as President Roosevelt suspended the gold standard. That is, the dollar prices of gold and foreign exchange began to rise. For example, between February and June, 1933, the British pound rose from $3.42 to $4.14, the Canadian dollar from 83.5 to 89.9 cents, and the French franc from 3.92 to 4.80 cents. It soon became evident that exchange rates might behave in a disorderly manner and that countries might even resort to competitive devaluation, each trying to lower the exchange rate on its own currency relative to

---

[3] This legislation was included in Title III of the Farm Relief Act approved by the President on May 12, 1933.

others in order to stimulate its exports and discourage imports. To deal with this and other issues, an international monetary conference was held in London in June, 1933. One proposal was that all important countries should enter into an agreement to return to some sort of gold standard. That many other countries would have agreed to this is doubtful. In fact, however, the proposal was killed when President Roosevelt refused, stating that to stabilize the dollar in gold was a far less important objective than that of raising the American price level to promote recovery and then stabilizing it. Soon thereafter he began vigorously to use his power to increase the dollar price of gold. From September 8 to October 24 the Secretary of the Treasury stood ready to buy newly mined domestic gold at a price equal to the best price available in free markets abroad. On October 24 this price was $29.80 per ounce, or 44 percent above the old mint price. Following President Roosevelt's instructions, the Reconstruction Finance Corporation began on October 25 to buy gold at gradually increasing prices. These month-end prices were:[4]

Date	RFC Purchase Price per Fine Ounce	Percentage of Old Mint Price ($20.67)
October 31, 1933	$32.12	155
November 29, 1933	33.93	164
December 30, 1933	34.06	165
January 31, 1934	34.45	167

Thus, by the end of January, 1934, the price of newly mined domestic gold had been raised 67 percent above the old mint price; the gold value of the dollar had been reduced about 40 percent.

It is clear that the gold-buying program to raise the price of gold was undertaken as part of the general program to raise commodity prices. This was emphasized in the President's October 22 radio address just before the RFC gold-buying program was begun.[5] What is not as clear, however, is the process by which the enhanced price of gold was expected to increase the prices of other goods and services. Some critics have accused the President of accepting fully the rather naïve theories held by one of his monetary advisers, Professor George F. Warren, regarding the relationship between gold and price levels. Professor Warren, pointing to alleged long-run correlations between the monetary value of gold stocks and the height of price levels, argued that an increase in the price of gold would raise domestic price levels in a short period of time and almost in proportion to the increase in the price of gold. With many qualifications, there is some tendency *in the long run* for the monetary value of gold stocks and price levels to move in a parallel manner.

[4] See Secretary of the Treasury, *Annual Report, 1934*, p. 205.
[5] This speech is reproduced in *The Public Papers and Addresses of Franklin D. Roosevelt*, vol. ii, pp. 420–427.

Even in the short run, an increase in the price of gold can be used to increase the monetary value of gold stocks and the size of bank reserves, thereby *permitting* an expansion of the money supply. But there is no assurance that the total money supply, being largely composed of bank deposits, will rise proportionally in the short run, or that an increase of the money supply, even if achieved, will increase spendings proportionally, or even that increased spendings will effect proportional changes in price levels. The extent to which the President was influenced by Professor Warren's theory is not known.

It seems likely, however, that a stronger motive for raising the dollar price of gold was the one mentioned earlier: the desire to lower the value of the dollar in terms of foreign money, thereby increasing the foreign demand for our exports, especially for farm products, and raising the prices of these goods in terms of dollars. This is indicated in the President's notes for his radio address on October 22, 1933.

At this point it may be said that the depreciation of foreign currencies, prior to 1933, had had the effect of making the dollar more expensive in terms of those foreign currencies. Thus it took more pounds, more francs or more marks to buy a dollar than it had formerly and, since the prices of our export products are determined in terms of dollars, it took more pounds, francs and marks to buy our export products. The effect of this had been to contribute to the serious decrease in our foreign trade, not because our own prices, in terms of dollars, had risen, nor because our own products were of an inferior quality, nor because we did not have sufficient products to export. But because, in terms of foreign currencies, our products had become so much more expensive, we were not able to obtain our fair share of the world's trade. It was, therefore, necessary to take measures which would result in bringing the dollar back to the position where a fair amount of foreign currency could again buy our products; that is, to make the dollar cheaper in terms of pounds, francs or marks. This was the process which commenced in March, 1933, and which had to be continued until that level was reached. It was not desirable to make this level too low, because then our own importers would find it difficult to buy foreign merchandise. But it was clear that the level had been too high, and we wanted to find the appropriate level.[6]

Table 55 shows the extent to which the increasing dollar price of gold was reflected in rising exchange rates on selected foreign currencies.

At the end of January, 1934, with the passage of the Gold Reserve Act, the United States reëstablished a gold standard. The principal provisions of this act were the following:

1. The President was authorized to fix the gold value of the dollar at not less than 50 percent nor more than 60 of the old level. This meant that he could define the dollar as not less than 11.61 grains nor more than 13.93 grains; the price of gold could be fixed at not more than $41.34 nor

---

[6] *Ibid.*, vol. ii, p. 428.

TABLE 55. Dollar Prices of Selected Foreign Moneys, February and September, 1933, and January, 1934

Money	Price in February, 1933	Price in September, 1933	Price in January, 1934	Percentage Increase, February, 1933, to January, 1934
English pound	$3.422	$4.665	$5.032	47
French franc	0.032	0.058	0.065	49
Australian pound	2.722	3.713	4.088	48
Canadian dollar	0.835	0.965	0.992	19

less than $34.45 an ounce—the latter being the price reached by January under the gold-buying program.

On January 31, 1934 the President set the price of gold at $35 an ounce, expressly reserving the right to alter it as the country's interest might require. Not until 1945 was this discretionary power repealed.[7] The gold content of the new dollar was 13.71 grains, a reduction of 40.94 percent. The Treasury reaped a handsome profit by raising the price of gold from $20.67 to $35 an ounce. It gained $14.33 on each of its nearly 196 million ounces of holdings, or $2805 million.

2. It nationalized all gold, provided that all profits or losses resulting from changes in the price of gold should accrue to the Treasury, and ended the domestic redeemability of currency in gold.

3. It ended the coinage of gold for domestic use and provided that all existing gold coins should be formed into bars.

4. It provided that gold might be held, transported, imported, exported, and otherwise dealt in only in accordance with regulations prescribed by the Secretary of the Treasury with the approval of the President. In practice these regulations permitted free imports and exports but limited domestic holding and dealing to "legitimate" commercial, industrial, artistic, and scientific purposes.

5. It provided that $2 billion of the gold profits should be used to establish an exchange stabilization fund under the Secretary of the Treasury. Thus, the Secretary was given broad powers to regulate foreign exchange rates and even to affect domestic credit conditions through his management of the exchange stabilization fund.

In summary, the nation had abolished the gold-coin standard, established a limited gold-bullion standard, decreased the gold content of the dollar 40.94 percent, and raised the price of gold 69.33 percent.

[7] The buying price is actually ¼ of 1 percent below $35 and the selling price is ¼ of 1 percent above it.

Silver Policies

By the end of 1932 the market price of silver had fallen to only 24.6 cents an ounce, a price that was hardly to the taste of the silver-mining interests and their spokesmen in Congress. These groups argued that a greater monetization of silver and an increase of its price would not only assist the silver-mining industry but also help bring the country out of depression and deflation. They even brought forth a new argument that Bryan had not used: we should raise the price of silver to help "the teeming millions in the Orient." They pointed out that as the price of silver fell the prices of Oriental silver money declined in terms of gold money, thereby—they argued erroneously—decreasing the purchasing power of Oriental countries in the world markets. Their remedy was as simple as it was fallacious; raise the price of silver, thereby raising the prices of Oriental silver money in foreign exchange markets and also raising the purchasing power of the Orient in world markets.

As already noted, the legislation of May, 1933, gave the President broad discretionary powers to accept silver in payment of war debts, to purchase the metal, to establish bimetallism, and to enter into international silver agreements. He did not establish bimetallism, and only limited amounts of silver were received in payment of war debts.[8] Nevertheless, the Treasury acquired very large amounts of silver under other programs. Senator Pittman, an ardent silverite and a United States delegate to the London Economic Conference in mid-1933, persuaded a number of silver-using and silver-producing countries to agree to measures raising the price of silver. The joker in the agreement was soon revealed. In effect, the United States had agreed to purchase annually an amount of silver equal to its entire domestic production while the commitments of other countries were small indeed. The President ratified the London Silver Agreement in December, 1933, ordering the Treasury to purchase the entire domestic output at 64.64 cents an ounce. This price was about 50 percent above that previously prevailing.

Still dissatisfied, the proponents of silver pushed through the Silver Purchase Act of 1934. This Act directed the Secretary of the Treasury to purchase silver at home and abroad until the monetary value of the silver stock should be equal to one third of the value of the monetary gold stock, or until the market price of silver should rise to the level of its monetary value ($1.29 an ounce). It also provided that in order to prevent excessive profits to speculators no more than 50 cents an ounce should be paid for silver located in the United States on May 1, 1934. The President implemented the latter provision in August by nationalizing all silver at this price. Fortunately the law

[8] For an excellent brief discussion of American silver policy, see G. Griffith Johnson, *The Treasury and Monetary Policy, 1932–1938,* Harvard University Press, Cambridge, pp. 161–200.

did not prescribe the speed of silver purchases by the Secretary of the Treasury. He therefore bought as slowly as political conditions permitted. Nevertheless, his purchases were very large. Table 56 shows that during the period 1934–1942 the Treasury purchased more than 2.6 billion ounces of silver at a total cost of more than $1.4 billion. It paid for the silver by issuing Treasury cur-

TABLE 56. Silver Production in the United States and Silver Purchases by the Government, 1934–1942

(In millions)

Year	Silver Production in the U.S. (Ounces)	Newly Mined Domestic Silver (Ounces)	(Dollars)	Nationalized Silver (Ounces)	(Dollars)	Foreign Silver (Ounces)	(Dollars)	Total Acquisitions (Ounces)	(Dollars)
1934	32.5	21.8	14.1	110.6	55.3	172.5	86.5	304.9	155.9
1935	45.6	38.0	27.3	2.0	1.0	494.5	318.2	534.1	346.5
1936	63.4	61.1	47.3	0.4	0.2	271.9	150.3	333.4	197.8
1937	71.3	70.6	54.6	—	—	241.5	108.7	312.1	163.3
1938	61.7	61.6	42.4	—	—	355.4	156.9	417.1	199.3
1939	63.9	60.7	40.1	—	—	282.8	120.5	343.5	160.6
1940	67.0	68.3	48.5	—	—	139.8	50.9	208.1	99.4
1941	71.1	70.5	50.1	—	—	72.6	27.1	143.1	77.2
1942	55.9	47.9	34.0	—	—	14.3	6.0	62.2	40.0
Total	532.4	500.5	358.4	113.0	56.5	2045.3	1025.1	2658.5	1440.0

SOURCE: *Treasury Bulletins.*

rency in the form of silver certificates. These silver acquisitions were of three types: (1) small amounts of nationalized silver purchased at 50 cents an ounce, (2) over 2 billion ounces of foreign silver purchased at an average price of 50.1 cents an ounce, and (3) about 500 million ounces of newly mined domestic silver. Newly mined domestic silver was from the beginning given preferential price treatment. But the initial price of 64.64 cents an ounce did not for long satisfy the silver groups. In 1939 they pushed through a law ordering the Secretary to pay 71.11 cents an ounce for all newly mined domestic silver offered to him. In 1946 they again entered the fray, raising the price to 90.5 cents an ounce. Since that time the Treasury has been purchasing most of the domestic output of silver, about 40 million ounces a year, at this price.

As massive United States purchases doubled the price of silver in world markets "the teeming millions in the Orient" wished that they might have fewer "helpful" friends. Rising exchange rates on silver currencies decreased the ability of these countries to export without drastic reductions in their domestic prices. This deflationary pressure was intensified as some of their silver money was melted and exported. In the end, most silver countries abandoned silver standards and adopted inconvertible standards or tied their money to the dollar or the British pound. Thus, the long-run effect of United States silver policy was to reduce still further the monetary use of silver abroad.

Other Relevant New Deal Measures

We cannot review here all the other New Deal measures that affected the structure and functioning of the monetary and financial system. Several of them related to the Federal Reserve. A number of amendments effected a greater centralization of authority in the System. For the first time the System was given legal authority to regulate margin requirements on security loans and to alter member bank reserve requirements.

Many new institutions were established to restore the flow of credit. Among the most important of these were the FDIC and many new agencies in the fields of housing and agricultural credit.

THE GOLDEN AVALANCHE

Monetary conditions in the United States prior to her entrance into World War II at the end of 1941 were largely dominated by the inflow of gold and silver resulting from the combination of United States policies and developments abroad. Largely reflecting silver purchases, Treasury currency outstanding rose about $1 billion between the end of 1932 and the end of 1941. This tended, of course, to increase directly both the public's money supply and member bank reserves. But far greater was the increase in the monetary gold stock. At the end of 1933 the United States monetary gold stock was at $4 billion; eight years later it was at $22.7 billion. This was an increase of $18.7 billion (see Table 57). A small part of this increase resulted from domestic gold production and melting of gold scrap; another part ($2805 million) resulted from the revaluation of the existing gold stock when the price of gold was increased in early 1934. But by far the largest part—more than $16 billion—came from net gold imports. Some of these gold imports reflected the excess of United States exports of goods and services over her imports but a very considerable part represented the movement of capital funds to the United States, many of them seeking safety from political and military threats abroad.

The period was one of greatly increased gold output in all gold-producing areas. This rise began early in the depression, even before the price of gold began to rise. With its price pegged by monetary authorities, gold was the only commodity whose production was enhanced by deflation. Declines in the prices of other things lowered the cost of producing gold. But marked increases in the price of gold while the prices of other things remained constant, or at least did not rise in proportion, enhanced gold production still

TABLE 57.   Monetary Gold Stock of the United States, 1929–1941[9]
(In millions of dollars)

End of	Monetary Value of Gold Stock	Increase During Year	Value of Domestic Gold Production	Net Gold Imports
1929	$ 3,997	—	—	—
1930	4,306	$ 309	$ 43	$ 280
1931	4,173	−133	46	145
1932	4,226	53	46	−446
1933	4,036	−190	47	−174
1934	8,238	4,202	93	1,134
1935	10,125	1,887	111	1,739
1936	11,258	1,132	132	1,117
1937	12,760	1,502	144	1,586
1938	14,512	1,751	149	1,974
1939	17,644	3,132	162	3,574
1940	21,995	4,351	170	4,744
1941	22,737	742	170	982
Addendum: Dec. 31, 1933– Dec. 31, 1941		$18,708	$1314	$16,655

TABLE 58.   World Gold Production

Period	Production in Millions of Fine Ounces	Index of Physical Gold Production, Average 1923–29 = 100	Value in Millions of Dollars ($20.67 an Ounce, 1933 and Earlier; $35 an Ounce in 1934 and Later)	Index of Value Average 1923–29 = 100
1923–1929 (annual average)	18.8	100	$ 388.6	100
1930	20.9	111	432.1	111
1931	22.3	119	460.7	119
1932	24.1	128	498.2	128
1933	25.4	135	525.1	135
1934	27.4	146	958.0	247
1935	30.0	160	1050.0	270
1936	32.9	175	1152.6	296
1937	35.1	187	1229.1	316
1938	37.7	201	1319.6	340
1939	39.5	210	1383.7	356
1940	41.1	219	1437.3	370
1941	36.2	193	1265.6	326

SOURCE: Board of Governors of the Federal Reserve System, *Banking and Monetary Statistics*, p. 542, and *Federal Reserve Bulletins*.

[9] For basic data and explanations of the contents of these figures, see Board of Governors of the Federal Reserve System, *Banking and Monetary Statistics*, Washington, 1943, pp. 522–525, 536.

more. Table 58 indicates that by the late 1930's the output of gold in ounces was double its level in the 1920's. And because of the increase in the price of gold the dollar value of current gold output was more than triple its level of a decade earlier.

The supply of gold for monetary purposes was further augmented from two other sources. Large but unknown amounts came from the melting of gold scrap as both the price and the purchasing power of gold rose. Larger amounts were released from hoards in the Orient. For example, during the relatively prosperous 1920's British India absorbed about 3½ million ounces of new gold each year. But as her own prosperity dwindled and as the purchasing power of gold abroad rose to unprecedented levels, she threw large amounts of the yellow metal on world markets. Her net exports for the period 1931–1940 amounted to 41 million ounces worth about $1.4 billion.

OTHER ASPECTS OF MONETARY POLICY, 1934–1941

As noted earlier, monetary conditions in the United States had again become relatively easy by the latter part of 1933. Member banks owed the Federal Reserve only about $100 million and held nearly $800 million of excess reserves. Then came the great inflow of funds from the Treasury's silver purchases and the golden avalanche. By mid-1934 member bank borrowings had fallen below $50 million. From that time until well after America's entrance into World War II, they rarely amounted to as much as $10 million. Banks did not need to borrow; they were swamped by excess reserves. The latter rose from less than $800 million in late 1933 to $2.9 billion in mid-1936. In the latter part of 1940 they were above $6.6 billion. Federal Reserve discount rates were of little importance under these conditions, but by mid-1935 they had been lowered to 1 percent at the New York and Cleveland Reserve Banks and to 1½ percent at the others. They were not raised again until after World War II.

By mid-1936, when the excess reserves of member banks had reached $2.9 billion and gold was still flowing in rapidly, Federal Reserve and Treasury officials feared that they might lose control of the situation and that inflation might occur. The country had not yet recovered fully from the depression. About 14 percent of the labor force was still unemployed and real national output was still about 5 percent below its level in 1929. Nevertheless, real output had already risen about 37 percent above its lowest level in 1933 and was still rising, and wholesale prices had risen 23 percent though they were still 16 percent below their levels in 1929. Federal Reserve and Treasury officials agreed that to protect against inflation in the future they should take some of the "slack" out of the system without going so far as to restrict credit currently.

They took two actions to this end. For one thing, the Board of Governors used for the first time its recently acquired power to change member bank reserve requirements. In three steps—the first on August 16, 1936, and the last on May 1, 1937—it doubled all these requirements, thereby setting them at the maximum level permitted by law. In addition, the Treasury embarked on a policy of "sterilizing" all gold imports. Between the end of 1936 and mid-1937 it sterilized about $1.3 billion of gold inflcws, thereby preventing this amount from augmenting the public's money supply, commercial bank reserves, and Federal Reserve bank reserves. It did this by selling government securities to get the funds with which to pay for the gold and then adding

TABLE 59.   Member Bank Reserve Requirements, 1936–1941

| | Percentages in Effect | | | | | |
	1917–Aug. 15, 1936	Aug. 16, 1936	Mar. 1, 1937	May 1, 1937	Apr. 16, 1938	Nov. 1, 1941
Demand deposits						
Central Reserve cities	13	19½	22¾	26	22¾	26
Reserve cities	10	15	17½	20	17½	20
Other	7	10½	12¼	14	12	14
Time deposits	3	4½	5¼	6	5	6

the gold to its own "cash holdings" without issuing gold certificates against it. In effect, it engaged in an offsetting open-market operation.

As a consequence of these Federal Reserve and Treasury actions, the excess reserves of member banks were reduced to $750 million by August, 1937. These excess reserves seem to have been widely distributed, for member bank borrowings did not rise above $24 million. Credit conditions tightened somewhat. In 1938, business activity declined sharply but briefly, reflecting largely a shift from inventory accumulation in 1937 to inventory decumulation in 1938. Both the Federal Reserve and the Treasury thereupon reversed their policies. On April 16, 1938, the Board of Governors lowered member bank reserve requirements (see Table 59). In the same month the Treasury "desterilized" about $1.2 billion of its idle gold holdings, adding that amount to both member bank reserves and Federal Reserve bank reserves. These actions, together with continued gold inflows, quickly brought excess member bank reserves above $3 billion, from which level they continued to rise.

Money market conditions were extraordinarily easy during the rest of this period. Short-term open-market rates were especially low. The yield on Treasury bills was usually less than ½ of 1 percent, sometimes much less. Yields on long-term governments gradually fell to less than 2 percent, far below their levels of more than 3½ percent in 1929 and 3⅓ percent in 1930.

This period witnessed a very important innovation in the objectives of Federal Reserve open-market operations in United States government securities—a change that proved to be highly significant both during World War II and in the postwar period. Prior to 1937, Federal Reserve purchases and sales of government securities were primarily for the purpose of affecting the reserve positions of member banks, thereby regulating general monetary and credit conditions. But in 1937, for the first time in its history, the Federal Reserve bought long-term government securities primarily because of the

TABLE 60.   Member Bank Reserve Positions on Selected
Dates, 1933–1941
(Averages of daily figures, in millions of dollars)

Period	Actual Reserve Balances	Required Reserves	Excess Reserves
Last quarter, 1933	$ 2,612	$1,839	$ 773
February, 1934	2,822	1,931	891
June, 1934	3,790	2,105	1,685
June, 1935	4,979	2,541	2,438
June, 1936	5,484	2,891	2,593
July, 1936	5,861	2,954	2,907
May, 1937	6,932	6,005	927
August, 1937	6,701	5,951	750
May, 1938	7,587	5,062	2,525
June, 1939	10,085	5,839	4,246
June, 1940	13,596	6,900	6,696
December, 1940	14,049	7,403	6,646
June, 1941	13,201	7,850	5,351
December, 1941	12,812	9,422	3,390

SOURCE: Board of Governors of the Federal Reserve System, *Banking and Monetary Statistics*, Washington, 1943, pp. 372–373.

direct effects of its purchases upon their market prices. In this case it bought long-terms to bolster their prices and sold short-terms to prevent the operation from increasing member bank reserves. Between this time and the entrance of the United States in World War II, it engaged in several operations of this sort. Sometimes it bought long-terms to bolster their prices; at other times it sold these securities to retard increases in their prices.

Federal Reserve officials insisted that they would not "peg" these prices at an inflexible level. They would allow the prices and yields of these securities to adjust themselves to levels consistent with the other objectives of monetary policy. The only purpose of Federal Reserve intervention, they insisted, was to prevent "disorderly" markets in these securities and to secure "orderly" adjustments of prices and yields. But it proved to be but a short step from a policy of maintaining "orderly markets" to one of pegging these security prices at inflexible levels, and this step was taken early in World War II.

FEDERAL FISCAL POLICIES

A brief look at federal fiscal policies during the 1930's will shed light on some aspects of the behavior of money during this period. After criticizing President Hoover for deficit financing and himself taking initial steps to reduce government expenditures, President Roosevelt soon embarked on a policy of increased expenditures and deficit financing. Even before the beginning of the defense program in 1940, federal expenditures had risen to more than three times their level in 1929. Some of the increase represented a rise of expenditures for public works and other goods and services, some transfer pay-

TABLE 61.   Federal Expenditures and Receipts, 1929–1941
(In billions)

Calendar Year	Purchases of Goods and Services	Other Expenditures	Total Expenditures	Receipts	Surplus (+) or Deficit (−)
1929	$ 1.3	$1.3	$ 2.6	$ 3.8	$+1.2
1930	1.4	1.4	2.8	3.0	+0.2
1931	1.5	2.7	4.2	2.0	−2.2
1932	1.5	1.7	3.2	1.7	−1.5
1933	2.0	2.0	4.0	2.7	−1.3
1934	3.0	3.4	6.4	3.5	−2.9
1935	2.9	3.6	6.5	4.0	−2.5
1936	4.8	3.7	8.5	5.0	−3.5
1937	4.6	2.6	7.2	7.0	−0.2
1938	5.3	3.2	8.5	6.5	−2.0
1939	5.2	3.8	9.0	6.7	−2.3
1940	6.2	3.9	10.1	8.6	−1.5
1941	16.9	3.6	20.5	15.4	−5.1

SOURCE: U.S. Department of Commerce, *National Income*, Washington, 1954, pp. 170–173.

ments to the public, and some grants to state and local governments. But these increased expenditures did not succeed in ending the depression before the United States embarked upon a massive armament program. For this there were many reasons, of which only a few can be noted. (1) The small scale of federal spending at the beginning of the depression. In 1929, when GNP was at about $104 billion, total federal expenditures were only $2.6 billion, or 2.5 percent of GNP. Thus even a large percentage rise of government expenditures from this level had but a small leverage effect relative to the capacity level of output. (2) The long delay in instituting the policy. The economy had been deteriorating for more than three years before any deliberately expansionary expenditures policy was adopted. (3) Increases of effective tax rates. Time and again old taxes were increased and new ones imposed. This is reflected in the rise of tax collections while GNP remained below its level in

1929. For example, in 1937 when GNP was still 13 percent below its level in 1929 federal tax collections were up 84 percent. A considerable part of the expansionary effects of increased government expenditures was absorbed by the increase of effective tax rates, which inhibited the rise of disposable private incomes. Government deficits during this period averaged about $2.5 billion a year, or less than 2½ percent of the 1929 level of GNP.

As a result of these fiscal policies the federal debt rose from $16 billion at the end of 1929 to $41.4 billion at the end of 1939, then to $57.5 billion by the end of 1941. A major part of the rise in the money supply during the latter part of the 1930's reflected increases in bank holdings of these obligations.

THE MONEY SUPPLY

Such liberalizing actions as were taken by the Federal Reserve in the early part of the depression did not succeed in preventing a large decrease in the money supply. Between mid-1929 and mid-1933 the money supply fell from $26.1 billion to $19.2 billion, a decline of $6.9 billion or 26 percent. Table 62 shows that the major reason for this was the $19 billion decrease of commercial bank loans and security holdings.

TABLE 62.　The Money Supply and Its Direct Determinants, 1929–1939
(In billions)

	Amount June 29, 1929	Amount June 30, 1933	Amount Dec. 30, 1939	Change 1929–33	Change 1933–39
Sources					
Monetary gold	$ 4.0	$ 4.0	$17.6	—	$+13.6
Treasury currency	2.0	2.3	3.0	$ +0.3	+0.7
Federal Reserve credit	1.4	2.2	2.6	+0.8	+0.4
Commercial bank credit					
Loans	35.7	16.3	17.2	−19.4	+0.9
U.S. government securities	4.9	7.5	16.3	+2.6	+8.8
Other securities	8.7	6.5	7.1	−2.2	+0.6
Total sources	$56.7	$38.8	$63.8	$−17.9	$+25.0
Competing uses					
Foreign deposits	$ 0.4	—	$ 1.2	$ −0.4	$ +1.2
U.S. government balances	0.6	$ 1.2	3.9	+0.6	+2.7
Time deposits	19.6	10.8	15.3	−8.8	+4.5
Capital accounts (net)	10.0	7.6	7.2	−2.4	−0.4
Total competing uses	$30.6	$19.6	$27.6	$−11.0	$ +8.0
Money supply (total)	26.1	19.2	36.2	−6.9	+17.0
Demand deposits	22.5	14.4	29.8	−8.1	+15.4
Currency outside banks	3.6	4.8	6.4	+1.2	+1.6

Between June, 1933, and the end of 1939 the money supply rose from $19.2 billion to $36.2 billion. Thus at the end of this period the money supply was 90 percent above its level at the bottom of the depression, and 40 percent above its level in 1929. This rise resulted largely from the rise of the monetary gold stock and increased commercial bank holdings of federal securities. This rise of the money supply was accompanied by a less than proportional rise in expenditures for output. While the money supply rose about 90 percent, GNP in current prices increased from $56.0 billion in 1933 to $91.1 billion in 1939, or an increase of 63 percent.

SUMMARY AND CONCLUSIONS

Monetary conditions in the United States during the period beginning in 1934 were far easier than any the country had ever seen prior to that time. The banking system was flooded with excess reserves. Yet the nation did not recover fully from the depression until about eight years later, after it had entered World War II. Should we conclude from this experience, as some have done, that monetary policy must always be ineffective in combating depression and unemployment? Only somewhat less sweeping and more tentative conclusions seem justified. One is that the effectiveness of an easy-money policy is likely to be seriously reduced if the policy is long delayed. The liberalizing policies employed in 1930 and the first eight months of 1931 were not aggressive; some member banks were still in debt to the Federal Reserve and others held only relatively small amounts of excess reserves. Few were in such condition that they felt excessively liquid and impelled to seek additional earning assets. Then came the 1931 episode and the restrictive policies accompanying it. The easy-money policy of 1932 lasted only a few months, terminated by the banking panic of early 1933. The depression had already been under way for more than three years before an aggressive easy-money policy of some duration was followed. By this time the economy was so depressed, the liquidity and solvency of borrowers so impaired, and excess capacity so widespread, that easy money was unlikely to bring a surge of recovery even if it slowed the decline.

Another important point suggested by this experience is that the effectiveness of monetary policy may depend greatly on the soundness of financial institutions. About 1350 commercial banks closed their doors in 1930, another 2300 in 1931, still another 1450 in 1932, and 4000 in 1933. Many other types of financial institutions were also failing. In such a situation the public became afraid to entrust its money to these institutions, and the institutions, fearing runs, were in many cases unwilling to make investable funds available. It is to be hoped that many of the institutions and practices adopted since the 1930's have made our financial system less vulnerable. Among these are better regulation of financial institutions and practices, the FDIC, the FSLIC, insurance of mortgages, the Federal Home Loan banks, and so on. But perhaps the best insurance against a collapse of financial institutions is to prevent the serious depressions that weaken them. This may require not only prompt and aggressive monetary policies but also prompter and more aggressive fiscal policies than were employed in the 1930's.

SELECTED READINGS

Beyen, J. W., *Money in a Maelstrom*, Macmillan, New York, 1949.

Hawtrey, R. G., *Bretton Woods for Better or Worse*, Longmans, Green, London, 1946.

Hodson, H. V., *Slump and Recovery, 1929–1937*, Oxford, London, 1938.

Johnson, G. G., Jr., *The Treasury and Monetary Policy, 1932–1938*, Harvard University Press, Cambridge, 1939.

Paris, J. D., *Monetary Policies of the United States, 1932–1938*, Columbia University Press, New York, 1938.

C H A·P T E R   2 2

Monetary Policy, 1941–1951

With the entrance of the United States into World War II in December, 1941, the Federal Reserve again became, as it had been during World War I, a servant of the government's fiscal policy. All conflicting objectives were pushed aside; its overriding objective became that of assuring that the nation's war effort would not suffer from any lack of money. Moreover, it was to assure that the huge war effort would be financed without any rise of interest rates above the low levels prevailing in early 1942.

WARTIME FISCAL POLICIES

The federal government's fiscal policy during this period followed the usual pattern for all-out war but on a huge scale. Its expenditures rose tremendously. Just before the beginning of the defense effort in mid-1940, they were at an annual rate of about $9 billion. By the fourth quarter of 1941 they had risen to an annual rate of more than $25 billion. By 1944 they were above $95 billion. Thus at the peak of the war effort federal expenditures were more than ten times their level before the beginning of the defense program and were themselves greater than total GNP at any time during the 1930's. More than 40 percent of the nation's output was being purchased for government purposes. Between mid-1940, when the accelerated defense program began, and mid-1946, when the wartime deficits ended, federal expenditures totaled more than $383 billion. This was more than twice as much as the federal government had spent during the preceding 150 years, nearly 100 times as much as it spent during the Civil War, and ten times as much as it spent during World War I.

Tax collections were increased greatly, but not nearly as much as expenditures. The result was, of course, huge deficits. These averaged more than $40 billion a year during the period of active participation of the United States in the war; in one year they were nearly $54 billion. For the six years following mid-1940 federal deficits totaled nearly $187 billion. The Treasury therefore faced the necessity of borrowing huge amounts to cover these deficits. In fact, its net borrowings during this six-year period were $199 billion, of which $187 billion was required to cover its deficits and $12 billion was used to increase its money balance.

TABLE 63.   Cash Operating Outgo, Income, and Deficits of the
Federal Government, 1940–1946
(In millions of dollars)

Fiscal Year Ending June 30	Cash Operating Outgo	Cash Operating Income	Cash Operating Deficit
1941	$ 14,060	$ 9,371	$ 4,689
1942	34,585	15,291	19,294
1943	78,979	25,245	53,734
1944	94,079	47,984	46,095
1945	95,986	51,051	44,935
1946	65,683	47,784	17,899
Total	$383,372	$196,726	$186,646

SOURCE: L. V. Chandler, *Inflation in the United States, 1940–1948*, Harper, New York, 1951, p. 62. Much of the material in this and the following chapter is taken from this book.

The Treasury again tried to borrow as much as it could in ways that would not involve an increase in the money supply. It used all the devices developed during World War I as well as new ones to sell securities to nonbank buyers: great bond-selling campaigns, pleas by movie stars and national heroes, 100 percent clubs, payroll deduction plans, and so on. It did succeed in getting nonbank investors to increase their holdings of Treasury obligations by $109 billion. But this was not enough; the commercial banks increased their holdings by $68.3 billion and the Federal Reserve banks by $21.3 billion.

WARTIME MONETARY POLICY

Federal Reserve assistance to Treasury financing during World War II differed in at least two important respects from that in World War I. In the earlier war the Federal Reserve itself bought very few Treasury obligations; it gave its assistance primarily by lending to banks. In World War II it lent very little to banks; it created additional money primarily by purchasing Treasury obligations, most of them in the open market rather than directly from the Treasury. It did establish very low preferential discount rates on loans collateraled by short-term Treasury obligations, but banks requested few loans. They did not need loans; they could get reserve money even more cheaply by selling short-term Treasury obligations to the Federal Reserve. Interest rate policies also differed markedly in the two wars. Interest rates were allowed to rise during World War I. In general, each new bond issue carried interest rates somewhat above those on earlier issues. During World War II interest rates were not allowed to rise at all.

In March, 1942, the Federal Open-Market Committee agreed with the Treasury that in general the level of interest rates and yields on government securities should not be allowed to rise during the war and pledged the full co-operation of the System to this end. This promise was fully kept. Interest rates in general were at that time low by historical standards, and short-term rates were abnormally low relative to longer-term rates. This was partly because of the low demand for investable funds during the depression, partly because of the huge volume of excess reserves in the banking system. At the end of 1941 the latter were still above $3 billion. The pattern of yields stabilized by

TABLE 64. Federal Borrowings, Their Use and Their Sources, 1940–1946
(In millions of dollars)

Fiscal Year Ending June 30	Federal Cash Operating Deficit	Increase or Decrease (−) of Treasury's General Fund Balance	Net Cash Borrowing	Net Increase in Amount of Federal Interest-Bearing Debt Held			
				By Nonbank Investors	By Federal Reserve and Commercial Banks	By Commercial Banks	By Federal Reserve Banks
1941	$ 4,689	$ 742	$ 5,431	$ 2,143	$ 3,318	$ 3,600	$−282
1942	19,294	358	19,652	12,869	6,761	6,300	461
1943	53,734	6,515	60,250	28,498	30,757	26,200	4,557
1944	46,095	10,662	56,757	32,913	23,899	16,200	7,699
1945	44,935	4,529	49,474	27,173	22,691	15,800	6,891
1946	17,899	−10,450	7,439	5,431	2,191	200	1,991
Total increase for period	$186,646	$12,356	$199,003	$109,027	$89,617	$68,300	$21,317

SOURCE: *Ibid.*, p. 72. This table was computed from various tables in *Treasury Bulletins*. It should be noted that the figures relating to debt reflect only the debt held outside the federal government itself; they do not include an increase of about $22 billion in federal debt held by government agencies and trust funds. These securities involved no borrowing outside the government itself; as the Treasury collected and spent social security taxes it issued to the trust funds under its control government securities indicating a future obligation to pay social security benefits.

the Federal Reserve during the war period reflected these conditions. On 90-day maturities this yield was ⅜ of 1 percent; on 9- to 12-month maturities it was ⅞ of 1 percent; on 5-year maturities it was 1½ percent; on 10-year maturities it was 2 percent; and on the longest marketable Treasury issues it was 2½ percent. The shape of this yield curve should be noted carefully, for it was to have important consequences.

The Federal Reserve's technique for preventing these various yields from rising—for preventing the prices of the securities from falling—was simple: it merely stood ready to buy without limitation all of these securities offered to it at the selected levels of prices and yields. In short, it stood ready to monetize, with high-powered reserve money, all the government securities offered to it by the banks and all other types of holders. As shown in Table 64, the System increased its holdings of Treasury obligations by $21.3 billion between the end of 1941 and June, 1946. Its purchases were concentrated in the short maturities; in fact, its holdings of the longer maturities actually declined during the latter part of the war. This was partly because of the very large Treasury issues of short maturities, partly because of the shape of the yield curve. Private investors tended to shun the short maturities with their low yields and to purchase the longer-term, higher-yield obligations. At their Federal Reserve support prices these longer-term obligations were just as liquid as the shortest maturities. They could be riskier than the short obligations only if purchased above the support price or if the support price were lowered or withdrawn. Most investors were confident that the latter would not happen during the war, and they suspected that support would be continued into the postwar period.

TABLE 65.   Maturities of Governments Held by the Reserve Banks, 1941–1946
(Last Wednesday of the month; in millions of dollars)

Date	Within 90 Days	90 Days to 1 Year	1 Year to 2 Years	2 Years to 5 Years	Over 5 Years	Total
Dec., 1941	$ 96	$ 97	$247	$ 477	$1,337	$ 2,254
Dec., 1942	1,199	886	242	1,408	2,254	5,989
Dec., 1943	7,256	2,457	224	488	1,190	11,615
Dec., 1944	12,703	4,064	760	620	918	19,065
Dec., 1945	15,839	7,000	0	508	691	24,038
June, 1946	17,877	4,436	46	449	582	23,390

This passive open-market policy had several important consequences, not only during the war but also in the postwar period. (1) The Federal Reserve thereby abandoned control over its volume of government holdings, the volume of bank reserves, and the money supply. To prevent yields from rising it had to buy all securities offered to it, regardless of the identity of the seller and regardless of the purpose for which the newly created money would be used. Thus banks and nonbank investors alike could get new money from the Federal Reserve at will, the only cost being the yield sacrificed on the securities sold. (2) The cost of getting such funds was the low yield on short-term government securities, for banks and all other types of financial institutions held billions of these. (3) By holding down interest rates on government securities, the Federal Reserve also held down interest rates on loans to private borrowers and assured a highly liberal supply of credit for private uses.

The reason was that all holders of governments retained complete freedom
to sell these holdings and shift to other assets. Thus not only banks but all
other lenders as well could get funds from the Federal Reserve to satisfy
private demands, and they would do so in great volume if yields on private
obligations tended to rise.

Table 66 shows that during the six years following 1939 the money supply
rose from $36.2 billion to $102.4 billion, for an increase of 183 percent. By
far the most important direct contributors to this increase were the $74.3

TABLE 66.   The Money Supply and Its Determinants, 1939–1945
(End-of-year figures, in billions)

	1939	1945	Net Increase 1939–1945
SOURCES			
Monetary gold stock	$17.6	$ 20.1	$ 2.5
Treasury currency	3.0	4.3	1.3
Total Federal Reserve credit	2.6	25.1	22.5
Commercial bank credit			
U.S. government securities	16.3	90.6	74.3
Loans	17.2	26.1	8.9
Other securities	7.1	7.3	0.2
Total sources	$63.9	$173.5	$109.6
Less: AMOUNTS ABSORBED BY COMPETING USES			
U.S. government deposits and cash holdings	$ 2.0	$ 25.9	$ 23.9
Time deposits	15.1	29.9	14.8
Other competing uses	10.6	15.3	4.7
Total competing uses	$27.7	$ 71.1	$ 43.4
Equals: THE MONEY SUPPLY			
Demand deposits	$29.8	$ 75.9	$ 46.1
Currency outside banks	6.4	26.5	20.1
Total money supply	$36.2	$102.4	$ 66.2

billion rise of commercial bank holdings of government securities and the
$22.5 billion increase of Federal Reserve holdings.

While following a passive general monetary policy, the authorities tried to
prevent or limit nonessential private borrowing by using selective credit controls. For example, in the autumn of 1941 the Federal Reserve imposed for the
first time a selective control over consumer credit, fixing maximum loan values
and maximum periods of repayment. Banks were admonished to refuse loans
for nonessential purposes. Authorities were established to pass upon the es-
sentiality of new security issues. But these and other selective credit controls
were far less effective in containing inflationary pressures, and even in limit-

ing the expansion of credit for private purposes, than were the great variety of direct controls imposed on the economy early in the war.

THE WARTIME ROLE OF DIRECT CONTROLS

It soon became evident that the government's fiscal policy would create strong inflationary pressure as output approached capacity levels, if not before. The huge rise of government expenditures directly increased the demand for output; it also contributed greatly increased amounts to private money incomes. Increased tax collections recovered some of this money from the private sectors, but not nearly enough to prevent disposable private incomes from increasing greatly. With greater disposable incomes consumers would, if left free to do so, increase their consumption demands. The multiplier would operate upward, perhaps raising consumer spending more than government spending was rising. Something of the same sort would happen to business spending. Prospects for profitable new investment were highly favorable, disposable business income was greatly increased, and credit was cheap. It became clear that something would have to be done to prevent consumers and business from spending as much as they wanted to spend and could afford to spend with their large and rising disposable money incomes. Inflationary pressures would have to be "repressed." This was not only to prevent or limit price inflation; it was also to prevent rising private demands from diverting productive resources away from the war effort.

A whole series of direct controls was used for these purposes. These included price ceilings on virtually every type of output, ceilings on wages, and ceilings on rents. It was illegal for anyone to charge or to pay more than these prices. Also included were many types of controls over the production, distribution, and use of output. In general, producers could buy equipment and supplies only if permitted to do so by the government, and the quantities that they could buy were limited. Thus total business spending was held down because the quantities of things business could buy were limited and the prices business could pay were limited by ceilings. In short, business was forced to spend less than it wanted to, many businesses were unable to spend all their current disposable incomes, and the inability of business to spend limited its demand for investable funds.

Consumer spending was similarly repressed. Consumers were forbidden to pay prices above the legal ceilings and the quantities of goods available was limited. Many were rationed. Many others, such as automobiles and most other consumer durables, simply were not being produced. Thus consumer spending was repressed and households were virtually forced to save far more than they would have done in the absence of direct controls.

The repression of private spending was not, of course, complete. Consumer spending did rise, as did also the wholesale and cost-of-living price indexes. The latter did not reflect actual price increases that occurred through up-grading, quality deterioration, and black markets. Yet the repression was re-markably successful in view of the strength of the inflationary pressures.

In short, the country had not been in the war very long before it was in a state of suppressed inflation, or widespread excess demands. The demand for output at existing prices had become far greater than the available supply. These inflationary pressures grew as the war progressed, partly because of the huge accumulation of private savings. For the years 1940 to 1945 inclusive, personal saving amounted to the huge sum of $132.6 billion and corporate net saving aggregated $28.5 billion. Total capital consumption accretions of $72.5 billion also enabled business to increase its liquidity to the extent that these funds could not be spent for replacement of plant and equipment. The private sectors used these huge savings in two principal ways. (1) To retire debt. Many households and businesses were enabled to retire their debts com-pletely or at least to reduce them markedly. (2) To acquire liquid assets. Be-tween the end of 1939 and the end of 1945, individual and business holdings of liquid assets rose from $69 billion to $227.5 billion, an increase of $158.5 billion. Not only the size of this increase but also the liquidity of the assets should be noted. Of the total increase, $59 billion was in holdings of money itself—demand deposits and currency. Another $21.4 billion was in time de-posits. Still another $75 billion was in highly liquid Treasury obligations. The nonmarketable issues, such as the E bonds, were redeemable at the Treasury on demand. The marketable issues were in effect redeemable on demand at the Federal Reserve at their support prices. The other $3.2 billion increase of liquid assets was in shares of savings and loan associations.

CONDITIONS AT THE END OF WORLD WAR II

The country had not escaped overt inflation during the war. By the end of 1945 consumer prices were 31 percent and wholesale prices 39 percent above their levels of six years earlier. Repressed inflationary pressures were very strong. The private sectors had accumulated a huge volume of liquid assets. Their money balances were now 183 percent above their level in 1939 and their total holdings of liquid assets were up 230 percent. Moreover, both business firms and households had accumulated unsatisfied wants in large volume. Many business firms that had spent little or nothing for investment purposes during the depression and had been prevented from spending dur-ing the war now wanted to replace, expand, or modernize their plants and equipment. Large numbers of families, feeling that they had lived like Spar-tans during the war, now wanted to go on a spending spree and to buy the cars and other things that had not been available during the war. The inflationary potential in increased private spending was large indeed.

But there was another side to the story, a side that led many to forecast deep depression and widespread unemployment rather than inflation for the postwar period. Many feared that the decrease of government spending following the cessation of hostilities would bring disaster. The sharp drop of federal expenditures from their level of almost $100 billion a year would directly decrease the demand for output, set off a downward multiplier effect on consumption, and leave industry with so much excess capacity that virtually no investment expenditures would be justified. Such gloomy forecasts were one, but by no means the only, reason for the early dismantling of direct controls. They were also a force making for a continued easy-money policy. When the predicted depression did not develop immediately after the war many continued to insist that it was "just around the corner."

As the war drew to a close the government quickly began to relax and remove the whole complex of direct controls. Rationing of consumers' goods was dropped almost immediately, and other controls over the use of raw materials and the production, distribution, and use of output were dismantled. Wage controls were abolished almost as soon as the war ended. Many goods and services were exempted from price controls immediately and other price ceilings were raised. By mid-1946 price controls were largely inoperative and in the autumn they were abolished. Rent ceilings remained as almost the only remnant of the wartime system of direct controls.

Prices rose immediately as direct controls were relaxed and removed. During 1946 alone wholesale prices rose more than they had during the entire 1939–1945 period, and the cost of living advanced two thirds as much as it had during the preceding six years. By August, 1948, when prices reached their first postwar peak, wholesale prices had risen 120 percent and the cost of living 76 percent since 1939. Two thirds of the total rise of wholesale prices and three fifths of the increase in the cost of living had occurred since the end of the war.

MONETARY POLICY, 1946–1948

Though direct controls over the economy were removed, Federal Reserve policies remained chained to their wartime objectives and methods of implementation. The System still used its powers to peg the prices and yields on Treasury obligations, and the pegged pattern of yields was for some time the same as it had been throughout the war. The range was from $\frac{3}{8}$ of 1 percent on 90-day maturities to a top of $2\frac{1}{2}$ percent on 25-year Treasury bonds. In short, during a period of full employment and inflation the Federal Reserve was pegging a general level and pattern of interest rates that had evolved during the nation's worst depression. Not until March, 1951, when the war had been over more than five years, did the Federal Reserve complete its escape from this pegging pattern.

This passive open-market policy of supplying additional Federal Reserve funds to anyone presenting securities at their pegged prices was potentially far more dangerous in the postwar period than it had been during the war. The wartime system of direct controls had effectively limited private demands for credit. As limitations on the quantities that they could purchase and on the prices they could pay limited their total spending, households and business firms limited their demands for credit. But as these limitations were removed, private buyers again became free to bid against each other for larger quantities, to pay higher prices, and to demand larger loans for the purpose. Moreover, all types of financial institutions were in a position to meet almost any foreseeable increase in private demands for credit and to do so at low interest rates as long as the Federal Reserve pegged yields on government securities, for they held huge amounts of these obligations. For example, at the end of 1945 commercial banks held $90.1 billion, life insurance companies $20.6 billion, mutual savings banks $10.7 billion, and savings and loan associations $2.4 billion. Households and nonfinancial business firms also had large holdings that they could sell to get money to lend to others or to finance their own spending.

Reasons for the Pegging Policy

Why did the Federal Reserve continue, despite inflation, to maintain easy-money conditions through its pegging policy? In part it was because of the widespread fear of unemployment. The long depression of the 1930's had left its indelible impression and almost a depression psychosis. Almost every year brought new forecasts of a coming decline. Moreover, the nation's new determination to promote the achievement and maintenance of "maximum employment, production, and purchasing power" was embodied in the Employment Act of 1946. Treasury and Federal Reserve officials were reluctant to take any action that might jeopardize the maintenance of prosperity. The policy was also made more acceptable by the current lack of faith in the efficacy of monetary policy. There was a widespread feeling that experience in the 1930's had proved that monetary policy was ineffective in combating depression. Many now asserted that it would be equally useless as an instrument for fighting inflation—that mildly restrictive policies would not be effective and that policies restrictive enough to halt price increases would throw the country into depression.

Concern for Treasury financing and for the prices of outstanding Treasury obligations was a major reason for continuing the policy. The Secretary of the Treasury was a strong and persistent advocate of pegging and a stubborn opponent of increases in interest rates. Several of the relevant arguments are worth noting. (1) Increased rates on the federal debt would add greatly to the already large interest burden. (2) Fluctuating prices and yields on governments would greatly complicate the Treasury's refunding operations, a serious matter with about $50 billion of the debt maturing within a year and nearly $100 billion within five years. (3) An increase of yields on governments, which without a rise of coupon rates would mean a decline of their prices, would impose capital depreciation on financial institutions and other holders and might lead to panicky selling and loss of confidence in financial institutions. Officials recalled the drastic decline of bond prices in 1920 when the federal debt was only $26 billion and pointed to the greater possibilities of panic now that the debt was nearly ten times as large and represented about 60 percent of all debt in the country. (4) Disturbances in the prices and yields of government securities would be transmitted to private securities and jeopardize prosperity. It was argued that not only low interest rates but also stability of interest rates and bond prices promoted prosperity.

Open-Market Policy

Until July, 1947, nearly two years after V-J Day, the Federal Open-Market Committee continued to prevent yields on government securities from rising above the pattern selected early in 1942. In 1946 and early 1947 the prices of long-term governments rose somewhat above the pegged level. This was primarily because the extremely low level of short-term rates led investors to "play the pattern of the rates" and to shift their purchases toward the longer-term obligations. The first break from the wartime pattern came in July, 1947, when the Federal Reserve persuaded the Treasury to allow it to eliminate the ⅜ of 1 percent buying rate on Treasury bills. The next break came the following month, when the Treasury agreed to the elimination of the ⅞ of 1 percent rate on 9- to 12-month certificates of indebtedness. But this did not mean that the Federal Reserve had ceased to limit increases of the yields on these shorter-term obligations. It had merely shifted its policy to one of maintaining the rates fixed by the Treasury on new issues.

Several aspects of open-market policy during the remainder of this period deserve emphasis. (1) Not until March, 1951, did the Federal Reserve permit the prices of long-term Treasury securities to fall below par or their yields to rise above 2½ percent. The prices of these obligations might rise above par, but the Federal Reserve intervened to the extent necessary to prevent their prices from falling below par. (2) In the last analysis it was the Secretary of the Treasury who set the yields on new issues and therefore the rates to be maintained by the Federal Reserve. And the Secretary consented to rate increases only reluctantly, belatedly, and to a limited extent. By the end of 1948, when the first postwar inflation had reached its peak, the yield on

Treasury bills had been allowed to rise only from ⅜ of 1 percent to 1.13 percent, and that on 9- to 12-month certificates from ⅞ per cent to 1¼ percent. These could hardly be considered high interest rates for a period of inflation. (3) This willingness of the Federal Reserve to buy government securities in unlimited amounts robbed its other instruments of all or most of their effectiveness for restrictive purposes. In effect it provided the banking system and others with a means of escape from other Federal Reserve attempts to restrict them.

Other Monetary Policies

The Federal Reserve employed two types of selective credit controls during this period. In 1946, as stock market activity began to rise markedly, the Board of Governors raised margin requirements on security loans to 100 percent, thereby putting the stock market on a "cash basis." This action probably inhibited the rise of stock prices and prevented a situation in which a highly speculative stock market might have enhanced inflationary expectations. It did not, of course, restrict the supply of credit for other purposes.

Regulation W, the selective control over consumer credit that had been imposed in the autumn of 1941 under the authority of an executive order of the President, was continued until November, 1947. It was then removed because Federal Reserve officials felt that they should exercise such a control only when specifically authorized by Congress to do so. They again imposed the control briefly following a temporary authorization by Congress in August, 1948. While it was in effect Regulation W probably retarded somewhat, though it did not stop, the growth of consumer credit.

The Federal Reserve also increased discount rates three times. The first came in the spring of 1946 when the Reserve banks eliminated the ½ of 1 percent preferential rate applicable to loans collateraled by short-term Treasury obligations, leaving in effect their 1 percent rate. This was raised to 1¼ percent in January, 1948, and to 1½ percent the following August. These rate advances probably exerted some influence toward firmness, but their effects were small, because the banks were largely out of debt to the Federal Reserve and were likely to remain so while they held so many short-term Treasury obligations that they could sell to the Federal Reserve at will.

From October, 1942, until February, 1948, the Board of Governors maintained member bank reserve requirements at the highest levels permitted by law, except that requirements against demand deposits in central reserve city banks were at 20 percent rather than the maximum level of 26 percent. It then raised these latter requirements to 22 percent in February, 1948, and to 24 percent in June. In August Congress enacted legislation giving the Board temporary permission to raise these requirements above the old maximum levels. The Board thereupon raised requirements against demand deposits at all classes of member banks by 2 percentage points and against time deposits by 1½ percentage points. In all, these 1948 increases raised required member bank reserves by about $2.5 billion. Such a large increase of requirements would ordinarily have restricted credit markedly. In this case the major effect was to evoke sales of an additional $2 billion of securities to the Federal Reserve. There was an accompanying slight increase of interest rates, but the effectiveness of the increases in reserve requirements was largely negated by the passive open-market policy.

The main argument of this section is not that these other Federal Reserve actions were wholly ineffective. It is only that the effectiveness of these restrictive actions was largely offset by the willingness of the Federal Reserve to supply reserve funds by purchasing Treasury obligations at relatively low and relatively stable yields.

MONETARY POLICY, 1949–MID-1950

After the first postwar peak of prices was reached in August, 1948, there followed more than a year of mild deflation. By the end of 1949 the cost of living had fallen 5 percent and wholesale prices were down 11 percent. In fact, the year 1949 was one of mild recession, with small declines of both production and employment. This was largely because net accumulations of business inventories in 1948 gave way to net decumulations of inventories in 1949. The Federal Reserve halted its vain attempts to restrict credit and initiated an easier money policy. Early in the spring of 1949 it eliminated its regulation of consumer credit. The temporary authorization to employ this type of regulation expired in June. It also lowered member bank reserve requirements. In several steps, beginning in May and ending in September, it lowered reserve requirements against demand deposits by 4 percentage points at all classes of member banks. Requirements against time deposits were reduced from 7½ to 5 percent. The Treasury lowered somewhat the yields on its new issues and the Federal Reserve stood ready to prevent market rates from rising above these lowered levels.

Under these conditions of mild deflation the controversy between the Federal Reserve and the Treasury died down. In such a situation there is no necessary conflict between the objective of promoting general economic stabilization, including stability of price levels, and the objectives of holding down interest costs on the national debt, facilitating Treasury financing operations, and preventing decreases in the prices of outstanding Treasury bonds.

By early 1950 the decline in business activity and prices had stopped and recovery was well under way. There was still some unemployment, but economic activity was at a high level. As to the future course of business activity and price levels, there was wide disagreement among economic forecasters.

The outbreak of fighting in Korea late in June, 1950, ended this uncertainty and ushered in a new upsurge of inflation.

MONETARY POLICY AFTER THE OUTBREAK
OF FIGHTING IN KOREA

The outbreak of fighting in Korea and this country's decision to intervene touched off a surge of buying by consumers and business firms. Remembering the scarcities and price increases of World War II, consumers rushed into the markets to get ahead of the hoarders. Business firms also hastened to replenish their inventories and make net additions to them. Only later, toward the end of 1950, did the rise of government expenditures for military purposes add its inflationary effects to the rise in private spending. Much of this latter increase was financed by sales of liquid assets, decreases in holdings of idle money balances, and expansions of credit. The velocity of money increased appreciably, redemptions of savings bonds rose, consumer credit expanded, and business loans increased markedly. Between May, 1950, and March, 1951, the cost of living rose 8 percent and wholesale prices 19 percent. During the rest of 1951 price levels remained relatively constant, the cost of living rising slightly and wholesale prices declining a little.

With the resurgence of inflation, the controversy between the Federal Reserve and the Treasury flared anew. The Federal Reserve wanted to restrict credit to curb the rise of prices, while the Treasury insisted that it continue to hold interest rates at an inflexibly low level. This controversy had begun to develop even before the Korean outbreak. Foreseeing a possible revival of inflation, the Federal Reserve had on two occasions—one late in 1949 and the other early in 1950—requested the Treasury to postpone public announcement of rates on its future short-term issues in order to see whether a rise in rates might be in order. On both occasions the Treasury responded by announcing immediately that the forthcoming issues would bear yields no higher than those currently being maintained in the market. And on both occasions the Federal Reserve obediently continued to hold market rates in line with those on the new Treasury issues. But in August, 1950, the controversy came out into the open and the Federal Reserve publicly defied the Treasury. On the same day and at almost the same hour the two issued conflicting public announcements. The Federal Open-Market Committee announced the System's determination to fight the current inflation and to use all its powers to this end. At the same time the Treasury announced a new $13-billion issue of short-term securities with yields no higher than those currently prevailing in the market. Despite this Treasury challenge, the Federal Reserve proceeded to tighten credit somewhat. To prevent the Treasury's financing from failing, the System purchased most of the new issue at the yields fixed by the Treasury. Then it sold some of its other holdings in the market on terms that raised the market yields of short-term obligations. It also raised its discount rates from 1½ to 1¾ percent. This controversy in 1950 related only to short-term issues; the Federal Reserve continued to prevent the prices of long-term government bonds from falling below par.

In early 1951 the controversy spread to the prices and yields on long-term Treasury bonds. A major reason for the Federal Reserve's rebellion was its fear that its other attempts to contain inflation would be ineffective so long as it had to peg the prices of these securities. In January it raised member bank reserve requirements against demand deposits by 2 percentage points. Acting under new congressional authorization, it reimposed selective controls on consumer credit and imposed a similar selective regulation on credit for residential construction. It also encouraged commercial banks, insurance companies, savings banks, and some other financial institutions to enter into a voluntary credit restraint program to prevent or lessen the extension of credit for "nonessential" purposes. But Federal Reserve officials doubted that these measures alone could stop the inflation. The policy of pegging Treasury bond prices at par would have to end.

The conflict between the Federal Reserve and the Treasury in early 1951 became dramatic. In January the Secretary of the Treasury publicly announced that during the defense period all the government's issues of marketable securities, for new money as well as for refunding purposes, would bear interest rates no higher than 2½ percent. He also implied, without stating it specifically, that the Federal Reserve had agreed to this policy. Reserve officials denied that this was true. The President and the Council of Economic Advisors then leaped into the fray to support the Treasury position. After a White House conference with Federal Reserve officials, the President publicly announced that the Federal Reserve had in effect agreed to the Treasury's announced policy. This the Federal Reserve publicly denied. Now that the controversy was out in the open and involved the President himself, it became a hotly debated issue in Congress, in the newspapers, and in financial circles. The Board of Governors finally informed the Treasury that as of February 19 it was no longer willing to maintain the existing situation in the government securities market. After further negotiations the Treasury and the Federal Reserve jointly announced on March 4, 1951, their now-famous "accord."

The Treasury and the Federal Reserve System have reached full accord with respect to debt-management and monetary policies to be pursued in furthering their common purpose to assure the successful financing of the Government's requirements and, at the same time, to minimize monetization of the public debt.

The Treasury–Federal Reserve accord of March 4, 1951, stands as a landmark in American monetary history, for it marked the end of inflexible pegging of the prices of Treasury obligations. Nine years after it had first adopted the policy in March, 1942, the Federal Reserve had finally regained at least some freedom to refrain from purchasing all securities offered to it, to limit its creation of bank reserves, and to restrict credit when necessary to prevent inflation. To the extent that it was freed from the task of supporting Treasury operations it could now direct them more toward promoting economic stability.

SELECTED READINGS

Brown, A. J., *The Great Inflation, 1939–1951*, Oxford, London, 1955.

Chandler, L. V., *Inflation in the United States, 1940–1948*, Harper, New York, 1951.

Fforde, J. S., *The Federal Reserve System, 1945–1949*, Oxford, London, 1954.

U.S. Congress, Joint Committee on the Economic Report:

Subcommittee on Monetary, Credit and Fiscal Policies,

Report, 1950.

Statements on Monetary, Credit, and Fiscal Policies, 1949.

Subcommittee on General Credit Control and Debt Management,

Monetary Policy and Management of the Public Debt, 1952.

(All published by Government Printing Office, Washington.)

CHAPTER 23

Monetary Policy Since the Accord

BACKGROUNDS

Though the Treasury–Federal Reserve accord of March, 1951, freed Federal Reserve officials from the shackles of an inflexible pegging policy and gave them greater latitude to develop new policy patterns, it did not provide them with new patterns. They now faced the task of developing new policy objectives and guides and new patterns of policy implementation. In doing so, they faced many problems, some of them quite unfamiliar. They were not hampered by any shortage of reserves or any lack of earning assets to sell for restrictive purposes. Holding more than $21 billion of gold certificates and with their actual reserve ratios nearly double the required level, the Reserve banks had ample capacity to expand credit whenever that might be appropriate. Their holdings of more than $22 billion of government securities at a time when total member bank reserves were about $19 billion gave them plenty of power to restrict credit. Their problem was not a lack of power; it was rather to decide how and for what purposes their power should be used.

A major purpose of the accord was to give the Federal Reserve greater freedom to restrict credit whenever such a policy was appropriate. But the Federal Reserve had not followed a really restrictive policy in about 20 years. Many, if not a majority, of Federal Reserve officials had never administered such a policy. Nor had most members of the financial community experienced really restrictive policies. Since 1934, or for 17 years, credit conditions had been easy, and interest rates low and relatively stable. How would the members of the financial community react to rising interest rates and falling bond prices? Would they become panicky, as some predicted? Or would they hold on to their bonds, as others forecast? No one could be sure.

It was expected that, with the abandonment of pegging, Federal Reserve discount policy would again become important. Unable to secure reserves on demand by selling government securities to the Federal Reserve, member banks would have to apply for loans. But for 17 years Federal Reserve lending had been of little importance. From 1934 until World War II member banks had been so swamped with excess reserves that very few had any need to borrow. Since that time most of them had adjusted their reserve positions by selling government securities. Many bankers had never applied for a loan and knew little or nothing about Federal Reserve lending policies. Moreover, Federal Reserve officials were by now inexperienced in the use of this instrument and needed to reconsider the whole problem of discount policy and discount rates.

The economic environment had changed markedly since the Federal Reserve had last followed really restrictive policies. For one thing, the federal debt was now far larger and more important. When the Federal Reserve took restrictive actions in the late 1920's, the federal debt was only $16.5 billion and made up only 8 percent of all debt in the country. No one then expected the System to stabilize the prices of government bonds or even to allow its policy to be influenced by the behavior of government bond prices. Now the federal debt held outside the Treasury was $219 billion and made up 45 percent of all debt in the country. A very large amount of it was short term and required frequent refinancing. Moreover, since 1937 the community had become accustomed to a Federal Reserve policy of stabilizing the prices of these obligations.

In the Employment Act of 1946 the nation had expressed its demand for a higher level of performance by the economy. Though the specific meaning of "maximum employment, production, and purchasing power" had not been defined, one thing was clear: the nation's tolerance for unemployment was far less than it had ever been before. The nation had also become acutely conscious of its capacity for economic growth and made continuous growth an important objective. At the same time it was developing less tolerance for price inflation. After 12 years of price increases that had raised the cost of living nearly 90 percent, it wanted a higher degree of price stability.

Thus the Federal Reserve faced the perplexing problem of reconciling its concern for the government securities market with its concern for economic stabilization. It also faced the no less perplexing problems of giving practical definitions to "maximum employment, production, and purchasing power" and "the highest sustainable rate of economic growth" and of reconciling this objective with that of promoting price level stability.

MONETARY AND DEBT MANAGEMENT POLICIES

During the period of pegging before March, 1951, the Federal Reserve entered the government securities market in two principal ways: (1) to stabilize the prices of securities that were already outstanding, and (2) to assist the Treasury in selling new issues, whether these were to secure new money to cover current deficits or to pay off maturing issues. For the latter purpose it frequently purchased a part of a new issue that others were not willing to buy at the yield rates fixed by the Treasury, and it sometimes bought outstanding issues of comparable maturities to "make room in the market" for the new Treasury issue.

The immediate purpose of the Federal Reserve at the time of the accord was not to withdraw completely from the government securities market and leave both the prices of outstanding Treasury obligations and current Treasury financing operations completely on their own. To withdraw support completely and abruptly after such a long period of pegging would have been both impossible and undesirable. Erratic and perhaps even panicky declines in the prices of outstanding securities would not only injure holders and jeopardize the future marketability of new long-term issues but might also disturb the markets for private obligations and upset economic stability. Nor could it immediately withdraw all support of Treasury financing operations. To permit a new issue to fail and perhaps force the Treasury to default on a part of the national debt was unthinkable. The Federal Reserve's immediate purpose, therefore, was merely to secure somewhat greater flexibility—to permit the prices and yields of outstanding government securities to vary more widely and to get the Treasury to put more realistic yields on its new issues and to rely less heavily on Federal Reserve support. However, its longer-run purpose was to work toward a situation in which its open-market policies would be shaped almost exclusively by economic stabilization objectives, and its purchases and sales would again be directed exclusively toward regulating the reserve position of the banking system rather than toward influencing directly the prices of Treasury obligations, new or old.

With respect to outstanding government securities, Federal Reserve policy for some time immediately following the abandonment of pegging was one of "maintaining an orderly market." Federal Reserve officials insisted that this did not mean that they would limit the extent to which the prices of these securities would be permitted to decline if the price decline was consistent with the attainment of other Federal Reserve objectives. It meant only that they would assist in keeping these adjustments "orderly" rather than "erratic" or "disorderly." The System then shifted to a policy of "preventing a disorderly market." This was not merely an exercise in semantics; it indicated a greater Federal Reserve tolerance of fluctuations in the prices of government securities, a lessened readiness to intervene to influence these prices directly, and a greater reliance on private purchasers and sellers to maintain "orderly" conditions. By the spring of 1953 the Federal Reserve had arrived at a new rule that would "normally" or "ordinarily" guide its open-market operations: it would not buy or sell longer-term Treasury obligations—those with maturities of more than a year—but would confine its operations to short maturities, preferably Treasury bills. This has come to be known popularly as "the bills-only doctrine." It also decided that thereafter it would not ordinarily engage in "swap operations," buying some maturities to raise their prices or to limit their price declines and selling others.

Federal Reserve officials had several closely related reasons for wanting to stay out of the market for long-terms and for confining their operations to bills and other short maturities where the direct effects of their purchases and sales on the prices of the securities would be much smaller. (1) They undoubtedly feared that if they continued to operate in the long-term market they might again be shackled by an inflexible pegging policy. A policy of pegging prices inflexibly at some point below par could be almost as shackling as pegging at par. (2) They wished to avoid possible charges that their sales of long-term securities, or even their refusal to buy, had unfairly imposed losses on holders. (3) The reason stressed most by Federal Reserve officials was their desire to create conditions in which private buyers and sellers would themselves develop an orderly and self-reliant market. They argued that as long as private operators in this market expected Federal Reserve intervention they would not perform the ordinary security market functions of taking speculative positions, buying when they thought prices were too low, selling short when they thought prices were too high, and arbitraging among the various issues to establish reasonable yield relationships. It was hoped that after the Federal Reserve's withdrawal from the long-term market private operators would themselves develop a "broad, deep, and resilient market."

The ability of the Federal Reserve to withdraw its support from current Treasury financing operations depended to a great extent on the attitudes and policies of the Treasury. If the latter persisted in fixing low rates on its issues, the Federal Reserve would either have to support them or risk being blamed for the failure of Treasury financing. In fact, however, the Treasury gradually adjusted its financing policies to the current monetary policies of the Federal Reserve and conscientiously tried to make the yields and other terms on its new issues such that they could be sold without Federal Reserve support. The Treasury's coöperation was sufficient to enable the Federal Reserve to adopt two more rules by the spring of 1953: ordinarily it would not buy any part of a new issue at the time of sale, and it would not buy at that time any outstanding issue of comparable maturity.[1]

Thus by the spring of 1953 the Federal Reserve had moved far from its policies during the period before March, 1951, and had developed four rules that would "ordinarily" or "normally" be followed: (1) It would not deal in securities with maturities in excess of a year and would confine its open-market operations to short maturities, preferably bills. (2) It would not engage in swap operations. (3) It would not buy any new Treasury issue at the time of

---

[1] This was not interpreted as preventing the Federal Reserve from taking a part of a new issue in exchange for its holdings of a maturing issue.

offering. (4) At the time of a new Treasury issue it would not buy any outstanding securities of comparable maturity.

The Federal Reserve departed from these "normal" rules only twice during the first five years after their adoption. The first time was in late 1955, when the System was following a restrictive policy and the Treasury offered a large new issue with a maturity in excess of a year. The Treasury believed the issue had been made sufficiently attractive to enable all of it to be sold to private purchasers, but it soon became apparent that some of the issue would remain unsold. The Federal Reserve thereupon violated three of its rules all at once; it bought some of the new longer-term issue and then sold some of its holdings of other maturities to mop up the reserves created by its purchases. The second departure occurred in July, 1958, after the dispatch of American troops to Lebanon following the revolution in Iraq. The prices of long-term governments, including prices on a recent issue, declined. Moreover, the Treasury had just announced a new issue, which was not finding purchasers in sufficient volume. The Federal Reserve intervened to purchase both some of the outstanding longer-term issue and some of the new issue. To mop up the reserves created by these purchases, it sold other maturities out of its portfolio.

These exceptions highlight two points. The fact that there were only two exceptions to the "normal" rules in over five years indicates how far the Federal Reserve had moved away from the policies it had followed before March, 1951. It also indicates how far the Treasury, in its debt management policies, was willing to depart from its old objective of borrowing at continuously low interest rates and to move toward adjusting its policies to the economic stabilization policies of the Federal Reserve. But these exceptions also highlight the fact that Federal Reserve policies cannot completely ignore federal debt management and that the problems of reconciling debt management and Federal Reserve policies directed toward economic stabilization could become even more serious in the future. It is not hard to imagine situations in which restrictive Federal Reserve policies to combat inflation might be seriously hampered by an unsympathetic Secretary of the Treasury faced with the problem of selling large new issues to meet maturing obligations and cover current deficits.

The bills-only doctrine has been a controversial issue both within and outside the Federal Reserve System. While respecting the reasons for its adoption, its critics believe that in refraining from dealing in long-term government securities the System is failing to take advantage of a useful means of promoting economic stabilization. They contend that by operating in the long-term market the Federal Reserve could more quickly alter the supply of long-term funds and the behavior of long-term interest rates. For example, when it wished to ease the long-term market it could directly tend to lower long-term rates by purchasing long-term securities. And it could directly tend to raise long-term rates by selling long-term securities. The advocates of the bills-only doctrine reply that the same results can be achieved through dealing exclusively in short maturities to regulate the reserve positions of banks. For example, the initial effect of purchasing bills and thereby increasing bank reserves may be to lower short-term rates. But as short-term rates fall the various types of investors tend to shift their purchases to longer obligations, thereby reducing yields in that market. On the other hand, sales of bills that reduce bank reserves may first raise short-term rates, but the induced shift of funds away from the long-term market will raise yields there. Such arbitrage among the various maturities undoubtedly occurs. But critics of the bills-only doctrine question whether it is quick enough or extensive enough to meet the needs of economic stabilization.

Let us now see how the Federal Reserve has used the freedom that it gained in March, 1951, to use its powers more flexibly to promote economic stability and growth.

FEDERAL RESERVE POLICIES, MARCH, 1951, TO THE SPRING OF 1953

The rise of prices touched off by the Korean conflict ended in March, 1951, with the cost of living up 8 percent and wholesale prices up 19 percent from their levels prior to the outbreak. There followed a period of more than four years of relative price stability. In mid-1955 the consumer price index was only 3 percent above its level in March, 1951. The wholesale price index actually declined 6 percent. This reflected a fall in the prices of farm products and some rise in other wholesale prices. The period up to early 1953 was one of high production and employment. GNP rose from $329 billion in 1951 to $347 billion in 1952 and to an annual rate of $369 billion in the second quarter of 1953. Unemployment was at a minimum. Out of a total labor force of more than 66 million, unemployment averaged only 1.9 million in 1951 and 1.7 million in 1952. In the spring of 1953 it fell to the extraordinarily low level of 1.3 million.

Under these conditions, the Federal Reserve allowed interest rates to rise somewhat during the remainder of 1951 and in 1952. It took no action to reduce the volume of bank reserves, but as the demand for bank credit rose it did not supply additional reserves by purchasing government securities. As a result, the excess reserves of member banks declined somewhat, and in 1952 member bank borrowings were often above $1 billion and at times rose to $1.5 billion. The prices of long-term government securities were about 4 percent below par by the end of 1952.

By early 1953 Federal Reserve officials began to fear a resumption of inflation. Prices had not begun to rise, but the economy was already operating at close to capacity levels, unemployment was at a minimum, demand was still rising, and Federal Reserve officials thought they detected a speculative building up of inventories. They therefore intensified their restrictive policy. For one thing, they allowed current gold exports and a reduction of Federal Reserve float to lower member bank reserves by about $1 billion. Member bank borrowings were kept above $1.2 billion during the first four months of the year. In January the discount rate was raised from 1¾ to 2 percent, its highest level since 1934. Interest rates rose to their highest levels in 20 years and the prices of long-term Treasury obligations fell about 10 percent below par. Credit stringency became severe as expectations of still tighter money and even higher interest rates led lenders to withhold funds and borrowers to rush in to anticipate their future needs.

In May, 1953, the Federal Reserve began to ease the situation. It now became evident that the immediate danger was not inflation but recession.

EASY MONEY, 1953–1954

The recession of 1953–1954 was short and relatively mild. GNP at annual rates declined from $369 billion in the second quarter of 1953 to $359 billion in the third quarter of 1954, a drop of 3 percent. This decline was entirely accounted for by a shift from inventory accumulation in early 1953 to inventory decumulation, and by an $11 billion decrease in federal expenditures for national security purposes. Other demands for output held up very well and consumption expenditures actually rose about $4 billion. The latter was due at least in part to a $5 billion tax reduction at the beginning of 1954 and to the automatic decrease of tax collections and the automatic rise of transfer payments in response to the fall of GNP. The number of unemployed rose above its extraordinarily low level of 1.3 million in the spring of 1953 but it did not quite reach 3.5 million or 5 percent of the labor force.

The Federal Reserve used all its major instruments to ease credit and combat the recession. Early in May, 1953, it began to buy short-term government securities in the open market; by the end of June it had increased its holdings nearly $1 billion. Though this action enabled banks to reduce their borrowings and increase their excess reserves, it did not succeed immediately in lowering interest rates. This failure was at least in part because the financial community did not believe that the Federal Reserve had really reversed its tight-money policy and was working toward easier credit conditions. Open-market purchases had not proved to be an effective means of announcing the change of policy. It was partly for this purpose that the Board of Governors reduced member bank reserve requirements against demand deposits at the beginning of July. Requirements against these deposits at central reserve city banks were decreased by 2 percentage points, and those at other member banks by 1 percentage point. This freed about $1.2 billion of reserves. The System then bought an additional $500 million of government securities, bringing the total increase since April to $1.5 billion.

The combined effect of these actions was to ease member bank reserve positions markedly. By November, 1953, member bank borrowings had fallen from their high level of about $1.2 billion in the early months of the year to about $500 million; excess reserves had risen from around $500 million to $700 million. In February, 1954, all the Reserve banks lowered their discount rates from 2 to 1¾ percent and in April they reduced them to 1½ percent.

In June and July, 1954, the Board again lowered member bank reserve requirements. This time it reduced requirements against time deposits by 1 percentage point, and requirements against demand deposits by 2 percentage points in central reserve cities and 1 percentage point at other member banks. This freed more than $1.5 billion of reserves. Simultaneously, however, the Federal Reserve absorbed about $1 billion of these released funds by selling government securities.

By mid-1954 credit conditions were very easy. Member bank borrowings were less than $200 million and excess reserves above $800 million. The money supply had risen about $3 billion during the preceding year. It rose another $6 billion during the latter half of 1954. Interest rates, which had fallen during 1953, declined still further. The yield on Treasury bills fell below ¾ of 1 percent. The prices of long-term government securities again rose above par.

This easy-money policy almost certainly helped shorten the recession, reduce its severity, and hasten recovery. It was especially helpful in stimulating residential construction. Expenditures for this purpose, which had been $11.1 billion in 1952 and $11.9 billion in 1953, rose to annual rates of $14 billion in the third quarter of 1954 and $15.9 billion in the first quarter of 1955.

Some Federal Reserve officials later wondered whether they had not eased credit too much, continued the easy-money policy too long, and provided both the public and the banking system with too much liquidity. Between the initiation of the easy-money policy in May, 1953, and the end of 1954 the public's money supply increased from $125 billion to $134 billion, a rise of 7.2 percent. Commercial banks were also put in a much more liquid condition. For one thing, they had been enabled to reduce their borrowings from $1.2 billion to $400 million and to increase their excess reserves from $500 million to $800 million. In addition, they had increased their holdings of government securities by more than $10 billion, and many of these were short-term obligations that could be sold quickly and with little loss by the banks. This greatly enhanced liquidity of both the public and the banks contributed to the subsequent rise of spending and prices. But it does not necessarily follow that the

TABLE 67. Commercial Bank Loans and Investments, 1953–1954
(In billions)

Date	Total	Loans	U.S. Government Securities	Other Securities
April 29, 1953	$138.5	$65.3	$58.9	$14.4
June 30, 1954	146.4	67.3	63.5	15.5
December 31, 1954	155.9	70.6	69.0	16.3

policies of 1953–1954 were too easy and too prolonged. Perhaps the error was in not moving more aggressively as business recovery approached an inflationary stage.

TIGHT MONEY, 1955–1957

The recession reached its trough in the second quarter of 1954 and was followed first by recovery and then by a boom that culminated in the third quarter of 1957. During this three-year period GNP at current prices rose $86.7 billion or 24.2 percent. Unemployment, which was about 3.4 million in mid-1954, averaged 2.6 million in 1955 and 1956 and fluctuated around this level during the first ten months of 1957. This represented less than 4 percent of the labor force.

Table 68 shows that increases in all the major categories of spendings for output contributed to the rise of GNP. In view of the widespread complaints

TABLE 68. GNP and Its Components, 1954–1957
(At annual rates in billions)

	Second Quarter 1954	1955	1956	Third Quarter 1957
GNP—Total	$358.9	$397.5	$419.2	$445.6
Personal consumption	236.5	256.9	269.4	288.3
Gross private domestic investment	47.2	63.8	68.2	66.7
Net foreign investment	−0.4	−0.4	1.3	3.6
Government purchases of goods and services, total	75.5	77.1	80.3	87.0
Federal	48.3	46.8	47.1	50.9
State and local	27.3	30.3	33.1	36.1

SOURCE: *Survey of Current Business,* July, 1958, pp. 5, 15.

against the Federal Reserve's "excessively restrictive" credit policy, it is interesting to note that spendings for gross private domestic investment purposes rose more than 40 percent during the three years following the third quarter of 1954 and that state and local expenditures, some of which were financed with borrowed money, rose 32 percent. Investable funds became "scarce," not because their supply was reduced but because the demand for them increased markedly.

Prices remained stable until mid-1955 and then began to rise, slowly at first and then more rapidly. By October, 1957, consumer prices had risen 5.6 percent and wholesale prices 6.6 percent.

The Federal Reserve began to reduce the degree of credit ease as business

TABLE 69. The Money Supply and Its Direct Determinants,
1954–1957
(In billions)

	December 31, 1954	October 31, 1957	Change, 1954–1957
SOURCES			
Monetary gold stock	$ 21.7	$ 22.7	+$ 1.0
Treasury currency outstanding	5.0	5.1	+ 0.1
Federal Reserve credit	25.3	24.1	− 1.2
Commercial bank credit			
Loans	70.6	93.0	+ 22.4
U.S. government securities	69.0	57.3	− 11.7
Other securities	16.3	17.6	+ 1.3
Total sources	$207.9	$219.8	+$11.9
Minus: COMPETING USES			
U.S. government cash and deposits	$ 5.9	$ 4.8	−$ 1.1
Foreign deposits, net	3.3	3.3	—
Time deposits	46.8	55.5	+ 8.7
Other accounts (net)	17.4	21.2	+ 3.8
Total competing uses	$ 73.4	$ 84.8	+$11.4
Equals: THE MONEY SUPPLY			
Demand deposits	$106.6	$107.2	+$ 0.6
Currency outside banks	27.9	27.8	− 0.1
Total money supply	$134.5	$135.0	+$ 0.5

activity started upward in the latter part of 1954 and then permitted tighter credit conditions to develop during the period from early 1955 to November, 1957. Its policy during this period may be characterized as almost purely defensive rather than aggressive. That is, it did not attempt to reduce the money supply despite the fact that the latter had risen more than 7 percent in the year and a half preceding 1955 and that the velocity of money had fallen during that period. Instead, it merely held the money supply approximately constant and refused to allow it to expand in response to increases in the demand for it. The 24 percent rise of GNP expenditures was financed almost entirely by an increase in the income velocity of money. And the rise of interest rates was due largely to the sharp rise in the demand for investable funds while the money supply was not permitted to rise.

Let us now see more specifically what the Federal Reserve did during this period. It did not raise member bank reserve requirements at all. Its most aggressive action was in the first part of 1955, when it sold over $1 billion of

TABLE 70.   Member Bank Reserves and Related Items, 1954–1957
(Averages of daily figures, in billions)

	December, 1954	October, 1957	Change, 1954–1957
Sources			
Federal Reserve credit			
U.S. government securities	$24.9	$23.4	−$1.5
Discounts and advances	0.4	0.8	+ 0.4
Float	1.0	1.1	+ 0.1
Total Federal Reserve credit	26.3	25.3	− 1.0
Monetary gold stock	21.7	22.7	+ 1.0
Treasury currency	5.0	5.1	+ 0.1
Total sources	53.0	53.1	+ 0.1
Competing uses			
Money in circulation	30.8	31.1	+ 0.3
Treasury cash and deposits at			
Federal Reserve	1.2	1.3	+ 0.1
Foreign deposits at Federal Reserve	0.4	0.3	− 0.1
Other deposits at Federal Reserve	0.4	0.3	− 0.1
Other Federal Reserve Accounts	0.9	1.1	+ 0.2
Total competing uses	33.7	34.1	+ 0.4
Member bank reserves	19.3	19.0	− 0.3
Addenda:			
Required reserves	18.6	18.6	0.0
Excess reserves	0.7	0.5	− 0.2

government securities, thereby forcing the banks to borrow more heavily and to draw down their excess reserves in order to support the existing money supply. Member bank borrowings, which had averaged less than $200 million for several months after July, 1954, averaged about $800 million during this period. In the latter part of the period they were close to $1 billion. And the excess reserves of member banks fell from $800 million to about $500 million. Federal Reserve discount rates, which had been lowered to 1½ percent in April, 1954, were raised to 1¾ percent in April, 1955, and then in six more steps to 3½ percent. The last increase, which occurred in August, 1957, brought these rates to their highest level since 1932.

This combination of a defensive Federal Reserve policy and the investment boom, which increased greatly the demand for investable funds, raised market rates of interest to their highest levels in 25 years.

We have already seen that these increases in interest rates did not prevent investment expenditures from rising more than 40 percent, that Federal Reserve policies did not prevent total expenditures for output from rising 24 percent, and that they did not prevent the cost of living from rising 5.6 percent and wholesale prices 6.6 percent. Does this prove, as some have asserted, that monetary policy cannot stop inflation? We cannot at this point speculate on the probable effects of a more aggressively restrictive policy, but a few comments on the actual events and policies of the period may be enlightening. In the first place, one should not expect a rise of interest rates to prevent a rise of investment expenditures when the rise of rates is itself produced by an upward shift of the investment demand schedule. The marginal efficiency of

TABLE 71.   Market Yields, 1954–1957
(In percentages)

Average for Period	3-Month Treasury Bills	Long-Term Treasury Bonds	Corporate Bonds, Aaa Quality
1954	0.94	2.55	2.90
1955	1.75	2.84	3.06
1956	2.66	3.08	3.36
Oct., 1957	3.60	3.73	4.10

capital schedule undoubtedly shifted sharply upward during this period, so that spenders for investment purposes were willing to spend much more at each level of interest rates or to spend the same amounts at much higher levels of interest rates. An actual rise of investment expenditures could have been prevented only by a sharp decrease in the supply of investable funds at each interest rate, and this did not occur.

In the second place, it would be unreasonable to expect that a policy of holding the money supply stable in the face of a sharp rise of investment demand schedules would succeed in preventing a rise of either investment spending or GNP. An induced rise of interest rates and the apparent "scarcity" of money almost inevitably lead some members of the community to find ways of "economizing" on their money balances—of holding smaller balances relative to their expenditures. This is especially true if the community enters the boom period with abnormally large balances relative to its current expenditures. We noted earlier that increases of interest rates were likely to reduce the quantity of money balances demanded. In practice this economizing of money balances can occur in several ways, of which the following are examples. (1) Households, enticed by higher interest rates and perhaps also by advertising campaigns by financial institutions, surrender some of their idle L_2 balances in exchange for securities or for claims against financial institutions, thereby making these balances available for L_1 purposes. (2) Business firms may do the same. For example, they may surrender money balances that they do not expect to spend in the near future and hold Treasury bills instead. Moreover, faced by higher interest rates on their own borrowings or by an unavailability of credit, they may maintain their expenditures by drawing down their money balances.

Commercial banks played a role in this process of activating idle balances or speeding up the income velocity of money. Table 69 showed that between the end of 1954 and the end of October, 1957, commercial banks reduced their holdings of Treasury obligations by $11.7 billion. Many of these sales were of shorter-term, highly liquid securities. The buyers of these securities paid for them by drawing down their deposit accounts, which lowered the required reserves of banks and enabled banks to expand their loans and holdings of other securities by an amount equal to the value of the Treasury securities that they had sold. Such transactions need not increase either the total supply of investable funds or the average velocity of money. For example, the buyers of Treasury obligations from the banks may pay for them with current savings, which would in any event have been made available for use. In this case the commercial banks merely act as intermediaries in transmitting current saving into investment. But the evidence indicates that in this period many of the Treasury obligations sold by the banks were paid for, not with current savings, but by relinquishing money balances—mostly deposits—that were previously idle. Thus the buyer gave up an idle deposit balance and enabled the banks to create for borrowers deposits that would be spent, at least in the first instance.

In short, a purely defensive policy of holding the money supply constant should not ordinarily be expected to prevent actual increases of investment expenditures and GNP in the face of upward shifts of investment demand schedules, for the induced rise of interest rates will lead to an economizing of money balances relative to expenditures—to a rise of expenditures relative to money balances. But in principle at least the Federal Reserve could have reduced the money supply enough to offset any unwanted effects of increases in the income velocity of money.

EASY MONEY, NOVEMBER, 1957–JULY, 1958

In November, 1957, the Federal Reserve relaxed its restrictive policy and again moved toward credit ease. For several months the various economic indicators had presented a confusing pattern. Several suggested a continuance of the boom and of price increases. GNP had increased from quarter to quarter, unemployment in October was at its lowest level in many months, and both the consumer price index and the wholesale index set a new high record almost every month. On the other hand, several indicators suggested that the boom was losing its vigor and might soon give way to recession. Industrial production had been falling for several months. The rate of growth of GNP was declining, as was also the rate of price increases. Late in the autumn, both official and private surveys revealed that business expenditures for plant and equipment, which had been at unprecedented levels in 1956 and the first three quarters of 1957, would begin to decline in the fourth quarter and would continue to fall through 1958.

The boom reached its peak in the third quarter of 1957 and gave way to recession. By the first quarter of 1958, GNP had fallen nearly $20 billion, or about 4.5 percent. This decline was slightly greater than those in the recessions of 1949 and 1953–1954. Unemployment, which had been 2.5 million in October, averaged above 5.1 million in the first quarter of 1958. Changes in business inventory policies were a major contributor to the recession. In the third quarter of 1957, business was adding to its inventories at an annual rate of $2.2 billion; in the first quarter of 1958 it reduced its inventories at an annual rate of $9.5 billion. This shift accounted for $11.7 billion of the decline of

TABLE 72.　GNP and Its Components, 1957–1958
(Seasonally adjusted annual rates in billions of dollars)

	Third Quarter 1957	First Quarter 1958	Change, Third Quarter 1957— First Quarter 1958
GNP, Total	$445.6	$425.8	−$19.8
Personal consumption	288.3	286.2	− 2.1
Gross private domestic investment	66.7	49.6	− 17.1
Residential construction (nonfarm)	16.9	17.1	+ 0.2
Other construction	19.7	19.2	− 0.5
Producers' durable equipment	28.0	22.9	− 5.1
Net change in business inventories	2.2	−9.5	− 11.7
Net foreign investment	3.6	0.5	− 3.1
Government purchases of goods and services	87.0	89.5	+ 2.5
Federal	50.9	50.9	—
State and local	36.1	38.6	+ 2.5

GNP. But as so often happens, the shift in business inventory policy was induced at least in part by more basic changes in the economy. For one thing, the predicted decline of business expenditures for plant and equipment began. For another, federal procurement policies in the autumn shifted expectations. Perhaps partly to combat inflation, but more for the purpose of holding its expenditures within the total budgeted for the fiscal year and to avoid raising the debt limit, the federal government sharply reduced its new orders for military equipment, reduced its progress payments for military equipment in process of production, and suggested to many firms that they stretch out their production over a longer period. Moreover, net foreign investment fell, largely because of a decrease in the foreign demand for United States exports. Personal consumption expenditures held up remarkably well, declining less than 1 percent. This was in large part because of the automatic decline of tax liabilities and the automatic rise of unemployment compensation and other transfer payments which bolstered disposable personal incomes.

It was under these conditions that the Federal Reserve relaxed credit restriction and moved toward easy money. In October, 1957, its open-market policy was designed to avoid a further tightening of the market and to ease it slightly. The first decisive move came in mid-November, when discount rates were reduced from 3½ to 3 percent. Market rates of interest, and especially long-term rates, immediately fell sharply. The Open-Market Committee cautiously purchased government securities to enable banks to reduce their borrowings and increase their excess reserves, as is shown in Table 73.

TABLE 73. Member Bank Borrowings and Excess
Reserves, 1957–1958
(Averages of daily figures, in millions of dollars)

	Borrowings	Excess Reserves	Net Borrowed Reserves (Member Bank Borrowings Minus Excess Reserves)	Net Free Reserves (Excess Reserves Minus Borrowings)
July, 1957	$ 917	$534	$383	
August	1,005	534	471	
September	988	522	466	
October	811	467	344	
November	804	512	292	
December	710	577	133	
January, 1958	451	573		$122
February	242	567		325
March	138	633		495
April	130	623		493
May	119	666		547

SOURCE: Federal Reserve Bulletins.

In February, March, and April the Board of Governors lowered member bank reserve requirements against demand deposits in several steps. The total reductions were 2 percentage points for central reserve city banks, 1½ for reserve city banks, and 1 for country banks. The effect was to lower required reserves by about $1.4 billion. These actions, together with those in the open market, enabled member banks to reduce their borrowings and increase their excess reserves. By March their excess reserves exceeded their borrowings by nearly $500 million, almost the reverse of the situation during the period of credit restriction. The Reserve banks lowered their discount rates three more times, bringing them down to 1¾ percent in mid-April.

These liberalizing Federal Reserve actions were accompanied by a sharp decline of short-term interest rates. The yield on Treasury bills, which had averaged about 3.6 percent in October, had fallen well below 1 percent by May. Long-term rates proved less responsive. After dropping sharply immediately after the first reduction of discount rates in mid-November, they began to drift downward much more slowly and by May had begun to rise. The very easy conditions prevailing in the short-term credit market were not evident in the long-term market. For this there were several reasons. One was the extraordinarily large volume of new long-term bond issues. State and local governments borrowed heavily, both to finance current expenditures and to retire short-term debt issued during the period of high interest rates. So did corporations. The federal government also floated several long-term issues, primarily to retire short-term debt. This became a highly controversial matter, for many believe that in periods of recession the Treasury should borrow only on short-term obligations and should refrain from issuing long-term securities that would compete with private long-term issues and tend to decrease the availability and increase the cost of long-term credit for private investment. These heavy borrowings in the long-term market while short-term loans were being repaid help to explain the disparity in the behavior of short-term and long-term interest rates. Some observers insisted that this was an occasion when the Federal Reserve should abandon the bills-only doctrine and buy long-term securities. A majority of Federal Reserve officials rejected this view.

Another factor was the growing expectation in financial circles that the easy-money policy would not long prevail. Federal Reserve policies during this recession had been considerably less liberal than in the recession of 1953–1954. Federal Reserve officials made no secret of their belief that they had eased credit too much and had maintained the easy-money policy too long during the earlier recession, and that they did not intend to repeat that mistake. Their resolve was strengthened by the behavior of prices during the recession. Instead of falling, the consumer price index actually rose a little over 2 percent between October and June; wholesale prices increased a little less than 2 percent.

It was against this background that the Federal Reserve again departed temporarily from its "normal" rules of open-market operations in July and early August. The market for longer-term Treasury obligations had shown signs of weakness for some time, and this weakness was accentuated by speculative activity in a recent longer-term issue. The dispatch of United States troops to Lebanon led to a sharp decrease in the demand for these obligations. On July 18 the Federal Reserve announced tersely that it would "buy Treasury securities other than short-term securities." This announcement, together with very small purchases of the long-term obligations, was sufficient to restore order in the market, and the Federal Reserve quickly withdrew. But soon thereafter the Treasury faced current financing problems. It feared that private buyers would not take all of a $13.5 billion August 1 issue of one-year 1⅝ percent certificates of indebtedness. The Federal Reserve purchased enough of these to assure the success of the issue. At the same time it sold enough of its other holdings to prevent an easing of the reserve position of the banks. After this episode it returned to its "normal" rules of open-market operations.

In August, 1958, the economic outlook was highly confusing. Some indicators suggested rapid recovery and a quickening of inflation. The recession had reached its lowest point in April and had given way to recovery. The rate of inventory liquidation had decreased. Personal consumption was rising slowly. Total construction expenditures were setting new records. Federal, state, and local expenditures were increasing. The stock market was booming. Both consumer and wholesale prices were advancing slowly. Talk of more rapid future inflation was widespread. But there was another side to the story. Business expenditures for plant and equipment were still falling and were expected to decline still more. The number of unemployed was still above 5 million and many others were working less than full time. GNP was still far below capacity levels.

Under these conditions, the Federal Reserve began to lessen the degree of monetary ease and to move toward restraint. The reader is invited to study subsequent developments and to judge the wisdom of this policy.

SOME CONTINUING PROBLEMS

A survey of United States experience during the period since the accord in March, 1951, shows that in its fiscal and monetary policies the nation still faces many unsolved problems. This applies both to choices of objectives and to methods of policy implementation. The problem of choosing objectives arises largely from their multiplicity. We have not just a single objective but many of them, and we find it difficult to choose among them when they appear to conflict with each other. For example, we have not yet given clear-cut answers to questions such as these: Just how much is it worth in terms of other objectives to hold down interest charges on the federal debt? How should we balance the objective of promoting price level stability against that of promoting "maximum employment, production, and purchasing power" and the "highest sustainable rate of economic growth"?

One reason for the nation's inability to answer this second question in a clear-cut fashion is that it does not know how much of one objective it can gain by a given sacrifice of another. Economists agree that price deflation is inconsistent with the maintenance of high levels of employment and output and that rapid price inflation is likely to add little or nothing to output. But within these limits there is wide disagreement. Some insist that maximum employment and output can be achieved only if the price level of output is allowed to rise slowly but continuously at a rate of 2 or 3 percent a year. Others claim that this is a short-sighted view and that output will average higher over a longer period if price levels are kept stable. In addition, there are continuing arguments over the harmfulness of continuing price increases because of their effects on the distribution of wealth and income.

Much of the disagreement arises out of differing theories as to the causes of modern peacetime inflations. Some economists distinguish between what they call "demand-pull" and "cost-push" types of inflation. Demand-pull inflations are those that occur as rising demands for output raise the prices of output, pull up employers' demand schedules for labor and other productive factors, and in effect pull up wages and the prices of other factors of production. This type of inflation, it is contended, can be dealt with satisfactorily by conventional monetary and fiscal policies. By preventing the emergence of excess demands for output, these instruments can eliminate the causes of both price increases and inflationary types of wage increases. And they may do so at little or no cost in terms of output and employment. But cost-push types of inflation, it is argued, are very different phenomena. These result from a combination of autonomous wage increases enforced by union demands and administered price policies by industries with strong monopoly power. Even in the midst of a considerable amount of unemployment, labor unions may insist on wage increases considerably in excess of increases in productivity, thereby raising cost schedules. Employers, with some previously unutilized monopoly power, then raise their prices at least enough to offset the rise of their labor costs. In effect, they will supply each amount of output only at higher prices. Faced with this market situation, the monetary and fiscal authorities have only two choices. (1) They may follow policies that will permit demands for output to rise sufficiently to maintain output and employment despite the rise of prices. In this case they will in effect validate the autonomous wage and price increases and create conditions favorable to another round. (2) They may refuse to allow demands for output to rise. In this case both output and employment must fall. Moreover, the restriction of demand will not prevent prices from rising. Thus, it is argued, conventional fiscal and monetary policies that operate by restricting demand are not only ineffective in preventing price increases but also reduce output and employment.

It is easy to show that many have overdrawn the distinction between demand-pull and cost-push elements in price inflation. In practice they are often difficult to distinguish because inflationary periods are usually characterized by both rising demands for output and aggressive union demands and rising wage rates. Whether one concludes that prices rose first or wages first often depends on the selection of the base date. Moreover, it is clear that both the size of union wage demands and the resistance of employers to such demands depend at least in part on their estimates of the future behavior of demand for the employers' output. A restriction of demands for output can both temper union wage demands and stiffen employers' opposition to them.

Even though the cost-push arguments are often exaggerated and wage demands are unrealistically considered to be completely independent of demands for output, these arguments cannot be dismissed. It may indeed turn out that both wage demands in excess of increases in average output per man-hour and the willingness of employers to grant such demands are so unresponsive to the state of demand for output that they can be held in check only by amounts of unemployment currently considered unacceptable. If this turns out to be the case, the nation will face three choices: (1) To follow fiscal and monetary policies liberal enough to maintain employment and output despite wage and price increases, thereby almost inevitably encouraging such increases. (2) To refuse to allow demands for output to rise enough to offset such wage and price increases and to maintain enough unemployment to end the upward spiral even though this turns out to require more unemployment than is currently considered acceptable. (3) To intervene in the wage and price-making processes to prevent the emergence of excessive wage increases and excessive price increases by firms with monopoly power. To do this effectively would probably require much more detailed intervention by the government than most Americans like to contemplate.

Conflicts of values and objectives also pose problems for the use of government fiscal policies for general stabilization purposes. The automatic variations of government revenues and expenditures have proved to be highly useful in reducing the breadth of fluctuations. In both the 1953–1954 and the 1957–1958 recessions the automatic decline of tax collections and the automatic rise of government transfer payments served to bolster disposable private incomes and private demands for output. Flexibility of the opposite type probably helped limit the rise of private demands during the 1955–1957 boom. Experience with respect to changes in the government's tax and expenditure programs has been less reassuring. The $5 billion decrease of taxes at the beginning of 1954 helped combat that recession. However, governmental processes for changing taxes and expenditure programs are so slow and preplanning is so limited as to make unlikely the use of these instruments in the early stages of a recession or depression. It seems likely that monetary policy, along with the automatic variations of government revenues and expenditures, will be the principal defenses used in the early stages of recession. Changes in tax and expenditure programs may, of course, come later.

Prospects for a timely and aggressive use of tax increases and of decreases in government expenditure programs to combat inflationary pressures are even less promising. Tax increases are delayed and limited not only by the time-consuming tax-making process and the inevitable wrangles over the question of who should pay the additional taxes but also by a widely held theory that tax rates are already so high that further increases would do irreparable harm to incentives and productivity. The fact that this hypothesis is not supported by such studies of it as have been made does not reduce its persuasiveness with legislators and government officials. Because of the strength of these forces, it will be difficult indeed to secure tax increases to fight inflation unless the rise of prices becomes rapid or prolonged. Reductions of government expenditure programs for this purpose are difficult to achieve because of the values attached to individual projects. There is a strong tendency to argue that every program is of such substantive importance that it cannot be curtailed or postponed.

These limitations on the timeliness and aggressiveness of fiscal policy measures leave a major role for monetary policy in promoting economic stabilization. Monetary policy is likely to have to bear a major part of the burden during the early stages of recession or depression, and in fighting inflation it may get little help in the form of tax increases or decreases of government expenditures unless the inflation is rapid or prolonged. But the aggressive use of monetary restriction to combat inflation also encounters active opposition. Much of this is because of its alleged drag on output, employment, and economic growth. However, during the 1955–1957 period of credit restriction, critics laid great stress on the alleged uneven impact of credit restriction on the various classes of borrowers. The Federal Reserve was not held directly responsible for this; it merely limited the total supply of credit and left the task of allocation and rationing to market processes. However, critics alleged that private lenders discriminated against some types of borrowers. Those who allegedly suffered most were borrowers for housing purposes, state and local governments, and small business. Housing credit was sharply curtailed, largely because of the policies of the FHA and the VA relative to the maximum interest rates that might be charged on mortgages insured by them. As interest rates on all other kinds of securities rose these agencies raised the allowable rates on insured mortgages only belatedly and inadequately. As a result, the flow of money into insured mortgages declined markedly. This situation could have been remedied easily by raising or eliminating the ceiling on allowable interest rates. Borrowing costs for state and local governments, including school authorities, rose sharply. This was partly because of the general rise of interest rates and partly because the great increase in the total supply of tax-exempt state and local securities during the postwar period raised yields on them relative to yields on taxable obligations. Did small and medium-sized business firms suffer from unfair discrimination? This charge has been neither proved nor disproved. But if it is true, the best remedy would seem to be a reform of the private lending and credit rationing mechanism rather than the maintenance of such a huge supply of credit that there will be enough for everybody no matter how large the total demand may be.

A major purpose of fiscal and monetary policies aimed at promoting economic stability is to regulate the behavior of the community. In recession it is to entice the community to spend more for output. In times of actual or threatened inflation it is to restrict spending. This cannot be achieved without restricting somebody, and one who is restricted from doing what he wants to do is not always properly appreciative. Some of those who listen with such sympathy to the complaints of everyone who is restricted by fiscal and monetary policies would do well to ponder the consequences of eliminating all such restraints.

SELECTED READINGS

U.S. Congress:
  Joint Economic Committee, various hearings and reports since 1952 on monetary and fiscal policies.
  Senate Committee on Finance,
    Investigation of the Financial Condition of the United States, 1958.
  (All published by Government Printing Office, Washington.)

CHAPTER 24

The Mechanism of International Payments

Most of the discussion up to this point has concentrated heavily on domestic aspects of money and monetary policy. This somewhat isolationist procedure was necessary for expositional purposes. Now, however, we shall broaden our perspective and explore such topics as these:

1. The functions of money in international transactions.
2. The mechanisms of international payments.
3. Exchange rates among national moneys.
4. International effects of domestic monetary policies.
5. International monetary policies and international monetary coöperation.

At the beginning we shall assume a system of free multilateral payments: that all individuals and business firms are permitted to make international payments as they see fit and to exchange at will any national money for any other. The various types of official restrictions on international payments will be considered later.

THE FUNCTIONS OF MONEY IN INTERNATIONAL TRANSACTIONS

The basic function of money in international trade is the same as in domestic trade—to facilitate specialization and exchange. Like domestic trade, international trade is essentially barter; in the final analysis goods and services are exchanged for goods and services. But barter would be at least as clumsy and inefficient in international transactions as in domestic trade—probably more so in view of the greater distances that are usually involved. The use of some sort of money as a medium of exchange or payments is essential to the full development of international trade and lending and of international specialization.

Moreover, international payments, like domestic payments, are facilitated by using types of money that can be transferred from payer to payee quickly, cheaply, and safely. It would, of course, be possible to make all international payments by shipping precious metals in the form of coin or bullion or by shipping paper money. This would be costly and inconvenient. Freight costs would be high, the risk of loss would be ever present, and the speed of transferring payments would depend on the speed of transport facilities. To avoid such costs and inconveniences, international payments, like domestic payments, are generally made by transferring debt (or credit) claims from payers to payees. The debts so transferred are usually deposit liabilities of banks. Many of these deposit transfers are made, as in domestic payments, by written orders. Some of these are ordinary checks written by bank customers. Some are certified checks. Some are checks or drafts drawn by a cashier or other bank official on his own bank or some other bank. Many payments, especially very large ones, are made with orders on banks transmitted by telegraph or cable.

THE BANKS AND INTERNATIONAL PAYMENTS

The process of making international payments is greatly facilitated by a network of banking offices within each country and by interrelationships among the banks of the different countries. We have already seen how the thousands of banks in the United States are intertwined in a nation-wide system for clearing and collection and in a correspondent banking system. Practically every bank in the country either has a correspondent relationship with a bank in New York or some other major financial center, or it has a correspondent relationship with some larger bank that in turn has a correspondent in New York. Thus virtually every bank, even a very small one, is enabled to provide its customers who wish to make payments abroad with checks drawn on a well-known New York or other metropolitan bank and even with checks drawn on foreign banks with which its city correspondent maintains close relations. In most other countries, similar results are achieved through nation-wide branch banking systems. Even small villages are served by branches of banks that have important offices, if not their head offices, in the nation's principal financial centers. Some countries have domestic correspondent banking systems similar to that in the United States.

These national financial centers and national commercial banking networks are interconnected in two principal ways: (1) Through foreign branches. A number of the larger banks in this country, such as the Chase Manhattan Bank, the First National City Bank, and the Guaranty Trust Company, operate foreign branches. Several British banks maintain branches in various parts of the world, as do banks in France, Holland, Canada, and some other countries. Each foreign branch usually becomes a member of the clearing and collection system of the country in which it is located, establishes relations with banks in that country, and engages in banking activity insofar as the laws of the country permit it. For the head office and its correspondents and customers, foreign branches perform many types of services. They supply credit and market information, draw and sell drafts, collect drafts, pay drafts, accept drafts, and so on. (2) Through international correspondent relationships.

The nature of these correspondent relationships can be illustrated by a hypothetical example in which the Chase Manhattan Bank of New York and the Midland Bank, Ltd., of London become correspondents of each other. Under such arrangements each performs many services for the other, compensation being fixed by the agreement or by later negotiation. (1) Each acts for the other and for the customers and correspondents of the other in collecting checks and other items, in presenting bills of exchange for acceptance, in buying and selling securities, and so on. (2) At least one of the banks maintains a deposit account with the other, and each may hold deposits with the other. For example, Midland may hold deposits with Chase, and Chase may hold deposits with Midland. (3) Each may agree to lend to the other up to a stipulated maximum amount. Suppose, for example, that you wish to buy £100,-000 at a time when the exchange rate is £1 = $2.80. Chase may sell you such a draft on the Midland Bank even though its deposit account with Midland is depleted at the time, and Midland will pay the draft. Chase may continue to owe Midland for a time, or it may immediately purchase claims against sterling and send them to Midland to replenish its account, or it may pay Midland by crediting $280,000 to its deposit account in New York.

It is easy to see how this vast network of correspondent relationships facilitates international payments. Americans are enabled to make payments abroad with written, telegraphic, or cable orders drawn by their banks on American banks or on foreign correspondent banks. And foreigners can make payments in the United States with written, telegraphic, or cable orders drawn by foreign banks on foreign or United States correspondent banks. It is interesting to note that a United States bank is even enabled to sell orders drawn on foreign banks with which it has no direct correspondent relationship. Suppose that you wish to make a £10,000 payment in Sydney, Australia, but neither Chase nor any other United States bank has a correspondent there. Chase might nevertheless sell you a £10,000 draft on a Sydney bank, informing that bank that when it makes payment its account with Midland in London will be credited by an equivalent amount. In effect, you pay Chase, Chase pays Midland, Midland pays the Sydney bank, and the Sydney bank pays the Australian payee. All these payments can be made by crediting and debiting deposit accounts.

Up to this point we have concentrated on commercial banks because it is through them that the great bulk of international payments is made. But we should not ignore the relevant roles of central banks, governments, and in some cases certain government agencies that deal in foreign exchange. We are interested here not in their function of domestic monetary management but in their function of providing means of international payments. (1) They sometimes supply some of the nation's own money to foreigners. For example, the Federal Reserve and the United States Treasury supply dollars to foreigners in exchange for gold purchased from them. In practice, the Federal Reserve and the Treasury buy foreign gold largely from foreign central banks, governments, and exchange stabilization funds or exchange control authorities rather than from private foreign sellers. These agencies that acquire dollars in this way can then use the dollars themselves or sell them to commercial banks or others who may use them in making payments. On occasion the Federal Reserve supplies dollars to foreigners by lending to foreign central banks, and sometimes by buying drafts or acceptances stated in foreign currencies. Similarly, foreign central banks, governments, and exchange authorities supply their own national moneys to foreigners by purchasing gold from them. They also supply their own money by purchasing claims against foreign moneys. For example, they buy checks on foreign banks, acceptances stated in foreign currencies, and so on. In such cases they not only supply their own national money but also demand foreign money. (2) They supply foreign money or the means of purchasing foreign money to their nationals and to others. For example, by selling gold to Americans for export the Federal Reserve and the Treasury provide them with a means of buying foreign currencies. By selling gold to foreign central banks or exchange authorities they enable these foreign institutions to acquire a means of purchasing any foreign moneys they may desire. Foreign central banks and exchange authorities do the same when they sell gold for export. Many of them also supply foreign money directly to their commercial banks or to others who wish to make foreign payments. For example, they may sell some of their own holdings of claims against dollars, sterling, or any other currency.

We shall see later how central banks, governments, and exchange authorities can use these powers to regulate exchange rates between their own money and foreign moneys, and even to peg them within narrow limits.

In some cases international payments are made with money of the payer's country. For example, most United States payments abroad are made with orders drawn on United States banks and stated in dollars. The recipient of these dollars may have deposit accounts in the United States to which the dollars can be added, and he may use them directly to make payments in the United States or elsewhere. Much more commonly, however, he sells the dollars in the exchange market—probably to his own bank or to the central bank or exchange authority of his country—in exchange for the money of his own country. In some other cases, international payments are made in the money of the payee's country. For example, a Swedish merchant would usually make payments to Britain in terms of sterling. If the payer does not himself have a sterling deposit in Britain, he will have to offer his own national money in the exchange market to buy claims on sterling.

A very large volume of international payments is made with the money of a third country. Two of the principal moneys used in this way are the United States dollar and the British pound sterling. For example, payments from Argentina to France may be made by transferring deposit credits on the books of New York banks. In effect, the Argentine payer uses pesos to buy an order on a New York bank and sends the order to pay dollars to the French payee, who sells the dollars for French francs. Someone in France may then buy the claims against dollars and use them to make payments to still other countries. It is partly to make payments to other countries as well as to the United States that foreign banks maintain large accounts in this country. In a similar way, many countries make payments to each other by transferring sterling claims against British banks. This includes not only most members of the British Commonwealth but also the Scandinavian countries and many others as well. For this and other purposes they maintain large accounts in London. Because of their widespread use in international payments, the dollar and the pound are often referred to as the great international currencies.

MULTILATERAL PAYMENTS AND MULTILATERAL TRADE

In the first chapter we noted that one of the great advantages of using money in trade is that it enables each person or firm to sell to those who offer the highest price and to buy from those who offer the best bargain. This not only enables each entity to make the most of his available resources but promotes maximum output by helping each person, firm, and region to specialize in the production of those things in which it has the greatest comparative advantage. This is just as true internationally as it is domestically. To make its maximum contribution to world trade and world productivity, an international monetary mechanism must enable buyers to purchase and sellers to sell in the most favorable markets; it must not force Nation A to buy from Nation B simply because the latter bought from it or lent to it.

Let us see how unrestricted exchange markets facilitate multilateral trade and multilateral payments. Suppose that the United States exports £1 million worth of wheat to England and receives sterling in return. Our exporters will sell the sterling claims to banks for dollars, and the banks are thus put in a position to sell sterling to others who wish to make payments abroad. The United States may not want to buy in England but does want Brazilian coffee, and may, therefore, buy checks or drafts on sterling deposits in London and remit them to Brazilan coffee exporters. These exporters sell their sterling claims to their banks for cruzeiros, and the Brazilian banks have sterling for sale. Brazilian importers may buy the sterling and use it to buy women's clothing in France. French exporters sell the sterling to French banks, which may then sell it to French importers, who use it to buy British industrial products. This example, admittedly simpler in its mechanics than many actual cases, illustrates the principles of multilateral trade and multilateral payments. No two of the countries balanced their trade with each other; England bought from us, we bought from Brazil, Brazil bought from France, and France bought from England. Through the unhindered exchange of money, each nation was enabled to sell in the most favorable market and to buy in the most favorable market the things it wanted most. This freedom of buyers also tended to cause producers to adjust their production to the desires of buyers and to locate the production of each commodity in the area or areas that could produce it most cheaply.

Free exchange markets also permit borrowers to use the proceeds of international loans in ways that they consider most advantageous and that will promote the most efficient types of specialization and production. Suppose, for example, that a French public utility company borrows $50 million in New York because interest rates are relatively low there. It may wish to buy only domestic labor and equipment and may therefore sell the dollar proceeds of the loan for francs. Other Frenchmen may remit the dollars to Argentina for needed foodstuffs and raw materials, and an Argentine railroad may use the dollars to buy United States locomotives. In the final analysis, the loan enabled France to increase its imports, but it imported what it wanted most and from the most favorable world market. Our loan to France increased our exports, but to Argentina rather than to France.

We shall see later how various types of exchange control inhibit the multilateral payments system, discourage multilateral trade, and impede international specialization.

EXCHANGE RATES AND EXCHANGE MARKETS

Most international payments involve trading or exchanging one national money for another. Thus, one making a payment abroad in a foreign money usually has to exchange some of the money of his own country for the foreign money, and one receiving payment in foreign money usually exchanges it for the money of his own country. Some international payment processes involve more than one such exchange of moneys. The various institutions involved in exchanging national moneys for each other are referred to collectively as "the exchange market" or "the foreign-exchange market." The principal foreign-exchange market in the United States is in New York, and commercial banks are its principal institutions.

Whenever things are exchanged for each other there must, of course, be a rate or ratio of exchange between them; there must be some sort of "price." By the "exchange rate" between two monetary units we mean simply the number of units of one money required to buy one unit of the other. Either monetary unit may be employed as the unit for stating the price of the other. For example, a situation in which two Philippine pesos exchange for one United States dollar could be stated either as $1 = 2 Philippine pesos or as 1 Philippine peso = ½ dollar. Also, a change in the exchange rate to $1 = 3 pesos can be expressed either as a rise in the exchange rate on the dollar relative to the peso, or as a decrease in the exchange rate on the peso relative to the dollar.

At a later point we shall discuss at some length the various determinants of the level of exchange rates at any time and of their changes through time. At this point we shall deal only with some structural relationships among exchange rates at a point of time. We shall assume here that there are no official restrictions on exchanging moneys.

The Structure of Exchange Rates in a Given Market at a Given Time

In our later discussion we shall find it convenient to speak of "the" exchange rate between two national moneys in a given market at a given time. In fact, however, there is not a single rate but a cluster of rates between the two, though all of them fall within a narrow range. These differentials are of three main types.

1. Differences between dealers' buying and selling prices. For example, a dealer may pay you only $2800 for a £1000 draft on a London bank at the same time that it would charge you $2804 for such a draft. It is out of this margin between selling and buying prices that exchange dealers pay their expenses and make profits.

2. Differences in maturities of the claims. At some given time the array of rates on sterling in the New York market might be as follows:

Cable rate	$2.80⅛
Sight rate (banker's demand drafts)	2.80
Rate for 60-day banker's bills	2.79⁵⁄₁₆

Thus at any time the cable rate is highest, followed by the rate on sight or demand drafts and then by the rate on time bills. This is because of differences in the time that sterling is paid out abroad. If a cable order is used, the selling bank loses that amount of its sterling balance almost immediately. If the bank sells a sterling demand draft, it does not lose its sterling balance until a few days later when the draft has traveled to London and been presented for payment. In effect, the bank has the use of the funds during the intervening period. Lowest of all is the exchange rate on time drafts or bills, for they are not payable until a future date. The rate on a sterling time draft is equal to the rate on sterling demand drafts less interest to the maturity of the time bill.

3. Differences in the degree of safety and liquidity of the claims. A claim on a well-known and highly regarded foreign bank will bring a higher price than a claim on a less highly regarded bank or on a nonbank debtor in whom confidence is not so high.

When we refer to "the" exchange rate between two moneys we shall, unless otherwise specified, mean the rate applicable to sight or demand drafts on highly regarded banks. It will be assumed that the prices of other claims cluster around this rate in their appropriate competitive positions.

EXCHANGE ARBITRAGE

Competition tends to establish one rate of exchange between two moneys in a given market at a given time. For example, the dollar price of sterling cables tends to be the same at all New York banks at a given moment. But may not exchange rates between two moneys be quite different in two widely separated markets, such as New York and London? This is impossible if movements between the markets are unrestricted, largely because of the possibility of arbitrage. By arbitrage we mean the simultaneous purchase of something in a cheap market and its sale in a dear market to profit from price differences between the markets. Arbitrage must not be confused with speculation, whose purpose is to profit from price differences between different points of time.

Exchange arbitrage is carried out through cable orders. Let us consider first what is usually called "two-point arbitrage." Suppose that the cable rate in New York is £1 = $2.81 at the same time that it is £1 = $2.80 in London. An arbitrageur—who might be the foreign-exchange department of a big New York bank—could make abnormally large profits out of this discrepancy. He could sell a £100,000 cable in New York for $281,000 and at the same time order his London correspondent to draw a $280,000 cable order on New York and sell it for £100,000. Thus in a matter of minutes the arbitrageur makes a gross profit of $1000; he sells in New York for $281,000 the sterling for which he paid in London only $280,000. The effect of these transactions is to equalize exchange rates in New York and London. The sale of sterling in New York tends to lower its dollar price there, and the offer of dollars for sterling in London tends to lower the dollar price of sterling in that market. Exchange rates must be practically the same in the two markets after arbitrageurs have completed their operations. In fact, discrepancies as large as the one assumed in our example could hardly occur in a market free of restrictions, for exchange arbitrageurs are always on the alert and can make good profits from very small margins. For this reason we can with little inaccuracy speak of one exchange rate between two moneys at a given time without specifying the market to which we are referring. This obviously is not possible if movements of funds between the markets are restricted.

The example above referred to two-point arbitrage in which arbitrageurs dealt in only two markets at once. But they can also deal in three or more markets simultaneously, thereby helping to establish at any given point of time a consistent network of exchange rates. For example, someone in the United States may purchase pounds directly with dollars, or he may first purchase some other money with dollars and then use that money to buy pounds. In unrestricted markets, arbitrageurs act in such a way as to make the cost of each money approximately the same whether it is purchased directly or through a series of exchange operations involving more than two moneys. To illustrate the principles of "three-point arbitrage," let us assume that the following exchange rates exist at some point of time:

$$£1 = \$2.81$$
$$1 \text{ Belgian franc} = 1.9 \text{ cents}$$
$$£1 = 139 \text{ Belgian francs}$$

An arbitrageur could make abnormal profits from this situation by doing simultaneously something like the following:

1. Sell £100,000 for $281,000
2. Pay $264,100 for 13,900,000 Belgian francs at 1.9 cents each
3. Use the 13,900,000 Belgian francs to buy £100,000 to cover his sales of sterling for dollars

In this way he would make a gross profit of $16,900, because he sold for $281,000 the sterling that he acquired for only $264,100 by the circuitous process of buying Belgian francs with dollars and using the francs to buy pounds. But his operations tend to erase the profitability of further operations of this type. His sale of sterling for dollars tends to lower the dollar price of sterling; his purchase of francs with dollars tends to raise the dollar price of the franc; and his purchase of pounds with francs tends to raise the price of the pound in terms of francs. Arbitrage transactions of this sort would not cease until each currency cost almost exactly the same whether purchased directly or through transactions in other moneys. The following exchange rates are consistent with each other:

$$£1 = \$2.80$$
$$1 \text{ Belgian franc} = 2 \text{ cents}$$
$$£1 = 140 \text{ Belgian francs}$$

In a system of unrestricted exchange markets, arbitrage operations of these types maintain mutually consistent relationships among the exchange rates of all moneys in all markets at any given time.

Exchange Speculation

Speculators buy and sell claims against money, just as they buy and sell securities and commodities, hoping to gain, or at least to avoid losses, from price changes through time. Exchange speculation occurs in two types of markets: forward exchange markets and spot markets. The forward exchange market is one in which sellers and buyers agree at one point of time to deliver and accept delivery of claims against some nation's money at a stipulated date in the future. The price or exchange rate is determined at the time of the agreement. For example, you might today agree to deliver to someone three months hence £10,000 at a price of $2.79 per pound. Your motive may be purely speculative; you may expect to be able to buy sterling at a lower price before the delivery date. But you might enter into such a contract because you are to receive a £10,000 payment in the future and want to protect yourself against the risk that the rate on sterling will fall below $2.79. On the other hand, you may today agree to accept delivery of £20,000 two months hence at a price of $2.80 per pound. You may do this for purely speculative purposes, hoping that you will be able to sell the sterling later at a price above $2.80, or you may buy now because you must make sterling payments later and want to protect yourself against the risk of having to pay a rate above $2.80.

A well-developed forward exchange market can perform a useful service by relieving international traders, lenders, and borrowers of exchange risks—of the risk that the foreign moneys that they own or owe will fall or rise in price. Suppose, for example, that an American, A, is to receive £10,000 two months hence. He runs the risk that the dollar price of sterling will fall. But B, another American, may be obligated to pay £10,000 in two months. He runs the risk that the dollar price of sterling will rise. Since these risks are of opposite types they may be eliminated if they can be matched or "married." Thus a broker or dealer may arrange for A and B to enter into a forward contract in which A agrees to deliver to B at a fixed price £10,000 two months hence. The same result is achieved if someone simultaneously agrees to accept future delivery from A and to make a future delivery to B at fixed prices. Risks that cannot be married may be borne by different speculators who agree to buy sterling from A and to sell to B at fixed prices. If the facilities available in forward exchange markets were adequate and cheap, they could go far toward preventing fluctuating exchange rates from inhibiting international trading, lending, and borrowing. Unfortunately, however, they are in many cases inadequate and speculators often charge a high price for bearing risks.

Spot exchange markets, which are the principal exchange markets and are far larger than forward markets, are those in which claims against money are bought and sold for immediate delivery. Speculation occurs in these markets in various forms. Suppose, for example, that the expectation arises that sterling may decline in terms of dollars or, to put it another way, that dollars may rise in terms of sterling. In various ways people may immediately offer more sterling for dollars and fewer dollars for sterling. Those who must make payments in sterling may postpone their purchases of sterling as long as possible. Those who must pay in dollars may rush to buy dollars with sterling. Foreigners may sell their holdings of sterling deposits and other claims stated in sterling. Some may borrow sterling and sell it immediately, hoping to buy later at lower prices to cover their sales. British nationals and others may offer more sterling to buy dollar deposits and other claims stated in dollars. On the other hand, a birth of expectations that sterling may rise in terms of dollars can bring about large immediate purchases of sterling and sales of dollars in exchange markets.

We shall be interested in three aspects of speculation in exchange markets. (1) Largely because of the possibility of speculation, expected coming events can cast their shadows before them. For example, an expectation that inflation or other future events will later lower the value of the French franc in exchange markets can lead not only foreigners but Frenchmen as well to offer immediately more French francs in exchange for other moneys. (2) During short periods, such speculative activities can influence markedly the behavior of exchange rates. (3) Speculation in currencies, like speculation in commodities or shares of stock, can be either stabilizing or destabilizing.

Suppose, for example, that speculators in a nation's money analyze realistically the trend of its exchange rate in the future and then buy the money when its exchange rate falls below this trend and sell it when its exchange rate rises above the trend. Such speculation tends to stabilize the exchange rate in the sense of narrowing its fluctuations. But some types of speculation in exchange markets, like those in stock and commodity markets, can aggravate and even create fluctuations in exchange rates. Suppose, for example, that the exchange rate on the French franc falls slightly and that speculators interpret this as a possible forerunner of further declines. They may rush to sell francs; this will push the franc exchange rate down still further; this further decline will create expectations of still further declines, and so on. "Bandwagon-hopping" types of speculation such as these may give rise to fluctuations of exchange rates that would not be justified by basic economic and financial conditions.

We shall see later that many countries now try to limit or prohibit speculative transactions in their moneys. They do this for two closely related reasons: (1) to prevent destabilizing effects on their exchange rates and to escape adverse effects on their economies, and (2) to inhibit speculative international movements of capital funds that might have deflationary or inflationary effects on their financial markets and might deflate or build up excessively their holdings of gold and other international reserves.

BALANCES OF INTERNATIONAL PAYMENTS

Now that we have surveyed briefly the mechanism of international payments and some of the mechanics of exchange markets, let us turn our attention to the types of transactions that give rise to international payments by the members of some countries and to receipts by the members of other countries. These international transactions are essentially the same as those within a country: purchases and sales of goods and services, purchases and sales of securities and claims of various kinds, gifts and other unilateral transfers, and purchases and sales of gold.

We have already looked at these transactions from one point of view when we were dealing with net foreign investment as a component of GNP. We found that a nation's net foreign investment for any period is that amount of its output that is used to change its net claims against the rest of the world. It may be expressed as follows:

Net foreign investment	equals	Exports of goods and services	minus	Imports of goods and services	minus	Net unilateral transfers to the rest of the world

We also found that a nation's net foreign investment during any period is equal to the change in its claims against foreigners plus the change in its gold holdings minus changes in foreign claims against it. It will now be convenient to rearrange these items and consider them as components of the nation's balance of international payments.

A NATION'S BALANCE OF PAYMENTS

This concept has been officially defined as follows: "The balance of payments of a country consists of the payments made, within a stated period of time, between the residents of that country and the residents of foreign countries. It may be defined in a statistical sense as an itemized account of transactions involving receipts from foreigners on the one hand and payments to foreigners on the other. Since the former relate to the international income of a country, they are called 'credits,' and since the latter relate to international outgo, they are called 'debits.' "[1]

Several points concerning a nation's balance of payments deserve emphasis. (1) It is not a balance sheet showing the nation's international assets and liabilities at a point of time. Instead, it shows *for some stated period of time* the *flow* of that nation's receipts from the rest of the world and of its payments

---

[1] U.S. Department of Commerce, *The Balance of Payments of the United States*, 1937, p. 1.

to the rest of the world. (2) Following the conventional rules of double-entry accounting that any entity must account for the use of all its receipts and must show all the sources of its payments, a nation's payments and receipts for any period must be exactly equal. Thus the payments side accounts for all the uses of the nation's receipts from the rest of the world, and the receipts side accounts for the sources of the funds used to make total payments to the rest of the world. We shall see later, however, that the methods used to equilibrate a nation's balance of payments may be of the utmost importance. (3) One nation's receipts are payments for the rest of the world, and its payments are receipts for the rest of the world.

To illustrate some of the principles involved, let us look at the balance of payments of the United States for the calendar year 1957. Receipts for mer-

TABLE 74.　United States Balance of International Payments, 1957
(In billions)

Receipts (or Credits)			Payments (or Debits)		
Exports of goods and			Imports of goods and		
services, total		$28.9	services, total		$20.7
Merchandise	$21.8		Merchandise	$16.4	
Services	4.2		Services	3.6	
Income on foreign			Foreign income		
investments	2.9		on investments		
			in the U.S.	0.7	
			Unilateral transfers		
			(net)		4.7
			U.S. capital flow (net)		3.6
			Long-term (net)	3.0	
			Short-term (net)	0.6	
Errors and omissions		0.9	Gold purchases (net)		0.8
Total receipts		$29.8	Total payments		$29.8

SOURCE: *Survey of Current Business*, June, 1958, p. 12.

chandise exports should need no elaboration. Exports of services were of many kinds: shipping services, banking and other financial services, services to foreign tourists in the United States, and so on. Income on foreign investments represented earnings on United States claims against foreign economies: on direct United States investments abroad, on United States holdings of foreign securities, and so on.

United States imports of merchandise should also require no elaboration. Imports of services were of many types. Services to United States tourists in foreign countries are the largest single item, but also included are United States purchases of shipping services, financial services, and so on. Foreign income on investments in the United States includes their earnings on direct investments in United States enterprises and on their holdings of long-term and short-term claims against United States entities. Unilateral transfers, usually shown as a net item, include all private and government gifts and grants. When we make such transfers to the rest of the world, we must pay in money or in kind.

International capital flows require more discussion. Though these are usually shown as net amounts, we shall show how they are derived. Let us look first at long-term international capital flows. By this we mean international receipts and payments because of sales and purchases of long-term claims. United States long-term capital outflows during any period, which would appear in the United States balance of payments as a payment item, are of three principal types: (1) United States direct investments abroad. These are investments during the period in new or enlarged facilities abroad by United States enterprises. (2) Purchases of long-term claims, either ownership or debt claims, against foreign countries. (3) Repurchases by United States buyers of long-term claims against the United States that were formerly owned by foreigners. All these purchases of long-term claims from foreigners during a stated period are obviously payment items in the United States balance of payments. They are receipt items for the rest of the world. But foreign purchases of such claims from the United States are receipt items in our balance of payments. Thus foreigners may during a period make direct investments in enterprises here, purchase long-term claims against United States entities, or repurchase claims against foreign countries that were formerly held by United States owners.

The net flow of long-term capital out of a country during a stated period is thus equal to its purchases of long-term claims from foreigners minus its sales of long-term claims to foreigners.

A nation may export short-term capital either by purchasing short-term claims against other countries or by repurchasing from foreigners the short-term claims that they formerly held against it. For example, the United States may export short-term capital during a given period: (1) by increasing its holdings of deposit claims against foreign banks or its holdings of short-term debt claims against other foreign entities, or (2) by decreasing its short-term debts to foreigners. In effect, it repurchases from them their short-term claims against United States banks and other United States entities. On the other hand, the United States can import short-term capital during a period by decreasing its holdings of short-term claims against foreign banks and other foreign entities or by increasing its short-term liabilities to foreigners. Net short-term capital flows out of or into a country are the resultant of these various transactions.

We shall later emphasize two aspects of these short-term international capital flows. (1) When the United States exports short-term capital by increasing its holdings of deposits or other short-term claims abroad or by decreasing its deposit liabilities and other short-term liabilities to foreigners, it provides the rest of the world with means of making payments to the United States. In effect, foreigners pay us with short-term claims against themselves or by surrendering short-term claims against the United States. (2) The extent to which other countries can balance their payments and receipts in this way depends on the size of their holdings of dollar deposits and other short-term dollar claims and on the extent to which the United States is willing to increase its holdings of deposit claims and other short-term claims against foreigners.

Gold purchases by a country are a payment item in its balance of payments, for it must pay for the gold. Gold sales by a country are a receipt item, for others must pay it for the gold.

Table 74 shows that in the balance of payments of the United States for 1957 unilateral transfers, long-term capital flows, short-term capital flows, and gold purchases were all net payment items. They were all net receipt items for the rest of the world. But one or more of these may, of course, be a net receipt item for a country. Unilateral transfers are net receipts for a country if it receives more gifts and grants than it makes. Long-term capital flows are net receipts when a country sells to others more long-term claims than it buys. Short-term capital flows are net receipts when a country decreases its net short-term claims against foreigners by reducing its short-term assets abroad or by increasing its short-term liabilities to foreigners. Gold flows are a net receipt item when a nation sells more gold to others than it buys from them.

BALANCES OF PAYMENTS AS ANALYTICAL DEVICES

Though balances of international payments are merely a form of *ex post* accounting showing the types and amounts of a nation's international receipts and payments during a stated period, they are highly useful for several types of analytical purposes. For one thing, they can be used to identify the sources of the supply of a nation's money in exchange markets and of the demand for it in those markets. For example, the payments side of the United States balance of payments shows all the sources of dollar receipts for the rest of the world. Foreigners can receive no more dollars than the United States pays for imports of goods and services, net long-term capital flows, net short-term capital flows, and net gold purchases. Thus United States payments may be considered as the supply of dollars in exchange markets. They may also be looked upon as the demand for foreign moneys in terms of dollars. If people of the United States make payments in foreign currencies, they must offer dollars for those currencies. If they pay in dollars, the foreign recipients usually sell the dollars and demand their own currencies.

On the other hand, the receipts side of the United States balance of payments shows all the sources of the demand for dollars by the rest of the world.

Foreigners demand dollars to pay for United States exports of goods and services. At times they may also demand dollars to make net purchases from us of long-term claims, of short-term claims, or of gold. The receipts side of the United States balance of payments also indicates the dollar value of foreign currencies supplied in exchange markets for dollars. If foreigners pay the United States with dollars they must offer their moneys in exchange markets for dollars. If they pay with their own moneys, the United States recipients exchange them for dollars.

In the next chapter we shall make extensive use of the fact that a nation's payments to the rest of the world constitute the supply of its money to the rest of the world and its demand for foreign moneys. Also, its receipts constitute the demand of the rest of the world for its money and the supply of foreign moneys for its money.

The fact that for any period the sum of a nation's receipts and the sum of its payments must be exactly equal makes it possible to highlight some interesting relationships among the components. For example, a nation's receipts and payments must always be equal only because we include net flows of gold and short-term capital. Suppose, for example, that a nation's other receipts exceed its other payments during some period by $1 billion. The balance is maintained by a $1 billion net payments item for gold and short-term capital flows. This could take the form of a net addition to its gold stock, a net addition to its holdings of deposits or other short-term claims abroad, or a reduction of its short-term liabilities to foreigners. The nation has clearly had an increase in its international liquidity position, for it has increased its holdings of gold and short-term foreign claims or it has reduced its short-term liabilities to foreigners.

Suppose, on the other hand, that during some period a nation's other payments exceed its other receipts by $2 billion. The balance is maintained by a $2 billion net receipts item for gold and short-term capital flow. This could take the form of a net reduction of its gold holdings, a net reduction of its deposits and other short-term assets abroad, or a net increase in its short-term debts to foreigners. The nation's international liquidity position is clearly worsened, for it has less gold and short-term assets abroad or is more deeply indebted to foreigners on short-term account.

Thus we find that though balances of payments always balance, they are not always in equilibrium. A nation's balance of payments is said to be "favorable" when it is balanced only by net gold purchases, net increases in the country's short-term assets abroad, or net decreases in its short-term liabilities to foreigners. The use of "favorable" in this sense is an old mercantilist coinage that ought to be abandoned. Such a situation need not be favorable even to the recipient country, to say nothing of others. On the other hand, a nation's balance of payments is said to be "unfavorable" when it is balanced only by net sales of gold, net decreases in its holdings of deposits and other short-term claims abroad, or net increases in its short-term debt to foreigners. The economic effects on a country need not be unfavorable if its international reserve and liquidity position is very strong. But it may be very unfavorable indeed if the country's gold and international reserves are drained away so that it must curtail its imports drastically, allow its exchange rate to decline, or take other distasteful actions.

We shall later discuss at length the problem of equilibrating international balances of payments—of bringing receipts and payments into balance without dangerous decreases of the international reserves of some countries and excessive increases in the international reserves of others.

ECONOMIC INTERRELATIONS

We shall also consider at some length at a later point the various interrelations among national economies: how economic developments in one country affect other countries and how that country's economy is affected by events elsewhere in the world. The balance of payments shows the various kinds of transactions through which impacts are transferred from one country to another: through purchases and sales of output, lending and borrowing, making and receiving gifts, and monetary transactions in the various international financial centers. Let us look first at some of the international effects of exporting and importing current outputs of goods and services. We have already touched upon this briefly in discussing net foreign investment. We found that net foreign investment, like gross private domestic investment, is a component of the total demand for our output and an offset to saving. Moreover, an upward shift of net foreign investment tends to have multiplier effects on GNP. Suppose, for example, that the foreign demand for United States exports, stated at an annual rate, rises by $2 billion. This will increase the incomes of those in the export industries, they will raise their consumption expenditures, this will raise incomes in the consumers' goods industries, and so on. A downward shift of the foreign demand for United States exports would, of course, have the reverse effects, multiplier and all. Similar shifts in foreign demands for the output of other countries would, of course, have similar effects.

INTERNATIONAL EFFECTS OF A RISE OF GNP IN THE UNITED STATES

It is therefore clear that a country's output, employment, and prices can be affected by shifts in the demand for its output by foreign countries. Let us now see how developments originating in one country can affect others. Suppose that GNP (or Y) in the United States initially rises by $10 billion because of changes in domestic conditions. This could have been initiated by a rise in the marginal efficiency of capital, an upward shift of the consumption function, the adoption of an expansionary fiscal policy, a more liberal Federal Reserve policy, or some combination of them. Suppose further that the price level of output remains unchanged so that the entire $10 billion rise of Y represents a rise of real output or real income in the United States. We make this second assumption in order to isolate the so-called *income effect* on the quantities of imports demanded by the United States. This $10 billion rise of real income is quite likely to increase the United States demands for imports. Some of the rise will be in the form of an increased demand for imported finished consumers' goods—for such things as foreign cars, perfumes, shoes, and so on. Some of it may be in the form of increased purchases of foreign finished goods by the government and business firms. Another part will be in the form of increased demands for imports of raw materials and semifinished materials for use in production processes: for such things as petroleum, lumber, tin, copper, zinc, iron ore, and so on. The change in the United States demand for imports relative to the rise of its income is called the "marginal propensity to import." This may be expressed as $\dfrac{\Delta M}{\Delta Y}$, where ΔM is the change in the demand for imports and ΔY the change in national income. If $\dfrac{\Delta M}{\Delta Y}$ is $\dfrac{1}{10}$, the $10 billion rise of Y will raise the United States demand for imports by $1 billion.

As soon as we introduce the responsiveness of the United States demand for imports to changes in its level of income, we have to modify somewhat our earlier multiplier analysis that implicitly assumed a closed national economy. We assumed earlier that domestic saving was the only "leakage" in the multiplier process. Now we find that purchases of imports constitute another leakage. To the extent that the nation uses some part of each increase of its income to purchase imported goods, the size of the multiplier effect on the level of its expenditures for domestic output tends to be reduced. But this is not by any means the end of the story. The increased United States demand for imports directly increases incomes in exporting industries abroad. With higher incomes, the members of those industries increase their consumption expenditures and an upward multiplier effect within their countries is under way. But their demand for imports is also likely to be responsive to increases in their level of income. The rise of their demand for imports will directly increase incomes in still more countries and tend to initiate multiplier processes there. This induced expansion of incomes in the rest of the world will tend, in turn, to raise the foreign demand for United States exports, thereby offsetting at least in part the "leakages" represented by the rise of United States spending for imports.

In summary, we find that a rise of real income in the United States tends to increase the United States demand for imports, to increase directly the incomes earned in foreign export industries, and to induce further increases in income not only in the countries that experience increased exports to the United States but also in other countries from which these countries increase their purchases. There are, however, two other effects that should be noted. (1) The increased United States demand for imports increases the supply of dollars offered in exchange markets. This tends to raise the exchange rates on foreign moneys in terms of the dollar. If the dollar prices of foreign moneys rise sharply, thereby making imports more expensive, this may inhibit the rise of United States imports. (2) The rise of the United States demand for imports may alter balances of payments in such a way as to have monetary effects in the United States, the rest of the world, or both. Thus, the United States may lose gold, which will tend to tighten credit unless the effects of the gold losses are offset. And the rest of the world may gain gold and dollar reserves, which will tend to ease monetary conditions there.

Up to this point we have assumed that price levels in the United States remained constant, so that the $10 billion rise of GNP was entirely a rise of real income. We did this to isolate the *income effect* on the United States demand for imports. However, a rise of the United States demand for domestic output may tend to raise United States price levels. If price levels in the United States rise relative to price levels abroad, this will tend to increase United States imports and to decrease United States exports.

INTERNATIONAL EFFECTS OF A FALL OF GNP IN THE UNITED STATES

A decline of GNP in the United States tends to have international effects that are in general the reverse of those described above. Suppose, for example, that the real income of this country declines by $10 billion. With lower real incomes, the members of the community will decrease their demand for imports, the size of the reduction varying with the marginal propensity to import, $\frac{\Delta M}{\Delta Y}$. The decreased demand for imports will apply not only to finished goods but also to materials used in the process of production. The reduced demand for their output will directly decrease incomes in foreign export industries and set off downward multiplier effects abroad, not only in the exporting countries but also in others that in turn suffer decreases in the demand for their exports. This induced decrease of incomes abroad will, in turn, decrease foreign demands for United States exports.

The decline of United States real income and of its demand for imports has two other effects worth noting: (1) It tends to decrease the supply of dollars offered to demand foreign currencies in exchange markets. This tends to raise the exchange rate on the dollar and to lower the dollar prices of foreign currencies. If the exchange rate on the dollar rises sharply, this will tend to decrease United States exports and stimulate United States imports. (2) The decline of the United States demand for imports may lead to gains of gold and international reserves by the United States and losses by the rest of the world. The resulting monetary effects may be important.

INTERNATIONAL CAPITAL FLOWS

Changes in conditions within one country can also affect the rest of the world by changing long-term and short-term international capital flows. Suppose, for example, that the United States initiates a very easy-money policy that is reflected in a marked decrease in United States interest rates. To the extent that this policy raises United States real incomes and prices it may encourage United States imports and thereby stimulate incomes abroad. It may also stimulate capital flows from the United States. With domestic yields lower, Americans may increase their long-term lending abroad. Moreover, the fall of short-term yields tends to discourage flows of short-term funds to the United States and perhaps even to induce an outflow of these funds. An increase of capital outflows from the United States would increase the supply of dollars in exchange markets and tend to lower the exchange rate on the dollar. It would also tend to increase the gold and dollar reserves of the rest of the world.

Higher interest rates in the United States would tend to have the reverse effects on the international flow of capital, the exchange rate on the dollar, and gold and dollar reserves.

SUMMARY AND CONCLUSIONS

This chapter has described the mechanism of international payments, the principal types of transactions giving rise to international payments, and some of the major ways in which economic developments in some countries affect others. In a system of international trading and lending, each nation is affected by developments in the rest of the world and affects developments in the rest of the world. Its own economy is affected by the demands of the rest of the world for its output, by the supply of imports from the rest of the world, by foreign supplies of capital to it and demands for capital from it, and by foreign effects on its money supply. In turn, it affects the rest of the world in all these ways.

SELECTED READINGS

International Monetary Fund, *Annual Reports* and *International Financial Statistics* (monthly), Washington.
Kindleberger, C. P., *International Economics*, Irwin, Homewood, Ill., 1953.

Lary, H. B., and associates, *The United States in the World Economy*, Government Printing Office, Washington, 1943.

Marsh, D. B., *World Trade and Investment*, Harcourt, Brace, New York, 1951.

U.S. Department of Commerce, *The Balance of International Payments of the United States* (annual), Government Printing Office, Washington.

Young, J. P., *The International Economy*, Ronald, New York, 3d ed., 1951.

CHAPTER 25

Exchange Rates and International Equilibrium

Most of this chapter will deal with exchange rates. It will consider such questions as these: What determines the level of the exchange rate on a nation's money at a point of time and changes of that rate through time? What sort of an exchange rate policy should a nation follow? Should it peg its exchange rate within narrow limits over a long period of time? Should it go to the other extreme and allow its exchange rate to vary freely in response to supply and demand forces in exchange markets? Should it follow some policy between these extremes? If so, what should that policy be?

We shall soon see, however, that exchange rate policy is only one aspect of the much broader problem of equilibrating balances of payments, of determining the response of a nation's economy to developments in the rest of the world, and of making international adjustments to developments within the country itself.

The reader is warned that an exhaustive treatment of the topics covered in this chapter would require at least a volume. Because of the necessity for brevity, our discussion must limit itself to a few major points. For simplicity of exposition, we shall assume a two-country world composed of the United States and Great Britain. We should, however, remember at all times the presence of other countries. Members of the United States can buy or sell in their own country, Great Britain, or the rest of the world. Members of Great Britain can buy or sell at home, in the United States, or the rest of the world. Similarly, other countries can buy or sell among themselves, in Great Britain, or in the United States. These decisions will be affected by relative prices in the various markets, and these prices as seen by purchasers and sellers will depend in part on exchange rates.

SOME EFFECTS OF CHANGES IN EXCHANGE RATES

An exchange rate is a means of converting a price stated in one national money into a price stated in another national money. For example, suppose that the British price of some commodity is £1. To United States buyers and sellers who base their decisions on prices stated in dollars this sterling price is meaningless until they know the dollar price of sterling. But as soon as they know the dollar value of a pound, they can make the translation. Suppose the exchange rate is £1 = 3. They can then quickly calculate that:

The dollar price of the commodity		The sterling price of the commodity		The dollar price of the pound
$3	=	£1	×	$3

Knowing that the dollar price of the commodity is $3, they can decide how much of it to buy or sell. Similarly, British buyers and sellers who base their decisions on prices stated in sterling would not know how to react if they knew only that the United States price of some commodity was $3. But if they knew that the exchange rate on the dollar was $1 = £⅓, they would know that the sterling price of the commodity was £1. That is,

The sterling price of the commodity		The dollar price of the commodity		The sterling price of the dollar
£1	=	$3	×	£⅓

They can then decide how much of it to buy or sell.

Since the exchange rate is a means of converting prices stated in one money into prices stated in another money, it should be evident that a change of the exchange rate can shift these price relationships.

An Increase in the Dollar Price of Sterling

Let us start with a situation in which the exchange rate is £1 = $3. Suppose that while other things remain unchanged, the exchange rate shifts to £1 = $4, or $1 = £¼. This may be stated either as a rise of the pound in terms of dollars or as a fall of the dollar in terms of pounds. How will this affect United States demands for British exports? With each pound costing ⅓ more than before, British goods will be ⅓ more expensive in terms of dollars than they were before if their sterling prices remain unchanged. Americans will therefore demand only a smaller quantity of British exports at their former sterling prices. To British producers who measure in terms of sterling this will appear as a downward shift of the foreign demand for their output. Faced with this decrease of demand, they may respond in either of two ways. (1) They may maintain the prices of their products in terms of sterling. In this case, the physical volume of their exports will fall, and the sterling value of their exports will also fall. In other words, the quantity of sterling demanded in exchange markets to pay for British exports will also fall. (2) They may lower the sterling prices of their exports to maintain their physical volume. Even if this succeeds, they will still suffer a loss in the sterling value of their exports because of the decreased sterling price per physical unit of exports. In other words, the quantity of sterling demanded in exchange markets to pay for British exports will be reduced.

In summary, an increase in the exchange rate on a nation's money tends to decrease the foreign demand for its exports at each price in that country, to decrease the physical volume of its exports, to decrease the total value of its exports as measured in its money, and to decrease the quantity of its money demanded in exchange markets.

How will the rise of the sterling rate from £1 = $3 to £1 = $4 affect British imports from the United States? To the British this will appear as a cheapening of the dollar from $1 = £⅓ to $1 = £¼. Thus United States products will be cheaper in sterling if their dollar prices remain unchanged. The British will therefore demand more United States exports at each dollar price. United States producers will view this as an upward shift of the foreign demand for their products. Thus the cheapening of United States exports in terms of sterling will increase the physical volume of British imports. It will also increase the sterling value of British imports if the British demand for imports is price-elastic, so that the decrease in the sterling price per unit is more than offset by the rise in the physical quantity of British imports. In other words, the rise of the exchange rate on the pound or the fall of the exchange rate on the dollar will increase the quantity of sterling supplied in exchange markets to pay for British imports.[1]

In short, we find that an autonomous rise of the exchange rate on a nation's money tends to have the following effects: (1) It shifts downward at each level of domestic prices the foreign demand for the nation's exports. Thus it is deflationary in the nation's export industries. (2) By cheapening foreign moneys, it makes imports less expensive in terms of the nation's money. This cheapening of imports tends to lower the prices at which the nation's import-competing industries must sell if they are to compete successfully. (3) It reduces the value of the country's exports in terms of its own money, and therefore reduces the quantity of its money demanded in exchange markets to pay for its exports. (4) If the nation's demand for imports is price-elastic, it increases the value of the nation's imports and the quantity of its money supplied in exchange markets to pay for its imports.

We shall later make considerable use of the fact that a rise of the exchange rate on a nation's money tends to decrease the quantity of its money de-

---

[1] We deal here only with the case in which the price elasticity of the British demand for imports is greater than unity. If the price elasticity is less than unity, the fall in the sterling price per unit of imports will not be offset by a sufficient rise in the quantity of imports, and the quantity of sterling offered in exchange markets will fall as the sterling price of dollars falls.

manded in exchange markets and to increase the quantity of its money supplied.

A Decrease in the Dollar Price of Sterling

Let us again start with the situation in which the exchange rate is £1 = $3. Suppose now that while other things remain unchanged, the rate shifts to £1 = $2, or $1 = £½. This may be stated as either a decline of the pound in terms of dollars or as a rise of the dollar in terms of pounds. The effects will, in general, be the reverse of those described above. With each pound costing ⅓ less than before, British goods will be ⅓ cheaper than before in terms of dollars if their sterling prices remain unchanged. Americans will therefore demand a larger volume of British exports at each price in terms of sterling. To British producers who measure in terms of sterling this will appear as an upward shift of the foreign demand for their products. They may react in either of two ways: (1) They may maintain the old prices of their products in terms of sterling. In this case the physical volume of their exports will rise, as will also the sterling value of the exports. The quantity of sterling demanded to pay for British exports will also rise. (2) They may raise the sterling prices of their exports. Even if they raise these prices enough to prevent any rise of their physical exports, the sterling value of their exports will rise. So will the quantity of sterling demanded in exchange markets to pay for British exports.

How will the fall of the pound from £1 = $3 to $1 = $2 affect British imports? To the British this will, of course, appear as a rise of the dollar from $1 = £⅓ to $1 = £½. United States goods will therefore be more expensive in terms of sterling. The British will therefore demand fewer United States exports at each level of their dollar prices. To United States producers this will appear as a downward shift of the foreign demand for their products. Thus the higher price of foreign products in terms of sterling will decrease the physical volume of British imports. If the British demand for imports is price-elastic, it will also decrease the sterling value of British imports and the quantity of sterling supplied in exchange markets to pay for imports.

Thus we find that a decline of the exchange rate on a nation's currency tends to have the following effects: (1) It shifts upward at each level of domestic prices the foreign demand for the nation's exports. Thus exporters can sell more exports at the same prices in their own money, they can sell the same quantity of exports at higher prices in terms of their own money, or they can follow some middle course. (2) By making foreign moneys more expensive, it raises the prices of imports in terms of the nation's money. The rise of import prices permits domestic import-competing industries to sell more at their old prices, to raise the prices of their output, or to follow a middle course. (3) It increases the value of the country's exports in terms of its own money and increases the quantity of the nation's money demanded in exchange markets. (4) If the nation's demand for imports is price-elastic, it decreases the value of its imports in terms of its own money and decreases the quantity of its money supplied in exchange markets to pay for imports.

A country may change its exchange rate for either aggressive or defensive purposes. Suppose, for example, that when its exchange rate is at £1 = $3, Britain has an equilibrium in her balance of payments, is not losing international reserves, and is not suffering serious unemployment. She might nevertheless lower her exchange rate to £1 = $2 in order to stimulate her exports, to discourage imports, to assist her import-competing industries, and to build up her international reserves. But she may also lower her exchange rate for defensive purposes. Suppose, for example, that because of a business depression in the United States and a consequent decline of the foreign demand for British exports, Britain should find that at the old exchange rate of £1 = $3 British exports were very low, the British balance of payments was adverse, and the nation was being drained of its international reserves. Britain might lower her exchange rate to £1 = $2 to combat the decline of her exports, to protect her import-competing industries against adverse effects of falling prices of foreign products, to equilibrate her balance of payments, and to protect her international reserves.

The Level of Exchange Rates

Let us now see how exchange rates are determined in the absence of restrictions on exchange dealings. We shall start with the case in which official agencies do not peg exchange rates or otherwise intervene but allow rates to be determined by free market forces. To illustrate the principles involved, we shall analyze the dollar price of the pound sterling.

Since an exchange rate is a price, we should be able to use an ordinary supply and demand analysis. By the supply of sterling we shall mean a function or schedule showing the quantities of sterling that would be supplied in exchange markets per period of time at each of the various possible dollar prices of sterling. The components of the supply of sterling are, of course, the payments items in the British balance of international payments. The purpose of such a schedule or function is the usual one of isolating the effect of price—in this case the exchange rate—on the quantities supplied. But to draw such a curve we must assume all other conditions affecting supply to be given and constant. Table 75 indicates some of the most important of these. Changes in these things can shift the supply function. That is, they can increase or decrease the quantity of sterling supplied at each exchange rate.

The supply schedule of sterling is indicated by the SS curve in Fig. 34. It is drawn on the assumption that the British demand for imports is price-elastic. It slopes upward to the right because a higher exchange rate on sterling

TABLE 75.   Some Principal Determinants of
the Supply Schedule of Sterling

I. The level of real income in Britain

II. The levels of prices and costs in Britain relative to those of other countries

III. Levels of interest rates in Britain relative to
those of other countries

IV. Expectations as to future exchange rates on
sterling

V. Tastes for British products relative to those
of other countries

VI. Other factors relevant to the productivity
and comparative costs of British and foreign
producers

---

tends to lower the sterling price of imports and thus to stimulate British
imports whereas a lower exchange rate on sterling tends to raise the sterling
price of imports and thus to discourage British imports.

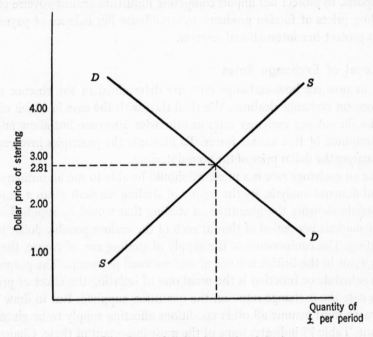

FIG. 34.   Demand for and Supply of Sterling.

By the demand for sterling we mean a schedule, curve, or function showing
the quantities of sterling that would be demanded at each of the various possible dollar prices of sterling. The components of this demand are the receipts
items in the British balance of payments. Again, our purpose in drawing such

a curve is to isolate the effect of changes in the exchange rate on the quantities of sterling demanded. To do so we must assume other conditions affecting the demand for sterling to be given and constant. Some of the most important of these are shown in Table 76. Shifts of these things can shift the demand

TABLE 76.   Some Principal Determinants of
the Demand Schedule for Sterling

I. The level of real income in the rest of the world

II. The levels of prices and costs in Britain relative to those of other countries

III. Levels of interest rates in Britain relative to those of other countries

IV. Expectations as to future exchange rates on sterling

V. Tastes for British products relative to those of other countries

VI. Other factors relevant to the productivity and comparative costs of British and foreign producers

curve for sterling. That is, they can increase or decrease the quantity of sterling demanded at each level of exchange rates.

The demand schedule for sterling is indicated by the DD curve in Fig. 34. It slopes downward to the right because a lower rate on sterling stimulates the demand for British exports whereas a higher sterling rate discourages the demand for British exports.

The exchange rate can be in equilibrium only when the quantity of sterling demanded is exactly equal to the quantity supplied, leaving neither an excess demand nor an excess supply. Fig. 34 shows that with the given DD and SS curves this can occur only at the exchange rate £1 = $2.81. At any higher exchange rate the supply of sterling would exceed the demand for it. The quantity of sterling demanded would be smaller because British exports would be more expensive to foreigners. The quantity of sterling supplied would be larger because British imports would be cheaper in terms of sterling. On the other hand, at any lower exchange rate the demand for sterling would exceed the supply of it. The quantity of sterling demanded would be larger because British exports would be cheaper to foreign buyers. The quantity of sterling supplied would be smaller because British imports would be more expensive in terms of sterling.

In short, as long as the SS and DD functions remain constant, the equilibrium exchange rate between the dollar and the pound will remain at $2.81. But the equilibrium rate can be shifted by anything that shifts the SS function, the DD function, or both.

Changes of Exchange Rates

Let us now consider a few of the most important developments that can shift the SS and DD functions for sterling.

1. A change in the level of British prices and costs relative to levels abroad. Suppose, for example, that Britain experiences a domestic inflation of her price and cost levels. As the sterling prices of British products rise, the demand curve for sterling will shift leftward and downward. Since the dollar cost of a British good is equal to its sterling price multiplied by the dollar price of sterling, British goods will now be more expensive at each level of exchange rates and British exports will be discouraged; or to put it another way, the dollar price of British exports can be prevented from rising only by a fall of the sterling exchange rate sufficient to offset the rise of British prices in terms of sterling.[2] The rise of British price levels will also shift downward and to the right the supply curve of sterling. As the prices of competing domestic products rise, the British will demand more imports at each exchange rate on the dollar. Also, they will now be willing to buy a given quantity of imports at a lower exchange rate on the pound, which they will see as a higher exchange rate on the dollar.

Thus we find that a rise of prices in Britain while prices elsewhere remain constant or rise less will tend to lower the exchange rate on sterling, both by shifting downward and to the left the demand function for sterling and by shifting downward and to the right the supply function of sterling. When a country inflates its domestic price levels while prices elsewhere remain relatively constant, it usually cannot balance its receipts and payments without reducing its exchange rate to maintain its exports and discourage imports.

It should be noted that the same result may occur if British prices remain constant while prices elsewhere fall. The decline of prices elsewhere will make British exports relatively expensive to foreign buyers unless the exchange rate on the pound is reduced sufficiently. Also, British imports will be cheaper in terms of sterling unless the fall of prices abroad is offset by a fall of the sterling exchange rate and a rise of exchange rates on foreign moneys. Note that Britain may be able to prevent her domestic price level from falling with price levels abroad if she reduces sufficiently the exchange rate on sterling so as to reduce the price of her exports in foreign moneys and to prevent a decline of the prices of her imports in terms of sterling.

A fall of British price levels relative to levels abroad would tend to raise the rate on sterling, both by increasing the demand for sterling at each exchange rate and by decreasing the supply of sterling at each exchange rate.

2. Changes in the level of real income in Britain. A rise of real income in Britain would tend to increase British imports at each level of exchange rates,

---

[2] It should be noted that we assume here that demands are price-elastic.

and thereby to increase the supply of sterling in exchange markets. It would therefore tend to lower the sterling exchange rate if the demand schedule for sterling remained constant. On the other hand, a fall of real income in Britain would tend to decrease the British demand for imports at each exchange rate, to decrease the supply of sterling at each exchange rate, and to raise the sterling rate in exchange markets.

3. Changes in the level of real income in the rest of the world. An increase of real incomes in the rest of the world tends to raise the demand for British exports at each exchange rate, to increase the demand for sterling at each exchange rate, and to raise the rate on sterling. Note that to the extent that the rise of foreign demands for British exports is allowed to raise the exchange rate on sterling, Britain may be enabled to escape inflationary effects on her domestic price level. The sterling prices of British exports need not rise, but the sterling prices of her imports may fall because each pound will now buy more foreign money.

On the other hand, a decline of real incomes abroad tends to decrease the demand for British exports at each exchange rate, to lower the demand for sterling at each rate, and to reduce the exchange rate on sterling. By allowing the sterling exchange rate to fall, thereby making British exports cheaper in foreign moneys, Britain may be able to reduce the extent to which the decrease of foreign demand will reduce British exports, and she may do this without reducing the sterling prices of her exports.

4. Changes in the level of interest rates in Britain relative to levels elsewhere. Suppose that British interest rates rise relative to those elsewhere. This will at least reduce capital outflows from Britain and may induce flows to Britain. Thus by decreasing the supply of sterling or increasing the demand for sterling it will tend to raise the sterling exchange rate. A fall of interest rates in Britain relative to levels elsewhere tends to have the opposite effect—to reduce the demand for sterling and increase the supply of sterling for international capital flow purposes.

5. Changes in expectations concerning future sterling exchange rates. Such changes may be very important in evoking speculative capital flows. Suppose, for example, that there arise expectations that the rate on sterling will fall sharply in the future. The demand curve for sterling may be shifted leftward and downward immediately as people postpone their purchases of sterling. The supply curve of sterling may be shifted rightward and downward as people sell sterling and buy foreign moneys. Both the decrease of the demand for sterling and the increase of its supply will bring about a decrease in the exchange rate on sterling. This decline of the sterling rate will, of course, stimulate British exports and discourage British imports.

What will be the economic effects of such a decline in the sterling rate induced by a speculative capital outflow from Britain? These depend in part on prevailing economic conditions. They may not be unwelcome if the British economy is depressed. The decline of the sterling rate will shift upward the demand schedule for British exports at each price level in terms of sterling and thus stimulate British export industries. Also, by making imports more expensive in terms of sterling, it will discourage British imports and enable import-competing industries to raise their prices. But suppose that the British economy is already under heavy inflationary pressure. The fall of the sterling exchange rate will intensify the pressure. The upward shift of foreign demands for British products will tend to raise their sterling prices. And the rise of the sterling prices of imports will add still further to British inflationary pressures.

On the other hand, newly created expectations of a future rise in the price of sterling can lead to an immediate decrease in the supply of sterling, an increase in the demand for sterling, and a rise of the sterling exchange rate. This will tend, of course, to discourage British exports and stimulate British imports. Such a development would hardly be welcome when Britain was in a state of unemployment.

This discussion indicates one reason why nations do not like speculative capital flows that make their exchange rates fluctuate in an erratic manner. Such fluctuations can have serious effects on their export industries, their import-competing industries, their price levels, and their entire economies.

Summary

This section has indicated how the exchange rate on a nation's money would be determined if that rate were not pegged or otherwise regulated by direct official intervention. In the following section we shall deal with pegged exchange rates. But much of the material in this section will be relevant. We shall be especially interested in the factors that determine the location of the demand and supply functions of a nation's money in exchange markets at any time, and that can increase and decrease the value of those functions at each exchange rate.

PEGGED EXCHANGE RATES

Historically, one of the most common exchange rate policies has been that of pegging exchange rates within narrow limits over considerable periods of time. The technique of pegging exchange rates, like that of pegging the price of wheat, the price of gold, or the price of a government security, is basically simple. A monetary authority or someone else stands ready to supply at some fixed price in exchange markets all the nation's money that is demanded from it at that price, and to demand at some fixed price all the nation's money that is offered to it at that price. Sometimes a monetary authority itself enters the exchange market and does the pegging. In other cases it merely provides others with a means of doing so. Let us consider the latter case first.

Methods of Exchange Rate Pegging

Private dealers in exchange will maintain virtually stable exchange rates between gold standard moneys if the nations issuing those moneys stand ready to buy and sell gold at a fixed price and to allow gold imports and exports. For example, suppose that at some time the dollar is defined as 13.71 grains of pure gold. This is equivalent to setting a gold price of $35 an ounce, for an ounce contains 480 grains. Suppose that at the same time the British define the pound as 38.39 grains of pure gold. This is the same as setting a gold price of £12.5 an ounce. The mint parity or par of exchange will be £1 = $2.80. This is because the gold content of the pound is 2.80 times that of the dollar; or to put the same thing another way, the dollar price of gold is 2.80 times the sterling price of gold. So long as both countries freely buy and sell gold at these fixed prices for international purposes, the dollar-sterling rate can deviate only slightly from this mint parity or parity of exchange. This is because exchange dealers can acquire sterling by using dollars to buy gold and then sell the gold for sterling, and they can use sterling to buy and sell the gold for dollars. For example, you may buy in New York 10,000 ounces of gold for $350,000. Suppose that the cost of shipping the gold to London, including your necessary profit, is $2500. The total cost of the gold delivered in London will be $352,500. You can sell the gold there for £125,000 at the official buying price. The cost of acquiring each pound in this way is $\frac{352,500}{125,000}$, or $2.82. The exchange rate on the pound cannot rise above this level, the exchange rate on the dollar cannot fall below this level, as long as dealers can freely get sterling by purchasing gold with dollars and using the gold to purchase sterling. At this rate on sterling, dealers will stand ready to supply all that may be demanded. The pound can rise further and the dollar can fall further if the United States ceases to sell gold freely at the fixed price for export or if the British cease to buy it freely at the fixed price.

Similarly, dealers can buy £125,000 in exchange markets, use it to buy 10,-000 ounces of gold in London, and sell the gold in New York for $350,000. Suppose that the cost and necessary profit to the dealer is $2500. His net realization will be $347,500, and his realization per pound will be $\frac{347,500}{125,000}$, or $2.78. The exchange rate on the pound cannot fall below this level, and the exchange rate on the dollar cannot rise above this level, as long as exchange dealers can freely secure dollars by purchasing gold with sterling and using the gold to buy dollars. At this rate on sterling, dealers will buy all offered to them. However, the dollar can rise further and the pound can fall further if Britain ceases to sell gold at a fixed sterling price or the United States ceases to buy gold.

Thus we find that under the old type of international gold standard the monetary authorities did not themselves have to enter exchange markets to maintain exchange rates within narrow limits. As long as they freely bought and sold gold at a fixed price, private exchange dealers stabilized rates. But note that a nation could prevent its exchange rate from falling only as long as it was both willing and able to supply sufficient gold for export at a fixed price.

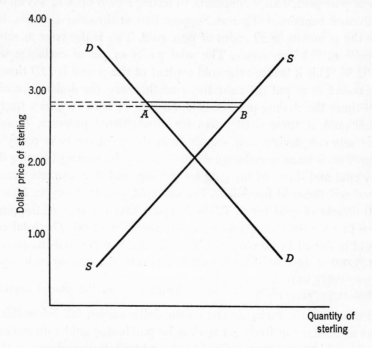

FIG. 35. Disequilibrium with Pegged Exchange Rates.

In recent years, techniques for pegging exchange rates within narrow limits have come to differ in at least two respects from those described above. In the first place, monetary authorities rely less on the activities of private exchange dealers to set the limits and intervene in the exchange markets themselves. In the second place, they do not always use gold as an intermediary. Instead, they often buy and sell foreign moneys directly. For example, an agency of the British government, the Exchange Equalization Account, prevents the exchange rate on sterling from rising above $2.82 and from falling below $2.78. Whenever the exchange rate on the pound rises to $2.82—that is, when the rate on the dollar falls to £1/2.82—it uses sterling to demand dollars. It may then continue to hold the dollars or it may sell them for gold. On the other hand, when the exchange rate on the pound falls to $2.78—the exchange rate on the dollar rises to £1/2.78—it sells dollars in exchange for sterling. For this purpose it needs a sufficient supply of dollars, of gold that can be sold for dollars, of some other currency that can be sold for dollars, or an ability to borrow dollars.

If other demands for sterling and other supplies of sterling are such as to equalize the demand for and the supply of sterling at some rate between $2.82 and $2.78, the government authority need not intervene at all. But the supply of sterling may exceed other demands for it at the support price. For example, at the rate £1 = $2.78, the supply of sterling may become greatly in excess of other demands for sterling, so that the authority must sell large amounts of its gold and foreign-exchange holdings to buy up the excess of the supply of sterling over other demands for it. Such a situation is depicted in Fig. 35. If this disequilibrium continues very long, Britain may be drained of all her holdings of gold and foreign exchange.

What policy should a nation follow when it faces a disequilibrium in its balance of international payments and is balancing its receipts and payments only by drawing down its holdings of gold and foreign assets or by building up large short-term debts to foreigners? This is one of the most important policy problems in the entire field of international finance. The nation may, of course, lower its exchange rate to equalize the demand for and supply of its money in exchange markets. Or it may resort to direct controls over its trade and payments in order to hold its payments down to the level of its receipts. Let us suppose, however, that Britain refuses to resort either to a depreciation of her exchange rate or to restrictions on the freedom of trade and payments. Instead, she insists on maintaining her old pegged exchange rate with freedom of trade and payments.

Equilibration of Receipts and Payments with Pegged Exchange Rates

The drain on Britain's international reserves at the pegged exchange rate of £1 = $2.78 can be ended only by developments that will shift the demand curve for sterling upward and to the right, shift the supply curve for sterling upward and to the left, or shift both to a sufficient extent to equalize the demand for sterling and the supply of sterling at a rate at or above £1 = $2.78. Several types of developments in other countries can assist in this process. (1) A rise of price levels abroad. Such a rise of prices abroad would increase the demand for sterling at each exchange rate by increasing the demand for British exports. It would also tend to reduce the supply of sterling by discouraging British imports. (2) A rise of real incomes abroad. By raising the demand for British exports this would shift the demand curve for sterling to the right. (3) A decrease of interest rates abroad. To the extent that this lessened capital flows out of Britain and induced or increased a flow of capital to Britain, it would reduce the supply of sterling and raise the demand for sterling. All these developments could help to raise the demand for sterling relative to the supply of it and to ease the drain on Britain's international reserves.

However, if these developments do not occur abroad or are not sufficiently strong to close the gap, one or more of the following things will have to happen in Britain: (1) A fall of British price levels. This would tend to increase the demand for sterling by cheapening British exports and to decrease the supply of sterling by reducing British imports. (2) A fall of real income. This would decrease British imports and the supply of sterling. (3) A rise of interest rates. To the extent that this reduced the outflow of capital from Britain or induced or increased capital inflows it would tend to reduce the supply of sterling or raise the demand for sterling.

Since all these developments in Britain would be at least anti-expansionary if not actually deflationary, it is easy to see why Britain might not relish this part of the adjustment process and might hope that most or all of the adjustment would come through increases of prices and real incomes and decreases of interest rates abroad. But one point must be emphasized: if such developments do not occur in Britain or the rest of the world, there is no reason to expect the drain on Britain's international reserves to end.

In an earlier chapter we saw how adherence to the old rules of the international gold standard game would tend to restore equilibrium in balances of payments without adjustments of exchange rates.[3] Suppose that the adverse balance for Britain arose because of a rise in British imports that increased the supply of sterling. This would have *income effects* in both Britain and the rest of the world. In Britain the diversion of a larger part of national income toward imports would tend to lower GNP and to have downward multiplier effects. The rise of exports by the rest of the world would increase GNP there and have upward multiplier effects. In addition to these income effects are the *monetary effects*. The loss of gold or its equivalent by Britain would tighten credit conditions there, while the gain of gold or its equivalent by the rest of the world would ease credit there. This would tend to induce capital flows to Britain, or at least to reduce capital outflows. Moreover, monetary restriction would tend to lower national money income in Britain while monetary expansion in the rest of the world would tend to raise national money incomes there. All these developments would tend to raise the demand for sterling relative to the supply of sterling and to end the drain on Britain's international reserves.

Nations were once willing to allow such adjustments to occur, and even to force them, in order to secure the advantages of stable exchange rates. They were so impressed by the advantages of free multilateral payments and exchange rate stability for promoting international trading and lending that

[3] See pp. 363–367.

they considered the cost of the adjustment process a modest price to pay. They did adjust their levels of incomes, prices, and interest rates and they did maintain stable exchange rates over very long periods. This objective of stable exchange rates is by no means obsolete. Yet many countries are no longer willing to pay whatever price may be involved to maintain both stable exchange rates and free multilateral payments.

The reasons for this change in attitude are numerous and complex. A basic factor has been the elevation of new objectives, and especially those related to the achievement and maintenance of full employment and rapid economic growth. In a few cases, countries have abandoned stable exchange rates and have raised their exchange rates in order to minimize or escape the importation of inflationary pressures. But in most cases in which countries have abandoned freedom of payments, or stability of exchange rates, or both, the motive has been to secure greater freedom to follow more expansionary or less contractionary types of economic policy at home. Some will not be deterred from following highly expansionary and inflationary monetary and fiscal policies to provide cheap financing for their governments, to maximize employment, or to strive for a rate of real investment that may be beyond their capacity. Others have abandoned stable exchange rates and have lowered their rates, not for the purpose of permitting price inflation at home, but to escape or minimize the importation of deflationary pressures as incomes and prices fell abroad. They were unwilling to allow stable exchange rates to transmit price declines abroad into domestic price declines or to permit the reductions of foreign demands for their products to be reflected fully in downward shifts of demand as measured in their own moneys. They hoped that a reduction of their exchange rates would serve both to bolster their exports and to maintain the prices of their exports in terms of their own moneys and also, by raising the costs of imports, to protect their import-competing industries.

Several other criticisms have been levied against a policy of maintaining stable exchange rates and free international payments and of equilibrating international receipts and payments through adjustments of relative national levels of income, prices, and interest rates. (1) Countries whose international receipts exceed their payments often do not allow their national money incomes and prices to rise and their interest rates to fall. This imposes a large part of the burden of adjustment on the countries suffering unfavorable balances of payments. (2) Costs and prices have become so inflexible downward that a policy of reducing domestic demands for output to bring international payments and receipts into equilibrium will be reflected largely in reduced employment and real income rather than in price reductions. (3) Even if price reductions can be achieved, the price elasticities of the foreign demand for the nation's exports and of the nation's demand for imports may be highly unfavorable to the adjustment process. Suppose, for example, that the foreign demand for the nation's exports is highly unresponsive to reductions in their prices and that the nation's demand for imports falls very little even though the prices of domestic import-competing goods fall. In this case a very large reduction of prices may be required to equilibrate the nation's receipts and payments. In extreme cases where the foreign demand for the nation's exports is highly price-inelastic, the reduction of prices may not equilibrate the nation's receipts and payments at all, for it may lower the nation's receipts for exports more than it reduces the nation's payments for imports.

CONCLUSIONS

The preservation of stable exchange rates over prolonged periods is still an important objective for many countries, and countries do adjust levels of money income, prices, and interest rates to promote stability of exchange rates. Yet loyalties to both freedom of international payments and stability of exchange rates over long periods have been impaired, largely because of the rising importance of objectives that sometimes compete with them. In the next chapter we shall consider some alternative policies.

SELECTED READINGS

Machlup, F., *International Trade and the National Income Multiplier*, Blakiston, Philadelphia, 1943.

Machlup, F., "The Theory of Foreign Exchanges," *Economica*, November, 1939; February, 1940. (Also reprinted in American Economic Association, *Readings in the Theory of International Trade*, Blakiston, Philadelphia, 1949.)

Nurkse, R., *Conditions of International Monetary Equilibrium*, Essays in International Finance, No. 4, International Finance Section of Princeton University, Princeton, 1945.

(See also readings at end of Chapter 24.)

CHAPTER 26

Exchange Rate Policies and Exchange Restrictions

As indicated earlier, there are three principal methods of equilibrating international receipts and payments: (1) adjustments of relative national levels of incomes, prices, and interest rates, (2) adjustments of exchange rates, and (3) direct controls over international transactions and payments. These may be employed in various combinations. In the preceding chapter we considered the case in which countries maintain stable exchange rates and rely solely on the first method, refusing to impose restrictions on transactions or payments. But a country may maintain stable exchange rates and employ both the first and third methods. Or it may abandon exchange rate stability and use all three methods together or any two of them.

This chapter will deal with two major topics: exchange rate policies other than those of pegging rates over very long periods and various types of restrictions on foreign exchange markets.

TYPES OF EXCHANGE RATE POLICIES

Once a nation abandons a policy of pegging its exchange rate at a fixed level over very long periods of time it has three major policy alternatives: (1) adjustable pegged rates, (2) free floating rates without official intervention, and (3) floating rates with official intervention. Any of these policies may be followed either with freedom of dealings in exchange markets or with restrictions on such dealings. In this section we shall assume that there are no restrictions on exchange operations so that at any time a single exchange rate on a nation's money will prevail. The effects of restrictions will be considered later.

Adjustable Pegged Rates

This is a policy of pegging rates in the fashion that we have already discussed but with this difference: the nation does not commit itself to maintain a particular pegged rate indefinitely and at whatever cost. The pegged level may be adjusted to correct a "fundamental disequilibrium." The nation will maintain a fixed rate and adjust its receipts and payments in other ways as long as these adjustments are not "excessively costly." But if it should appear that the stable rate could be defended only at excessive costs in terms of inflation or of unemployment and deflation, it will adjust the pegged rate to correct the fundamental disequilibrium and then maintain the new pegged rate until it becomes too costly to defend. We shall see later that this is the exchange rate policy embodied in the Bretton Woods agreements. The precise meaning of such a policy varies from country to country. Some countries will make great sacrifices to defend a pegged rate; others will drop the peg whenever its defense becomes slightly painful.

The advantages claimed for this policy are that it affords a country the benefit of stable exchange rates in the short run while protecting it against excessively costly adjustments of its levels of income, prices, and interest rates. But it also has disadvantages. (1) Fear that a country may lower the peg may inhibit the flow of capital to it. This can be serious for a country that aspires to be an important international financial center and for a country that wishes to borrow heavily abroad. (2) The country may suffer serious speculative capital outflows and losses of international reserves if people come to suspect that it may lower its exchange rate.

Free Floating Rates

Under this policy there is no official pegging of exchange rates and no official intervention to influence their behavior; they are determined by the market forces of supply and demand. The great advantage claimed for this policy is the freedom it affords a nation in its domestic policies. Undeterred by considerations relating to stability of its exchange rate and the status of its international reserves, the nation can promote to the utmost its domestic objectives and allow appropriate adjustments of its exchange rates to equilibrate its international receipts and payments.

Some economists believe that under such a policy exchange rates would behave in an orderly way and that speculation would be predominantly of a stabilizing type. Others are far less optimistic; they fear that speculative movements would be erratic and often destabilizing, and that in the absence of effective control of capital movements or official intervention, sharp and erratic fluctuations of exchange rates would occur and would be highly disturbing to a nation's economy.

Floating Rates with Official Intervention

Under this type of policy the authorities do not peg exchange rates, but they do intervene at times to buy and sell the nation's money in exchange markets to influence the behavior of its exchange rate. These operations are usually carried out by a nation's government, central bank, or exchange authority.

Official purchases and sales in the exchange market may have the very limited objective of preventing erratic or disorderly fluctuations of exchange rates without altering the basic level or trend of those rates. But they may also be used to lower or raise the level of rates over a longer period. For example, an authority may sell large amounts of its nation's money in exchange markets in order to keep its exchange rate lower than it would otherwise be. The only limitation on its ability to do this may be its willingness to accumulate gold and claims against foreign moneys. On the other hand, it may purchase large amounts of its own money to keep its exchange rate higher than it would otherwise be. Its ability to do this is, of course, limited by its ability to command gold and foreign moneys.

EXCHANGE RATE ADJUSTMENTS

Changes in exchange rates are sometimes a highly useful device for equilibrating international receipts and payments. They are especially appealing to a nation as a method of escaping or minimizing the importation of inflationary or deflationary pressures from the rest of the world. Suppose, for example, that at a time when the British economy is already operating at practically full employment levels, a highly inflationary situation develops in the United States and several other economically powerful countries. If Britain maintained stable exchange rates, the sterling prices of her imports would rise proportionally with price levels abroad, as would also the sterling prices of her exports. Britain could escape at least some of these inflationary pressures by raising the exchange rate on the pound. Suppose that foreign price levels double. The sterling price of British imports need not rise at all if the exchange rate on the pound is also doubled—that is, if the pound will buy twice as many units of foreign money. Moreover, the doubling of the exchange rate on sterling would make British exports twice as expensive in foreign moneys without any increase in their sterling prices.

Suppose, on the other hand, that the rest of the world slides into depression with falling price levels and that its demands for British exports, as expressed in foreign moneys, shift sharply downward. If the exchange rate on sterling remains unchanged, the sterling prices of British imports will fall, thereby putting British import-competing industries under deflationary pressure. Also, the decline of foreign demand for British exports will be fully reflected in a corresponding downward shift at each level of sterling prices for exports. However, an appropriate decrease of the sterling exchange rate, reflected in a rise in the sterling cost of foreign moneys, may prevent the sterling prices of imports from falling. It will also cheapen British exports in terms of foreign moneys without a decrease in their sterling prices and offset at least in part the decline of foreign demands.

Variable exchange rates are not, however, without their disadvantages and possibilities of abuse. For one thing, they increase the risk of international trading and lending. Sellers who accept claims against foreign moneys in payment run the risk that the exchange value of those moneys will fall. Buyers who must pay in foreign moneys run the risk of having to pay higher prices for those moneys. Forward exchange markets and speculative activities in them can lessen the burden of these risks, but these facilities are often inadequate and expensive. They are usually not available at all to bear the exchange risks on long-term lending and borrowing.

Members of a nation whose money is expected to depreciate in exchange markets find it very difficult to secure foreign loans in return for their promises to pay interest and principal in terms of their own money. For example, United States investors would be most reluctant to lend in return for promises to pay Brazilian cruzeiros or Argentine pesos in the future. Loans repayable in dollars may not solve the problem. For one thing, a Brazilian borrower may be unwilling to commit himself to pay dollars in the future when there is a possibility that the cruzeiro price of dollars will rise more than the cruzeiro price of the assets that he purchased with the loan. Moreover, this possibility may cause United States lenders to consider the borrower less credit-worthy.

Variations of exchange rates can also be abused. For example, nations may engage in competitive exchange depreciation in attempts to achieve nationalistic goals. This can occur even in times of prosperity. Accepting the old mercantilist doctrine that it is more blessed to export than to import, Nation A may drive down its exchange rate to promote its exports and to give greater protection to its import-competing industries. Nations B, C, and D may retaliate. All may do this despite the fact that their balances of international payments are in equilibrium or are quite favorable. Such competitive exchange depreciation is more likely in times of unemployment. Suppose, for example, that because of purely domestic developments, such as a decline of domestic investment, Nation A slides into a depression. It could combat the decline with measures increasing domestic demand. But it chooses instead to try to solve its domestic problem by driving down its exchange rate, thereby promoting its exports and decreasing its imports. This obviously tends to reduce Nation A's demands for the output of other countries and to divert demands from other countries to the export industries of A. Other countries may retaliate, each trying to make its exports cheaper than the others and to give still more protection to its import-competing industries. This is a game in which everyone cannot win but everyone can lose if the result is to demoralize world trade.

Under some conditions, changes of exchange rates can be a costly and even an ineffective method of equilibrating a nation's receipts and payments. To illustrate the principles involved, let us consider a case in which Britain lowers the sterling exchange rate to eliminate an excess of her international payments over her international receipts. In this case we shall measure both British payments and British receipts in terms of dollars. Note that this action operates through the price elasticity of the British demand for imports and the price elasticity of the foreign demand for British exports. One purpose is to reduce the dollar value of British imports by making imports more expensive in terms of sterling. The other is to increase the dollar value of British exports by making these exports cheaper in terms of dollars. This process may operate quite smoothly if both price elasticities are high. If the British demand for imports is highly price-elastic, a small rise of the exchange rate on the dollar may decrease markedly both the physical volume of British imports and the dollar value of her imports. If the foreign demand for British exports has a price elasticity far above unity, a small reduction of their dollar prices will be much more than off-set by the increase in their physical volume so that the dollar value of British exports will rise markedly. In such a case only a small reduction of the sterling exchange rate may be sufficient to eliminate the excess of British dollar payments over her dollar receipts.

At the other extreme, a reduction of the sterling exchange rate may actually increase the excess of British dollar payments over her dollar receipts. Suppose that the British demand for imports is highly price-inelastic, so that each rise of the exchange rate on the dollar reduces very little the volume and dollar value of British imports. Suppose also that the price elasticity of the foreign demand for British exports is far below unity. The decrease in the dollar price per unit of British exports will not be compensated by a sufficient increase of their volume, and British dollar receipts for exports will fall. British dollar receipts may be reduced more than her dollar payments, so that the excess of her payments is accentuated.

In intermediate cases, price elasticities may be such that a nation's payments and receipts can be equilibrated by a reduction of its exchange rate, but only by a very large reduction. In such cases the nation may suffer a serious worsening of its "barter terms of trade." By this we mean the quantity of real imports that it can buy with each unit of its real exports. Its barter terms of trade vary with the ratio:

$$\frac{\text{The price of exports}}{\text{The price of imports}}$$

Suppose, for example, that as Britain lowers the sterling exchange rate, the dollar prices of her imports change hardly at all but that the dollar prices of her exports fall almost proportionally with the exchange rate on sterling. (This would happen if the sterling price of exports remained constant.) If the sterling exchange rate has to be reduced drastically to equilibrate Britain's receipts and payments, the result may be to lower drastically the dollar prices of her exports relative to the dollar prices of her imports. Her barter terms of trade could be worsened so much that even a much greater real volume of exports would buy only a smaller real volume of imports. The result can be a lowering of the country's standard of living even though its physical output is sustained or increased. Fear of such a worsening of barter terms of trade is one reason why countries may be reluctant to lower their exchange rates to equilibrate their receipts and payments.

EXCHANGE RESTRICTIONS AND OTHER DIRECT CONTROLS

Our discussion of methods of equilibrating balances of international payments has assumed up to this point that there are no official restrictions on international transactions and payments. However, governments can take various types of direct action that affect the nation's payments, receipts, exchange rates, and international reserves. In some cases these actions are taken primarily for other reasons, and their effects in exchange markets are incidental. In others they are taken primarily because of their effects in exchange markets.

These direct actions are of various types, of which the following are merely examples: (1) Increased tariffs on imports. By increasing the cost of imports these may reduce the nation's imports and its demand for foreign moneys. (2) Quantitative restrictions on imports. These take various forms. A nation may merely put a few types of imports under quota, or it may go as far as to prohibit all imports except those specifically licensed by the government. (3) Taxes on exports, subsidies on exports, quotas on exports, and so on. (4) Restrictions on exchange transactions. These merit more detailed consideration.

Exchange Restrictions

This term applies to any departure from a system of free multilateral international payments. It therefore includes all restrictions on the types of transactions in exchange markets, the prices that may be received or paid for moneys, the use of receipts from abroad, the purposes for which international payments may be made, and so on. The first widespread use of exchange restrictions in peacetime came during the great depression of the 1930's. Many nations adopted them as world trade shrank, capital movements became disorderly, balance of payments problems multiplied, and exchange rate stability was threatened. During World War II, all the belligerents and most neutral countries instituted comprehensive systems of exchange control. In the typical case, receipts from abroad had to be surrendered at a fixed price to the central bank or an official exchange control authority, no one could make a foreign payment without official permission, and both the types and amounts of foreign payments were strictly limited. At the end of the war, many countries were exercising strict control over all exchange transactions and were pegging exchange rates at levels that could not be supported if freedom of international payments were restored. One of the major problems since World War II has been that of lessening these restrictions to restore greater freedom of trading and lending.

Exchange restrictions vary greatly as to their comprehensiveness and their severity. In the early 1930's their initial purpose in many cases was only to prevent abnormal capital flows out of a country—to prevent speculative flights into foreign moneys. Countries often insisted that they wished to preserve normal short-term and long-term capital movements to finance international trade and investment. These restrictions had several closely related purposes: to protect the size of the country's international reserve, to enable it to use these reserves for more important purposes, and to prevent or lessen the decline of the nation's exchange rate.

The problem of preventing "abnormal" capital movements while maintaining "normal" capital movements turned out to be extremely difficult. (1) In practice it is often virtually impossible to distinguish between normal and abnormal capital transactions. (2) As soon as a nation refuses to allow foreign withdrawals of funds, its ability to attract new funds from abroad is greatly reduced. (3) These restrictions can be enforced effectively only with a large organization and strict supervision of all exchange dealings, for funds can be withdrawn from a country in many ways. For example, funds were smuggled out of Germany by such devices as these: People made automobile parts and accessories out of gold and silver, painted them over, and drove the cars to Switzerland. They smuggled jewelry out of Germany and sold it abroad. German exporters underbilled their foreign buyers and made arrangements for the excess funds to be placed in accounts abroad. German importers overpaid their foreign suppliers and arranged for the extra funds to be held abroad for them. And so on.

But the difficulty of regulating capital exports was but one reason why many nations came to apply exchange restrictions to virtually all types of international transactions. Perhaps more important was the feeling that these supplied a useful method of defending exchange rates, of protecting their international reserves, of protecting home industries, and of regulating all types of international trading and lending. A complete exchange control system usually includes the following: (1) The government fixes the exchange rate on its money considerably above the level that would prevail in a free market. (2) Exchange dealings are centralized in the government and its authorized agencies. (3) All recipients of payments from abroad are required to sell them to the exchange authority at the official rates. (4) No payment can be made abroad for any purpose without a permit, and in most cases an allocation of exchange, from the exchange authority.

Almost uniformly, an exchange rate pegged under a system of exchange controls overvalues the nation's money; the pegged rate is above that which would prevail with freedom of payments. For example, a South American country may peg its exchange rate at 1 peso = \$0.20 or \$1 = 5 pesos when the market rate would be \$1 = 10 pesos if the market were free of restrictions. At the pegged rate, the supply of pesos will exceed the demand for pesos; the demand for foreign money will exceed the supply of it. Such a situation has important implications: (1) The overvaluation of the peso, which makes the country's exports more expensive to foreign buyers, is likely to depress the nation's total export earnings. And since its capacity to pay for imports may be limited to the value of its exports, its imports are also depressed. (2) Since the demand for foreign money exceeds the available supply, the exchange authority faces a rationing problem. (3) The presence of exchange restrictions and an excess demand for foreign moneys makes likely the development of a black market in foreign exchange. Those whose demands are not fully met by allocations from the exchange authority may seek additional supplies elsewhere and be willing to pay higher prices for them.

Exchange Rationing

Let us now look at some of the problems of exchange rationing, assuming that the authorities are largely successful in maintaining a single exchange rate. Faced with an excess of demands for foreign exchange over available supplies, the exchange authorities must give practical answers to questions such as these: How much do we allocate to each individual, business firm, and governmental agency wanting to make payments abroad? How much do we allocate for each general type of payment—how much for payment of debts abroad, how much for payments of interest and dividends, how much for foreign investment, how much for foreign travel, how much for each of the various types of goods and services that might be imported? Should we merely ration by type of payment, or should we also ration payments to individual countries? If the latter, how many payments should we permit to be made to each country?

Both practices and experience with exchange control and exchange rationing have varied from country to country, but the following have been some of the most common problems. One is that of maintaining fairness and honesty in rationing foreign exchange among competing individuals and business firms. When the total value of imports is limited, an allocation of foreign exchange can be extremely valuable. For example, an importer might buy an American car for \$2500 and sell it in his own country for the equivalent of \$15,000 if but little foreign exchange is allocated for auto imports. If the government does not capture this excess profit with an import tax, the importer may share it with government officials. Friendships, family ties, political affiliations, and financial generosity to government employees and officials have too often played an important role in exchange rationing.

In general, countries have severely restricted exchange allocations for payments of foreign debts and transfers of interest and dividends. They have classified some types of imports as "essentials" and given them preferential allocations while discriminating against "nonessentials." Domestic political considerations often influence these classifications. For example, imports that would compete with the output of politically powerful domestic industries are discriminated against, whereas exchange allocations for imports that are noncompetitive are more generous.

Exchange allocation policies have also been used as an instrument for forcing bilateral trade balancing. Thus Argentina has favored payments to Britain over payments to the United States because the British are better customers for its exports. Germany used exchange rationing for political and military purposes. Payments to countries evidencing "the proper attitude" were permitted on a liberal scale, but payments to other countries were niggardly.

These examples should suggest how powerfully exchange rationing policies can influence a nation's internal structure of production and prices and the types and directions of its international trade.

Multiple Exchange Rates

We noted earlier that there can be but one exchange rate on a nation's money at any time if exchange dealings are free of restrictions. But more than one rate becomes possible as soon as restrictions are imposed; those whose demands for foreign money are not fully satisfied at the official rate may be willing to pay a higher rate. In our example above, those whose demands for dollars are not fully met at the official rate of $1 = 5 pesos may be willing to pay 10 pesos or even more for extra dollars. Also, some of those who own or can get dollars will try to avoid selling them at the official price of 5 pesos and will make them available in the black market at some higher price. In many cases these black markets become well organized even though they are illegal. Let us suppose that the black market rate becomes $1 = 10 pesos. The initial reaction of exchange control authorities toward black markets is usually one of strong opposition; they want the entire supply of foreign money surrendered to them. After a time, however, some of them come to believe that the black market rate provides a useful way of stimulating exports. For example, some of the nation's exporters may not be able to compete successfully if they have to sell their dollar receipts at the official rate of 5 pesos to the dollar, but they will increase their exports markedly if they can sell their dollars at the black market price of 10 pesos. The exchange authority may therefore wink at such an "informal depreciation" of the peso in a limited number of transactions. Later it may formally set up a legal multiple exchange rate system.

Some of these multiple exchange rate systems are extremely complex. Let us use a simple system to illustrate the principles involved. Suppose that the South American country retains the "official rate" of $1 = 5 pesos and establishes two additional rates: an "export rate" of $1 = 7 pesos and a "free rate" of $1 = 10 pesos. If demands for dollars are not fully met at these prices, another higher black market rate on dollars may appear. The exchange authorities then define the types of dollar receipts and payments to which each of the official rates applies. Multiple exchange rates are a powerful instrument.

Let us see first how multiple buying prices for dollars can be used to influence the nation's dollar receipts and exports. If the exchange authority wishes to discourage its nationals from borrowing abroad, it may force them to sell borrowed dollars at the official rate of 5 pesos, but if it wishes to encourage capital inflows, it may purchase borrowed dollars at the export rate of 7 pesos or even at the free rate of 10 pesos. The rates paid for dollars received for exports usually depend on the type of export involved. Dollars received for some types of exports must be surrendered at the relatively low official price of 5 pesos. These are usually exports which can compete successfully at that rate and for which the foreign demand is believed to be relatively price-inelastic. The authorities may believe that the nation's dollar earnings will be greater if foreigners must pay 20 cents for each peso than they would be if fewer cents would buy a peso. Dollar receipts for certain other types of exports may be purchased at the export rate of 7 pesos. This may both raise the peso price of the exports and lower their dollar prices. Dollar receipts for certain highly favored types of exports may be purchased at the high free rate of 10 pesos.

Multiple exchange rates also affect a nation's payments and imports. If the authority wishes to encourage a certain type of payment, it supplies foreign money at a low price; if it wishes to discourage a certain type of payment, it charges a high price for the foreign money. For example, if it wishes to discourage payments of foreign debt and transfers of interest and dividends, it may sell dollars for the purpose only at the high free rate of 10 pesos. Thus it is enabled to repay a given peso obligation with fewer dollars. To encourage certain types of "essential" imports and to hold down their peso prices, it may sell dollars at the low official rate of 5 pesos. These may be things imported for government use, machinery or supplies to promote economic development, raw materials used in producing exports, or essentials that enter into the cost of living. But dollars to pay for other imports may be available only at the export rate of 7 pesos or at the free rate of 10 pesos. These imports may be discriminated against because they are "nonessentials," or their peso prices may be forced up to help import-competing industries. For example, dollars to pay for steel imports may have to be bought at the free rate of 10 pesos to afford protection to the nation's budding steel industry.

Multiple selling rates have also been used to regulate the sources of imports. To encourage imports from selected countries, the authority provides foreign exchange at a low price. To discourage imports from other areas, it provides foreign exchange only at very high prices.

Summary

Brief and incomplete as it is, this account of exchange restrictions should indicate the power and breadth of their influence. They are indeed a wide departure from the old system of free multilateral international payments. Their original purpose was primarily to equilibrate international receipts and payments, to protect international reserves, and to avoid or lessen the extent of exchange rate depreciation. But once they were highly developed and made applicable to virtually every type of international transaction, they came to be used for many other purposes as well: not only to limit total imports, but to regulate the types and sources of imports and the relative prices of imports; to protect import-competing industries in varying degrees and to build up new domestic industries; to regulate the types of exports and to subsidize or penalize various types of exports; to bargain with other countries and force bilateral balancing of trade and payments; and so on. The very existence of these restrictions and the possibility of their use to prevent or limit repayments of foreign debt and transfers of interest and dividends is a drag on international capital movements. Such restrictions not only reduce the total volume of world trade but also misdirect it and prevent the achievement of the most efficient types of regional specialization in production. It is, therefore, easy to see why those who value highly the advantages to the world of free multilateral trade and payments work toward elimination of exchange restrictions and toward reliance on other methods of equilibrating international receipts and payments.

CONCLUSIONS

There are only three major ways of achieving and maintaining equilibrium in international payments and receipts: (1) adjustments of relative levels of national incomes, price levels, and interest rates, (2) adjustments of exchange rates, and (3) direct controls of international receipts and payments. These may be used singly, in various combinations, and in varying degrees. None is without its costs and disadvantages. One of the world's major monetary problems is to determine the extent of its reliance on each of these general methods of equilibrating international payments. But policies in this area are clearly interrelated with domestic monetary and fiscal policies.

Historically, one of the most common policies has been that of pegging exchange rates, maintaining relatively free multilateral international payments, and relying on adjustments of relative national levels of incomes, prices, and interest rates to equilibrate international payments. The major criticism of this policy is that it unduly limits expansionary domestic policies and exposes a nation's economy to deflationary pressures originating abroad. The greatest enemies of this system have undoubtedly been depression and threats of depression. Various things can be done to lessen the costs of maintaining such a system. Among these are the following: (1) Eliminate serious business depressions that reduce demands for output, and do this by means that sustain domestic demands. As the world's greatest economic power, the United States can help the world's economy in many ways, but one of the most important is by avoiding depression and maintaining and expanding its demands for the output of other nations. The same principle applies to other major nations. (2) Establish the principle that nations with favorable balances of payments have some responsibility for assisting in the adjustment process, so as to reduce the restrictiveness in nations with adverse balances of payments. (3) Provide larger sources of international reserves so that countries with adverse balances of payments will not be forced quickly into highly restrictive policies.

Such measures would reduce the cost of maintaining stable exchange rates and free exchange markets. But even if they were put into operation, some nations might still feel that their freedom to follow expansionary domestic policies was too restricted and might therefore resort to adjustments of their exchange rates, to restrictions on international transactions and payments, or both. Nations that have adopted rapid and continuous inflation as a way of life cannot maintain stability of exchange rates and freedom of payments unless they can persuade others to inflate as rapidly.

We have seen that neither fluctuating exchange rates nor exchange restrictions present a wholly attractive alternative as a world-wide system. A particular country may find exchange restrictions useful, but a widespread use of such restrictions may throttle world trading and lending and injure almost everyone, including the nation that started them. A country may help itself by adjusting its exchange rate, but it may be seriously injured if other countries adjust their exchange rates for nationalistic purposes. "Orderly" and "appropriate" adjustments of exchange rates may be generally beneficial, but nations may not agree on the meaning of these terms or accept adjustments that harm them or are less beneficial than other rates might be. This is clearly an area in which nationalistic rivalries may produce results that are far from ideal for anyone.

SELECTED READINGS

Bell, P. W., *The Sterling Area in the Postwar World*, Clarendon Press, Oxford, 1956.

Gordon, M., *Barriers to World Trade*, Macmillan, New York, 1941.

Harrod, R., *The Dollar*, Macmillan, London, 1953.

International Monetary Fund:
    Annual Reports.
    Annual Reports on Exchange Restrictions.
    Staff Papers (published at various intervals).

CHAPTER 27

International Monetary Policies Since World War II

This chapter will deal with the reëstablishment of international payments systems after World War II, discussing briefly the principal problems, the leading policy alternatives, the institutions and processes involved, and some of the remaining unresolved issues.

CONDITIONS AT THE END OF THE WAR

As World War II drew to a close, all international transactions of belligerent countries, and those of most neutrals as well, were under strict government control. Governments were determining the types and amounts of both exports and imports, and were exercising equally strict controls over all international receipts and payments. They were pegging their exchange rates, some at prewar levels and some at levels reached during the early part of the war. It was evident that these exchange rates would not equilibrate international payments and receipts if these and international trade were freed of official restrictions. The existing system was clearly one of repressed disequilibrium.

Developments since the outbreak of the war had differed greatly from country to country. (1) Differences in the extent of open and repressed inflation. Some nations had permitted their price levels to rise only about as much as those in the United States; others had experienced much larger price increases. The extent of repressed inflation also differed greatly. To an even greater extent than in the United States, the people of many countries had accumulated huge holdings of money and other liquid assets that they were eager to spend. If permitted to do so, they would increase their demand for imports and themselves consume abnormal amounts of exportable goods. (2) Differences in changes in ability to produce. The United States economy emerged from the war more productive than ever. It had escaped damage from military attack and had enjoyed a large increase in its stock of productive capital during the defense and war period. On the other hand, the productive capacities of some countries had been seriously reduced in many ways: by death, injury, disease, and malnutrition of workers; by direct military destruction; by unrepaired depreciation of equipment; by lack of fertilizer; by depletion of raw material inventories; by economic disorganization; and so on. These reductions of domestic productive capacities affected balances of payments in at least two ways. In the first place, they reduced the ability of nations to export and earn foreign exchange. In the second place, they created urgent needs to increase imports to reconstruct capital, to rebuild inventories, and to meet essential consumption needs. (3) Differences in international reserves and international liquidity. The United States did decrease its gold reserves by about $2.5 billion during the war to increase its imports. Nevertheless, it emerged from the war with gold reserves of more than $20 billion, nearly two thirds of the world's monetary gold, and with only a small volume of international debt. Many other countries were not as fortunate; they had seriously depleted their international reserves and accumulated large debts to other countries. Britain had borrowed billions abroad to secure imports to meet military and essential civilian needs, and much of this debt was short term.

Thus nations faced many complex interrelated questions at the end of the war. What should be their policies relative to exchange controls and other direct controls over international transactions? Should they relax these quickly and move toward a system of free multilateral trade and payments? Should they go to the other extreme and make such controls a permanent instrument for regulating not only their balances of payments but also the types and amounts of their exports and imports? Or should they follow some intermediate policy? What should their exchange rate policies be? Should they continue to peg existing rates, change their rates and then peg them indefinitely at the new level, adopt a policy of adjustable pegging, permit flexible rates without official intervention, or permit flexible rates but intervene officially to regulate their behavior? What should be their policies relative to their levels of money incomes, prices, and interest rates? Should these be regulated with a view to equilibrating international receipts and payments at some selected exchange rate? Or should they be determined by other objectives?

As nations faced these questions at the end of World War II, they did so with philosophies and attitudes far different from those that had guided their decisions a quarter of a century earlier at the end of World War I. In the earlier period there was a widespread desire to restore a system of relatively free multilateral trade and multilateral payments with stable exchange rates over a prolonged period of time. Most nations then were quite reluctant to lower the gold values of their currencies. Most of these loyalties were seriously weakened during the great depression of the 1930's. Many nations became reluctant to commit themselves to pegged exchange rates over a long period, to forgo the various advantages of exchange controls and other direct controls over international transactions, and to adapt the behavior of their money incomes, prices, and interest rates to the maintenance of stable exchange rates and free international payments. In part this was because these objectives might conflict with others that they considered highly important. Economic reconstruction was an urgent need. Moreover, many nations adopted policies similar to that expressed in the Employment Act of 1946; they, too, were determined to avoid serious depressions and to "maximize employment, production, and purchasing power." They also came to share the desire to achieve "the highest sustainable rate of economic growth," and sometimes an even higher rate. But reluctance to accept the principles of international monetary reconstruction that were followed after World War I did not mean that nations were agreed upon a new set of guiding principles. Striving toward these has proved to be a long and laborious process involving both controversies within countries and differences of outlook and policies among countries.

The environment after World War II differed in another important respect from that following World War I: Governments had now become willing to coöperate in the process of monetary reconstruction. After the earlier war they had remained largely aloof, leaving the leadership in this process to central banks. Perhaps most striking was the shift of United States government policy. After World War I the United States had refused to join the League of Nations, to grant any financial aid above a minimum amount to prevent actual starvation, to cancel the large war debts of its former allies, to use its influence to hold down the volume of reparations to be paid by the vanquished, or to participate officially in international monetary conferences. Now it shared the lead in establishing the United Nations and participated heavily in its work, used its influence to minimize the extraction of reparations from defeated countries, did not request repayment for materials and services furnished to its allies, supplied tens of billions of government grants and loans, and helped establish and finance two new international institutions to promote international monetary and economic reconstruction.

These two new institutions are often called the Bretton Woods institutions, because they resulted from plans agreed upon in July, 1944, at Bretton Woods, New Hampshire, by experts from 44 nations. Their formal names are the International Monetary Fund and the International Bank for Reconstruction and Development. The latter is also popularly known as the World Bank. The United States and many other nations approved the Bretton Woods proposals with unexpected dispatch and both institutions were in operation before the end of 1946.

THE INTERNATIONAL MONETARY FUND

The broad purposes of the Fund, as stated in Article I of the Bretton Woods agreements, are:

1. To promote international monetary coöperation through a permanent institution which provides the machinery for consultation and collaboration on international monetary problems.
2. To facilitate the expansion and balanced growth of international trade, and to contribute thereby to the promotion and maintenance of high levels of employment and real income and to the development of the productive resources of all members as primary objectives of economic policy.
3. To promote exchange stability, to maintain orderly exchange arrangements among members, and to avoid competitive exchange depreciation.
4. To assist in the establishment of a multilateral system of payments in respect of current transactions between members and in the elimination of foreign-exchange restrictions which hamper the growth of world trade.
5. To give confidence to members by making the Fund's resources available to them under adequate safeguards, thus providing them with opportunity to correct maladjustments in their balance of payments without resorting to measures destructive of national or international prosperity.
6. In accordance with the above, to shorten the duration and lessen the degree of disequilibrium in the international balances of payments of members.

Structure and Control

The Fund, whose membership included 60 nations in 1958, has its principal office in Washington, D.C. Its assets are derived primarily from "quotas" subscribed by member nations. The sizes of national quotas vary widely, as is

TABLE 77.   National Quotas Subscribed to the International Monetary Fund, and National Voting Power, as of April 30, 1957

	Size of Quota (in millions)	Percent of Total Quotas	National Voting Power	Percent of Total Voting Power
United States	$2,750.0	30.8	27,750	26.6
United Kingdom	1,300.0	14.6	13,250	12.7
China	550.0	6.2	5,750	5.5
France	525.0	5.9	5,500	5.3
India	400.0	4.5	4,250	4.1
Germany (West)	330.0	3.7	3,550	3.4
Canada	300.0	3.4	3,250	3.1
Netherlands	275.0	3.1	3,000	2.9
Belgium	225.0	2.5	2,500	2.4
Australia	200.0	2.2	2,250	2.2
Italy	180.0	2.0	2,050	2.0
Brazil	150.0	1.7	1,750	1.7
Other nations	1,746.5	19.6	29,465	28.2
Total	$8,931.5	100.0	104,315	100.0

SOURCE: International Monetary Fund, *Annual Report*, 1957, pp. 147–149.

shown in Table 77. Of the total quota of $8.9 billion, the United States subscribed 30.8 percent and the United Kingdom 14.6 percent.

Each nation must pay a part of its quota in gold. This part is the smaller of the following: 25 percent of its quota, or 10 percent of its net official holdings of gold and United States dollars as of the date that the Fund announced its readiness to begin exchange transactions. The remainder can be paid in gold or in the nation's own money, the latter usually being in the form of a deposit claim against the nation's central bank. However, if the Fund does not need some part of a nation's money for its operations, it may accept obligations that are nonnegotiable, noninterest-bearing, and payable on demand at their par value to the Fund's depository in the country. If a nation devalues its currency in terms of gold, it must pay into the Fund an additional quantity of its money sufficient to protect the Fund against loss in terms of gold. Each member nation has agreed to place no restrictions on the use of its money held by the Fund. The Fund's assets are used primarily to help members meet temporary drains on their international reserves and stabilize their exchange rates.

Control and management of the Fund are by a Board of Governors, the Executive Directors, and a Managing Director. All powers of the Fund are vested in the Board of Governors, which is composed of one appointee from each member nation. As indicated in Table 77, the voting powers of the governors are roughly proportioned to the size of their nation's quotas. Each governor has 250 votes plus one additional vote for each $100,000 of his nation's quota.[1] Thus, the governor from the United States is entitled to cast 27,750 votes, the governor from the United Kingdom 13,250 votes, and the governor from El Salvador 275 votes. The Board of Governors delegates all except a few of its most important functions to the Executive Directors, of whom there must be at least twelve. Each of the five nations with the largest quotas appoints one executive director; the other seven are elected by groups of countries. Each executive director casts a number of votes equal to the number of votes possessed by the country or countries that selected him. The chief executive officer, the managing director, is usually selected from a small country, such as Belgium or Sweden.

Initial Exchange Rates

The Bretton Woods agreement provided that each member nation should establish with the Fund an initial exchange rate. There were, however, wide differences of opinion as to when and under what conditions these initial par values should be established.

Many people, including some outstanding economists, contended that these should not be fixed until economic conditions had been restored to "normal," trade and payments restrictions relaxed, price levels stabilized, and information gathered concerning the structure of exchange rates that would equili-

---

[1] The voting power of each governor is altered by adding one vote for each $100,000 of his nation's currency sold by the Fund and by subtracting one vote for each $100,000 of foreign money purchased by his nation from the Fund.

brate international payments. The Fund did not follow this course. On December 18, 1946, it announced initial par values for virtually all member moneys. Table 78 shows these for some of the principal moneys as well as par values in July, 1958.

Officials of the Fund were fully aware that many of the initial exchange rates

TABLE 78.   Initial Par Values and Par Values in Effect on July 16, 1958, for Some of the World's Principal Currency Units
(In U.S. cents per currency unit)

Country	Currency Unit	Initial Par Value	Par Value as of July 16, 1958	Percentage Depreciation, Dec., 1946— July 16, 1958
United States	Dollar	100.0000	100.000	0.0
United Kingdom	Pound	403.0000	280.000	30.5
France	Franc	0.8396	(a)	—
Canada	Dollar	100.0000	(a)	—
Netherlands	Guilder	37.6953	26.3158	30.2
Belgium	Franc	2.2817	2.0000	12.4
Denmark	Krone	20.8376	14.4778	30.5
Chile	Peso	3.2258	0.9091	71.8
India	Rupee	30.2250	21.0000	30.5
Norway	Krone	20.1500	14.0000	30.5
Union of South Africa	Pound	403.0000	280.0000	30.5
Philippines	Peso	50.0000	50.0000	0.0
Mexico	Peso	20.5975	8.0000	61.2
Colombia	Peso	57.1433	51.2825	10.3
Peru	Sol	15.3846	(a)	—

a Exchange value not fixed on this date.

would prove to be inappropriate, yet for the reasons indicated in their press release they believed the Fund should begin operations as soon as possible.

This is the first time that a large number of nations have submitted their exchange rates to consideration by an international organization and thus a new phase of international monetary coöperation has begun. The major significance of the present step is not in the particular rates of exchange which are announced, but in the fact that the participating nations have now fully established a regime wherein they are pledged to promote exchange stability, to make no changes in the par values of their currencies except in accordance with the Fund Agreement, and to assist each other in attaining the general objectives of the Fund.

The initial par values are, in all cases, those which have been proposed by members, and they are based on existing rates of exchange. The acceptance of these rates is not, however, to be interpreted as a guarantee by the Fund that all the rates will remain unchanged. As the Executive Directors of the Fund stated in their First Annual Report, issued in September: "We recognize that in some cases the initial par values that are established may later be found incompatible with the maintenance of a balanced international payments position at a high level of domestic economic activity. . . . When this occurs, the Fund will be faced with new problems of adjustment and will have to recognize the unusual circumstances under which the initial par values were determined. It is just at such times that the Fund can be most useful in seeing that necessary exchange adjustments are made in an orderly manner and competitive exchange depreciation is avoided."

The Fund realizes that at the present exchange rates there are substantial disparities in price and wage levels among a number of countries. In present circumstances, however, such disparities do not have the same significance as in normal times. For practically all countries, exports are being limited mainly by difficulties of production or transport, and the wide gaps which exist in some countries between the cost of needed imports and the proceeds of exports would not be appreciably narrowed by changes in their currency parities. In addition, many countries have just begun to recover from the disruption of war, and efforts to restore the productivity of their economies may be expected gradually to bring their cost structures into line with those of other countries. Furthermore, for many countries now concerned with combating inflation there is a danger that a change in the exchange rate would aggravate the internal tendencies toward inflation.

In view of all these considerations, the Fund has reached the conclusion that the proper course of action is to accept as initial par values the existing rates of exchange.

Adjustments of Exchange Rates

The temporary and experimental nature of the initial exchange rates accepted by the Fund emphasizes the importance of subsequent adjustments of these rates. But what principles should be applied in adjusting them? On this question there were wide differences of opinion. At one extreme were those who wanted complete fixity of exchange rates over long periods of time, as under the gold standards. At the other extreme were those who would adjust these rates to remedy practically every disequilibrium in a nation's balance of international payments. The formula accepted by the Fund represents a compromise between these views. Exchange rates are to be "stable" but not "rigid."

The general principle is that the exchange value of a currency shall be altered only "to correct a fundamental disequilibrium." Though these broad terms have not yet been given a specific meaning, a few conclusions are warranted. (1) A nation is not supposed to alter its exchange rate to correct a merely temporary disequilibrium in its balance of payments. Temporary difficulties are to be met by borrowing from the Fund or by other means. Only persistent disequilibrium is to be remedied by exchange rate adjustments. (2) A nation is not to adjust its exchange rate to offset a disequilibrium in its balance of payments resulting from a capital flight. Such a disturbance is to be met by direct control of capital movements or by other means. (3) A nation may alter its exchange rate if pressure on its balance of payments is such as to bring about unemployment of a chronic or persistent character. This was made clear in an interpretation given to the United Kingdom in September, 1946.

The Executive Directors interpret the Articles of Agreement to mean that steps which are necessary to protect a member from unemployment of a chronic or persistent character, arising from pressure on its balance of payments, are among the measures necessary to correct a fundamental disequilibrium; and that in each instance in which a member proposes a change in the par value of its currency to correct a fundamental disequilibrium the Fund will be required to determine, in the light of all relevant circumstances, whether in its opinion the proposed change is necessary to correct the fundamental disequilibrium.[2]

(4) Each member nation agrees to avoid competitive exchange alterations. · By following such principles the Fund hopes to facilitate exchange rate adjustments that will remedy fundamental disequilibria and at the same time avoid frequent, temporary, and harmful fluctuations.

The Fund also provides an orderly procedure for the adjustment of exchange rates. A change in the par value of a member's currency may be made only if proposed by the member and only after consultation with the Fund. The Fund may not force a member to make such an alteration, and the member may not act without first consulting the Fund. If the change proposed by a member nation, together with all previous changes, does not exceed 10 percent of the initial par value, the Fund may not object to it. If, however, the proposed change plus previous changes is greater than 10 percent of this value, the Fund may either concur or object. A member that changes the par value of its money despite objection by the Fund is subject to penalties. Unless specifically permitted to do so, it may not use the resources of the Fund, and it may be forced to withdraw.

After the par value of a nation's money has been established, the nation undertakes to maintain actual exchange rates within a narrow range. Countries are to prevent exchange rates from rising above or falling below the selected par by more than 1 percent. It is important to note that most foreign-exchange transactions are not carried on through the Fund. Private individuals, business firms, and banks are expected to operate in the foreign-exchange market in the ways described earlier. The Fund does not deal directly with private individuals and firms; it deals only with the Treasury, central bank, stabilization fund, or other fiscal agency designated by a member nation. National central banks and stabilization funds still have a function to perform in buying and selling exchange in order to maintain exchange rates within the limits mentioned above. For example, the British pound now has a par value of $2.80. Under the Fund agreement Britain is obligated to prevent the exchange rate on the pound from rising above or falling below par by more than 1 percent. If the pound should tend to rise more than 1 percent above this level, the British Exchange Equalization Account or some other designated agency is to offer

[2] *Report of the First Annual Meeting of the Board of Governors of the International Monetary Fund,* Washington, 1946, pp. 105–106.

pounds in the market in sufficient volume to arrest the rise. It is to be assumed that the British can always supply enough pounds to terminate a rise in sterling. If, on the other hand, the pound should tend to fall more than 1 percent below par, the British are to buy sterling, offering gold or foreign money in payment, in sufficient volume to halt the decline. If their holdings of gold and foreign exchange are adequate, they need not use the Fund's resources. But if they have an inadequate supply of gold and foreign exchange they may borrow foreign money from the Fund and sell it to halt the rise of foreign-exchange rates.

Financial Aid by the Fund

As noted earlier, the Fund has assets of nearly $9 billion resulting from the quotas subscribed by member nations. About 20 percent of these are in the form of gold that can be used to buy the money of any nation; the other 80 percent is in the form of claims against the moneys of member nations. For example, the Fund owns over 2 billion of United States dollars and could get more by selling some of its $1.7 billion of gold. The Fund uses these assets to help countries that need foreign money. Though in effect it lends foreign currency to a nation, transactions are in the form of sales of foreign money by the Fund in exchange for an equal value of a nation's own money. Thus Britain may buy dollars with pounds. It must later sell dollars to the Fund to buy back the pounds. For this type of aid the Fund collects a service charge of ½ of 1 percent a year on the amount of foreign money owed by a member.

To conserve the assets of the Fund, to promote its broad purposes, and to protect countries whose moneys may be sold by the Fund, several safeguards have been provided. (1) The Fund may sell a nation's money only with the permission of that nation. (2) A member may use the Fund's resources only for purposes that are consistent with the provisions of the agreement. As the Executive Directors stated in September, 1946, ". . . Authority to use the resources of the Fund is limited to use in accordance with its purposes to give temporary assistance in financing balance of payments deficits on current account for monetary stabilization operations." Two aspects of this interpretation are important. In the first place, the Fund's resources are to be used only for temporary assistance; prolonged and chronic deficits in a nation's balance of payments are to be met through devaluation of its money or by other methods. Nations are expected to repay within 3 to 5 years. And in the second place, the resources may be used to meet only balance of payments deficits on "current account"—that is, deficits on account of current international transactions in goods and services. They may not be used to meet large or sustained capital outflows from a nation. "A member may not make net use of the Fund's resources to meet a large or sustained outflow of capital, and the Fund may request a member to exercise controls to prevent such use of

TABLE 79. Purchases and Sales of National Currencies by the
International Monetary Fund from Its Inception to May 31, 1958
(All values stated in millions of United States dollars)

Member Nation	Value of Currencies Sold to Member by IMF	Value of Member's Currency Sold by IMF
Argentina	$ 75.0	
Australia	50.0	
Belgium	83.0	$ 11.4
Bolivia	7.5	
Brazil	206.0	
Burma	15.0	
Chile	58.6	
Colombia	40.0	
Costa Rica	1.2	
Cuba	47.5	
Czechoslovakia	6.0	
Denmark	44.2	
Ecuador	5.0	
El Salvador	2.5	
Ethiopia	0.6	
Finland	9.5	
France	452.5	
Haiti	1.0	
Honduras	6.2	
India	300.0	
Indonesia	70.0	
Iran	46.0	
Israel	3.8	
Japan	249.0	
Mexico	45.0	
Netherlands	144.1	5.0
Nicaragua	6.1	
Norway	9.6	
Paraguay	6.4	
Peru	0.0	
Turkey	15.0	
Union of South Africa	48.5	
Egypt	35.0	
United Kingdom	861.5	191.7
Yugoslavia	31.9	
Canada		15.0
Germany		26.4
United States		2,766.7
Total	$3,016.0	$3,016.0

SOURCE: IMF, *International Financial Statistics*, August, 1958, p. 3.

the resources of the Fund. If, after receiving such a request, a member fails to
exercise appropriate controls, the Fund may declare the member ineligible to
use the resources of the Fund."[3] (3) Limits are placed on each nation's net

[3] Article VI, Section 1 (a).

purchase of foreign money from the Fund. Unless these limitations are specifically waived by Fund officials, the Fund may not increase its holdings of a nation's money during any twelve-month period by an amount exceeding 25 percent of that nation's quota, and its total holdings of a nation's money may not at any time exceed 200 percent of that nation's quota. The Fund has often waived the first limitation in recent years but never the second. (4) To discourage members from using the Fund's resources for excessively long periods or in excessive amounts, the Fund imposes charges that are graduated with both the size of a member's drawings relative to its quota and the length of time that the Fund holds the member's currency.

Members often complained during the early years of the Fund that they could not plan ahead with assurance because they did not know whether the Fund would aid them, or on what terms. The Fund has taken two steps to remedy this situation. In the first place, the Fund now assures each member that all doubts will be resolved in its favor when it applies for drawings not in excess of its quota. In the second place, the Fund instituted in 1952 a policy of entering into stand-by arrangements with members. These assure a member that drawings upon Fund resources up to specified limits and within an agreed period may be made without reconsideration of the member's position at the time of drawing. The total value of these commitments between 1952 and mid-1958 was $1.6 billion.

Table 79 shows that from its inception to May 31, 1958, the Fund sold to its members slightly more than $3 billion of foreign moneys. More than 90 percent of these sales were in the form of United States dollars. The only other currencies sold were those of the United Kingdom, Germany, Canada, Belgium, and the Netherlands. At the end of this period the Fund also had outstanding $884 million of commitments under stand-by arrangements.

Elimination of Exchange Restrictions

A major purpose of the Fund is to promote the elimination of exchange restrictions, multiple exchange rates, and discriminatory monetary practices and to move toward a system of free multilateral payments. All member nations pledge themselves to remove exchange restrictions on current transactions as soon as conditions permit and to employ them thereafter only in accordance with the Fund agreement. It is important to note that the use of exchange restrictions is not completely outlawed. (1) It was recognized that the elimination process would require some time. The Fund makes annual reports on exchange restrictions, confers with members that retain restrictions, attempts to persuade them to move toward greater freedom of payments, and offers both technical and financial assistance to this end. If the Fund finds that a member persists in maintaining restrictions that are inconsistent with the purposes of the Fund it may force that nation to withdraw from membership.

Almost never is this drastic step taken. (2) The purpose of the Fund is not to eliminate all exchange restrictions, but only those relative to "transfers for current international transactions": payments for goods and services, interest and other net income on international investments, moderate amortization of loans, and moderate remittances for family living expenses. Exchange restrictions aimed at controlling abnormal capital movements are not disapproved; in fact, the Fund may request members to impose them to control capital flights. (3) Members may restrict transactions in a national money that the Fund has declared to be "scarce." It is not to declare a money "scarce" unless the supply of it is so small relative to the demand for it that the Fund's ability to meet the demand is seriously threatened. For example, dollars might become scarce as a result of large foreign demands for them when the United States purchased and lent abroad in inadequate amounts. Even in this case, however, a member that restricts purchases of dollars is pledged to make the restrictions no more stringent than is necessary to equalize demand and supply, and to relax them as rapidly as conditions permit.

Summary

We find, then, that the International Monetary Fund has the following long-run purposes: (1) To reëstablish a system of free multilateral payments, except that nations may continue to restrict capital movements. This would end multiple exchange rates and exchange rationing for current transactions purposes. (2) To maintain "stable" but not "rigid" exchange rates. Members would alter their rates only to correct "a fundamental disequilibrium." (3) To encourage each country to follow domestic monetary and fiscal policies that will enable it to balance its international payments and receipts without recourse to exchange restrictions on current transactions and without recourse to frequent adjustments of its exchange rate.

We shall see later how successful or unsuccessful the Fund has been in promoting these objectives.

THE INTERNATIONAL BANK FOR RECONSTRUCTION AND DEVELOPMENT

The primary function of the World Bank is supplementary to that of the Fund; it is to facilitate the international flow of loans to promote the reconstruction of damaged areas, the development of backward areas, and the solution of problems relating to balances of payments over a longer period. The purpose of the World Bank is not to displace private international lending or to solve all the problems of reconstruction. In the first place, other loans such as the United States and Canadian loans to Britain, the United States loans to Greece and Turkey, Marshall Plan aid, and several other forms of financial assistance for reconstruction and development have been granted, and more are likely in the future. And in the second place, banks, business concerns, and individuals still make international loans without using the World Bank in any way. The Bank is designed to supplement, not replace, other flows of international loans.

Structure and Control

Like the Fund, the World Bank has its principal office in Washington and in 1958 had 60 members. No nation may join the Bank without being a member of the Fund. The Bank is controlled in almost exactly the same manner as the Fund: by officials bearing the same titles, selected in the same way, and exercising voting power determined in the same way. Thus the nations with large capital subscriptions have a dominant voting power.

TABLE 80.   National Subscriptions to the International Bank
for Reconstruction and Development as of June 30, 1957
(In millions of dollars)

Nation	Subscriptions	Percent of Total Subscriptions
United States	$3,175.0	34.3
United Kingdom	1,300.0	14.0
China	600.0	6.5
France	525.0	5.7
India	400.0	4.3
Germany	330.0	3.6
Canada	325.0	3.5
Netherlands	275.0	3.0
Japan	250.0	2.7
Belgium	225.0	2.4
Australia	200.0	2.2
Italy	180.0	1.9
Brazil	150.0	1.6
Indonesia	110.0	1.2
All other countries	1,223.4	13.1
	$9,268.4	100.0

SOURCE: *Annual Report of the International Bank for Reconstruction and Development*, 1956–1957, p. 50.

The capital of the Bank is derived from subscriptions by its member nations. Only a part of its subscribed capital has been paid in but the remainder is subject to call. For example, at the end of 1957 when the Bank's total capital was $9.3 billion, only $1.9 billion had been paid in. The functions of its capital will become clear as we look at the methods employed by the Bank to facilitate international loans.

Methods Used by the Bank in Making or Facilitating Loans

The Bank is empowered to augment the flow of international loans in three ways:

1. By making direct loans to borrowers out of its own capital and surplus. In making these loans the Bank may act alone or it may participate with others.
2. By making direct loans, either alone or with others, out of funds borrowed by the Bank itself in the loan markets of member countries. For this purpose the Bank is empowered to issue and sell its own bonds and other debt obligations.
3. By guaranteeing in whole or in part loans made by private investors through the usual investment channels.

The total of the Bank's outstanding loans and guarantees of loans may not at any time exceed its subscribed capital plus any accumulated surplus. And its direct loans out of its capital and surplus are limited to 20 percent of its subscribed capital plus any accumulated surplus. The purpose of the remaining 80 percent of its subscribed capital is to "guarantee" the bonds it issues as well as the loans of others that are insured by it.

The provisions governing payment of capital subscribed by member countries are consistent with the lending and loan-guaranteeing functions of the Bank. Each original member had to pay 2 percent of its subscription within 60 days after the Bank began operations, another 8 percent was subject to call within a year after that time, and a further 10 percent is subject to call whenever the Bank needs the funds for its operations. The remaining 80 percent of the subscription is callable only when needed by the Bank to meet its own debts to those from whom it has borrowed or to compensate private investors whose loans it has guaranteed. This balance will therefore be called only to the extent that borrowers fail to meet their obligations to the Bank or to lenders whose loans are guaranteed by it.

Conditions Under Which the Bank May Make or Guarantee Loans

To understand some of the limitations placed on the Bank's operations, it is necessary to mention some of the fears aroused by the proposal for its establishment. The principal ones were: (1) That the Bank would replace the normal channels of international lending, thereby injuring the institutions previously operating in this field. (2) That the loans made or guaranteed by the Bank would be used for outright relief purposes, for uneconomic projects, for rearmament, or for other purposes that would not contribute to international reconstruction, peace, and security. (3) That the Bank would assume excessive risks and endanger its capital. (4) That the Bank's operations in lending or borrowing countries would disturb their domestic economies. (5) That the Bank's financial power would be used for "political" purposes.

To avoid these results, the articles of agreement placed several restrictions on the Bank's loans and guarantees. (1) The Bank may lend or guarantee loans only if it is satisfied that the borrower will otherwise be unable to obtain the loan under reasonable conditions. This provision plus the Bank's commission charges will encourage borrowers to seek funds through normal channels. (2) Except in special circumstances, loans made or guaranteed by the Bank shall be for specific projects for reconstruction or development. A competent committee is to study and make a written report on each loan application, and in extending or guaranteeing a loan the Bank must pay due regard to the ability of the borrower or his guarantor to meet the obligations created by the loan. (3) When the member nation in whose territory the project is located is not itself the borrower, the Bank may not make or guarantee the loan unless the member's government, its central bank, or some other comparable agency

TABLE 81.   Loans Disbursed by the IBRD by Borrowing Country
from the Beginning of Operations to June 30, 1958
(In millions of dollars)

Borrower	Amount of Loan	Percent of Total Loans
Australia	$ 300.0	10.7
India	276.7	9.9
France	250.0	8.9
Netherlands	236.5	8.5
Brazil	167.2	6.0
Union of South Africa	148.4	5.3
Mexico	146.3	5.2
Italy	112.8	4.0
Colombia	92.2	3.3
Japan	79.2	2.8
Iran	75.0	2.7
Belgium	69.7	2.5
U.K.: Rhodesia-Nyasaland	69.3	2.5
Yugoslavia	60.7	2.2
Pakistan	59.4	2.1
All others	651.3	23.3
Total	$2,794.7	100.0

Source: IMF, *International Financial Statistics.*

that is acceptable to the Bank fully guarantees payment of the principal and interest and all other charges on the loan. Thus, the securities issued or insured by the Bank should be relatively safe, for they will carry the guarantee not only of itself but also of the country in which the project is located and, in some cases, of the borrowing business concern or political subdivision. (4) Each member country is to deal with the Bank only through its treasury, central bank, stabilization fund, or other similar fiscal agency, and the Bank is to deal with members only through the same agencies. Moreover, it may lend the money subscribed for capital by a member country, borrow in a member country, or guarantee loans floated in a member country, only with that country's consent.[4] These provisions prevent the Bank from influencing a nation's money markets and balance of payments position without its knowledge and consent. They may also, of course, permit a country to impede the Bank's operations. For example, its usefulness could be seriously impaired by our refusal to allow it to lend our dollar subscriptions, to borrow in this country, or to guarantee dollar loans. (5) The Bank may not require that the proceeds of a loan be spent in the territory of any particular member or members.

Table 81 summarizes the Bank's lending activities from its inception to June 30, 1958. Though $2.8 billion is not a negligible amount, the Bank's lending policies have been criticized as overly conservative. Table 82 shows that more than three quarters of the loans were in United States dollars.

TABLE 82. Loans by the IBRD by Currency Lent from the
Beginning of Operations to June 30, 1958
(In millions of dollars)

Currency Lent	Amount	Percent of Total
U.S. dollars	$2,127.5	76.1
Pounds sterling	143.5	5.1
Swiss francs	134.9	4.8
Canadian dollars	106.5	3.8
Deutsche marks	64.9	2.3
Netherlands guilders	41.8	1.5
French francs	36.8	1.3
Italian lire	28.4	1.0
Belgian francs	27.4	1.0
Japanese yen	20.8	0.7
All other	62.2	2.2
Total	$2,794.7	100.0

SOURCE: IMF, *International Financial Statistics.*

ACHIEVEMENTS OF THE FUND AND THE BANK

As a first step toward evaluating the work of the Fund let us look briefly at some of the major developments in the postwar period.

This period was not, as many feared it would be, one of depression and unemployment. Rather, it was a period of high employment interrupted by only minor brief recessions and characterized by widespread inflationary pressures. Many factors contributed to these pressures: excess liquidity carried over from the war period, easy-money policies, large expenditures for reconstruction, full employment policies, ambitious development programs, fiscal ineptitude,

[4] There is one exception to this general rule. After its subscribed capital has been entirely called, the Bank cannot be prevented from using a country's money to meet the Bank's contractual liabilities arising out of its own borrowings or loan guarantees.

and so on. But both the types and degrees of inflation varied greatly from country to country. Some countries quickly dropped their wartime direct controls and permitted open price inflation. Others continued for years to repress inflationary pressures with price ceilings and many other types of direct controls. In some countries inflationary pressures were little greater than those in the United States; in others they were many times as great. Such great differences in the behavior of the various national levels of money incomes and prices were important contributors to widespread disequilibrium in balances of payments and to widespread retention of exchange restrictions.

An outstanding characteristic of the period was the large and persistent "dollar shortage." Other countries wanted far more dollars than were made available to them by United States imports, foreign investment, and unilateral transfers. This reflected huge foreign desires for United States exports of goods and services. Table 83 shows that foreign countries drew down their holdings

TABLE 83.   Gold and Dollar Reserves of Foreign
Countries, 1945–1957 (Excluding USSR)
(In billions of dollars)

End of	Total	Reported Gold Reserves of Central Banks and Governments	Foreign Holdings of Short-Term Claims on Dollars
1945	$20.6	$13.7	$ 6.9
1947	15.2	10.3	4.9
1950	18.2	11.3	6.9
1955	25.3	13.6	11.7
1957	28.6	14.7	13.6

Source: Computed from data in *Federal Reserve Bulletin*.

of gold and dollars by $5.4 billion in the two years following 1945. But this does not reflect the full extent of the excess demand for dollars that was held in check by official rationing of dollar exchange and by import restrictions. Foreign countries increased their gold and dollar holdings by $13.4 billion during the ten years following 1947, but they did this in part by continuing to ration dollars and to restrict imports from dollar areas. Moreover, many countries did not share in this rise of reserves.

A major obstacle to the restoration of free multilateral payments over most of the world has been the position of Britain and the sterling area. The term "sterling area" is applied to a group of countries that hold a major part of their international reserves in the form of claims on London, pay each other largely with British sterling, and maintain relatively free payments among themselves. The members of the sterling area are the United Kingdom and its dependencies, Australia, New Zealand, India, the Union of South Africa, and a few other countries. In the early postwar years, Britain restricted payments to other members of the area and they restricted payments among themselves. Gradually, however, the members of the sterling area came to restore freedom of payments among themselves except for capital movements. But the area as a whole continued to suffer a dollar shortage; it did not feel that it possessed enough gold and dollars to permit sterling to become freely exchangeable or convertible into dollars.

In the autumn of 1949 Britain, the other members of the sterling area, and a few other countries reduced the dollar prices of their moneys about 30 percent. They hoped this would improve their balance of payments positions and eliminate, or at least reduce, their dollar shortage by increasing their sales to dollar areas and by diverting not only their own purchases but also the purchases of other countries away from dollar areas. Though the action was helpful it did not enable them to eliminate their rationing of dollars or their restrictions on imports from dollar areas. Britain and the other members of the sterling area have gradually built up their gold and dollar reserves and have decreased markedly their restrictions on dollar payments. But in 1958 they had not yet reached full convertibility of sterling into dollars for current transactions purposes.

At the end of 1958, more than 13 years after World War II, the Fund had not yet achieved all its stated objectives. Exchange restrictions were still widely used. In some countries restrictions were mild and applied to only a few types of transactions; in others they were highly restrictive. Many of these countries were still maintaining multiple exchange rates and engaging in discriminatory monetary practices.

The Fund has not succeeded in getting all its members to maintain par values for their currencies and to maintain their actual exchange rates within 1 percent of those levels. In 1958 a total of 17 members had no par values; these included such important countries as Canada, France, and Italy. Moreover, several members have altered their exchange rates after only nominal consultation with the Fund.

In short, the Fund has not succeeded in reaching its objectives, and some nations question the desirability of those objectives. There is not yet full agreement as to the desirability of free multilateral payments on current account or as to the relative roles of direct controls, adjustments of exchange rates, and adjustments of relative levels of national incomes, prices, and interest rates in equilibrating international payments. These issues are likely to remain unresolved for some time. Yet it would be a mistake to play down achievements in this field since World War II, and the contributions of the Fund. The task of monetary and economic reconstruction proved to be much greater than was expected during the war and it has been made more difficult by international tensions, minor wars, and the threat of another major war. In most countries exchange restrictions have been relaxed greatly, more and more nations have adopted fiscal and monetary policies that have lessened their balance of payments problems, and in recent years the international reserve positions of foreign countries have been improving. The Fund has played a useful role in this process not only by providing financial assistance but also by serving as a medium for international consultation and as a source of technical assistance.

INTERNATIONAL RESERVES

Some economists believe that the world's future international monetary policies and practices will depend greatly on the adequacy of the supply of international reserves. They fear that if these reserves are inadequate, nations will persist in using exchange restrictions to equilibrate their balances of payments and perhaps even tighten these restrictions, will resort to predatory reductions of exchange rates, and will experience serious deflationary pressures. On the other hand, the future may see far different policies if the supply of international reserves is kept "adequate." Unfortunately, these arguments are often ambiguous, partly because they employ terms that are not clearly defined. For example, they do not define clearly the purposes for which international reserves are demanded, the composition of these reserves, or the criteria for judging "adequacy." We can discuss here only a few of the issues involved, and those only briefly.

For what purposes does a nation demand gold and other international reserves? We found earlier that nations once demanded them not only to meet excesses of their international payments over their international receipts but also to redeem their currencies domestically and to limit the size of their domestic money supply, the last being accomplished by limiting central bank liabilities to some multiple of gold and foreign-exchange holdings. These latter functions of international reserves have now largely but not completely disappeared, so that the principal remaining function of international reserves is to meet excesses of a nation's international payments over its international receipts. How much international reserves does a nation need for this purpose? No one has yet given a satisfactory general answer to this question. Nevertheless, it is clear that if a nation feels that its international reserve is inadequate, it is likely to follow restrictive monetary and credit policies to improve its balance of payments, to lower its exchange rate, to impose or tighten exchange and trade restrictions, or to take some combination of these actions. If large numbers of countries did so simultaneously the results could be adverse.

International reserves are of three general types. (1) The world's monetary gold stock. (2) Central bank and government holdings of short-term claims against the moneys of other countries. Table 84 shows that at the end of 1957 when the total gold and foreign-exchange reserves of foreign central banks and governments were \$30.2 billion, more than half, or \$16 billion, was in the form of foreign exchange. Of these, \$8.3 billion were short-term claims against dollars and \$5.8 billion short-term claims against British pounds. (3) Lines of

TABLE 84.   Gold and Foreign Exchange Holdings of Central Banks, Treasuries, and Other Governmental Institutions, 1937–1957
(In billions of United States dollars)

End of Year	World Total	U.S. Gold	Total Gold and Foreign Exchange	Gold	Total Foreign Exchange	U.S. Dollars	U.K. Sterling	Other Foreign Exchange
					All Other Countries[a]			
1937	\$27.7	\$12.8	\$14.8	\$12.6	\$ 2.3	\$ —	\$—	\$ —
1950	47.2	22.8	24.4	10.8	13.6	4.5	7.8	1.3
1955	50.8	21.8	29.0	13.2	15.8	7.9	6.6	1.3
1957	53.1	22.9	30.2	14.2	16.0	8.3	5.8	2.0

[a] Excludes the USSR.
SOURCE: IMF, *International Financial Statistics*, August, 1958, pp. 14–17.

credit or drawing rights in terms of foreign money. For example, an assured right to draw upon the International Monetary Fund or some foreign central bank may be as useful as holdings of foreign assets for making international payments. However, the usefulness of this source is reduced to the extent that stigma is attached to foreign borrowing or the availability of borrowings is left uncertain.

Those who believe that the world faces a shortage of international reserves and that this should be remedied by increasing the price of gold advance two general lines of argument. In the first place, the world faces a shortage of reserves even if we include at their face value not only gold but also all official holdings of foreign exchange and all international drawing rights. The money value of world trade has risen greatly since the prewar period. This is in part because of the great world-wide inflation of prices during and following World War II. This inflation may have been unfortunate but prices cannot be lowered again without devastating effects on the world's output and production. The future growth of world trade and production may be impeded if international reserves do not grow roughly proportionally with the world's capacity to produce.

Their second argument is that official holdings of foreign exchange are an inferior and undependable form of international reserves. Admitting that countries were willing to increase greatly their holdings of reserves in this form after the end of World War II, they express doubt that countries will continue this trend indefinitely. Countries may even decide to convert their foreign-exchange holdings into gold and hold the gold themselves. This might not force the United States to follow a deflationary policy, impose exchange controls, or devalue the dollar, but it could have devastating effects on Britain and indirectly on the world.

The scarcity of reserves can best be remedied, some argue, by a world-wide action raising the price of gold. Suppose, for example, that all countries simultaneously double the price of gold, in effect raising it from $35 to $70 an ounce. This would increase in three principal ways the money value of the world's international reserves in the form of gold. (1) It would automatically double the money value of existing monetary gold stocks. (2) It would increase the money value of current gold output. Each ounce produced would have a doubled money value, and physical output would rise. (3) It would reduce nonmonetary uses of gold. A larger part of current output would flow into monetary uses and some inflow of gold from other uses might be induced.

An increase in the price of gold would indeed increase international reserves and may be justified if there is in fact a shortage of international reserves and if no better remedy proves acceptable. But it would be a costly and clumsy remedy. For one thing, it would involve real costs because a larger part of the world's resources would be diverted to gold mining. Much more importantly, however, it would not distribute the increase of reserves on the basis of need. The increased money value of existing gold stocks, which in the short run would represent a major part of the increase in international reserves, would be distributed among nations in proportion to their gold holdings. To them that hath shall be given! Thus, about two thirds of the increase of reserves would accrue to the gold-rich United States and another significant part to West Germany and Switzerland, which are already rich in reserves and in comfortable balance of payments positions. Switzerland alone would gain more reserves than the center country of the sterling area, the United Kingdom, and almost as much as the whole of Latin America. Increased reserves from current gold production would in the first instance accrue to a few gold-producing countries. More than two thirds would accrue to Africa, most of this to South Africa. Much of the rest would accrue to Canada.

What are the alternatives? That the world in fact faces a shortage of international reserves has not yet been established. But if it does there are at least two alternative remedies. One is to develop still further the practice of holding foreign moneys as international reserves. For example, the rest of the world might hold little gold and use dollar and sterling claims to an even greater extent. Another alternative is to enlarge greatly the scope of the International Monetary Fund, or to establish a new international monetary institution, and permit it to create claims that will serve as international reserves for member countries. In effect, it would be an international central bank with the power to create a medium of payments that would be generally acceptable in international transactions.

Such an institution could operate in various ways, some of which would involve no use of gold. Let us suppose, however, that it issues a monetary unit that is kept at a constant value in terms of gold and that it holds gold reserves. The following steps might be taken. (1) The International Central Bank (the ICB) creates a monetary unit, "the bancor," equal to one ounce of gold. (2) Each nation contributes to the ICB some part of its monetary gold stock,

TABLE 85. Monetary Gold Stocks and Gold Production, 1957
(In millions of dollars)

A. Monetary gold stocks, end of 1957

United States	$22,857
Germany	2,541
Switzerland	1,718
United Kingdom	1,600
Canada	1,100
IMF	1,180
All other	7,654
World total	$38,650

B. Gold production during 1957

Africa	$ 656
Canada	155
United States	63
Australia	38
All other	125
Total	$ 1037

SOURCES: IMF, *International Financial Statistics*, August, 1958, p. 15. Also, *Federal Reserve Bulletin*, September, 1958, p. 1130.

taking in return an equal value of bancor deposit credits at the ICB. (3) Each nation agrees to accept bancor deposits at the ICB in international payments and to refrain from demanding gold from the ICB except under certain clearly defined and restricted circumstances. In return, each nation is assured that others will accept bancor deposits in payment. Thus net payments among countries can be effected by transferring deposit claims against the ICB. (4) The ICB is empowered to create bancor deposits up to several times—such as four or five times—its gold reserves. It may do this by making loans to central banks and governments or by purchasing securities in the open market in the various countries.

Thus the ICB could create international reserves in much the same way that national central banks create reserves within their own countries. Similarly, it could regulate the supply of international reserves in such a way as to promote the achievement of selected objectives.

Whether and how far the world is prepared to move in this direction, either by expanding the scope and functions of the International Monetary Fund or by other means, remains to be seen.

SELECTED READINGS

European Payments Union, *Annual Reports*, Organization for European Economic Coöperation, Paris.

Harrod, R. F., *The Pound Sterling, 1951–1958*, Essays in International Finance, No. 30, International Finance Section of Princeton University, Princeton, 1958.

International Bank for Reconstruction and Development, *Annual Reports*, and various other publications, Washington.

International Monetary Fund, *Annual Reports*, and various other publications, Washington.

Kindleberger, C. P., *The Dollar Shortage*, Wiley, New York, 1950.

Kriz, M., *The Price of Gold*, International Finance Section of Princeton University, Princeton, 1952.

Tew, B., *International Monetary Coöperation*, Hutchinson House, London, 1952.

CHAPTER 28

The Future

Monetary and banking institutions and policies may appear to be slow-moving and almost static if one looks only at their changes over a span of a year or two. But if one compares the structures, policies, and attitudes of today with those of 50 or even 30 years ago the contrast is striking indeed. Those of 1929 seem far away, those of 1913 almost alien. But what of the future? It will almost certainly bring further controversies and changes. Some of these will relate to issues that are already with us and are as yet unresolved; others will be generated by developments not yet foreseen. Let us look at some of the issues that will probably continue to confront the nation.

INTERNATIONAL POLICIES

No matter how isolationist we may be in our domestic policies we cannot ignore their relationships to the policies of the rest of the world. Both the nature of our monetary policies and their effects are inevitably influenced by those elsewhere; in turn, the policies of such a powerful nation as the United States greatly influence the rest of the world. But in what direction will the international monetary system move? Will it be toward reëstablishing the system prevailing before 1913, with its emphasis on free multilateral payments, relatively free multilateral trade, free capital movements, stable exchange rates over long periods, and unvarying gold values for the various national monetary units? That many nations will restore this system in its pure form seems unlikely. To do so successfully they would have to give up many direct controls over international trade and capital movements and jeopardize such domestic objectives as those of maintaining continuous full employment and promoting rapid economic growth. But there is not yet agreement on the nature of the international monetary system of the future. Direct restrictions on international payments, trade, and capital movements have their costs as well as their national advantages and are in a state of flux. Nor have nations yet reached agreement as to the appropriate behavior of exchange rates, the criteria for setting and changing rates, or coöperative procedures that would prevent individual countries from following exchange rate policies that would injure others. Still at issue are the relative responsibilities of countries with international deficits and those with international surpluses for equilibrating international payments.

The future international role of the dollar is still uncertain. Will it maintain or increase its relative importance, or will it lose ground to sterling or some other currency? Will other nations continue to hold a large part of their international reserves in the form of dollars or even increase the portion of their reserves in this form? Or will they cease to hold dollars and instead hold gold, some other foreign currency, or claims against the International Monetary Fund or some other international financial institution? The United States unquestionably has great power over the volume of gold and dollar reserves of the rest of the world. To what extent should its policy be influenced by the objective of regulating the size of these reserves?

Also uncertain are the future monetary roles of gold. We found that since 1914 gold has lost most of its importance as a component of the actual circulating medium, as a means of redeeming moneys domestically, and as regulator of domestic monetary policies. Will it in the future gain or lose importance in these roles? Nor is its future role as an international reserve clear. Will it lose relative importance to such substitutes as claims against dollars, sterling, other foreign currencies, and international institutions? Or will nations turn away from such substitutes and hold a larger part of their international reserves in the form of gold? Closely related is the question of the future price of gold. Even at present prices, the monetary gold stock of the United States seems adequate for the foreseeable future. But if it should turn out that the rest of the world faces a shortage of international reserves, should the United States join in a world-wide increase in the price of gold? Or should it seek to solve the problem by providing more dollar reserves to the rest of the world, or by helping to establish an international institution that could supply such reserves?

DOMESTIC ISSUES

No less numerous and perplexing are the unresolved domestic issues relating to both economic objectives and methods of implementation. One of the outstanding events of recent decades has been the government's assumption of greater responsibility for the overall behavior of the economy. Prior to 1914 the United States had no central bank; the government's policy was not the classic one of laissez faire but it was certainly one of limited intervention and did not include assuming any responsibility for regulating the overall level of output and employment. This government policy was maintained without major change through the 1920's. The newly established Federal Reserve sought to promote stability of price levels and business activity, but its objectives were then quite limited by present-day standards. Now the federal government has taken what would earlier have been considered a revolutionary step in assuming responsibility for promoting "maximum employment, production, and purchasing power." Many, though not all, assume that this also implies responsibility for promoting the highest sustainable rate of economic growth and stability of price levels.

However, the enunciation of these ambitious objectives has left many unresolved questions. There is not yet agreement as to the practical definitions of these objectives, as to the extent to which they are mutually consistent or contradictory, as to their relative importance, and as to which should be sacrificed when they appear to conflict. How will these objectives be weighed in the future? Will full employment and economic growth be promoted to such a degree that continuous price inflation will become a way of life? Will price stability be maintained even at some cost in terms of employment and growth? Or will these objectives happily turn out to be mutually consistent?

Expectations concerning the adaptability of cost and price structures have changed in an almost revolutionary way. In the period of the old international gold standard, cost and price levels were expected to adjust to the extent necessary to equilibrate balances of international payments, and this included downward as well as upward adjustments. By the 1930's many had concluded that downward adjustments were no longer feasible because they were too costly in terms of output and employment. Now many argue that price level stability is too costly, that labor unions have become so strong and are so aggressive in their wage demands and so many industries have strong monopoly power in setting their prices that continuous price increases of 2 or 3 percent a year are necessary to yield acceptable results in terms of employment and output. But is this actually the situation? If it is, what are the policy implications? Should it be dealt with solely by fiscal and monetary policies that regulate the demand for output? Or should it evoke government intervention to reduce monopoly power in the markets for labor and output or to regulate in a detailed way the wage- and price-making processes?

This elevation of new objectives and the assumption of increased responsibilities by government have inevitably been accompanied by important changes in methods of implementation. Fiscal policy has come to be a powerful instrument. But many important fiscal policy issues remain unresolved. What should be the relative roles of fiscal and monetary policies in regulating output, employment, and price levels? How can the other objectives of tax and expenditure policies be reconciled with that of promoting stability? What should be the relative roles of taxes and expenditures in such a program? How feasible is it to speed up the processes of changing tax and expenditure programs? All these and other similar questions bear upon the nature and size of the task of monetary policy.

Federal debt management policies have undergone great changes. The Treasury recognizes that its policies affect monetary and credit conditions and for some years now has ceased to demand continuously easy money and low interest rates to facilitate its financing operations. But there is not as yet any clear formulation of either the objectives or the principles of debt management. May not debt management be made into a powerful instrument for economic stabilization? If both its objectives and its operations were made consistent with and supplementary to those of monetary policy, might it not be employed usefully to regulate credit conditions and interest rates? No permanent solution of the relationship between debt management and monetary policies has yet been evolved.

THE FEDERAL RESERVE

Changes during recent decades have affected the Federal Reserve System in many ways. Perhaps most important has been the rise of new economic objectives accepted and sanctioned by the government. The Federal Reserve cannot deviate far from these or for long; it is a creature of Congress, can be directed by Congress, and is through many channels influenced by the values and attitudes of the nation. It therefore faces tasks far more difficult and exacting than those set for it at the time of its establishment or even in the 1920's. And because its responsibilities are of great social importance, its policies and actions are now scrutinized much more closely than ever before by both the public and the government.

Such changes in national objectives and in the responsibilities assumed by government could lead to changes in the structure and control of the Federal Reserve. Under somewhat similar circumstances many other countries have ended the "independence" of their central banks and placed them under the jurisdiction of the executive branch of government. May something similar happen to the Federal Reserve? If it does, how will monetary policy be affected? And what would be the other implications for the Federal Reserve? Would the twelve separate Reserve banks be continued or would they be merged into one? Would their stock remain with member banks or be purchased by the government?

Whether or not its relation to the executive branch of the government is altered significantly, the Federal Reserve may undergo further internal changes. In its early years much stress was laid on regional autonomy and adaptation of policies to regional differences in credit conditions. Since then the emphasis has shifted toward a single national credit policy, and with this has occurred a shift of power away from the regional Reserve banks and toward a centralized authority. Control of open-market operations has been centralized, the Board of Governors has acquired greater power over discount rates, and it was to the Board rather than to the Reserve banks that Congress delegated new powers to fix and alter member bank reserve requirements and to administer margin requirements on security loans and other selective controls. Will this trend toward centralization continue?

Nor is it safe to assume that the instruments available to the Federal Reserve for regulatory purposes will remain unchanged. What will be the future of selective controls? Will the Federal Reserve again be given the power to regulate consumer credit and perhaps also similar powers over residential construction and some other types of credit? If so, what will be the relative roles of general monetary management and selective controls in the future? Even its instruments for general monetary management may be altered. In the 1930's the System was given an important new instrument—the power to vary member bank reserve requirements. This has been severely criticized. What will its future be? Will this power of the Federal Reserve be eliminated or curtailed? Or may it be expanded? For example, may it be extended to all commercial banks, member and nonmember alike, as many have advocated? May it, or some similar instrument, be extended to cover financial institutions other than commercial banks? In the past the primary purpose of general monetary and credit management has been to regulate the quantity of credit and money supplied by institutions that have the power to create and destroy money. But with the institutionalization of savings and the huge flows of funds through such entities as life insurance companies, savings banks, and savings and loan associations, some have come to argue that it would be useful to regulate the volume of investable funds supplied by these institutions. Will these views prevail?

The relationship of the Federal Reserve to other regulatory agencies in the banking field may also come under scrutiny. There are three such agencies at the federal level: the Federal Reserve, the Comptroller of the Currency, and the Federal Deposit Insurance Corporation. Their jurisdictions overlap in many ways. Through informal agreement, the Comptroller now has primary responsibility for examining and regulating national banks, the Federal Reserve for state member banks, and the Federal Deposit Insurance Corporation for nonmember insured state banks. But these arrangements leave much to be desired. For example, representatives of the FDIC have even been known to advise banks to remain outside the Federal Reserve System. There also remain many problems of reconciling the attitudes and policies of these federal agencies with those of state banking authorities.

THE FINANCIAL STRUCTURE

The whole structure of financial institutions in the United States has undergone tremendous changes since 1914. Perhaps most striking has been the rise of institutions sponsored in one way or another by the federal government:

for example, the whole complex of farm credit institutions, the many new institutions in the housing credit field, and the Small Business Administration. It cannot be taken for granted that this structure will or should remain static. Even if fully justified at the time of their establishment, some of them may already have become, or will in the future become, unnecessary or even harmful. On the other hand, similar institutions may be established in other fields.

The structure of the commercial banking system has already changed greatly and continues to change. In 1920 the nation had more than 28,000 commercial banks. In the late 1950's, despite large increases in population and even greater increases in real wealth and income, it had less than half that number. But multiple office banking has grown markedly. In 1920 there were fewer than 1300 branch banking offices; in 1958 there were more than 8000. Moreover, group banking—the ownership and control of two or more banks through a holding company—has expanded in the interim. The pressure toward multiple office banking continues to be strong and persistent. Many banks want to acquire branches either by establishing *de novo* offices or by absorbing other banks and converting them into branches. In addition, group banking would expand rapidly if undeterred by official restrictions.

Many public policy issues in this field remain unresolved. Some pertain to bank chartering. Fearing "overbanking," the Comptroller of the Currency and most state banking commissioners have abandoned the old principle of free banking and now grant new charters only if a community is found to be without "adequate banking facilities." Other issues relate to the granting of permits for *de novo* branches, for absorption of other banks in mergers, and for establishing and expanding bank holding companies. The decisions issued by the authorities usually refer to such criteria as the adequacy of banking facilities, the quality of banking services, and the avoidance of undue monopoly power in banking. Yet many of these decisions leave one with the uncomfortable feeling that they are not solidly based on a realistic analysis of alternatives and a clear understanding of the effects of the banking structure on the functioning of the system.

Other unresolved issues relate to jurisdiction over decisions affecting the banking structure. Is the division of authority between three federal agencies and forty-nine state agencies conducive to the development of the most efficient and effective banking structure, however that may be defined? Should promoters who are denied a national bank charter be able to get a charter for a state bank, or vice versa? Should the federal government continue to deny to a national bank any more liberal branching powers than those possessed by banks chartered by the state in which it is located? Should a national bank located in California be permitted to establish a state-wide system of branches while a national bank in Illinois may not have a single branch regardless of the size of its resources or the growing demand for banking services in nearby areas? These are but a few aspects of the broader issue of the relative responsibilities of the federal government and state governments for regulating the structure and practices of the commercial banking system.

CONCLUSIONS

This chapter has not attempted to catalogue all the existing unresolved issues in this field, still less to forecast those that may develop in the future. But incomplete as it is, it should have succeeded in making one major point: there is no reason to believe that the process of change in our monetary and banking objectives, structures, policies, and practices is nearing an end. A wise commentator once observed, "To some problems there is no solution, only an outcome." He might have added, "And the outcome is unlikely to be permanent."

Index